T0173483

The Right to be Forgotten

Second Edition

Dedication

To Eileen R

A loving light and inspiration to us all. Love and fondness.

The Right to be Forgotten

Second Edition

Dr Paul Lambert

BA, LLB, LLM, TMA, CTMA, Qualified Lawyer, CDPO, PhD,
Consultant, Visiting Professor, Manchester Metropolitan University
Visiting Research Fellow, Institute of Advanced Legal Studies, University of London

Bloomsbury Professional

LONDON • DUBLIN • EDINBURGH • NEW YORK • NEW DELHI • SYDNEY

BLOOMSBURY PROFESSIONAL
Bloomsbury Publishing Plc
50 Bedford Square, London, WC1B 3DP, UK
1385 Broadway, New York, NY 10018, USA
29 Earlsfort Terrace, Dublin 2, Ireland

BLOOMSBURY and the Diana logo are trademarks of Bloomsbury Publishing Plc

© Bloomsbury Professional 2022

All rights reserved. No part of this publication may be reproduced or transmitted in any form or by any means, electronic or mechanical, including photocopying, recording, or any information storage or retrieval system, without prior permission in writing from the publishers.

While every care has been taken to ensure the accuracy of this work, no responsibility for loss or damage occasioned to any person acting or refraining from action as a result of any statement in it can be accepted by the authors, editors or publishers.

All UK Government legislation and other public sector information used in the work is Crown Copyright ©. All House of Lords and House of Commons information used in the work is Parliamentary Copyright ©. This information is reused under the terms of the Open Government Licence v3.0 (http://www.nationalarchives.gov.uk/doc/open-government-licence/version/3) except where otherwise stated.

All Eur-lex material used in the work is © European Union, http://eur-lex.europa.eu/, 1998–2022.

British Library Cataloguing-in-Publication Data

A catalogue record for this book is available from the British Library.

ISBN:	HB	978 1 52652 193 4
	ePDF	978 1 52652 195 8
	ePub	978 1 52652 194 1

Typeset by Evolution Design and Digital Ltd (Kent)
Printed and bound by CPI Group (UK) Ltd, Croydon, CR0 4YY

To find out more about our authors and books, visit www.bloomsburyprofessional.com. Here you will find extracts, author information, details of forthcoming events and the option to sign up for our newsletters.

'The Court case heard around the world – *Google Spain*.'[1]

These 'are novel questions, which have never yet been considered in this Court. They arise in a legal environment which is complex, and has developed over time'.[2]

Individual data subjects 'have the right to obtain from the controller the erasure of personal data concerning him or her without undue delay and the controller [must] erase personal data without undue delay'.[3]

'Customers need to be given control of their own data.'[4]

1   JP Eckart, 'The Court Case Heard Around the World – *Google Spain SL v Agencia Espanola de Proteccion de Datos* – The Right to Be Forgotten and What It May Mean to the United States' *Dartmouth Law Journal* (Spring 2017) (15:1) 42.
2   *NT1 & NT2 v Google LLC* [2018] EWHC 799 (QB) (13 April 2018) Warby J, at para 10.
3   GDPR Art 17(1).
4   Tim Berners-Lee, 'Customers need to be given control of their own data'. Available at: www. brainyquote.com/authors/tim_bernerslee.

Contents

Preface

The issue of the Right to be Forgotten (RtbF) and the partial, but necessary, solution it presents to certain increasingly evident internet problems is an important societal and legal issue. While strictly speaking the right to takedown and forgetting existed under the previous data protection regime evident under the DPD 95/46,[5] it is now more expressly evident under the General Data Protection Regulation (GDPR). Indeed, recent official hearings and proposals for new internet laws make it even more clear than at the time of the first edition that RtbF tools and solutions are required. While debate may arise in relation to particular aspects from time to time, the overall need is difficult to doubt.

Without doubt there are problems evident on the internet which were not originally envisaged, especially in the original utilitarian vision – prior to the explosion of activities from the advent of the so-called Internet 2.0 onwards. We have now moved well past Internet 2.0 and experts are talking of Internet 3.0 – and some are even envisaging Internet 4.0. Unlike the original internet which, at its core, focused as a utilitarian communications medium largely between academics, vast amounts of different activities, both commercial and non-commercial, occur both *on* and *via* the internet. Even on the internet, a vast amount of activity is hidden.[6]

For many lawyers, the very topic of personal data, data protection and privacy is new. The same can unfortunately be said for many business and non-commercial organisations. Notwithstanding that there has been a Council of Europe Convention on data protection since 1981[7] and the DPD 95/46 in the EU since 1995,[8] many organisations are starting to appreciate the importance and necessity of data protection in light of the massive worldwide attention which focused upon the go-live or commencement of the GDPR in May 2018.

Without doubt, there is greater attention being focused on data protection and privacy (DPP), and the security requirement of the data protection regime, as a

---

5   Directive 95/46; Directive 95/46/EC of the European Parliament and of the Council of 24 October 1995 on the protection of individuals with regard to the processing of personal data and on the free movement of such data (OJ 1995 L 281, p 31).
6   For example, so-called 'dark web' activities are on websites which are not obviously accessible given that they are not 'indexed' in internet mapping collections by the larger commercial search engines, and hence they are not listed.
7   Council of Europe Convention on data protection, No 108 of 1981. Note that the Council of Europe has over 40 Member States and so is wider than the European Union.
8   Directive 95/46.

result of the growing list of significant data breach instances.[9] The number[10] and scale[11] of these are increasing, which is a significant problem in itself.[12] These are also noteworthy in that some of the entities suffering data breaches are large brand-name companies, as well as official and government entities. There are a number of reasons for suggesting that official organisations should be expected to be more considered and better aligned to best practice. Sony and the NHS are just two examples. The personal liability and contract obligations of directors and officers for data protection and privacy compliance and breaches is also in focus.[13] The vicarious liability issues of companies are also being scrutinised, even judicially.[14]

Fortunately, there is increasing legal attention being paid to data protection and the GDPR. However, there is much less legal attention and commentary being focused on the RtbF aspect of the GDPR. Arguably, more commercial attention is being devoted to more 'commercial' issues, such as increases in fines and penalties,[15] data transfer issues,[16] etc., whereas public and individual data subject issues are somewhat backgrounded.

---

9 P Lambert, 'Equifax Data Breach, 143 Million Only Tip of the Iceberg,' *International Journal for the Data Protection Officer, Privacy Officer and Privacy Counsel (IDPP)* (2017) (2:1) 30; A Tantleff, 'Applying the GDPR Rules to the Equifax 143m Data Breach' *International Journal for the Data Protection Officer, Privacy Officer and Privacy Counsel (IDPP)* (2018) (2:2) 8.

10 Number or volume of data breach events.

11 Number of individuals affected in each data breach event.

12 One issue in this regard is the question of whether penalties for hacking and data breaches are sufficient and proportionate and, if not, whether they need to be increased. A related issue is the establishment of an interface mechanism for considering data breach under data protection and privacy rules and criminal law rules in relation to data breaches at the same time. As the problem of data breaches is increasing, consideration may be warranted to enhance these penalties. Companies may point to the fact that there has been a significant increase in fines and penalties for organisations under the GDPR, yet there is no consequent increase in penalties and deterrents for hackers and those responsible for data breaches. Companies may also point to the fact that they can be penalised for data breaches, but data breach attackers do not face increased consequences. While some data protection law does contain criminal offences, many criminal hacking type offences are contained in discrete criminal laws. The increase in data breaches might suggest a need for review.

13 G Wade, 'Directors: When Company Law and Data Protection Law Collide' *International Journal for the Data Protection Officer, Privacy Officer and Privacy Counsel* (IDPP) (2018) (2:8) 19.

14 M Everett, and L McAlister, 'Court of Appeal Confirms First Successful UK Class Action for Data Breach' *International Journal for the Data Protection Officer, Privacy Officer and Privacy Counsel (IDPP)* (2018) (2:11) 8, referring to the *Morisson's* case.

15 L Loftis, 'GDPR Violations – Hefty Fines or Broken Reputations, Which Is Worse?' *Information-Management.com*, 3 June 2018, p 1; HA Wolff, Prof Dr, 'The Implementation of Administrative Fines Under the General Data Protection Regulation from the German Perspective,' *International Journal for the Data Protection Officer, Privacy Officer and Privacy Counsel (IDPP)* (2018) (2:11) 11.

16 PM Schwartz, and Karl-Nikolaus, 'Transatlantic Data Privacy Law' *Georgetown Law Journal*, (2017) (106:1) 115; W Krouse, 'The Inevitable Demise of Privacy Shield, How to Prepare' *The Computer and Internet Lawyer* (2018) (36:6) 19; P Fischer, 'From the Safe Harbor to the Privacy Shield: Selected Aspects of the EU–US Privacy Shield' *International Business Law Journal* (2018) (2) 143. Also see Christoper Kuner, *Transborder Data Flows and Data Privacy Law* (Oxford University Press, 2013).

There has also been greater legal attention over a longer period to intellectual property rights (eg, copyright and trade marks) and related online content disputes and online infringements.[17] As part of this there has been focused attention on targeting online infringements – including methods for takedown of problem infringing content. Largely (albeit not exclusively) these infringing problem issues are commercial or corporate in nature.

In contrast, the problem issues which the RtbF and related solutions seek to address concern problem content online of a more personal and individual nature. Effects range from embarrassment, personal, and psychological damage, career and financial damage to life-affecting situations.

This is in contrast to quite a large amount of media commentary referring to the RtbF;[18] and an even larger amount of media attention referring to some of the problem issue aspects of the internet – including the need for personal-takedown and forgetting (PTF), online abuse (OA) and aspects of OA such as attacks, coordinated group attacks, abuse, trolling, revenge porn, blackmail, extortion, sextortion, viral publication of personal content (whether directly or third party posted)[19] and the sometimes adult suicides[20] and child and teenage suicides resulting from OA.[21]

There are increasing examples of internet of things (IoT) devices being vulnerable to attack. Consider video images of your baby being uploaded to the internet as a result of an IoT device being hacked. As a parent you may well be concerned to have such images taken down and forgotten. This may not be an OA attack but is similarly an issue with which the RtbF can assist. Upskirting images online may not be linked to sextortion, demands or attacks, but is another problem area where the victim may wish to avail of the solution offered by the RtbF.

The internet and IT technical issues have sometimes been considered less relevant or too technical by courts and lawyers. This reticence is thankfully decreasing

---

17 R Giblin, *Code Wars: 10 Years of P2P Software Litigation* (Elgar, 2011). Interestingly, in terms of online music and film copyright infringement and peer-to-peer sharing, the issue of the problem infringing content soon took a backstep as the focus increased on the technologies of distribution, routes of distribution and solution issues. Arguably, the RtbF discussion is still more focused on the right per se and less on the technologies of distribution, routes of distribution and tools and application of the RtbF solution (eg Are the current tools being applied as user friendly as they should be? Are the RtbF tools less consumer focused than initial sign-up interfaces? Is every service provider providing the same RtbF and the same level of accessibility?).

18 K Lillington, 'Right to be Forgotten Key Regulatory Scrutiny of Tech Giants' *Irish Times*, 13 September 2018; M Scott, '"Right to be Forgotten" Should Apply Worldwide – EU Panel' *New York Times*, 26 November 2014.

19 Which can be personally posted, or posted by a third party, which can range from personal and private, to embarrassing, harmful, intrusive, shaming, demands and blackmail.

20 'Asley Madison, "Suicides" Over Website Hack' *BBC*, 2 August 2015; I Thomson, 'More Deaths Linked to Asley Madison Hack as Scammers Move In' *TheRegister.co.uk*, 24 August 2015.

21 'Rise in Teen Suicide Connected to Social Media Popularity: Study' *New York Post*, 14 November 2017. Also S Knapton, 'Cyberbullying Makes Young People Twice as Likely to Self-harm or Attempt Suicide' *Telegraph*, 22 April 2018.

as technology and the internet pervades almost every aspect of society. There is often a criticism that, all too often, the law lags behind technology and current events.

However, in some respects the European Court of Justice (ECJ) or, as it has more recently been called, the Court of Justice of the European Union (CJEU) has demonstrated that it is not just familiar with modern concerns such as data protection and privacy but is sometimes ahead of the curve.

These are also some of the reasons why there is a lack of resources available to lawyers and other interested parties who need to consider RtbF academic issues. It is quite clear that PTF and OA problem issues are increasing, as will the instances where individuals seek to utilise the RtbF solution mechanism provided for in the GDPR.

The number of applications for RtbF to websites and other companies, complaints to data protection supervisory authorities when individuals are not satisfied with the response (and even lack of response in some instances) and calls to expand the RtbF, are naturally going to increase. There will be increasing case law and scrutiny of the problem issues and the GDPR RtbF.

Consider, for example, the current problem issues linked with current technology and applications with which the RtbF can assist. The ongoing march of technology means that there will likely be new situations and scenarios giving rise to additional problem content issues; these may need an expanded RtbF or new RtbFs.

There is, therefore, a need for guidance and information in the form of a legal textbook in relation to the RtbF specifically.[22] The problem issues while increasing (in volume) are relatively new; the GDPR RtbF only went live in May 2018; the number of RtbF applications are increasing; and naturally lawyers and other interested parties will need to be able to refer to formal considerations of these issues and not just what may exist in media commentary.

While this work will necessarily continue to expand over time, this first edition seeks to assist courts, lawyers, individuals, policymakers and other interested parties in relation to the following:

---

22 In relation to data protection more generally, see, eg, P Lambert, *A User's Guide to Data Protection* 3rd edition (Bloomsbury, 2018); R Jay, *Data Protection Law and Practice* (Sweet & Maxwell, 2012). In relation to internet legal issues see, eg, P Lambert (ed) *Gringras, The Laws of the Internet* 5th edition (Bloomsbury, 2018). In relation to social media legal issues see, eg, P Lambert, *International Handbook of Social Media Laws* (Bloomsbury, 2014); *Social Networking: Law, Rights and Policy* (Clarus Press, 2014); V Mayer-Schönberger, *Delete: The Virtue of Forgetting in the Digital Age* (Princeton University Press, 2009).

Problem:	the underlying internet problem issues giving right to the need for personal-takedown and forgetting (PTF) and the RtbF.
Solution:	the reaction and solution of the RtbF. One aspect is to look at the problem issues and whether these can be assisted by the RtbF; how successfully this solution in achieved; how user friendly and how fair and transparent the mechanisms and tools for implementing the RtbF actually are. Might there be impediments to using the RtbF?
Interpretation:	aiming to cover interpretation and description of Right to be Forgotten, RtbF in the GDPR – and national statute examples;
Practice:	practice impact and issues for judiciary and practitioner, including from claimant and respondent perspectives.
Case law:	such as when cases can and cannot be taken; rights and nuances; and defences.
Post-Brexit change:	The is a variety of post-Brexit changes being proposed in relation to data protection, the internet, and potentially the RtbF. These all need to be considered as these may affect some of the contours of this new and expanding legal right (but to clarify, will not prevent it).

Paul Lambert

March 2022

Table of Statutes

Table of EC Materials and International Conventions

Table of Cases

Abbreviations

CJEU	Court of Justice of the European Union
Commission	the EU Commission
controller	the organisation collecting, processing and holding the personal data (previously called the data controller)(see DPD 95/46 and the GDPR detailed definitions below)
data subject	the individual who the personal data relates to (see DPD 95/46 and the GDPR detailed definitions below)
Directive	see DPD 95/46
DPA	Data Protection Act
DPA 1998 (UK)	Data Protection Act 1998 (UK)
DPA 2018 (UK)	Data Protection Act 2018 (UK)
DPA 2018 (IE)	Data Protection Act 2018 (Ireland)(IE)
DPC	Data Protection Commission (previously the Data Protection Commissioner) (Ireland)
DPD 95/46	EU Data Protection Directive 1995 Directive 95/46 Directive 95/46/EC of the European Parliament and of the Council of 24 October 1995 on the protection of individuals with regard to the processing of personal data and on the free movement of such data
DPO	Data Protection Officer
EEA	European Economic Area, comprising the EU plus Iceland, Liechtenstein and Norway (Note, Switzerland has a similar type of arrangement with the EU.)
ECJ	European Court of Justice (now also referred to as CJEU)
EDPB	European Data Protection Board (pursuant to the GDPR)
GDPR	EU General Data Protection Regulation Regulation (EU) 2016/679 of the European Parliament and of the Council of 27 April 2016 on the protection of natural persons with regard to the processing of personal data and on the free movement of such data and repealing Directive 95/46/EC (General Data Protection Regulation) (Text with EEA relevance) OJ L 119, 4.5.2016, pp 1–88
	(The GDPR replaces DPD 95/46 and is directly effective throughout the EU without the need for separate sets of national implementing legislation.)
ICO	Information Commissioner's Office (UK)
Member State	Member State of the European Union (EU)
OA	online abuse

personal data	any data or information identifying or relating to the individual data subject (see DPD 95/46 and the GDPR detailed definitions below)
processor	an outsourced third-party organisation or related entity carrying out certain defined outsourced activities for and on behalf of the main data controller with the personal data eg outsourced payroll, outsourced direct marketing, etc (previously called the data processor)(see DPD 95/46 and the GDPR detailed definitions below)
Regulation	see the GDPR
RtbF	Right to be Forgotten Right to (takedown), erasure and forgetting as referred to under the GDPR Article 17(3)
RtbFs	Rights to be Forgotten
WP 29	the Article 29 Working Party on Data Protection (replaced by EDPB)

PART A

BACKGROUND

CHAPTER 1

The Problem of Time

I INTRODUCTION

1.1   In the modern internet environment, it is inevitable that many people will want to have online and digital content containing information about them taken down as a range of actual or potential problems can arise as a result of this content being accessible to others. This can be on a simple discretionary choice basis (ie, no fault).

That, however, is not to suggest that the internet and its general content is problematic *per se*. However, there are problem areas. In terms of our current review, we are focusing closely on one of these issues – Right to be Forgotten (RtbF) and the type of public content containing personal information and data in relation to identified or identifiable individuals. (This may also expand into less publicly available data as we learn more of problematic issues that can also arise with such data).

2 THE PROBLEM OF TIME

1.2   These important and timely issues cannot be divorced from time. The problem with time, however, is that it never stands still. Tempus fugit.[1] The contemporary discussion of erasure, forgetting and takedown of content relating to individuals must be placed in context. The context is historical insofar as the now recently historic EU Data Protection Directive (DPD 95/46) and similar laws and rules neither expressly contemplated the current problems with content issues nor expressly provided for them. In addition, the trajectory of these issues makes clear (see below) that when the modern commercial internet was initially adopted, the current erasure, forgetting and takedown problems did not exist, nor did the current explosion of technologies and services with which internet users are now familiar.

3 A WHOLE NEW WORLD

1.3   The date of the DPD 95/46 is 24 October 1995. Yet, there has been a world of changes since then. The commercial internet really arrived after 1995 in the late 1990s/early 2000s. Web 2.0 came post-1995. A great many events, internet developments and now familiar websites simply did not exist. Compare the date of the directive to later developments in relation to the following sample timeline.

---

1   The Latin phrase meaning 'time flies'.

Timeline	
Timeline	
1995:	Data Protection Directive (DPD 95/46)[2]
	and since ...
1996:	3D dancing baby viral video
1996:	Hotmail
1998:	Google
1999:	Napster
2003:	Skype
2003:	LinkedIn
2003:	iTunes
2004:	*World of Warcraft* online gaming
2004:	Facebook
2004:	Gmail
2005:	Broadband surpasses dial up
2005:	Reddit
2005:	YouTube
2006:	Twitter
2007:	iPhone
2008:	App Store
2009:	Uber
2009:	Bing
2010:	Pinterest
2010:	Instagram
2010:	Facebook reaches 400m members
2011:	Social media and Arab Springs
2011:	Snapchat
2012:	Facebook 1b monthly users
2013:	Edward Snowden reveals
2013:	Majority of Americans use online banking
2016:	TikTok
2016:	Google Assistant
2018:	Tim Berners-Lee calls for regulation and rights

---

2   Directive 95/46/EC of the European Parliament and of the Council of 24 October 1995 on the protection of individuals with regard to the processing of personal data and on the free movement of such data (Directive 95/46/EC) OJ 1995 L 281, p 31.

Obviously, this is not an exhaustive list. In addition, we see that from 2015 onwards, issues such as web 2.0, the Internet of Things (IoT) and devices,[3] drones, body cameras, vehicle number plate readers, facial recognition, state hacking, blockchain,[4] etc came about well after DPD 95/46.[5]

Importantly for present purposes, online abuse (OA), trolling and the very 'permanent' type of massive worldwide exposure that problem internet posting can bring were not issues or considerations in 1995, certainly not to the extent that they are now.

As Justice Warby indicates in *NT1* and *NT2*, '[m]any of the legislative provisions date back to before the advent of the internet and well before the creation of [internet search engines (ISEs)]. As often happens, statute has not kept pace with technical developments'.[6]

4   TWO DECADES FAR, FAR AWAY

1.4   The DPD of 1995,[7] while referring to deletion, was quite old and some would say outdated. Others might say that it was inadequate for the task of dealing with numerous issues which were small in scale or non-existent over 20 years ago. While it is sometimes possible for the legal draftsperson to look to the future, it is altogether different to have to predict the technologies that will become commonplace. It would be difficult to fully predict the increase in the number of data breaches or the massive increase in the mountains of personal data that would be breached in many of the new breach incidents, nor predict the range and severity of OA incidents that would arise.

5   INCREASING REACH

1.5   There are also other issues more pertinent to the issue at hand. In *Google Spain*, a Spanish national made a complaint to the Spanish Data Protection Agency (AEPD) against La Vanguardia newspaper, Google Spain and Google Inc, about newspaper articles which appeared in Google search results if his name was

---

3   SK Mizrahi, 'Ontario's New Invasion of Privacy Torts: Do They Offer Monetary Redress For Violations Suffered via the Internet of Things?' *Western Journal of Legal Studies* (Jan 2018) (8:1) COV2, 37.

4   B Verma, 'Blockchains in the GDPR Era' *International Journal for the Data Protection Officer, Privacy Officer and Privacy Counsel (IDPP)* (2018) (2:6) 15.

5   Directive 95/46/EC (OJ 1995 L 281, p 31).

6   *NT1 & NT2 v Google LLC* [2018] EWHC 799 (QB) (13 April 2018) Warby J, at para 10. The Information Commissioner was also an intervenor party to the proceedings. There are also calls for more regulation and less self-regulation, of particular online service providers. See A Matthews-King, 'Social Media Companies Need "Legal Duty of Care" to Protect Young Users, MPs Say' *Independent* (31 January 2019); C Hymas, 'Web Giants Face Legal Duty of Care for Children' *Daily Telegraph* (31 January 2019); each referring to the UK Parliamentary Science and Technology Committee investigations.

7   Directive 95/46/EC(OJ 1995 L 281, p 31).

put in. The pages mentioned a real estate auction following proceedings for the recovery of Mr González's social security debts. The AEPD rejected the claim against La Vanguardia stating that its information had been lawfully published, but it upheld the complaint against Google and requested that it withdrew the personal data from its search indexes. *Google Spain*[8] highlights the modern reality that once certain information is published online – sometimes by third parties and sometimes directly – it can be seen worldwide. Sometimes immediately, on other occasions over time, that online content can have adverse effects for the individual in question. It can impact personal relationships, personality, well-being, school and college applications and/or later employment.

6   RANGE

1.6   The full range of reasons and justifications as to why individuals want to have online content removed, as well as the full range of the nature of the particular content, will vary widely. Some will have stronger motivation than others; some may well be more urgent than others.

In some instances, it can be alarming. The range of damage can vary and, in some instances, be most severe. While it can apply to adults, teenagers and children, there may be greater relevance to younger people (eg, OA arising from class peers).

7   INCREASING PROBLEMS

1.7   Another important point is that any current discussion of erasure, forgetting and takedown issues, should recognise that an individual may be interested in these issues from the perspective of individual choice (ie, discretionary, no fault, subject to their current wishes) or from the perspective of making problem-related content unavailable on or via the internet. Factors contributing to each of these perspectives are the increasingly pervasive (and global public) nature of the availability of internet problem content relating to the individual once uploaded; the increasing avenues and instances for identifying harmful or otherwise problem content relating to the individual being available online; and also the increasing propensity for content once online to often be available in a permanent manner. Some commentators will often say things such as: 'once content is online it is permanent' or that 'once online, it can never come down'. This is not always or universally correct, however.

---

8   *Google Spain SL, Google Inc v Agencia Española de Protección de Datos (AEPD), Mario Costeja González*, Court of Justice (Grand Chamber), Case C-131/12, 13 May 2014. This relates to outdated results from search engines.

8   REAL EFFECTS

1.8   Once published online, other types of content can be used to undermine and attack the individual who is the subject of the data. People have lost their jobs in companies or have been refused employment in the first instance. Teachers have lost their positions. Students have been refused places in schools and colleges. Individuals have, no doubt, also been refused promotions. In some instances, this can occur without the individual even knowing. In even more serious instances, people have committed suicide as a result of the publication of personal data online (see Appendix 1). There is an unfortunate misconception that this only relates to children and teenagers. However, there are also examples of adults committing suicide as a result of material about them being published online (see below).

9   TRAGIC EFFECTS

1.9   At least two adults have committed suicide after the adult dating/adultery website Ashley Madison was hacked and customer lists and personal data was published online.[9] The damage was compounded when many individual victims then became the target of blackmail based on this leaked personal information.

The example of Amanda Todd, the Canadian teenager, who committed suicide after she was repeatedly attacked, trolled, and victimised online after an intimate picture was repeatedly posted, is just one of many illustrating the problems faced by teenagers. Sadly, increasing numbers of child and teenage suicides are being linked to the internet and OA.[10]

Both cases are examples of why there is a need for an ability for harmful personal data online to be taken down, deleted or forgotten, or even urgently taken down in some instances. On this trajectory comes Right to be Forgotten (RtbF) in the new General Data Protection Regulation (GDPR).[11] This provides one potential solution to the ongoing problem of OA, such as in the Amanda Todd type case or harmful outdated personal data, such as the individual in *Google Spain*.[12] (There is also policymaker discussion in relation to more mandatory regulatory

---

9   'Asley Madison, "Suicides" Over Website Hack', *BBC* (2 August 2015); I Thomson, 'More Deaths Linked to Asley Madison Hack as Scammers Move In', *TheRegister.co.uk* (24 August 2015).

10   'Rise in Teen Suicide Connected to Social Media Popularity: Study' *New York Post* (14 November 2017). See also S Knapton, 'Cyberbullying Makes Young People Twice as Likely to Self-harm or Attempt Suicide' *Telegraph* (22 April 2018). Another example is the death of Molly Russell, see for example, reference in C Hymas, 'Web Giants Face Legal Duty of Care for Children' *Daily Telegraph* (31 January 2019).

11   Regulation (EU) 2016/679 of the European Parliament and of the Council of 27 April 2016 on the protection of natural persons with regard to the processing of personal data and on the free movement of such data, repealing Directive 95/46/EC (General Data Protection Regulation) (Text with EEA relevance) OJ L 119, 4 May 2016, pp 1–88.

12   *Google Spain SL, Google Inc v Agencia Española de Protección de Datos (AEPD), Mario Costeja González*, Court of Justice (Grand Chamber), Case C-131/12, 13 May 2014.

protection solutions and less self-regulation, for internet companies, as well as online safety regulation (eg, UK).)[13]

So, we can see that the trajectory and escalation leading to the GDPR RtbF is of real-life import. It is in that sense everything but legalese, academic, or niche. The more written research and consideration of the RtbF and the underlying issues the better.

10 RTBF SOLUTION

1.10   RtbF is one potential solution or tool – or one aspect of the solution – to these problem content issues. The right to erasure, forgetting and takedown (RtbF) issues are very important legal, policy, and societal matters. Indeed, given technological developments and the increasing popularity of the internet and related technologies, devices, and services, the importance is growing. Revenge porn and Gamergate[14] are just two of many examples.

The importance of erasure, forgetting, and takedown of content (increasingly problem content) – primarily from the internet – relating to individuals is becoming increasingly relevant to both individuals, commentators, individual rights organisations, legal policymakers and those interested in the importance of individuality, personality, privacy and data protection. It goes without saying that these issues are now important subjects for consideration with courts and national data regulators (also referred to as data protection supervisory authorities).

11 INCREASING ADOPTION

1.11   The touchstones in the wider RtbF discussion is the GDPR and the decision in *Google Spain*.[15] However, the increasing rolling acceptance, implementation, and application of RtbF amongst online service providers is also very important.

---

13   An example comes from the (UK) parliamentary Science and Technology Committee, see A Matthews-King, 'Social Media Companies Need "Legal Duty of Care" to Protect Young Users, MPs Say' *Independent* (31 January 2019); C Hymas, 'Web Giants Face Legal Duty of Care for Children' *Daily Telegraph* (31 January 2019); 'Social Media Companies Must be Subject to Legal "Duty of Care"' Science and Technology Committee (31 January 2019) at www.parliament.uk/business/committees/committees-a-z/commons-select/science-and-technology-committee/news-parliament-2017/impact-of-social-media-young-people-report-published-17-19/. More recently, see, for example, J Waterson and D Milmo, 'Facebook Whistleblower Frances Haugen Calls for Urgent External Regulation' *Guardian* (25 October 2021); C Lima, 'A Whistleblower's Power: Key Takeaways From the Facebook Papers' *Washington Post* (26 October 2021).
14   Referring to OA attacks, harassment and sexism directed at female electronic game players and female games developers.
15   *Ibid.*

Following on from this, there should be a small number of RtbF notices which come to be disputed (compared to the total number of RtbF notices which should not be controversial). For example, a given service provider may not (yet) have online tools and procedures through which to file a RtbF notice. There may be examples where a service provider does not reply and action a RtbF notice or does not do so on a timely basis. (Obviously, these instances should reduce over time as greater adoption and compliance is achieved.)

A service provider in some instances may decide not to comply with a RtbF notice. Only some of these refusal decisions may be correct. The basis of and policy behind such refusal decisions will need to be considered. However, this should only apply to a small number of RtbF notices.

Therefore, in some instances, an unsatisfactory response in the refusal subset from a service provider in relation to a given RtbF notice may mean that it is referred or escalated to the national data protection supervisory authority who will assess the fairness of the refusal as well as its lawful basis. Normally, one would expect that some decisions will be upheld while others will not. In the latter instance, the complaint referral from the individual data subject will be upheld and the service provider will be directed by the national data regulator to comply with the RtbF notice.

Where a refusal has occurred or if there is no response from the service provider, an additional option is available. The individual data subject may escalate the matter to a court by way of legal action instead of making an escalation complaint to the national data protection supervisory authority. An example of this appears to be the successful *NT2*[16] case in the related UK High Court decision. This relates to an application to erase, forget and takedown old outdated case details which were still available on a search engine.

There is also another avenue through which a case may reach the courts. A national data regulator may decide in favour of the individual data subject, but the service provider refuses to comply with the RtbF notice. In such instances, the national data protection supervisory authority can issue proceedings against the service provider. Effectively, the national data protection supervisory authority will be seeking an order and directions against the service provider to comply.

By way of variation, it should be remembered that the various national data regulators have a variety of legal enforcement tools at their disposal. It may make an appropriate order, direction or notice to the service provider, which will contain specific directions as to the compliance actions which it must take to comply with the RtbF notice. In general, companies prefer to comply with an official enforcement notice but there will be some instances where the service provider refuses to comply. (Over time, we will come to see whether there is

---

16 *NT1 & NT2 v Google LLC* [2018] EWHC 799 (QB) (13 April 2018) Warby J. This is understood to be the first such successful case, in the UK High Court. The related case (insofar as being heard and decided at the same time, but otherwise unrelated), *NT1* was unsuccessful.

a higher level of non-compliance with RtbF official enforcement notices, as compared to other types of official enforcement notices that may issue from data regulators.) In those instances, the national data protection supervisory authority will bring legal proceedings against the service provider.

It will be recalled that *Google Spain* arose as a result of the national data protection supervisory authority taking the matter to court.

12 CONCLUSION

1.12   We will now consider in detail the increasing importance and necessity in the view of individuals, to have online content erased, forgotten or taken down – whether for personal so-called discretionary no-fault reasons (eg, it is no longer current; I no longer like it or no longer like it being available: X photograph was taken when I was a child and I do not want it online anymore; or Y photograph was from the office Christmas party over four years ago and is out of date; some of my college photographs may be better left offline as I have now graduated and am applying for employment positions and recruiters may see them; or potential problem issues are evident or have actually arisen in relation to particular online content).

The point is that the variety and nuances of why someone may wish online content erased, forgotten or taken down will vary. So too can the urgency. In addition, the service provider responsible for the website on which the content is available may be amenable instantly upon notice to assist the individual by complying with that notice. In other instances, the service provider may be reluctant. There are many nuances to considering the legitimacy of such a refusal. The refusal may be valid. It may also be invalid. There are also particular considerations in relation to past and current legal instruments which may need to be taken into account. Courts and national data regulators (and indeed other interested parties) are only starting to grapple with the issues and nuances.

What may become clearer by the end of this work is that:

- the right to erasure, forgetting and takedown (as provided for in the GDPR) should not be considered simply as RtbF is bad, full stop;[17]

- RtbF is good or necessary full stop; that it is fault or problem-based only; or that all individuals should be considered the same;[18]

---

17 This 'RtbF is Bad, Full Stop' attitude, regardless of any consideration of some of the justification and need for a RtbF (even revenge porn, child porn, rape, blackmail or other exploitative content) was originally suggested by Jimmy Wales, the Wikipedia founder. Subsequently, however, Wikipedia refined its position recognising that the issues were more nuanced than a simple bald 'Bad Full Stop' approach.

18 For example, consider whether children have a greater interest in having a RtbF or whether victims of online abuse have a greater interest in having a RtbF.

- all RtbF individuals filing RtbF notices have the same interests and exact same entitlements;

- the timeline for dealing with RtbF notices are all the same and that the same procedures must be followed for all;[19]

- all RtbF notices to media organisations are the same; ... or assume that *there is only one RtbF* (in the GDPR) or only one interest in making RtbF notices; or

- additional *Rights to be Forgotten* may not exist, not be needed and or may not be added in future.

After all, the range of and motivation in relation to problem content and other personal data content varies across a wide range. Equally, the age, stage in life and interest of individuals making RtbF notices will also vary widely. The importance of achieving takedown varies, is nuanced, and will reflect the nature of the personal effects, or potential effects, for the individual. Importantly, the lesson for organisations should be that they cannot sit back and wait for RtbF notices to arrive; or worse, assume that the organisation, for whatever reason, is unlikely to receive such a notice. Nor should it be assumed that nothing needs to be done in advance by way of preparation as the process, procedures, and identification of such notices differentiate them from other notices that may be received, such as individual data subject access notices.

One final lesson for organisations is that they cannot assume that knowing that there is a RtbF provision in the GDPR is enough on its own. Organisations and other interested parties must remain familiar with ongoing events such as most current official guidance, case law and developments at a national, EU, and even international level.[20]

Tempus fugit. Our consideration of these issues cannot remain static, as the content, problems and technology also change.

---

19   The temporal nature of RtbF notices and getting particular content removed from the internet will vary. Non-descript photographs which the individual simply wants taken down is altogether different from a live threat or blackmail scenario. The nature of whether, for example, RtbF notices regarding revenge porn necessitate different procedures, treatment and responses from other notices will need to be considered from an organisational and policy perspective. In addition, the availability of interim or injunctive type reliefs will ultimately also need to be considered. In time, these issues will no doubt be considered in greater detail by researchers as well as organisations, national data protection supervisory authorities and respective courts.
20   Those in the UK must still remain familiar with EU developments, regardless of the new DPA 2018 and UK GDPR.

CHAPTER 2

Big Bang

I INTRODUCTION

2.1   As Julia P Eckart correctly indicates, Google Spain[1] is certainly the case that was 'heard around the world'.[2] An interesting factor is the frequent surprise, if not astonishment, with which the case has been received in many quarters. *Google Spain*, in conjunction with RtbF contained in the General Data Protection Regulation (GDPR), have sometimes been regarded as so new and novel that they have created a 'Big Bang' effect, changing the existing legal order.

2 'BIG BANG' OVER-REACTION

2.2   *Google Spain* has been greeted with unwarranted surprise in many quarters. Some responses have been a clear over-reaction, others have adopted a critical knee-jerk reaction. It is interesting to consider some of these responses and where they may be coming from. There have been some extreme comments, for example, saying that the case and RtbF is a threat to the very internet itself.[3] Meg Ambrose suggests that it creates the risk of a digital dark age.[4] There have also been calls to amend and narrow the EU RtbF.[5] (Strictly speaking there was a *Google Spain* RtbF, and then later a GDPR RtbF).[6]

Why has there been such a reaction? There are various reasons. For one, some of the comments come from those who are narrowly focused on one issue or sector and who may be less familiar with some of the concerns and problem issues which exist. Surprisingly, some of these comments have come from people who are experts in certain aspects of the internet. Other comments can be discerned as being somewhat geographical; located in a somewhat (but not wholly) different legal and historical regime. Many of these later queries and

---

1   *Google Spain SL, Google Inc v Agencia Española de Protección de Datos (AEPD), Mario Costeja González*, Court of Justice (Grand Chamber), Case C-131/12, 13 May 2014.
2   JP Eckart, 'The Court Case Heard Around the World – *Google Spain SL v Agencia Espanola de Proteccion de Datos* – The Right to Be Forgotten and What It May Mean to the United States' *Dartmouth Law Journal* (2017) (15:1) 42.
3   'A Threat to the Internet' *Bloomberg Businessweek* (10 August 2018) (Issue 4587) 10.
4   ML Ambrose, 'A Digital Dark Age and the Right to Be Forgotten' (cover story) *Journal of Internet Law* (2013) (17:3) 1.
5   EA Shoor, 'Narrowing the Right to be Forgotten: Why the European Union Needs to Amend the Proposed Data Protection Regulation' *Brooklyn Journal of International Law* (2014) (39:1) 487.
6   Strictly speaking still, the *Google Spain* RtbF is really an RtbF under the then Data Protection Directive, ie, Directive 95/46.

attacks[7] are US centred. That is in no way to suggest that all discussion in and from the US is negative towards RtbF or the decision in *Google Spain*. Some of the negative commentary can also be seen to be sector specific. In some other instances it is possibly discernible that one interested sector may be seeking to rope in other sectors to add to the criticism or otherwise to bolster its position. So, it is necessary to examine from whom and where the criticism is coming. It is respectfully suggested that some of the more extreme responses are less than appropriate or warranted.

3   LESS 'BIG BANG', MORE PROGRESS

2.3   It is suggested that, in a large number of instances where there has been criticism, it is more surprise-based, than a deep-seated fundamental or principle-based criticism. One can also suggest that when many initial critics take a step back and begin to understand that individuals are facing real issues with problem content online and that it is fair or appropriate to seek to address some or all of these issues, the criticisms recede. They certainly become more nuanced. This is not to suggest that all criticism will disappear, but once properly considered it is difficult to postulate that there should be no RtbF at all. Such general criticism is all too blinkered.

While there have been adverse reactions, these recede or become more limited once it is seen that RtbF in the GDPR is less 'Big Bang' and more the result of progression in data protection and privacy laws.

EU data protection laws,[8] as illustrated in the many texts on the issue,[9] have long sought to protect individuals and the personal data of individual data subjects. It is also clear that these laws have a wide concept of what is personal

---

7   A Bunn, 'The Curious Case of the Right to be Forgotten' *Computer Law & Security Review* (2015) (31:3) 336; K Byrum, *The European Right to be Forgotten: The First Amendment Enemy* (Lexington, 2018); LE Minora, 'US Courts Should Not Let Europe's "Right to be Forgotten" Force the World to Forget' *Temple Law Review* (2017) (89:3) 609; McKay Cunningham, 'Privacy Law That Does Not Protect Privacy, Forgetting the Right to Be Forgotten' *Buffalo Law Review* (2017) (65:3) 495; GF Frosio, 'The Right to Be Forgotten: Much Ado About Nothing' *Colorado Technology Law Journal* (2017) (15:2) 307. Also note ND Costescu, 'Google Spain Decision – An Analysis of the Right to Be Forgotten – A Regression From Past Interpretations of ECJ' *Analele Universitatii din Bucuresti: Seria Drept* (2016) 64.

8   A Hartkamp, C Sieburgh, and W Devroe, *Cases, Materials and Text on European Law and Private Law* (Hart, 2017).

9   A Iftimiei, 'Protection of Personal Data: Aspects of European Law' *Analele Stiintifice Ale Universitatii Alexandru Ioan Cuza Din Iasi Stiinte Juridice* (2018) (64:1) 273; O Lynskey, *The Foundations of EU Data Protection Law* (OUP, 2015). I Sammut, *Constructing Modern European Private Law: A Hybrid System* (Cambridge Scholars Publishing, 2016); P Lambert, Understanding the New European Data Protection Rules (Routledge, 2018); P Lambert, Understanding the New EU Data Fine Rules (Kortext, 2021); P Lambert, A User's Guide to Data Protection (Bloomsbury, 2020).

data and data protection.[10] Complying with data protection and privacy laws[11] is important for all organisations, online or otherwise. Data protection and related researchers have long noted the increase in threats and content issues arising for individuals in the online environment. Data regulators have long been interested in assisting individuals and groups of individuals wherever possible. Recall also that even *Google Spain*, prior to the GDPR, was based on a data protection law originating from 1995.[12] Therefore, it is fair to suggest that the GDPR RtbF is the emanation of the advancement and progression of data protection and data protection laws, as compared to a perceived unforeseen, anomalous 'Big Bang' case.

4   ON POINT

2.4   Most of the commentary and reaction to *Google Spain* and the later GDPR RtbF, is considered commentary. It is on point and reflective of the view that problem content and online abuse (OA) both exists and is on the increase. It recognises that RtbF is fair, reasonable, balanced, and proportionate. Seeking particular takedowns from the internet is a fair issue to have addressed. There are real problems being created for individuals by certain categories of online content and a remedy is needed. The growing commentary also elucidates that there are a variety of different problem content issues and that different concerns are being raised by individuals. This discussion is both welcome and positive.

Even the general commentary in other countries is more balanced and reflective of the wide individual concerns underlying RtbF.[13] Overall, US reaction has

10   N Purtova, 'The Law of Everything: Broad Concept of Personal Data and Future of EU Data Protection Law' *Innovation and Technology* (2018) (10:1) 40.

11   L Determann, *Determann's Field Guide to Data Privacy Law: International Corporate Compliance* (Elgar, 2015); P Lambert, *Understanding the New European Data Protection Rules* (Taylor & Francis, 2017); P Lambert, Data Fines, Understanding the New EU Data Fine Rules (Kortext, 2021)

12   Namely, the DPD 95/46.

13   ML Rustad and S Kulevska, 'Reconceptualizing the Right to be Forgotten to Enable Transatlantic Data Flow' *Harvard Journal of Law* (2015) (28:2) 349; '*Google Spain SL v Agencia Espanola de Proteccion de Datos*' *Harvard Law Review* (128:2) 735; S Singleton, 'Balancing a Right to be Forgotten with a Right to Freedom of Expression in the Wake of *Google Spain v AEPD*' *Georgia Journal of International* Law (2015) (44:1) 165; S Alessi, 'Eternal Sunshine: The Right to be Forgotten in the European Union After the 2016 General Data Protection Regulation' *Emory International Law Review* (2017) (32:1) 145; MT Andrus, 'The Right to Be Forgotten in America: Have Search Engines Inadvertently Become Consumer Reporting Agencies' *Business Law Today* (2016) (5) 1; HJ McCarthy, 'All the World's a Stage: The European Right to be Forgotten Revisited from a US Perspective' *Journal of Intellectual Property Law* (2016) (11:5) 360.

become more balanced[14] and has focused on specific nuanced issues,[15] such as RtbF effects on domestic,[16] and international business[17] – and even whether there can be a positive benefit and opportunity.[18] Given the significance of relations and commerce between the US and EU, there has obviously been a comparison of the approaches to the issues around RtbF.[19] Cayce Myers compares US and EU concerns around social media policy issues.[20] Others ask whether the US has an answer to RtbF or what its response should be to the EU RtbF.[21] John W Dowdell refers to 'An American Right to be Forgotten'.[22] Others try to reconcile US and EU perspectives on RtbF.[23] Savanna Shuntich praises the 'long-awaited resurrection of privacy' and 'how Americans can reclaim their lives from the internet with' a RtbF'.[24] Various revelations during 2021 in relation to online harms and given how websites operate, also push the momentum towards federal privacy legislation (US) and online safety legislation (eg, US, UK).

5   SIMILARITY

2.5   While the GDPR RtbF is EU based, it is at the forefront of the focus seeking to assist and address the increasing problems individuals are having in particular with certain content in the modern internet environment. It is important to recall that these issues are causing problems for children, teenagers and adults worldwide, not merely those in the EU.

---

14   MJ Kelly and D Satolam, 'The Right to Be Forgotten' *University of Illinois Law Review* (2017) (1) 1; J Tashea, 'A New Era: Companies and their Lawyers are Bracing for a Wide-Ranging EU Data-Privacy Law That Takes Effect in May' *ABA Journal* (2018) (104:3) 34; A Forde, 'Implications of the Right To Be Forgotten' *Tulane Journal of Technology & Intellectual Property* (2015) (18) 83; JD Brougher, 'The Right to Be Forgotten: Applying European Privacy Law to American Electronic Health Records' *Indiana Health Law Review* (2016) (13:2) 510.

15   Rustad and Kulevska, 'Reconceptualizing the Right to be Forgotten to Enable Transatlantic Data Flow' above at 349.

16   A Seucan, 'The EU "Right to be Forgotten"' *Perspectives of Business Law Journal* (2014) (3:1) 336; J Lee, 'What the Right to be Forgotten Means to Companies: Threat or Opportunity?' *Procedia Computer Science* (2016) (91) 542; C Manny, 'The European Union's "Right to be Forgotten"' *Business Law Review* (2015) (48) 51.

17   F Gilbert, 'The Right of Erasure or Right to be Forgotten: What the Recent Laws, Cases and Guidelines Mean for Global Companies' *Journal of Internet Law* (2015) (18:8) 1.

18   Lee, 'What the Right to be Forgotten Means to Companies: Threat or Opportunity?' above at 542.

19   SW Royston, 'The Right to Be Forgotten: Comparing US and European Approaches' *St Mary's Law Journal* (2016) (48:2) 253.

20   C Myers, 'Digital Immortality vs "The Right to be Forgotten"': A Comparison of US and EU Laws Concerning Social Media Privacy' *Romanian Journal of Communications and Public Relations*, (2016) (16:3) 47.

21   ARW Hughes, 'Does the United States Have an Answer to the European Right to Be Forgotten' *Landslide* (2014) (7:1) 18.

22   JW Dowdell, 'An American Right to be Forgotten' *Tulsa Law Review* (2017) (52:2) 311.

23   SC Bennett, 'The "Right to Be Forgotten": Reconciling EU and US Perspectives' *Berkeley Journal of International Law* (2012) (30:1) 161.

24   S Shuntich, 'The Life, the Death and the Long-Awaited Resurrection of Privacy: How Americans can Reclaim their Lives from the Internet with a Right to be Forgotten' *Human Rights* (2016) (41:4) 2.

As would be expected, there have been calls for similar RtbFs in other jurisdictions including calls for a US version.[25]

Kimberly Peaslee, for example, asks if it is time for the US to have a RtbF.[26] There have been various calls for a US EU-style federal data protection framework,[27] taking aspects of the GDPR and including calls for a RtbF. There is also additional research into reconciling EU and US privacy enforcement differences[28] and there have been efforts to bridge the divide in common interest between EU and US privacy interests.[29]

Erin Cooper suggests that the US 'should adopt' a US RtbF – but in relation to the victims of crime.[30] Some commentary also seeks to consider a basis for a US RtbF (eg, James Lavelle asks if America can accept a RtbF as a publicity right).[31] US reaction to RtbF has both a general impact[32] and an impact on more sector-specific issues such as health data,[33] international data transfers,[34] search engine issues,[35] and even existing case law.[36] A RtbF in the US is also recognised

---

25 KAW Peaslee, 'Does the United States Need a "Right to Be Forgotten"?' *Computer & Internet Lawyer* (2016) (33:5) 12. Dowdell, 'An American Right to Be Forgotten' above at 311.

26 Peaslee, *ibid*, 12.

27 C Pope, 'Biometric Data Collection in an Unprotected World: Exploring the Need for Federal Legislation Protecting Biometric Data' *Journal of Law and Policy* (2018) (26:2) 769; R Davies, '"Conditioning an Entire Society": The Rise of Biometric Data Technology' Guardian (26 October 2021); JM Myers, 'Creating Data Protection Legislation in the United States: An Examination of Current Legislation in the European Union' *Case Western Reserve Journal of International Law* (1997) (29:1) 109; S Cutler, 'The Face-Off Between Data Privacy and Discovery: Why US Courts Should Respect EU Data Privacy Law when Considering the Production of Protected Information' *Boston College Law Review* (2018) (59:4) 1512.

28 N Narielwala, 'Post-Digital Era Reconciliation Between United States and European Union Privacy Law Enforcement' *Washington University Global Studies Law Review* (2018) (17:3) 707.

29 See, for example, *Privacy Bridges: EU and US Privacy Experts in Search of Transatlantic Privacy Solutions*, report (Massachusetts Institute for Technology Computer Science and Artificial Intelligence Laboratory and the Institute for Information Law of the University of Amsterdam, 21 October 2015); see also https://privacybridges.mit.edu/.

30 E Cooper, 'Following in the European Union's Footsteps: Why the United States Should Adopt Its Own Right to Be Forgotten Law for Crime Victims' *John Marshall Journal of Information Technology and Privacy Law* (2015) (32:3) 185.

31 JJ Lavelle, 'Search Query: Can America Accept a Right to Be Forgotten as a Publicity Right' *Brooklyn Law Review* (2018) (83:3) 1115.

32 Eckart, 'The Court Case Heard Around the World – *Google Spain SL v Agencia Espanola de Proteccion de Datos* – The Right to Be Forgotten and What It May Mean to the United States' above at 42.

33 Brougher, 'The Right to Be Forgotten: Applying European Privacy Law to American Electronic Health Records' above at 510.

34 Rustad and Kulevska, 'Reconceptualizing the Right to be Forgotten to Enable Transatlantic Data Flow' above at 349.

35 MT Andrus, 'Constitutional Issues in Granting Americans a "Right to Dispute" Personal Information With Search Engines Akin to the Existing Remedy Afforded to Europeans Via Europe's Right to Be Forgotten' *Business Law Today* (2016) (Nov) 1.

36 R Titiriga, 'Right to Privacy & Right to Be Forgotten (on Internet): A New Reading of Gonzales Case' *Law Series of the Annals of the West University of Timisoara* (2018) (1) 49; CD Tobin and CN Walz, 'Right to be Forgotten: Expungement Laws Raise New Challenges on the 40th Anniversary of *Cox Broadcasting v Cohn*' *Communications Lawyer* (2015) (31:4) 4.

as being (one of the) solution(s) for personal data breaches.[37] There is also commentary in terms of the need for guidance in implementing a US RtbF[38] and related discussion in terms of the existing Federal Trade Commission (FTC) and its ambit in terms of privacy issues.[39] There has even been a call for an inter-American approach to RtbF.[40] However, some have recognised the need for a RtbF in the US and how it helps to restore privacy interests for individuals. This may restore the balance which had shifted too far in favour of corporate interests. It has been described as a 'resurrection' of privacy and a way that individuals (in the US) can 'reclaim their lives from the internet with a Right to be Forgotten'.[41]

Steven Bennett, for example, asks if 'America is ready for the Right to Be Forgotten'.[42] Others refer to a US RtbF[43] and also whether the EU's RtbF could exist in the US[44] and whether there is a need for one.[45] Others refer to the case for US privacy and RtbF.[46] Some commentators (eg, Antani) ask whether the EU version of RtbF could exist in the US.[47]

Mackenzie Olson refers to the Ashley Madison (marketed as an affair dating website) data breach case and 'the Federal Trade Commission as executor of a narrow Right to Be Forgotten in the United States'.[48] Of course, at the end of the day individuals generally have the same interests and the same concerns. People in both the US and the EU all have data protection and privacy interests.[49]

---

37 A Stenning, 'Gone But Not Forgotten: Recognizing the Right to Be Forgotten in the US to Lessen the Impacts of Data Breaches' *San Diego International Law Journal* (2016) (18:1) 129.
38 HC Webb, '"People Don't Forget": The Necessity of Legislative Guidance in Implementing a US Right to Be Forgotten' *George Washington Law Review* (2017) (85:4) 1304.
39 CJ Hoofnagle, *Federal Trade Commission Privacy Law and Policy* (CUP, 2016); DJ Solove and W Hartzog, 'The FTC and the New Common Law of Privacy' *Columbia Law Review* (2014) (114:3) 583.
40 M Garrido Villareal, 'The Grey Digital Divide and the Right to be Forgotten: An Inter-American Approach' *Asia Pacific Journal of Health Law & Ethics* (2017) (11:1) 83.
41 Shuntich, 'The Life, the Death and the Long-Awaited Resurrection of Privacy: How Americans can Reclaim their Lives from the Internet with a Right to be Forgotten' above at 2
42 SC Bennett, 'Is America Ready for the Right to Be Forgotten' *New York State Bar Association Journal* (2016) (88:1) 11.
43 Dowdell, 'An American Right to be Forgotten' above at 311; K Vick, 'The Right to be Forgotten in the US' *The Los Angeles Daily Journal*, 7 November 2017 (130:216) 1.
44 R Antani, 'The Resistance of Memory: Could the European Union's Right to Be Forgotten Exist in the United States' *Berkeley Technology Law Journal, Annual Review 2015* (2015) (30) 1173.
45 Peaslee, 'Does the US Need a "Right to be Forgotten"?' above at 6.
46 R Belbin, 'When Google Becomes the Norm: The Case for Privacy and the Right to Be Forgotten' *Dalhousie Journal of Legal Studies* (2017) (26) 17.
47 Antani, 'The Resistance of Memory: Could the European Union's Right to Be Forgotten Exist in the United States' above at 1173.
48 M Olson, 'Equitable Recovery for Ashley Madison Hack Victims: The Federal Trade Commission as Executor of a Narrow Right to Be Forgotten in the United States' *Washington Journal of Law, Technology & Arts* (2016) (12:1) 61.
49 MA Weiss and K Archick, *Data Privacy and Protection in the EU and the United States* (Congressional Research Service: Report: 2/12/2016) 1.

EU and California state data protection interests[50] and rules are actually quite similar and are certainly interested in seeking to recognise and protect the rights and interests of individual data subjects. It may be that an express US RtbF is state-based before it is federal based. However, there is increasing pressure in the US for a federal privacy law. This is gaining added momentum with the increasing vocal support for such a law from technology companies, including Apple,[51] Facebook, Microsoft, and Twitter.

6 CONCLUSION

2.6   The US perspective on the EU RtbF[52] ranges from commentary,[53] assessments,[54] Bode and Jones refer to US attitudes to RtbF,[55] the consideration of data transfers[56] between the EU and US (a logical niche area for consideration), search engines and RtbF,[57] implications for existing case law,[58] US constitutional issues,[59] US privacy issues and laws,[60] EU and US norms,[61] US and EU data

---

50 D Vogel and J FM Swinnen, *Transatlantic Regulatory Cooperation: The Shifting Roles of the EU, the US and California* (Elgar, 2011).

51 T Cook, 'Apple Tim Cook Privacy Speech at ICDPPC 2018' *International Journal for the Data Protection Officer, Privacy Officer and Privacy Counsel (IDPP)* (2018) (2:10) 8.

52 McCarthy, 'All the World's a Stage: The European Right to be Forgotten Revisited from a US Perspective' above at 360.

53 Kelly and Satola, 'The Right to be Forgotten' above at 65.

54 D Lyons, 'Assessing the Right to be Forgotten' *Boston Bar Journal* (2015) (59:4) 26.

55 L Bode and M Jones, 'Ready to Forget: American Attitudes Toward the Right to be Forgotten' Information Society (2017) (33:2) 76.

56 C Kuner, *Transborder Data Flows and Data Privacy Law* (OUP, 2013); P Schwartz and K-N Peifer, 'Transatlantic Data Privacy Law' Georgetown Law Journal (2017) (106) 115; Rustad and Kulevska, 'Reconceptualizing the Right to be Forgotten to Enable Transatlantic Data Flow' above at 349; J-S Berge, Stephane Grumbach and V Zeno-Zencovich, 'The Datasphere, Data Flows Beyond Control and the Challenges for Law and Governance' *European Journal of Comparative Law and Governance* (2018) (5:2) 144

57 Andrus, 'The Right to Be Forgotten in America: Have Search Engines Inadvertently Become Consumer Reporting Agencies?' above at 1; A Slane, 'Search Engines and the Right to Be Forgotten: Squaring the Remedy with Canadian Values on Personal Information Flow' *Osgoode Hall Law Journal* (2018) (55:2) 349.

58 Tobin and Walz, 'Right to be Forgotten: Expungement Laws Raise New Challenges on the 40th Anniversary of *Cox Broadcasting v Cohn*' above at 4.

59 Andrus, 'Constitutional Issues in Granting Americans a "Right to Dispute" Personal Information with Search Engines Akin to the Existing Remedy Afforded to Europeans Via Europe's Right to Be Forgotten' above at 1.

60 Myers, 'Creating Data Protection Legislation in the United States: An Examination of Current Legislation…' above at 109; C Schreiber, 'Google's Targeted Advertising: An Analysis of Privacy Protections in an Internet Age' *Transnational Law* (2014) (24:1) 269; Hoofnagle, *Federal Trade Commission Privacy Law and Policy*; Solove and Hartzog, 'The FTC and the New Common Law of Privacy' above at 583; W Hartzog, *Privacy Blueprint, the Battle to Control Design of New Technologies* (Harvard University Press, 2018); W Hartzog, 'Are Privacy Laws Deficient?' *International Journal for the Data Protection Officer, Privacy Officer and Privacy Counsel (IDPP)* (2018) (2:10) 17; N Richards and W Hartzog, 'Taking Trust Seriously in Privacy Law' *Stanford Technology Law Review* (2016) (19:3) 431.

61 G de Búrca and J Scott, *Law and New Governance in the EU and the US* (Hart, 2006).

protection laws,[62] and US–EU data protection issues and protections.[63] Some of these reactions are disproportionate. Some may be self-interested. Importantly, they need to consider the interests of individuals and the problem content issues facing individuals. These problem issues and solutions, need to be put into proper context.

62 Vogel and Swinnen, *Transatlantic Regulatory Cooperation: The Shifting Roles of the EU, the US and California.*
63 Prof Dr HC Burkhard Hess and Dr CM Mariottini, *Protecting Privacy in Private International and Procedural Law and by Data Protection: European and American Developments* (Nomos, 2015); RA Miller, *Privacy and Power: A Transatlantic Dialogue in the Shadow of the NSA-Affair* (CUP, 2017); CJ Bennett and CD Raab, 'The Adequacy of Privacy: The European Union Data Protection Directive and the North American Response' *Information Society* (1997) (13:3) 245; Berge, Grumbach and Zeno-Zencovich, 'The Datasphere, Data Flows Beyond Control and the Challenges for Law and Governance' above at 144; Schwartz and Peifer, 'Transatlantic Data Privacy Law' above at 115.

CHAPTER 3

Problems Facing Individuals

I INTRODUCTION

3.1   One of the predominant reasons[1] as to why RtbF is topical at this time is because there are increasing examples of problem content being uploaded to the internet, in many instances by parties other than the individual data subject. RtbF is referred to in greater detail below, but it is useful at this stage to highlight that there are new enhanced provisions which can be applicable to individual data subjects who are concerned with particular online content and who may wish to seek to have it removed either entirely or from more specific public access.

The nature of the internet has changed immensely since 1995. The risk to individuals in relation to their personal data being published online has greatly increased over the past two decades and new risks have arisen, and continue to arise. This offers context as to the need for RtbF.

The problem of time demonstrates a need for new data protection rules per se. Old static rules can become outdated and need updating, or as can often arise with new technologies, there can be gaps in the law and a lack of solutions even where discernible risks arise. However, the scale of technological internet changes and developments also demonstrate the need for new rights to address particular problem issues, in harmful problem content online. RtbF is just one such example to assist in the takedown of personal data which does not need to be online and which may be outdated or should never have been there in the first place. In addition, certain types of personal data can have consequential and harmful effects once online. This increases the imperative for solutions such as removal.

Some of the new problem content risks are referred to below.[2] It is important to note that there is no defined and delimited list of risks and problem content online as these issues for individuals continue to grow. The examples below are illustrative. Also see reference to new problem issues developing, as referred to

---

1   There are, of course, other reasons. These include the new GDPR which expressly refers to and provides for RtbF; the momentous *Google Spain* decision; the surprise with which many received the announcement of the decision (not least being Google, which Professor Jonathan Zittrain of Harvard University describes, after discussion with Google, as a 'WTF' response reaction (ie, 'WTF just happened'); and the global attention which accompanied the decision. For those unfamiliar with the above acronym, the author will leave it up to readers to look up in an internet search.
2   However, no list such as this will be fully complete, or will remain static in a dynamic technological environment.

below and in Ch 26 and 26.7 below. As the sensitivity and risk of the personal data increases (eg, family data protection, sexual preferences, illnesses and privacy interests – and increasingly data on political preferences)[3] so too does the level of interest in getting problem content taken down from the internet.

2   MEMORY AND 'PERMANENCE'

3.2   One of the problems facing individuals is that information, once online, can become almost permanent. At least that is the common perception. This can have implications for the remainder of their life. Where the information becomes problem content, whether by reason of inaccuracy, malicious posting, becoming outdated, viral attack, etc, the individual is justified in proactively seeking to have it removed. Ângela Pereira et al refer to the need to examine the 'ethics of memory in a digital age'.[4] They also refer to these issues in the context of RtbF.[5] The EU Commission also highlights certain data ethics and data protection issues.[6]

Consideration of memory and forgetting[7] in relation to online content issues will need continuing focus. Authors such as Viktor Mayer-Schönberger in his groundbreaking publication *Delete: The Virtue of Forgetting in the Digital Age*,[8] poignantly highlights, by way of examples, the damage that can occur and the need for solutions to online forgetting and permanence issues. These examples serve as a precursor to the ultimate RtbF contained in the General Data Protection Regulation (GDPR).

While there is merit to the suggestion that there can be an almost permanent character to the personal data and information once online, like so many things, this is not an absolute. Nor should it be. Content online can recede from prominence and importantly, it can be taken down. We should be circumspect in terms of over-generalising.

---

3   R Matefi, 'Interference in the Exercise of the Right to Private and Family Life in the Context of National and European Regulations and ECHR Jurisprudence' *Bulletin of the Transilvania University of Braşov: Series VII: Social Sciences, Law* (2018) (11:60) 65.

4   Â Pereira, A Ghezzi and L Vesnic-Alujevic, *The Ethics of Memory in a Digital Age: Interrogating the Right to be Forgotten* (Palgrave Macmillan, 2014).

5   *Ibid.*

6   EU Commission, *Ethics and Data Protection* (14 November 2018).

7   R Antani, 'The Resistance of Memory: Could the European Union's Right to Be Forgotten Exist in the United States' *Berkeley Technology Law Journal*, Annual Review (2015) (30) 1173.

8   V Mayer-Schönberger, *Delete: The Virtue of Forgetting in the Digital Age* (Princeton, 2011). Also see P Lambert, *International Handbook of Social Media Laws* (Bloomsbury, 2014); P Lambert, *Social Networking: Law, Rights and Policy* (Clarus Press, 2014); D Wright and P de Hert, *Enforcing Privacy: Regulatory, Legal and Technological Approaches* (Springer, 2016); P Lambert, Data Fines, Understanding the New EU Data Fine Rules (Kortext, 2021); P Lambert, Data Protection, Privacy Regulators and Supervisory Authorities (Bloomsbury, 2020).

In some instances, references to the so-called 'permanence' and 'genie out of the bottle'-type arguments can be made by an interested party, as opposed to a disinterested observer. The 'permanence' argument is a tactic or stratagem sometimes used to suggest that it is futile to try to do anything. As such, it must be considered critically. This argument also ignores the fact that individuals can suffer damage; and can have a fair and legitimate interest in seeking to have problem content taken down – and non-problem content personal data.

Also, the interest of individual data subjects can have a contemporary focus in mind, but can also be future focused in terms of wanting to proactively prevent future damage occurring, each of which are also legitimate pursuits.

3   DIGITAL MEMORY AND AUTOMATION

3.3   A further developing issue relates to how digital memory may be utilised in an automated manner. Elena Esposito refers to 'algorithmic memory' and RtbF issues. She notes for example and by way of contextualisation, that '[w]hat distinguishes digital memory is … its ability to process information without understanding'.[9] There are increasing risk and safety considerations which mirror the interests sought to be protected via RtbF. The UK, for example, is considering a new internet and digital safely law.

There are also vastly increased amounts of digital information available which contains personal information, whether in live database or online accessible archives.[10] Politicians and the wider public are only starting to discover the importance of data signals collections and profiling categorisation.

The GDPR carries additional obligations and restrictions where personal data is to be used in an automated or automated processing manner (and which may impact the individual).[11] The main provision provides, inter alia, that:

> The data subject shall have the right not to be subject to a decision based solely on automated processing, including profiling, which produces legal effects concerning him or her or similarly significantly affects him or her.[12]

---

9   E Esposito, 'Algorithmic Memory and the Right to be Forgotten on the Web' *Big Data & Society* (2017) (4) 1.

10   A Mkadmi, Archives in the Digital Age: Preservation and the Right to be Forgotten (Wiley, 2021); I Jiménez-Castellanos Ballesteros, 'The Conflict Between the Right to be Forgotten of the Criminal History and Freedom of Information: Digital Newspaper Archives (In this Respect the Spanish Constitutional Court Judgment of June 4, 2018 and the European Court of Human Rights' Judgment in the M.L. and W.W. vs. Germany Case, June 28, 2018)' Revista de Derecho Político (2019) (1:106) 137; C Quelle, 'GC and Others v CNIL on the Responsibility of Search Engine Operators for Referring to Sensitive Data: The End of 'Right to be Forgotten' Balancing?' European Data Protection Law Review (EDPL) (2019) (5:3) 438.

11   See GDPR Art 22 (re automated individual decision making, including profiling) and Art 21 (right to object).

12   GDPR Art 22.

Genevieve Laura Silvanus refers to the 'the ethics of memory in a digital age'.[13] She also refers to RtbF. Also consider the EU document in relation data ethics and data protection.[14]

Previous considerations of internet and IT law generally[15] and past internet dispute issues[16] may need to give way to increased protection for personal data[17] to cover new risks and new problem issues.

Databases and Data Pools

3.4 Compounding the potential for risk and problem content for individuals is the fact that electronic or digital data is increasingly stored in ever larger

13 G Laura Silvanus, 'The Ethics of Memory in a Digital Age – Interrogating the Right to be Forgotten' *Records Management Journal* (2016) (26:1) 102.

14 EU Commission, *Ethics and Data Protection* (14 November 2018). Also see CR La Roche, 'The "Right to Be Forgotten": An Ethical Dilemma' Journal of Leadership, Accountability & Ethics (2020) (17:3) 36; LT Price, K Sanders and WN Wyatt (eds), The Routledge Companion to Journalism Ethics (Routledge, 2021); CE Clark, KK Chang and SP Melvin, Business and Society: Ethical, Legal, and Digital Environments (Sage, 2020); G Aitchison and S Meckled-Garcia, 'Against Online Public Shaming: Ethical Problems with Mass Social Media' Social Theory (2021) (47:1) 1; M Odlanicka-Poczobutt and A Szyszka-Schuppik, 'The Right to be Forgotten as an Element of the Personal Data Protection System in the Organisation' Organization & Management Quarterly (2020) (51:3) 57; N Hodge, 'Getting Smart About Artificial Intelligence: How Can Companies Avoid the Risks and Regulatory Pitfalls of Artificial Intelligence-Based Technology?' Risk Management (2021) (68:8) 20; DW Linna Jr and WJ Muchman, 'Ethical Obligations to Protect Client Data When Building Artificial Intelligence Tools: Wigmore Meets AI' Professional Lawyer (2020) (27:1) 27; I Jiménez-Castellanos Ballesteros, 'The Conflict Between the Right to be Forgotten of the Criminal History and Freedom of Information: Digital Newspaper Archives (In this respect the Spanish Constitutional Court Judgment of June 4, 2018 and the European Court of Human Rights' Judgment in the M.L. and W.W. vs. Germany case, June 28, 2018)' Revista de Derecho Político (2019) (1:106) 137; A Trites, 'Black Box Ethics: How Algorithmic Decision-Making is Changing How We View Society and People: Advocating for the Right for Explanation and the Right to be Forgotten in Canada' Global Media Journal: Canadian Edition (2020) (12:1) 18; A Olteanu, J Garcia-Gathright, M de Rijke and M Ekstrand, ' FACTS-IR: Fairness, Accountability, Confidentiality, Transparency, and Safety in Information Retrieval' SIGIR Forum (2019) (53:2) 20.

15 L Edwards, *Law, Policy and the Internet* (Hart, 2019); GJH Smith, *Internet Law and Regulation* (Sweet and Maxwell, 2019); A Murray, *Information Technology Law* (OUP, 2019); R Kennedy and MH Murphy, *Information and Communications Technology Law in Ireland* (Clarus, 2017); C Reed, *Making Laws for Cyberspace* (OUP, 2012); C Reed, *Computer Law* (OUP, 2011); I Kerr, *Lessons From the Identity Trail* (OUP, 2009); D Kelleher, *Information Technology Law in Ireland* (Bloomsbury, 2007). Also D Bainbridge, *Information Technology and Intellectual Property Law* (Bloomsbury, 2019).

16 E Katsh and O Rabinovich-Einy, *Digital Justice, Technology and the Internet of Disputes* (OUP, 2017).

17 C Pope, 'Biometric Data Collection in an Unprotected World: Exploring the Need for Federal Legislation Protecting Biometric Data' *Journal of Law and Policy* (2018) (26:2) 769; R Davies, '"Conditioning an Entire Society": The Rise of Biometric Data Technology' Guardian (26 October 2021); N Purtova, *Property Rights in Personal Data, A European Perspective* (Kluwer, 2012) at 53; P Lambert, 'IP and PI Takedowns: Comparing and Contrasting the Right to be Forgotten' European Intellectual Property Review (2019) (41:6) 381.

databases. A significant portion of such data in these databases is information which is personal data identifying or relating to individuals (or which can be linked to such information).

Many modern activities also mean that some databases are also expanding exponentially. Ever more personal data is held. An example of this is the process of live signals data collections on social media websites.

Until relatively recently, the risk attached to a given database may reduce gradually over time as it becomes less necessary for current or live activities, and graduated more to an archive of past records. As such it comes to be less accessible internally.

New software intelligence capabilities are being promoted to businesses, yet there can still be important commercial meaning or insights to be gathered even from older databases or archives. Applications now mean that what were once older and restricted access databases (in practice, and as a result of data laws) now become increasingly live or used for current activities. The memory of individuals' personal information in old databases and archives is no longer receded with time.

Some modern internet activities also mean that there is in practice an always-on database. The content, activities, and communications of individual users, and what an internet company may (1) pull from such data, (2) push to individuals, and (3) push to advertisers, are effectively constant activities. Nothing falls into old non-live archives or forgetting. Every activity, every insight, every preference, every profile (whether correct or otherwise) compounds – as will the potential for risks and problems arising for individuals. Social media is a good example of this, but it is by no means so exclusive.

The need for solutions, including RtbF, in relation to databases[18] and archives[19] for when problems arise becomes ever greater, and also ever more apparent. This is leading to increasing policymaker scrutiny on harmful effect issues, eg, US hearings, UK hearings, EU hearings and policymaker investigations.[20] The UK is also proposing specific online safety laws, and which may come to be influential as a trend elsewhere.

---

18 S Shastri, V Banakar, M Wasserman, A Kumar and V Chidambaram, 'Understanding and Benchmarking the Impact of GDPR on Database Systems' Proceedings of the VLDB Endowment (2020) (13:7) 1064; P Lambert, 'The Right to be Forgotten: Context and the Problem of Time' Communications Law (2019) (24:2) 74.
19 A Mkadmi, Archives in the Digital Age: Preservation and the Right to be Forgotten (Wiley, 2021); Lambert, 'The Right to be Forgotten: Context and the Problem of Time', ibid.
20 For example, see C Duffy, 'State Attorneys General Launch Investigation into Meta-owned Instagram's Impact On Kids', CNN, 18 November 2021.

Tagging and Linking

3.5　　The issue of digital memory and its (perceived) near permanence is compounded further by the separate issues of tagging and linking. These tools now mean that it is very easy to identify and find content relating to an individual online.[21] It is possible that people are visible online in photographs uploaded to social media which they do not want. They may not have consented to the image or content, nor to being tagged, linked or otherwise identified in the content.

In addition, social media websites can permit people to be tagged and labelled in uploaded photographs, without their consent. (On some sites, there are now options to set consent mechanisms or tools and/or to notify individuals if they are being tagged in advance and possibly to seek consent in advance.) There is also the separate issue of historic online images in which individuals may have been tagged previously.

Current tagging and linking capabilities are now being surpassed by even more enhanced capabilities to search, locate and link data which was not previously linkable or identifiable, part of the chain of information[22] which relates to identified and identifiable individuals. Even if only a part of this relates to problem content, that is still significant. Various internet companies have enhanced identification, linking and tagging tools. Facebook, for example, has developed an enhanced capacity to link, index and reveal information and photographs from its website using the Facebook Graph Search tool as well as new facial recognition applications. There has been some controversy as to which jurisdictions these types of tools may be applied.

An increasing variety of companies are also developing and utilising facial recognition technologies. Facial recognition tools on Facebook were originally activated and then turned off in the EU as a result of official concerns raised in an audit investigation by the (then) Irish Data Protection Commissioner.[23]

However, it should be noted that Facebook announced in 2021 that it would cease using facial recognition tools and would delete associated data.

It is also noted that users were requested to submit nude photographs to be scanned in such a manner as to aid in dealing with revenge porn attacks.[24] By submitting such photographs and presumably furnishing associated specific terms

---

21　Tagging, without getting too technical, refers largely to the ability to tag or label particular content or more particularly to tag, label and name particular identified individuals in that content, eg tagging, labelling, naming or otherwise identifying an individual in a photograph or video.

22　Purtova, *Property Rights in Personal Data* at 37.

23　Data Protection Commissioner, *Facebook Ireland Limited, Report of Re-Audit* (21 September 2012). Since the Data Protection Act 2018 (IE), the Irish data protection supervisory authority has become the Data Protection Commission.

24　For example, being so requested by Facebook.

and acknowledgements, there may be an intention to obtain not just consent, but explicit consent.

These concerns are even more enhanced as the ability to identify, link and tag individuals and their personal data and information (including photographs, videos, and facial images) increases with advances in technology and the development of more identification tools. The more we move towards the Cloud and Big Data[25] and their interface with social media,[26] online activities and online content, the greater the need for examination of identification, takedown, forgetting and RtbF. One writer refers to how linking, association, and public references can impact a person's career.[27]

One of the problems arise because humans (often) eventually forget, but machines and computers – and the internet – remember. The rise of artificial intelligence (AI) has increased computer and internet memory and enhanced it with the ability to connect more and more dots to make data chains identifying increasing amounts of personal data relating to individuals. This has implications in terms of RtbF[28] in making it more timely, reasonable and justified.

25 W Kuan, Hon, J Hörnle and C Millard, 'Data Protection Jurisdiction and Cloud Computing – When Are Cloud Users and Providers Subject to EU Data Protection Law? The Cloud of Unknowing' *International Review of Law, Computers & Technology* (2012) (26:2/3) 129. Also see V Mayer-Schönberger and Kenneth Cukier, *Big Data* (John Murray, 2013).

26 S Rogerson, 'Wireless and Social Media Influence' *International Journal for the Data Protection Officer, Privacy Officer and Privacy Counsel (IDPP)* (2018) (2:7) 12.

27 JJ Brennan, 'Guilt by Association – Public References and Their Impact on Your Security Career' Security: Solutions for Enterprise Security Leaders (2020) (57:2) 20.

28 E Fosch Villaronga, P Kieseberg and T Li, 'Humans Forget, Machines Remember: Artificial Intelligence and the Right to Be Forgotten' *Computer Law & Security Review* (2018) (34:2) 304. Also see T Sérgio Cabral, 'Forgetful AI: AI and the Right to Erasure under the GDPR' *European Data Protection Law Review* (EDPL) (2020) (6:3) 378; M Odlanicka-Poczobutt and A Szyszka-Schuppik, 'The Right to be Forgotten as an Element of the Personal Data Protection System in the Organisation' *Organization & Management Quarterly* (2020) (51:3) 57; N Hodge, 'Getting Smart About Artificial Intelligence: How Can Companies Avoid the Risks and Regulatory Pitfalls of Artificial Intelligence-Based Technology?' *Risk Management* (2021) (68:8) 20; I Jiménez-Castellanos Ballesteros, 'The Conflict Between the Right to be Forgotten of the Criminal History and Freedom of Information: Digital Newspaper Archives (In this respect the Spanish Constitutional Court Judgment of June 4, 2018 and the European Court of Human Rights' Judgment in the M.L. and W.W. vs. Germany case, June 28, 2018)' *Revista de Derecho Político* (2019) (1:106) 137; A Trites, 'Black Box Ethics: How Algorithmic Decision-Making is Changing How We View Society and People: Advocating for the Right for Explanation and the Right to be Forgotten in Canada' *Global Media Journal: Canadian Edition* (2019) (11:2) 18; HJ Watson, 'Avoid Being Creepy in the Use of Personal Data and Algorithms' *Business Intelligence* (2019) (24:2) 5; I Pilving and M Mikiver, 'Kratt as an Administrative Body: Algorithmic Decisions and Principles of Administrative Law' *Juridica International* (2020) (29) 47; A Kesa and T Kerikmäe, 'Artificial Intelligence and the GDPR: Inevitable Nemeses?' *TalTech Journal of European Studies* (2020) (10:3) 67; C Wendehorst, 'Strict Liability for AI and Other Emerging Technologies' *Journal of European Tort Law* (2020) (11:2) 150; Quang-Vinh Dang, 'Right to Be Forgotten in the Age of Machine Learning' chapter in *Advances in Digital Science* (ICADS, 2021) 403; 'Professor Calls For Access to Facebook Algorithms and Data' *Yahoo! Finance*, 6 October 2021, referring to Sinan Aral, David Austin Professor of Management at the MIT Sloan School of Management and MIT Initiative on Digital Economy.

Social Media

3.6   Social media websites are increasingly seen as the location – and also the cause – of significant risks and problem content for individuals.[29] Of course it goes without saying that there can be many genuine and even beneficial outcomes from social media. In addition, social media is a broad term. Even social networking can mean somewhat different things depending on the context ranging from social networking activities on social media websites to computer social network analysis, of which the the latter can sometimes have nothing at all to do with internet activities.

It would be remiss, however, to ignore the current controversies involving whistleblower disclosures revealing internal company research indicating that WhatsApp can be harmful to the health and wellbeing of quite significant numbers of users who are teenage girls.

Separate disclosures also suggest that Facebook was aware of material harmful effects involving its social network but chose to ignore, and/or not fix, these problem issues for profit motives. One Washington Post article refers to the '[h]arm [c]aused by Facebook.'[30]

The nature of the various problems arising with social media can be different, and can vary from one company to another, but recent spotlights from disclosures and congressional and parliamentary hearings are suggested by regulators, media commentators, and other interested parties, as pointing to an enhanced need for new regulations, updated regulations (eg, curtailing or removing so called internet defences), more regulator investigations[31] (eg, data regulators, consumer regulators, competition regulators), and for more legal and technical solutions to be made available to individuals.[32]

While RtbF can certainly be one of these tools – and is already expressly provided for in many countries already – more research and greater understanding of some of the implications of the internet company documents and research disclosed,

---

29   C Duffy, 'State Attorneys General Launch Investigation into Meta-owned Instagram's Impact On Kids', CNN, 18 November 2021.

30   I Tharoor, 'The Indisputable Harm Caused by Facebook' Washington Post (26 October 2021). Also see T Knowles, 'Facebook Whistleblower Frances Haugen: Children Can't Escape From Instagram Bullies' Times (25 October 2021); C Duffy, 'The Facebook Papers May be the Biggest Crisis in the Company's History' CNN (26 October 2021); R Lerman and C Lima 'TikTok, Snap, YouTube to Defend How They Protect Kids Online in Congressional Hearing, TikTok and Snap Are Facing Congress For the First Time' Washington Post (26 October 2021).

31   For example, see C Duffy, 'State Attorneys General Launch Investigation into Meta-owned Instagram's Impact On Kids', CNN, 18 November 2021.

32   R Colvin, 'Senators Say New Social Media Laws Could be on the Way – Sooner Than Later' Washington Post (26 October 2021); J Waterson and D Milmo, 'Facebook Whistleblower Frances Haugen Calls for Urgent External Regulation' Guardian (25 October 2021); C Lima, 'A Whistleblower's Power: Key Takeaways From the Facebook Papers' Washington Post (26 October 2021); A Rochefort, 'Regulating Social Media Platforms: A Comparative Policy Analysis' Communication Law (2020) (25:2) 225.

may point the trajectory of additional tailored solutions in addition to RtbF. Indeed, it may seem obvious now, but to look only at the external public facing manifestations of a social media problem issue can sometimes miss the other half of the pertinent documentation needed to solve that problem. The internal documentation is also needed to appreciate the entire nature of the problem and to come up with appropriate tailored solutions that work.[33]

Non Problem, No Fault Discretionary RtbF

3.7   There are obvious examples of problem-type content for which RtbF can be of assistance and in many instances will provide a solution – at least insofar as there is particular content online in a particular location. However, as indicated above, there are also RtbF notices which have nothing to do with any identified or known problem content. This separate category is discussed below.

There are various discretionary (non-problem) reasons why someone may wish to have content erased, forgotten or taken down ie, essentially a no-fault basis.

Some examples (but by no means a complete list) of the personal so-called discretionary no-fault reasons include:

- it is no longer current;

- I no longer like it or no longer like it being available; X photograph was taken when I was a child and I do not want it online any more; or

- Y photograph was from the office Christmas party two years ago and is out of date as I will have photographs from this year's Christmas party; or

- some of my college photographs may be better offline, or restricted, as I have now graduated and am applying for jobs and potential employers and recruiters may see them; or

---

33   More generally, see Z Sujon and HT Dyer, 'Understanding the Social in a Digital Age' *New Media* (2020) (22:7) 1125. A Rochefort, 'Regulating Social Media Platforms: A Comparative Policy Analysis' *Communication Law* (2020) (25:2) 225; G Aitchison and S Meckled-Garcia, 'Against Online Public Shaming: Ethical Problems with Mass Social Media' *Social Theory* (2021) (47:1) 1; B Schneider, TG Ford and L Perez-Felkner, 'Social Networks and the Education of Children and Youth' *Social and Emotional Aspects of Learning* (2010) 705; E Georgiades, 'Down the Rabbit Hole: Applying a Right to Be Forgotten to Personal Images Uploaded on Social Networks' *Fordham Intellectual Property, Media & Entertainment Law Journal* (2020) (30:4) 1111; G Cintra Guimarães, *Global Technology and Legal Theory Transnational Constitutionalism: Google and the European Union* (Taylor and Francis, 2019); P Lambert, 'The Right to be Forgotten: Context and the Problem of Time' *Communications Law* (2019) (24:2) 74; F Fabbrini and E Celeste, 'The Right to Be Forgotten in the Digital Age: The Challenges of Data Protection Beyond Borders' *German Law Journal*, Special Issue (2020) (21) 55; R Normey, 'The Rise of the Digital Robber Barons: Is Government Up to the Task at Hand?' *LawNow* (2020) (44:6) 19.

- the image is of my old girlfriend/boyfriend and I am in a new relationship; or

- potential problem issues are evident (or have actually arisen) regarding particular content online and it is best to have it taken down as a precaution.

Online Abuse

3.8   The problem of online abuse (OA) is incontrovertible, with increasing numbers of suicides. If anyone is still unclear about the devastation caused to victims and families, the video posted by Canadian teenager Amanda Todd is required viewing. Indeed, it should be required viewing for all parents, educators and policymakers.

It is disappointing, therefore, that even some otherwise well-informed people would completely ignore the existence of OA and its very real effects on individuals, sometimes the most vulnerable in society and suggest that there is no basis whatsoever for any RtbF, there is no need for it and that it should not exist.[34]

4   REAL TIME

3.9   One of the problems is that OA happens in real time. It is very different to a defamatory statement in a book or in a newspaper. It is online and available to more people. The audience has the potential to keep growing; in a viral online abuse situation the audience will certainly increase significantly. In the worst cases, a viral online abuse incident can attract attention from countries worldwide.

When seeking to deal with these issues there are various real-time issues. These are emphasised if the problem content is going viral in some way and gaining more and more online attention (so-called (if not ironically) 'popularity'). Once problem content has gone viral it may mean that it was originally on one website but is now being repeated on many others. That makes it difficult for the victim to identify where the problem content is and it is more difficult to have it taken down as it is on an expanding stage. It also means that there is a greater urgency to deal with the problem, as the victim is desperate to stop it spreading. This creates added pressure. It also demonstrates that historic problem content is a different issue from new live problem content which is starting to go viral. Edward Lee refers to some of the real time issues now arising and RtbF.[35]

While these differences have not been overly referred to in the jurisprudence as yet, it may be that deference many be given in future to the live real-time online abuse problems that victims face.

---

34   The founder of Wikipedia, Jimmy Wales, originally voiced this view. However, Wikipedia did subsequently refine this position and added more nuance.

35   E Lee, 'Recognizing Rights in Real Time: The Role of Google in the EU Right to Be Forgotten' *UC Davis Law Review* (2016) (49:3) 1017.

While most jurisdictions have interim and injunctive-type temporary remedies, it may be that some of the traditional aspects of these procedural stage remedies do not fully align to tackling online abuse. The requirements of certain of these longstanding procedural remedies may be onerous for (certain) victims. Potentially, over time, they may be tailored or ameliorated for (certain) victims of online abuse.

This also raises the separate issue of sometimes needing to have a record of how many people saw the problem content, where, over what period, etc. Some of these details may be available online, while others may need to be requested from the relevant website service provider(s), who may not be facilitative, or in an urgent real-time scenario.

A related point is that the victim is put in the difficult position of having to document and record the details of the abuse which may have been posted online, as well as the ballooning take up and comments from third parties, redistribution, amendments, etc. This can be a very onerous task – and even technical in some respects also. It is equally difficult to be fully definitive in some respects (eg, the full extent of what occurred or is currently visible via a given search engine) whereas this may be easier in other examples such as defamation cases. There are many differences between OA and RtbF, on the one hand and traditional defamation laws and cases and injunctive rules, on the other.

5 CHILDREN

3.10   RtbF has particular added relevance for children and child data. As children are younger than adults, the issues of permanence hold added risk. Child data has the potential to stay online much longer than it would if it was adult data. If problem content is online longer, there is added risk.

In future, we will have more examples of children using RtbF to ensure that images and other content that they or their parents may have uploaded is taken down. A parent may think that it a great idea to place pictures of their babies or children online, but in years to come those children may like to make their own decisions and may want to have these images, videos, etc, removed. These issues are starting to be referred to as the problems of over-sharing and sharenting.[36]

There will also be similar problems where a parent may have consented to some third party taking a picture or video of their child (eg, at an event or partaking in some leisure activity), and later publishing this content in some way. Newspaper photographers frequently seek to take images of people and children enjoying summer activities, for example, swimming or eating ice cream. Years later, the child may not want that photograph on the internet or on a publicly accessible online newspaper archive.

---

36   A Azurmendi, C Etayo and A Torrell, 'Sharenting and Digital Rights of Children and Teenagers' Profesional de la Informacion (2021) (30:4) 10.

An interesting, but perhaps not typical, example of this occurred when the baby on the Nevermind music album cover of the band Nirvana decided that he no longer consented to his image being used.[37] The baby was now an adult. One added factor may have been that the album cover photo was of the baby naked. While some discussions may centre on consent, parental consent, and payments (if any), this is clearly a set of facts which fit within the RtbF universe. RtbF issues arise directly with the band and record company – but also with the many images online where third parties have copied the album cover photo.

Another aspect of certain online abuse is that the problem content and the victim refers to a child. This adds an extra dimension to the issue. There is obviously an additional sensitivity in relation to such content relating to or identifying children.

The sensitivities in relation to child issues are already recognised in many areas of law and policy. Notwithstanding that the data is personal data, regardless of the data subject being a child (or an adult), the content online is personal data. In addition, the GDPR expressly refers to children, children's personal data concerns and certain additional protection.[38] (One future issue will be whether RtbF needs to be more expressly expanded in relation to children issues.)

Any form of OA referring to children should bear additional scrutiny and importance given its natural sensitivity. It may also, depending on the circumstances, bear enhanced urgency.

Roger Levesque, for example, refers to adolescence, privacy and developmental issues, which of course deserve protection, but because it is child related it may require additional considered protection.[39] Yun Li-Reilly, in what will no doubt not be the only research referring to this issue, refers to RtbF using descriptions such as 'remembering, forgetting, reinvention and freedom' for children.[40] Children's data protection, privacy[41] and RtbF interests will receive increasingly separate and individualised attention. Again, the outlier critics of having any RtbF at all, ignore child and OA concerns entirely.

Additional considerations arise when seeking to use child data generally[42] and even more issues arise when internet and digital media activities are involved.

---

37   M Savage, 'Nirvana Sued by the Baby from Nevermind's Album Cover', BBC, 25 August 2021; S Reardon, 'Baby on Nirvana's "Nevermind" Album Cover Sues Band For Child Porn' CNSNews, 26 August 2021.

38   The GDPR variously refers to children but see, in particular, Art 8.

39   RJR Levesque, *Adolescence, Privacy and the Law: A Developmental Science Perspective* (OUP, 2016).

40   Yun Li-Reilly, 'Remembering, Forgetting, Reinvention and Freedom: Social Media and Children's Right to Be Forgotten' *Advocate* (Vancouver Bar Association) (2017) (75:5) 661.

41   H Hancock, '*Weller & Ors v Associated Newspapers Ltd* [2015] EWCA Civ 1176. Weller Case Highlights Need for Guidance on Photography, Privacy and the Press' *Journal of Media Law* (2016) (8:1) 17.

42   S-D Schiopu, 'Brief Considerations on Processing a Child's Personal Data' Jus et Civitas (2019) (6:2) 23.

Until relatively recently, most of the consideration was front loaded, concentrating on consent, parental consent, age mandates, age verification, and policies. We are coming to realise that as more risk issues and problems arise, a holistic view is required of many more issues, factors and time points.[43] The recent Facebook disclosures by whistleblowers refer to how design and feature issues can be very impactful on the health and wellbeing of users, in this case teenage girls using WhatsApp. A variety of solution tools will be required. Child RtbF is one of these tools, and an important one.[44] Indeed, we may only be coming to realise how RtbF may be somewhat future proofed to the extent that it will apply to some of these issues. (There can be benefits in seeking to draft laws in a neutral and future friendly manner.)[45] Child RtbF will become increasingly important. In fact, some of the reasons for the use of child RtfF will be quite different from adult usage.

It is increasingly recognised that when online abuse arises for children and teenagers, this can be persistent and follows them home and into the bedroom 24/7, and no longer ends at the school yard. It is constant and persistent, with no safe spaces or off-time. RtbF is apt and appropriate.

6   SPECIAL PERSONAL DATA

3.11   The data protection regime has already recognised that there are different forms of personal data. The GDPR refers to general personal data and special personal data.[46] It is recognised that additional sensitivity is deserving of protection. This will have to be carried through into the consideration, application and implementation of RtbF.

The GDPR identifies the following as deserving of additional protections, namely, personal data revealing:

---

43   M JS Beauvais and BM Knoppers, 'Coming Out to Play: Privacy, Data Protection, Children's Health, and COVID-19 Research' Frontiers in Genetics (2021) (11); A Azurmendi, C Etayo and A Torrell, 'Sharenting and Digital Rights of Children and Teenagers' Profesional de la Informacion (2021) (30:4) 10; L Green, D Holloway, K Stevenson, T Leaver and L Haddon (eds), The Routledge Companion to Digital Media and Children (Routledge, 2020); B Schneider, TG Ford and L Perez-Felkner, 'Social Networks and the Education of Children and Youth' Social and Emotional Aspects of Learning (2010) 705.

44   Some sample fledgling literature includes A Bunn, 'Children and the "Right to be Forgotten": What the Right to Erasure Means for European Children, and Why Australian Children Should be Afforded a Similar Right' Media International Australia (2019) (170:1) 37; E Lievens and CV Maelen, 'A Child's Right to be Forgotten: Letting Go of the Past and Embracing the Future?' Latin American Law Review (2019) (2) 61.

45   J Wong and T Henderson, 'The Right to Data Portability in Practice: Exploring the Implications of the Technologically Neutral GDPR' International Data Privacy Law (2019) (9:3) 173.

46   Special data was previously referred to as sensitive personal data under the previous DPD 95/46. Also see comparisons in M Wang and Z Jiang, 'The Defining Approaches and Practical Paradox of Sensitive Data: An Investigation of Data Protection Laws in 92 Countries and Regions and 200 Data Breaches in the World' International Journal of Communication (2017) (11) 3286. Also, C Quelle, 'GC and Others v CNIL on the Responsibility of Search Engine Operators for Referring to Sensitive Data: The End of "Right to Be Forgotten" Balancing?' European Data Protection Law Review (EDPL) (2019) (5:3) 438.

- racial or ethnic origin;

- political opinions;

- religious or philosophical beliefs;

- trade union membership;

- genetic data;

- biometric data;

- health data; and

- sex life or sexual orientation.[47]

The *GC* RtbF case (lesser known to the *Google Spain* case) refers to RtbF for sensitive data issues. The case held that '[t]he provisions of Article 8(1) and (5) of Directive 95/46 must be interpreted as meaning that the operator of a search engine is in principle required ..., subject to the exceptions provided for by the directive, to accede to requests for de-referencing in relation to links to web pages containing personal data falling within the special [data] categories.'[48]

Increasing Sensitivity

3.12   One aspect of modern life is the increasing interface, some might suggest intrusion, by devices, into our zones of personal activity such as home, family life and interactions, entertainment viewing, exercise, sleeping, etc. Increasingly, devices are directly – or indirectly – collecting and storing some of our personal details. These details are then subject to misuse, unintended usage and data breach and can inadvertently end up available to the public online. For example, if your home viewing habits are released online, should you be able to get them taken down? If one has personal sensitive information collected by a home device and released online, should one be able to have this deleted? Should images of one's baby placed online without permission be removed? Just because increasing amounts of data, including personal data, are in the Cloud,[49] does not mean that

---

47   See GDPR Art 9.

48   See *GC and Others v CNIL*, CJEU, C-136/17 (24 September 2019), para 2 of decision holding; D De Conca, 'GC et al v CNIL: Balancing the Right to Be Forgotten with the Freedom of Information, the Duties of a Search Engine Operator' European Data Protection Law Review (EDPL) (2019) (5:4) 561; C Quelle, 'GC and Others v CNIL on the Responsibility of Search Engine Operators for Referring to Sensitive Data: The End of "Right to Be Forgotten" Balancing?' European Data Protection Law Review (EDPL) (2019) (5:3) 438; J Globocnik, 'The Right to Be Forgotten is Taking Shape: CJEU Judgments in GC and Others (C-136/17) and Google v CNIL (C-507/17)' GRUR International: Journal of European (2020) (69:4) 380.

49   O Kilgore, 'Your Head Is in the Cloud: The Application of Outdated Privacy Law to Rapidly Changing Technologies' *Drake Law Review Discourse* (2017, 2018) (67) 101; ASY Cheung and RH Weber, *Privacy and Legal Issues in Cloud Computing* (Elgar, 2015); Purtova, *Property Rights in Personal Data* at 38; Kuan, Hörnle and Millard, 'Data Protection Jurisdiction and Cloud Computing – When are Cloud Users and Providers Subject to EU Data Protection Law? The Cloud of Unknowing' at 129.

it is immune from being hacked or otherwise released publicly or released to third parties.

Some may suggest that there is an increasing argument for expanding the list of special personal data as exists under data laws. The increasing instances of what was intended to be private family information and from locations in the home, collected (indirectly) by AI devices[50] but which through a variety of unintended circumstances are released publicly or to third parties without consent, may well increase the case for expanding the protection of special personal data to the zone of family and home.

A further consideration may well be whether data from inside the home should be classed as special or sensitive personal data automatically and/or should automatically require express explicit consent and higher transparency.

Increasing Risk and Locus

3.13   The above highlights just some of the home and family risks that are distilling presently. There are, however, increasing risks in other areas too. The internet of things (IoT),[51] while present in the home, can also extend to devices on the body and to vehicles.

New devices and applications collect biometric data.[52] This is private and personal to individuals. Sometimes it can relate to health, insurance and the like, but in other instances the collection and use of biometric data is presented as a simple consumer family-tree or ancestry type product/service.

Face-recognition technology is increasingly being sought to be used – sometimes without transparency,[53] It is then just one step further to seek to analyse facial emotions. Some uses are official security and terror related, others are advertising/marketing, tracking stalkers at a Taylor Swift concert[54] or mere data gathering for

---

50 Purtova, *Property Rights in Personal Data* above at 38.
51 S Varadi, G Varkonyi, G Gultekin and A Kertesz, 'Law and IoT: How to See Things Clearly in the Fog' *2018 Third International Conference on Fog and Mobile Edge Computing (FMEC)* (2018) (April) 233; SK Mizrahi, 'Ontario's New Invasion of Privacy Torts: Do They Offer Monetary Redress for Violations Suffered Via the Internet of Things?' *Western Journal of Legal Studies* (2018) (8:1) COV2, 37.
52 Pope, 'Biometric Data Collection in an Unprotected World: Exploring the Need for Federal Legislation Protecting Biometric Data' above at 769. The GDPR now expressly refers to biometric data, see GDPR Art 4(1) (14).
53 P Lewinski, J Trzaskowski and J Luzak, 'Face and Emotion Recognition on Commercial Property Under EU Data Protection Law' *Psychology & Marketing* (2016) (33:9) 729.
54 G Canon, 'Surveillance Fears Grow After Taylor Swift Uses Face Recognition Tech on Fans' *Guardian*, 14 December 2018; S Knopper, 'Why Taylor Swift is Using Facial Recognition at Concerts' *Rolling Stone*, 13 December 2018; J Stanley, 'The Problem with Using Face Recognition on Fans at a Taylor Swift Concert' *ACLU.org*, (America Civil Liberties Union) 14 December 2018.

mere possible future use. The discontinuance of facial recognition (and associated deletions) by Facebook exemplifies that there are important risk issues arising.

Insurance companies are acutely aware that there are increasing data opportunities in terms of people's activities in their vehicles. Some are now offering so-called 'connected car insurance' and 'car insurance tracking' where a device monitors the individual driver. (Some insurance companies now offer discounts if you allow it to track your Fitbit device on your wrist.[55])

Employment law raises many important issues.[56] However, it presents another zone of measuring and monitoring via the employee sphere.[57] This includes communication, internet, social media and vehicular use.[58]

As general technology developments increase,[59] new relationships and data flows[60] are established between entities which previously were neither connected nor partnered. We see this in the health sphere,[61] where there are increasing partnerships and sharing of data. This includes live health data, profiling health data and historic genetic and ancestry data (but with a variety of future applications).

There is also a discussion which needs to be had in relation to the numerous examples of mass data collection, data mining and data mining for possible future applications, and *live* data not just for beta testing but *development* stage research and testing. Incorrect data is sometimes being released in inappropriate circumstances and its usage is questionable in terms of law, data protection, privacy and ethics (eg, data ethics and business ethics).

Data mining[62] ethics and proportionality are not being considered as much as they should be and – perhaps alarmingly – not in advance of the go-live of certain projects with live data. There can, of course, be benefits, but the search should

---

55 L Mearian, 'Insurance Company Now Offers Discounts – If You Let It Track Your Fitbit' *Computer World* (15 April 2015).

56 Just by way of sample example, see S Bloch, QC and K Brearley, *Employment Covenants and Confidential Information: Law, Practice and Technique* (Bloomsbury, 2018); D Ashton, PW Reid and Snaith, *Ashton & Reid on Clubs and Associations* (Bloomsbury, 2019).

57 F Hendrick, 'Privacy, Data Protection and Measuring Employee Performance: The Triggers of Technology and Smart Work' *European Labour Law Journal* (2018) (9:2) 99.

58 Lambert, *International Handbook on Social Medial Laws*; A Etgen Reitz, J Rudolph and PM Berkowitz, *Social Media and Employment Law, An International Survey* (Kluwer, 2015); P Lambert, *A Users Guide to Data Protection* (Bloomsbury, 2018). C Manara and C Roquilly, 'The Risk of Brand Equity Erosion in the Social Media: The Efficacy and Limitations of Legal Instruments' *Recherche et Applications en Marketing* (English Edition) (AFM c/o ESCP-EAP) (2011) (26:3) 93

59 Purtova, *Property Rights in Personal Data, A European Perspective* above at 18; P Lambert, 'IP and PI Takedowns: Comparing and Contrasting the Right to be Forgotten' European Intellectual Property Review (2019) (41:6) 381.

60 Purtova, *ibid*, at 39.

61 G Comande and G Schneider, 'Regulatory Challenges of Data Mining Practices: The Case of the Never-Ending Lifecycles of Health Data' *European Journal of Health Law* (2018) (25:3) 284.

62 *Ibid*.

not (always) be speculative when live data, special data and large data sets are involved. In addition, we should also be willing to question whether 'perfect knowledge'[63] is (always) possible and whether unlimited access to increasing data sets for data mining for perfect knowledge is always warranted and, if not, then in what more limited circumstances and conditions it may be. It is always legitimate to scale back a project or speculative research where it is clear that there is no clear defined purpose for collecting all of the potential data sets that may be potentially available. It may be that the Facebook facial recognition discontinuance and deletions is an example of this.

OA Problem Content Increasing

3.14   Bad and problem content are increasing. Problem political content and so-called 'fake news' is a large issue in contemporary political, media and policymaker focus.[64] It is also clear that personal OA problem issues are significant and appear to be increasing. Pierre Trudel, for example, notes that the risks to individuals increase from many online activities, including in relation to data protection, safety, etc.[65] The Olympics in London brought to the fore the disadvantages of social media, where social networks such as Twitter, Facebook, etc, can be used for online abuse.[66] There is a growing and troubling number of instances of suicides arising as a result of OA and threats occurring on social media websites. Social networks and other websites also contain controversial material in relation to self-harm. Worryingly, disclosures during 2021 appears to indicate that Facebook (now Meta) was aware through internal research that there was disproportionate harm to teenage female users of Instagram (a Facebook (now Meta) group company).

It will be interesting to see how much is increasing and how much is there already. In either event, there is a need for greater statistical knowledge to inform policy and assist in dealing with these issues. There is a specific need for baseline

63   Purtova, *Property Rights in Personal Data* above at 47.
64   For example, voter manipulation, disinformation, radicalisation profiling, targeting. See International Grand Committee on Disinformation and Fake News hearings. Commons Select Committee, hearings beginning on 23 November 2018. Available at: www.parliament. uk/business/committees/committees-a-z/commons-select/digital-culture-media-and-sport-committee/news/grand-committee-evidence-17-19/. Also see Y Benkler, R Faris and H Roberts, *Network Propaganda, Manipulation, Disinformation and Radicalization in American Politics* (OUP, 2018); CJ Bennett, 'Voter Databases, Micro-Targeting and Data Protection Law: Can Political Parties Campaign in Europe as They Do in North America?' *International Data Privacy Law* (2016) (6:4) 261. Related problems include issues with dissemination, manipulation and inequality, see Purtova, *Property Rights in Personal Data* above at 50.
65   P Trudel, 'Privacy Protection on the Internet: Risk Management and Networked Normativity' in S Gutwirth, Y Poullet, P de Hert, C de Terwange and S Nouwt, *Reinventing Data Protection?* (Springer, 2009) 317.
66   J Rosenberg, 'Tom Daley, Twitter Abuse and the Law' *Guardian* (31 July 2012); S James, 'Man Cautioned After Mark Halsey Twitter Abuse' *Guardian* (27 September 2012); LL Baughmanm, 'Friend Request or Foe? Confirming the Misuse of Internet and Social Networking Sites by Domestic Violence Perpetrators' *Widener Law Journal* (2010)(19) 933. Generally, also see JJ Ator, 'Got Facebook?' *GPSolo* (2009) (March) 4.

research and baseline statistics. Website A cannot suggest that it has improved if no baseline year statistics are gathered and made available against which to compare year on year; nor suggest with baseline statistics and follow on annual statistics that it is fully responsive and fully compliant in this area.

Some OA Examples

3.15   The problem of OA is increasingly evident. It is also evident that it comprises more than one neat problem issue. These variety of consequences can apply to children and teenagers as well as adults. While the consequences may vary as between these categories, some of the examples include the following:

- cyberbullying;

- revenge porn;

- doxing (exposing private personal details online);

- threats of identification, doxing, and similar;

- shaming;

- trolling;

- defamation;

- blackmailing children and teenagers;

- blackmailing adults;

- threats;

- hate threats;

- harassment;

- stalking;

- grooming;

- breach of data protection and privacy; and

- over sharing by parents.

The increasing data protection and privacy challenges from emerging technologies and collections which includes OA, cannot be ignored.[67]

In the current political climate, there are increasing examples of online public shaming and political related shaming.[68] This is even extending to school board

---

67 N Witzleb, D Lindsay, M Paterson and S Rodrick, *Emerging Challenges in* Privacy Law*: Comparative Perspectives* (CUP, 2014). Purtova, *Property Rights in Personal Data* above at 45; P Billingham and T Parr, 'Online Public Shaming: Virtues and Vices' *Journal of Social Philosophy* (2020) (51:3) 371.

68 G Aitchison and S Meckled-Garcia, 'Against Online Public Shaming: Ethical Problems with Mass Social Media' Social Theory (2021) (47:1) 1.

members, teachers, doctors, restaurant staff and owners, airline employees and executives, and others.

There is even discussion of online persecution[69] and intentional humiliation of others with online content.[70]

These forms of new enhanced political related problem content are a live problem area raising a number of issues. While the full extent, implications and effects are still to be fully documented, RtbF style tools may provide one avenue for dealing with the removal of categories of this problem content (but certainly not all). In many respects, the individuals that are being attacked are not political nor public figures in the normal understanding of these labels, which further inclines this towards RtbF solutions.

Cyberbullying

3.16   The problem of cyber bullying is incontrovertible. We have had many, some high-profile, suicides involving cyberbullying.

Copying and utilising personal data to abuse and blackmail children, teenagers, etc, is an issue which must be considered by all organisations, as well as policymakers. No country is immune, as we have all-too-painfully discovered with teenagers falling victim to cyberbullies almost everywhere. However, this is part of a greater problem. Cyberbullying, or in this instance, the cyberbullying of teenagers, is just one facet of online abuse.

We should also consider the term 'cyber bullying' and 'cyberbullying'. Too much focus on 'cyber' can sometimes mask the fact that OA can extend into the real world, both offline and online. Virtual trolls can be real-life bullies to the victim. Online abusers can also gain, or perceive, encouragement online which may not occur offline.

7   REVENGE PORN

3.17   The internet has both positive and negative traits. So, too, has social media.[71] It would seem, however, that recent discussion highlights how social

---

69   LMJ Cooper, 'Social Media and Online Persecution' Georgetown Immigration Law Journal (2021) (35:3) 749.
70   D Nash, 'Politics of Humiliation – How do we Save us from our Liberal Selves?' Cultural History (2021) (10:2) 275; J Israel, Living With Hate in American Politics and Religion: How Popular Culture Can Defuse Intractable Differences (Columbia University Press, 2019); I Down and KJ Han, 'Far Right Parties and "Europe": Societal Polarization and the Limits of EU Issue Contestation' Journal of European Integration (2021) (43:1) 65; M Goldmann, 'As Darkness Deepens: The Right to Be Forgotten in the Context of Authoritarian Constitutionalism' *German Law Journal*, Special Issue (2020) (21) 45.
71   Rogerson, 'Wireless and Social Media Influence' *International Journal for the Data Protection Officer, Privacy Officer and Privacy Counsel (IDPP)* above at 12.

media may have more dark sides than the internet more generally. The dark side of social media[72] interfaces with many aspects of OA. In terms of revenge porn and data protection,[73] it is noted that if images of a person in a sexual or suggestive manner in a personal private setting are subsequently published by an ex-partner in a deliberate and malicious manner (sometimes even after threats and blackmail), the images are personal data[74] under the data protection regime. Revenge porn can include consensual but private images but can also extend to non-consensual sexual images.[75]

The problem and the need for solutions to revenge porn is one of the stronger imperatives pointing to the necessity of RtbF, which is a valuable and practical solution. Criminal laws, existing and new, as well as associated penalties are another aspect of the solution. No doubt other solutions may also exist[76] or may be identified in the future, some of which may need explicit legislation.[77] There are increasing calls for express explicit revenge porn laws where they do not exist already, (e.g. country or federal criminal laws).[78] One consideration is the extent to which an act of uploading revenge porn may fall within pre-existing harassment prohibitions.[79] Personal rights, privacy and data protection and human rights may all be infringed.[80]

---

72   A Close Scheinbaum, *The Dark Side of Social Media: A Consumer Psychology Perspective* (Routledge, Taylor & Francis, 2018).

73   BA Genn, 'What Comes Off, Comes Back to Burn: Revenge Pornography as the Hot New Flame and How It Applies to the First Amendment and Privacy Law' *American University Journal of Gender, Social Policy & the Law* (2014) (23:1) 163.

74   K Benedick, 'Eradicating Revenge Porn: Intimate Images as Personal Identifying Information' *Lewis & Clark Law Review* (2018) (22:1) 231.

75   N Suzor, B Seignior and J Singleton, 'Non-Consensual Porn and the Responsibilities of Online Intermediaries' *Melbourne University Law Review* (2017) (40:3) 1057.

76   J Brown, 'Revenge Porn and the *Actio Iniuriarum*: Using Old Law to Solve New Problems' *Journal of the Society of Legal Scholars* (2018) (38:3) 396.

77   A Hamilton, 'Is Justice Best Served Cold?: A Transformative Approach to Revenge Porn' *UCLA Women's Law Journal* (2018) (25:1) 1.

78   A Greene, 'The Ill of Misogyny on the Internet: Why Revenge Porn Needs Federal Criminalization' *Colorado Technology Law Journal* (2017) (16:1) 175; KM Brady, 'Revenge in Modern Times: The Necessity of a Federal Law Criminalizing Revenge Porn' *Hastings Women's Law Journal* (2017) (28:1) 3; E Souza, '"For His Eyes Only": Why Federal Legislation Is Needed To Combat Revenge Porn' *UCLA Women's Law Journal* (2016) (23:2) 101. R Budde Patton, 'Taking the Sting Out of Revenge Porn: Using Criminal Statutes to Safeguard Sexual Autonomy in the Digital Age' *Georgetown Journal of Gender and the Law* (2015) (16:2) 407; A Jacobs, 'Fighting Back Against Revenge Porn: A Legislative Solution' *Northwestern Journal of Law and Social Policy* (2016) (12:1) 69; R Hill, 'Cyber-Misogyny: Should Revenge Porn Be Regulated in Scotland and If So, How?' *SCRIPTed: A Journal of Law, Technology and Society* (2015) (2:2) 117.

79   A Lai, 'Revenge Porn as Sexual Harassment: Legislation, Advocacies and Implications' *Journal of Gender, Race and Justice* (2016) (19:2) 251.

80   M Run Bjarnadottir, 'Does the Internet Limit Human Rights Protection: The Case of Revenge Porn' *Journal of Intellectual Property, Information Technology and Electronic Commerce Law* (2016) (7:3) 204.

There are also calls to make it easier for victims to bring civil actions.[81] Copyright law can also be used in certain circumstances to help victims to file notices and/ or to take appropriate action.[82]

An additional problem, separate to the malicious poster of the problem image(s) online, are websites dedicated to hosting images of revenge porn and claims by their operators that they are immune from liability (and responsibility) under so-called e-commerce-type defences[83] or free speech-type defences.[84]

In the absence of a dedicated revenge porn law, there is a strong argument that there is insufficient victim protection and remedy.[85]

Sometimes, we can get too caught up about a definitive solution, in this instance breach of data protection and privacy on the one hand, or criminal threat or harassment on the other.[86] But the result and solution is more important from the victim's perspective. The egregious nature of this dark side issue[87] should mean that we are result-solution orientated. A wrong needs to be righted or – more correctly – needs to be minimised in terms of seeking to prevent the damage continuing on an ongoing basis. There are, of course, various potential solutions and even many different types of legislative solutions.[88] (Some RtbF critics do not engage with issues of OA and problem content issues, thus undermining their criticism.) However, we should not expect that there will be one 'magic bullet' solution. Rather, the problem demands a variety of solutions, each complementing each other in a blended, layered approach. For example, an immediate RtbF or an

---

81 JM Pollack, 'Getting Even: Empowering Victims of Revenge Porn with a Civil Cause of Action' *Albany Law Review* (2016) (80:1) 353.

82 C Varriale, 'What's Love Got to Do With It: Copyright Laws and Revenge Porn' *Entertainment and Sports Lawyer* (2018) (34:3) 34. Also see P Lambert, 'IP and PI Takedowns: Comparing and Contrasting the Right to be Forgotten' European Intellectual Property Review (2019) (41:6) 381; A O'Connell and K Bakina, 'Using IP Rights to Protect Human Rights: Copyright for "Revenge Porn" Removal' Legal Studies (2020) (40:3) 442; A Aseri, 'Juxtaposing Right to be Forgotten and Copyright Law' Journal of Intellectual Property Rights (2020) (25:3/4) 100; D Schwalbe, 'An Introduction to the GDPR for IP Professionals in the United States' Licensing Journal (2020) (40:1) 10.

83 Z Franklin, 'Justice for Revenge Porn Victims: Legal Theories to Overcome Claims of Civil Immunity by Operators of Revenge Porn Websites' *California Law Review* (2014) (102:5) 1303; R Setterfield, 'The Bare Truth About Revenge Porn: Revealing the Regulatory Challenges Exposed by an Exploration of Revenge Porn's Roots in Pornography and Technology' *Edinburgh Student Law Review* (2017) (3:2) 38.

84 PJ Larkin, Jr, 'Revenge Porn, State Law and Free Speech' *Loyola of Los Angeles Law Review* (2014) (48:1) 57; Hill, 'Cyber-Misogyny: Should Revenge Porn Be Regulated in Scotland and If So, How?' *SCRIPTed: A Journal of Law, Technology and Society* at 117.

85 M Fay, 'The Naked Truth: Insufficient Coverage for Revenge Porn Victims at State Law and the Proposed Federal Legislation to Adequately Redress Them' *Boston College Law Review* (2018) (59:5) 1839.

86 S Pegg, 'A Matter of Privacy or Abuse? Revenge Porn in the Law' *Criminal Law Review* (2018) (7) 512.

87 A Close Scheinbaum, *The Dark Side of Social Media: A Consumer Psychology Perspective* (Routledge, 2017).

88 J Haynes, 'Legislative Approaches to Combating 'Revenge Porn': A Multijurisdictional Perspective' *Statute Law Review* (2018) (39:3) 319.

immediate injunction may provide a solution. Thereafter, it may be appropriate for a criminal investigation and prosecution to follow. If the police can intervene positively earlier, well and good. However, sometimes, case-complaint officers need to call in and/or rely on police forensic experts who may be unable to act immediately due to lack of resources or other work commitments. Jurisdictions should also engage in appropriate research to discern where gaps may exist in their legal solutions and to address these shortcomings.[89]

In addition to the above, a large consideration in the event of proceedings having to issue, is whether the victim must be identified by name, further compounding the invasions which the victim may feel.[90]

DeepFakes

3.18   Even as new criminal laws are expanding to expressly encompass the problem of revenge porn, new problems are arising with new technology. Technology now makes it relatively easy for anyone with basic technical capabilities to produce or make porn videos and to superimpose the image of a person onto the video. Unlike copy and pasting a still photographic image, it is now possible to place a face image into a moving video. The superimposed image looks like it was the original person in the video and is indistinguishable (without some forensic analysis).

This creates a new problem in relation to fake news and fake political stories, but it also creates a follow-on problem in revenge porn. Errant individuals are creating porn videos using images of famous women and then uploading and distributing them. Others are also inserting the images of teenagers and adults they know into these altered porn videos, thus making it appear that the target individual was actually in a sex video. These fake image-superimposed videos are being called 'DeepFake 'videos.[91]

A follow-on problem is that errant individuals may also seek to blackmail the victim or to pay money to have the doctored videos taken down, or not to be put online. They often threaten that if their demands are not met, the video will be uploaded, disseminated to more websites or even sent to parents, friends,

---

89 N Neris, J Pacetta Ruiz and M Giorgetti Valente, 'Comparative Analysis of Strategies to Face Revenge Porn Around the World' *Brazilian Journal of Public Policy* (2017) (7:3) 334.

90 E Brown, 'Protecting Does and Outing Mobsters: Recalibrating Anonymity Standards in Revenge Porn Proceedings' *Duke Journal of Gender Law & Policy* (2018) (25:2) 155.

91 D Harwell, 'Fake-Porn Videos Are Being Weaponized to Harass Women: "Everybody Is A Potential Target"' *Washington Post* (31 December 2018); R Khalaf, 'If You Thought Fake News Was a Problem, Wait For "Deepfakes"' *FT.com* (25 July 2018); A Shermoen, 'Deepfakes Strip Dignity' *University Wire* (18 February 2018); M-H Maras and A Alexandrou, 'Determining Authenticity of Video Evidence in the Age of Artificial Intelligence and In the Wake of Deepfake Videos' *International Journal of Evidence and Proof* (2018) (October); R Black, 'What Can the Law Do About "Deepfake"?' *Mondaq Business Briefing* (29 March 2018).

work colleagues, employers, etc. There are troubling examples of each of these occurring.

It is difficult to respond that RtbF should not be available as one of the remedies for the victims. (There is also a separate argument to create new laws or to expand the existing revenge porn laws.)

Overlapping OA

3.19   There are also overlaps. The cyberbulling of children can involve harassment, threats, verbal abuse, defamation, etc, or, in the case of Amanda Todd, privacy and data protection breaches later extending to threats. There may also be elements of deliberation and planning involved. These issues add extra complexity as to how to deal with these OA issues. Examples can range from threats to defamation, harassment to stalking, grooming and breaches of data protection and privacy.

OA Locus

3.20   Much of this OA occurs on social media websites.[92] It also occurs via mobile phones and smartphones, through social media, and also by text message. An article in the Guardian states that the 'mobile internet is now just the internet'.[93] It notes how we increasingly access the internet and social media and other websites via mobile wireless devices.

It is natural that some of the solutions include RtbF. Others are directed to social media, internet search engines, etc, and takedown from these websites.

8   OA REMEDY AND SOLUTION ISSUES

3.21   The solutions are multifaceted. Certain commentary points to education, educators and parents. While correct, this is only one aspect. In addition, the source of such commentary may sometimes be queried, especially if it is for overly commercial or defensive reasons. Social media is often central to these activities. We cannot ignore issues of RtbF, identification, timeliness, tools for making RtbF notices, follow through after the notices are received, statistics on solutions, time taken, etc; and statistics on whether problem content is increasing or decreasing year on year and on each given website.

RtbF is a solution for the victims of OA – and the associated issues arising from permanence and forgetting online (including attacks, data breaches, etc). Recall

---

92   Rogerson, 'Wireless and Social Media Influence' at 12. Also see K Ahmad, *Social Computing and the Law: Uses and Abuses in Exceptional Circumstances* (CUP, 2018).
93   J Naughton, 'Mobile Internet is Now Just the Internet' *Guardian*, 27 December 2015. Rogerson, 'Wireless and Social Media Influence' above at 12.

the data breaches involving dating websites, such as Ashley Madison, where personal membership details were subsequently posted online; in some instances, the victims committed suicide.[94] The required solutions are multifaceted. Some of these are referred to below.

- *RtbF*: For example, the GDPR RtbF. This, like the on-site reporting of complaints is also online on the same or a related website of the service provider in question.

- *Criminal laws and remedies*: Online abusers can face criminal consequences.

- *Civil laws and remedies*: Online abusers can face civil consequences.

- *On-site complaint*: Reporting if and when there is a complaint or report button or similar function available – and transparent – on the website(s) holding the problem content.

- *Police*: Police reporting (if and when effective, which unfortunately it is not always so).

- *Official reporting:* Reporting to data regulators.

- *New laws*: Express legal protections for the victims of crime.[95] There are, for example, increasing numbers of express criminal revenge porn laws across the world.

- *Security for data*: Security and the protection of personal data.[96]

- *Education*: Much of the recent commentary correctly points to education, educators and parents. Some of this discussion may also be motivated in terms of commercial motivation, defence and or diversion. However, this is only one aspect of the solution.

- *Compensation and damages*: The GDPR enhances the ability of individual data subjects to obtain compensation and damages.[97] There are comparative laws in other countries. Ontario, for example, has a new invasion of privacy tort.[98]

Some of these solutions and related issues arising are discussed in more detail below.

---

94   M Olson, 'Equitable Recovery for Ashley Madison Hack Victims: The Federal Trade Commission as Executor of a Narrow Right to Be Forgotten in the United States' *Washington Journal of Law, Technology & Arts* (2016) (12:1) 61.

95   M Groenhuijsen, 'Protection of Crime Victims by Legal Means: International and European Law and Policy' *Temida* (2015) (18:1) 3.

96   G Gonzalez Fuster, 'Security and the Future of Personal Data Protection in the European Union' *Security & Human Rights* (2013) (23:4) 331.

97   GDPR, Art 82.

98   Mizrahi, 'Ontario's New Invasion of Privacy Torts: Do They Offer Monetary Redress for Violations Suffered Via the Internet of Things?' above at 37.

9   ON-SITE ABUSE REPORTING

3.22   Much of this abuse occurs on social networking websites. It also occurs via mobiles and smartphones. As regards social networking websites, some – but not all – provide some level of 'tools' or 'reporting processes'. However, it would be perceptive to suggest that many social networking websites and indeed other Web 2.0 websites, do not do all that they can to deal with these issues. Even some of the largest social networking websites have been slow to implement reporting procedures for certain forms of abuse and other issues. Some websites also have tools available which they use but are reluctant to extend to abuse victims.

It would also be a perceptive observation to suggest that, no matter how many 'report' buttons are featured on a website, they are entirely useless without protocols, policies and procedures behind the scenes to follow up on reports that are made. Reports and complaints are also meaningless unless there are enough people to investigate them.

It would be interesting to examine and compare the number of people employed in abuse investigation teams on various social networking websites. Should there be a minimum number of employees required per number of users? Should there be a minimum number of such employees per number of abuse reports on a given website?

It is all well and good to scale commercially, geographically, by user-base, by advertising, turnover, etc, but life, death and quality of user experience also requires social networking (and other) websites to prioritise proper abuse reporting mechanisms and effective processing of such reports. If that requires more staff, so be it. The level of turnover of such websites can easily absorb hiring more staff.

A further point arises regarding social media and related websites. Some such websites are commercially happy to publish significant statistics on the level of reports and complaints relating to copyright infringement. This arguably appears to be commercially driven. There is significantly less 'transparency' as to the complaints of abuse made to social media and similar websites, nor how and how quickly these are resolved.

As much as we are presently shocked by the dark side of internet abuse, cyberbullying and its terrible consequences, we would be further shocked at the scale of abuse reporting (if and when available). That may be a useful line of enquiry for anyone officially concerned. It could also be useful to consider that whatever a website may say at first blush, may not always be the whole picture.

Policymakers and courts are beginning to realise that, on occasion, social media and other websites can not only be unhelpful but can be positively obstructive. They can also be positively aggressive and combative to victims of abuse. The White House can now be added to this list, eg in relation to vaccine misinformation issues.

10   REPORTING TO POLICE

3.23   Victims of OA can report problem content to the police. Sometimes the police are of great assistance, sometimes not. It goes without saying the police must follow-up reports. Media commentary suggests that the UK police are proactive in this area. It is also welcome that official authorities call for victims to report these matters to the police.

Identifying Abusers: Police

3.24   The law sometimes provides that the police, by way of a specified demand procedure or at a certain level of seniority, may sometimes demand that an organisation discloses user and identification details. The law sometimes provides that the police, by way of a court order may seek the disclosure of user details, including identification details, from relevant website and service providers.

Identifying Abusers: Victims

3.25   Online abusers can face civil as well as criminal consequences. However, in order to do so, the abuser must be identified or traced. Frequently, online abusers and the public generally may feel that using a different profile name or some form of anonymity can hide the abuser from justice.

A victim can be forgiven for thinking that unless the abuser provides their real name and location, that nothing can be done and that there can be no consequences for their actions. This is sometimes compounded by websites which may indicate that they either will not or cannot identify their users. Ironically, this is indicated to be based upon data protection grounds. Note, however, that some websites state in their terms and/or user agreements, that they may be required to disclose user details in response to a court request. Others provide that they may, on a discretionary basis, without court order, disclose user details if there is a breach of the website's policies.

One point often missing from the current discussion is that it is legally possible to find even the most abusive or determined anonymous abusers.

Victims can apply to court for the disclosure of user details from relevant websites and service providers. This may involve slightly different procedures in different jurisdictions. In the UK and elsewhere, these applications are frequently known as *Norwich Pharmacal*[99] applications.

---

99   Named after *Norwich Pharmacal v Customs and Excise Commissioners* [1974] AC 133, [1973] 2 All ER 943.

The law provides victims and the police, with the ability to apply to court for the disclosure of user details from relevant websites and service providers. These orders are frequently known as *Norwich Pharmacal* orders.

Parents and victims of online abuse can find and trace the abusers to ensure that they stop or are pursued as appropriate. The point is that no abuser is immune from being found and identified. That is not, however, to say that the process will not be both difficult, time consuming, and/or costly.

11 IMAGE COPYRIGHT

3.26 Data and property rights in data is also looked at as a solution for individuals.[100] Some people have sought to rely on owning their own copyright in problem images online.[101] In McKeogh,[102] the plaintiff also obtained the copyright of the images in question from the original image owner. This can sometimes assist in the successful takedown of problem content. One advantage is that where this is possible, it may be treated differently by some of the online service providers and there may potentially be easier takedown mechanisms than those under RtbF. This raises policy issues in and of itself, as to why some victims may be treated differently.

Security

3.27 There is a need to deal with and improve security[103] including, but not exclusively, to tackle the problem issue of data breaches.[104] It is also suggested that there should be RtbF to help deal with and reduce the negative effects of data breaches.[105]

Drones

3.28 There is a lot of attention focusing on the development of drone technology and such valuable use applications as pizza and book deliveries.

---

100 Purtova, *Property Rights in Personal Data* at 23; see also Chapter 10 'The Property Rights Solution' at 245 and Chapter 3, 'The Personal Data Problem: Concerns' at 43.
101 Chapter 9 refers to copyright and rights to one's image issues, in NA Moreham and Sir Mark Warby, Tugendhat and Christie, *The Law of Privacy and the Media* (OUP, 2016) at 389.
102 *McKeogh v Doe and Others* [2012] IEHC 95.
103 H Wong, *Cyber Security: Law and Guidance* (Bloomsbury, 2018); PTJ Wolters, 'The Security of Personal Data Under the GDPR: A Harmonized Duty or a Shared Responsibility?' *International Data Privacy Law* (2017) (7:3) 165; M Schallbruch and S Isabel, *Cybersecurity in Germany* (Springer, 2018).
104 J Cellerini and C Lang, 'Cyber Liability: Data Breach in Europe' *Defense Counsel Journal* (2018) (85:3) 1.
105 A Stenning, 'Gone But Not Forgotten: Recognizing the Right to Be Forgotten in the US to Lessen the Impacts of Data Breaches' *San Diego International Law Journal* (2016) (18:1) 129.

While these commerce and purchase applications still involve personal data and data protection, there are altogether more important drone privacy issues that need to be considered.[106]

The issue of drone privacy invasions is developing. However, consider that a nosy neighbour regularly takes drone photos and videos of their own home environment but in so doing they also include images of their neighbour. The nosy neighbour may place all their content online – even live. But are they allowed to? And are they obliged to take some of the content down if the neighbour objects? What if the drone operator is a retail outlet in the area, not a resident, whose website and social media pages have many thousands of followers? Maybe an estate agent in endeavouring to sell House A, takes drone pictures and unintentionally includes images of a neighbour in House C sunbathing and includes this in both hard copy and online brochures. Should someone be able to operate drones over junior schools or playgrounds and be permitted to post these images of children online? Should private investigators acting for financial institutions be permitted to use drones to capture images relating to a target customer?

Are the paparazzi able to take drone images of a famous person's house and property; to seek to peer inside the windows of a house or building; or to hover over a sporting arena to see a closed non-public team training session, for a news story and where images will be published online?

What is clear, however, is that this type of invasion and conflict will escalate in future, especially as drones become smaller, silent, and even more unobtrusive. Drones are already responsible for new forms of problem content online, which will become the subject of RtbF notices.

WP 29, EDPB and Online Issues

3.29   The WP 29 data regulator body (now, of course, replaced by the European Data Protection Board (EDPB)) in the context of online behavioural advertising[107] indicates that an icon in itself can be insufficient. In that context it was particularly concerned with consent issues. However, significant research remains to be undertaken to properly assess the adequacy of icons, notices, tools, information, information notices, report buttons, reports processes, report teams, response times, resolutions times, etc, in relation to online abuse and social media websites. There is, as yet, a distinct shortage of research and literature on

---

106 See, for example, D Butler, 'The Dawn of the Age of the Drones: An Australian Privacy Law Perspective' *University of New South Wales Law Journal* (2014) (37:2) 434; C Pauner Chulvi, 'El Uso Emergente de Drones Civiles en España. Estatuto Jurídico e Impacto en el Derecho a la Protección de Datos / The Emerging Use of Civilian Drones in Spain. Legal Status and Impact on the Right to Data Protection' *Revista de Derecho Político* (2016) (1:95) 83.
107 WP 29, *Opinion 2/2010 on Online Behavioural Advertising*, WP 171 (22 June 2010).

this topic despite media reports of online abuse and many examples of its tragic consequences.

Designing Harm/Designing Safety

3.30   With the increasing focus on new technologies it may be useful to consider how technology can be designed to increase risks and harms. There are increasing suggestions that data protection and privacy (and consumer[108]) laws should consider how technology creates risks and influences behaviour.[109] There are also calls for laws to influence technology – particularly its design – to increase safety and to protect individuals.[110]

12   ON-SITE TOOL DESIGN AND ASSESSMENT

3.31   We are starting to see greater scrutiny of the availability, design, accessibility, transparency, user friendliness, and effectiveness of different on-site tools that may be needed to assist individuals to deal with online problem issues.

Much of this attention is directed to on-site reporting tools, but the examination is becoming much more nuanced (as it needs to be) as greater understanding of the problem issues, and the internal resources available in given internet and social media companies, develops.

As interested parties learn more about a particular problem issue, they may consider that there is a legal tool gap or on-site tool gap in relation that problem.

Assessments may be made as to whether a given company is dedicating tools to identified problem issues, and if and where tools exist, whether those tools are sufficient and adequately resourced. In light of recent discussion, another question that may be asked is whether an individual company has sufficiently operationalised and escalated a given tool.

---

108 The link and relationship between consumer law and data protection law is increasing in focus. N Helberger, F Zuiderveen Borgesius and A Reyna, 'The Perfect Match? A Closer Look at the Relationship Between EU Consumer Law and Data Protection Law' *Common Market Law Review* (2017) (54:5) 1427.

109 K Hughes, 'A Behavioural Understanding of Privacy and its Implications for Privacy Law' *Modern Law Review* (2012) (75:5) 806. Note also the various Facebook disclosures during 2021, and consequent Congressional and Parliamentary hearings.

110 W Hartzog, *Privacy's Blueprint, The Battle to Control the Design of New Technologies* (Harvard University Press, 2018); DJ Solove and W Hartzog, 'The FTC and the New Common Law of Privacy' *Columbia Law Review* (2014) (114:3) 583; W Hartzog, 'Are Privacy Laws Deficient?' *International Journal for the Data Protection Officer, Privacy Officer and Privacy Counsel (IDPP)* (2018) (2:10) 17; N Richards and W Hartzog, 'Taking Trust Seriously in Privacy Law' *Stanford Technology Law Review* (2016) (19:3) 431.

New social media activities, and new more general technological advances, can raise new problems in and of themselves, but also potentially compound some pre-existing problem issues.[111]

RtbF tools are one very important part, but not the only part, of the solutions-mix. But RtbF tools also need to be scrutinised from time to time as to whether they are working smoothly and efficiently.

New digital tools may needed from time to time, and so too may new digital rights.[112]

13 CONCLUSION

3.32   While the issues of digital memory and additional technologies such as tagging, labelling and linking are all relevant – and important – there is an altogether different avenue to consider in terms of both RtbF and problem content specifically and reducing OA more generally. If the tools are not available, or

---

111 L Green, D Holloway, K Stevenson, T Leaver and L Haddon (eds), The Routledge Companion to Digital Media and Children (Routledge, 2020); RG Aydin and IA Nazim, 'The Impact of New Technologies on Human Rights in the Context of the Right to Be Forgotten and the Right to Privacy' Law of Ukraine: Legal Journal (Ukrainian) (2021) (2) 125; Z Sujon and HT Dyer, 'Understanding the Social in a Digital Age' New Media (2020) (22:7) 1125; 'Digital Media and the Right to be Forgotten' Lawyer (18 May 2020) 1-1; M Maroni, 'Lawless: The Secret Rules That Govern Our Digital Lives' European Journal of Risk Regulation (2021) (12:1) 264; F Fabbrini and E Celeste, 'The Right to Be Forgotten in the Digital Age: The Challenges of Data Protection Beyond Borders' German Law Journal, Special Issue (2020) (21) 55; R Childress, 'Tech Talk: 25 Technology Terms Everyone Should Know' Associations Now (2019) (15:3) 50; P Bernal, The Internet, Warts and All. Free Speech, Privacy and Truth (Cambridge University Press, 2019); A Koltay, 'The Internet, Warts and All. Free Speech, Privacy and Truth: by Paul Bernal, Cambridge University Press' Review, Journal of Media Law (2019) (11:2) 165; C Goanta, 'New Technologies and EU Law' European Journal of Risk Regulation (2019) (10:1) 236; AF Douhan, 'Adapting the Human Rights System to the Cyber Age' Max Planck Yearbook of United Nations Law (2020) (23:1) 251; E Georgiades, 'A Right That Should've Been: Protection of Personal Images on the Internet' IDEA: The Intellectual Property Law Review (2021) (61:2) 275; C Kwak, J Lee and H Lee, 'Could You Ever Forget Me? Why People Want to be Forgotten Online' Journal of Business Ethics (2021) (February) 1; ME Gilman, 'Five Privacy Principles (From the GDPR) the United States Should Adopt To Advance Economic Justice' Arizona State Law Journal (2020) (52:2) 368.

112 A Rallo Lombarte, 'A New Generation of Digital Rights' Revista de Estudios Politicos (2020) (187) 101; G Cintra Guimarães, Global Technology and Legal Theory Transnational Constitutionalism: Google and the European Union (Taylor and Francis, 2019); C Kwak, J Lee and H Lee, 'Could You Ever Forget Me? Why People Want to be Forgotten Online' Journal of Business Ethics (F2021) (February) 1; AF Douhan, 'Adapting the Human Rights System to the Cyber Age' Max Planck Yearbook of United Nations Law (2020) (23:1) 251; D Wakabayashi, 'U.S. Antitrust Suit Is Existential Threat To an Internet Giant' New York Times (22 October 2020) (170:58854) B1-B7; A Satariano and D McCabe, 'The Unlikely Alliance Working to Rein In Tech's Biggest Names' New York Times (22 October 2020) (170:58854) B1-B7; S Changqing, T Sourdin and L Bin, 'The Smart Court – A New Pathway to Justice in China?' International Journal for Court Administration (2021) (12:1) 1; ME Gilman, 'Five Privacy Principles (From the GDPR) the United States Should Adopt To Advance Economic Justice' *Arizona State Law Journal* (2020) (52:2) 368.

some of the tools and interfaces for availing of RtbF (and other remedies) are under-designed, under-resourced or understaffed, or notices are not properly followed up, the effectiveness of RtbF is likely to be less than satisfactory. The victims of OA will often want to have problem content taken down, removed and forgotten – regardless of jurisdiction and location.[113] RtbF is welcome, but it cannot always be considered in isolation. It must be complemented by associated issues and strategies. Greater research, baselines and statistics can go a long way to improve efforts to deal with and eventually diminish problems with online abuse.

There are emerging challenges to the data protection and privacy of individuals – including as consumers – as well as emerging challenges to the data protection and privacy laws.[114] New developments will continue to bring increasing threats to data, information, and privacy.[115] These issues are enhanced when there is a lack of transparency and accountability[116] – whether generally or at the launch of new applications.

The phenomena of increasing attacks and diminishing zones of personal privacy[117] must be considered. There is concern about the growing number of victims being subjected to OA and the increasing number of individuals who are becoming potentially subject to some form of it. As threats increase, respective solutions must also keep pace – this is why there is a need for RtbF.

We need to consider data protection and privacy interests in the new internet, device. and information technology society.[118] Sometimes, the question arises as to whether, when and whether law shapes technology or vice versa,[119] but we cannot ignore increasing risks and new threats. The concepts of privacy, personality, confidentiality[120] and personal data and information[121] as previously understood are being tested. Our traditional zones of privacy and data protection are not as safe as they once were. The risk of personal data ending up online has vastly increased since 1995. Some discussion centres on how data protection

---

113 Erin Cooper, for example, suggests that the US 'should adopt' a US RtbF in relation to the victims of crime. E Cooper, 'Following in the European Union's Footsteps: Why the United States Should Adopt Its Own Right to Be Forgotten Law For Crime Victims' *John Marshall Journal of Information Technology and Privacy Law* (2015) (32:3) 185. Also note C Myers, 'Digital Immortality vs "The Right to be Forgotten": A Comparison of US and E.U. Laws Concerning Social Media Privacy' *Romanian Journal of Communications and Public Relations* (2016) (16:3) 47.

114 Witzleb, Lindsay, Paterson and Rodrick, *Emerging Challenges in Privacy Law: Comparative Perspectives*.

115 M Schachter, *Information and Decisional Privacy* (Carolina Academic Press, 2003).

116 Purtova, *Property Rights in Personal Data* above at 51.

117 LL Llanillo and KY Baustista, 'Zones of Privacy: How Private?' *Defense Counsel Journal* (2017) (84:3) 1.

118 P Leith, *Privacy in the Information Society* (Routledge, 2016).

119 D Flint, 'Law Shaping Technology: Technology Shaping the Law' *International Review of Law*, Computers & Technology (2009) (23:1/2) 5.

120 E Christie Reid, *Personality, Confidentiality and Privacy in Scots Law* (W Green/Thomson Reuters, 2010).

121 R Wacks, *Personal Information: Privacy and the Law* (Clarendon, 1989).

and privacy laws have become outdated.[122] Urs Gasser of Harvard believes that we need to 'recode' (data protection and) privacy law(s).[123] Increasingly, international perspectives and comparisons are possible as the same risks apply to individuals regardless of location.[124] Brimblecombe and Phillipson, amongst others, suggest that RtbF can help individuals in 'regaining digital privacy'[125] and data protection. Many may also suggest that it is a necessary solution. One cannot discuss RtbF without also considering online problem content issues.[126]

122 Kilgore, 'Your Head Is in the Cloud: The Application of Outdated Privacy Law to Rapidly Changing Technologies' above at 101.
123 U Gasser, 'Recoding Privacy Law: Reflections on the Future Relationship Among Law, Technology and Privacy' *Harvard Law Review* (2016) (130:2) 61.
124 L Bygrave, *Data Privacy Law: An International Perspective* (OUP, 2014).
125 F Brimblecombe and G Phillipson, 'Regaining Digital Privacy: The New Right to Be Forgotten and Online Expression' *Canadian Journal of Comparative and Contemporary Law* (2018) (4) 1.
126 P Lambert, 'The AG Opinion in Google Franc, An Adequate Remedy?' International Journal for the Data Protection Officer, Privacy Officer and Privacy Counsel (IDPP) (2019) (3:3).

CHAPTER 4

Online Tools

I INTRODUCTION

4.1   The discussion in relation to online tools is often less developed than it needs to be. There is quite a lot of media commentary in relation to there being a lack of tools or inadequate tools for the takedown of online problem content relating to individuals. There is also some publicity when a company announces that it is either introducing or improving a given tool on its website. When a website has announced a stream of individual 'improvements', over 12 or 18 months, one question that arises is whether there were poor safety and takedown options originally.[1] Frequently media commentary also highlights that there is a perception that complaints by individuals are often ignored entirely. Despite the media commentary, there is a lack of more detailed academic research around online tools. This is also relevant for particular court disputes.

2   NEED FOR RULES AND TOOLS

4.2   There is a wider discussion about the need to regulate technologies and future technologies.[2] Data protection and privacy laws are a legitimate avenue to do so (albeit, not the only one[3]). There is an increasing need for identifying, takedown and forgetting and legislating for risks arising with new technologies.[4] RtbF is a core part of assisting and protecting individuals in this regard.

---

1   As an example, see: A Banerjea and A Wilson, 'Facebook Releases Safety Check Crisis Response Tool for Workplace' 9 October 2008. Available at: https://code.fb.com/web/safety-check-for-workplace; S Perez, 'Facebook Rolls Out New Anti-Bullying Tools and An Appeals Process' *TechCrunch*, 2 October 2018; J Karaian and H Kozlowska, 'Facebook Is Rushing Out A New Design for Privacy Settings' *QZ.com*, 28 March 2018; E Wills, 'Facebook Launches Anti-harassment Tools to Prevent Unwanted Messages and Unwanted Friend Requests' *Evening Standard*, 19 December 2017. More recently, see C Duffy, 'The Facebook Papers may be the Biggest Crisis in the Company's History' CNN (26 October 2021). It is useful to trace safety improvement announcements over time from technology companies such as Twitter and Uber. The question arises when looking at these timelines as to whether some or more of these should have been in place sooner. The New Zealand mosque shooting also involved takedown speeds.
2   G Hornung, 'Regulating Privacy Enhancing Technologies: Seizing the Opportunity of the Future European Data Protection Framework' *Innovation: The European Journal of Social Sciences* (2013) (26:1/2) 181.
3   For example, criminal law.
4   G van Calster, 'Risk Regulation, EU Law and Emerging Technologies: Smother or Smooth?' *NanoEthics* (2008) (2:1) 61.

There is a need for protection against overly invasive technologies.[5] The technology for identifying, categorising, and profiling personal data[6] is outpacing the ability of most individuals to stay aware of how that data can be used in the future and how it is currently being used.

RtbF is just one of these tools. As we begin to further appreciate it, we need to know more about how it can be used for different types of online abuse (OA); and the effectiveness of RtbF online reporting tools and other forms of online reporting tools. Part of this exercise and research is the ability of the public, data regulators and the courts to be able to see in a transparent manner how the mechanisms of reporting can be effected and how reports are dealt with once they are received by the service provider websites, as well as what tools are available, how they operate, effectiveness of given tools, and also tool gaps. Courtney Brewer, in a different context, asks if companies have the right tool-sets in place for making proactive safety decisions.[7] This question also applies in the online environment. Indeed, whistleblower' disclosures concerning Instagram issues regarding safety and wellbeing of girls just emphasises the need for tool scrutiny – of which RtbF is just one part.

Indeed, the extent to which a given company or website is deemed to have insufficient safety tools (including RtbF tools) and processes, data fines will increasingly come into focus.[8]

Ultimately, relevant parties need to be able to establish if complaints about problem content and related reports are increasing or decreasing and how the practices of website X compare to websites Y and Z, in part to see if website X is implementing standards and respect for data rights that are less stringent than other websites.

As we increasingly focus on digital memory and issues of digital forgetting, we may also consider forgetting by design (FbD) or digital forgetting by design (DFbD). Alternatively, there might be a need for planned forgetting in particular contexts (eg, social media websites). If there was a policy of obsolescence and forgetting in relation to old personal data, might RtbF be part of this social media FbD? Might reminder and choices be given to individuals in relation to whether they wish to store or delete old data or restrict access or availability? Might there be options to set defaults to delete certain types of data or certain databases after,

---

5   T Hale-Kupiec, 'Immortal Invasive Initiatives: The Need for a Genetic Right to Be Forgotten' *Minnesota Journal of Law, Science and Technology* (2016) (17:1) 441; J Valentino-Devries, N Singer, MH Keller and A Krolik, 'Your Apps Know Where You Were Last Night, and They're Not Keeping It Secret' *New York Times* (10 December 2018).

6   Note, profiling does not always go as planned. See, eg, J Archer, 'Facebook and Twitter Apologise After Mother Who Suffered a Stillbirth is Bombarded With Baby Ads' *Telegraph* (13 December 2018).

7   C Brewer, 'Do Companies Have the Right Tools to Make Proactive Safety Decisions?' Hydrocarbon Processing (2021) (100:1) 19.

8   A recent example is A White, 'Google gets Record Belgian Privacy Fine Over "Right to Be Forgotten"' Bloomberg.com (14 July 2020). Also see P Lambert, Data Fines, Understanding the New EU Data Fine Rules (Kortext, 2021).

say, five years, 10 years, 15 years or even on events such as graduating from university?

Privacy by design (PbD) (now called privacy and security by design) and data protection by design (DPbD) are important, the latter of which is explicitly required in the new General Data Protection Regulation (GDPR).[9] These are also increasingly discussed for their positive commercial effects, as well as in particular contexts, such as PbD/DPbD for Big Data.[10] There would, of course, be benefits to social media and related websites considering better design and early embedded design from the earliest opportunity to assist in reducing problem content online.

Just as PbD and DPbD can create positive commercial benefits for organisations, where it becomes evident that a given organisation has ignored better practices, best practice and the very safety of its customers and users, this can have a detrimental effect on the reputation of the organisation.[11]

In terms of considering the tapestry of online problem content from a policy perspective, of which RtbF is a part, we should not ignore focus on methods to identify current – and future – threats to individuals. Once threats exist, we need to be able to recognise them as soon as possible.[12]

As a result of foreign interference in the 2016 US presidential election and subsequently, there are new channels of communication between many social media websites and official authorities in the US to report or communicate new identified threats as soon as they arise.

Given their specialist knowledge, experience, and position, it may be that social media websites have an obligation to report new forms or escalations of OA to the appropriate authorities, including to the data regulators.

While RtbF is an evolution of takedown and respect for personal data we may, in time, need to recognise that it needs further expanded development.

In future, the increase in 'smart' devices and internet of things (IoT) will put pressure on what was once home, family, and private space. This will inevitably increase the amount of problem content which individuals will need to have taken down, erased, and forgotten from the internet.

9   JE Giannakakis, '"Privacy By Design (PbD) and Transparency Requirements Under the General Data Protection Regulation (GDPR) as Fraud Prevention Tools' *International Journal for the Data Protection Officer, Privacy Officer and Privacy Counsel (IDPP)* (2017) (1:2) 8.
10   E Everson, 'Privacy by Design: Taking CTRL of Big Data' *Cleveland State Law Review* (2017) (65:1) 27.
11   See generally, for example, C Manara and C Roquilly, 'The Risk of Brand Equity Erosion in the Social Media: the Efficacy and Limitations of Legal Instruments' *Recherche et Applications en Marketing* (English Edition) (AFM c/o ESCP-EAP) (2011) (26:3) 93.
12   Payton and Claypoole refer to the need to identify threats. TM Payton and T Claypoole, *Privacy in the Age of Big Data: Recognizing Threats, Defending Your Rights and Protecting Your Family* (Rowman, 2014).

The increasing ability of more and more devices to record images and sound in public spaces will also put pressure on individuals as the amount of what can then become problem content increases.[13]

The current remedies against interference with the right to private and family life under national, European, and ECHR rules[14] may not be sufficient for future events and problem content. Just as there was a problem of time with the DPD 95/45, it may be that the speed of developments mean that we cannot wait over 20 years to address future online problem content and forgetting issues.

Slow Roll Out

4.3   Some social media sites provide 'tools' or 'reporting processes'. However, many of them and indeed other Web 2.0 sites, do not do all they can to deal with these issues. Even some of the largest social media websites have been slower to implement reporting procedures for certain forms of OA than should be the case.

Blinkered

4.4   Some websites also have tools available which they use for certain activities but are reluctant to extend to OA victims. For example, certain tools already exist which help the victims of copyright infringement (eg, identifying infringing problem content; blocking and keeping problem content down to prevent re-uploads). These can also assist the victims of online abuse, but providers are refusing to use them, even when these have been specifically requested.[15] There is also an imbalance in that corporate victims receive more assistance from certain online service providers than do individuals.

Front End Follow Up

4.5   No matter how many 'report buttons' there are on a given website, they are entirely useless without protocols, policies and procedures behind the scenes to follow up on complaints that are made. A complaints procedure is meaningless unless there are enough people to investigate reports of online abuse.

---

13 On public space issues generally, see T Timan, B Clayton Newell and B- Koops, *Privacy in Public Space: Conceptual and Regulatory Challenges* (Elgar, 2017).

14 R Matefi, 'Interference in the Exercise of the Right to Private and Family Life in the Context of National and European Regulations and ECHR Jurisprudence' *Bulletin of the Transilvania University of Braşov: Series VII: Social Sciences, Law* (2018) (11:60) 65.

15 Some of these were requested and refused, in *McKeogh v Dow & Others* [2012] IEHC 95. Also note EJ George, 'The Pursuit of Happiness in the Digital Age: Using Bankruptcy and Copyright Law as a Blueprint for Implementing the Right to Be Forgotten in the US' *Georgetown Law Journal* (2018) (106:3) 905. Note also P Lambert, 'IP and PI Takedowns: Comparing and Contrasting the Right to be Forgotten' European Intellectual Property Review (2019) (41:6) 381.

Number of Employees Needed

4.6   We need to examine and compare the number of people employed in OA teams across various social media websites. We need better metrics to consider whether or not they are adequate and, importantly, when there are deficiencies to identify this, increase the numbers, improve the safety measures and complaint processes and procedures.

Reporting Detailed Statistics

4.7   A further point arises. Some social media and related websites are happy to publish statistics about the level of reports and complaints they have received relating to copyright infringement. This appears commercially driven. There is significantly less 'transparency' as regards the level of OA reports and complaints made to social media websites. We do not have transparency around how and how quickly these reports are resolved. What one website may say is resolved may not equate with what another website defines as a resolution.

We may be shocked at the scale of online abuse being reported, when full transparency is available. That may be a useful line to pursue for anyone who is officially concerned about this issue.

Transparent and User Friendly; Non-transparent and Not User Friendly

4.8   Social media frequently appears to value membership numbers over fully transparent, obvious and user-friendly privacy protection and complaint tools. The on-site tools (if they are present) are 'frequently unobvious or difficult to use. The cynical might imagine that this is because … the revenue stream from the SNS comes from third parties – advertisers – having access to as much data, on as many profiles, as possible'.[16]

One solution is to have privacy and friend-restricted access as the default model for social media websites. This is suggested, particularly in relation to children, by the Home Office Code of Conduct for Social Networks.[17]

There is frequent criticism in relation to problems with online policies and complaint reporting tools. Even being able to leave social media websites and cancel one's account is not an easy or transparent task.

Equally, policymakers and courts must start to look at the design of websites when considering certain issues in relation to RtbF notices and cases when disputes arise.

---

16   L Edwards and C Waelde, *Law and the Internet* (Hart, 2009) 483. Also see Gringras, The Laws of the Internet (Bloomsbury, 2021),
17   In 2008. Available at: www.gov.uk/government/uploads/system/uploads/attachment_data/file/251456/industry_guidance_social_networking.pdf.

Woodrow Harzon points out that:

> There are a number of issues regarding the implementation of this right, but the largest so far has been the uncertainty around the decision making and actual takedown process for the links.[18]

He is also puzzled that, too often, courts have ignored these wider relevant issues.[19] This may change in future.

Improvements and Tracking

4.9   Popular social media[20] websites, such as Twitter and Reddit, are recognising that more needs to be done to address issues of OA and have been implementing changes to deal with the problem. (That various changes are made by a given website does not mean that there is not more to do.) It would also assist if websites maintained a dedicated page listing all their improvements over time.

YouTube and Google also embrace 'real name' posting policies (in part). Such policies may assist in reducing trolling and attacks online, as well as their unfortunate consequences.[21]

It can sometimes be difficult, however, to keep track of the statements, changes, improvements (and regressions) in terms of the activities, policies, and tools on websites. It is not easy for observers to identify that there has been a safety improvement or reduction in complaints or a more efficient resolution of complaints, without baseline year statistics which would allow comparison in future years and also between different websites.

Online Takedown Codes of Conduct

4.10   There are also business case advantages to improving safety, trust, forgetting, etc. The EU Commission and websites have agreed a Code of Conduct initiative for certain online takedowns (namely, online hate).[22] A further Code of Practice on Online Disinformation has subsequently been drawn up

---

18 W Hartzon, *Privacy's Blueprint: The Battle to Control the Design of New Technologies* (Harvard University Press, 2018) 165.

19 *Ibid*, 171. *McKeogh v Doe and Others*, an online abuse (and related issues) case did refer to some of the wider concerns and design issues in addition to policies.

20 S Rogerson, 'Wireless and Social Media Influence' *International Journal for the Data Protection Officer, Privacy Officer and Privacy Counsel (IDPP)* (2018) (2:7) 12.

21 Generally note, for example, B Kane, 'Balancing Anonymity, Popularity, & Micro-Celebrity: The Crossroads of Social Networking & Privacy' *Albany Law Journal of Science and Technology* (2010)(20) 327.

22 European Commission, 'European Commission and IT Companies Announce Code of Conduct on Illegal Online Hate Speech' *Press Release* (31 May 2016). Available at: http://europa.eu/rapid/press-release_IP-16-1937_en.htm. This is directed at 'hate' content but crosses over and can include OA.

between the EU Commission and online service providers.[23] The wide concept of personal data and data protection[24] may further assist individuals in terms of the effectiveness of these Codes. However, at present, these codes appear to be voluntary; enforcement and adherence issues will have to be reviewed in due course.

Knowledge Gaps

4.11 Unfortunately, there are large gaps in our knowledge, research, and understanding of these developing issues, the scale of OA, and statistics on report actions (once a complaint is made by an individual) and demonstrated statistical improvements year on year. More research is needed to understand potential solutions and policy decisions as well as assisting websites to fully engage their own (corporate, moral, ethical, and legal) responsibilities and functional capabilities. The more information we have on baselines, statistics, improvements, etc, the better equipped companies, courts, and regulators are to tackle these problems.

23 European Commission, *Code of Practice on Online Disinformation* (26 September 2018). Further details are available at: https://ec.europa.eu/digital-single-market/en/news/code-practice-disinformation. The Code is available at: file:///C:/Users/dell/Downloads/1CodeofPrac ticeonDisinformation.pdf. This appears more directed at 'fake news' and online disinformation but can have potential relevance and assistance in terms of OA.

24 N Purtova, 'The Law of Everything: Broad Concept of Personal Data and Future of EU Data Protection Law' *Innovation and Technology* (2018) (10:1) 40.

CHAPTER 5

Legal Backdrop

I INTRODUCTION

5.1 The backdrop and background of the data protection regime and some of the most relevant rules in the context of RtbF must also be considered. These set the tapestry against which the current interests and notice of individuals will be successfully dealt with (or otherwise) depending on the nature of the notice and/ or the industry of the service provider responsible for the website in question.

2 FUNDAMENTAL RIGHT OF DATA PROTECTION

5.2 Personal data protection is recognised as a fundamental right for individuals. It is expressly recognised in:

- the new GDPR[1] (and UK GDPR);

- the EU Charter of Fundamental Rights, Lisbon Treaty;[2] and

- the Council of Europe Convention.[3]

The Charter refers to personal data as a fundamental right in Article 8(1) as follows:

Protection of Personal Data

Everyone has the right to the protection of personal data concerning him or her.

The Lisbon Treaty refers to personal data as a fundamental right in Article 16(1), as follows:

Everyone has the right to the protection of personal data concerning them.

---

1   Regulation (EU) 2016/679 of the European Parliament and of the Council of 27 April 2016 on the protection of natural persons with regard to the processing of personal data and on the free movement of such data and repealing Directive 95/46/EC (General Data Protection Regulation) (Text with EEA relevance) OJ L 119, 4.5.2016, p 1. See P Lambert, A User's Guide to Data Protection (Bloomsbury, 2020); P Lambert, 5 Essential GDPR Context Lists (Kortext, 2021); P Lambert, Essential GDPR Index (Kortext, 2021); P Lambert, The UK GDPR Annotated (Kortext, 2021).
2   Treaty on the Functioning of the European Union.
3   Council of Europe Convention on data protection, No 108 of 1981. Note that the Council of Europe contains over 40 Member States and so is wider than just the European Union.

3 EU LAW AND DATA PROTECTION LAWS

5.3 Part of the inevitable backdrop to this discussion is, of course, the wider European law regime.[4] This focuses on EU data protection law[5] and commentary.[6] Complying with data protection and privacy laws and the manner of compliance is an important aspect of the data protection regime.[7] The wide concept of personal data and data protection is an integral part of any such consideration.[8]

There is a growing list of academic references to EU data protection law[9] and an increasing number of textbooks dedicated to EU data protection laws.[10]

Complying with data protection and privacy laws is also increasingly the focus of scholars and professional guidance and intelligence firms.[11]

---

4 See, eg, texts such as R Schütze and T Tridimas, *Oxford Principles of European Union Law* (OUP, 2018); N Foster, Foster on *EU Law* (OUP, 2019); E Kirk, *EU Law* (Pearson, 2021); T Tridimas, *General Principles of EU Law* (OUP, 2019); R Schütze, *An Introduction to European Law* (CUP, 2020); E Jones, A Menon and S Weatherill, *The Oxford Handbook of the European Union* (OUP, 2014); C Barnard and S Peers, *European Union Law* (OUP, 2020); D Chalmers, G Davies and G Monti, *European Union Law* (CUP, 2019); P Craig and G de Búrca, *The Evolution of EU Law* (OUP, 2021); C Barnard, *The Substantive Law of the EU, The Four Freedoms* (OUP, 2019); TC Hartley, *European Union Law in a Global Context* (CUP, 2004); P Raworth, *Introduction to the Legal System of the European Union* (Oceana, 2001); JA Usher, *EC Institutions and Legislation* (Longman, 1998): Chapter 8 'Consequences of EC Legislation: The Direct Effect and Indirect Effect' at 144; P Craig and C Harlow, *Law Making in the European Union* (Kluwer, 1998); A Reinisch, *Essential Questions in EU Law* (CUP, 2009); S Szabo, 'European Values, Fundamental Rights and the Private International Law of the European Union' *Hungarian Yearbook of International Law and European Law* (2014) 307; A Hartkamp, C Sieburgh and W Devroe, *Cases, Materials and Text on European Law and Private Law* (Hart, 2017); M Macchia, 'Research Handbook on EU Administrative Law' *Italian Journal of Public Law* (2017) (9:2) 420; R Gordon QC and R Moffat, *EU Law in Judicial Review* (OUP, 2014); Lambert, Data Fines, Understanding the New EU Data Fine Rules; P Lambert, Data Protection, Privacy Regulators and Supervisory Authorities (Bloomsbury, 2020).
5 Hartkamp, Sieburgh and Devroe, *Cases, Materials and Text on European Law and Private Law*.
6 A Iftimiei, 'Protection of Personal Data: Aspects of European Law' *Analele Stiintifice Ale Universitatii Alexandru Ioan Cuza Din Iasi Stiinte Juridice* (2018) (64:1) 273; O Lynskey, *The Foundations of EU Data Protection Law* (OUP, 2015). I Sammut, *Constructing Modern European Private Law: A Hybrid System* (Cambridge Scholars Publishing, 2016).
7 L Determann, *Determann's Field Guide to Data Privacy Law: International Corporate Compliance* (Elgar, 2015); P Lambert, *Understanding the New European Data Protection Rules* (Taylor & Francis, 2017); P Lambert, 'Complying with the Data Protection Regime' *International Journal for the Data Protection Officer, Privacy Officer and Privacy Counsel (IDPP)* (2018) (2:7) 17.
8 N Purtova, 'The Law of Everything: Broad Concept of Personal Data and the Future of EU Data Protection Law' *Innovation and Technology* (2018) (10:1) 40.
9 Hartkamp, Sieburgh and Devroe, *Cases, Materials and Text on European Law and Private Law*.
10 Iftimiei, 'Protection of Personal Data: Aspects of European Law' *Analele Stiintifice Ale Universitatii Alexandru Ioan Cuza Din Iasi Stiinte Juridice* at 273; Lynskey, *The Foundations of EU Data Protection Law*; Sammut, *Constructing Modern European Private Law: A Hybrid System*; Lambert, A User's Guide to Data Protection; P Lambert, Data Fines, Understanding the New EU Data Fine Rules (Kortext, 2021).
11 Determann, *Determann's Field Guide to Data Privacy Law*; Lambert, *Understanding the New European Data Protection Rules*.

How data protection laws exist and are used generally in the different EU Member States is also the focus of dedicated texts. This also includes reference to these issues after commencement of the GDPR. Just some of the Member State examples are:

- Germany;[12]

- Spain;[13]

- Italy;[14]

- Denmark;[15]

- Ireland;[16]

---

12 AF von dem Bussche and P Voigt, *Data Protection in Germany: Including EU General Data Protection Regulation 2018* (Beck, 2017); Lambert, Data Fines, Understanding the New EU Data Fine Rules; HA Wolff, 'The Implementation of Administrative Fines Under the General Data Protection Regulation From the German Perspective' *International Journal for the Data Protection Officer, Privacy Officer and Privacy Counsel (IDPP)* (2018) (2:11) 11; M Göoman 'The New Territorial Scope of EU Data Protection Law: Deconstructing a Revolutionary Achievement' *Common Market Law Review* (2017) (54:2) 567; L Essers, 'Facebook Must Comply with German Data Protection Law, Court Rules' *Good Gear Guide* (18 February 2014) 4; N English and F Bieker, 'Upholding Data Protection Law Against Multinational Corporations: German Administrative Measures Relating to Facebook' *German Yearbook of International Law* (2012) (55) 587; T Hoeren, 'The New German Data Protection Act and Its Compatibility with the European Data Protection Directive' *Computer Law & Security Review* (2009) (25:4) 318; G Bachmann, P Bialski and M Hansen, 'The Terms of Anonymity: An Interview With Marit Hansen, German Data Protection Expert' *Ephemera: Theory & Politics in Organization* (2017) (17:2) 421; M Schallbruch and S Isabel, *Cybersecurity in Germany* (Springer, 2018); J Kirchner, PR Kremp and M Magotsch, *Key Aspects of German Employment and Labour Law* (Springer-Verlag, 2018): Chapter 12 'Data Protection and Monitoring' by V Grentzenberg and J Kirchner; Chapter 18 'Compliance' by PR Kremp and J Kirchner. N Studt, 'Germany: Data Protection Law Scuppers Archive on Serial Litigants' *Venulex Legal Summaries* (2010 Q2, Special section) 14; A de Hingh, 'Some Reflections on Dignity as an Alternative Legal Concept in Data Protection Regulation' *German Law Journal* (2018) (19:5) 1269.

13 M Recio, 'Spain: Preparations for a New Law on Data Protection to Implement the GDPR' *European Data Protection Law Review (EDPL)* (2017) (3:3) 376; AM Leiva, 'Data Protection Law in Spain and Latin America: Survey of Legal Approaches' International Law News (2012) (41:4) 16; C Álvarez, '"Perspectives on the GDPR: Spanish Privacy Professionals Association' *International Journal for the Data Protection Officer, Privacy Officer and Privacy Counsel (IDPP)* (2018) (2:3) 14.

14 NCN Hampson, 'The Internet is Not a Lawless Prairie: Data Protection and Privacy in Italy' *Boston College International and Comparative Law Review* (2011) (34:2) 477; G Ziccardi, *Cyber Law in Italy* (Turpin, 2011); S Bologna, A Bellavista, PP Corso and G Zangara, *Electronic Health Record in Italy and Personal Data Protection* (Brill, 2016); F Di Ciommo, 'Privacy in Europe after Regulation (EU) No 2016/679: What Will Remain of the Right to Be Forgotten' *Italian Law Journal* (2017) (3:2) 623; GM Riccio, 'Perspectives on the GDPR, A View from Italy' *International Journal for the Data Protection Officer, Privacy Officer and Privacy Counsel (IDPP)* (2018) (2:3) 24; A Soro, President Italian Data Protection Authority, 'Perspectives on the GDPR: Italian Data Protection Authority' *International Data Protection Officer, Privacy Officer and Privacy Counsel (IDPP)* (2018) (2:3) 13.

15 P Blume, 'The Data Protection Directive and Danish Law' *International Review of Law, Computers & Technology* (1997) (11:1) 65.

16 P Lambert, *Data Protection Law in Ireland, Sources and Issues* (Clarus, 2019); E O'Dell, 'Compensation for Breach of the General Data Protection Regulation' *Dublin University Law Journal* (2017) (40:1) 97.

- Greece;[17]

- UK[18] (notwithstanding Brexit issues);

- Scotland[19] (but part of UK).

Data protection laws in other countries are also referred to, for example:

- Canada;[20]

- New Zealand;[21]

- Mexico;[22]

- Brazil;[23]

- El Salvador;[24]

- South Africa;[25]

- Columbia;[26]

---

17 M Katrakazi, 'Road to GDPR Compliance: Developments in Greece' *International Journal for the Data Protection Officer, Privacy Officer and Privacy Counsel (IDPP)* (2018) (2:3) 23.

18 E Denham, UK Information Commissioner, 'Perspective on the GDPR and Current Issues from the UK Information Commissioner' *International Journal for the Data Protection Officer, Privacy Officer and Privacy Counsel (IDPP)* (2018) (2:3) 12. HJ Cremer, *Human Rights and the Protection of Privacy in Tort Law: A Comparison Between English and German Law* (Routledge-Cavendish, 2011); Lambert, The UK GDPR Annotated.

19 E Christie Reid, *Personality, Confidentiality and Privacy in Scots Law* (W Green/Thomson Reuters, 2010).

20 Privacy Commissioner of Canada, 'A Canadian Perspective on Modernizing Privacy Legislation' *International Journal for the Data Protection Officer, Privacy Officer and Privacy Counsel* (2018) (2:3); S Morgan, 'Private Sector Privacy Audits, Undertaken by the Privacy Commissioner of Canada and the Impact of Impending Privacy Regulations' *International Journal for the Data Protection Officer, Privacy Officer and Privacy Counsel (IDPP)* (2017) (1:1) 11; S Morgan, 'Preparing for the Canadian Data Breach Reporting Requirements' *International Journal for the Data Protection Officer, Privacy Officer and Privacy Counsel* (2018) (2:7) 8.

21 David Harvey, Hon Judge and Professor, 'Perceptions to the GDPR: New Zealand' *International Journal for the Data Protection Officer, Privacy Officer and Privacy Counsel (IDPP)* (2018) (2:3) 10; A Roos, 'Personal Data Protection in New Zealand: Lessons for South Africa?' *Potchefstroom Electronic Law Journal* (2008) (11:4) 61.

22 L Determann and S Legorreta, 'New Data Privacy Law in Mexico' *Computer & Internet Lawyer* (2010) (27:12) 8.

23 F Bousso, 'Perspectives of the European General Data Protection Regulation (GDPR) in Brazil' *International Journal for the Data Protection Officer, Privacy Officer and Privacy Counsel (IDPP)* (2018) (2:3) 31; R Opice Blum and C Rioja, 'Brazil's "GDPR" Sanctioned' *International Journal for the Data Protection Officer, Privacy Officer and Privacy Counsel (IDPP)* (2018) (2:9) 12.

24 R Bonilla, '"Perspectives for Supranational Digital Regulation in Developing Countries' *International Journal for the Data Protection Officer, Privacy Officer and Privacy Counsel (IDPP)* (2018) (2:3) 21.

25 C Yav, '"Perspectives on the GDPR From South Africa' *International Journal for the Data Protection Officer and Privacy Counsel (IDPP)* (2018) (2:3) 19.

26 D Peña, '"The Future of Data Protection After the New Government in Colombia' *International Journal for the Data Protection Officer, Privacy Officer and Privacy Counsel (IDPP)* (2018) (2:6) 18.

- US;[27]
- US states eg California.[28]

Data protection is also sometimes referred to on a regional basis, for example:
- Central Europe;[29]
- Latin America;[30]
- Asia;[31]
- Africa;[32]
- Middle East.[33]

There is also some comparison of issues between different countries.[34] This also extends to how EU law applies in national systems[35] and how different implementation routes can exist. Indeed, this is evidenced by the previous data protection regime (namely, that implemented via the DPD 95/46) as opposed to the new data protection regime (implemented in the form of the GDPR).

27 KK Dort, JT Criss and R Thakrar, 'Trends in Cybersecurity Law, the Privacy Shield and Best Practices for Businesses Operating in the Global Marketplace' *International Journal for the Data Protection Officer, Privacy Officer and Privacy Counsel (IDPP)* (2017) (1:1) 15. SK Katyal, 'Perceptions to the GDPR: US' *IDPP* (2018) (2:3) 16; A Tantleff, 'Perceptions to the GDPR: US' *IDPP* (2018) (2:3) 16; D Reynolds, 'Perceptions to the GDPR: US' (*IDPP*) (2018) (2:3) 17; G Nojeim, 'Wider Implications of *Carpenter v United States*' *International Journal for the Data Protection Officer, Privacy Officer and Privacy Counsel (IDPP)* (2018) (2:6) 8.

28 A Lee, 'Enforcement of Calif. Data Privacy Law Begins' WWD: Women's Wear Daily (2 July 2020) 3-3; M McGinnis Stine and S Kilian, 'Deletion Completion Under the CCPA' Computer & Internet Lawyer (2020) (37:5) 3; S Shatz and SE Chylik, 'The California Consumer Privacy Act of 2018: A Sea Change in the Protection of California Consumers' Personal Information' Business Lawyer (2020) (75:2) 1917; ME Gilman, 'Five Privacy Principles (From the GDPR) the United States Should Adopt To Advance Economic Justice' Arizona State Law Journal (2020) (52:2) 368.

29 L Majtenyi, 'Ensuring Data Protection in East-Central Europe' *Social Research* (2002) (69:1) 151.

30 AM Leiva, 'Data Protection Law in Spain and Latin America: Survey of Legal Approaches' *International Law News* (2012) (41:4) 16.

31 G Greenleaf, *Asian Data Privacy Laws* (OUP, 2017).

32 AB Makulilo, 'The GDPR Implications for Data Protection and Privacy Protection in Africa' *International Journal for the Data Protection Officer, Privacy Officer and Privacy Counsel (IDPP)* (2017) (1:2) 12.

33 B Meenagh and O Elsayed, 'The GDPR from Saudi Arabia and United Arab Emirates' *International Journal for the Data Protection Officer, Privacy Officer and Privacy Counsel (IDPP)* (2018) (2:3) 26.

34 Cremer, *Human Rights and the Protection of Privacy in Tort Law: A Comparison Between English and German Law.*

35 M Bobek, 'The Effect of EU Law in the National Legal Systems' in Barnard and Peers, *European Union Law* at 143; A-M Slaughter, A Stone Sweet and JHH Weiler, *The European Court and National Courts: Doctrine and Jurisprudence* (Bloomsbury, 1998); Chapter 8 'Consequences of EC Legislation: The Direct Effect and Indirect Effect' in Usher, *EC Institutions and Legislation* at 144; Macchia, 'Research Handbook on EU Administrative Law' at 420. Also in national systems such as Varju-Varnay (eds) The Law of the European Union in Hungary (HVG-ORAc, 2014) *Hungarian Yearbook of International Law and European Law* (2016) 745; C Beatrice Gabriela, 'ENE-DINU, The Impact of Preliminary Rulings Pronounced by the Court of Justice of the European Union on the Activity of the Romanian Courts of Law', *Challenges of the Knowledge Society* (2017) (7) 440.

4 DATA PROTECTION AND LEGAL INSTRUMENTS

5.4   As mentioned in various instances, EU law can be embodied in a variety of EU legal instruments. The origin or source of these instruments can also differ somewhat. In terms of the EU data protection regime we need to consider the two primary legislative routes adopted: Directives and Regulations.

The DPD 95/46 was a Directive:[36] 'Directives are normative acts addressed to the Member States, which are then required, within a specified deadline, to adopt the necessary national provisions to give effect to ("transpose") the policy objectives set out in the directive and to notify the Commission of their transposition measures.'[37]

The GDPR, in contrast and partly to ensure a more uniform application of EU data protection rules across the EU Member States, is a Regulation:[38] 'A Regulation is in effect the equivalent of a statute or law in a national legal order.'[39]

A Regulation has direct effect[40] in Member States without any further implementation being necessary.[41] (However, Directives can also have direct effect in certain circumstances.[42])

Data Protection Regime and Rules

5.5   The data protection regime provides or enshrines a number of rights to individuals in relation to their informational data and informational privacy and related obligations on both organisations and companies. RtbF is one of these important rights – and will become increasingly important as the amount of online personal

---

36   TFEU, Art 288, para 3. Usher, *EC Institutions and Legislation* at 131; Barnard and Peers, *European Union Law* at 100; Chapter 8 'Consequences of EC Legislation: The Direct Effect and Indirect Effect' in Usher, *EC Institutions and Legislation* at 144; Halsbury, *EU Legislation Implementator 2018: The Guide to the Implementation of Directives* (LexisNexis: 2018). Also J Dickson, 'Directives in EU Legal Systems: Whose Norms Are They Anyway?' *European Law Journal* (2011) (17:2) 190.

37   Barnard and Peers, *European Union Law* above at 100.

38   TEU, Art 288, para 2. See, eg, Usher, *EC Institutions and Legislation* at 128, 129; C Barnard and Peers, *European Union Law* at 99; Chapter 8 'Consequences of EC Legislation: The Direct Effect and Indirect Effect' in Usher, *EC Institutions and Legislation* at 144.

39   Barnard and Peers, *European Union Law* above at 99.

40   R Schütze, 'Direct Effect and Indirect Effects of Union Law' in Schütze and Tridimas, *Oxford Principles of European Union Law* above at 265.

41   However, in terms of the practicalities of the application of the GDPR in respective Member States, many have also introduced national data protection legal measures, in some instances to repeal past national laws implemented previously to implement and comply with the DPD 95/6; or in some instances also to deal with certain national law nuances that needed to be tailored to align with the new GDPR.

42   M Rasmussen, 'How to Enforce European Law? A New History of the Battle Over the Direct Effect of Directives, 1958–1987' *European Law Journal* (2017) (23:3/4) 290; D Carolin Hübner, 'The Decentralized Enforcement of European Law: National Court Decisions on EU Directives With and Without Preliminary Reference Submissions' *Journal of European Public Policy* (2018) (25:12) 1817.

content continues to grow. The wide definition of personal data[43] and the wide concept of personal data and data protection[44] will help in considering RtbF. There are also additional concepts to consider. Transparency and consent are very important aspects of respecting and enabling such fundamental rights to be vindicated, utilised, and enforced by individual data subjects. Individual data subjects have a right of access to personal data, which may, on occasion, be utilised simultaneously with the exercise of RtbF. There are also time limits, to be complied with by a data controller, in relation to replying to an individual data subject access notice (ie, a notice to access or obtain a copy of the personal data that the organisation holds).

5 GDPR

5.6   The new General Data Protection Regulation (GDPR)[45] refers to personal data as an important fundamental right. The GDPR recitals refer to fundamental rights at: Recitals 1, 2, 3, 4, 10, 16, 47, 51, 52, 53, 69, 73, 102, 104, 109, 111, 113, 114, 153, 159, 166 and 173. The GDPR Articles refer to fundamental rights at: Articles 2, 4 (24), 6, 9, 23, 45, 50, 51 and 88.

In addition, the GDPR expressly states in the background recitals, for example:

- *Recital 1*: The protection of natural persons in relation to the processing of personal data is a fundamental right. Article 8(1) of the Charter of Fundamental Rights of the European Union (the 'Charter') and Article 16(1) of the Treaty on the Functioning of the European Union (TFEU) provide that everyone has the right to the protection of their personal data.

- *Recital 2*: The principles of and rules on the protection of natural persons with regard to the processing of their personal data should, whatever their nationality or residence, respect their fundamental rights and freedoms, in particular their right to the protection of personal data.

- *Recital 4*: The GDPR respects all fundamental rights and observes the freedoms and principles recognised in the Charter as enshrined in the Treaties, in particular the respect for private and family life, home and communications, the protection of personal data, freedom of thought, conscience and religion, freedom of expression and information, freedom to conduct a business, the right to an effective remedy and to a fair trial and cultural, religious and linguistic diversity.

- *Recital 10*: Consistent and homogenous application of the rules for the protection of the fundamental rights and freedoms of natural persons with regard to the processing of personal data should be ensured throughout the Union.

---

43   GDPR Art 4(1).
44   Purtova, 'The Law of Everything: Broad Concept of Personal Data and Future of EU Data Protection Law' above at 40.
45   Generally, see Lambert, 5 Essential GDPR Content Lists; Lambert, Essential GDPR Index; and P Lambert, The UK GDPR Annotated. Also, Lambert, A User's Guide to Data Protection; and Gringras, The Laws of the Internet (Bloomsbury, 2022).

- *Recital 47*: The legitimate interests of a controller – including those of a controller to which the personal data may be disclosed – or of a third party, may provide a legal basis for processing, provided that the interests or the fundamental rights and freedoms of the data subject are not overriding, taking into consideration the reasonable expectations of data subjects based on their relationship with the controller ... The interests and fundamental rights of the data subject could in particular override the interest of the data controller where personal data are processed in circumstances where data subjects do not reasonably expect further processing.

- *Recital 51*: Personal data which are, by their nature, particularly sensitive in relation to fundamental rights and freedoms merit specific protection as the context of their processing could create significant risks to the fundamental rights and freedoms.

- *Recital 52*: '... so as to protect personal data and other fundamental rights ...'

- *Recital 111*: Fundamental rights of the data subject.

- *Recital 113*: '... protect fundamental rights and freedoms of natural persons with regard to the processing of their personal data'.

- *Recital 114*: '... benefit from fundamental rights and safeguards'.

- *Recital 116*: '... to protect the fundamental rights and freedoms of natural persons and in particular their right to the protection of personal data'.

In the Articles, the GDPR states:

- *Article 2*: The GDPR protects fundamental rights and freedoms of natural persons, in particular their right to the protection of personal data.

- *Article 6*: Fundamental rights and freedoms of the data subject which require protection of personal data, in particular where the data subject is a child.

- *Article 50*: Appropriate safeguards for the protection of personal data and other fundamental rights and freedom.

- *Article 51*: To protect the fundamental rights and freedoms of natural persons in relation to processing.

The data protection regime relies on its foundation definitions as important building blocks. The steps in understanding the data protection regime can be described as follows:

- the definition;
- the principles of data protection;
- the lawful processing conditions or grounds;
- the special (or sensitive) lawful processing conditions or grounds;
- additional lawful processing conditions for children's personal data; and
- the various rights of individual data subjects.

Principles of Data Protection

5.7　　The principles, or principles of data protection,[46] require that personal data are:

(1)　processed lawfully, fairly and transparently;

(2)　purpose limited;

(3)　minimised;

(4)　accurate;

(5)　storage limited;

(6)　secure; and

(7)　accountable.

The new GDPR expresses the principles as requiring that personal data are:

- processed lawfully, fairly and in a transparent manner in relation to the data subject (lawfulness, fairness and transparency);[47]

- collected for specified, explicit and legitimate purposes and not further processed in a way incompatible with those purposes; further processing for archiving purposes in the public interest, scientific and historical research purposes or statistical purposes shall, in accordance with Article 89(1), not be considered incompatible with the initial purposes (purpose limitation);[48]

- adequate, relevant and limited to what is necessary in relation to the purposes for which they are processed (data minimisation);[49]

- accurate and, where necessary, kept up to date; every reasonable step must be taken to ensure that personal data that are inaccurate, having regard to the purposes for which they are processed, are erased or rectified without delay (accuracy);[50]

- kept in a form which permits identification of data subjects for no longer than is necessary for the purposes for which the personal data are processed; personal data may be stored for longer periods insofar as the data will be processed solely for archiving purposes in the public interest, scientific or historical research purposes or statistical purposes in accordance with Article 89(1) subject to implementation of the appropriate technical and organisational measures required by the GDPR to safeguard the rights and freedoms of the data subject (storage limitation);[51]

- processed in a manner that ensures appropriate security of the personal data, including protection against unauthorised or unlawful processing and against accidental loss, destruction or damage, using appropriate technical or organisational measures (integrity and confidentiality).[52]

46　Previously, prior to the GDPR, referred to as the data protection principles.
47　GDPR Art 5(1)(a).
48　*Ibid* Art 5(1)(b).
49　*Ibid* Art 5(1)(c).
50　*Ibid* Art 5(1)(d).
51　*Ibid* Art 5(1)(e).
52　*Ibid* Art 5(1)(f).

The controller must be responsible for and be able to demonstrate compliance (accountability).[53]

Rights for Individual Data Subjects

5.8   The data protection rules contain several important rights for individuals in respect of their personal data, such as:

- RtbF;

- prior information that must be given to them by data controllers;

- access to personal data;

- the right to object to processing;

- not being forced to make an access request as a condition of recruitment, employment or provision of a service; and

- not being subjected to 'automated decision-making processes'.[54]

Individuals also have a right to prevent data processing for direct marketing (DM) purposes.

The individual data subject has a right to prevent processing likely to cause damage or distress.

A further right relates to automated decision taking,[55] which relates to automated decisions being taken without human oversight or intervention. The traditional example often used is adverse credit decisions being taken automatically. However, it can equally encompass such adverse decisions and activities as so-called neutral algorithmic processing and arranging of information and result outputs. Examples could include search rankings and priorities; search suggestions; search prompts; autosuggest; and autocomplete, etc. Other examples could arise in relation to profiling and advertising related activities.

Importantly for present purposes, individual data subjects have specific rights in relation to rectification, blocking, erasure, and destruction and what is becoming known as the Right to be Forgotten (RtbF). This has added significance and attention following the Court of Justice decision in the landmark case of *Google Spain*.[56]

---

53   *Ibid* Art 5(2).

54   G Malgieri and G Comande, 'Why a Right to Legibility of Automated Decision-Making Exists in the General Data Protection Regulation' *International Data Privacy Law* (2017) (7:4) 243. Also note E Esposito, 'Algorithmic Memory and the Right to be Forgotten on the Web' *Big Data & Society* (2017) (4) 1.

55   Malgieri and Comande, *ibid*.

56   *Google Spain SL, Google Inc v Agencia Española de Protección de Datos (AEPD), Mario Costeja González*, Court of Justice (Grand Chamber), Case C-131/12, 13 May 2014.

Individual data subjects are also entitled to compensation and damages, as well as being entitled to complain to the national data protection supervisory authority and to the courts to obtain judicial remedies.

The EU GDPR refers to individual data subject rights; principles of fair and transparent processing; prior information requirements; right of access; right of rectification and right to be forgotten (RtbF); right to complain to single data protection supervisory authority; and automated processing.[57]

One difficulty, however, in dealing with individual data subject rights is that the rights set out in the GDPR can have certain derogations, amendments and exemptions set out in Member State national data protection laws.[58]

Overall, the rights are expanding and becoming more explicit. It is important that organisations keep abreast of their increasing obligations. The data protection rights enshrined in the data protection regime for individuals are set out in the principles of data protection and elsewhere in the data protection rules. They include the following:

- individuals have a right to be informed by organisations as to their identity when they are collecting and processing the individual's personal data;

- the organisation must disclose to the individual the purpose for which it is collecting and processing the individual's personal data;

- if the organisation is forwarding on the personal data to third-party recipients, it must disclose this to the individual as well as identify the third-party recipients. If it is permitted to transfer the personal data outside of the country, the organisation must then also identify which third-party country will be receiving the personal data; and

- organisations must answer and comply with requests from the individual in relation to their data protection rights.

This includes requests for access to a copy of the personal data held in relation to the individual. This is known as a personal data access request.

The important rights of individual data subjects for present purposes can be summarised as:

- right to rectification, blocking, erasure and forgetting and destruction; and

- right to notification of erasure and for getting to third parties, etc.

---

57   Malgieri and Comande, 'Why a Right to Legibility of Automated Decision-Making Exists in the General Data Protection Regulation' at 243.

58   The UK Data Protection Act 2018 (DPA 2018) is one example of national law which applies derogations, amendments and exemptions from the GDPR, as is permitted. These are, however, not always easy to immediately discern given the complexity of the DPA 2018, including the extensive materials included in the Schedules to the Act. It may come to pass that some of these may be tested in court as not fulfilling or implementing the GDPR or departing from its requirements.

There are also additional rights of individual data subjects which can be summarised including:

- right of access;

- right to establish if personal data exists;

- right to be informed of the logic in automatic decision taking;

- right to prevent processing likely to cause damage or distress;

- right to prevent processing for direct marketing;

- right to prevent automated decision taking;[59]

- right to compensation;

- right to rectify inaccurate data;

- right to complain to the national data protection supervisory authority; and

- right to go to court.

Recipients of Right

5.9   The recipients of the rights of data protection, including RtbF, are important to understand and may be wider than some might think.

There are referred to below in greater detail.

6   NATIONAL REFERENCE, REACTION AND ADAPTATION OF RTBF

5.10   There are increasing references to RtbF after *Google Spain* and the GDPR. This includes, for example, in countries such as:

- Germany;[60]

- Spain;[61]

---

59   Malgieri and Comande, 'Why a Right to Legibility of Automated Decision-Making Exists in the General Data Protection Regulation' at 243.

60   H Tomlinson and A Wills, '*ML and WW v Germany* – Article 8 Right to be Forgotten and the Media' *Entertainment Law Review* (2018) (29:7) 232; A Bobić, 'Developments in The EU-German Judicial Love Story: The Right To Be Forgotten II' German Law Journal, Special Issue (2020) (21) 31; C Rauchegger, 'National Constitutional Courts as Guardians of the Charter: A Comparative Appraisal of the German Federal Constitutional Court's Right to Be Forgotten Judgments' Cambridge Yearbook of European Legal Studies (2020) (22) 258; P Frield, 'A New European Fundamental Rights Court: The German Constitutional Court on the Right to Be Forgotten' European Papers (2020) (5:1) 447.

61   M Peguera, 'In the Aftermath of *Google Spain*: How the 'Right to be Forgotten' is Being Shaped in Spain by Courts and the Data Protection Authority' *International Journal of Law* (2015) (23:4) 325; Mª. B López Portas, 'La Configuración Jurídica del Derecho al Olvido en el Derecho Español a Tenor de la Doctrina del Tjue / The Right to be Forgotten in Spanish Law Due to the CJEU Doctrine' *Revista de Derecho Político* (2015) (1:93) 143; J María Martínez

- France;[62]

- Italy;[63]

- Netherlands;[64]

- Romania;[65]

- Canada;[66]

Otero, 'El Derecho al Olvido en Internet: Debates Cerrados y Cuestiones Abiertas Tras la STJUE Google vs AEPD / 'The Right to be Forgotten on the Internet: Closed Debates and Open Questions after the CJEU's Decision On the Case Google vs AEDP' *Revista de Derecho Político* (2015) (1:93) 103; A Azurmendi, 'Por un "Derecho al Olvido" Para los Europeos: Aportaciones Jurisprudenciales de la Sentencia del TJUE Del Caso Google Spain y Su Recepción Por la Sentencia de la Audiencia Nacional de 29.12.2014 / In support to a "Right to be Forgotten,"' *Revista de Derecho Político* (2015) (0:91) 273; J Martínez Bavière, 'Spain: Extraterritorial Application of "Right to be Forgotten" Contrary to International Law' *Computer Law Review International* (2018) (19:2) 62; I Jiménez-Castellanos Ballesteros, 'The Conflict Between the Right to be Forgotten of the Criminal History and Freedom of Information: Digital Newspaper Archives (In this Respect the Spanish Constitutional Court Judgment of June 4, 2018 and the European Court of Human Rights' Judgment in the M.L. and W.W. vs. Germany case, June 28, 2018)' Revista de Derecho Político (2019) (1:106) 137.

62 WG Voss, 'After *Google Spain* and Charlie Hebdo: The Continuing Evolution of European Union Data Privacy Law in a Time of Change' *Business Lawyer* (2015/2016) (71:1) 281; DA Nadeem, 'Territorial Limits to the European Union's Right to Be Forgotten: How the CNIL Ignores Jurisdictional Basics in Its March 10, 2016 Decision Against Google' *Creighton International and Comparative Law Journal* (2017) (8:2) 182; S-D Schiopu, 'The Territorial Scope of the Right to be Forgotten (Right to De-referencing) in the Light of the Request for a Preliminary Ruling from the Conseil d'Etat (France)' *Pandectele Romane* (2018) (1) 61; Z Kharazian, 'Yet Another French Exception: The Political Dimensions of France's Support for the Digital Right to Be Forgotten' *European Data Protection Law Review (EDPL)* (2017) (3:4) 452; P Sayer, 'France Rejects Google's Appeal on Right to be Forgotten' *CIO* (13284045) (21 September 2015) 1.

63 Di Ciommo, 'Privacy in Europe after Regulation (EU) No 2016/679: What Will Remain of the Right to Be Forgotten' *Italian Law Journal* above at 623.

64 AJ Verheij, 'The Right to be Forgotten – a Dutch Perspective' *International Review of Law, Computers* (2016) (30:1/2) 32.

65 A Serban, 'The Enactment of the Right to Be Forgotten' *Analele Stiintifice Ale Universitatii Alexandru Ioan Cuza Din Iasi Stiinte Juridice* (2017) (63:2) 327; 'An Example of Romanian Case Law on the Digital Right to be Forgotten' *Bulletin of the Transilvania University of Braşov: Series VII: Social Sciences, Law* (2016) (11:60:1) 175.

66 F Brimblecombe and G Phillipson, 'Regaining Digital Privacy: The New Right to Be Forgotten and Online Expression' *Canadian Journal of Comparative and Contemporary Law* (2018) (4) 1; E Gratton and J Polonetsky, 'Droit a L'oubli: Canadian Perspective on the Global "Right to be Forgotten" Debate' *Colorado Technology Law Journal* (2017) (15:2) 337; A Slane, 'Search Engines and the Right to Be Forgotten: Squaring the Remedy with Canadian Values on Personal Information Flow' *Osgoode Hall Law Journal* (2018) (55:2) 349; M Wagner and Yun Li-Reilly, 'The Right to Be Forgotten' *Advocate* (Vancouver Bar Association) (2014) (72:6) 823; K Eltis, 'The Anglo-American/Continental Privacy Divide: How Civilian Personality Rights Can Help Reconceptualize the Right to Be Forgotten Towards Greater Transnational Interoperability' *Canadian Bar Review* (2016) (94:2) 355; IN Cofone, The Right to be Forgotten: A Canadian and Comparative Perspective (Taylor and Francis, 2020); A Trites, 'Black Box Ethics: How Algorithmic Decision-Making is Changing How We View Society and People: Advocating for the Right for Explanation and the Right to be Forgotten in Canada' Global Media Journal: Canadian Edition (2019) (11:2) 18.

- Brazil;[67]

- Israel;[68]

- New Zealand;[69]

- South Africa;[70]

- Hong Kong;[71]

- Puerto Rico;[72]

- China;[73]

- Russia;[74]

- Argentina;[75]

- Australia;[76]

67 C Rosa Pereira de Lima, 'The Data Processing Concept After *Google Spain* and its Influence on Brazilian Society' *Conpedi Law Review* (2016) (1:9) 117; B de Lima Acioli, Ehrhardt de Albuquerque and M Augusto Junior, 'An Agenda for the Right to Be Forgotten in Brazil' *Brazilian Journal of Public Policy* (2017) (7:3) 384; A Antonio Bruno da Silva, Maciel da Costa and N Marlea, 'Right to Be Forgotten: Is There Space in the Informal Society for the Epilogue of the Kafkanian Torture Machine' *Brazilian Journal of Public Policy* (2017) (7:3) 454; J Augusto Fontoura Costa and Geraldo Miniuci, 'Do Not Even Try to Forget: A Study on the Right to Be Forgotten' *Brazilian Journal of Public Policy* (2017) (7:3) 412; G Fachetti Silvestre, C Biazatti Borges and N Schades Benevides, 'The Procedural Protection of Data De-Indexing in Internet Search Engines: The Effectiveness in Brazil of the So-Called "Right to be Forgotten" Against Media Companies' Revista Jurídica (2019) (1:54) 25.

68 C Rosa Pereira de Lima and U Volovelsky, 'The Right to be Forgotten: The Israeli Version' *Computer Law & Security Review* (2018) (34:4) 824.

69 M Karlsens, 'Forget Me, Forget Me Not: a 'Right to be Forgotten' in New Zealand's Information Society?' *New Zealand Law Review* (2016) (3) 507; F Gollogly, 'The Blemish on the Clean Slate Act: Is There a Right to Be Forgotten in New Zealand?' Auckland University Law Review (2019) (25) 129; K Jackson-Cox, 'A 21st Century Right? An Analysis of the Extent to Which New Zealand's Privacy Act 1993 Provides A Right to be Forgotten' New Zealand Universities Law Review (2019) (28:4) 561.

70 M Parmar, 'Memorialising 40 Years Since Idi Amin's Expulsion: Digital "Memory Mania" to the "Right to be Forgotten"' *South Asian Popular Culture* (2014) (12:1) 1.

71 G Cheng, 'Latest Developments on the Right to Be Forgotten – Is the Time Ripe for Hong Kong?' *Hong Kong Law Journal* (2017) (47:3) 847.

72 W Irizarry Toro, 'El Derecho al Olvido, (The Right to Be Forgotten): Una Propuesta Innovadora par la Proteccion Digital a la Intimidad' *Revista de Derecho Puertorriqueno* (School of Law, Catholic University of Puerto Rico) (2016) (56:1) 61.

73 M Ning Yan, 'Protecting the Right to Be Forgotten: Is Mainland China Ready?' *European Data Protection Law Review* (2015) (1:3) 190.

74 E Andryushchenko, 'Right to be Forgotten on the Internet in Europe and Russia' *Conhecimento* (2016) (8:15) 14.

75 EL Carter, 'Argentina's Right to be Forgotten' *Emory International Law Review* (2013) (27:1) 23.

76 M Susi, 'The Right to be Forgotten' *Australian Law Journal* (2014) (88:9) 608; A Bunn, 'Children and the "Right to be Forgotten": What the Right to Erasure Means for European Children, and Why Australian Children Should be Afforded a Similar Right' Media International Australia (2019) (170:1) 37.

- US;[77]

- US states;[78]

- Columbia;[79]

- Greece;[80]

- Slovenia;[81]

- Turkey;[82]

77 Editorial Board, 'The "Right to be Forgotten" vs. the Right to Erase' Washington Post (24 September 2019); ME Gilman, 'Five Privacy Principles (From the GDPR) the United States Should Adopt To Advance Economic Justice' Arizona State Law Journal (2020) (52:2) 368; J Buckley, 'Congress Needs to Hurry Up On Data Protection' American Banker (31 October 2019) (184:210) 1; J Friesen, 'The Impossible Right to Be Forgotten' Rutgers Computer and Technology Law Journal (2021) (47:1) 173; H Criscione, 'Forgetting the Right to Be Forgotten: The Everlasting Negative Implications of a Right to Be Dereferenced on Global Freedom in the Wake of Google v. CNIL' Pace International Law Review (2020) (32:2) 315; S Shatz and SE Chylik, 'The California Consumer Privacy Act of 2018: A Sea Change in the Protection of California Consumers' Personal Information' Business Lawyer (2020) (75:2) 1917; J Adam Holland, 'Contemporary Practical Alternatives to a "Right To Be Forgotten" in the United States' Latin American Law Review (2019) (2) 23; R Pfenninger, 'The Right to Be Forgotten Has Not Found Its Home in United States Law: A Comparison of Law Between the European Union and the United States' Willamette Journal of International Law and Dispute Resolution (2021) (28:2) 291; RV Distante, 'Reconciling U.S. Banking and Securities Data Preservation Rules With European Mandatory Data Erasure Under GDPR' Fordham Journal of Corporate Law (2019) (25:1) 195; A Lee, 'Enforcement of Calif. Data Privacy Law Begins' WWD: Women's Wear Daily (2 July 2020) 3-3; HG Cohen and M Zalnieriute, 'Personal Data – Right to be Forgotten – Internet Search Engine Operators – De-Referencing of Search Results – Territorial Scope of Application – Data Privacy – General Data Protection Regulation (EU)' American Journal of International Law (2020) (114:2) 261; OJ Gstrein, 'Right to be Forgotten: European Data Imperialism, National Privilege, or Universal Human Right?' Review of European Administrative Law (2020) (13:1) 125; G Cintra Guimarães, Global Technology and Legal Theory Transnational Constitutionalism: Google and the European Union (Taylor and Francis, 2019); BW Cramer, 'Privacy Exceptionalism Unless it's Unexceptional: How the American Government Misuses the Spirit of Privacy in Two Different Ways to Justify Both Nondisclosure and Surveillance' Ohio State Technology Law Journal (2020) (17:1) 306; 'Is Erasure the Right Technique for U.S. History?' Wall Street Journal (29 June 2020) N.PAG-N. PAG.
78 M McGinnis Stine and S Kilian, 'Deletion Completion Under the CCPA' Computer & Internet Lawyer (2020) (37:5) 3; ME Gilman, 'Five Privacy Principles (From the GDPR) the United States Should Adopt To Advance Economic Justice' Arizona State Law Journal (2020) (52:2) 368.
79 SO Peralta, 'Search Engines in Colombia: Legal Review and Study of the Muebles Caqueta vs. Google Inc Case' Revista de Direito, Estado e Telecomunicações (2020) (12:2) 1.
80 M Tsirintani, M Serifi M and S Binioris, 'Digital Oblivion (The Right to Be Forgotten): A Big Challenge for the Public Hospital Management in Greece' Studies in Health Technology and Informatics (2019) 91.
81 M Milosavljević, M Poler and R Čeferin, 'In the Name of the Right to be Forgotten: New Legal and Policy Issues and Practices Regarding Unpublishing Requests in Slovenian Online News Media' Digital Journalism (2020) (8:6) 780.
82 ME Karakas, 'Removal of Digital History from Internet Access "Right to Be Forgotten" and Appearance in Turkish Law' Necmettin Erbakan Universitesi Hukuk Fakultesi Dergisi (2020) (3:2) 262; O Canyaş and A Bayata Canyaş, 'Approach Towards the Right to be Forgotten Under Turkish Law in Comparison With EU and US Laws: A Need For a Reform?' Juridical Tribune

- Ukraine;[83]

- Peru;[84]

- Japan;[85]

- and many more.

There are also various references in the UK in relation to RtbF[86] and, in addition, specific RtbF issues,[87] including Brexit and post Brexit.[88] RtbF is also increasingly referred to in sectors and regions, including for example:

- Europe;

- Asia;[89]

/ Tribuna Juridica (2021) (11:2) 174; S Atalar, 'Does GDPR Cover The Expectations After DPD?' Law (2019) (10:19) 55.

83   O Posykaliuk, 'Scientific Commentary on the Judgment of the Court of Justice of the European Union in the Case of Google Spain SL and Google Inc. v. the Spanish Data Protection Agency (AEPD) and Mario Costeja Gonzalez (regarding the Right to Be Forgotten)' Law of Ukraine: Legal Journal (Ukrainian) (2019) (4) 209; RG Aydin and IA Nazim, 'The Impact of New Technologies on Human Rights in the Context of the Right to Be Forgotten and the Right to Privacy' Law of Ukraine: Legal Journal (Ukrainian) (2021) (2) 125.

84   DF Garcia and A Quintanilla Perea, 'The Protection of Personal Data and the Right to Be Forgotten in Peru. On the Purpose of the International Standards of the Inter-American Human Rights System' Derecho PUCP (2020) (84) 271.

85   F Zufall, 'Challenging the EU's Right to Be Forgotten: Society's Right to Know in Japan' European Data Protection Law Review (EDPL) (2019) (5:1) 17.

86   P O'Callaghan and S de Mars, 'Narratives About Privacy and Forgetting in English Law' *International Review of Law, Computers & Technology* (2016) (30:1/2) 42; J Townend, 'Data Protection and the "Right to be Forgotten" in Practice: A UK Perspective' *International Journal of Legal Information* (2017) (45:1) 28; D Erdos, 'Data Protection and the Right to Reputation: Filling the "Gaps" After the Defamation Act 2013' *Cambridge Law Journal* (2014) (73:3) 536; O Lynskey, 'The "Europeanisation" of Data Protection Law' *Cambridge Yearbook of European Legal Studies* (2017) (19) 252; P Lambert, *A Users Guide to Data Protection Law* (Bloomsbury, 2018). In relation to data protection and privacy interests also see H Hancock, 'Weller & Ors v Associated Newspapers Ltd [2015] EWCA Civ 1176. Weller Case Highlights Need for Guidance on Photography, Privacy and the Press' *Journal of Media Law* (2016) (8:1) 17; LA Bygrave, 'A Right to Be Forgotten?' *Communications of the ACM* (2015) (58:1) 35; House of Lords European Union Committee, *EU Data Protection Law: A 'Right to be Forgotten'* (Stationery Office, 2014); C Dibene, 'Sir, the Radar Sir, It Appears to Be … Jammed: The Future of "The Right to Be Forgotten" in a Post-Brexit United Kingdom' *San Diego International Law Journal* (2017) (19:1) 161; P Lambert, 'The Right to be Forgotten: Context and the Problem of Time' Communications Law (2019) (24:2) 74; S Aidinlis, 'The Right to be Forgotten as a Fundamental Right in the UK After Brexit' Communications Law (2020) (25:2) 67.

87   'British Library Exempted from "Right to Be Forgotten" Rule' *Information Management Journal* (2017) (51:6) 16; Dibene, 'Sir, the Radar Sir, It Appears to Be … Jammed: The Future of "The Right to Be Forgotten" in a Post-Brexit United Kingdom' at 161.

88   For example, S Aidinlis, 'The Right to be Forgotten as a Fundamental Right in the UK After Brexit' Communications Law (2020) (25:2) 67.

89   F Werro, The Right to Be Forgotten: A Comparative Study of the Emergent Right's Evolution and Application in Europe, the Americas, and Asia (Springer, 2020); M José Reymond, 'The Future of the European Union "Right to be Forgotten"' Latin American Law Review (2019) (2) 81.

- Americas.[90]

7 CONCLUSION

5.11   We cannot ignore the wider context nor the building blocks of the data protection regime when considering RtbF. These will be considered variously in the future disputes and cases that will arise as regards this legislation.

---

90 DF Garcia and A Quintanilla Perea, 'The Protection of Personal Data and the Right to Be Forgotten in Peru. On the Purpose of the International Standards of the Inter-American Human Rights System' Derecho PUCP (2020) (84) 271; F Werro, The Right to Be Forgotten: A Comparative Study of the Emergent Right's Evolution and Application in Europe, the Americas, and Asia (Springer, 2020); ME Gilman, 'Five Privacy Principles (From the GDPR) the United States Should Adopt To Advance Economic Justice' Arizona State Law Journal (2020) (52:2) 368; M José Reymond, 'The Future of the European Union "Right to be Forgotten"' Latin American Law Review (2019) (2) 81; CT Bavitz, 'The Right to be Forgotten and Internet Governance: Challenges and Opportunities' Latin American Law Review (2019) (2) 1; F Werro, The Right to Be Forgotten: A Comparative Study of the Emergent Right's Evolution and Application in Europe, the Americas, and Asia (Springer, 2020); G Fachetti Silvestre, C Biazatti Borges and N Schades Benevides, 'The Procedural Protection of Data De-Indexing in Internet Search Engines: The Effectiveness in Brazil of the So-Called "Right to be Forgotten" Against Media Companies' Revista Jurídica (2019) (1:54) 2; SO Peralta, 'Search Engines in Colombia: Legal Review and Study of the Muebles Caqueta vs. Google Inc Case' Revista de Direito, Estado e Telecomunicações (2020) (12:2) 1.

CHAPTER 6

The Parties of Data Protection

1   INTRODUCTION

6.1   The wider concepts of personal data and data protection,[1] such as the building blocks of what is personal data[2] and the respective rights of individual data subjects under the GDPR[3] are all important. We must not forget, however, that there are also various parties to be aware of in relation to any consideration of data protection. These are referred to below.

2   MAIN PARTIES

6.2   The main parties to consider are:

*   *The individual data subject*: This is the individual to whom the personal data relates.

*   *The controller*: This is the entity, company, or organisation which has collected or obtained the personal data relating to the individual data subject. It intends to collect, process and hold the personal data.[4]

*   *The processor*: An outsourced entity which has obtained the personal data from the controller and whom is acting for and on behalf of the controller and generally performing some outsourced data processing task for the controller.[5]

The Individual Data Subject

6.3   The individual data subject is at the centre of data protection and privacy.[6] This is no different for the RtbF. The data protection regime and RtbF regime, confer rights[7] on the individual data subjects – and corresponding obligations

---

1   N Purtova, 'The Law of Everything: Broad Concept of Personal Data and Future of EU Data Protection Law' *Innovation and Technology* (2018) (10:1) 40.
2   GDPR Art 4(1).
3   PTJ Wolters, 'The Control by and Rights of the Data Subject Under the GDPR' *Journal of Internet Law* (2018) (22:1) 1.
4   Previously, prior to the GDPR, referred to as the data controller.
5   Previously, prior to the GDPR, referred to as the data processor.
6   Wolters, 'The Control by and Rights of the Data Subject under the GDPR' above.
7   *Ibid.*

to be respected and accomplished by the other parties involved, particularly the controller and processor.[8]

The consideration of RtbF must be considered in context of the wide concept of personal data and data protection[9] wide description and definitions of personal data[10] and related rights.[11]

The data protection regime was created in part to recognise and protect the interests of individuals in relation to their personal information and data – in particular that held in electronic form. The recipient of the rights is known as the individual data subject.

The data protection rights apply generally in relation to any individuals whose personal data are being collected and processed. In terms of RtbF considerations, obvious examples are registered members of websites. However, it is much wider. Many websites allow non-members to access them and in some instances also to heavily engage with the controller and its services. So, there are registered members and non-members who may be interested in having information or content taken down under RtbF.

However, we also need to be open to considering individual data subjects in a much wider context than mere members and users of a given website. In the modern internet context, information can be published or uploaded online directly relating to and/or identifying a specific individual data subject which may be of concern to that individual.

The individual data subject in *Google Spain*,[12] for example, was concerned with old and outdated content originating from official sources and published in the online version of a newspaper. The victim of revenge porn may be concerned with the takedown and forgetting of intimate images from a private setting uploaded by errant, if not criminal, third parties. For example, an ex-partner may deliberately have uploaded pictures or videos to try to hurt, damage, embarrass, and intimidate an individual. Sometimes, these images may have been from an original consensual context – but strictly on the basis that they were private, personal, intimate, and would never be uploaded, published, or otherwise distributed.

On other occasions the photographs or video may have been taken surreptitiously without the victim even knowing. Amada Todd did not have a RtbF where she lived and appeared to be unaware of potential routes that may have helped her. It is also

---

8 In terms of controller and processors see, eg, R Fielding, 'The Concept of Controller and Processor Data Entities' *International Journal for the Data Protection Officer, Privacy Officer and Privacy Counsel (IDPP)* (2018) (2:8) 8.

9 Purtova, 'The Law of Everything: Broad Concept of Personal Data and Future of EU Data Protection Law' above.

10 GDPR Art 4(1).

11 GDPR Chapter III (rights) and GDPR Chapter VIII (remedies). Wolters, 'The Control by and Rights of the Data Subject under the GDPR' above at 1.

12 *Google Spain SL, Google Inc v Agencia Española de Protección de Datos (AEPD), Mario Costeja González*, Court of Justice (Grand Chamber), Case C-131/12, 13 May 2014.

unclear if her counsellors or teachers were aware of these options. However, this points to the need for greater understanding of online harms and RtbF amongst professional groups such as data regulators and children's groups who should be watching out for victims of online abuse. They have a responsibility to publicise these issues and demonstrate how RtbF may be able to assist.

There is also a very high obligation on relevant controllers to publicise RtbF and other matters and to implement it in as easy a manner as possible – especially as children may be among the individual data subjects who may wish to have problem content removed and forgotten.

It is also important to consider that RtbF can be utilised by individual data subjects. Therefore, it is helpful to consider how wide the net of data subjects actually is. A data subject is defined as 'an identified or identifiable natural person':[13]

> who can be identified, directly or indirectly, in particular by reference to an identifier such as a name, an identification number, location data, an online identifier or to one or more factors specific to the physical, physiological, genetic, mental, economic, cultural or social identity of that natural person.[14]

Readers also need to consider the wide definition of what amounts to personal data, namely:

> "personal data" means any information relating to an identified or identifiable natural person.[15]

References such as 'identifiable', 'any', 'indirectly', 'in particular', 'such as' are important in understanding that the number of individual data subjects who may potentially wish to avail of RtbF is great indeed.

We have mentioned registered members, non-registered users, general data subjects who may have had problem content posted online about them and how wide the relevant definitions in the GDPR can be. More specifically, we might also consider individual data subjects such as:

- members;

- users;

- employees and employee data protection issues, including internet and device usage;[16]

- other workers such as contractors, temps, casual staff;

- agency staff;

- ex-employees and retired employees;

---

13   GDPR Art 4(1).
14   *Ibid.*
15   *Ibid.*
16   R Blanpain, 'Protection of Employees' Personal Information and Privacy' *JILPT Comparative Labor Law Seminar* (12th: 2014, Tokyo, Japan); 'Proposed German Bill Would Prohibit Employers From Using Social Networks for Background Checks' *Venulex Legal Summaries* (2010 Q3) (Special section) 5.

- spouses and family members;

- job applicants, including unsuccessful applicants;

- volunteers;

- apprentices and trainees;

- customers and clients;

- prospective customer and clients;

- suppliers;[17] and

- any other individuals.

This merely exemplifies that individual data subjects can fall into many different categories and organisations should not be narrowly focused in relation to just one set of data subjects in terms of their preparation and consideration of RtbF.

The Controller

6.4   We now consider some of the responsibilities of controller entities.[18] It is the controller who received RtbF notice in relation to problem content on its website or services. Chapter IV of the GDPR refers to controllers. Chapter IV, Section 1 refers to general obligations.

Taking into account the nature, scope, context and purposes of the processing as well as the risks of varying likelihood and severity for the rights and freedoms of individuals, the controller shall implement appropriate technical and organisational measures to ensure and be able to demonstrate that the processing of personal data is performed in compliance with GDPR. Those measures shall be reviewed and updated where necessary.[19]

Where proportionate in relation to the processing activities, the measures referred to in Article 24(1) of GDPR must include the implementation of appropriate data protection policies by the controller.[20]

Adherence to approved codes of conduct[21] or an approved certification mechanism[22] may be used as an element to demonstrate compliance with the controller's obligations.[23] As yet, there are no codes or certification mechanisms in relation to RtbF.

---

17 LAC MacDonald, *Data Protection: Legal Compliance and Good Practice for Employers* (Tottel, 2008) 41.
18 See generally Fielding, 'The Concept of Controller and Processor Data Entities' above at 8.
19 GDPR Art 24(1).
20 *Ibid* Art 24(2).
21 Pursuant to GDPR Art 40.
22 *Ibid* Art 42.
23 *Ibid* Art 24(3).

The WP 29 also refers to controller issues.[24] In future, it will be the European Data Protection Board (EDPB) which will issue guidance in this regard.

The Joint Controller

6.5   We also have to consider these issues in terms of a new category: the joint controller.[25] The issues involving joint controllers are only starting to be considered in greater detail,[26] but may well have certain impacts in terms of considering the proliferation and copies of problem content and joint control or operation of websites, services and or activities in relation to given websites.

The GDPR now provides for a new category of controller, namely, the joint controller. This was not previously expressly included under the data protection regime. This has several implications. It recognises the increasing instances where there can be more than one controller involved and that there can be increasingly complicated commercial relationships, joint ventures, etc, where the traditional description of one pure controller is no longer wholly reflective of all the circumstances. There is also increasing reliance by organisations on online services, cloud services and storage, etc, which can mean that there is sometimes more than one prime controller-type party and/or more than one category of controller-type processing activities being undertaken. In addition, many larger entities providing online services, hosting, storage, etc, may seek to reserve the ability to themselves to carry out data analysis or other activities of a processing nature which hold the potential to change them from – at least for some activities – what was traditionally understood as processor-type activities to controller-type activities. Yet, under the traditional model, their customer would have been viewed as the controller to their own customers and users.

This all has potential implications for those who may hold personal data and who may be asked to delete, take down, and/or forget personal data as notified by an individual data subject.

Where two or more controllers jointly determine the purposes and means of the processing of personal data, they are joint controllers. They shall, in a

---

24   WP 29, Opinion 1/2010 on the concepts of 'controller' and 'processor'.
25   See GDPR Art 26; and generally G Zanfir-Fortuna, 'Personal Data for Joint Controllers and Exam Scripts' *International Journal for the Data Protection Officer, Privacy Officer and Privacy Counsel (IDPP)* (2018)(2:8) 12.
26   See, eg, the so-called Facebook Fanpage case, *Unabhängiges Landeszentrum für Datenschutz Schleswig-Holstein v Wirtschaftsakademie Schleswig-Holstein GmbH*, CJEU, Case C-210/16, 5 June 2018. Also R Hopkins, 'The CJEU's "Facebook Fan Page" Judgement: Joint Data Controllers, Cookies and Targeted Advertising' *International Journal for the Data Protection Officer, Privacy Officer and Privacy Counsel (IDPP)* (2018) (2:5) 13; N Blanc, '*Wirtschaftsakademie Schleswig-Holstein*: Towards a Joint Responsibility of Facebook Fan Page Administrators for Infringements to European Data Protection Law' *European Data Protection Law Review (EDPL)* (2018) (4:1) 120; G Zanfir-Fortuna, 'Personal Data for Joint Controllers and Processor Data Entities' *International Journal for the Data Protection Officer, Privacy Officer and Privacy Counsel (IDPP)* (2018) (2:8) 12.

transparent manner, determine their respective responsibilities for compliance with the obligations under GDPR, in particular as regards the exercising of the rights of the individual data subject and their respective duties to provide the information,[27] by means of an arrangement between them unless and in so far as, the respective responsibilities of the controllers are determined by EU or state law to which they are subject. The arrangement may designate a point of contact for individual data subjects.[28]

The arrangement shall duly reflect the joint controllers' respective effective roles and relationships vis-à-vis individual data subjects. The essence of the arrangement shall be made available for the individual data subject.[29]

Irrespective of the terms of the arrangement,[30] the individual data subject may exercise their rights under GDPR in respect of and against each of the controllers.[31]

The Processor

6.6　　The issue of processors acting on behalf of the main controller may also need to be considered in relation to RtbF. These issues are perhaps less developed in comparison to the main controller issues. However, given the nature of the internet and internet services and the sometimes complex and interrelated activities of group entities – sometimes on the same website – these issues will likely be considered in greater detail in future.

Chapter IV of GDPR refers to processors. Chapter IV, Section 1 refers to general obligations.[32] Where processing is to be carried out on behalf of a controller, the controller shall use only processors providing sufficient guarantees to implement appropriate technical and organisational measures in such a manner that the processing will meet the requirements of the GDPR and ensure the protection of the rights of the individual data subject.[33]

The processor must not engage another processor without the prior specific or general written authorisation of the controller. In the case of general written authorisation, the processor shall inform the controller of any intended changes concerning the addition or replacement of other processors, thereby giving the controller the opportunity to object to such changes.[34]

27　Referred to in GDPR Arts 13 and 14.
28　*Ibid* Art 26(1).
29　*Ibid* Art 26(2). Generally see J Mäkinen, 'Data Quality, Sensitive Data and Joint Controllership as Examples of Grey Areas in the Existing Data Protection Framework for the Internet of Things' *Information & Communications Technology Law* (2015) (24:3) 262.
30　Referred to in GDPR Art 24(1).
31　*Ibid* Art 24(3).
32　See, eg, Fielding, 'The Concept of Controller and Processor Data Entities' above at 8.
33　GDPR Art 28(1).
34　*Ibid* Art 28(2).

The carrying out of processing by a processor shall be governed by a contract or other legal act under EU or state law, that is binding the processor with regard to the controller and that sets out the subject-matter and duration of the processing, the nature and purpose of the processing, the type of personal data and categories of individual data subjects and the obligations and rights of the controller. The contract or other legal act shall stipulate, in particular, that the processor:

- process the personal data only on documented instructions from the controller, including with regard to transfers of personal data to a third country or an international organisation, unless required to do so by EU or state law to which the processor is subject; in such a case, the processor shall inform the controller of that legal requirement before processing the data, unless that law prohibits such information on important grounds of public interest;

- ensure that persons authorised to process the personal data have committed themselves to confidentiality or are under an appropriate statutory obligation of confidentiality;

- take all measures required pursuant to Article 32;

- respect the conditions referred to in Article 28(2) and (4) for engaging another processor;

- taking into account the nature of the processing, assists the controller by appropriate technical and organisational measures, insofar as this is possible, for the fulfilment of the controller's obligation to respond to requests for exercising the individual data subject's rights laid down in Chapter III;

- assist the controller in ensuring compliance with the obligations pursuant to Articles 32 to 36 taking into account the nature of processing and the information available to the processor;

- at the choice of the controller, deletes or returns all the personal data to the controller after the end of the provision of services relating to processing and deletes existing copies unless EU or state law requires storage of the personal data;

- make available to the controller all information necessary to demonstrate compliance with the obligations laid down in this Article and allow for and contribute to audits, including inspections, conducted by the controller or another auditor mandated by the controller. (With regard to this point, the processor shall immediately inform the controller if, in its opinion, an instruction breaches the GDPR, EU or state data protection provisions.)[35]

Where a processor engages another processor to carry out specific processing activities on behalf of the controller, the same data protection obligations as set out in the contract or other legal act between the controller and the processor[36] shall be imposed on that other processor by way of a contract or other legal act

---

35   *Ibid* Art 28(3).
36   *Ibid*.

under EU or state law, in particular providing sufficient guarantees to implement appropriate technical and organisational measures in such a manner that the processing will meet the requirements of the GDPR. Where that other processor fails to fulfil its data protection obligations, the initial processor shall remain fully liable to the controller for the performance of that other processor's obligations.[37]

Adherence of the processor to an approved code of conduct[38] or an approved certification mechanism[39] may be used as an element to demonstrate sufficient guarantees.[40]

Without prejudice to an individual contract between the controller and the processor, the contract or the other legal act[41] may be based, in whole or in part, on standard contractual clauses,[42] including when they are part of a certification granted to the controller or processor.[43]

The Commission may lay down standard contractual clauses for certain matters,[44] and a national data protection supervisory authority may adopt standard contractual clauses for certain matters.[45]

The contract or the other legal act[46] must be in writing, including in an electronic form.[47]

Without prejudice to other provisions,[48] if a processor infringes GDPR by determining the purposes and means of data processing, the processor will be considered to be a controller in respect of that processing.[49] This may involve detailed analysis of activities, revenues and even contracts, amongst other things.

Organisations acting as processor should also bear in mind that while they may indeed be processors, they can also at the same time be a controller in relation to different sets of personal data. This only adds to the potential complexity.

A further concept is that of processing under authority of controller and processor. The processor and any person acting under the authority of the controller or of

37 *Ibid* Art 28(4).
38 Pursuant to GDPR Art 40.
39 Pursuant to GDPR Art 42.
40 Sufficient guarantees as referred to in GDPR Art 28(1), (4) and (5).
41 As referred to in GDPR Art 26(3) and (4).
42 As referred to in GDPR Art 28(7) and (8).
43 Certification pursuant to GDPR Arts 42 and 43. GDPR Art 28(6).
44 The matters referred to in Art 28(3) and (4) and in accordance with the examination procedure referred to in Art 93(2). GDPR Art 28(7).
45 The matters referred to in Art 28(3) and (4) and in accordance with the consistency mechanism referred to in Art 63. GDPR Art 28(8).
46 Referred to in GDPR Art 28(3) and (4).
47 GDPR Art 28(9).
48 Expressly Arts 82, 83 and 84.
49 GDPR Art 28(10).

the processor who has access to personal data shall not process them except on instructions from the controller, unless required to do so by EU or state law.[50]

The WP 29 also refers to processor issues.[51] As indicated above, these issues will in future be considered by the EDPB.

Representatives of Controllers Not Established in EU

6.7 Where Article 3(2) applies, the controller or the processor shall designate in writing a representative in the EU.[52]

This obligation shall not apply to:

- processing which is occasional, does not include, on a large scale, processing of special categories of data as referred to in Article 9(1) or processing of personal data relating to criminal convictions and offences referred to in Article 10 and is unlikely to result in a risk for the rights and freedoms of natural persons, taking into account the nature, context, scope and purposes of the processing; or

- a public authority or body.[53]

The representative shall be established in one of the Member States where the individual data subjects whose personal data are processed in relation to the offering of goods or services to them, or whose behaviour is monitored, are located.[54]

The representative shall be mandated by the controller or the processor to be addressed in addition to or instead of the controller or the processor by, in particular, supervisory authorities and individual data subjects, on all issues related to the processing, for the purposes of ensuring compliance with the GDPR.[55]

The designation of a representative by the controller or the processor shall be without prejudice to legal actions which could be initiated against them.[56]

3   NATIONAL DATA REGULATOR

6.8 While not mentioned above, another party to consider is the data regulator (also referred to as the national data protection supervisory authority)

---

50   *Ibid* Art 29.
51   WP 29, Opinion 1/2010 on the concepts of 'controller' and 'processor'.
52   GDPR Art 27(1).
53   *Ibid* Art 27(2).
54   *Ibid* Art 27(3).
55   *Ibid* Art 27(4).
56   *Ibid* Art 28(5).

which promotes, implements, and polices compliance with the data protection regime and rules in respective Member States. The national data regulators are important because they are the bodies to which an individual data subject can complain in the event that a given controller (eg, a website) refuses to reply to or adequately address a RtbF notice. The data regulator can take up the notice and refusal with the website controller to progress the matter.

Indeed, readers will recall that it was the data regulator[57] which assisted the individual data subject in *Google Spain*.[58]

It is also interesting to consider the particular issue and impact of official cooperation in dealing with RtbF problems. The national data regulators may cooperate.[59] There can also be judicial cooperation.[60]

4 COURTS

6.9   The Court of Justice of the European Union (CJEU) [61] and respective national courts will also be instrumental in the vindication of rights and obligations relating to RtbF.

---

57   The Agencia Española de Protección de Datos (AEPD).

58   See *Google Spain.*

59   See GDPR Arts 60–62 in relation to cooperation issues involving different data protection supervisory authorities. P Lambert, Data Protection, Privacy Regulators and Supervisory Authorities (Bloomsbury, 2020).

60   E Mak, N Graaf and E Jackson, 'The Framework for Judicial Cooperation in the European Union: Unpacking the Ethical, Legal and Institutional Dimensions of "Judicial Culture"' *Utrecht Journal of International and European Law* (2018) (34:1) 24. Also note KPE Lasok, *Lasok's European Court Practice and Procedure* (Bloomsbury, 2017); Lambert, Data Protection, Privacy Regulators and Supervisory Authorities.

61   T Tridimas, 'The Court of Justice of the European Union' in R Schütze and T Tridimas, *Oxford Principles of European Union Law* (OUP, 2018) at 581; B Wägenbaur, *Court of Justice of the European Union* (Beck, Hart, Nomos, 2013); A Arnull, *The European Union and Its Court of Justice* (OUP, 2006); G de Búrca and JHH Weiler, *The European Court of Justice* (OUP, 2001); N March Hunnings, *The European Courts* (Cartermill, 1996); Miguel Poiares Maduro, *We The Court, the European Court of Justice and the European Economic Constitution* (Hart 1998); A Stone Sweet, 'The European Court of Justice' in P Craig and G de Búrca, *The Evolution of EU Law* at 121; A-M Slaughter, A Stone Sweet and JHH Weiler, *The European Court and National Courts: Doctrine and Jurisprudence* (Hart, 1998); L Azoulai and R Dehousse, 'The European Court of Justice and Legal Dynamics of Integration' in E Jones, A Menon and S Weatherill, *The Oxford Handbook of the European Union* (OUP, 2014) at 350; S Saurugger and F Trepan, *The Court of Justice of the European Union and the Politics of Law* (Palgrave, 2017); JA Usher, *EC Institutions and Legislation* (Longman, 1998); M Szabo, 'General Principles of Law in the Practice of International Courts and the European Court of Justice' *Hungarian Yearbook of International Law and European Law* (2016) 135; Lasok, *Lasok's European Court Practice and Procedure.* Also, Lambert, Data Protection, Privacy Regulators and Supervisory Authorities.

Institutional Parties

6.10   There are various interested institutional parties. In a wider context, there can also be consideration of the different institutions of the EU which are interested in RtbF issues of policy and legislation, such as the EU Commission[62] and the EU Parliament,[63] or how wider EU laws are interpreted judicially including cases before the CJEU.[64]

5   CONCLUSION

6.11   These are the parties we need to consider when looking at RtbF issues (and data protection more widely). It is likely that the issues between respective joint controllers will have to be resolved as much as possible in advance, as issues involving both controllers will come to the fore in certain disputes in the future. This has not yet been an issue, in part because the concept of joint controller is first expressly referred to in the GDPR.

---

62   N Nugent and M Rhinard, *The European Commission* (Palgrave, 2015); SK Schmidt and A Wonka, 'European Commission, in E Jones, A Menon and S Weatherill, *The Oxford Handbook of the European Union* at 336; M Cini, *The European Commission* (Manchester University Press, 1996); Usher, *EC Institutions and Legislation*.

63   K Bradley, 'The European Parliament' in R Schütze and T Tridimas, *Oxford Principles of European Union Law* at 457; T Raunio, 'The European Parliament' in E Jones, A Menon and S Weatherill, *The Oxford Handbook of the European Union* at 365; Usher, *EC Institutions and Legislation*.

64   Tridimas, 'The Court of Justice of the European Union' in R Schütze and T Tridimas, *Oxford Principles of European Union Law* at 581; Wägenbaur, *Court of Justice of the European Union*; Arnull, *The European Union and Its Court of Justice*; de Búrca and Weiler, *The European Court of Justice*; Hunnings, *The European Courts*; M Poiares Maduro, *We The Court, the European Court of Justice and the European Economic Constitution* (Hart 1998); A Stone Sweet, 'The European Court of Justice' in P Craig and G de Búrca, *The Evolution of EU Law* at 121; Slaughter, Stone Sweet and Weiler, *The European Court and National Courts: Doctrine and Jurisprudence*; Azoulai and Dehousse, 'The European Court of Justice and Legal Dynamics of Integration' in E Jones, A Menon and S Weatherill, *The Oxford Handbook of the European Union* at 350; Saurugger and Trepan, *The Court of Justice of the European Union and the Politics of Law*; Usher, *EC Institutions and Legislation*; Szabo, 'General Principles of Law in the Practice of International Courts and the European Court of Justice' *Hungarian Yearbook of International Law and European Law* at 135; Lasok, *Lasok's European Court Practice and Procedure*. Also, Lambert, Data Protection, Privacy Regulators and Supervisory Authorities.

CHAPTER 7

Forgetting and Other Rights

I INTRODUCTION

7.1   The General Data Protection Regulation (GDPR) provides for an express RtbF for the first time in EU data protection law. This will provide assistance to individual data subjects when facing the issue of problem online content (both actual and prospective). This is highlighted below. The wider updates to the data protection regime are also relevant (and are discussed in Chapter 8).

2 THE RTBF RIGHT

7.2   One of the more important extensions and enhancements relates to the expanded RtbF, which includes the 'right to be forgotten and to erasure, which consists of securing from the controller the erasure of personal data as well prevention of any further dissemination of his data'.[1] (It is also indicated to interface with the new right to data portability.[2])

The erasure and forgetting right is even more enhanced where personal data was originally disclosed or collected when the individual data subject was a child. Some commentators refer to the need for an entire 'clean slate' – whether generally or for children specifically.[3]

> The use of data from social networks in employment contexts is a representative example. Personal data such as photos taken in private contexts have been used to refuse job positions and fire people. But forgetfulness is larger. It is one dimension of how people deal with their own history, being related not only to leaving the past behind but also to living in the present without the threat of a kind of "Miranda" warning, where whatever you say can be used against you in the future. In this sense the [RtbF] is closely related to entitlements of dignity and self-development. Once again, privacy appears as the pre-requisite of our liberties, assuring the possibility to freely express ourselves and move freely on the street ...[4]

Erasure, takedown, and forgetting is most clearly associated and related to the following in particular:

---

1   See L Costa and Y Poullet, 'Privacy and the Regulation of 2012' *Computer Law & Security Review* (2012)(28) 254, at 256.
2   *Ibid.*
3   *Ibid* at 257.
4   *Ibid.*

- where the personal data is no longer necessary in relation to the purposes for which they were originally collected and processed (and the associated finality principle);

- where the individual data subject has withdrawn their consent for processing;

- where individual data subject objects to the processing of the personal data concerning them; and

- where the processing of the personal data does not comply with the GDPR.[5]

The GDPR and the erasure and forgetting right 'amplifies the effectiveness of data protection principles and rules'.[6]

Individual data subjects can have their data erased under RtbF when there is no compliance, in addition to instances where they simply withdraw their consent.[7] User control and individual data subject control are, therefore, to that extent, enhanced.

The new right creates compliance obligations, such as:

- erasing personal data and not processing it further;

- informing third parties that the individual data subject has notified the deletion of the personal data; and

- taking responsibility for publication by third parties under the controller's authority.[8]

3   RECTIFICATION RIGHT

7.3   Chapter III, Section 3 of the new GDPR refers to rectification and erasure. The new GDPR provides that the individual data subject shall have the right to obtain from the controller without undue delay the rectification of inaccurate personal data concerning them. Taking into account the purposes of the processing, the individual data subject will have the right to have incomplete personal data completed including by the provision of a supplementary statement.[9]

4   ERASURE AND FORGETTING RIGHT

7.4   Chapter III, Section 3 of the new GDPR refers to rectification and erasure. The new GDPR provides that the individual data subject shall have the

---

5   *Ibid* at 254–262.
6   *Ibid*.
7   *Ibid* at 257.
8   *Ibid* and referring to GDPR Arts 17, 2 and 8.
9   GDPR Art 16.

right to obtain the erasure of personal data concerning them from the controller where one of the following grounds applies:

- the data are no longer necessary in relation to the purposes for which they were collected or otherwise processed;

- the individual data subject withdraws consent – which was the basis on which the processing was based according to Article 6(1)(a) or Article 9(2)(a) and where there is no other legal ground for the processing;

- the individual data subject objects to the processing pursuant to Article 21(1) and there are no overriding legitimate grounds for the processing, or the individual data subject objects to the processing pursuant to Article 21(2);

- the personal data have been unlawfully processed;

- the personal data must be erased for compliance with a legal obligation in EU or State law to which the controller is subject; and

- the data have been collected in relation to the offering of information society services referred to in Article 8(1).[10]

Where the controller has made the personal data public and is obliged, pursuant to paragraph 1 to erase it, the controller, taking account of available technology and the cost of implementation, shall take reasonable steps, including technical measures, to inform controllers who are processing the personal data, that the individual data subject has notified the erasure by such controllers of any links to, or copy or replication of that personal data.[11]

Article 17(1) and (2) shall not apply to the extent that processing is necessary:

- for exercising the right of freedom of expression and information;

- for compliance with a legal obligation which requires processing by EU or State law to which the controller is subject or for the performance of a task carried out in the public interest or in the exercise of official authority vested in the controller;

- for reasons of public interest in the area of public health in accordance with Article 9(2)(h) and (i) as well as Article 9(3);

- for archiving purposes in the public interest, scientific or historical research purposes or statistical purposes in accordance with Article 89(1) in so far as the right referred to in paragraph 1 is likely to render impossible or seriously impair the achievement of the objectives of that processing; and

- for the establishment, exercise or defence of legal claims.[12]

10 *Ibid* Art 17(1).
11 *Ibid* Art 17(2).
12 *Ibid* Art 17(3).

Tatiana-Eleni Synodinou[13] refers to the 'right to oblivion' and notes in relation to her research that media rights are not immune from the right to be forgotten. Examples are given where cases have been successful in preventing particular media stories dragging up past events long after they had occurred, including court cases.[14] Indeed, many countries already obscure party names from decisions and judgments so as to render them anonymous (eg, Germany, Austria, Greece, Finland, Belgium, Hungary, the Netherlands, Poland and Portugal).[15] The right to be forgotten has also been recognised in France and Belgium.[16] A UK case also granted anonymity to the plaintiff,[17] as did the Canadian Supreme Court in an online abuse case.[18] To be successful, however, it can also be important to change party initials.[19]

5 GDPR: ARTICLE 16

7.5   Article 16 of the GDPR provides that '[t]he data subject shall have the right to obtain from the controller without undue delay the rectification of inaccurate personal data concerning him or her'. There is no need for the data in question to be causing actual harm or damage. The individual data subject is entitled and may simply file the notification accordingly.

6 GDPR: ARTICLE 17

7.6   Article 17 of the GDPR provides for the erasure, forgetting, and takedown right. It sets out instances when the individual data subject can request the controller to comply with RtbF notices. One of these is simply that the individual 'data subject withdraws consent on which the processing is based'.[20] There is no requirement that the data in question is causing actual harm or damage. The individual data subject is entitled and may simply file the notification accordingly.

13   T-E Synodinou, 'The Media Coverage of Court Proceedings in Europe: Striking a Balance Between Freedom of Expression and Fair Process' *Computer Law & Security Review* (2012) (28) 208, at 217. Also see P Lambert, Television Courtroom Broadcasting Effects, The Empirical Research and the Supreme Court Challenge (American University Press, 2015); P Lambert, Television Courtroom Broadcasting, Distraction Effects and Eye Tracking (Intellect, 2012); P Lambert, Twitter and Television Cameras in Court (Bloomsbury, 2011).
14   *Ibid* at 218.
15   *Ibid* and fn 106 at 218.
16   *Ibid* at 218–219, at 218
17   See *XY v Facebook*, which also said that the website was a publisher. *XY v Facebook*, McCloskey J [2012] NIQB 96, 30 November 2012.
18   *AB v Bragg Communications*, 27 September 2012. Available at: http://scc-csc.lexum.com/scc-csc/scc-csc/en/item/10007/index.do.
19   For example, while the parties and director defendants in a Berlin Facebook data protection case were reduced to initials, reducing one party's name to 'MZ' may not have been fully effective. See *The Federal Association of Consumer Organisations and Consumer Groups, Federal Consumer Association, GB v Facebook Ireland Limited, MA, JB, DG, PT and the Chairman* [names redacted], [redacted].
20   Provided for in GDPR Article 17(1)(b). See actual provision for full details and context.

In addition, by way of further example, the GDPR provides that the controller must comply when the individual data subject simply 'objects to the processing'.[21] There is again no requirement that the data in question is causing actual harm or damage. The individual data subject is entitled and may simply file the notification accordingly.

7 OTHER COMPLEMENTARY RIGHTS

Processing Restriction Right

7.7   There are additional alternative and even complementary rights provided for in the GDPR in addition to RtbF. Article 18 of the GDPR refers to the right to restriction of processing.

> The individual data subject shall have the right to obtain from the controller the restriction of the processing where one of the following applies:

> * the accuracy of the data is contested by the individual data subject, for a period enabling the controller to verify the accuracy of the personal data;

> * the processing is unlawful and the individual data subject opposes the erasure of the personal data and requests the restriction of their use instead;

> * the controller no longer needs the personal data for the purposes of the processing, but they are required by the individual data subject for the establishment, exercise or defence of legal claims;

> * the individual data subject has objected to processing pursuant to Article 21(1) pending the verification whether the legitimate grounds of the controller override those of the individual data subject.[22]

Where processing has been restricted under Article 18(1), such personal data shall, with the exception of storage, only be processed with the individual data subject's consent or for the establishment, exercise or defence of legal claims or for the protection of the rights of another natural or legal person or for reasons of important public interest of the EU or of a state.[23]

An individual data subject who obtained the restriction of processing pursuant to Article 18(1) shall be informed by the controller before the restriction of processing is lifted.[24]

Notification Follow Through Obligation

7.8   There are additional alternative and even complementary rights provided for in the GDPR in addition to RtbF. The new GDPR provides a notification

---

21   *Ibid* Art 17(1)(c). See actual provision for full details and context.
22   GDPR Art 18(1).
23   *Ibid* Art 18(2).
24   *Ibid* Art 18(3).

obligation regarding rectification, erasure or restriction actions. The controller shall communicate any rectification or erasure of personal data or restriction of processing carried out in accordance with Articles 16, 17(1) and 18 to each recipient to whom the personal data have been disclosed, unless this proves impossible or involves disproportionate effort. The controller shall inform the individual data subject about those recipients if the individual data subject requests it.[25]

Transparency Measures

7.9   Article 5 of the GDPR provides important transparency measures. It provides that the personal data shall be 'processed … in a transparent manner in relation to the data subject'. Transparency:

> require[s] greater awareness among citizens about the processing going on: its existence, its content and the flows generated in and out by using terminals.

> Transparency also relates to security of data and risk management.[26]

Some commentators have suggested the GDPR could go further. It has been suggested that 'the greater the flow of information systems the more opaque it becomes in modern information systems and with new ICT applications. In that case the right to transparency must increase alongside these new processes'.[27]

Article 5 of the new GDPR in the principles of data protection (first principle) now reads that personal data shall be:

> processed lawfully, fairly and in a transparent manner in relation to the data subject ("lawfulness, fairness and transparency").

Article 12 refers to transparent information, communication and modalities for exercising the rights of the individual data subject.

The controller shall take appropriate measures to provide any information referred to in Articles 13 and 14 and any communication under Articles 15–22 and 34 relating to processing to the individual data subject in a concise, transparent, intelligible and easily accessible form, using clear and plain language, particularly for any information addressed specifically to a child. The information shall be provided in writing or by other means where appropriate (eg, in electronic form). When notified by the individual data subject, the information may be provided orally, provided that the identity of the individual data subject is proven by other means.[28]

---

25   *Ibid* Art 19.
26   L Costa and Y Poullet, 'Privacy and the Regulation of 2012' *Computer Law & Security Review* above at 256.
27   *Ibid*.
28   GDPR Article 12(1).

Ultimately, however, it may have to be considered whether RtbF offered (where it is offered) by the controller is fully compliant; is fully available (eg, can a controller refuse a RtbF complaint received other than on a clunky non-user friendly, hard to find web page); whether there are adequate staff or adequate processes and procedures to deal with the complaint in a timely and proper manner; or whether genuine RtbF complaints are being refused; etc.

The controller shall facilitate the exercise of individual data subject rights under Articles 15–22. In cases referred to in Article 11(2), the controller shall not refuse to act on the notice of the individual data subject for exercising their rights under Articles 15–22, unless the controller demonstrates that it is not able to identify the individual data subject.[29]

The controller shall provide information on action taken on a notice under Articles 15–22 to the individual data subject without undue delay and in any event within one month of receipt of the notice. That period may be extended by two further months when necessary, considering the complexity and the number of the notices. The controller shall inform the individual data subject of any such extension within one month of receipt of the notice, together with the reasons for the delay. Where the individual data subject makes the notice request by electronic means, the information shall be provided by electronic means where possible, unless otherwise notified by the individual data subject.[30]

If the controller does not act after the notice of the individual data subject, the controller shall inform the individual data subject without delay and at the latest within one month of receipt of the notice of the reasons for not taking action and on the possibility of lodging a complaint to a supervisory authority and seeking a judicial remedy.[31]

Information provided under Articles 13 and 14 and any communication and any actions taken under Articles 15–22 and 34 shall be provided free of charge. Where notification requests from an individual data subject are manifestly unfounded or excessive, in particular because of their repetitive character, the controller may either charge a reasonable fee, considering the administrative costs for providing the information or the communication, taking the action notified or refusing to act on the notice. The controller shall bear the burden of demonstrating the manifestly unfounded or excessive character of the notice.[32]

Without prejudice to Article 11, where the controller has reasonable doubts concerning the identity of the natural person making the notice request referred to in Articles 15–21, the controller may request the provision of additional information necessary to confirm the identity of the individual data subject.[33]

---

29   *Ibid* Art 12(2).
30   *Ibid* Art 12(3).
31   *Ibid* Art 12(4).
32   *Ibid* Art 12(4).
33   *Ibid* Art 12(6).

The information to be provided to individual data subjects pursuant to Articles 13 and 14 may be provided in combination with standardised icons to give in an easily visible, intelligible and clearly legible manner, a meaningful overview of the intended processing. Where the icons are presented electronically, they shall be machine readable.[34]

The Commission shall be empowered to adopt delegated acts in accordance with Article 92 for the purpose of determining the information to be presented by the icons and the procedures for providing standardised icons.[35]

Right to Object

7.10 Chapter III, Section 4 of the GDPR refers to the right to object and automated individual decision making. The individual data subject shall have the right to object, on grounds relating to his or her situation, at any time to the processing of personal data concerning him or her which is based on Article 6(1) (e) or (f), including profiling based on these provisions. The controller shall no longer process the personal data unless the controller demonstrates compelling legitimate grounds for the processing which override the interests, rights and freedoms of the individual data subject or for the establishment, exercise or defence of legal claims.[36]

Where personal data are processed for direct marketing purposes, the individual data subject shall have the right to object at any time to the processing of personal data concerning him or her for such marketing, which includes profiling to the extent that it is related to such direct marketing.[37]

Where the individual data subject objects to the processing for direct marketing purposes, the personal data shall no longer be processed for such purposes.[38]

At the latest at the time of the first communication with the individual data subject, the right referred to in Article 21(1) and (2) shall be explicitly brought to the attention of the individual data subject and shall be presented clearly and separately from any other information.[39]

---

34 *Ibid* Art 12(7).
35 *Ibid* Art 12(8). Prior to the new GDPR, many data protection supervisory authorities issued recommendations in relation to privacy notices. As an example, the ICO in the UK issued the following guidance, namely: *Getting It Right: Collecting Information about Your Customers* and *Privacy Notices Code of Practice*. These types of guidance now need to be read in light of the GDPR changes. No doubt there will be future guidance from data protection supervisory authorities following the GDPR and ultimately following the ePrivacy Regulation once finalised.
36 GDPR Art 21(1).
37 *Ibid* Art 20(2).
38 *Ibid* Art 21(3).
39 *Ibid* Art 21(4).

In the context of the use of information society services and notwithstanding Directive 2002/58/EC,[40] the individual data subject may exercise his or her right to object by automated means using technical specifications.[41]

Where personal data are processed for scientific or historical research purposes or statistical purposes pursuant to Article 89(1), the individual data subject, on grounds relating to his or her particular situation, shall have the right to object to processing of personal data concerning him or her, unless the processing is necessary for the performance of a task carried out for reasons of public interest.[42]

Right Against Automated Individual Decision Making, Including Profile

7.11   Chapter III, Section 4 of the GDPR refers to the right to object and automated individual decision making. There is often a wide concern as to the data protection impact of increased profiling techniques.[43] The new GDPR provides that the individual data subject shall have the right not to be subject to a decision based solely on automated processing,[44] including profiling,[45] which produces legal effects concerning him or her or similarly significantly affects him or her (Article 22(1)).

Article 22(1) shall not apply if the decision:

* is necessary for entering into, or performance of, a contract between the individual data subject and a controller;

* is authorised by EU or state law to which the controller is subject and which also lays down suitable measures to safeguard the individual data subject's rights and freedoms and legitimate interests; or

* is based on the individual data subject's explicit consent.[46]

In cases referred to in Article 22(2)(a) and (c) the controller shall implement suitable measures to safeguard the individual data subject's rights and freedoms

---

40   Directive 2002/58/EC of the European Parliament and of the Council of 12 July 2002 concerning the processing of personal data and the protection of privacy in the electronic communications sector (Directive on privacy and electronic communications).
41   GDPR Art 21(5).
42   *Ibid* Art 21(6).
43   This is in the EU as well as the US (and elsewhere). For a US perspective, see N Roethlisberger, 'Someone is Watching: The Need for Enhanced Data Protection' *Hastings Law Journal* (2011) (62:6) 1793.
44   G Malgieri and G Comande, 'Why a Right to Legibility of Automated Decision-Making Exists in the General Data Protection Regulation' *International Data Privacy Law* (2017) (7:4) 243.
45   See, eg, M Hildebrandt, 'Who is Profiling Who? Invisible Visibility' in S Gutwirth, Y Poullet, P de Hert, C de Terwange and S Nouwt, *Reinventing Data Protection?* (Springer, 2009) 239.
46   GDPR Art 22(1).

and legitimate interests, at least the right to obtain human intervention on the part of the controller, to express his or her point of view and to contest the decision.[47]

Decisions referred to in Article 22(2) shall not be based on special categories of personal data referred to in Article 9(1), unless Article 9(2)(a) or (g) applies and suitable measures to safeguard the individual data subject's rights and freedoms and legitimate interests are in place.[48]

Access Right

7.12   Another complementary right that may sometimes assist the individual data subject in instances of takedown and online abuse (OA) (and in other instances), is the right of access to personal data. This allows the individual to demand from the controller a copy of their personal data, or more specifically a copy of more relevant personal data related to the problem content in question. This can, for example, assist the victim to see the extent of the OA in relation to them and as a result to better tackle the problem.

Article 15 of the GDPR provides that:

> The data subject shall have the right to obtain from the controller confirmation as to whether or not personal data concerning him or her are being processed and, where that is the case, access to the personal data.[49]

In addition, the access right also obliged the controller to provide the following information, namely:

- the purposes of the processing;

- the categories of personal data concerned;

- the recipients or categories of recipient to whom the personal data have been or will be disclosed in particular, recipients in third countries;

- where possible, the envisaged period for which personal data will be stored, or if this is not possible, the criteria used to determine that period;

- the existence of the right to request from the controller rectification or erasure of personal data or restriction or processing of personal data concerning the data subject or to object to such processing;

- the right to lodge a complaint with the data protection supervisory authority;

- where the personalised data are not collected from the individual data subject, any available information as to their source; and

- the existence of automated decision making, including profiling and at least in those cases, meaningful information about the logic involved, as well as

47   *Ibid* Art 22(3).
48   *Ibid* Art 22(4).
49   *Ibid* Art 15(1).

the significance and the envisaged consequences of such processing for the individual data subject.[50]

In addition, where the personal data is transferred to a third country, the individual data subject has the right to be informed of the appropriate safeguards relating to the transfer.[51]

Article 15(3) adds that '[t]he controller shall provide a copy of the personal data undergoing processing'.[52]

---

50 *Ibid* Art 15(1)(a)–(h).
51 *Ibid* Art 15(2). Also see Art 46 in relation to appropriate safeguards.
52 Note that Art 15(4) provides that '[t]he right to obtain a copy referred to in paragraph 3 [ie Article 15(3)] shall not adversely affect the rights and freedoms of others'.

CHAPTER 8

Enhanced Regime

I   INTRODUCTION

8.1   RtbF is contained in the new General Data Protection Regulation (GDPR).[1] However, the wider context of new enhanced GDPR regime also needs to be considered as it provides a valuable context for this (new) solution for individuals who wish to have materials and content removed from the internet and in the context of a variety of settings and justifications. This includes the definition of personal data itself [2] and the wide concept of personal data and data protection.[3] The GDPR also contains detailed provisions, namely, right to rectification;[4] right to erasure/right to be forgotten;[5] right to restriction of processing;[6] and notification regarding rectification or erasure or restriction of processing.[7]

2   CHANGES AND EXPANSIONS

8.2   Some of the key changes are referred to below. In some respects, these could also be seen as advantages of the new GDPR data protection regime:

- enhanced RtbF will improve the position of individual data subjects and the ability to delete data;

- administrative costs are to be reduced with a single EU-wide set of rules and obligations;

- there may be less need to interact with the national data regulator, as more responsibility and accountability is passed to the organisational level;

- the consent requirement is clarified as to mean explicit consent (whereas previously there were references to different categories of consent);

- rights are improved with easier access to personal data, as well as its transferability;

---

1   Generally, see P Lambert, 5 Essential GDPR Content Lists (Kortext, 2021); P Lambert, Essential GDPR Index (Kortext, 2021); and P Lambert, The UK GDPR Annotated (Kortext, 2021).
2   GDPR Art 4(1).
3   N Purtova, 'The Law of Everything: Broad Concept of Personal Data and Future of EU Data Protection Law' *Innovation and Technology* (2018) (10:1) 40; P Lambert, A User's Guide to Data Protection (Bloomsbury, 2020).
4   GDPR Art 16.
5   *Ibid* Art 17.
6   *Ibid* Art 18.
7   *Ibid* Art 19.

- the EU data protection regime will apply to non-EU entities operating with regard to EU personal data and EU citizens; and

- the national authorities will be able to impose fines based on a percent of global turnover[8] (see below).

The GDPR also enhances and expands the various powers of the national data regulators, and the UK GDPR for the Information Commissioner's Office (ICO).

3 GENERAL WELCOME

8.3 The various data protection supervisory authorities all welcome the GDPR. As an example, the UK national data regulator (the ICO) welcomed the GDPR, stating:

> it strengthens the position of individuals, recognises important concepts such as privacy by design and privacy impact assessments and requires organisations to be able to demonstrate that they have measures in place to ensure personal information is properly protected.[9]

4 EU COMMISSION

8.4 The EU Commission's press statement issued once the new GDPR text was agreed notes that the GDPR 'will enable people to better control their personal data. At the same time modernised and unified rules will allow businesses to make the most of the opportunities of the Digital Single Market by cutting red tape and benefiting from reinforced consumer trust'.[10]

The EU Commission also refers to the benefits of the changes. It states:

> The reform will allow people to regain control of their personal data. Two-thirds of Europeans (67%), according to a recent Eurobarometer survey, stated they are concerned about not having complete control over the information they provide online. Seven Europeans out of ten worry about the potential use that companies may make of the information disclosed. The data protection reform will strengthen the right to data protection, which is a fundamental right in the EU and allow them to have trust when they give their personal data.

> The new rules address these concerns by strengthening the existing rights and empowering individuals with more control over their personal data. Most notably, these include,

---

8   In Brief, *Communications Law* (2012) (17) 3. HA Wolff, Prof Dr, 'The Implementation of Administrative Fines Under the General Data Protection Regulation from the German Perspective' *International Journal for the Data Protection Officer, Privacy Officer and Privacy Counsel (IDPP)* (2018) (2:11) 11.

9   Referred to in In Brief, *Communications Law*.

10 European Commission, Press Release, 'Agreement on Commission's EU Data Protection Reform Will Boost Digital Single Market' Brussels (15 December 2015).

- easier access to your own data: individuals will have more information on how their data is processed and this information should be available in a clear and understandable way;

- a right to data portability: it will be easier to transfer your personal data between service providers;

- a clarified [RtbF]: when you no longer want your data to be processed and provided there are no legitimate grounds for retaining it, the data will be deleted;

- the right to know when your data has been hacked: For example, companies and organisations must notify the national supervisory authority of serious data breaches as soon as possible so that users can take appropriate measures.

Clear modern rules for businesses

In today's digital economy, personal data has acquired enormous economic significance, in particular in the area of big data. By unifying Europe's rules on data protection, lawmakers are creating a business opportunity and encouraging innovation.

One continent, one law: The [GDPR] will establish one single set of rules which will make it simpler and cheaper for companies to do business in the EU.

One-stop-shop: businesses will only have to deal with one single supervisory authority. This is estimated to save €2.3 billion per year.

European rules on European soil: companies based outside of Europe will have to apply the same rules when offering services in the EU.

Risk-based approach: the rules will avoid a burdensome one-size-fits-all obligation and rather tailor them to the respective risks.

Rules fit for innovation: the [GDPR] will guarantee that data protection safeguards are built into products and services from the earliest stage of development (Data protection by Design (DPbD)). Privacy-friendly techniques such as pseudonymisation will be encouraged, to reap the benefits of big data innovation while protecting privacy.

Benefits for big and small alike

The data protection reform will stimulate economic growth by cutting costs and red tape for European business, especially for small and medium enterprises (SMEs). The EU's data protection reform will help SMEs break into new markets. Under the new rules, SMEs will benefit from four reductions in red tape:

- No more notifications: Notifications to supervisory authorities are a formality that represents a cost for business of €130 million every year. The reform will scrap these entirely.

- Every penny counts: Where requests to access data are manifestly unfounded or excessive, SMEs will be able to charge a fee for providing access.

- Data protection officers: SMEs are exempt from the obligation to appoint a data protection officer insofar as data processing is not their core business activity.

- Impact assessments: SMEs will have no obligation to carry out an impact assessment unless there is a high risk.

...

Better protection of citizens' data

Individuals' personal data will be better protected, when processed for any law enforcement purpose including prevention of crime. It will protect everyone – regardless of whether they are a victim, criminal or witness. All law enforcement processing in the Union must comply with the principles of necessity, proportionality and legality, with appropriate safeguards for the individuals. Supervision is ensured by independent national data protection authorities and effective judicial remedies must be provided.

The Data Protection Directive for Police and Criminal Justice Authorities provides clear rules for the transfer of personal data by law enforcement authorities outside the EU, to ensure that the level of protection of individuals guaranteed in the EU is not undermined.[11]

In one survey, 72 per cent of internet users were concerned that they gave away too much personal data.[12] However, red tape reduction and economic growth are also considered under the new regime. New technological changes are also recognised and encompassed. European harmonisation issues are also a central consideration.

GDPR Recitals

8.5   The recitals to the new GDPR are also instructive in relation to the purposes and themes covered. They refer to, for example: the DPD 95/46 being repealed; the WP 29/EDPB; background and rationale; obligations; security; processing; rights; proceedings; establishment; transfers; supervisory authorities; new bodies; lawful processing and consent; online identifiers; sensitive personal data; children; and health data. The importance of data protection and health data is also referred to by the OECD.[13]

5   MAIN PROVISIONS AND CHANGES

8.6   The main new GDPR provisions and changes are referred to below.

Repeal of DPD

8.7   The DPD 95/46 was repealed with effect from 25 May 2018.[14] References to the repealed DPD 95/46 shall be construed as being references to the GDPR.[15]

---

11   *Ibid*.
12   Eurobarometer, 'Attitudes on Data Protection and Electronic Identity in the EU' (June 2011).
13   *Strengthening Health Information Infrastructure for Health Care Quality Governance: Good Practices, New Opportunities and Data Privacy Protection Challenges*, OECD (2013).
14   GDPR Art 94(1).
15   *Ibid* Art 94(2).

New Definitions

8.8   Article 4 of the new GDPR sets out the definitions for the new data protection regime.[16]

The WP29 and European Data Protection Board

8.9   A new European Data Protection Board (EDPB) has been established. This effectively replaces the WP 29. References to the previous WP 29 shall be construed as references to the EDPB established by the GDPR.[17] Chapter IV, Section 3 of the GDPR provides for the EDPB. The EDPB is established as a body of the EU and shall have legal personality.[18] The EDPB is composed of the head of one supervisory authority of each Member State and of the European Data Protection Supervisor, or their respective representatives.[19] The EDPB acts independently when performing its tasks or exercising its powers pursuant to Articles 70 and 71.[20]

Context of GDPR

8.10   The initial provisions refer to the context of the GDPR, namely, the subject matter and objectives;[21] material scope;[22] and territorial scope.[23]

New Processing Rules: Obligations

8.11   The new processing rules as set out in the new GDPR regime are set out below.

The recitals refer to the following: data processing must be lawful and fair;[24] processing necessary for a contract;[25] processing for a legal obligation;[26] processing necessary to protect life;[27] and the legitimate interests of the controller.[28]

---

16 Prior to the new GDPR, the various data protection supervisory authorities issued recommendations and guidance in relation to personal data, definitions, etc. The UK data protection supervisory authority (the ICO), for example issued the following documentation, namely: *Determining What is Personal Data*; *What is 'Data' for the Purposes of the DPA?*; *What is Personal Data? – A Quick Reference Guide*. These now need to be read in light of the GDPR changes, as well as future guidance post the GDPR. Note the GDPR version in the UK is now the UK GDPR post Brexit. See Lambert, The UK GDPR Annotated.
17 GDPR Art 94(2).
18 *Ibid* Art 68(1).
19 *Ibid* Art 68(3).
20 *Ibid* Art 69(1).
21 *Ibid* Art 1.
22 *Ibid* Art 2.
23 *Ibid* Art 3.
24 *Ibid* Art 39.
25 *Ibid* Art 40.
26 *Ibid* Art 40.
27 *Ibid* Art 46.
28 *Ibid* Art 47.

Principles of Data Protection

8.12   Article 5 of the GDPR sets out the new principles relating to data protection. Personal data must be:

- processed lawfully, fairly and in a transparent manner in relation to the data subject (lawfulness, fairness and transparency);

- collected for specified, explicit and legitimate purposes and not further processed in a manner that is incompatible with those purposes; further processing for archiving purposes in the public interest, scientific or historical research purposes or statistical purposes shall, in accordance with Article 89(1), not be considered to be incompatible with the initial purposes (purpose limitation);

- adequate, relevant and limited to what is necessary in relation to the purposes for which they are processed (data minimisation);

- accurate and, where necessary, kept up to date; every reasonable step must be taken to ensure that personal data that are inaccurate, having regard to the purposes for which they are processed, are erased or rectified without delay (accuracy);

- kept in a form which permits identification of data subjects for no longer than is necessary for the purposes for which the personal data are processed; personal data may be stored for longer periods insofar as the personal data will be processed solely for archiving purposes in the public interest, scientific or historical research purposes or statistical purposes in accordance with Article 89(1) subject to implementation of the appropriate technical and organisational measures required by the GDPR to safeguard the rights and freedoms of the data subject (storage limitation); and

- processed in a way that ensures appropriate security of the personal data, including protection against unauthorised or unlawful processing and against accidental loss, destruction or damage, using appropriate technical or organisational measures (integrity and confidentiality).

The controller must be responsible for and be able to demonstrate compliance with the above (accountability).

These can be summarised as:

- data lawfulness, fairness and transparency requirement;

- data purpose limitation requirement;

- data minimisation requirement;

- data accuracy requirement;

- data storage limitation requirement;

- data security, integrity and confidentiality requirement; and

- demonstrate data compliance and accountability requirements.

Lawfulness of Processing: Legitimate Processing Conditions

8.13   Article 6 of the GDPR sets out the new provisions in relation to the lawfulness of processing. Processing of personal data is lawful only if and to the extent that at least one of the following applies:

- the individual data subject has given *consent* to the processing of their personal data for one or more specific purposes (see section below and also Article 7);

- processing is necessary for the performance of a contract to which the individual data subject is party or to take steps at the request of the individual data subject prior to entering into a contract;

- processing is necessary for compliance with a legal obligation to which the controller is subject;

- processing is necessary to protect the vital interests of the individual data subject or of another natural person;

- processing is necessary for the performance of a task carried out in the public interest or in the exercise of official authority vested in the controller; and

- processing is necessary for the purposes of the legitimate interests pursued by the controller or by a third party, except where such interests are overridden by the interests or fundamental rights and freedoms of the individual data subject which require protection of personal data, in particular, where the individual data subject is a child. This shall not apply to processing carried out by public authorities in the performance of their tasks.[29]

States may maintain or introduce more specific provisions to adapt the application of the rules of the GDPR with regard to the processing of personal data for compliance with Article 6(1)(c) and (e) by determining more precisely specific requirements for the processing and other measures to ensure lawful and fair processing including for other specific processing situations as provided for in Chapter IX.[30] The basis for the processing referred to in Article 6(1)(c) and (e) must be laid down by EU law, or state law to which the controller is subject.

The purpose of the processing shall be determined in this legal basis or as regards the processing referred to in Article 6(1)(e), shall be necessary for the performance of a task carried out in the public interest or in the exercise of official authority vested in the controller. This legal basis may contain specific provisions to adapt the application of rules of the GDPR, inter alia, the general conditions governing the lawfulness of processing by the controller, the type of data which are subject to the processing, the individual data subjects concerned; the entities to and the purposes for which the data may be disclosed; the purpose limitation; storage periods and processing operations and processing procedures, including

29   *Ibid* Art 6(1).
30   *Ibid* Art 6(2).

measures to ensure lawful and fair processing, such as those for other specific processing situations as provided for in Chapter IX. EU law or the state law must meet an objective of public interest and be proportionate to the legitimate aim pursued.[31]

Where the processing for another purpose than the one for which the data have been collected is not based on the individual data subject's consent or on EU or state law which constitutes a necessary and proportionate measure in a democratic society to safeguard the objectives referred to in Article 23(1), the controller shall, in order to ascertain whether processing for another purpose is compatible with the purpose for which the personal data are initially collected, take into account, inter alia:

- any link between the purposes for which the data have been collected and the purposes of the intended further processing;

- the context in which the personal data have been collected, in particular regarding the relationship between individual data subjects and the controller;

- the nature of the personal data, in particular whether special categories of personal data are processed, pursuant to Article 9 or whether personal data related to criminal convictions and offences are processed, pursuant to Article 10;

- the possible consequences of the intended further processing for individual data subjects; and

- the existence of appropriate safeguards, which may include encryption or pseudonymisation.[32]

Consent for Processing: Conditions for Consent

8.14   Consent is an important issue under the new GDPR.[33] Lawful processing and consent are referred to in recital 40. The WP 29 also refers to consent issues.[34]

Article 7 of the GDPR refers to conditions for consent as follows: 'Where processing is based on consent, the Controller shall be able to demonstrate that

---

31   *Ibid* Art 6(3).
32   *Ibid* Art 7(4). Prior to the new GDPR, the various data protection supervisory authorities issued guidance and recommendations in relation to marketing personal data issues. The UK data protection supervisory authority (the ICO), for example, issues the following guidance, namely: *Direct Marketing*; *Direct Marketing Checklist – Ideal for Small Businesses*; *Companies Receiving Unwanted Marketing*; *Guidance on Political Campaigning*. These now need to be read in light of the GDPR changes and also subsequent guidance as may be issued post the GDPR.
33   JP Vandenbroucke and J Olsen, 'Informed Consent and the New EU Regulation on Data Protection' *International Journal of Epidemiology* (2013) (42:6) 1891.
34   WP 29, Opinion 15/2011 Consent; Working Document 02/2013 providing guidance on obtaining consent for cookies, 201; Opinion 04/2012 on Cookie Consent Exemption.

the individual data subject has consented to the processing of their personal data.'[35]

If the individual data subject's consent is given in the context of a written declaration which also concerns other matters, the request for consent must be presented in a manner which is *clearly distinguishable* from other matters, in an *intelligible and easily accessible form*, using *clear and plain language*. Any part of such a declaration which constitutes an infringement of the GDPR shall not be binding.[36]

The individual data subject shall have the *right to withdraw his or her consent at any time*. The withdrawal of consent shall not affect the lawfulness of processing based on consent before its withdrawal. Prior to giving consent, the individual data subject shall be informed thereof. It shall be as easy to withdraw consent as to give consent.[37]

When assessing whether consent is freely given, utmost account shall be taken of the fact whether, inter alia, the performance of a service, is conditional on consent to the processing of personal data that is not necessary for the performance of this contract.[38]

Children

8.15   The issue of children in the data protection regime has been steadily rising. The increased use of social media and Web 2.0 services enhance the exposure and risk for children and the uninitiated.[39]

This has included children's groups, regulators and also the EDPB (previously the WP 29). The WP 29 issued Opinion 2/2009 on the Protection of Children's Personal Data (General Guidelines and the Special Case of Schools) in 2009 and also Working Document 1/2008 on the Protection of Children's Personal Data (General Guidelines and the Special Case of Schools). Schools are being encouraged to be proactive and to have in place appropriate codes and policies for children's social media and internet usage.[40]

---

35   GDPR Art 7(1).
36   *Ibid* Art 7(2).
37   *Ibid* Art 7(3).
38   *Ibid* Art 7(4).
39   See, eg, D Gourlay and G Gallagher, 'Collecting and Using Children's Information Online: The UK/US Dichotomy' SCL *Computers and Law*, 12 December 2011.
40   Note generally, eg, JS Groppe, 'A Child's Playground or a Predator's Hunting Ground? – How to Protect Children on Internet Social Networking Sites' *CommLaw Conspectus* (2007) (16) 215; EP Steadman, 'MySpace, But Who's Responsibility? Liability of Social Networking Websites When Offline Sexual Assault of Minors Follows Online Interaction' *Villanova Sports and Entertainment Law Journal* (2007) (14) 363; DC Beckstrom, 'Who's Looking at Your Facebook Profile? The Use of Student Conduct Codes to Censor College Students' Online Speech' *Willamette Law Review* (2008) 261.

There is now an explicit acknowledgement of children's interests in the EU data protection regime, unlike with DPD 95/46 which contained no explicit reference to them. The GDPR refers to a 'child' as a person below the age of 16. This is significant amongst other things in relation to consent, contracting, etc. It is also significant for social networks which have significant numbers of children. Up until now it was common for certain social networks to purport to accept users only over the age of 13. A child was defined in the first and draft version of the GDPR as up to 18 years of age. Therefore, the potential implications will require careful assessment. This includes, for example, social contracts, consent, notices, terms of use, contract terms, payment and purchase issues, related process models, sign-ups, social media, internet, etc.[41]

Article 8 of the original proposal for the GDPR contained provisions in relation to the processing of personal data of a child. The final version of Article 8(1) provides that where Article 6(1)(a) applies, in relation to the offer of information society services directly to a child, the processing of the personal data of a child shall be lawful where the child is at least 16 years old. Where the child is below the age of 16, such processing shall be lawful only if and to the extent that consent is given or authorised by the holder of parental responsibility over the child. The original Article 8(1) proposal provided that it shall not affect the general contract law of states, such as the rules on the validity, formation or effect of a contract in relation to a child. Under the original Article 8(3) the Commission is empowered to adopt delegated acts in accordance with Article 86 for the purpose of further specifying the criteria and requirements for the methods to obtain verifiable consent referred to in Article 8(1). In doing so, the Commission shall consider specific measures for micro, small and medium-sized enterprises (original draft Article 8(3)). In addition, the Commission under may lay down standard forms for specific methods to obtain verifiable consent referred to in Article 8(1). Those implementing acts shall be adopted in accordance with the examination procedure referred to in Article 87(2).[42]

The explicit reference to children is new and some would argue overdue. Increasingly, the activities of children on the internet and on social media, poses risks and concerns.[43] This has been further emphasised of late with tragic events involving online abuse, in particular cyber bullying. Risks arise obviously from their activities online (eg, inappropriate content, cyber bullying, but also from the collection and use of their personal data online and collected online, sometimes without their knowledge or consent). Their personal data and privacy is more vulnerable than that of older people.

---

41 Note, however, that the respective Member States may vary or derogate from the age 16 requirement and may specify a lower age. The UK, for example, has adopted a change whereby it specifies the age as being 13 in the UK: Data Protection Act 2018, s 9. UK data protection laws are subject to further potential change, and an official change consultation process was announced in 2021.
42 Original draft Art 8(4).
43 See, eg, L McDermott, 'Legal Issues Associated With Minors and Their Use of Social Networking Sites' *Communications Law* (2012) (17) 19.

It is important for organisation to note the 'child' provisions in the GDPR. This will have implications in how organisations:

- consider the interaction with children and what personal data may be collected and processed; and

- ensure that there is appropriate compliance for such collection and processing for children as distinct from adults.

Child's Consent Online

8.16   The processing of children's personal data is referred to in Recital 38. Article 8 of the GDPR makes new provisions in relation to conditions for children's consent for Information Society services. Where Article 6(1)(a) applies, in relation to the offer of information society services directly to a child, the processing of the personal data of a child shall be lawful where the child is at least 16 years old. Where the child is below the age of 16 years, such processing shall only be lawful if and to the extent that consent is given or authorised by the holder of parental responsibility over the child.[44]

The controller shall make reasonable efforts to verify in such cases that consent is given or authorised by the holder of parental responsibility over the child, taking into consideration available technology.[45] This shall not affect the general contract law of states such as the rules on the validity, formation or effect of a contract in relation to a child.[46]

Special Personal Data

8.17   Sensitive personal data are referred to in recitals 10 and 51 and special categories of personal data are referred to in recitals 10, 51, 52, 53, 54, 71, 80, 91 and 97.

Article 9 refers to the processing of special categories of personal data. The processing of personal data, revealing racial or ethnic origin, political opinions, religious or philosophical beliefs, or trade-union membership and the processing of genetic data, biometric data for the purpose of uniquely identifying a natural person, data concerning health or data concerning a natural person's sex life and sexual orientation shall be *prohibited*.[47]

The above shall not apply if one of the following applies:

---

44   GDPR Art 8(1).
45   *Ibid* Art 8(2).
46   *Ibid* Art 8(3).
47   *Ibid* Art 9(1). In relation to genetic data generally, see eg D Hallinan, PJA de Hertand M Friedewald, 'Genetic Data and the Data Protection Regulation: Anonymity, Multiple Subjects, Sensitivity and a Prohibitionary Logic Regarding Genetic Data?' *Computer Law and Security Review* (2013) (29:4) 317.

- the individual data subject has given *explicit consent* to the processing of those personal data for one or more specified purposes, except where EU law or state law provide that the above prohibition may not be lifted by the individual data subject;

- processing is necessary for the purposes of carrying out the obligations and exercising specific rights of the Controller or of the individual data subject in the field of employment and social security and social protection law in so far as it is authorised by EU law or state law or a collective agreement pursuant to state law providing for adequate safeguards for the fundamental rights and the interests of the individual data subject;

- processing is necessary to protect the vital interests of the individual data subject or of another natural person where the individual data subject is physically or legally incapable of giving consent;

- processing is carried out in the course of its legitimate activities with appropriate safeguards by a foundation, association or any other not-for-profit-seeking body with a political, philosophical, religious or trade union aim and on condition that the processing relates solely to the members or to former members of the body or to persons who have regular contact with it in connection with its purposes and that the personal data are not disclosed outside that body without the consent of the individual data subjects;

- processing relates to personal data which are manifestly made public by the individual data subject;

- processing is necessary for the establishment, exercise or defence of legal claims or whenever courts are acting in their judicial capacity;

- processing is necessary for reasons of substantial public interest, based on EU or state law which shall be proportionate to the aim pursued, respect the essence of the right to data protection and provide for suitable and specific measures to safeguard the fundamental rights and the interests of the individual data subject;

- processing is necessary for the purposes of preventive or occupational medicine, for the assessment of the working capacity of the employee, medical diagnosis, the provision of health or social care or treatment or the management of health or social care systems and services on the basis of EU law or state law or pursuant to contract with a health professional and subject to the conditions and safeguards referred to in Article 9(3);

- processing is necessary for reasons of public interest in the area of public health, such as protecting against serious cross-border threats to health or ensuring high standards of quality and safety of health care and of medicinal products or medical devices, on the basis of EU law or state law which provides for suitable and specific measures to safeguard the rights and freedoms of the individual data subject, in particular professional secrecy; or

- processing is necessary for archiving purposes in the public interest, scientific or historical research purposes or statistical purposes in accordance with

Article 89(1) based on EU or state law which shall be proportionate to the aim pursued, respect the essence of the right to data protection and provide for suitable and specific measures to safeguard the fundamental rights and the interests of the individual data subject.[48]

Personal data referred to in Article 9(1) may be processed for the purposes referred to in Article 9(2)(h) when those data are processed by or under the responsibility of a professional subject to the obligation of professional secrecy under EU or state law or rules established by national competent bodies or by another person also subject to an obligation of secrecy under EU or state law or rules established by national competent bodies.[49]

States may maintain or introduce further conditions, including limitations, with regard to the processing of genetic data, biometric data or health data.[50]

Processing of Criminal Convictions and Offences Data

8.18   Article 10 refers to processing of data relating to criminal convictions and offences. Processing of personal data relating to criminal convictions and offences or related security measures based on Article 6(1) shall be carried out only under the control of official authority or when the processing is authorised by EU law or state law providing for adequate safeguards for the rights and freedoms of individual data subjects. Any comprehensive register of criminal convictions may be kept only under the control of official authority.[51]

6 SECURITY

8.19   While security was already an obligation under the previous data protection regime, the GDPR enhances it. Now, both 'the controller and the processor shall implement appropriate technical and organisational measures to ensure a level of security appropriate to the task'.[52] Illustrative examples are

---

48   GDPR Art 9(2).
49   *Ibid* Art 9(3).
50   *Ibid* Art 9(5).
51   A Lytvynenko, 'The Application of the Right to Be Forgotten in the Context of Criminal Records Expungement: The Case Law of the European Court of Human Rights and the Case Law of the US Courts' Law Review of Kyiv University of Law (2019) (4) 379; K Faisal, 'Balancing Between Right to Be Forgotten and Right to Freedom of Expression in Spent Criminal Convictions' Security (2021) (4:4) 1; I Jiménez-Castellanos Ballesteros, 'The Conflict Between the Right to be Forgotten of the Criminal History and Freedom of Information: Digital Newspaper Archives (In this respect the Spanish Constitutional Court Judgment of June 4, 2018 and the European Court of Human Rights' Judgment in the M.L. and W.W. vs. Germany case, June 28, 2018)' Revista de Derecho Político (2019) (1:106) 137; AJ Pitts, 'Challenging the Carceral Imaginary in a Digital Age: Epistemic Asymmetries and the Right to Be Forgotten' International Journal of Political Philosophy / Las Torres de Lucca (2021) (10:19) 3.
52   *GDPR* Art 31(1).

given. The term 'including, inter alia' confirms that the list is not closed. The examples specified are:

• the pseudonymisation and encryption of personal data;

• the ability to ensure the ongoing confidentiality, integrity, availability and resilience of processing systems and services;

• the ability to restore the availability and access to personal data in a timely manner in the event of a physical or technical incident; and

• a process for regularly testing, assessing and evaluating the effectiveness of technical and organisational measures for ensuring the security of the processing.[53]

There are various issues which the controller and processor can and should take into account.[54]

7 GDPR ANALYSIS

8.20　There is now growing analysis in relation to the GDPR, from the history and genesis, Commission proposal stage,[55] negotiations and legislative process,[56] lobbying,[57] legislative stages and final GDPR text[58] – all of which are warranted and appropriate.

---

53 *Ibid* Art 32(1)(a)–(d).

54 *Ibid* Arts 31(1), 32(2), 32(3) and 32(4).

55 P van Eecke, C Craig and J Halpert, 'The First Insight into the European Commission's Proposal for a New European Union Data Protection Law' *Journal of Internet Law* (2012) (15:8) 19.

56 WG Voss, 'The Right to be Forgotten in the European Union: Enforcement in the Court of Justice and Amendment to the Proposed General Data Protection Regulation' *Journal of Internet Law* (2014) (18:1) 3.

57 At the time of the GDPR drafting, there was some criticism by privacy advocates of some of the lobbying activities, including claims that certain politicians were presenting letter officially which were, in part, copy pastes of materials supplied by lobbyists. See also G Christou and I Rashid, 'Interest Group Lobbying in the European Union: Privacy, Data Protection and the Right to be Forgotten' Comparative European Politics (2021) (19:3) 380.

58 R Jay, *A Guide to the General Data Protection Regulation* (Sweet and Maxwell, 2017); C Kuner, LA Bygrave, C Docksey, *General Commentary on EU General Data Protection Regulation* (OUP, 2019); P Lambert, *Understanding the New European Data Protection Rules* (Taylor & Francis, 2017); A Linder, *European Data Protection Law, General Data Protection Regulation 2016* (2018); R Jan Pohle, Data Privacy Legislation in the EU Member States – Part Two of the Practical Overview: How EU Member States Have Adjusted Their Domestic Data Privacy Law to the GDPR – Update' *Computer Law Review International* (2018) (19:5) 133; RL Gutwirth and P de Hert, *Reforming European Data Protection Law* (Springer, 2015); CJ Bennett, S Ae Chun, NR Adam and B Noveck, 'The European General Data Protection Regulation: An Instrument for the Globalization of Privacy Standards?' *Information Polity: The International Journal of Government & Democracy in the Information Age* (2018) (23:2) 239. Also Gringras, The Laws of the Internet (Bloomsbury, 2022); Lambert, A User's Guide to Data Protection; P Lambert, Understanding the New EU Data Fine Rules (Kortext, 2021).

There is also research beginning the review of the GDPR following a period of enactment.[59] One of the intentions of the GDPR and the regulation format, is greater harmonisation and baselines. The success of this strategy will be assessed both in the short and longer term.[60] The success of the individual components of the GDPR will also require individual assessment over time, including the GDPR RtbF.

Other areas for consideration for analysis include the:

- Member State GDPR implementation or adjustment;[61]

- general reaction and business reaction to the GDPR;[62]

- legal reasoning and interpretation[63] of specific GDPR components;

- the GDPR as an instrument for globalising data protection and privacy standards and norms,[64] and wider international data protect texts;[65]

---

59 WG Voss, 'Looking at European Union Data Protection Law Reform Through a Different Prism: The Proposed EU General Data Protection Regulation Two Years Later' *Journal of Internet Law* (2014) (17:9) 1; J Globocnik, 'The Right to Be Forgotten is Taking Shape: CJEU Judgments in GC and Others (C-136/17) and Google v CNIL (C-507/17)' GRUR International: Journal of European (2020) (69:4) 380; S Atalar, 'Does GDPR Cover the Expectations after DPD?' Law (2019) (10:19) 55; S-D Şchiopu, 'Divergent Views on the Right to be Digitally Forgotten: The Opinions of the General Advocates Vs. The Decisions of the Court of Justice Of The European Union' Law Review: Judicial Doctrine (2020) (10:2) 18; L Caddy, 'The "Right to be Forgotten" Four Years on from Google Spain – A Practitioner's View' Entertainment Law Review (2019) (30:1) 3; D Erdos, 'Disclosure, Exposure and the "Right to be Forgotten" After Google Spain: Interrogating Google Search's Webmaster, End User and Lumen Notification Practices' Computer Law & Security Review (2020) (38) 24; S Uncular, 'The Right to Removal in the Time of Post-Google Spain: Myth or Reality Under General Data Protection Regulation?' International Review of Law, Computers & Technology (2019) (33:3) 309; CM Wulff, 'The Right to be Forgotten in Post-Google Spain Case Law: An Example of Legal Interpretivism in Action?' Comparative Law Review (2020) (26) 255; P Lambert, 'The AG Opinion in Google Franc, An Adequate Remedy?' International Journal for the Data Protection Officer, Privacy Officer and Privacy Counsel (IDPP) (2019) (3:3).

60 An example of the former is G Thüsing and J Traut, 'The Reform of European Data Protection Law: Harmonisation at Last?' *Intereconomics* (2013) (48:5) 271.

61 Pohle, 'Data Privacy Legislation in the EU Member States – Part Two of the Practical Overview: How EU Member States Have Adjusted Their Domestic Data Privacy Law to the GDPR – Update' above at 133.

62 N Ghibellini, 'Some Aspects of the EU's New Framework for Personal Data Privacy Protection' *Business Lawyer* (2017) (73:1) 207; Augusto Sebastio, 'The Online Right to be Forgotten in the European Justice Evolution' International Journal of Management, Knowledge and Learning (2015) (4:1) 59.

63 In relation to European interpretation and reasoning, see, eg, AIL Campbell and M Voyatzi, *Legal Reasoning and Judicial Interpretation of European Law: Essays in Honour of Lord Mackenzie-Stuart* (Trenton, 1996). Also, Lambert, Essential GDPR Index.

64 Bennett, Chun, Adam and Noveck, 'The European General Data Protection Regulation: An Instrument for the Globalization of Privacy Standards?' *Information Polity: The International Journal of Government & Democracy in the Information Age* at 239.

65 LA Bygrave, *Data Privacy Law, An International Perspective* (OUP, 2014); P Schiff Berman, *The Globalization of International Law* (Routledge, 2017); B Van Vooren and RA Wessel, *EU External Relations Law: Text, Cases and Materials* (CUP, 2014); J Orbie, *Europe's Global Role: External Policies of the European Union* (Ashgate, 2009).

- EU data protection becoming the international norm or baseline;[66]

- EU international influence;[67]

- expanding data protection rights for new data problems, including RtbF;[68]

- RtbF in EU and national courts;[69]

- an international RtbF or international baseline for RtbF;[70]

66 Bennett, Chun, Adam and Noveck, 'The European General Data Protection Regulation: An Instrument for the Globalization of Privacy Standards?' *Information Polity: The International Journal of Government & Democracy in the Information Age* at 239; McKay Cunningham, 'Diminishing Sovereignty: How European Privacy Law Became International Norm' *Santa Clara Journal of International Law* (2013) (11:2) 421.

67 D Kochenov and F Amtenbrink, *The European Union's Shaping of the International Legal Order* (CUP, 2013); Orbie, *Europe's Global Role: External Policies of the European Union*; TC Hartley, *European Union Law in a Global Context* (CUP, 2004); G de Búrca and J Scott, *Law and New Governance in the EU and the US* (Hart, 2006); MA Weiss and K Archick, *Data Privacy and Protection in the EU and the United States* (Congressional Research Service: Report: 2/12/2016) 1; Schiff Berman, *The Globalization of International Law*; Van Vooren and Wessel, *EU External Relations Law: Text, Cases and Materials*; I Sammut, *Constructing Modern European Private Law: A Hybrid System* (Cambridge Scholars Publishing, 2016); M Szabo, 'General Principles of Law in the Practice of International Courts and the European Court of Justice' *Hungarian Yearbook of International Law and European Law* (2016) 135.

68 P Lambert, The Right to be Forgotten (Bloomsbury, 2019); A Bobic, 'Developments in the EU-German Judicial Love Story: The Right to Be Forgotten II,' German Law Journal, Special Issue (2020) (21) 31; F Werro, The Right to be Forgotten: A Comparative Study of the Emergent Right's Evolution and Application in Europe, the Americas, and Asia (Springer, 2020).

69 P Frield, 'A New European Fundamental Rights Court: The German Constitutional Court on the Right to Be Forgotten,' *European Papers* (2020) (5:1) 447; Bobic, 'Developments in the EU-German Judicial Love Story: The Right to Be Forgotten II'; 'Better in than Out: When Constitutional Courts Rely on the Charter' *European Constitutional Law Review* (2020) (16:1) 1; OJ Gstrein, 'Right to be Forgotten: European Data Imperialism, National Privilege, or Universal Human Right?' *Review of European Administrative Law* (2020) (13:1) 125; C Rauchegger, 'National Constitutional Courts as Guardians of the Charter: A Comparative Appraisal of the German Federal Constitutional Court's Right to be Forgotten Judgments,' *Cambridge Yearbook of European Legal Studies* (2020) (22) 258.

70 D Erdos and K Garstka, 'The "Right to be Forgotten" Online within G20 Statutory Data Protection Frameworks' *International Data Privacy Law* (2020) (10:4) 294; D Erdos 'The "Right to be Forgotten" Beyond the EU: An Analysis of Wider G20 Regulatory Action and Potential Next Steps' *Journal of Media Law* (2021) (13:1) 1; F Werro, *The Right to Be Forgotten: A Comparative Study of the Emergent Right's Evolution and Application in Europe, the Americas, and Asia* (Springer, 2020); J Ausloos, *The Right to Erasure in EU Data Protection Law: From Individual Rights to Effective Protection* (OUP, 2020); P Lambert, Understanding the New EU Data Fine Rules (Kortext, 2021); P Lambert, 'The AG Opinion in Google Franc, An Adequate Remedy?' *International Journal for the Data Protection Officer, Privacy Officer and Privacy Counsel* (IDPP) (2019) (3:3); J Kaganoff, 'Send the Word Over There: An Offshore Solution to the Right to Be Forgotten' *Northwestern Journal of International Law & Business* (2021) (41:2) 245; KG Vazquez, 'The Right to be Forgotten does not Apply Outside the European Union: A Proposal for Worldwide Application' *Southwestern Journal of International Law* (2021) (27: 1) 146; ML Rustad and TH Koenig, 'Towards A Global Data Privacy Standard' *Florida Law Review* (2019) (71:2) 365.

- need to consider, or rather include, personal data consideration, in international instruments and transactions;[71]

- EU legal and policy values;[72]

- European values,[73] rights and norms, including fundamental rights;[74]

- wider EU (and international) human rights law and its interaction with personal data and data protection;[75]

- Charter rights;[76]

71 S Yakovleva, 'Should Fundamental Rights to Privacy and Data Protection Be a Part of the EU's International Trade Deals' *World Trade Review* (2018) (17:3) 477. Note the discussion of trade issues in the UK data law change consultation of 2021.
72 A Williams, *The Ethos of Europe, Values, Law and Justice in the EU* (CUP, 2010).
73 S Szabo, 'European Values, Fundamental Rights and the Private International Law of the European Union' *Hungarian Yearbook of International Law and European Law* (2014) 307.
74 Szabo, *ibid*; S Morano-Foadi and L Vistors, *Fundamental Rights in the EU* (Hart 2015); P Craig and G de Búrca, *Fundamental Rights in Europe* (OUP, 2014); S Douglas-Scott, 'The European Union and Fundamental Rights' in R Schütze and T Tridimas, *Oxford Principles of European Union Law* (OUP, 2018) at 383; E Spaventa, 'Fundamental Rights in the European Union' in C Barnard and S Peers, *European Union Law* (OUP, 2014) at 227; Chapter 7, 'Fundamental Rights' in T Tridimas, *The General Principles of EU Law* (OUP, 2006); Chapter 6 'Protecting Fundamental Rights with the Community' in A Reinisch, *Essential Questions in EU Law* (CUP, 2009) at 88; S Aidinlis, 'The Right to be Forgotten as a Fundamental Right in the UK After Brexit' Communications Law (2020) (25:2) 67; 'Better in than Out: When Constitutional Courts Rely on the Charter'; OJ Gstrein, 'Right to be Forgotten: European Data Imperialism, National Privilege, or Universal Human Right?' Review of European Administrative Law (2020) (13:1) 125.
75 G de Búrca, 'The Evolution of EU Human Rights Law 'in P Craig and G de Búrca, *The Evolution of EU Law* at 465; HG Shermers, 'European Remedies in the Field of Human Rights' in C Kilpatrick, T Novitz and P Skidmore, *The Future of Remedies in Europe* (Hart, 2000) at 205; AS Hartkamp, *European Law and National Private Law: Effect of EU Law and European Human Rights Law on Legal Relationships Between Individuals* (Intersentia, 2016); J Nergelius and Eleanor Kristoffersson, *Human Rights in Contemporary European Law* (Hart, 2015); M Arden, *Human Rights and European Law: Building New Legal Orders* (OUP, 2015); RG Aydin and IA Nazim, 'The Impact of New Technologies on Human Rights in the Context of the Right to Be Forgotten and the Right to Privacy' Law of Ukraine: Legal Journal (Ukrainian) (2021) (2) 125; M Nastić, 'The Impact of the Informational and Communication Technology on the Realization and Protection of Human Rights,' Balkan Social Science Review (2021) (17) 75; DF Garcia and A Quintanilla Perea, 'The Protection of Personal Data and the Right to be Forgotten in Peru. On the Purpose of the International Standards of the Inter-American Human Rights System' Derecho PUCP (2020) (84) 271; 'Better in than Out: When Constitutional Courts Rely on the Charter'; OJ Gstrein, 'Right to be Forgotten: European Data Imperialism, National Privilege, or Universal Human Right?' Review of European Administrative Law (2020) (13:1) 125; E Corcione, 'The Right to Be Forgotten, Between Web Archives and Search Engines: Further Steps at the European Court of Human Rights' European Data Protection Law Review (EDPL) (2019) (5:2) 262; AF Douhan, 'Adapting the Human Rights System to the Cyber Age' Max Planck Yearbook of United Nations Law (2020) (23:1) 251; A O'Connell and K Bakina, 'Using IP Rights to Protect Human Rights: Copyright for "Revenge Porn" Removal' Legal Studies (2020) (40:3) 442.
76 C Rauchegger, 'National Constitutional Courts as Guardians of the Charter: A Comparative Appraisal of the German Federal Constitutional Court's Right to Be Forgotten Judgments,' Cambridge Yearbook of European Legal Studies (2020) (22) 258.

- the protection of private and family life;[77]

- wider EU (and international) consumer law;[78]

- private law rights and personality rights for individuals;[79]

- EU law and the individual,[80] personal dignity[81] and freedoms;[82]

- data protection supervisory authority cooperation[83] and judicial cooperation[84] in relation to data protection;

- national authorities and regulators[85] which, of course, includes national data protection supervisory authorities;

77 R Matefi, 'Interference in the Exercise of the Right to Private and Family Life in the Context of National and European Regulations and ECHR Jurisprudence' *Bulletin of the Transilvania University of Braşov: Series VII: Social Sciences, Law* (2018) (11:60) 65.

78 H-W Micklitz, 'European Consumer Law' in E Jones, A Menon and S Weatherill, *The Oxford Handbook of the European Union* (OUP, 2014) at 526; G Howells, 'European Consumer Law' in Barnard and Peers, *European Union Law* at 686; Chapter 5, 'Consumer Protection Law' in F Wilman, *Private Enforcement of the EU Law Before National Courts* (Elgar, 2015) at 146; A Bosco and M Hutsebau, *Social Protection in Europe* (European Trade Union Institute (ETUI), 1997); C Llaneza, 'An Analysis on Biometric Privacy Data Regulation: A Pivot Towards Legislation Which Supports The Individual Consumer's Privacy Rights in Spite of Corporate Protections' St Thomas Law Review (2020) (32:2) 177; C Kwak, J Lee and H Lee, 'Could You Ever Forget Me? Why People Want to be Forgotten Online' Journal of Business Ethics (2021) (February) 1.

79 Szabo, 'European Values, Fundamental Rights and the Private International Law of the European Union' *Hungarian Yearbook of International Law and European Law* at 307; A Hartkamp, C Sieburgh and W Devroe, *Cases, Materials and Text on European Law and Private Law* (Hart, 2017); R Matefi, 'The Balance Between the Right to Freedom of Expression and the Protection of the Personality Rights from the Jurisprudence Perspective' Jus et Civitas (2019) (6:1) 1.

80 FG Jacobs, *European Law and the Individual* (North-Holland Publishing, 1976); Hartkamp, Sieburgh and Devroe, *Cases, Materials and Text on European Law and Private Law*.

81 A de Hingh, 'Some Reflections on Dignity as an Alternative Legal Concept in Data Protection Regulation' *German Law Journal* (2018) (19:5) 1269; T Reed, 'Indigenous Dignity and the Right to be Forgotten' Brigham Young University Law Review (2021) (4) 1119; D Nash, 'Politics of Humiliation–How do We Save Us From Our Liberal Selves?' Cultural History (2021) (10:2) 275.

82 C Barnard, *The Substantive Law of the EU, The Four Freedoms* (OUP, 2019); S O'Leary, 'Free Movement of Persons and Services' in Craig and de Búrca, *The Evolution of EU Law*.

83 See GDPR Arts 60–62 in relation to cooperation issues involving different data protection supervisory authorities. T Devine and M Eliantonio, 'EU Soft Law in the Hands of National Authorities: The Case Study of the UK Competition and Markets Authority' *Review of European Administrative Law* (2018) (11:1) 49. O Andreea Ştefan, 'European Competition Soft Law in European Courts: A Matter of Hard Principles?' *European Law Journal* (2008) (14:6) 753.

84 E Mak, N Graaf and E Jackson, 'The Framework for Judicial Cooperation in the European Union: Unpacking the Ethical, Legal and Institutional Dimensions of "Judicial Culture"' *Utrecht Journal of International and European Law* (2018) (34:1) 24. Also note KPE Lasok, *Lasok's European Court Practice and Procedure* (Bloomsbury, 2017).

85 P Lambert, Data Protection, Privacy Regulators and Supervisory Authorities (Bloomsbury, 2020); Devine and Eliantonio, 'EU Soft Law in the Hands of National Authorities: The Case Study of the UK Competition and Markets Authority' above at 49.

- enforcement of data protection and privacy;[86]

- administrative fines, penalties and sanctions;[87]

- remedies for data issues, particularly breach of data protection rights;[88]

- private remedies and enforcement;[89]

- anonymity;[90]

- proportionality;[91]

- legitimate expectations;[92]

- transparency rights;

- explanation rights (which is increasingly apt in terms of recent discussions regarding access to code, algorithms, and the like);[93]

86   D Wright and Paul de Hert, *Enforcing Privacy: Regulatory, Legal and Technological Approaches* (Springer, 2016). Also, Lambert, Understanding the New EU Data Fine Rules; Lambert, Data Protection, Privacy Regulators and Supervisory Authorities .

87   A de Moor-van Vugt, 'Administrative Sanctions in EU Law' *Review of European Administrative Law* (2012) (5:1) 5; M Macchia, 'Research Handbook on EU Administrative Law' *Italian Journal of Public Law* (2017) (9:2) 420. T Whitaker, 'The BA Data Breach' *International Journal for the Data Protection Officer, Privacy Officer and Privacy Counsel (IDPP)* (2018) (2:10) 15; Wolff, 'The Implementation of Administrative Fines Under the General Data Protection Regulation from the German Perspective' *International Journal for the Data Protection Officer, Privacy Officer and Privacy Counsel (IDPP)* (2018) (2:11) 11. Also Lambert, Understanding the New EU Data Fine Rules.

88   JNE Varuhas and N Moreham, *Remedies for Breach of Privacy* (Hart, 2018); A Biondi and M Farley, 'Damages in EU Law' in Schütze and Tridimas, *Oxford Principles of European Union Law* at 1040; Kilpatrick, Novitz and Skidmore, *The Future of Remedies in Europe*; Shermers, 'European Remedies in the Field of Human Rights' in Kilpatrick, Novitz and Skidmore, *The Future of Remedies in Europe* at 205; Lambert, Understanding the New EU Data Fine Rules.

89   Wilman, Chapter 10, 'The How, When and Why of EU Legislation on Private Enforcement' in Wilman, *Private Enforcement of the EU Law Before National Courts* at 393; J Lonbay and A Biondo, *Remedies for Breach of EU Law* (Wiley, 1997); Lambert, Understanding the New EU Data Fine Rules.

90   G Bachmann, P Bialski and M Hansen, 'The Terms of Anonymity: An Interview With Marit Hansen, German Data Protection Expert' *Ephemera: Theory & Politics in Organization* (2017) (17:2) 421.

91   T Tridimas, 'The Purpose of Proportionality' in Schütze and Tridimas, *Oxford Principles of European Union Law* at 243; Chapters 3–5 in Tridimas, *The General Principles of EU Law*; Tor-Iinge Harbo, 'Introducing Procedural Proportionality Review in European Law' *Leiden Journal of International Law* (2017) (30:1) 25; N Emiliou, *The Principle of Proportionality in European Law: A Comparative Study* (Kluwer, 1996).

92   Chapter 6 'Legal Certainty and Protection of Legitimate Expectations' in Tridimas, *The General Principles of EU Law*.

93   A Trites, 'Black Box Ethics: How Algorithmic Decision-Making is Changing How We View Society and People: Advocating for the Right for Explanation and the Right to be Forgotten in Canada' Global Media Journal: Canadian Edition (2019) (11:2) 18. Note also the Facebook whistleblower disclosures, and related hearings.

- transfers,[94] in particular international third-country transfers from the EU to the US and wider EU–US data protection and privacy law interests;[95]

- international views and reactions;[96]

- promotion of data protection and privacy internationally (which one might consider to be already a success);

- more need to be proactive, and not reactive;

- more risk assessment, design and preparation in advance; and

- effective rules and effective tools.

94 C Kuner, *Transborder Data Flows and Data Privacy Law* (OUP, 2013). xxxx
95 PM Schwartz and K-N Peifer, 'Transatlantic Data Privacy Law' *Georgetown Law Journal* (2017) (106:1) 115.
96 Weiss and Archick, *Data Privacy and Protection in the EU and the United States* at 1; D Vogel and JFM Swinnen, *Transatlantic Regulatory Cooperation: The Shifting Roles of the EU, the US and California* (Elgar, 2011); Lambert, Data Protection, Privacy Regulators and Supervisory Authorities.

CHAPTER 9

Responses

I INTRODUCTION

9.1 There have been a wide variety of reactions and responses in response to both the initial Google Spain[1] case and ultimately to the RtbF contained in the General Data Protection Regulation (GDPR). Some of these disparate issues are referred below. No doubt, however, as the practice of RtbF further expands, new responses will become evident, new arguments will be developed and new considerations will arise. This is particularly so where new risks issues become visible. Examples of the latter may focus on new problem issues online as they arise and also the very nuances of the technical tools and interfaces available to users to make RtbF notices. Broadly speaking, some of the main issues and responses arising are particular issues, reactions and sectorial issues and responses.

2 HEADLINE ISSUES RAISED

9.2 As indicated above, there is increasing attention being paid to specific and more nuanced issues arising in relation to RtbF. Some of these are referred to below. There is some focus on whether RtbF may apply to information on company registers.[2] Issues include:

- *Public registers*: There is also discussion of RtbF in the context of applying to information on public registers.[3]

- *Public sphere*: There is also some discussion and consideration of RtbF and data in the public sphere.[4]

- *General implications*: The general implications of RtbF are sometimes discussed.[5]

1   *Google Spain SL, Google Inc v Agencia Española de Protección de Datos (AEPD), Mario Costeja González*, Court of Justice (Grand Chamber), Case C-131/12, 13 May 2014.
2   E Caravà, 'Personal Data Kept in Companies Registers: The Denial of the "Right to be Forgotten"' *European Data Protection Law Review* (EDPL) (2017) (3:2) 287.
3   A Mantelero, 'Right to Be Forgotten and Public Registers – A Request to the European Court of Justice for a Preliminary Ruling' *European Data Protection Law Review (EDPL)* (2016) (2:2) 231.
4   RC Post, 'Data Privacy and Dignitary Privacy: Google Spain, The Right to be Forgotten and the Construction of the Public Sphere' *Duke Law Journal* (2018) (67:5) 981.
5   A Forde, 'Implications of the Right to Be Forgotten' *Tulane Journal of Technology and Intellectual Property* (2015) (18:1) 83; D Midorović Sloboda, 'The Right to Erasure of Personal Data Available on the Internet' Zbornik Radova Pravnog Fakulteta u Nišu (2019) (58:84) 281; R Bailey, 'Right to be Forgotten,' Reason (2020) (51:8) 61; P Coe, 'The Right to be Forgotten,' Communications Law (2019) (24:3) 137; D Shefet, 'The Right to be Forgotten'

- *Heath data and health records*: RtbF is particularly relevant to special or sensitive data such as health data and heath records data.[6]

- *Medical research issues*: Data protection and medical research[7];

- *Consent*: RtbF has also been referred to in relation to consent-type issues.[8]

- *Economics*: RtbF issues are also references in terms of the economics of RtbF[9] or the so-called cost of complying with RtbF notices. In many instances, however, the recipients of the notices are large and well-resourced businesses.

SciTech Lawyer (2020) (16:3) 26; P Lambert, 'The Right to be Forgotten: Context and the Problem of Time' Communications Law (2019) (24:2) 74; S DiBella, 'Ctrl+Z: The Right to Be Forgotten' Surveillance (2020) (18:3) 428; A Tasar and M Atas, 'The Right to Be Forgotten Under Protection of Personal Data Law' GSI Articletter (2020) (23) 10; G Fachetti Silvestre, C Biazatti Borges and N Schades Benevides, 'The Procedural Protection of Data De-Indexing in Internet Search Engines: The Effectiveness in Brazil of the So-Called "Right to be Forgotten" Against Media Companies' Revista Jurídica (2019) (1:54) 25; M Flyverbomm, R Deibert, D Matten, J-M Chenou and R Radu, 'The "Right to Be Forgotten": Negotiating Public and Private Ordering in the European Union' Business and Society (2019) (58:1) 74; A Bobić, 'Developments in The EU-German Judicial Love Story: The Right To Be Forgotten II' German Law Journal (2020) (Supplement) (21) 31; Editorial Board, 'The "Right to be Forgotten" vs. the Right to Erase' Washington Post (24 September 2019); P Lambert, The Right to be Forgotten (Bloomsbury, 2019); A O'Connell, 'The Right to be Forgotten, by Paul Lambert' Review, International Journal of Law (2020) (28:1) 88.

6   JD Brougher, 'The Right to Be Forgotten: Applying European Privacy Law to American Electronic Health Records' *Indiana Health Law Review* (2016) (13:2) 510; M Correia, G Rego and R Nunes, 'The Right to be Forgotten Versus the Right to Disclosure of Gamete Donors' ID: Ethical and Legal Considerations' Acta Bioéthica (2021) (27:1) 69; E Balistri, F Casellato, C Giannelli and C Stefanelli, 'BlockHealth: Blockchain-Based Secure and Peer-to-Peer Health Information Sharing With Data Protection and Right to be Forgotten' ICT Express (2021) (7:3) 308; M Correia, G Rego, R and R Nunes, 'Gender Transition: Is There a Right to Be Forgotten?' Health Care Analysis (2 May 2021) 18; H Iannucci, '"Erasing Transgender Public Figures" Former Identity with the Right to Be Forgotten' Federal Communications Law Journal (2021) (73:2) 259; S Suzuki, K Mizoguchi, H Watanabe, T Nakamura and Y Deguchi, 'Privacy-Aware Data-Lifetime Control NAND Flash System for Right to be Forgotten with In-3D Vertical Cell Processing' Asian Solid-State Circuits Conference (A-SSCC) (2019) (November) IEEE, 231; G Scocca and F Meunier, 'A Right to be Forgotten for Cancer Survivors: A Legal Development Expected to Reflect the Medical Progress in the Fight Against Cancer' Journal of Cancer Policy (2020) 25; C Llaneza, 'An Analysis on Biometric Privacy Data Regulation: A Pivot Towards Legislation Which Supports The Individual Consumer's Privacy Rights in Spite of Corporate Protections' St Thomas Law Review (2020) (32:2) 177; M JS Beauvais and BM Knoppers, 'Coming Out to Play: Privacy, Data Protection, Children's Health, and COVID-19 Research' Frontiers in Genetics (2021) (11); M Tsirintani, M Serifi and S Binioris, 'Digital Oblivion (The Right to be Forgotten): A Big Challenge for the Public Hospital Management in Greece' Studies in Health Technology and Informatics (2019) 91; C Cicchini, M Mazzeo, D Livoli, A Simone, V Valeriano and F Pugliese, 'The Right to be Protected, the Right to be Forgotten: The European General Data Protection Regulation 679/2016 in Emergency Medicine' Italian Journal of Emergency Medicine (2020) (9:1) 41.

7   D Beyleveld, D Townsend, S Rouillé-Mirza and J Wright, *Implementation of the Data Protection Directive in Relation to Medical Research in Europe* (Routledge, 2018).

8   C Bartolini and L Siry, 'The Right to be Forgotten in the Light of the Consent of the Data Subject' *Computer Law & Security Review* (2016) (32:2) 218.

9   B- Kim and JY Kim, 'The Economics of the Right to Be Forgotten' *Journal of Law* (2017) (60:2) 335.

- *Philosophy*: Stepping back somewhat there is also developing examination of RtbF from a philosophical perspective.[10]

- *History*: Stepping back further, there is also contextualisation of RtbF from a historical perspective.[11]

- *Back-up storage*: RtbF and data located in back-up storage.[12] The vast amounts of data which may be located in back-up storage, as opposed to live usage, is an interesting issue to consider in terms of RtbF notices. However, as personal data access requests can include data in backup storage, this may not prove to be a justified reason to limit or restrict compliance with a given RtbF notice.[13]

- *Re-examining existing law*: Re-examining current law to see if there is a RtbF or similar already included.[14]

- *Case law examined*: Re-examining past cases to see if there is an impact on RtbF or if it impacts past cases.[15]

- *Self-regulation*: Examining issues of self-regulation and self-policy by organisations, business and service providers in terms of applying RtbF.[16]

- *RtbF compliance*: Compliance implications for RtbF compliance.[17]

- *Practice*: Best practice requirements for dealing with RtbF.[18]

---

10 L Floridi, 'The Right to Be Forgotten: A Philosophical View' *Jahrbuch fur Recht und Ethik / Annual Review of Law and Ethics* (2014) (23) 163.

11 A De Baets, 'A Historian's View on the Right to be Forgotten' *International Review of Law, Computers* (2016) (30:1/2) 57.

12 E Politou, A Michota, E Alepis, M Pocs, *et al*, 'Backups and the Right to be Forgotten in the GDPR: An Uneasy Relationship' *Computer Law & Security Review* (2018) (34:6)1247.

13 However, the issue of backup data and responses to data subject access requests may sometimes be treated a little differently in some Member States.

14 For example, M Rosenstock, 'Is There a "Right to be Forgotten" in Canada's Personal Information Protection and Electronic Documents Act (PIPEDA)?' *Canadian Journal of Law & Technology* (2016) (14:1) 131.

15 CD Tobin and CN Walz, 'Right to Be Forgotten, Expungement Laws Raise New Challenges on the 40th Anniversary of *Cox Broadcasting v Cohn*' *Communications Lawyer* (2015) (31:4) 4. Also note A Lytvynenko, 'The Role of *Sidis v F-R Publishing Co* in the Formation of Right to be Forgotten' *Teise/Law* (2017) (105) 188.

16 M Santín, 'The Problem of the Right to be Forgotten From the Perspective of Self-Regulation in Journalism' *El Profesional de la Información* (2017) (26:2) 303.

17 A Schildhaus, 'EU's General Data Protection Regulation (GDPR): Key Provisions and Best Practices' *International Law News* (2018) (46:2) 11.

18 *Ibid.*

- *Data flows and transfers and related international relations*: Data flows and transfers are a consideration for some in relation to the fulfilment of RtbF.[19] Most of this literature refers to the EU and US.[20]

19 SD Schiopu, 'The Territorial Scope of the Right to be Forgotten (Right to De-referencing) in the Light of the Request for a Preliminary Ruling from the Conseil d'Etat (France)' *Pandectele Romane* (2018) (1) 61; ML Rustad and S Kulevska, 'Reconceptualizing the Right to be Forgotten to Enable Transatlantic Data Flow' *Harvard Journal of Law* (2015) (28:2) 349; D Meyer, 'The "Right to Be Forgotten" Globally? How Google Is Fighting to Limit the Scope of Europe's Privacy Law' *Fortune.com* (9 November 2018) 1; RH Weber and Dr DN Staiger, 'Transatlantic Data Protection in Practice – Revisited' *International Journal for the Data Protection Officer, Privacy Officer and Privacy Counsel (IDPP)* (2018) (2:5) 16; PTJ Wolters, 'The Territorial Effect of the Right to be Forgotten After Google v CNIL' International Journal of Law & Information Technology (2021) (29:1) 57; J Kaganoff, 'Send the Word Over There: An Offshore Solution to the Right to Be Forgotten' Northwestern Journal of International Law & Business (2021) (41:2) 245; M Samonte, 'Google v. CNIL: The Territorial Scope of the Right to be Forgotten Under EU Law,' European Papers (2019) (4:3) 839; G Bevilacqua, 'The Territorial Scope of the Right to be Forgotten Online in the Opinion of the Advocate General on the Case Google CNIL' European Papers (2019) (4:2) 655; Y Padova, 'Is the Right to be Forgotten a Universal, Regional, or "Global" Right?' International Data Privacy Law (2019) (9:1) 15; 'Right to be Forgotten Likely to be EU-Based' Emerald Expert Briefings (Emerald, 2019); 'Geographical Range of the "Right to be Forgotten"' GRUR International: Journal of European (2020) (69:4) 430; M Hall, 'EU Court Holds Right to be Forgotten Applies Only In EU' Business Law Today (2019) (September) 2; 'EU Court Limits "Right to be Forgotten" in Google Case' Telecommunications Reports (9/27/2019) (58:17) 32; D Busvine, P Blenkinsop and P Maushagen, 'Google can Limit "Right to be Forgotten" to EU Says Top Court Adviser' CIO (1 December 2019) 2-2; A Satariano, 'Decision Limits Europe's "Right To Be Forgotten"' New York Times (25 September 2019) (169:58461) B1-B5; W Wright, 'EU Citizens' Right to be Forgotten by Google does not Apply Outside Europe, Court Rules' Daily Telegraph (London) (25 September 2019) 13; F Fabbrini, E Celeste and J Quinn (ed), Data Protection Beyond Borders: Transatlantic Perspectives on Extraterritoriality and Sovereignty (Hart, 2021); A White, 'Google's Right-to-be-Forgotten Fine Toppled by French Court' Bloomberg.com (27 March 2020); A White, 'Google Wins EU Court Fight Making It Harder to be Forgotten' Bloomberg.com (24 September 2019); F Fabbrini and E Celeste, 'The Right to be Forgotten in the Digital Age: The Challenges of Data Protection Beyond Borders' German Law Journal, Special Issue (2020) (21) 55; G Aleksandra, 'Can the Internet Forget? – The Right to be Forgotten in the EU Law and its Actual Impact on the Internet. Comparison of the Approaches Towards the Notion and Assessment of its Effectiveness' Wroclaw Review of Law, Administration and Economics (2020) (9:1) 86; 'EU: Territorial Scope of De-Referencing Search Engine Results Based on "Right to be Forgotten"' Computer Law Review International (2019) (20:5) 151; HG Cohen and M Zalnieriute, 'Personal data – right to be forgotten – internet search engine operators – de-referencing of search results – territorial scope of application – data privacy – General Data Protection Regulation (EU)' American Journal of International Law (2020) (114:2) 261; SC Lewis, 'EU's Top Court Limits "Right To Be Forgotten"' New York Law Journal (15 October 2019) (262:74); D Meyer, 'Google Likely to Win Fight Against Global Censorship of EU "Right to be Forgotten"' Fortune.com (10 January 2019).

20 F Fabbrini, E Celeste and J Quinn (eds), Data Protection Beyond Borders: Transatlantic Perspectives on Extraterritoriality and Sovereignty (Hart, 2021); R Pfenninger, 'The Right to Be Forgotten Has Not Found Its Home in United States Law: A Comparison of Law Between the European Union and the United States, Willamette Journal of International Law and Dispute Resolution (2021) (28:2) 291; HG Cohen and M Zalnieriute, 'Personal Data – Right to be Forgotten – Internet Search Engine Operators – De-Referencing of Search Results – Territorial Scope of Application – Data Privacy – General Data Protection Regulation (EU)' American Journal of International Law (2020) (114:2) 261; VP Muskin, 'The Right to Be Forgotten: Are Europe and America on a Collision Course?' New York State Bar Association Journal (2019) (91:2) 36; OJ Gstrein, 'Right to be Forgotten: European Data Imperialism, National

126

- *Anonymity*: There is reason for a policy of anonymity.[21] in relation to an applicant requesting RtbF in relation to problem online content, particularly where formal litigation proceedings must be issued. Indeed, there is a policy of anonymity in several countries already more generally in relation to, for example, data protection-type cases, which one would assume will now also include RtbF.

The consideration of RtbF also cannot be ignored against the existing backdrop of the rules and norms of the data protection regime. Some of these include:

- wide concept of personal data and data protection;[22]

- definition of personal data;[23]

- data protection compliance;[24]

- data protection contract issues;[25]

- data protection remedies;[26]

- rights of individual data subjects under the GDPR;[27]

- damages;[28]

Privilege, or Universal Human Right?' Review of European Administrative Law (2020) (13:1) 125; J Penney, 'Chilling Effects and Transatlantic Privacy' European Law Journal (2019) (25:2) 122; Editorial Board, 'The "Right to be Forgotten" vs. the Right to Erase' Washington Post (24 September 2019).

21 G Bachmann, P Bialski and M Hansen, 'The Terms of Anonymity: An Interview With Marit Hansen, German Data Protection Expert' *Ephemera: Theory & Politics in Organization* (2017) (17:2) 421.

22 N Purtova, 'The Law of Everything: Broad Concept of Personal Data and Future of EU Data Protection Law' *Innovation and Technology* (2018) (10:1) 40.

23 GDPR Article 4(1). Purtova, 'The Law of Everything: Broad Concept of Personal Data and Future of EU Data Protection Law' above at 40.

24 S van Gulijk and J Hulstjin, 'Ensuring Data Protection by Private Law Contract Monitoring: A Legal and Value-Based Approach' *European Review of Private Law* (2018) (26:5) 63; Beyleveld, Townsend, Rouillé-Mirza and Wright, *Implementation of the Data Protection Directive in Relation to Medical Research in Europe*.

25 van Gulijk and Hulstjin, 'Ensuring Data Protection by Private Law Contract Monitoring: A Legal and Value-Based Approach' above at 63.

26 A Galetta and P De Hert, 'The Proceduralisation of Data Protection Remedies Under EU Data Protection Law: Towards a More Effective and Data Subject Orientated Remedial System' *Review of European Administrative Law* (2015) (8:1) 125.

27 PTJ Wolters, 'The Control by and Rights of the Data Subject under the GDPR' *Journal of Internet Law* (2018) (22:1) 1.

28 A Biondi and M Farley, *The Right to Damages in European Law* (Kluwer, 2009); T Heukels and A McDonnell, *The Action for Damages in Community Law* (Kluwer, 1997); Chapter 7, 'Actions for Damages and Actions for Injunctions' in F Wilman, *Private Enforcement of the EU Law Before National Courts* (Elgar, 2015) at 255; M Hoskins, 'The Relationship Between the Action for Damages and the Award of Interim Measures' in T Heukels and A McDonnell, *The Action for Damages in Community Law* (Kluwer, 1997), at 259; C von Bar, *The Common European Law of Torts. Vol 2, Damage and Damages, Liability for and Without Personal Misconduct, Causality and Defences* (Clarendon, 2000). See in particular P Lambert, Understanding the EU Data Fine Rules (Kortext, 2021).

- torts[29] and civil law;

- interim remedies;[30]

- joint liability;[31] and

- anonymity.[32]

There is also additional research referring to technologies to assist or enhance the application of RtbF. Xiaojuan, Weiming, Xianjun and Keyang discuss how images may be watermarked in a technical manner, which can assist RtbF identification and takedown.[33]

3   GENERAL REACTIONS

9.3   The reactions to RtbF[34] are wide and varied. They include a vast array of responses across many different media outlets. There is also now an increasing academic focus on RtbF. There have been many research seminars and conferences in the wake of the decision in *Google Spain* and RtbF.[35] As

29   E Hondius, 'Tort Law in the European Union' *European Journal of Comparative Law and Governance* (2018) (5:2) 203; A Ahmeti and F Musliu, 'The European Law of Torts, Case Study: Regulation No 864/2007 of the European Union' *Acta Universitatis Danubius: Juridica* (2018) (14:1) 75; C von Bar, *The Common European Law of Torts. Vol 2, Damage and Damages, Liability for and Without Personal Misconduct, Causality and Defences* (Clarendon, 2000); C von Bar, *The Common European Law of Torts. Vol 1, The Core Areas of Tort Law, Its Approximation in Europe and Its Accommodation in the Legal System* (Clarendon, 1998); H-J Cremer, *Human Rights and the Protection of Privacy in Tort Law: A Comparison Between English and German Law* (Routledge-Cavendish, 2011); Lambert, Understanding the EU Data Fine Rules.

30   I Goldrein, *Privacy Injunctions and the Media: A Practice Manual* (Hart, 2012); E Sharpston, 'Interim Relief in the National Courts' in J Lonbay and A Biondo, *Remedies for Breach of EU Law* (Wiley, 1997) 47; MH Chisholm, 'Some Observations on the Use of Injunctions and Interdicts in the Enforcement of EU Law' in J Lonbay and A Biondo, *Remedies for Breach of EU Law* (Wiley, 1997) at 73; M Hoskins, 'The Relationship Between the Action for Damages and the Award of Interim Measures' in T Heukels and A McDonnell, *The Action for Damages in Community Law* (Kluwer, 1997) at 259; Lambert, Understanding the EU Data Fine Rules.

31   In relation to joint liability referring to the Community and Member States, see P Oliver, 'Joint Liability of the Community and the Member States' in Heukels and McDonnell, *The Action for Damages in Community Law* above at 285; Lambert, Understanding the EU Data Fine Rules.

32   Bachmann, Bialski and Hansen, 'The Terms of Anonymity: An Interview with Marit Hansen, German Data Protection Expert' above at 421.

33   D Xiaojuan, Z Weiming, H Xianjun and L Keyang, 'A Cloud-User Watermarking Protocol Protecting the Right to Be Forgotten for the Outsourced Plain Images' *International Journal of Digital Crime* (2018) (10:4) 118.

34   C Manny, 'The European Union's "Right to be Forgotten"' *Business Law Review* (2015) (48) 51; Ashish S Joshi, 'Leave Me Alone! Europe's "Right to be Forgotten"' *Litigation* (2015) (41:2) 15; A Sebastio, 'The Online Right to be Forgotten in the European Justice Evolution' *International Journal of Management, Knowledge and Learning* (2015) (4:1) 59.

35   For example, S Collins, 'Remember Me? The Right to be Forgotten, The Law Society Public Debate 15th October 2014' *Entertainment and Sports Law Journal* (2014) (12) 6; S Kanamori, K Kawaguchi and H Tanaka, 'Study on a Scheme for the Right to be Forgotten' 2014 International Symposium on Information Theory and its Applications Information Theory and its Applications (ISITA) (2014) (October); R Leenes, R van Brakel, S Gutwirth and P De Hert,

time passes, an increasing number of cases are being made to respective data protection supervisory authorities. Where these matters are not resolved, either at the direct notice stage to the appropriate service provider or as a result of escalating to the data protection supervisory authority, the number of legal cases that will be filed in court will also increase. Some examples of general RtbF commentary are referred to further in the attached footnote.[36] While there is some RtbF comparative[37] commentary, this will be further enhanced over time.

4 POSITIVE REACTIONS

9.4   Commentators such as Lyndsay Cook refer positively to how RtbF is 'a step in the right direction'[38] and offer support for RtbF.[39] Meg Leta Ambrose states that it is timely, even overdue. She refers to RtbF in the context of 'information life cycles' and forgetting issues.[40] Kieron O'Hara and Nigel Shadbolt suggest that RtbF may have a role in enhancing a 'coherent privacy regime'.[41] Thomas Hale-Kupiec suggests the need for a 'generic' RtbF.[42] Herman Nys[43] refers to the

---

'Data Protection and Privacy: The Age of Intelligent Machines' Computers, Privacy and Data Protection (Conference) (10th: 2017: Brussels, Belgium); M Leta Jones, E Zeide, J-E Mai, E Jones, Jill Dupre, *et al*, 'The Right to be Forgotten' *Proceedings of the Association for Information Science* (2015) (52:1) 1; I Igglezakis and D Politis, 'Digital Forgetting in the Age of On-Line Media: The Forensics for Establishing a Comprehensive Right to Cyber-Oblivion' *2014 International Conference on Communication Technologies and Learning (IMCL)* (2014) (November) 274.

36 P O'Callaghan and S de Mars, 'Narratives About Privacy and Forgetting in English Law' *International Review of Law, Computers & Technology* (2016) (30:1/2) 42; Jef Ausloos, 'Ctrl+Z: The Right to Be Forgotten' *European Data Protection Law Review (EDPL)* (2017) (3:1) 138; D McGoldrick, 'Developments in the Right to Be Forgotten' *Human Rights Law Review* (2013) (13:4) 761; PJ Williams, 'The Right to Be Forgotten' *Nation* (10 June 2014) (299:14) 10; R Knez, 'Right to be Forgotten – Indeed a New Personal Right in Digital EU Market?' *InterEULawEast: Journal for International & European Law, Economics & Market Integrations* (2016) (3:1) 31; N Pahwa, 'Right to be Forgotten in the Online World' *Alive* (2018) (August) 32; L Owings, 'The Right to be Forgotten' *Akron Intellectual Property Journal* (2015) (9) 45; S Alessi, 'Eternal Sunshine: The Right to be Forgotten in the European Union After the 2016 General Data Protection Regulation' *Emory International Law Review* (2017) (32:1) 145; L Feiler, N Forgó, M Weigl, 'The EU General Data Protection Regulation (GDPR): A Commentary' *Globe* (2018).

37 M Shim and Hye-Kyeong Ko, 'A Comparative Study of the Differences in Legal Requirements and Technical Coverage for the Right to Be Forgotten in the GDPR Era' *Indian Journal of Public Health Research* (2018) (9:8) 507.

38 L Cook, 'The Right to be Forgotten: A Step in the Right Direction for Cyberspace Law and Policy' *Journal of Law, Technology & the Internet* (2015) (6:1) 121.

39 'Dataguise Supports GDPR Right of Erasure/Access' *Computer Security Update* (2017) (18:11) 7.

40 M Leta Ambrose, 'It's About Time: Privacy, Information Life Cycles and the Right to be Forgotten' *Stanford Technology Law Review* (2013) (February) 369.

41 K O'Hara and Nigel Shadbolt, 'The Right to Be Forgotten: Its Potential Role in a Coherent Privacy Regime' *European Data Protection Law Review (EDPL)* (2015) (1:3) 178.

42 T Hale-Kupiec, 'Immortal Invasive Initiatives: The Need for a Genetic Right to Be Forgotten' *Minnesota Journal of Law, Science and Technology* (2016) (17:1) 441.

43 H Nys, 'Towards a Human Right "to Be Forgotten Online"?' *European Journal of Health Law* (2011) (18:5) 469.

human rights aspect of RtbF or RtbF as a human right. Michele E Gilman refers to five GDPR principles that the US should adopt.[44] Anna Bunn refers to the GDPR RtbF for children and how it should be extended or introduced elsewhere (referring specifically to Australia).[45] Kwak et al refer to why individuals wish to be forgotten online[46] – which is only likely to increase further over time.

Other countries also benchmark their own law against the GDPR, follow GDPR rules in their own laws, and compare the GDPR in order to assess gaps in their own data laws. This includes in relation to RtbF issues.[47]

5   NEGATIVE REACTIONS

9.5   Some people have made arguments against RtbF,[48] raising problems and criticisms.[49] Some criticisms have also been apocalyptic, referring, for example, to a 'digital dark age' potentially arising from RtbF.[50] This was in 2013 and it might be suggested that such pessimism in relation to RtbF has not been realised. One of the sectors affected closely with certain of RtbF notices is the newspaper and media industry. However, we are arguably in the middle of a golden age of journalism.[51] Other critics refer to the so-called 'shaky grounds' for RtbF.[52] One article suggests that there may be a need to limit its geographical scope.[53] This, however, ignores that the ambit and effect, including damage, of problem online content does not respect neatly defined borders. There is also increasing discussion, in the EU and elsewhere, that for RtbF to be effective, it must be more than national and possibly global in effect.[54] Further research may also delve

---

44   ME Gilman, 'Five Privacy Principles (From the GDPR) the United States Should Adopt To Advance Economic Justice' Arizona State Law Journal (2020) (52:2) 368.

45   A Bunn, 'Children and the "Right to be Forgotten": What the Right to Erasure Means for European Children, and Why Australian Children Should be Afforded a Similar Right' Media International Australia (2019) (170:1) 37.

46   C Kwak, J Lee and H Lee, 'Could You Ever Forget Me? Why People Want to be Forgotten Online' Journal of Business Ethics (2021) (February) 1.

47   O Canyaş and A Bayata Canyaş, 'Approach Towards the Right to be Forgotten Under Turkish Law in Comparison with EU and US Laws: A Need For a Reform?' Juridical Tribune / Tribuna Juridica (2021) (11:2) 174; F Werro, The Right to Be Forgotten: A Comparative Study of the Emergent Right's Evolution and Application in Europe, the Americas, and Asia (Springer, 2020).

48   Alessi, 'Eternal Sunshine: The Right to be Forgotten in the European Union after the 2016 General Data Protection Regulation' above at 145.

49   Santín, 'The Problem of the Right to be Forgotten from the Perspective of Self-Regulation in Journalism' above at 303.

50   M Leta Ambrose, 'A Digital Dark Age and the Right to be Forgotten' Journal of Internet Law (2013) (17:3) 1.

51   This is particularly so since 2016 and notwithstanding such issues as false 'fake' news attacks and separate commercial issues as between online and offline media content.

52   M Peguera, 'The Shaky Ground of the Right to be Delisted' Vanderbilt Journal of Entertainment & Technology Law (2016) (18:3) 507.

53   D Jerker and B Svantesson, 'Limitless Borderless Forgetfulness: Limiting the Geographical Reach of the Right to Be Forgotten' Oslo Law Review (2015) (2:2) 116.

54   For example, the view of the French and Swedish national data protection supervisory authorities.

into whether certain problem content, notices and individual data subjects have reason for wider geographical protection than others.

One author refers to the threat of the EU RtbF to US interests, in particular the US constitutional interest contained in the First Amendment. RtbF is dramatically described as an 'enemy'.[55] Those who seek to criticise RtbF frequently refer to jurisdiction and applicable law issues in relation to the data protection and the GDPR generally,[56] as well as in relation to RtbF.[57] The issue of data transfers,[58] particularly international third-country transfers from the EU to the US and wider EU–US data protection and privacy law interests are also raised.[59] Jurisdiction[60] and extraterritoriality considerations[61] and data law conflicts[62] can also be referenced. It is also suggested by Friesen that RtbF effort is an '[i]mpossible [r]

55   K Byrum, *The European* Right to be Forgotten: *The First Amendment Enemy* (Lexington, 2018).

56   M Gömann, 'The New Territorial Scope of EU Data Protection Law: Deconstructing a Revolutionary Achievement' *Common Market Law Review* (2017) (54:2) 567; J Chen, 'How the Best-Laid Plans Go Awry: The (Unsolved) Issues of Applicable Law in the General Data Protection Regulation' *International Data Privacy Law* (2016) (6:4) 310; M Gömann, 'The New Territorial Scope of EU Data Protection Law: Deconstructing a Revolutionary Achievement' *Common Market Law Review* (2017) (54:2) 567.

57   J Čošabić, 'Territorial Implications of the "Right to be Forgotten"' *Psychosociological Issues in Human Resource Management* (2015) (3:2) 53; Rustad and Kulevska, 'Reconceptualizing the Right to be Forgotten to Enable Transatlantic Data Flow' at 349. Also note J Martínez Bavière, 'Spain: Extraterritorial Application of "Right to be Forgotten" Contrary to International Law' *Computer Law Review International* (2018) (19:2) 62; DA Nadeem, 'Territorial Limits to the European Union's Right to Be Forgotten: How the CNIL Ignores Jurisdictional Basics in Its March 10, 2016 Decision Against Google' *Creighton International and Comparative Law Journal* (2017) (8:2) 182.

58   C Kuner, *Transborder Data Flows and Data Privacy Law* (OUP, 2013).

59   PM Schwartz and Karl-Nikolaus Peifer, 'Transatlantic Data Privacy Law' *Georgetown Law Journal* (2017) (106:1) 115; Weber and Staiger, 'Transatlantic Data Protection in Practice – Revisited' at 16.

60   C Kuner, LA Bygrave and C Docksey, *General Commentary on EU General Data Protection Regulation* (OUP, 2019); D Jerker and B Svantesson, *Solving the Internet Jurisdiction Puzzle* (OUP, 2017); Schiopu, 'The Territorial Scope of the Right to be Forgotten (Right to De-referencing) in the Light of the Request for a Preliminary Ruling from the Conseil d'Etat (France)' at 61; W Kuan Hon, J Hörnle and C Millard, 'Data Protection Jurisdiction and Cloud Computing – When are Cloud Users and Providers Subject to EU Data Protection Law? The Cloud of Unknowing' *International Review of Law, Computers & Technology* (2012) (26:2/3) 129; D Vogel and JFM Swinnen, *Transatlantic Regulatory Cooperation: The Shifting Roles of the EU, the US and California* (Elgar, 2011).

61   D Jerker and B Svantesson, 'The Extraterritoriality of EU Data Privacy Law – Its Theoretical Justification and Its Practical Effect on US Businesses' *Stanford Journal of International Law* (2014) (50:1) 53. Also Martínez Bavière, 'Spain: Extraterritorial Application of "Right to be Forgotten" Contrary to International Law' at 62; Kuan Hon, Hörnle and Millard, Data Protection Jurisdiction and Cloud Computing – When are Cloud Users and Providers Subject to EU Data Protection Law? The Cloud of Unknowing' at 129; A Azzi, 'The Challenges Faced by the Extraterritorial Scope of the General Data Protection Regulation' *Journal of Intellectual Property, Information Technology and Electronic Commerce Law* (2018) (9:2) 126.

62   M Brkan, 'Data Protection and Conflict-of-Laws: A Challenging Relationship' *European Data Protection Law Review* (EDPL) (2016) (2:3) 324.

ight.'[63] Hunter Criscione refers to '[e]verlasting [n]egative [i]mplications' from the the RtbF (after Google v CNIL).[64]

RtbF is overall described as '[s]quare [p]egs in [t]riangular [s]paces' by Vishv Priya Kohli.[65] It is also queries as to whether it amounts to legal 'imperialism' or a '[u]niversal [h]uman [t]ight' in Gstrein.[66] Carsten M Wulff asks whether post *Google Spain* there is '[l]egal [i]nterpretivism in [a]ction.'[67]

Focusing on the EU-US angle, Jonathon Penney queries whether there may be potential chilling effect issues[68]; and Victor P Muskin asks whether the US and EU may be on some form of collision course.[69]

There is also pronouncement by R Pfenninger that the (EU) RtbF has not found a home in US law.[70] Frederike Zufall seeks to do similarly in Japan.[71]

6 BUSINESS REACTIONS

9.6 Data laws require that businesses at a macro level engage in legal compliance activities.[72] It also applies to managers and employees, which raises additional considerations.[73]

There have been a number of business reactions to the GDPR itself from the worlds of both business and commerce to RtbF issues.[74] More business reactions, such as in the Business Law Review, also relate to the decision in *Google Spain*

---

63 J Friesen, 'The Impossible Right to be Forgotten' Rutgers Computer and Technology Law Journal (2021) (47:1) 173.
64 H Criscione, 'Forgetting the Right to be Forgotten: The Everlasting Negative Implications of a Right to be Dereferenced on Global Freedom in the Wake of Google v. CNIL' Pace International Law Review (2020) (32:2) 315.
65 VP Kohli, 'Square Pegs in Triangular Spaces: Right to be Forgotten' European Intellectual Property Review (2020) (42:2) 75.
66 OJ Gstrein, 'Right to be Forgotten: European Data Imperialism, National Privilege, or Universal Human Right?' Review of European Administrative Law (2020) (13:1) 125.
67 CM Wulff, 'The Right to be Forgotten in Post-Google Spain Case Law: An Example of Legal Interpretivism in Action?' Comparative Law Review (2020) (26) 255.
68 J Penney, 'Chilling Effects and Transatlantic Privacy' European Law Journal (2019) (25:2) 122.
69 VP Muskin, 'The Right to be Forgotten: Are Europe and America on a Collision Course?' New York State Bar Association Journal (2019) (91:2) 36;
70 R Pfenninger, 'The Right to be Forgotten has not Found its Home in United States Law: A Comparison of Law Between the European Union and the United States, Willamette Journal of International Law and Dispute Resolution (2021) (28:2) 291.
71 F Zufall, 'Challenging the EU's Right to Be Forgotten: Society's Right to Know in Japan' European Data Protection Law Review (EDPL) (2019) (5:1) 17.
72 A Stone, 'Practical Privacy' Government Technology (2019) (32:5) 14; P Lambert, A User's Guide to Data Protection (Bloomsbury, 2020); Gringras, The Laws of the Internet (Bloomsbury, 2022); S Carr, 'Now You See Me, Now You Don't: Client Information and the GDPR' Procurement Lawyer (2019) (44:3) 8.
73 See P Lambert, The Manager's Data Protection Duties (Clarus Press, 2020).
74 S Seo, "Perspective on GDPR from the Technology Sector' *International Journal for the Data Protection Officer, Privacy Officer and Privacy Counsel* (IDPP) (2018) (2:3) 15.

initially and later to RtbF in the GDPR.[75] There is increasing commentary on what RtbF means for companies[76] and organisations generally, with wide reference to data protection implications for businesses and organisations.[77] RtbF implications for organisations and businesses,[78] compliance with RtbF requirements[79] and best practice for dealing with RtbF[80] are issues referenced for business.

This must all fit within existing modalities and procedures for commercial corporate compliance[81] and continued commercial business transfers between the EU and the US.[82] This is additional to other past and ongoing issues and challenges, arising for such data transfers. There is also reference to how this may increase compliance costs and may be even somewhat difficult to comply with.[83] On a wider note, there is increasing examination of the personal liability and contract obligations of directors and officers for data protection and privacy compliance and breaches, as well as company vicarious liability.[84]

75 Manny, 'The European Union's "Right to be Forgotten"' at 51; Joshi, 'Leave Me Alone! Europe's "Right to be Forgotten"' at 15; Sebastio, 'The Online Right to be Forgotten in the European Justice Evolution' at 59.
76 J Lee, 'What the Right to be Forgotten Means to Companies: Threat or Opportunity?' *Procedia Computer Science* (2016) (91) 542.
77 van Gulijk and Hulstjin, 'Ensuring Data Protection by Private Law Contract Monitoring: A Legal and Value-Based Approach' at 63; Beyleveld, Townsend, Rouillé-Mirza and Wright, *Implementation of the Data Protection Directive in Relation to Medical Research in Europe*.
78 Schildhaus, 'EU's General Data Protection Regulation (GDPR): Key Provisions and Best Practices' above at 11.
79 *Ibid*. M Odlanicka-Poczobutt and A Szyszka-Schuppik, 'The Right to be Forgotten as an Element of the Personal Data Protection System in the Organisation' Organization & Management Quarterly (2020) (51:3) 57; H Yaish, 'Forget Me, Forget Me Not: Elements of Erasure to Determine the Sufficiency of a GDPR Article 17 Request' Journal of Law, Technology & the Internet (2019) (10:1) 1; CR La Roche, 'The "Right to be Forgotten": An Ethical Dilemma' Journal of Leadership, Accountability & Ethics (2020) (17:3) 36.
80 *Ibid*; P Lambert, 'Complying with the Data Protection Regime' *International Journal for the Data Protection Officer, Privacy Officer and Privacy Counsel (IDPP)* (2018) (2:7) 17.
81 L Determann, *Determann's Field Guide to Data Privacy Law: International Corporate Compliance* (Elgar, 2015); P Lambert, *Understanding the New European Data Protection Rules* (Taylor & Francis, 2017).
82 Rustad and Kulevska, 'Reconceptualizing the Right to be Forgotten to Enable Transatlantic Data Flow' at 349; Weber and Staiger, 'Transatlantic Data Protection in Practice – Revisited' at 16.
83 SM LoCascio, 'Forcing Europe to Wear the Rose-Colored Google Glass: The "Right to Be Forgotten" and the Struggle to Manage Compliance Post Google Spain' *Columbia Journal of Transnational Law* (2015) (54:1) 296.
84 G Wade, 'Directors: When Company Law and Data Protection Law Collide' *International Journal for the Data Protection Officer, Privacy Officer and Privacy Counsel (IDPP)* (2018) (2:8) 19; M Everett and L McAlister, 'Court of Appeal Confirms First Successful UK Class Action for Data Breach' *International Journal for the Data Protection Officer, Privacy Officer and Privacy Counsel (IDPP)* (2018) (2:11) 8. Also P Lambert, The Manager's Data Protection Duties (Clarus Press, 2020).

Related issues that business must consider, in conjunction with growing RtbF issues, include data risks,[85] data ethics,[86] biometric privacy,[87] artificial intelligence (AI),[88] each of which have RtbF implications.

7 SECTORIAL REACTIONS

9.7 There is increasing literature on business sector and business specific data protection issues.[89] RtbF also can have implications for different sectors and/or may be considered differently depending on the sector in question.[90] Different sectors may feel that they have more need to be aware of RtbF as they may be the focus of notices being made, as compared to other sectors. Virginia Dressler and Cindy Kristof refer to RtbF and its implications for those involved with Digital Collections. They also refer to a study on the issue amongst ARL member institutions.[91] Naturally, there is focus on the issues of transatlantic data flows. This is also flagged as possibly being impacted by RtbF.[92] There is also a discussion on the need for an extraterritorial protection element of RtbF as part of the solution.[93] Sebastian Schweda refers to the issues from the perspective of how RtbF applies to online news archives,[94] as does Jiménez-Castellanos Ballesteros.[95] Don Reisinger refers to the implications on web searches.[96] Ronald V Distante refers to how banking and financial institutions will comply with the

---

85 H Tuttle, '2020 Cyberrisk Landscape' Risk Management (2020) (67:1) 18.

86 CE Clark, KK Chang and SP Melvin, Business and Society: Ethical, Legal, and Digital Environments (Sage, 2020).

87 C Llaneza, 'An Analysis on Biometric Privacy Data Regulation: A Pivot Towards Legislation which Supports the Individual Consumer's Privacy Rights in Spite of Corporate Protections' St Thomas Law Review (2020) (32:2) 177.

88 N Hodge, 'Getting Smart About Artificial Intelligence: How Can Companies Avoid the Risks and Regulatory Pitfalls of Artificial Intelligence-Based Technology?' Risk Management (2021) (68:8) 20.

89 As just one example see A Sofia Ferrão *et al*, 'Surveying the Issues Facing Data Protection Officers, Privacy Officers and Counsel in Different Industry Sectors' *International Journal for the Data Protection Officer, Privacy Officer and Privacy Counsel (IDPP)* (2017) (1:1) 9.

90 A Nicole Vavra, 'The Right to Be Forgotten: An Archival Perspective' *American Archivist* (2018) (81:1) 100.

91 V Dressler and C Kristof, 'The Right to Be Forgotten and Implications on Digital Collections: A Survey of ARL Member Institutions on Practice and Policy' *College* (2018) (79:7) 972.

92 Rustad and Kulevska, 'Reconceptualizing the Right to be Forgotten to Enable Transatlantic Data Flow' above at 349.

93 Schiopu, 'The Territorial Scope of the Right to be Forgotten (Right to De-referencing) in the Light of the Request for a Preliminary Ruling from the Conseil d'Etat (France)' **above** at 61.

94 S Schweda, 'Right to Be Forgotten Also Applies to Online News Archive, Supreme Court Rules' *European Data Protection Law Review (EDPL)* (2015) (1:4) 301.

95 I Jiménez-Castellanos Ballesteros, 'The Conflict Between the Right to be Forgotten of the Criminal History and Freedom of Information: Digital Newspaper Archives (In this respect the Spanish Constitutional Court Judgment of June 4, 2018 and the European Court of Human Rights' Judgment in the M.L. and W.W. vs. Germany case, June 28, 2018)' Revista de Derecho Político (2019) (1:106) 137.

96 D Reisinger, 'The Implications of the EU "Right to Be Forgotten' Law on Web Searches' *eWeek* (8 July 2015) 1.

RtbF.[97] Tsirintani et al refer to the hospital and healthcare sector and how RtbF compliance will occur.[98]

8   REACTIONS FROM THE US

9.8   There have been both positive and negative comments and reactions in the US. Some welcome the EU RtbF but in addition suggest how a similar right and solution is much-needed in the US. Others offer criticism – some reasoned, some melodramatic. Some is based on cultural differences, some on principled differences and others, perhaps, from a sectorial or interest perspective. Soon after *Google Spain*, there were immediate questions as to whether such a right should apply in the US and whether it is 'ready for the Right to Be Forgotten'.[99] In the Washington Law Review, Amy Gajda refers to RtbF and general issues of the press and privacy in the US.[100] Kristie Byrum,[101] while referring to the principle of the right to freedom of expression as contained in the US First Amendment, dramatically describes RtbF as being the 'enemy' of the First Amendment. One should not forget that there are also journalism and freedom of expression interests in the EU. Such interests are neither absent nor ignored in Europe. Charles Tobin and Christine Walz refer to how past cases and policy may be affected, referring specifically to Cox[102] and the so-called 'expungement laws'.[103]

Other comments appear to be more personally dismissive of the original personal applicant in *Google Spain*.[104] Robert Lee Bolton III suggest that the RtbF is a case of 'forced amnesia', but respectfully also nods to this being in the context of the 'technological age'.[105] One of many US articles asks if there should simply

---

97   RV Distante, 'Reconciling U.S. Banking and Securities Data Preservation Rules with European Mandatory Data Erasure Under GDPR' Fordham Journal of Corporate Law (2019) (25:1) 195.

98   M Tsirintani, M Serifi and S Binioris, 'Digital Oblivion (The Right to be Forgotten): A Big Challenge for the Public Hospital Management in Greece' *Studies in Health Technology and Informatics* (2019) 91.

99   SC Bennett, 'Is America Ready for the Right to Be Forgotten' *New York State Bar Association Journal* (2016) (88:1) 11.

100 A Gajda, 'Privacy, Press and the Right to be Forgotten in the United States' *Washington Law Review* (2018) (93:1) 201.

101 Byrum, *The European* Right to be Forgotten*: The First Amendment Enemy*.

102 *Cox Broadcasting Corp v Cohn* 420 US 469 (1975).

103 Tobin and Walz, 'Right to Be Forgotten, Expungement Laws Raise New Challenges on the 40th Anniversary of *Cox Broadcasting v Cohn*' above at 4.

104 MD Goldhaber, 'Unforgettable: How a 27-Year-Old Lawyer and a Client Miffed About an Old Legal Notice Successfully Led the Fight for the Right to be Forgotten' *American Lawyer* (2015) (37:10) 84.

105 R Lee Bolton III, 'The Right to be Forgotten: Forced Amnesia in a Technological Age' *John Marshall Journal of Information Technology and Privacy Law* (2015) (31:2) 132.

be a RtbF for internet users,[106] suggesting they should forget about 'your' RtbF.[107] Another US critic suggests that the basis for the RtbF is 'shaky'.[108]

9   SEARCH ENGINES AND SOCIAL MEDIA

9.9   There is comment on the wider implications and compliance obligations of RtbF for search engines generally,[109] as well as comment on Google and RtbF.[110] Cayce Myers compares US and EU social media policy issues.[111] Mark T Andrus refers to US constitutional issues in terms of granting a US 'right to dispute' online personal information 'akin' to the EU RtbF.[112] However, referring to a 'right to dispute' appears, in essence, something less than the GDPR RtbF. Sylvia de Mars and Patrick O'Callaghan also seem to refer to a downgraded RtbF, namely 'contextualizing', which seems less than erasure and forgetting.[113]

There is also discussion as to whether search engines have become so influential that they are now more powerful in terms akin to 'consumer reporting agencies'.[114] This would have added weight in terms of rules that may need to apply, but also in terms of an ability to erase and forget such as RtbF. There are various references to the impact that an extraterritorial RtbF may have on search engines which are non-EU based.[115] Julia Kerr suggests that the CJEU omitted to ask what a search engine is in *Google Spain*.[116] However, Google often sets out detailed descriptions of what it services and activities are, when it comes to issuing inter-party correspondence in contentious situations. This includes reference to its

---

106 D Sidhu and J Simpson, 'Should Internet Users Have a "Right to be Forgotten"?' *US News Digital Weekly* (26 December 2014) (6:52) 16.

107 D Winder, 'Forget Your Right to be Forgotten' *PC Pro* (1 September 2014) (239) 71.

108 Peguera, 'The Shaky Ground of the Right to be Delisted' above at 507.

109 Reisinger, 'The Implications of the EU "Right to Be Forgotten' Law on Web Searches"' at 1; D Lindsay, 'The "Right to be Forgotten" by Search Engines Under Data Privacy Law: A Legal Analysis of the *Costeja* Ruling' *Journal of Media Law* (2014) (6:2) 159; LoCascio, 'Forcing Europe to Wear the Rose-Colored Google Glass: The "Right to Be Forgotten" and the Struggle to Manage Compliance Post Google Spain' at 296.

110 H Kranenborg, 'Google and the Right to Be Forgotten' *European Data Protection Law Review (EDPL)* (2015) (1:1) 70.

111 C Myers, 'Digital Immortality vs "The Right to be Forgotten": A Comparison of US and E.U. Laws Concerning Social Media Privacy' *Romanian Journal of Communications and Public Relations*, (2016) (16:3) 47.

112 MT Andrus, 'Constitutional Issues in Granting Americans a "Right to Dispute" Personal Information with Search Engines Akin to the Existing Remedy Afforded to Europeans Via Europe's Right to Be Forgotten' *Business Law Today* (2016) 1.

113 S de Mars and Patrick O'Callaghan, 'Privacy and Search Engines: Forgetting or Contextualizing?' *Journal of Law & Society* (2016) (43:2) 257.

114 MT Andrus, 'The Right to Be Forgotten in America: Have Search Engines Inadvertently Become Consumer Reporting Agencies' *Business Law Today* (2016) (5) 1.

115 S Tassis and Margarita Peristeraki, 'The Extraterritorial Scope of the Right to Be Forgotten and How This Affects Obligations of Search Engine Operators Located Outside the EU' *European Networks Law and Regulation Quarterly* (ENLR) (2014) (3) 244.

116 J Kerr, 'What is a Search Engine? The Simple Question the Court of Justice of the European Union Forgot to Ask and What it Means for the Future of the Right to be Forgotten' *Chicago Journal of International Law* (2016) (17:1) 217.

own description of its search activities. In most instances, this would be available to the court in the relevant paper pleadings. David Meyer refers to how Google is seeking to curtail the scope of the GDPR RtbF, particularly in terms of its potential global effect.[117] There is also reference to Google and its approach to cases dealing with RtbF.[118] Ryan Belbin refers to Google as the 'norm' and suggests this as an added reason for RtbF, data protection and privacy.[119] Whether search engines or social media, service providers, often describe themselves as such (as opposed to websites) and intermediaries[120] in terms of falling within the eCommerce Directive defences Diana Sancho-Villa notes that the developing area of search engine law is also more than just a RtbF issue.[121]

There is also reference to general social media, including Facebook (now Meta).[122] English and Bieker refer to data protection law and multi-nationals and the applicability of German law to Facebook (Meta).[123] Facebook (Meta) has faced cases in Austria[124] and Germany[125] as to whether it must comply with the respective data protection laws there, as opposed to the law in Ireland. Marc Benioff of Salesforcedescribed Facebook as the 'new tobacco'.[126] Nicolas Blanc discusses *Wirtschaftsakademie*, the Facebook (Meta) fan page case, where the operator of the fan page was held to be a Joint Controller with Facebook,[127] as do

---

117 Meyer, 'The 'Right to Be Forgotten' Globally? How Google Is Fighting to Limit the Scope of Europe's Privacy Law' at 1.

118 J Vijayan, 'Google Changes Approach to EU "Right to Be Forgotten" Mandate' *eWeek* (3 July 2016) 4; P Sayer, 'France Rejects Google's Appeal on Right to be Forgotten' *CIO* (13284045) (21 September 2015) 1.

119 R Belbin, 'When Google Becomes the Norm: The Case for Privacy and the Right to be Forgotten' *Dalhousie Journal of Legal Studies* (2018) (26) 17.

120 D Erdos, 'Intermediary Publishers and European Data Protection: Delimiting the Ambit of Responsibility for Third-Party Rights Through a Synthetic Interpretation of the EU Acquis' *International Journal of Law and Information Technology* (2018) (26:3) 189; Kuan Hon, Hörnle and Millard, 'Data Protection Jurisdiction and Cloud Computing – When are Cloud Users and Providers Subject to EU Data Protection Law? The Cloud of Unknowing' at 129; J Bezerra de Menezes and H Silva Colaço, 'Right to be Digital Forgotten and Civil Liability of Internet Search Providers: Interface Between the Civil Mark, National and Foreign Experience and the Law Projects N° 7881/2014 AND N° 1676/2015' *Revista de Direito, Governança e Novas Tecnologias* (2015) (1:1) 1; N Ni Loideain, 'The End of Safe Harbor: Implications for EU Digital Privacy and Data Protection Law, *Journal of Internet Law* (2016) (19:8) 8.

121 D Sancho-Villa, 'Developing Search Engine Law: It Is Not Just about the Right to Be Forgotten' *Legal Issues of Economic Integration* (2015) (42:4) 357.

122 N English and Felix Bieker, 'Upholding Data Protection Law Against Multinational Corporations: German Administrative Measures Relating to Facebook' *German Yearbook of International Law* (2012) (55) 587; C Carugati, 'The 2017 Facebook Saga: A Competition, Consumer and Data Protection Story' *European Competition and Regulatory Law Review (CoRe)* (2018) (2:1) 4. 'Delimitation of National Data Protection Laws Reflected By Recent EU Case Law on Facebook' *Computer Law Review International* (2017) (18:10) 10.

123 *Ibid* English and Bieker.

124 *Maximilian Schrems v Facebook Ireland Limited*, CJEU, C-498/16, Judgment of the Court (Third Chamber) 25 January 2018.

125 L Essers, 'Facebook Must Comply with German Data Protection Law, Court Rules' *Good Gear Guide* (18 February 2014) 4.

126 M Benioff, 'Facebook is the New Tobacco' *CNN* (4 December 2018).

127 Case C-210/16 Unabhängiges Landeszentrum für Datenschutz Schleswig-Holstein v Wirtschaftsakademie Schleswig-Holstein GmbH ECLI:EU:C:2018:388, 05/06/2018. Nicolas

barrister Robin Hopkins,[128] Rowenna Fielding,[129] and Gabriela Zanfir-Fortuna.[130] There are also some references to the RtbF in terms of Twitter.[131]

10 UNINTENDED CONSEQUENCES

9.10 Unintended consequences can sometime result from data protection and privacy litigation.[132] On one level, one can say that *Google Spain* was an unexpected and unintended consequence for the company concerned. It is also an unintended consequence for the wider search engine sector. There are wider implications for many other technology sectors. It is important to assess potential ripple effects to litigation before embarking upon it, because these can sometimes be more than one bargained for and can also contain wider unintended consequences. These factors should also be considered.

11 FOUNDATION DISCUSSIONS

9.11 There are various descriptors being used to refer to RtbF:

- Andrew Neville refers to RtbF in terms of considering whether RtbF is a 'human right';[133]

- Rajko Knez refers to RtbF as a 'new' 'personal right';[134]

- Silviu-Dorin Schiopu refers to RtbF as the 'Right to be Forgotten (Right to De-referencing)';[135]

Blanc, 'Wirtschaftsakademie Schleswig-Holstein: Towards a Joint Responsibility of Facebook Fan Page Administrators for Infringements to European Data Protection Law' *European Data Protection Law Review (EDPL)* (2018) (4:1) 120.

128 R Hopkins, 'The CJEU's "Facebook Fan Page" Judgment: Joint Data Controllers, Cookies and Targeted Advertising' *International Journal for the Data Protection Officer, Privacy Officer and Privacy Counsel (IDPP)* (2018) (2:5) 13.

129 R Fielding, 'The Concept of Controller and Processor Data Entities' *International Journal for the Data Protection Officer, Privacy Officer and Privacy Counsel (IDPP)* (2018) (2:8) 8.

130 G Zanfir-Fortuna, 'Personal Data for Joint Controllers and Exam Scripts' *International Journal for the Data Protection Officer, Privacy Officer and Privacy Counsel (IDPP)* (2018) (2:8) 12.

131 Y Shuzhe, Anabel Quan-Haase and Kai Rannenberg, 'The Changing Public Sphere on Twitter: Network Structure, Elites and topics of the #righttobeforgotten' *New Media & Society* (2017) (19:12) 1983.

132 H Jacqueline Brehmer, 'Data Localization: The Unintended Consequences of Privacy Litigation' *American University Law Review* (2018) (67:3) 927. Also note CC Goldfield, '"The Right to be Forgotten" and its Unintended Consequences to Intelligence Gathering' Florida Journal of International Law (2020) (32:2) 183.

133 A Neville, 'Is It a Human Right to Be Forgotten: Conceptualizing the World View' *Santa Clara Journal of International Law* (2017) (15:2) 157.

134 R Knez, 'Right to be Forgotten – Indeed a New Personal Right in Digital EU Market?' *InterEULawEast: Journal for International & European Law, Economics & Market Integrations* (2016) (3:1) 31.

135 Schiopu, 'The Territorial Scope of the Right to be Forgotten (Right to De-referencing) in the Light of the Request for a Preliminary Ruling From the Conseil d'Etat (France)' **above** at 61.

- Bonnici Mifsud *et al* refer to 'forgetting', 'deleting' and 'de-listing';[136]

- R George Wright refers to RtbF as 'voluntary recall';[137]

- Robert Lee Bolton III refers to RtbF as 'forced amnesia';[138]

- Miquel Peguera refers to the 'right to be delisted';[139]

- Lyndsay Cook refers to cyberspace law and policy and how RtbF aptly fits within this setting.[140]

- Ray et al refer to forgetting and interpersonal signals.[141]

There is some discussion on the basis, underpinning and conceptual understanding of RtbF. We should consider its conceptual understanding and rationalisation. There is discussion and consideration of the basis and concepts behind RtbF in the GDPR[142] – and the need to 'search for the concept of protection'. Andrew Neville refers to the need for 'conceptualising'[143] RtbF. There is also some discussion in relation to data in the public sphere.[144] Some of the analysis has begun to consider RtbF in the context of personal data protection in the context of the ECHR.[145] It is also suggested that it could be considered as a human right.[146] Rolf Weber, for example, refers to 'the search for an adequate scope' of RtbF.[147] Others might prefer to reconceptualise such research more as the (best) basis and (best) underpinning scope. Maximilian Von Grafenstein and Wolfgang Schulz refer to RtbF's 'search for the concept of protection'.[148] Kieron O'Hara

---

136 B Mifsud, P Jeanne and AJ Verheij, 'On Forgetting, Deleting, De-listing and Starting Afresh!' *International Review of Law, Computers & Technology* (2016) (30:1/2) 1.
137 R George Wright, 'The Right to Be Forgotten: Issuing a Voluntary Recall' *Drexel Law Review* (2015) (7:2) 401.
138 R Lee Bolton III, 'The Right to be Forgotten: Forced Amnesia in a Technological Age' *John Marshall Journal of Information Technology and Privacy Law* (2015) (31:2) 132.
139 Peguera, 'The Shaky Ground of the Right to Be Delisted' above at 507.
140 L Cook, 'The Right to Be Forgotten: A Step in the Right Direction for Cyberspace Law and Policy' *Case Western Reserve Journal of Law, Technology and the Internet* (2015) (6) 121.
141 DG Ray, S Gomillion, AI Pintea and I Hamlin, 'On Being Forgotten: Memory and Forgetting Serve as Signals of Interpersonal Importance' Journal of Personality and Social Psychology (2019) (116:2) 259.
142 M Von Grafenstein and Wolfgang Schulz, 'The Right to be Forgotten in Data Protection Law: A Search for the Concept of Protection' *International Journal of Public Law and Policy* (2015) (5:3) 249.
143 Neville, 'Is It a Human Right to Be Forgotten: Conceptualizing the World View' above at 157.
144 Post, 'Data Privacy and Dignitary Privacy: Google Spain, The Right to be Forgotten and the Construction of the Public Sphere' above at 981.
145 M Klarić, 'Protection of Personal Data and "ECHR,"' *Zbornik Radova Pravnog Fakulteta u Splitu* (2016) (53:4) 973; J Nergelius and Eleanor Kristoffersson, *Human Rights in Contemporary European Law* (Hart, 2015); Cremer, *Human Rights and the Protection of Privacy in Tort Law: A Comparison Between English and German Law*; M Szabo, 'General Principles of Law in the Practice of International Courts and the European Court of Justice' *Hungarian Yearbook of International Law and European Law* (2016) 135.
146 Nys, 'Towards a Human Right "to Be Forgotten Online"?' above at 469.
147 RH Weber, 'On the Search for an Adequate Scope of the Right to Be Forgotten' *Journal of Intellectual Property, Information Technology and Electronic Commerce Law* (2015) (6:1) 2.
148 Von Grafenstein and Schulz, 'The Right to be Forgotten in Data Protection Law: A Search for the Concept of Protection' above at 249.

and Nigel Shadbolt refer to how the it may have a role in enhancing a 'coherent privacy regime'.[149] There is also some discussion of the influence of national data protection supervisory authorities and courts in interpreting RtbF.[150]

Some research also refers to possible subjectivity issues in terms of RtbF.[151] This potential extends from individual service providers, to data protection supervisory authorities, individual courts and individual subjectivity decisions and opinions on what should be taken down in a given instance. There will be large areas which should be uncontroversial in terms of RtbF takedown and erasure. For example, problem content which is inaccurate, having been maliciously posted by a third party, content which is sexual in nature, private content, content involving elements of OA, defamatory content, etc, will often be less controversial and routine RtbF notices.

Questions have also been raised as to who decides what is forgotten or taken down under RtbF and what implications this might have.[152] Lawrence Siry refers to two different 'paradigms' or forms of RtbF and the need for these to be reconciled.[153] There are some, perhaps surprisingly, who contextualise RtbF against an historical backdrop. Antoon De Baets refers to RtbF from a historian's point of view,[154] while others use the historical reference that 'whomever controls the present, also controls the past'.[155] Following this theme, Giovanni Sartor hints at the interests which arise, how they may change over the passage of time and how an original balance may have to be recalibrated in later years or given the 'flux of time'.[156] Karen Eltis refers to how civil personality rights may help to reconceptualise the understanding of RtbF and effect greater interoperability and acceptance.[157] One line of review refers to RtbF in the stream of private law enforcement mechanisms.[158]

---

149 O'Hara and Shadbolt, 'The Right to Be Forgotten: Its Potential Role in a Coherent Privacy Regime' above at 178.

150 M Peguera, 'In the Aftermath of Google Spain: How the 'Right to be Forgotten' Is Being Shaped in Spain by Courts and the Data Protection Authority' *International Journal of Law & Information Technology* (2015) (23:4) 325.

151 S Lindroos-Hovinheimo, 'Legal Subjectivity and the "Right to be Forgotten": A Rancièrean Analysis of Google Law' *Law and Critique* (2016) (27:3) 289.

152 P Sánchez Abril and Jacqueline D Lipton, 'The Right to be Forgotten: Who Decides What the World Forgets?' *Kentucky Law Journal* (2015) (103:3) 363.

153 L Siry, 'Forget Me, Forget Me Not: Reconciling Two Different Paradigms of the Right to Be Forgotten' *Kentucky Law Journal* (2014/2015) (103:3) 311.

154 De Baets, 'A Historian's View on the Right to be Forgotten' above at 57.

155 A Vertes-Olteanu and Codruta Guzei-Mangu, 'The Right to Be Forgotten – He Who Controls the Present Controls the Past' *Analele Stiintifice Ale Universitatii Alexandru Ioan Cuza Din Iasi Stiinte Juridice* (2017) (63:2) 203.

156 G Sartor, 'The Right to be Forgotten: Balancing Interests in the Flux of Time' *International Journal of Law & Information Technology* (2016) (24:1) 72.

157 K Eltis, 'The Anglo-American/Continental Privacy Divide: How Civilian Personality Rights Can Help Reconceptualize the Right to Be Forgotten Towards Greater Transnational Interoperability' *Canadian Bar Review* (2016) (94:2) 355.

158 TFE Tjong Tjin Tai, 'Right to Be Forgotten – Private Law Enforcement' *International Review of Law, Computers & Technology* (2016) (30:1-2) 76.

Others are more reductive and limit comment to how RtbF is a compliance issue and that there may be a 'struggle to manage compliance'.[159] Prior to the GDPR RtbF, Miquel Peguera[160] referred to how the Spanish courts and the Spanish data protection supervisory authority are involved in 'shaping' RtbF. This is to the extent that CJEU cases result in guideline answers to the queries raised to it by the national court. It is then for the national court to 'apply' or implement the CJEU ruling on the original questions to the facts of the case. In a not dissimilar stream, Abril and Lipton then ask who decides what the world forgets under RtbF.[161] As stated above, both of these articles appeared before the 'go-live' of the GDPR RtbF, which is on a different, more harmonised and directly effective identical basis throughout all Member State countries. However, this still suggests a stream of interesting research in terms of comparing applications and decisions in national courts and at national data protection supervisory authorities in terms of researching patterns and differences where they may apply. The need for RtbF comparative[162] research will continue.

In contrast to some of the criticisms, Kieron O'Hara acknowledges that there is a need for positive aspects, but that there are some negative aspects too, describing them as 'the good, the bad and the ugly'.[163] RtbF is also used as an example of private law enforcement;[164] this offers further avenues for research consideration. Pereira, Ghezzi and Vesnic-Alujevic[165] highlight the issue of memory, especially ethical issues. This can provide further understanding of the need for a RtbF. Amanda Cheng reacts by suggesting other concepts and interests and conceptualises a 'right to be different'.[166] Ryan Belbin suggest another basis and the need to have a RtbF in an age when a single company become so powerful that it becomes the norm or status quo.[167] W Gregory Voss and Celine Castets Renard refer to the need for analysis and an 'international taxonomy' of the various different 'forms of' RtbF. They refer to the study of the 'convergence of norms'.[168]

---

159 LoCascio, 'Forcing Europe to Wear the Rose-Colored Google Glass: The "Right to Be Forgotten" and the Struggle to Manage Compliance Post Google Spain' above at 296.
160 Peguera, 'In the Aftermath of *Google Spain*: How the Right to Be Forgotten Is Being Shaped in Spain by Courts and the Data Protection Authority' above at 325.
161 Sánchez Abril and Lipton, 'The Right to be Forgotten: Who Decides What the World Forgets?' above at 363.
162 For example, Shim and Ko, 'A Comparative Study of the Differences in Legal Requirements and Technical Coverage for the Right to Be Forgotten in the GDPR Era' above at 507.
163 K O'Hara, 'The Right to Be Forgotten: The Good, the Bad and the Ugly' *Internet Computing IEEE* (2015) (19:4) 73.
164 Tjong Tjin Tai, 'The Right to be Forgotten – Private Law Enforcement' above at 76.
165 Â Pereira, A Ghezzi and L Vesnic-Alujevic, *The Ethics of Memory in a Digital Age: Interrogating the Right to be Forgotten* (Palgrave Macmillan, 2014). Also see G Laura Silvanus, 'The Ethics of Memory in a Digital Age – Interrogating the Right to be Forgotten' *Records Management Journal* (2016) (26:1) 102.
166 A Cheng, 'Forget About the Right to be Forgotten: How About a Right to be Different?' *Auckland University Law Review* (2016) (22) 106.
167 Belbin, 'When Google Becomes the Norm: The Case for Privacy and the Right to be Forgotten' above at 17.
168 W Gregory Voss and C Castets-Renard, 'Proposal for an International Taxonomy on the Various Forms of the Right to Be Forgotten: A Study on the Convergence of Norms' *Colorado Technology Law Journal* (2016) (14:2) 281.

Tim Berners-Lee, the inventor of the World Wide Web, rstates that given developments, 'customers need to be given control of their own data'.[169] He has also made a statement in terms of a need for greater rights for internet users and a Magna Carta for the internet. Berners-Lee also refers separately to design considerations, the implications of design and comments that 'the Web is now philosophical engineering'.[170] He adds that 'IT professionals have a responsibility to understand the use of standards and the importance of making Web applications that work with any kind of device'.[171]

This emphasis on the real impacts of technological, internet and website design is a growing area for consideration. There is the suggestion that laws increasingly need to be cognizant of design impacts on data protection and privacy – and that they may need to expressly include design mandates in new laws and regulations.[172] John Samons and Michael Cross suggest that we need to focus beyond technology and instead on real people using the technology.[173]

Tim Cook of Apple also made a famous speech in Brussels which advocates better tech responsibility, data protection and privacy.[174] This has been broadly welcomed.[175] It is also noted that many US tech companies have now announced their support for a US federal privacy law. However, as always, the devil will be in the detail. The concept of personal dignity is also being considered in terms of an additional basis of, or separate justification for, individual rights and remedies.[176]

---

169 T Berners-Lee, 'Customers Need to be Given Control of Their Own Data', available at: www.brainyquote.com/authors/tim_bernerslee.
170 T Berners-Lee, 'The Web is Now Philosophical Engineering', available at: www.brainyquote.com/authors/tim_bernerslee.
171 T Berners-Lee, 'IT Professionals Have a Responsibility to Understand the Use of Standards and the Importance of Making Web Applications That Work With Any Kind of Device.' Available at: www.brainyquote.com/authors/tim_bernerslee.
172 See W Hartzog, *Privacy Blueprint, the Battle to Control Design of New Technologies* (Harvard University Press, 2018); W Hartzog, 'Are Privacy Laws Deficient?' *International Journal for the Data Protection Officer, Privacy Officer and Privacy Counsel (IDPP)* (2018) (2:10) 17; N Richards and W Hartzog, 'Taking Trust Seriously in Privacy Law' *Stanford Technology Law Review* (2016) (19:3) 431; DJ Solove and W Hartzog, 'The FTC and the New Common Law of Privacy' *Columbia Law Review* (2014) (114:3) 583.
173 'Chapter 9: Beyond Technology – Dealing with People' in John Samons and Michael Cross, *The Basics of Cyber Safety* (Syngree, 2017).
174 T Cook, 'Apple Tim Cook Privacy Speech at ICDPPC 2018' *International Journal for the Data Protection Officer, Privacy Officer and Privacy Counsel (IDPP)* (2018) (2:10) 8.
175 European Data Protection Supervisor, 'Reactions and Comments to Apple Tim Cook ICDPPC Privacy Speech' *International Journal for the Data Protection Officer, Privacy Officer and Privacy Counsel (IDPP)* (2018) (2:10) 12; Data Protection Commission Ireland, 'Reactions and Comments to Apple Tim Cook ICDPPC Privacy Speech' *IDPP* (2018) (2:10) 12; P Raether, 'Reactions and Comments to Apple Tim Cook ICDPPC Privacy Speech' *IDPP* (2018) (2:10) 12; D Fernández, 'Reactions and Comments to Apple Tim Cook ICDPPC Privacy Speech' *IDPP* (2018) (2:10) 12; P Bartel, 'Reactions and Comments to Apple Tim Cook ICDPPC Privacy Speech' *IDPP* (2018) (2:10) 12; J Farley, 'Reactions and Comments to Apple Tim Cook ICDPPC Privacy Speech' *IDPP* (2018) (2:10) 12; L Landes-Gronowski, 'Comment on Tim Cook Brussels Speech' *IDPP* (2018) (2:11) 25.
176 A de Hingh, 'Some Reflections on Dignity as an Alternative Legal Concept in Data Protection Regulation' *German Law Journal* (2018) (19:5) 1269.

12   CONCLUSION

9.12   John Samons and Michael Cross refer to how we might sometimes better consider matters in terms of 'beyond technology' thus remembering that products, services and companies are still dealing with actual people.[177] Christopher Hodges refers to the need for a new focus on trust and ethics to deliver data protection and privacy,[178] and the EU Commission has also highlighted the interrelated nature of data ethics and data protection.[179]

---

177 'Chapter 9: Beyond Technology – Dealing with People' in Samons and Cross, *The Basics of Cyber Safety*.

178 C Hodges, 'Delivering Data Protection: Trust and Ethical Culture' *European Data Protection Law Review (EDPL)* (2018) (4:1) 65.

179 See EU Commission, *Ethics and Data Protection* (14 November 2018).

Practical Issues Facing Individuals

I INTRODUCTION

10.1   There are various practical issues facing individuals seeking to have problem content taken down, including via RtbF. As the practice of individuals availing of RtbF and making RtbF notices to service providers develops further, we will have more insight into how these impediments to individuals are continuing, increasing or decreasing. We will also need to consider if new impediment issues also begin to arise.

2 RESPONSIBILITY

10.2   One issue facing individuals is responsibility. In the first instance, the responsibility is placed on individuals to become aware of problem content; they then have to find and navigate the RtbF notification process. The location of the respective RtbF application filing site/page may not always be easy to find. It may not always be clear how to make the application. There may not be clear information on what an individual data subject needs to do, what happens once an application is filed, or the relevant timeframe. Some application forms may contain specific legal-type wording whether from the General Data Protection Regulation (GDPR) RtbF and/or *Google Spain*,[1] which may be obvious to lawyers but will be less so to applicants. It may also be the case that some websites do not have a RtbF procedure in place at all. An interesting area for future research, if not litigation, will be how effective and user-friendly RtbF application sites or pages are. A critic might suggest that certain RtbF filing processes are designed to be less easy to find and use and less effective than they should otherwise be. Where a particular RtbF process of a service provider is under-developed or under-resourced and where there may also be a deliberate calculated element to this, it could be argued that there is a lack of compliance, or full compliance with *Google Spain* and the GDPR RtbF.

The evaluation of the responsibility issues is also interesting from the defence perspective. It may be that certain defensive actions and strategies of service providers are directed in some part by a reluctance on the part of the service provider to be deemed as being in some way responsible for problem content on its website. This follows the line of an entity being described as a so-called

---

1   *Google Spain SL, Google Inc v Agencia Española de Protección de Datos (AEPD), Mario Costeja González*, Court of Justice (Grand Chamber), Case C-131/12, 13 May 2014.

'neutral platform' and wishing to fall within one of the three ISP defences[2] as referred to in the eCommerce Directive.[3]

3 PASSING THE BUCK

10.3 The victims of online abuse (OA) sometimes feel that the service providers of the main websites where OA exists and is perpetuated are less than helpful in terms of preventing the attacks occurring, dealing with the attacks once they occur and helping individual victims once they have been notified.

In addition, there are many instances where a service provider will effectively respond that they do not have an issue with the problem content and that it is the victim's responsibility to contact the person who is perpetuating or posting the content. Sometimes the perpetrator may be known to them, sometimes they will not, but there is always a user name or 'handle', which leaves the name, identity and location of the bad actor. This is all unknown to the victim. Even where a victim contacts the person in question, the attacker can ignore them, may even choose to make this communication public or even escalate the attack.

Worse still are situations where there are several attackers; this is worse again when the matter has gone viral. This is much more difficult for an individual victim to deal with, especially when the service provider – or one of several service providers – which is the locus of the problem content, is passing the buck.

It remains to be seen how effectively the response of service providers will assist or enable RtbF to function properly. Only time will tell whether, even within RtbF, there is an element of 'passing the buck' by a service provider or group of service providers.

4 DISPARITY

10.4 Related to the above points is the fact that there is a disparity in resources and numbers. There is a clear disparity in the size and resources of an individual victim of OA or other individual data subjects when dealing with a large, sometimes multi-national, service provider in seeking to have problem content taken down, erased and forgotten.

There is also the disparity of resources to consider for an individual victim. In large-scale and or viral examples of OA, the victim is not dealing with one

---

2   Namely, caching (Article 13), hosting (Article 14) and mere conduit (Article 15) of the eCommerce Directive.
3   Directive 2000/31/EC of the European Parliament and of the Council of 8 June 2000 on certain legal aspects of information society services, in particular electronic commerce, in the Internal Market (Directive on Electronic Commerce) (aka the eCommerce Directive).

comment or one image, but rather a vast number of comments, images, copies of images, etc, across a variety of different locations.

5 EVIDENCE

10.5 When an individual is dealing with RtbF filings to service providers, complaints to data protection supervisory authorities and/or court applications, the victim of OA or other respective data subject, they must rely on evidence. This can be to a greater or lesser extent depending on the issues, facts and history. So, again, a great onus is placed on the individual. The service provider may view an application strictly with a legal lens and apply legal evidentiary standards. This is a more expert level of knowledge and appreciation than the individual themselves may possess.

The individual, often on their own, may not appreciate the legal evidential value of particular statements, postings, etc. They may also not understand that evidence can change quickly and that if something online is not saved or printed off, it may not be there in future. In addition, it can sometimes be necessary to save a copy of the actual RtbF filing being made to a service provider and the online receipt (if there is one). An online receipt is not guaranteed to be emailed to the individual, depending on the service provider. Receipts may also not specify the exact time that a RtbF notice was filed. It can also be beneficial to keep copies of any communication sent to the culprit(s) as they may be referred to in evidence.

Individuals need to be aware of the danger either of losing or not saving evidence which may later be argued to be a defect in the application by the service provider, regulator or the court. Arguably, there is a need for greater dissemination of information on these issues by the respective data regulators (also known as data protection supervisory authorities) and other interested organisations.

6 REPORT, REPORT, REPORT

10.6 One lesson which may not be familiar to individual data subjects and especially to victims of OA is that is vital to report, report, report. There is often a criticism from victims and consumer and victim organisations that service providers are not doing enough and/or do not respond or act in response to individual online reports or online complaint reports (which may include RtbF reports).

However, continuous reporting of the issue can be important as this may be required to demonstrate to the service provider, data protection supervisory authority or court that a complaint was made at a specific time on a certain date and similarly so for each subsequent report or complaint. It may also be necessary to show that X number of reports or complaints were made and that there was no response and/or no action from the service provider.

Continuous reporting is also recommended for another reason. There is a suggestion that certain service providers only act or act more swiftly, if they receive lots of reports about a specific item of problem content compared to instances where they receive only a single complaint. The suggestion is that the manual and/or automated processes escalate the issue the more complaints are received. To that extent, therefore, there may be benefit in making as many reports as possible. Also, it is sometimes suspected that certain complaints are dealt with (or more swiftly) if the compliant is made by a number of people as opposed to just one person.

Again, however, the responsibility appears to have been wholly shifted to the individual. This may not be clear or transparent to them. However, this also becomes more difficult for the individual where there are several examples of problem content and/or several perpetrators and/or the attack is going viral in some manner. In addition, these issues are also more difficult to deal with from the individual's perspective when the issue is live and possibly growing, as opposed to an historic problem.

There is an argument, therefore, that individuals in certain situations may need more assistance than is currently recognised, available or being provided by service providers.

7 US, NOT US

10.7 Across these issues is the internal perception or external argument from a given service provider that the problem content is always third party and therefore not content of, or from, a specific website. The service provider may argue that it is not responsible, in the sense of being liable and that this extends to there being no responsibility (legally, ethically or otherwise) to assist the individual. However, this is eliding two entirely different concepts, namely, liability and responsibility. Both concepts exist independently and should be considered in relation to problem online content.

8 TRANSPARENCY OF RTBF

10.8 Some may feel that there is a lack of transparency in relation to there being a RtbF available in relation to each given service provider. For example, RtbF filing mechanisms may not be expressly referred to on the main website. Referring to 'take down' or 'reporting' (generally) only, may mask the fact that RtbF is available. Should this be expressly referred to and highlighted separately in addition to general take down? If RtbF is referred to on the main website, is it buried or backgrounded as compared to other information and content? How transparent is RtbF process from start to finish? These are ample areas for research as they potentially have a great impact on how effective RtbF compliance by a given website actually is.[4]

---

4   Also see A Olteanu, J Garcia-Gathright, M de Rijke and M Ekstrand, 'FACTS-IR: Fairness, Accountability, Confidentiality, Transparency, and Safety in Information Retrieval' SIGIR Forum (2019) (53:2) 20.

9 RELIABILITY OF INTERNET SOURCES

10.9   One of the advantages of the internet over other information sources is that it is quick and simple to retrieve vast quantities of data about almost any subject, including living individuals. There is no quality control, however, over this data. It is as easy for individuals to publish unsubstantiated personal data on the internet as it is for organisations who prudently vet their data. It is therefore unwise, and probably unreasonable, for a controller to compile data about individuals using unsubstantiated material from the internet. This reinforces the issue that the important details about data extracted from the internet are the actual sources, which can be checked for unreliability, potentially under a verification enquiry, not simply the URL of the material on the internet. The issues of online abuse, revenge porn, sextorting, etc, heighten the importance of the virtue of digital forgetting, RtbF and *Google Spain*.[5]

RtbF has also now been recognised in the UK. In the case of *NT2*, a businessman was successful in obtaining an order that Google delete the notified references to him relating to a conviction ten years ago in relation to conspiracy to intercept communications. Google had refused the original notice. (A case relating to another individual at the same time was unsuccessful[6].)

10 INTERNET DATA SOURCES AND LOCATIONS

10.10   Particularly on the internet, the location of data may be only one aspect of its source. For example, the data held on the home page may be stored in a directory that is within a parent directory. This is its location. Its source, in contrast, may include the person who uploaded that data onto the home page. This person's identity, together with the URL, may forms the source of the information.

The source may therefore not be the place where the data are stored or from where they are retrieved, but the person who supplied the data to the data user. If a data user obtains personal data from a particular book, it will not be enough to include as its source its location in a library; the publisher and author will be its source. By analogy, if personal data are obtained from a particular home page, it will not be enough to include as the source the URL on the internet; the controller and creator of the home page will also be the source.

---

5   See, for example, P Lambert, *International Handbook of Social Media Laws* (Bloomsbury, 2014); P Lambert, *Social Networking: Law, Rights and Policy* (Clarus Press, 2014); V Mayer-Schönberger, *Delete: the Virtue of Forgetting in the Digital Age* (Princeton University Press, 2009); *Google Spain*; P Lambert, Understanding the EU Data Fine Rules (Kortext, 2021). Also see Olteanu, Garcia-Gathright, de Rijke and Ekstrand, 'FACTS-IR: Fairness, Accountability, Confidentiality, Transparency, and Safety in Information Retrieval' above.
6   *NT1 and NT2 v Google* [2018] EWHC 799 (QB) 13 April 2018, Warby J.

11 CLOUD

10.11 The popularity of cloud computing and virtualisation services with users, companies and increasingly official organisations is ever increasing. However, there are real concerns in relation to data protection, data security,[7] continuity, discovery, liability, record keeping, etc.[8] One commentator refers to cloud computing as 'the privacy storm on the horizon'.[9] Any organisation considering cloud services needs to carefully consider both the advantages, disadvantages and any assessments and contract assurances that will be required. Such organisations, as well as the service operators, also need to acquaint themselves with how they ensure data protection compliance and can respond to RtbF complaints.

12 INTERNET OF THINGS

10.12 The beginning of the so-called Internet of Things (IoT) or connected devices,[10] is now well publicised. However, the full consideration of the data protection implications are yet to be fully appreciated. Organisations need to appreciate the implications for employees, users and their compliance systems. Manufacturers must assist in identifying and reducing these risks as the new risk and assessment tools of the GDPR.

13 ON-SITE/OFF-SITE

10.13 Organisations must tackle the issues presented by employees not just working on-site, but also travelling and working at home or other locations off-site. This can impact, for example, both the security and security risks regarding the personal data collected and processed by the organisation. It also means that devices may be taken off-site and or that third-party devices may exist which are utilised to access the organisation's systems remotely.

---

7   See, eg, C Soghoian, 'Caught in the Cloud: Privacy, Encryption, and Government Back Doors in the Web 2.0 Era' *Journal of Telecommunications & High Technology Law* (2010) (8) 359. Also note U Pagallo, 'Robots in the Cloud With Privacy: A New Threat to Data Protection?' *Computer Law & Security Report* (2013) (29:5) 501.

8   ICO, *Guidance on the Use of Cloud Computing.* Available at: https://ico.org.uk; Article 29 Working Party, *Opinion 05/2012 on Cloud Computing,* WP 196, 1 July 2012; P Lanois, 'Caught in the Clouds: The Web 2.0, Cloud Computing, and Privacy?' *Northwestern Journal of Technology and Intellectual Property* (2010)(29:9); FM Pinguelo and BV Muller, 'Avoid the Rainy Day: Survey of US Cloud Computing Caselaw' *Boston College Intellectual Property & Technology Forum* (2011) 1; IR Kattan, 'Cloudy Privacy Protections: Why the Stored Communications Act Fails to Protect the Privacy of Communications Stored in the Cloud' *Vandenburg Journal of Entertainment and Technology Law* (2010–2011)(13) 617.

9   AC DeVere, 'Cloud Computing: Privacy Storm on the Horizon?' *Albany Law Journal* (2010) (20) 365.

10 SK Mizrahi, 'Ontario's New Invasion of Privacy Torts: Do They Offer Monetary Redress for Violations Suffered Via the Internet of Things?' *Western Journal of Legal Studies* (2018) (8:1) COV2, 37.

14   GDPR AND DIRECTIVE: ENHANCED PROVISIONS

10.14   One of the more important extensions and enhancements relates to RtbF; the 'right to be forgotten and to erasure, which consists of securing from the [data] controller the erasure of personal data as well prevention of any further dissemination of his data'.[11] It is also said to interface with the new right to data portability[12]). RtbF is even more enhanced in instances where the personal data was originally disclosed when the individual data subject was a child.[13]

Some commentators refer to the option of an entire 'clean slate'.[14]

> The use of data from social networks in employment contexts is a representative example. Personal data such as photos taken in private contexts have been used to refuse job positions and fire people. But forgetfulness is larger. It is one dimension of how people deal with their own history, being related not only to leaving the past behind but also to living in the present without the threat of a kind of "Miranda" warning, where whatever you say can be used against you in the future. In this sense the [RtbF] is closely related to entitlements of dignity and self-development. Once again, privacy appears as the pre-requisite of our liberties, assuring the possibility to freely express ourselves and move freely on the street ...[15]

---

11   *Ibid* at 254–262 at 256.
12   *Ibid.*
13   GDPR, Art 17(1)(f).
14   *Ibid* at 254–262 at 257. In terms of criminal convictions and the issue of deletion note, see *Chief Constable of Humberside v Information Commissioner and another* [2009] EWCA Civ 1079 where a deletion notice was refused, largely on crime policy issues. However, the ECHR has held that there was a breach in the context of an historical disclosure of a person's caution record in the context of an employment application. In this instance there was also an intervening change in weeding policy and certain police records which were previously weeded, were no longer weeded. The ECHR held that '[t]he cumulative effect of these shortcomings is that the Court is not satisfied that there were, and are, sufficient safeguards in the system for retention and disclosure of criminal record data to ensure that data relating to the applicant's private life have not been, and will not be, disclosed in violation of her right to respect for her private life. The retention and disclosure of the applicant's caution data accordingly cannot be regarded as being in accordance with the law. There has therefore been a violation of Article 8 of the Convention in the present case'. *MM v The United Kingdom*, ECHR (Application No. 24029/07) 13 November 2012, para. 207. The ECHR also held a violation in relation to the retention of fingerprint and DNA samples of persons acquitted of offences, in *S and Marper v The United Kingdom*, ECHR (Applications nos 30562/04 and 30566/04) 4 December 2008. See also *Goggins and others v The United Kingdom*, ECHR (Applications nos 30089/04, 14449/06, 24968/07, 13870/08, 36363/08, 23499/09, 43852/09 and 64027/09), 19 July 2011; Protection of Freedoms Bill and Protection of Freedoms Act 2012; Police and Criminal Evidence Act 1984 (PACE); Retention Guidelines for Nominal Records on the Police National Computer 2006 drawn up by the Association of Chief Police Officers in England and Wales (ACPO); Human Rights Act 1998; *R (on the application of GC) v The Commissioner of Police of the Metropolis* and *R (on the application of C) v The Commissioner of Police of the Metropolis* ([2011] UKSC 21 on 18 May 2011. Note proposals for a Digital Safety Act in the UK. Also note F Gollogly, 'The Blemish on the Clean Slate Act: Is There a Right to Be Forgotten in New Zealand?' *Auckland University Law Review* (2019) (25) 129.
15   L Costa and Y Poullet, 'Privacy and the Regulation of 2012' *Computer Law & Security Review* (2012) (28) 254 at 257.

RtbF is associated with the following:

- where the personal data is no longer necessary in relation to the purposes for which they were originally collected and processed (and the associated finality principle);

- where the individual data subject has withdrawn their consent for processing;

- where individual data subjects object to the processing of the personal data concerning them; and

- where the processing of the personal data does not comply with the GDPR.[16]

The GDPR and RtbF 'amplifies the effectiveness of data protection principles and rules'.[17]

Individual data subjects can have their data erased under RtbF when there is no compliance as well as where they simply withdraw their consent.[18] User control and individual data subject control are, therefore, enhanced.

The GDPR and RtbF create the following compliance obligations, namely:

- erasing personal data and not processing it further;

- informing third parties that the individual data subject has notified the deletion of the personal data; and

- taking responsibility for publication by third parties under the controller's authority[19] (see Articles 17, 2 and 8).

The GDPR also enhances and expands the various powers of the national data protection supervisory authorities.[20]

Pursuant to Article 17 of the GDPR, individual 'data subjects have the right to obtain from the controller the erasure of personal data concerning them without undue delay and the controller must erase personal data without undue delay where particular grounds apply'. The grounds are:

- the personal data are no longer necessary for the purposes collected;

- consent is withdrawn;

- the individual data subject objects per Article 21(1) (right to object) and there is no overriding legitimate grounds or the individual data subject objects per Article 21(2);

- the personal data was unlawfully processed;

---

16   *Ibid.*
17   *Ibid.*
18   *Ibid.*
19   *Ibid.*
20   *Ibid* at 260.

- there is a legal obligation to erase; and

- the personal data is that of a child in relation to an information society service under Article 8(1).

Under Article 17(2), it is provided that where the controller made the personal data public and must erase as above, the controller, taking account of available technology and costs of implementation, must take reasonable steps including technical measures to inform controllers processing the personal data that erase is notified.

In addition, under Article 17(3), there are limited carveouts. These are where 'to the extent that the processing is necessary':

- for the exercising the right of freedom of expression and information;

- compliance with a legal obligation or performance of a public interest task or under official authority;

- public health public interest;

- archiving purposes in the public interest, scientific or historical research purposes or statistical purposes; and

- establishment, exercise or defence of legal claims.

There is a significant stress on the proposed carve out being 'necessary'. If it is not necessary, it will not apply. In addition, the carve outs should not be seen as absolute, particularly where issues of alternatives, proportionality and layers or graduated processing or takedown may apply. The first carveout, it is suggested, may well transpire to be more nuanced than media entities might have first envisaged. This might include, for example, redactions, takedown of photographs, addresses, etc., where a media organisation seeks to maintain the data material in question. This will no doubt be an area of further elucidation through case law.

15 PROBLEM CONTENT

10.15 The field of deletion of online problem materials will continue to gather pace. This is particularly so as greater understanding of the harm which can occur through certain online content and activities, especially forms of online abuse. One aspect of this relates to the deletion of personal data. While *Google Spain* has received a lot of attention,[21] both academic and from the media, it merely reflected existing law under the DPD 95/46, not the more recent GDPR. Arguably, the GDPR expands this deletion or RtbF requirement. However, given the-then existing DPD 95/46, one can query the level of surprise at the decision.

---

21 J Jones, 'Control-Alter-Delete: The "Right to be Forgotten" – *Google Spain SL, Google Inc v Agencia Espanola de Proteccion de Datos' European Intellectual Property Review* (2014) (36) 595.

As individuals become more familiar with the GDPR, there will undoubtedly be an increase in notices under RtbF; where individuals' notices are refused, there will be an increase in complaints both to data protection supervisory authorities and to the courts.

16 ACCURATE

10.16 There are various principles required to be complied with by controller. One of these refers to an obligation that personal data must be accurate and kept up to date.[22]

Controllers must be careful when searching the internet for personal data to add to an existing data record. One should certainly record details of the source of the data. *Google Spain* and the GDPR also lay emphasis on the data accuracy issue and, where data is inaccurate, the individual data subject is assisted in their RtbF notification.

17 NOTIFICATION OF INACCURACY

10.17 If an individual data subject finds inaccurate personal data, they may commence an action for the court to order rectification, erasure or restriction of the data.

In *Google Spain*, the ECJ/CJEU held that:

> Article 12(b) and subparagraph (a) of the first paragraph of Article 14 of [the DPD 95/46] are to be interpreted as meaning that, in order to comply with the rights laid down in those provisions and in so far as the conditions laid down by those provisions are in fact satisfied, the operator of a search engine is obliged to remove from the list of results displayed following a search made on the basis of a person's name links to web pages, published by third parties and containing information relating to that person, also in a case where that name or information is not erased beforehand or simultaneously from those web pages, and even, as the case may be, when its publication in itself on those pages is lawful.[23]

18 CONCLUSION

10.18 These issues will be sure to develop in future as problem content issues continue to manifest themselves. The imperative to have solutions – and solutions which work – must clearly be met.

---

22 GDPR Art 5(1)(d).
23 *Google Spain*.

PART B

RIGHT TO BE FORGOTTEN: THE DETAILS

GDPR Article 17

Right to erasure (right to be forgotten)

1. The data subject shall have the right to obtain from the controller the erasure of personal data concerning him or her without undue delay and the controller shall have the obligation to erase personal data without undue delay where one of the following grounds applies:

    (a) the personal data are no longer necessary in relation to the purposes for which they were collected or otherwise processed;

    (b) the data subject withdraws consent on which the processing is based according to point (a) of Article 6(1), or point (a) of Article 9(2) and where there is no other legal ground for the processing;

    (c) the data subject objects to the processing pursuant to Article 21(1) and there are no overriding legitimate grounds for the processing, or the data Subject objects to the processing pursuant to Article 21(2);

    (d) the personal data have been unlawfully processed;

    (e) the personal data have to be erased for compliance with a legal obligation in Union or Member State law to which the controller is subject;

    (f) the personal data have been collected in relation to the offer of information society services referred to in Article 8(1).

2. Where the controller has made the personal data public and is obliged pursuant to paragraph 1 to erase the personal data, the controller, taking account of available technology and the cost of implementation, shall take reasonable steps, including technical measures, to inform controllers which are processing the personal data that the data subject has requested the erasure by such controllers of any links to, or copy or replication of, those personal data.

3. Paragraphs 1 and 2 shall not apply to the extent that processing is necessary:

    (a) for exercising the right of freedom of expression and information;

    (b) for compliance with a legal obligation which requires processing by Union or Member State law to which the controller is subject or for the performance of a task carried out in the public interest or in the exercise of official authority vested in the controller;

    (c) for reasons of public interest in the area of public health in accordance with points (h) and (i) of Article 9(2) as well as Article 9(3);

(d) for archiving purposes in the public interest, scientific or historical research purposes or statistical purposes in accordance with Article 89(1) in so far as the right referred to in paragraph 1 is likely to render impossible or seriously impair the achievement of the objectives of that processing; or

(e) for the establishment, exercise or defence of legal claims.

GDPR Recital 65

A data subject should have the right to have personal data concerning him or her rectified and a 'right to be forgotten' where the retention of such data infringes this Regulation or Union or Member State law to which the controller is subject. In particular, a data subject should have the right to have his or her personal data erased and no longer processed where the personal data are no longer necessary in relation to the purposes for which they are collected or otherwise processed; where a data subject has withdrawn his or her consent or objects to the processing of personal data concerning him or her; or where the processing of his or her personal data does not otherwise comply with this Regulation. That right is relevant in particular where the data subject has given his or her consent as a child and is not fully aware of the risks involved by the processing and later wants to remove such personal data, especially on the internet. The data subject should be able to exercise that right notwithstanding the fact that he or she is no longer a child. However, the further retention of the personal data should be lawful where it is necessary, for exercising the right of freedom of expression and information, for compliance with a legal obligation, for the performance of a task carried out in the public interest or in the exercise of official authority vested in the controller, on the grounds of public interest in the area of public health, for archiving purposes in the public interest, scientific or historical research purposes or statistical purposes, or for the establishment, exercise or defence of legal claims.

Recital 66

To strengthen the right to be forgotten in the online environment, the right to erasure should also be extended in such a way that a controller who has made the personal data public should be obliged to inform the controllers which are processing such personal data to erase any links to, or copies or replications of those personal data. In doing so, that controller should take reasonable steps, taking into account available technology and the means available to the controller, including technical measures, to inform the controllers which are processing the personal data of the data subject's request.

157

CHAPTER 11

The Right

Article 17 Right to Erasure (Right to Be Forgotten)

1.   The data subject shall have the right to obtain from the controller the erasure of personal data concerning him or her without undue delay and the controller shall have the obligation to erase personal data without undue delay where one of the following grounds applies …

I INTRODUCTION

11.1   Now we consider the specific GDPR Article specifying the erasure and forgetting right for individual data subjects. This is referred to below and in the following chapters. Article 17 of the GDPR provides that all individual data subjects have a right to erasure, also referred to as a right to be forgotten (RtbF), in relation to their personal data, in effect the GDPR RtbF[1] (and as may be distinguished from the earlier *Google Spain* RtbF and decision).

Readers when considering these issues will have to consider Article 17, as well as the definition of personal data,[2] the wide concept of personal data and data protection,[3] relevant case law, academic guidance on textual legal reasoning and interpretation[4] as well as the problem issues facing individuals.

The individual data subject has the 'right to obtain from the controller the erasure of personal data concerning him or her without undue delay' and the controller has the obligation to 'erase' personal data without undue delay. In the internet environment, this effectively includes the takedown of (problem) content.

2 RIGHT TO ERASURE/RIGHT TO BE FORGOTTEN (RTBF)

11.2   Chapter III, Section 3 of the GDPR is headed '[r]ectification and erasure'. This was already an important and topical issue and is now even more

---

1   M Magdziarczyk, 'Right to be Forgotten in Light of Regulation (EU) 2016/679 of the European Parliament and of the Council of 27 APRIL 2016 on the Protection of Natural Persons with Regard to the Processing of Personal Data and on the Free Movement of Such Data, and Repeali' *International Multidisciplinary Scientific Conference on Social Sciences* (2019) (6) 177.
2   GDPR Art 4(1).
3   N Purtova, 'The Law of Everything: Broad Concept of Personal Data and Future of EU Data Protection Law' *Innovation and Technology* (2018) (10:1) 40.
4   In relation to European interpretation and reasoning, see, eg, AIL Campbell, and M Voyatzi, *Legal Reasoning and Judicial Interpretation of European Law: Essays in Honour of Lord Mackenzie-Stuart* (Trenton, 1996).

important on foot of *Google Spain*[5] (see below) and also issues such as online abuse.

The individual data subject shall have the right to obtain from the controller the erasure of personal data concerning them without undue delay where one of the following grounds applies:

- the personal data are no longer necessary in relation to the purposes for which they were collected or otherwise processed;

- the individual data subject withdraws consent on which the processing is based according to Article 6(1)(a), or Article 9(2)(a) and where there is no other legal ground for the processing;

- the individual data subject objects to the processing of personal data pursuant to Article 21(1) and there are no overriding legitimate grounds for the processing, or the individual data subject objects to the processing of personal data pursuant to Article 21(2);

- the personal data have been unlawfully processed;

- the personal data must be erased for compliance with a legal obligation in EU or Member State law to which the controller is subject; and

- the data have been collected in relation to the offer of information society services referred to in Article 8(1).[6]

Where the controller has made the personal data public and is obliged pursuant to Article 17(1) to erase the personal data, the controller, taking account of available technology and the cost of implementation, shall take reasonable steps, including technical measures, to inform controllers which are processing the personal data that the individual data subject has requested the erasure by such controllers of any links to, or copy or replication of those personal data.[7]

Article 17(1) and (2) shall not apply to the extent that processing is necessary:

- for exercising the right of freedom of expression and information;

- for compliance with a legal obligation which requires processing of personal data by EU or Member State law to which the controller is subject or for the performance of a task carried out in the public interest or in the exercise of official authority vested in the controller;

- for reasons of public interest in the area of public health in accordance with Article 9(2)(h) and (i) as well as Article 9(3);

---

5   *Google Spain SL, Google Inc v Agencia Española de Protección de Datos (AEPD), Mario Costeja González*, Court of Justice (Grand Chamber), Case C-131/12, 13 May 2014.
6   GDPR Art 17(1).
7   *Ibid* Art 17(2).

- for archiving purposes in the public interest, or scientific and historical research purposes or statistical purposes in accordance with Article 89(1) in so far as the right referred to in Article 17(1) is likely to render impossible or seriously impair the achievement of the objectives of that processing; or

- for the establishment, exercise or defence of legal claims.[8]

In *Google Spain*, the CJEU held that:

> Article 2(b) and (d) of [the DPD 95/46] ... are to be interpreted as meaning that, first, the activity of a search engine consisting in finding information published or placed on the internet by third parties, indexing it automatically, storing it temporarily and, finally, making it available to internet users according to a particular order of preference must be classified as "processing of personal data" within the meaning of Article 2(b) when that information contains personal data and, second, the operator of the search engine must be regarded as the "controller" in respect of that processing, within the meaning of Article 2(d).

> Article 4(1)(a) of [the DPD 95/46] is to be interpreted as meaning that processing of personal data is carried out in the context of the activities of an establishment of the controller on the territory of a Member State, within the meaning of that provision, when the operator of a search engine sets up in a Member State a branch or subsidiary which is intended to promote and sell advertising space offered by that engine and which orientates its activity towards the inhabitants of that Member State.[9]

This case arises under the prior DPD 95/46 prior to the GDPR. However, it clarifies and confirms on the instant facts that a search engine website service is processing and can be required (even under the DPD 95/46) to delete particular personal data.[10] This continues to apply under the GDPR.

The CJEU in *Google Spain* further clarifies and confirms that an entity or organisation can be responsible under the data protection regime by virtue of a subsidiary promoting (or 'intended to promote') and sell advertising for the entity (in this instance a search engine) which targets ('orientates its activity towards') people in a Member State.[11]

---

8   *Ibid* Art 17(3). In relation to the original draft, etc, see, eg, G Sartor, 'The Right to be Forgotten in the Draft Data Protection Regulation' *International Data Privacy Law* (2015) (5:1) 64. Also A Mantelero, 'The EU Proposal for a General Data Protection Regulation and the Roots of the "Right to be Forgotten"' *Computer Law and Security Report* (2013) (29:3) 229.
9   See *Google Spain SL and Google Inc v Agencia Española de Protección de Datos and Mario Costeja González*. Also, see P Lambert, *International Handbook of Social Media Laws* (Bloomsbury 2014); P Lambert, *Social Networking: Law, Rights and Policy* (Clarus Press 2014); V Mayer-Schönberger, *Delete: the Virtue of Forgetting in the Digital Age* (Princeton, 2009).
10   *Google Spain SL and Google Inc v Agencia Española de Protección de Datos and Mario Costeja González*.
11   *Ibid.*

3 ERASURE AND FORGETTING

11.3

> *Right to erasure ("right to be forgotten")*[12]

The heading to the provision refers to the right to be forgotten in brackets after a description of what the right is, namely, being a right to erasure. The right permits individual data subjects to seek and obtain the erasure or forgetting of their personal data.

The individual data subject shall have the right to obtain from the controller the erasure of personal data concerning him or her without undue delay and the controller shall have the obligation to erase personal data without undue delay.

The section heading refers to the right as being a 'right to erasure'. The data in question must be deleted by erasure. The reference to the 'right to be forgotten' only comes after reference to the 'right to erasure' and furthermore is in brackets. These both signify that the predominant takeaway is that the right is the right to erasure. The reference also could suggest that the right to erasure can also be known as the right to be forgotten, but that the right to be forgotten is not separate, outside or stand alone from the *erasure* right.

Notwithstanding that the public and the media may prefer to use the term right to be forgotten, from the legal perspective the provision is more appropriately described as the erasure right.

4 TO WHOM? THE INDIVIDUAL DATA SUBJECT

11.4

> *The data subject shall have the right*[13]

It is important to always assess who may invoke a particular right and to whom the right applies. In this instance, the provision makes clear that this particular right applies to and is directed for the benefit of the individual 'data subject.'

An individual data subject is defined in the GDPR to mean the following:

> an identified or identifiable natural person.

> (GDPR Article 4(1)).

This concept is further described as follows:

> an identifiable natural person is one who can be identified, directly or indirectly, in particular by reference to an identifier such as a name, an

---

12 Heading to GDPR Art 17.
13 GDPR Art 17(1).

162

identification number, location data, an online identifier or to one or more factors specific to the physical, physiological, genetic, mental, economic, cultural or social identity of that natural person.

(GDPR Article 4(1)).

It is also clear that by referring to a natural person, the right may not apply to corporations or companies. This might also extend to other types of entities such as bodies and official organisations, departments or entities. However, in the case of small trading entities and sole traders, the individual may be difficult to separate from the 'entity' and one can see the argument that it is legitimate to include additional content in what might be legitimate to erase or forget.

In addition, it can be the impact or adverse impact on the trade, profession or business of the individual that is the main reason leading to the notice for erasure or forgetting. Indeed, this appears to be the case in *Google Spain* where the professional needed the old outdated content taken down as it was adversely impacting his present-day business.

5   ERASURE AND FORGETTING OF WHAT? PERSONAL DATA

11.5

the erasure of personal data[14]

The right requires that the personal data of the individual data subject must be deleted, erased and forgotten pursuant to a request made. The definition of personal data[15] and the wide concept of personal data and data protection[16] will also be relevant to consider.

6   WHO MUST ACT? THE CONTROLLER

11.6

to obtain from the controller the erasure[17]

The provision makes clear that the required action is directed at the controller. The controller must act and action the erasure and forgetting.

Organisations as controller should ensure provisions internally for recognising RtbF notices once received and for considering, complying with and responding to same as appropriate. On foot of the above case, this includes those entities

---

14   *Ibid.*
15   *Ibid* Art 4(1).
16   Purtova, 'The Law of Everything: Broad Concept of Personal Data and Future of EU Data Protection Law' above at 40.
17   GDPR Article 17(1).

which collect and index personal data and provide search results containing or containing reference and/or access to such personal data.

Additionally, such organisations should consider the extent to which processors acting on their behalf may or may also be processing such personal data. It may be that by virtue of the controller furnishing the data in question to the processor or the processor otherwise acting for the controller, the controller should also be responsible for the erasure and forgetting of such data. This might be copies of the data or depending on the circumstances may be original data.

Therefore, it is not expressly directed at the processor who may be acting for and at the direction and engagement of a controller. The individual data subject should make contact with the controller, not the processor acting for the controller.

To the extent that certain activities may be happening at the instigation, operation or technical control of a processor and there is associated content at issue, it would still be the controller whom engaged the processor to act for them, whom is the appropriate party to contact. The controller would then be required to review their own content and that of the processor in terms of dealing appropriately with the erasure and forgetting issue.

There can, of course, be instances where a processor is acting as a processor for a third-party controller; but also be a controller in their own right for other unrelated content or activities.

The circumstances will dictate who the controller and processor are in relation to particular content, who should be contacted and who has direct responsibility to act.

7   WHAT MUST HAPPEN? ERASURE AND FORGETTING

11.7

> *to obtain from the controller the erasure of personal data concerning him or her*[18]

What must a controller do when a notice comes in from an individual data subject? The provision provides that the controller must arrange 'the erasure of personal data concerning' the individual data subject. The controller must have the data erased and forgotten.

It is prudent, if not required, for the organisation to have in place appropriate processes, procedures, systems, training and resources *in advance of* any such RtbF notice arising from an individual data subject.

---

18   *Ibid.*

It is important to note that the right is express and clear. It is not possible to deny this right and respond ultimately to a different separate right. The controller cannot, based on its own decision and discretion, answer, fulfil or otherwise act in relation to a right which the individual data subject has not requested to be acted upon, instead of resolving the RtbF notice. A response to another right does not fulfil the controller's obligations under RtbF.

Unfortunately, there are examples where controllers are in breach of RtbF by way of the above, namely, ignoring RtbF request and making a change as a response to some other right. More worryingly perhaps, there are also examples where a controller may threaten the individual data subject who has filed a RtbF request, that if the individual persists, the controller will amend the problem content online but in a way that the individual may not want, has not requested and which may amplify the problem content: the controller will not be refusing the notice, but to all intent and purposes, will be materially ignoring it. One would hope that, over time, these problem instances will decrease and that RtbF will be fully and effectively complied with.

8 WHEN MUST IT HAPPEN? NO DELAY

11.8

> *without undue delay*[19]

As indicated above, the controller must ensure that the data are erased. The next question is how quickly must the data be erased? The requirement of the right is that the data must be erased and forgotten 'without undue delay'. The controller must not delay. However, if there is a delay it must not be an 'undue delay'.

The query arises as to what circumstances might exist for a delay to be a permissible delay and what circumstances are an 'undue' or non-permissible delay.

It will be clear that 'due' delay cannot be indefinite. One can also suggest unreasonableness or unreasonable delay would not be permissible. In addition, one should not assume that a delay is permissible if the delay is for a separate motive or merely not wishing to comply. An intention to delay and to be otherwise difficult or non-facilitative to a particular individual data subject (or worse individual data subjects more generally) would take the organisation away from what may potentially be due or reasonable delay.

Recital 59 provides further assistance. It states that:

> Modalities should be provided for facilitating the exercise of the data subject's rights under this Regulation, including mechanisms to request and, if applicable, obtain, free of charge, in particular, access to and rectification or

---

19 *Ibid.*

erasure of personal data and the exercise of the right to object. The controller should also provide means for requests to be made electronically, especially where personal data are processed by electronic means. The controller should be obliged to respond to requests from the data subject without undue delay and at the latest within one month and to give reasons where the controller does not intend to comply with any such requests.

The controller is obliged to respond to requests (which must include notices under the erasure and forgetting right) from the individual data subject 'without undue delay and at the latest within one month'.

There is, therefore, a one-month boundary placed on complying and/or responding to the notice. This will commence on the date that the notice is received by the controller.

Recital 85 and Article 33 of the GDPR refers specifically to the notification of data breaches to the appropriate data protection supervisory authority. It states that breaches must be notified 'without undue delay and, where feasible, not later than 72 hours'. One might suggest that a 'due delay' as regards complying with the erasure and forgetting right may occur within 72 hours. However, that should not mean that there might be other relevant circumstances to consider. If the matter can be dealt with sooner, it may become unreasonable to further delay.

Notifications regarding data breaches should also be made to the individual data subject affected. Recital 86 and Article 34 state that the communication should be 'without undue delay'. This 'should be made as soon as reasonably feasible' according to Recital 86.

'[U]ndue delay' 'should be established taking into account in particular the nature and gravity of the personal data breach and its consequences and adverse effects for the data subject'. This is referred to in recital 87. So, in terms of data breach notifications at least, some of the factors in considering and understanding 'undue delay' should include:

- the nature and gravity of the personal data breach;

- its consequences; and

- adverse effects for the individual data subject.

The latter tends to be ignored or underappreciated, it would seem, by many controllers in their consideration of these issues.

The use of the phrase 'in particular' also indicates that the items listed are merely examples, albeit emphasised for importance and that other factors and examples may be relevant in a particular instance and may be relevant generally. However, what these additional factors may be require further elucidation, whether by way of official advice, case law and or further expansion. It may be imprudent, however, for a controller organisation to make an assumption that a particular issue will not be a relevant factor (see 11.10 below).

9 OBLIGATION ON THE CONTROLLER: ERASURE AND FORGETTING

11.9

and the Controller shall have the obligation to erase personal data[20]

It has already been indicated above that it is the controller who must act. The right exists 'to obtain from the controller the erasure' requested. This part of the provision is absolute in terms of the obligation: the controller 'shall'. (There are other issues to also consider, however, see below.)

To reiterate, the provision also states that 'the controller [has] the obligation to erase personal data' in accordance with the erasure and forgetting right. This also characterises the right further, by providing 'the obligation to erase'.

The obligation remains with the controller, as opposed to a processor who acts for a controller. The individual data subject must identify the controller as regards the request to be made.

10 TIMING: NO DELAY

11.10

without undue delay[21]

As indicated above (11.8) the controller must act and comply without undue delay.

Obviously, a breach may occur by virtue of the controller not responding as required. However, there may also be a breach if the response was not in a timely manner.

That gives rise to consideration, however, of what may amount to so called 'due delay' and the expressly prohibited 'undue delay'.

An organisation may consider itself somewhat insulated by the phrase as regards delays of days if not weeks. In due course, the EDPB and/or respective data protection supervisory authorities may provide more specific guidance.

However, organisations should guard against an assumption that 'undue delay' may be some ubiquitous standard wholly subject to whatever uniform process(es) exist internally within the organisation. As highlighted elsewhere, RtbF notices as may be presented will range across a spectrum of interests, necessity and urgency. Some may be quite urgent and should be dealt with accordingly. There may, therefore, be actual 'undue delay' in the absence of immediate expedition. It

20 *Ibid.*
21 *Ibid.*

is not inconceivable that some circumstances require expedition in days or even hours. Such examples, however, may be less than the predominant or typical type of RtbF notice.

11 CONDITIONAL OR SPECIFIC RIGHT(S)

11.11

> *where one of the following grounds applies*[22]

The erasure and forgetting right is not an absolute general or overarching right. It is a right which is specified to apply to specific circumstances. The provision states that the right arises 'where one of the following grounds applies': So the right requires one of a specific set of circumstance to apply when the right can be exercised.

The provision is clear that only 'one' of the specified qualifiers need apply to enable the right to be exercised.

Therefore, an individual data subject should consider which one of the qualifying conditions applies. It may, of course, be the case that depending on the circumstances more than one of the conditions can be satisfied.

The individual data subject should also consider these in advance in case the controller may ask which ground is most applicable.

The grounds which need to be considered and one of which must exist for availing the right, are that either:

- the personal data are no longer necessary in relation to the purposes for which they were collected or otherwise processed;

- the individual data subject withdraws consent on which the processing is based according to point (a) of Article 6(1), or point (a) of Article 9(2) and where there is no other legal ground for the processing;

- the individual data subject objects to the processing pursuant to Article 21(1) and there are no overriding legitimate grounds for the processing, or the individual data subject objects to the processing pursuant to Article 21(2);

- the personal data have been unlawfully processed;

- the personal data must be erased for compliance with a legal obligation in EU or Member State law to which the controller is subject; and

- the personal data have been collected in relation to the offer of information society services referred to in Article 8(1).[23]

---

22 *Ibid.*
23 *Ibid* at (a)–(e).

12 DIFFERENT POTENTIAL RIGHTS

11.12 There are a number of different rights, grounds or streams of RtbF notices which may potentially arise. RtbF should not be considered solely as a single composite application or right. A number of different scenarios are expressly included in the GDPR provision, hence a level of added nuance and complexity arises. However, the intended availability of an erasure and forgetting solution to individual data subjects should not be discounted or glossed over. The presumption is that there is such a right unless ... an exemption trigger arises and is made out; not that only if an individual can surmount all the exemption issue might a possible RtbF situation arise to assist them.

In terms of considering the different potential rights, readers might consider the following:

* where the purpose has expired;

* where there is no longer consent;

* where there is an objection;

* where there is unlawful processing;

* where there is a legal obligation of erasure and forgetting;

* where there is data relating to a child (in particular, child information society services data);

* where there is an additional obligation; and

* to ensure specific and appropriate follow on or follow through actions.

Again, just as with certain other concepts, there should be a wide purposeful perspective and scope taken.[24]

13 THE SPECIFIC RIGHT(S) TO BE FORGOTTEN

11.13 There is merit in considering that there is a need for more than one RtbF. A child has more interest in erasure, forgetting and takedown than an adult might have. The exuberance of youth and student life also leans in favour of the need for such a right.

There can also be degrees of sensitivity and importance for adults. Private nude or sexually related images of an adult which may have been uploaded by way of a revenge porn attack would have to have a stronger claim of interest in erasure, forgetting and takedown than, say, an unflattering double chin image of a politician in a public political setting.

---

24 Purtova, 'The Law of Everything: Broad Concept of Personal Data and Future of EU Data Protection Law' above at 40; GDPR Art 4(1).

These types of attacks, namely revenge porn, are also emphasised by way of an increasing number of criminal offences relating to the act of a revenge porn in an increasing number of countries world-wide. In these and other instances where a criminal statute may have been breached, one might consider that there are strong grounds or interests in having erasure, forgetting and takedown.

However, it might also be considered that having an independent right to erasure and forgetting, while important in and of itself, is important especially because a criminal law or other solution is not available to the injured data subject. This may be the best available remedy to meet the needs and interests of the individual victim or data subject.

Similarly, strong claims might exist in the unfortunate examples where an individual may be being blackmailed with images. 'Sextortion' can arise where an individual may have been duped or tricked into providing a revealing image or video chat. Typically, an errant person deliberately poses as a romantic friend or online match. After an individual has been tricked, the attacker blackmails them, either demanding that they pay money or undertake certain actions; if they refuse, the attacker threatens to publish the images on the internet or, in some instances, to send the images to their family and/or school or employer. There are several examples where this has occurred. There are also several examples where people have taken their own lives because of this type of online abuse (OA).

One can easily see the need to have a right or remedy to get material taken down from the internet – even where the culprit is not directly identified or within reach.

There are several potential crimes applicable to sextortion, but that in no way undermines the need or appropriateness for a separate erasure, forgetting or takedown solution being available to victims.

One of the issues which will need to be increasingly examined is the need to recognise that there is justification to ensure *rights* to erasure, forgetting or takedown, not just one composite right. While this is not expressed in Article 17, one might argue that it is implied that there is more than one right to erasure and forgetting. Even where there might be disagreement on this point, it is quite clear that the Article's provision does go some way towards recognising that there are different interests and gravity of interest in obtaining the solution which erasure, forgetting or takedown can affect for an individual. For example, the erasure, forgetting or takedown interests of children are separate and distinct in clause (f) from other interests or needs referred to.

Just as there is a wide definition of personal data[25] and wide concepts of personal data and data protection,[26] the rights may also be interpreted somewhat widely.

---

25 *Ibid* Art 4(1).
26 Purtova, 'The Law of Everything: Broad Concept of Personal Data and Future of EU Data Protection Law' above at 40.

The intention must be to protect individual data subjects in a meaningful and purposeful manner.

14   QUALIFYING FACTORS

11.14   The qualifying factors for the right are:[27]

(a)   the personal data are no longer necessary in relation to the purposes for which they were collected or otherwise processed;

(b)   the data subject withdraws consent on which the processing is based according to Article 6(1)(a), or Article 9(2)(a) and where there is no other legal ground for the processing;

Article 6(1)(a) refers to consent and the lawfulness of processing for general personal data. It states '[p]rocessing shall be lawful only if and to the extent that at least one of the following applies: ... (a) the data subject has given consent to the processing of his or her personal data for one or more specific purposes'.

Article 9(2)(a) refers to explicit consent and processing for special categories of personal data. It states 'the data subject has given explicit consent to the processing of those personal data for one or more specified purposes except where Union or Member State law provide that the prohibition [on processing special categories of personal data] may not be lifted by the data subject'.

(c)   the data subject objects to the processing pursuant to Article 21(1) and there are no overriding legitimate grounds for the processing, or the data subject objects to the processing pursuant to Article 21(2);

Article 21(1) refers to the right to object. It states that the individual 'data subject shall have the right to object, on grounds relating to his or her particular situation, at any time to processing of personal data concerning him or her which is based on point (e) or (f) of Article 6(1), including profiling based on those provisions. The controller shall no longer process the personal data unless the controller demonstrates compelling legitimate grounds for the processing which override the interests, rights and freedoms of the data subject or for the establishment, exercise or defence of legal claims'.

(d)   the personal data have been unlawfully processed;

(e)   the personal data must be erased for compliance with a legal obligation in EU or Member State law to which the controller is subject;

(f)   the personal data have been collected in relation to the offer of information society services referred to in Article 8(1).

---

27   GDPR Art 17(1)(a)–(e).

Article 8 refers to conditions applicable to child's consent in relation to information society services. Article 8(1) states: '[w]here point (a) of Article 6(1) applies, in relation to the offer of information society services directly to a child, the processing of the personal data of a child shall be lawful where the child is at least 16 years old. Where the child is below the age of 16 years, such processing shall be lawful only if and to the extent that consent is given or authorised by the holder of parental responsibility over the child.' It adds that 'Member States may provide by law for a lower age for those purposes provided that such lower age is not below 13 years.'

15 CONCLUSION

11.15 EU laws are typically divided into 'recitals' and 'Articles'. An Article provides the main legal provisions and measures. Recitals are not legal provisions, but rather provide background and guidance on the aim of the legal provisions. The recitals are often used in legal cases to help interpret the legal provisions and to understand the intentions of the legislators. The GDPR (and UK GDPR) contains Articles and recitals, which help to explain the main Article provisions. These are referred to in greater detail below. There are also certain exceptions to consider in relation to RtbF (see Chapter 14 below for further details). There are also certain additional rights to consider, such as the right to rectification (see Chapter 13 below for further details).

CHAPTER 12

The RtbF Rights and Streams

Article 17

[T]he ... right [exists] where one of the following ... applies:

(a) the personal data are no longer necessary in relation to the purposes for which they were collected or otherwise processed;

(b) the data subject withdraws consent on which the processing is based according to point (a) of Article 6(1), or point (a) of Article 9(2) and where there is no other legal ground for the processing;

(c) the data subject objects to the processing pursuant to Article 21(1) and there are no overriding legitimate grounds for the processing, or the data subject objects to the processing pursuant to Article 21(2);

(d) the personal data have been unlawfully processed;

(e) the personal data have to be erased for compliance with a legal obligation in Union or Member State law to which the controller is subject;

(f) the personal data have been collected in relation to the offer of information society services referred to in Article 8(1).

2. Where the controller has made the personal data public and is obliged pursuant to paragraph 1 to erase the personal data, the controller, taking account of available technology and the cost of implementation, shall take reasonable steps, including technical measures, to inform controllers which are processing the personal data that the data subject has requested the erasure by such controllers of any links to, or copy or replication of, those personal data.

I INTRODUCTION

12.1 The different General Data Protection Rights (GDPR) rights or grounds for RtbF are referred to in greater detail below. These will need to be considered carefully in each instance, as well as other wider issues such as the Charter, case law (eg, Google Spain[1]), the definitions (eg, the definition of personal data[2]) and

---

1 *Google Spain SL, Google Inc v Agencia Española de Protección de Datos (AEPD), Mario Costeja González*, Court of Justice (Grand Chamber), Case C-131/12, 13 May 2014.
2 GDPR Art 4(1).

the wider concepts of personal data and data protection.[3] In addition, it is noted that this remains a developing area, notwithstanding history and context going back to 2000,[4] 1995,[5] and even earlier.

2 DIFFERENT POTENTIAL RIGHTS

12.2 In the first instance it should be noted that RtbF erasure, forgetting and takedown can be requested on a no-fault basis regardless of a specific problem issue arising. An individual can decide themselves that they do not want it or that it is better to stop the processing of certain personal data. It can also be precautionary to take certain material down because of general safety concerns.

There are several different rights, grounds or streams of RtbF and RtbF notices which may potentially arise. RtbF should not be considered solely as a single composite stream or right. A number of different scenarios are expressly included in the GDPR provision, hence a level of added nuance and complexity arises. However, the intended purpose of the availability of and to an erasure, forgetting and takedown solution to individual data subjects should not be discounted or glossed over. The presumption is that there is such a right … unless an exemption trigger arises and is made out; not that RtbF only arises if an individual can surmount all the exemption issues first. In addition, practitioners and interested parties should not focus solely on Article 17 of the GDPR and without consideration of the Charter, case law and even other provisions of the GDPR (such as the right to object;[6] right to restriction of processing;[7] etc).

3 HEADLINE GDPR RIGHTS AND STREAMS

12.3 In terms of considering the different potential rights, grounds and streams of GDPR RtbFs, readers might consider the following circumstances as recognised in the GDPR:[8]

- where the purpose has expired;[9]

- where there is no longer consent;[10]

---

3   N Purtova, 'The Law of Everything: Broad Concept of Personal Data and Future of EU Data Protection Law' *Innovation and Technology* (2018) (10:1) 40. Also see P Lambert, 5 Essential GDPR Content Lists (Kortext, 2021); P Lambert, Essential GDPR Index (Kortext, 2021); and P Lambert, The UK GDPR Annotated (Kortext, 2021).
4   The date of the Charter of Fundamental Rights of the European Union.
5   The date of the DPD 95/46.
6   GDPR Arts 21 and 22.
7   GDPR Art 18.
8   GDPR Art 17. Also see Lambert, 5 Essential GDPR Content Lists; Lambert, Essential GDPR Index; and Lambert, The UK GDPR Annotated.
9   GDPR Art 17(1)(a).
10 *Ibid* Art 17(1)(b).

- where there is an objection;[11]

- where there is unlawful processing;[12]

- where there is a legal obligation of erasure and forgetting;[13]

- where there is particular data relating to a child (in particular child information society services data[14]); and

- where there is an additional obligation and right to ensure specific and appropriate follow on or follow through actions.[15]

4 DIFFERENT RIGHTS TO BE FORGOTTEN

12.4   *Google Spain* must be scrutinised as it highlights different or additional rights and streams in terms of RtbF, separate to the above streams as referred to in the GDPR. A real consideration is the extent to which a RtbF arises per *Google Spain* and per the Charter, separate to the GDPR. Recall that the decision in *Google Spain* expressly refers to the Charter as a basis for a RtbF – in addition to the then DPD 95/46.[16] While the DPD 95/45 has been replaced by the GDPR, the Charter remains.

There are different and separate streams for exercising erasure, forgetting and takedown. Given the different problem scenarios, there is some justification for suggesting there are, or are effectively, different Rights to be Forgotten (RtbFs). As we have also seen from earlier discussion, the interests of the individual filing a RtbF notice can be quite different. Adults can have relatively different interests than children. Online abuse (OA) can raise different interests and perspectives than other content. There can also be significant difference between outdated problem content and a live problem issue such as revenge porn which is going viral or being placed live on a growing number of websites. There can also be issues as between an instant live problem content issue on one website versus one where there is a viral or group element (eg, 'vigilante'/group attacks, 'Gamergate' type online attacks on female gamers or attacks on female game developers,[17] etc).

---

11 *Ibid* Art 17(1)(c).
12 *Ibid* Art 17(1)(d).
13 *Ibid* Art 17(1)(e).
14 *Ibid* Art 17(1)(f).
15 *Ibid* Art 17(2).
16 See *Google Spain*, decision point 4, at para 100(4).
17 See, eg, TE Mortensen, 'Anger, Fear and Games: The Long Event of #GamerGate' *Games and Culture* (2018) (13:8) 787; M Salter, 'From Geek Masculinity to Gamergate: The Technological Rationality of Online Abuse' *Crime, Media, Culture: An International Journal* (2018) (14:2) 247.

5 PROBLEM CONTENT

12.5   There is merit in considering that there is a need for more than one GDPR RtbF. A child may have more interest in erasure, forgetting and takedown than an adult. They have more of their lives ahead of them. Problem content can create more damage, over a longer period, for a child. The exuberance of youth and student life also leans in favour of the need for such a right being stronger than an adult, at least in certain circumstances and policy scenarios.

There can also be content with degrees of sensitivity and importance for adults, as opposed to other content. Private nude or sexual related images of an adult, which may have been hacked or uploaded by way of a revenge porn attack, one may expect, may have a stronger claim of interest in erasure, forgetting and takedown than, say, in an unflattering double chin image of a politician in a public setting.[18]

The importance of attacks such as revenge porn[19] are also emphasised by the increasing number of criminal offences relating to the act in countries around the world.[20] That this problem content is increasingly being criminalised reflects societal and policy attitudes towards revenge porn. In these and other instances where a criminal statute may have been breached, one might consider that there are strong grounds or interests in having erasure, forgetting and takedown in relation to the problem content online. (That is not to say criminal laws can fully replace RtbF laws. Both do different things and both are required.)

However, it might also be considered that having an independent right to erasure, forgetting and takedown while important in and of itself, it can be important especially because there is not a criminal law or other solution available to the injured data subject. RtbF may be the best available remedy to solve the needs and interests of the individual victim or data subject. Recall that the GDPR RtbF law is relatively recent. Also, not all forms of OA are expressly criminalised as offences (ie, in the sense of having a modern express offence created in their name).[21]

---

18 This is even if the politician is upset by the image. Note R Boost, 'Trump Calls Out NBC for Double Chin Pictures' *DigitalRev.com* (23 November 2016); A Dejean, 'Donald Trump Asked Media Not to Publish Unflattering Pictures. So the Internet Did This' *SplinterNews.com* (27 November 2016); E Wanshel, 'Trump Is Insecure About His Double Chin, Internet Takes It To Task' *HuffPost* (1 December 2016).

19 One description of revenge porn is 'the distribution of a private sexual image of someone without their consent and with the intention of causing them distress'. Referred to at UK Government, 'New Law to Tackle Revenge Porn' *GovUK*, Press Release (12 October 2014).

20 By way of example note the new revenge porn offence in the UK contained in the Criminal Justice and Courts Act 2015, s 33. The section heading refers to: 'Disclosing Private Sexual Photographs and Films with Intent to Cause Distress'. Note also the comments of Chris Grayling, the then Justice Secretary who states that 'we want those who fall victim to this type of behaviour to know that we are on their side. That is why we will change the law and make it clear to those who act in this way that they could face prison' referred to at N Titchener, 'What is the Revenge Porn Law?' *LawtonsLaw.co.uk* (19 September 2017).

21 On occasion, a new OA errant activity and content may be pigeon-holed into an old offence under pre-existing law. This is not always ideal. It may not always work. In addition, where an old offence does not have a modern activity name on it, there is likely going to be some element of under-use or under-prosecution. There may also be some element of under-reporting.

Similarly, strong claims might exist in the unfortunate examples where an individual may be being blackmailed with images. 'Sextortion'[22] can arise where an individual may have been duped or tricked into a revealing image or video which a third party obtains and uses to blackmail them. Often the person deliberately poses as a romantic friend or online match. After an individual has been tricked, the attacker blackmails the victim, demanding that they pay money or carry out certain actions; if they do not, their attacker threatens to publish the images on the internet or send the images to their family and/or school or employer. There are examples where this has occurred.[23] There are also examples where people have taken their own lives after this type of online attack.

One can easily appreciate the need and interest in having a right or remedy to get material taken down from the internet – even where the culprit is not directly identified or within reach. A fully effective remedy may in some circumstances require action inside and outside of the EU.

There are a number of potential crimes applicable to sextortion, but that in no way undermines the need or appropriateness for a separate erasure, forgetting and takedown solution being available to victims.[24]

One of the issues is the need to recognise that there is the justification to ensure *rights* to erasure, forgetting and takedown, not just one composite right. While *plural* per se is not expressed in Article 17, one might argue that it is expressly implied that there is more than one right to erasure, forgetting and takedown. Even where there might be disagreement on this point, it is quite clear that the Article's provision does go some way to recognising that there are different interests and gravity of interests in obtaining the solution which erasure, forgetting and takedown can affect for an individual. For example, the erasure, forgetting and takedown interests of children are separate and distinct in clause (f)[25] from other interests, needs and RtbF streams referred to.

Just as there is a wide definition of personal data[26] and wide concepts of personal data and data protection[27] provided for, the rights may also be interpreted somewhat widely, and in certain circumstances exception viewed narrowly.

---

22 See generally, C McGlynn and E Rackley, 'Image-Based Sexual Abuse' *Oxford Journal of Legal Studies* (2017) (37:3) 534; JF Clark, 'Growing Threat: Sextortion' *US Attorneys Bulletin* (2016) (64:3) 41; B Wittes, 'Cyber Sextortion and International Justice' *Georgetown Journal of International Justice* (2017) (48:3) 941.

23 There are increasing examples of the police calling to homes to notify parents that sexually explicit images of their child have been posted online. This is occurring in many countries.

24 It was an unfortunate use of language when a Facebook executive, Andrew Bosworth, said that 'maybe it costs someone a life' in a memo, taken by many to be at least insensitive, or worse, ignoring victims of online abuse and attacks. See, eg, R Sandler, 'Mark Zuckerberg Says a Facebook Exec's Memo Justifying Deaths in Order to Grow the Network was a "Provocative' Thing He Disagreed With" *Business Insider* (29 March 2018).

25 GDPR Art 17(1)(f) and referring to Art 8.

26 *Ibid* Art 4(1).

27 N Purtova, 'The Law of Everything: Broad Concept of Personal Data and Future of EU Data Protection Law' above at 40.

The intention must be to protect individual data subjects in a meaningful and purposeful manner, as opposed to a limited and strict manner which would be of little, if any, use to individuals.

In addition, the implications of the Charter and what rights – including RtbF rights – are created or arise must also be taken into account. After all, in *Google Spain*, the CJEU expressly referred to the Charter in the context of RtbF.

Further still, the use, interoperability, complementary and/or separate nature of the right to object,[28] etc, and the GDPR RtbF[29] may need to be considered.

6 PRE- AND POST-GDPR COMPARISON

12.6 Set out below is a comparison of the legal provisions referred to in *Google Spain* and the situation post the GDPR.

Google Spain and GDPR

Reference to legal provisions compared

	Pre-GDPR Article	*Pre-GDPR Specific Article*	*Pre-GDPR Heading/ Scope*	*Post-GDPR Article*	*Post-GDPR Heading/ Scope*
DPD 95/46	Article 2	Article 2(b)	Definitions	Article 4	Definitions
		Article 2(d)			
	Article 4	Article 4(1)(a)	National law applicable	Article 3	Territorial scope
		Article 4(1)(c)			
	Article 12	Article 12(b)	Right of access	Article 15	Right of access by the data subject
	Article 14	Article 14 first paragraph, subparagraph (a)	The data subject's right to object	Article 21	Right to object
NA	NA	NA	NA	GDPR Article 17	Right to erasure (right to be forgotten)

---

28 See right to object under DPD 95/45 Art 14 and GDPR Art 21.
29 GDPR Art 17.

	Pre-GDPR Article	Pre-GDPR Specific Article	Pre-GDPR Heading/ Scope		Post-GDPR Article	Post-GDPR Heading/ Scope
Charter	Article 7	Everyone has the right to respect for his or her private and family life, home and communications.	Respect for private and family life		Charter Article 7	Respect for private and family life
	Article 8	1. Everyone has the right to the protection of personal data concerning him or her.	Protection of personal data		Charter Article 8	Protection of personal data
		2. Such data must be processed fairly for specified purposes based on the consent of the person concerned or some other legitimate basis laid down by law. Everyone has the right of access to data which has been collected concerning him or her, and the right to have it rectified.				
		3. Compliance with these rules shall be subject to control by an independent authority.				

This indicates that the Charter and the Charter rights referred to are most important. These must be included in the consideration of erasure, forgetting, and takedown, noting that the Charter is separate to the GDPR. *Google Spain* both referred to and relied heavily on the Charter – in addition to the then DPD 95/46. It would be remiss, therefore, to simply refer to Article 17 of the GDPR when considering the ability and entitlement of a given individual in seeking erasure, forgetting, and takedown. It should not, at this remove, be automatically assumed that the Charter can be ignored, is not relevant or that issues of erasure, forgetting and takedown do not arise under the Charter separately or regardless of GDPR Article 17 right(s),[30] or GDPR Article 21 right(s)[31], etc.

Note further that the WP 29 states that the erasure, forgetting and takedown rights as acknowledged in *Google Spain* are 'recognised by the CJEU in the light of the fundamental rights granted under Articles 7 and 8 of the EU Charter of Fundamental Rights …'[32]

We shall now refer below to each of the respective rights and streams referred to under Article 17 of the GDPR.

Regulators and individuals may take a dim view of controllers or controller trends which seek to refuse RtbF requests or restrict the basis or volume of requests. For example, if a controller was to say there was no prior withdrawal of consent or objection (ie, 'you never asked us'; 'you never notified us') and RtbF request is refused.

GDPR RtbF Right I/Stream I: Purpose Expired

12.7   There is a RtbF where:

> *the personal data are no longer necessary in relation to the purposes for which they were collected or otherwise processed.*[33]

GDPR

12.8   The individual data subject can obtain and the controller is obliged to ensure erasure, forgetting and takedown where the 'personal data are no longer necessary in relation to the [original] purposes' (emphasis added).

Personal data must only be collected and processed in relation to a previously identified purpose and generally identified in advance of the collection and processing. As with all identified purposes, this should have a natural timeframe

---

30   That is, GDPR RtbF rights.
31   That is, GDPR right to object rights.
32   WP 29, guidance list of Common Criteria for the Handling of Complaints by European data protection supervisory authorities. WP 29, *Guidelines on the Implementation of the Court of Justice of the European Union Judgment on 'Google Spain and Inc v Agencia Espanola de Proteccion de Datos (AEPD) and Mario Costeja Gonzalez'* C-131/12, WP 225 (26 November 2014) 12.
33   GDPR Art 17(1)(a).

and expiry date. Once the activity and purpose has reached its expiry, the processing should cease and the personal data should be deleted.

However, deletion does not always occur for a variety of reasons, such as non-compliance, lack of procedures, third-party issues as the processing is automated and is not reviewed. The existing complaint cases to data protection supervisory authorities give examples of where controllers overhold or over-use personal data beyond its original purpose, when that purpose is now expired and spent.

In this instance, if the individual data subject feels that the data purpose has been spent or expired, they are able to ask that the controller to erases and is obliged to erase, the data in question.

The provision also refers to the data being 'necessary'.

If the data were never 'necessary' for a pre-identified legitimate purpose, then issues arise as to whether they were ever validly collected and processed in the first instance. This would emphasise that there is also no current valid basis to hold the data. The data should not be stored or processed and should be deleted. This would be an example of overbroad or unjustified collection and processing of personal data *per se*. This, however, is a separate point to that which arises in relation to the right provided for under this provision of the GDPR.

In terms of this particular right, the reference to 'necessary' suggests that at one stage there was a legitimate processing need for the use of the original personal data purpose in question – but that is now no longer valid. Once the legitimate purpose necessity has expired, there is an automatic right for the individual data subject to demand erasure, forgetting or takedown, and corresponding obligation on the controller to ensure the right is complied with.

If the controller wishes to contest the request under this right, it would have to be able to show that the data and the processing is still 'necessary processing'. One might consider whether 'necessary' is in some way a higher standard to meet than say 'legitimate' processing. If 'necessary' or 'necessity' processing is different from more general permissible processing, a controller might have to demonstrate a greater need to process the data requested to be erased, forgotten or taken down.

Recitals can often provide further interpretative assistance in relation to the meaning and understanding of the Article's legal provisions. Recital 66 of the GDPR states that '[i]n particular, a data subject should have the right to have his or her personal data erased and no longer processed where the personal data are no longer *necessary* in relation to the purposes for which they were collected or otherwise processed'[34] (emphasis added). 'Necessary' is a higher standard than, say, 'helpful' or 'useful' for processing. This notes that the data are no longer necessary and also that 'necessary' is in relation to the purpose(s) 'for which [the data] were collected'. This places the basis of when the purpose

---

34   It remains to be seen what 'or otherwise processed' may mean in this context.

is evaluated as being the original purpose at the time the data was originally collected.[35] Therefore, for example, if the data were only collected originally for Purpose 1, that does not equate to leakage or expansion years later to wishlist new Purposes 2, 3, 4 and 5. They are outside the original (permitted) purpose. Also, if the activities of Purposes 2–5 did not exist originally and are only being organised contemporaneously, they are outside the scope of the original purpose. If Purpose 1 has now expired or was otherwise time limited, there would appear to be no basis or permitted purpose justification to continue to use, process or store the data in question. It is also counter to understood norms (eg, fairness, transparency, prior notice, etc) for Purposes 1–5 to be so loose and fluid that one is not able to distinguish them and to know when one purpose ends and related deletions should occur.

Readers should also consider the principles of data protection, in particular, the principle of purpose limitation,[36] principle of data minimisation[37] and principle of storage limitation.[38] These may have added relevance on when personal data is necessary, when it becomes non-necessary; when a purpose is legitimate or not and when it expires.

Charter

12.9   While the DPD 95/46 has now been repealed, and replaced by the GDPR, the Charter[39] remains. The Charter was also relevant and was relied upon in the *Google Spain* ruling. Parties will be required to consider the Charter provisions referred to Articles 7 and 8.[40] These are set out below.

- *Article 7: Respect for Private and Family Life*

  Everyone has the right to respect for his or her private and family life, home and communications.

- *Article 8: Protection of Personal Data*

  8(1): Everyone has the right to the protection of personal data concerning him or her.

  8(2): Such data must be processed fairly for specified purposes and on the basis of the consent of the person concerned or some other legitimate basis laid down by law. Everyone has the right of access to data which has been collected concerning him or her, and the right to have it rectified.

  8(3): Compliance with these rules shall be subject to control by an independent authority.

---

35 That is, the original purpose, not a later additional new or extended purpose.
36 GDPR Art 5(1)(b).
37 *Ibid* Art 5(1)(c).
38 *Ibid* Art 5(1)(e).
39 Charter of Fundamental Rights of the European Union, 2012/C 326/02.
40 See generally S Peers, T Hervey, J Kenner and A Ward, *The EU Charter of Fundamental Rights, A Commentary* (Beck, Hart and Nomos, 2014).

These rights and provisions will continue to be relevant in RtbF disputes. The CJEU expressly refers and relies on the Charter rights either as a basis for or for part of the deletion, erasure, forgetting and takedown referred to in *Google Spain*. The extent to which these are standalone or complementary to the GDPR must be considered. No doubt these will be relevant in future cases, both before national data protection supervisory authorities and courts.

DPD 95/45

12.10   Prior to the GDPR, Article 14 of the DPD 95/46 entitled 'The data subject's right to object' provided:

> Member States shall grant the data subject the right:
>
> (a) at least in the cases referred to in Article 7(e) and (f), to object at any time on compelling legitimate grounds relating to his particular situation to the processing of data relating to him, save where otherwise provided by national legislation. Where there is a justified objection, the processing instigated by the Controller may no longer involve those data; …

This sets out a right to the individual data subject to object to the data processing and such data may 'no longer' be processed. Processing can include online processing. Note that this provides that this right arises 'in at least' the specified cases, so there can be other cases or instances where the right arises and can also be exercisable by the data subject. There is an interesting exercise of comparison, therefore, as to whether DPD 95/45 Article 14 is wider in this respect than GDPR Article 17(1) which appears to contain (at least in the GDPR) a fixed (a)–(e) list or vice versa.[41]

It should also be recalled that the GDPR RtbF of erasure, forgetting and takedown is contained in Article 17. The CJEU in *Google Spain* refers, inter alia, to the right to object contained in DPD 95/46 Article 14. The GDPR also contains a right to object, as contained in GDPR Article 21. Therefore, there is comparison to also be had in relation to DPD 95/46 Article 14 and GDPR Article 21. This is in addition to the GDPR Article 17. The GDPR Article 21 provides as follows:

> 1.   The data subject shall have the right to object, on grounds relating to his or her particular situation, at any time to processing of personal data concerning him or her which is based on point (e) or (f) of Article 6(1), including profiling based on those provisions. The controller shall no longer process the personal data unless the controller demonstrates compelling legitimate grounds for the processing which override the interests, rights and freedoms of the data subject or for the establishment, exercise or defence of legal claims.
>
> [2] [3] [4] [5][42]

---

41   However, perhaps the direct comparison in this instance is with GDPR Art 21, as both refer to a right to object.

42   Sub-paras 2 and 3 refer to direct marketing processing; sub-para 4 refers to information notices and transparency issues; and sub-para 5 refers to the use of automated objection filing.

6.   Where personal data are processed for scientific or historical research purposes or statistical purposes pursuant to Article 89(1), the data subject, on grounds relating to his or her particular situation, shall have the right to object to processing of personal data concerning him or her, unless the processing is necessary for the performance of a task carried out for reasons of public interest.

In some respects, this may initially appear somewhat more limited than DPD 95/46 Article 14. Separately, one might also consider in relation to paragraph 6 that in terms of media online, there can be commercial imperatives and reasons at stake.

GDPR Article 6(1)(e) and (f) refers as follows:

(e)   processing is necessary for the performance of a task carried out in the public interest or in the exercise of official authority vested in the controller;

(f)   processing is necessary for the purposes of the legitimate interests pursued by the controller or by a third party, except where such interests are overridden by the interests or fundamental rights and freedoms of the data subject which require protection of personal data, in particular where the data subject is a child.

Arguably (e) is quite limited and specific to official type activities. It may be limited from more general application.

Point (f) refers to the legitimate interest lawful processing ground. To that extent, it is also somewhat specific, albeit relating to all general controllers (and not limited to official activity only). However, the provision and right is also wide. It refers to processing based on point (e) plus profiling. It also refers to point (f) plus profiling. In addition, it also refers to 'personal data concerning him or her', thus any personal data; and which while linked in some way to (e) and (f) individually, the onus may be on the controller to establish that data was otherwise obtained and processed. If there is not a prior separate documented stream of collections, use and purposes and perhaps separate segregated databases, the controller may have difficulty in pointing to separation. It may also be necessary to consider whether there can be a temporal element and limitation to legitimate interest processing. In the context of erasure, forgetting and takedown and other objections, the circumstances may lead an individual to argue that their fundamental rights increase over time and are a more significant interest over time as compared to a gradually reducing claim of legitimate interest. Individual data subjects will also be aware that personal data held by a controller may not be permanent and that a mandated policy of purpose limitation,[43] storage limitation,[44] lifecycle and deletion is necessary (as per the principles of data protection). It is also wide in the sense that the motivation – or part of the motivation – of the individual data

---

43   The purpose limitation principle while contained in the GDPR, as previously, it also now introduces a concept of certain archiving which may also need to be considered in particular circumstances. See GDPR Art 5(1)(b).

44   GDPR Art 4(1)(e).

subject can relate to 'grounds relating to his or her particular situation' and which will vary both with the individual circumstances and widely across the range of potential activities and circumstances which may apply to various individuals.

However, the extent to which there may be differences as between the DPD 95/45 and the GDPR (respectively Articles 14 and 21), may be overtaken somewhat by the fact that there is an express GDPR Article 17 containing a RtbF or RtbFs. The individual data subject can avail themselves of GDPR Articles 17 *and* 21. In addition and noting the CJEU's references to the Charter in *Google Spain*, the individual data subject may also refer to these rights.

To the extent that the DPD 95/46 Article 14 has been viewed or interpreted as being or enabling a prior RtbF and the new GDPR RtbF is contained in a new Article 17 separate to the GDPR right to object (in Article 21), it remains to be seen what the linkage or continuity between them may be. It also remains to be seen what the past interpretation of DPD 95/46 Article 14 (including in *Google Spain*) may mean in terms of interpreting the new GDPR Article 17 – if indeed the same is possible in terms of continuity of like-for-like provisions. However, given *Google Spain*, it may be imprudent to assume that there is not a takedown or erasure and forgetting issue to consider under Article 21 and/or the Charter.

One might also consider whether some controllers may seek to refuse a given object notice if, for example, it is made in or as part of a RtbF notice. Consideration also arises as to whether online contact templates of a controller allow for different notices to be made simultaneously. The question arises whether users should be notified of other options on the page of each complaint or notice page. Possible design issues can adversely impact rights and their take up by individuals.

DPD 95/46 Article 12 (prior to the GDPR), entitled 'Right of access' provided:

> 'Member States shall guarantee every data subject the right to obtain from the controller: …
>
> (b) as appropriate the rectification, *erasure* or blocking of data the processing of which does not comply with the provisions of this Directive, in particular because of the incomplete or inaccurate nature of the data; …

Google Spain

12.11 In terms of the GDPR Article 17 RtbF Right 1/Stream 1 (Purpose Expired), it is also useful to review what the CJEU decided in the leading *Google Spain* case (relying on the DPD 95/46 and the Charter). The case held that:

> Article 2(b) and (d) of Directive 95/46/EC of the European Parliament and of the Council of 24 October 1995 on the protection of individuals with regard to the processing of personal data and on the free movement of such data are to be interpreted as meaning that, first, the activity of a search engine consisting in finding information published or placed on the internet by third parties, indexing it automatically, storing it temporarily and finally, making it available to internet users according to a particular order of preference

must be classified as 'processing of personal data' within the meaning of Article 2(b) when that information contains personal data and second, the operator of the search engine must be regarded as the 'controller' in respect of that processing, within the meaning of Article 2(d);[45]

This is directed at confirming online data on or via search engines can be personal data as referred to under the data protection regime and that the search engine is the controller as regards same. Similarly, other online service providers and websites will have personal data and will also be controllers. These activities are also, in general, commercial. There is also a differentiation between behind the scenes processing and public processing activities.

As regards erasure, forgetting, and takedown when the purpose has expired, this is the original purpose, not any subsequent additional purposes or activities. Any original purpose, even if permitted, does not equate to permitting or extending to additional later purposes.

The discussion in relation to the original purpose as regards website 1 and indexing and/or copying (and publication) by a third-party website or entity is not expressly included in this part of the decision. Equally, this does not engage the point of an original purpose expiring or becoming spent. The various issues engaged by third parties considering an original purpose, purpose timeline and expiry, are not promulgated upon in this instance.

Google Spain also held that:

Article 4(1)(a) of Directive 95/46 is to be interpreted as meaning that processing of personal data is carried out in the context of the activities of an establishment of the controller on the territory of a Member State, within the meaning of that provision, when the operator of a search engine sets up in a Member State a branch or subsidiary which is intended to promote and sell advertising space offered by that engine and which orientates its activity towards the inhabitants of that Member State.[46]

This more clearly refers to location issues and commercial activities. While this decision was quite predictable, it should also be borne in mind in terms of the new more expansive GDPR on this point and also in terms of anti-avoidance planning. This decision refers to the instant service provider, namely the search engine and does not need to delve into purpose, original purpose and third parties. Once the original collection purpose has expired, erasure, forgetting and takedown arises.

Google Spain also held that:

Article 12(b) and subparagraph (a) of the first paragraph of the DPD 95/46 Article 14 are to be interpreted as meaning that, in order to comply with the rights laid down in those provisions and in so far as the conditions laid down by those provisions are in fact satisfied, the operator of a search engine is

---

45   *Google Spain*, ruling, para 100(1).
46   *Ibid* para 100(2).

obliged to remove from the list of results displayed following a search made on the basis of a person's name links to web pages, published by third parties and containing information relating to that person, also in a case where that name or information is not erased beforehand or simultaneously from those web pages, and even, as the case may be, when its publication in itself on those pages is lawful.[47]

This confirms that removal, erasure, forgetting and takedown must occur. Interestingly perhaps, this refers to removal from the list displayed. It may be the case that there is also a need and circumstance for additional removals by, in this instance, the search engine provider. If any basis for list display must give way to removal, erasure, forgetting and or takedown, an individual might suggest there can be no separate internal use, nor any use other than that of a listing display, and that such uses in addition to *public listing* must also cease.

If the purpose has expired, there could be no purpose or other basis for use or processing and the main display 'purpose' use has expired, some may query whether there can possibly be any secondary personal data use purpose.

While this part of the decision highlights the obligation for removal, etc and highlights that this arises even where the original website may have the same obligation under this stream where the purpose has expired, this should be the original collection purpose by the original website. Thus, the purpose expiring may be argued to apply to both websites, primary and secondary.

Google Spain also held that:

> Article 12(b) and subparagraph (a) of the first paragraph of Article 14 of the DPD 95/46 are to be interpreted as meaning that, when appraising the conditions for the application of those provisions, it should *inter alia* be examined whether the individual data subject has a right that the information in question relating to him personally should, at this point in time, no longer be linked to his name by a list of results displayed following a search made on the basis of his name, without it being necessary in order to find such a right that the inclusion of the information in question in that list causes prejudice to the individual data subject. As the individual data subject may, in the light of his fundamental rights under Charter Articles 7 and 8, request that the information in question no longer be made available to the general public on account of its inclusion in such a list of results, those rights override, as a rule, not only the economic interest of the operator of the search engine but also the interest of the general public in having access to that information upon a search relating to the individual data subject's name. However, that would not be the case if it appeared, for particular reasons, such as the role played by the individual data subject in public life, that the interference with his fundamental rights is justified by the preponderant interest of the general public in having, on account of its inclusion in the list of results, access to the information in question.[48]

---

47   *Ibid* para 100(3).
48   *Ibid* para 100(4).

This refers to the 'point in time' at which the data exists and implicitly purpose issues and that the time and purpose and purpose expiry are relevant in terms of no longer linking, deletion, erasure, forgetting and takedown. It also makes clear that a finding of actual prejudice is not necessary.

One could opine that the types, forms and nuances are increasing and are more involved than in perhaps other areas of law and loss.

This also refers to the economic (commercial) interests of the controller being overridden, as well as those of the public.

There is reference to public figures; however, the standard is high referring to a 'preponderance' level.

Official Guidance: WP 29

12.12   It is always important to look at the official guidance which may be issued from time to time on data protection issues. In the European context, this is often issued by the European Data Protection Board (EDPB).[49] The EDPB includes representatives from all the respective data protection supervisory authorities. However, prior to the creation of the EDPB, the previous advisory body, the Article 29 Working Party (WP 29), issued assistive guidance following *Google Spain*.

The WP 29 guidance included a list of common criteria for the handling of complaints by European data protection supervisory authorities.[50] Some of these are potentially relevant to this RtbF right stream of the GDPR. The following WP 29 Common Criteria Questions or issues may need to be considered, in particular:

* *Condition 7*:

  Is the data up to date? Is the data being made available for longer than is necessary for the purpose of the processing?[51]

* *Condition 10*:

  In what context was the information published?

  (a)   Was the content voluntarily made public by the data subject?

  (b)   Was the content intended to be made public? Could the data subject have reasonably known that the content would be made public?[52]

---

49   See GDPR Arts 68–76. Guidance may also arise from the European Data Protection Supervisor (EDPS) and respective national data protection supervisors.
50   WP 29, guidance list of Common Criteria for the Handling of Complaints 12–20.
51   *Ibid* criteria 7.
52   *Ibid* criteria 10.

Note, however, that consent can be withdrawn. Content can also be something that can be made available online to a small group of friends, but subsequently be made available to many, many more, even in a viral manner. All the subsequent activity can be non-voluntary or without any intention by the data subject that it should be so additionally made available. It may even gain wider publicity a long time after the initial act. Even after there is wider publicity, the data subject may not become immediately aware of it. There may be consent for one limited purpose but not for any other activity or wider purpose. (See the next right in relation there no longer being consent.)

Note also that service providers can change their terms, policy as well as engineer, tools and settings over time. It is not unknown that what might have been restrictively set by a an individual, inadvertently becomes available to others when the service provider changes settings unknown to the individual. There are also examples where the individual may place viewing restrictions to only those they choose, but changes by the service provider reveals the private content to a wider or public setting, thus revealing the nature of some of the private content in a manner which the individual never intended or to which they did not consent.

The timeline and nature of changes by a service provider does not appear to be highlighted in detail as yet in the jurisprudence in relation to RtbF, but may become more important in future cases, as the implications and relevance come into greater focus. The nature of how content can become online problem content, notwithstanding limited intention and/or limited appreciation by the individual, due wholly or in part to the system changes of a service provider should not be ignored when considering Condition 10.

Amplification issues which may not be fully known to the individual and information which may not even be in the general public domain as yet (eg, internal to the service provider), may also be relevant issues in particular cases.

GDPR RtbF Right 2/Stream 2: No Longer Consent

12.13   There is a RtbF where:

> *The data subject withdraws consent on which the processing is based according to point (a) of Article 6(1) [ie consent], or point (a) of Article 9(2) [ie explicit consent], and where there is no other legal ground for the processing.*[53]

GDPR

12.14   This is a multi-faceted provision with different potential applications. It is useful to review if there ever was consent (or other lawful basis) to collect and process and, if there was not, there should be no reason to have the personal data

---

53   GDPR Art 17(1)(b).

in the first instance and it should be deleted per se and per this ground. It should no longer be processed.

The individual data subject is entitled to exercise their right to erasure, forgetting and takedown and the controller is obliged to comply where the individual data subject withdraws consent. However, this is complicated by adding the words 'on which the processing is based according to'.

This might mean that consent in terms of this right is limited. For example, it might mean that this right only refers to withdrawing consent to Article 6(1) (a) processing or Article 9(2)(a) processing. Therefore, potentially consent cannot be withdrawn to enable erasure, forgetting and takedown to be invoked for processing outside of Article 6(1)(a) processing or Article 9(2)(a) processing if and where this may be possible. Article 6(1)(a) refers to consent for general personal data processing; Article 9(2)(a) refers to explicit consent for special categories of personal data processing.

One might consider whether a user can withdraw consent, but other than under Articles 6(1), 9(2) or if the controller refuses this instant RtbF request.

The provision also adds another proviso, namely 'and where there is no other legal ground for the processing'. This suggests that even where consent is withdrawn as provided above, it may still be possible for a controller not to have to comply with an erasure, forgetting, and takedown right notice if there is some other legal processing ground. It is unclear as to whether this stems from a legal obligation on the controller or whether it includes some other basis for processing as contained in the GDPR.

However, the controller cannot invent a new later lawful basis if consent was the basis originally relied upon. From the individual's perspective it is now too late. Also, where consent is withdrawn, to permit a new processing basis could amount to a right to be undermined and circumvented.

Take a transaction example where a controller may feel that they need to maintain a record of the transaction for a certain identified period. While that may be the case, if consent was used and is withdrawn, the processing for any other purposes should certainly cease. Also, the record keeping processing is a non-live record state and access must be restricted for other uses.

This might require particular attention. For example, if consent is relied upon as the processing basis, then legitimate interest may not be appropriate. In addition, it has sometimes been recommended to rely on another lawful basis for processing other than consent; where no other ground is more appropriate than to consider relying on consent (assuming that it is – and could be – obtainable).

It may be that certain personal data is used for purpose 1, but some of the data is also used for purpose 2. But in terms of purpose 1, it is unlikely that there would be both consent and legitimate interest processing at the same time. Therefore, in those instances where consent is withdrawn, it may be rare for there to be some other basis to continue processing and upon which to seek to avoid complying with erasure or forgetting.

However, the same or overlapping personal data may sometimes be used for more than one purpose, eg purpose 1, purpose 2, etc. If consent applied for purpose 1 and purpose 3, then when consent is withdrawn and a request for erasure, forgetting and takedown is made, then it being unlikely for there to be any additional basis for purpose 1 and purpose 3, then the personal data should be deleted (ie, erasure, forgetting, and takedown) in relation to purposes 1 and 3.

An issue that may then arise is whether erasure, forgetting, and takedown for purpose and activities 1 and 3, that also means erasure and forgetting is required for purpose 2. In this example, consent was not used as the basis for the purpose 2 processing activities. Therefore, consent was not used and is not appropriate to be withdrawn – unless it is ever decided that consent can still be withdrawn even for, for example, legitimate interest processing. That is, consent can be withdrawn, but was not originally requested. Might it be argued that express consent was not requested under the consent ground, but any implied consent under legitimate interests can be validly withdrawn or withdrawn in the sense of being objected to. These are issues that may be considered in greater detail as more notices are considered under these provisions.

Another issue should be pointed out, namely, the reference to withdrawing consent. The individual data subject is required to withdraw any consent previously given to exercise the erasure, forgetting, and takedown right. It is not clear whether the consent needs to be withdrawn *prior* to making the erasure and forgetting notice or whether the consent can be withdrawn as part of and at the same time as the erasure, forgetting, and takedown right notice. In addition, it may be that either of these can occur at the instance of the individual data subject.

One possibility that may arise is for a particular controller to be somewhat glib and seek to refuse requests where there is no recorded prior consent withdrawal. It would be even worse if the same controller simply refused such a notice, did not request the consent withdrawn/consent withdrawn confirmation and did not advise the individual that the withdrawal has a requirement or prerequisite of the consent being withdrawn. So, the individual would have their RtbF notice refused, but without knowing why. A court or data protection supervisor authority to whom an individual data subject can refer the matter may not be sympathetic to such a glib reductive approach by a controller.

Recitals can often provide further interpretative assistance in relation to the meaning and understanding of the Article's legal provisions. Recital 66 of the GDPR states that '[i]n particular, a data subject should have the right to have his or her personal data erased and no longer processed ... where a data subject has withdrawn his or her consent'. It is not clear if this adds anything. However, issues arise such as whether consent withdrawal is implied by a RtbF notice per se; whether it can be included; whether it needs to be so included; or whether there must be some temporal difference between the two.

Consideration may also be directed to whether the legitimate interest ground can act as a fall-back processing basis subsequent to collection where consent was the original basis of data collection. So, for example, might an individual data subject be met with the argument for refusal to a RtbF notice filing on or after withdrawing consent, that the controller decides at its discretion that it wants to process via legitimate interest and not consent.

Charter

12.15   While the DPD 95/46 has now been repealed and replaced by the GDPR, the Charter[54] remains. The Charter was also relevant and relied upon in the *Google Spain* ruling. Parties will also be required to consider the Charter provisions referred to, namely, Articles 7 and 8.[55] These are set out below.

- *Article 7: Respect for Private and Family Life*

   Everyone has the right to respect for his or her private and family life, home and communications.

- *Article 8: Protection of Personal Data*

   8(1): Everyone has the right to the protection of personal data concerning him or her.

   8(2): Such data must be processed fairly for specified purposes and on the basis of the consent of the person concerned or some other legitimate basis laid down by law. Everyone has the right of access to data which has been collected concerning him or her, and the right to have it rectified.

   8(3): Compliance with these rules shall be subject to control by an independent authority.

These rights and provisions will continue to be relevant in RtbF disputes including this right stream.

DPD 95/46

12.16   The DPD 95/46 Article 12 (prior to the GDPR), entitled 'Rights of access', provided:

   Member States shall guarantee every data subject the right to obtain from the Controller: …

   (b)   as appropriate the rectification, erasure or blocking of data the processing of which does not comply with the provisions of this Directive, in particular because of the incomplete or inaccurate nature of the data; …

---

54   Charter of Fundamental Rights of the European Union, 2012/C 326/02.
55   See generally Peers, Hervey, Kenner and Ward, *The EU Charter of Fundamental Rights, A Commentary.*

The DPD 95/46 Article 14 (prior to the GDPR), entitled 'The data subject's right to object' provided:

> 'Member States shall grant the data subject the right:
>
> (a) at least in the cases referred to in Article 7(e) and (f), to object at any time on compelling legitimate grounds relating to his particular situation to the processing of data relating to him, save where otherwise provided by national legislation. Where there is a justified objection, the processing instigated by the controller may no longer involve those data; ...'

Google Spain

12.17   In terms of the GDPR Article 17 RtbF Right 2/Stream 2 (No Longer Consent), it is also useful to review what the CJEU decided in the leading *Google Spain* case (relying on the DPD 95/46, and the Charter).

The comments referred to above made in relation to Right 1/Stream 1 and *Google Spain* should be considered in addition to the comments below.

It was held that:

> Article 2(b) and (d) of Directive 95/46/EC of the European Parliament and of the Council of 24 October 1995 on the protection of individuals with regard to the processing of personal data and on the free movement of such data are to be interpreted as meaning that, first, the activity of a search engine consisting in finding information published or placed on the internet by third parties, indexing it automatically, storing it temporarily and finally, making it available to internet users according to a particular order of preference must be classified as "processing of personal data" within the meaning of Article 2(b) when that information contains personal data and, second, the operator of the search engine must be regarded as the "controller" in respect of that processing, within the meaning of Article 2(d).[56]

In the context of consent and explicit consent, there may not have been any direct contact or relationship between individual data subject and in the above case, the search engine controller. One issue which may arise then is whether a controller or search engine controller might seek to refuse a request by arguing that there never was consent, consent was not its basis of processing and therefore the issue of withdrawing a non-existent consent does not arise. Note that the right does not refer to primary processing (as then collected or copied by the search engine crawlers) and secondary processing by the search engine (by way of publication online via search), nor respective consent. However, courts and policymakers may not be amenable to a restrictive view that the individual must evidence a withdrawal to the original processor and or to the search engine to avail of RtbF. Bear in mind also the higher obligations and higher interests when the data is special personal data and express consent is referred to.

---

56   *Google Spain*, ruling, para 100(1).

Article 4(1)(a) of Directive 95/46 is to be interpreted as meaning that processing of personal data is carried out in the context of the activities of an establishment of the controller on the territory of a Member State, within the meaning of that provision, when the operator of a search engine sets up in a Member State a branch or subsidiary which is intended to promote and sell advertising space offered by that engine and which orientates its activity towards the inhabitants of that Member State.[57]

This does not expressly refer to consent issues.

Article 12(b) [re rectification, erasure and blocking] and subparagraph (a) of the first paragraph of the DPD 95/46 Article 14 [re objection right] are to be interpreted as meaning that, in order to comply with the rights laid down in those provisions and in so far as the conditions laid down by those provisions are in fact satisfied, the operator of a search engine is obliged to remove from the list of results displayed following a search made on the basis of a person's name links to web pages, published by third parties and containing information relating to that person, also in a case where that name or information is not erased beforehand or simultaneously from those web pages, and even, as the case may be, when its publication in itself on those pages is lawful.[58]

Article 14 as referred to above includes a previous right to object. This confirms that erasure, forgetting and takedown must occur with the search engine controller in at least the manner referred. This leaves open that there may be other information held. However, some may query whether the erasure, forgetting, and takedown needs to be even more extensive, or at least in certain circumstances. Where there is an objection this is generally not going to be so segmented as to differentiate between each form of use. Nor does it appear that same is required by RtbF tools available from controllers currently post *Google Spain*. Consideration will also arise as to whether the GDPR is at least the same as referred to above or even more extensive as many have suggested.

Article 12(b) and subparagraph (a) of the first paragraph of Article 14 of the DPD 95/46 are to be interpreted as meaning that, when appraising the conditions for the application of those provisions, it should inter alia be examined whether the individual data subject has a right that the information in question relating to him personally should, at this point in time, no longer be linked to his name by a list of results displayed following a search made on the basis of his name, without it being necessary in order to find such a right that the inclusion of the information in question in that list causes prejudice to the individual data subject. As the individual data subject may, in the light of his fundamental rights under Charter Articles 7 and 8, request that the information in question no longer be made available to the general public on account of its inclusion in such a list of results, those rights override, as a rule, not only the economic interest of the operator of the search engine but also the interest of the general public in having access to that information upon a search relating to the individual data subject's name. However, that would not be the case if it appeared, for particular reasons, such as the role

---

57   *Ibid* para 100(2).
58   *Ibid* para 100(3).

played by the individual data subject in public life, that the interference with his fundamental rights is justified by the preponderant interest of the general public in having, on account of its inclusion in the list of results, access to the information in question.[59]

As noted elsewhere there is no prejudice requirement, and there is a suggestion that the interest in some circumstances can increase over time. By comparison, where the original consent (where relevant) was a long time ago and now well after a once-off (or last) transaction there may be a suggestion that the right and imperative to erase, forget and takedown after consent is withdrawn (or otherwise) increases.

Official Guidance: WP 29

12.18 It is always important to look at the official guidance which may be issued from time to time on data protection issues. In the European context this is often issued by the EDPB.[60] The EDPB includes representatives from the respective data protection supervisory authorities. However, prior to the GDPR the previous advisory body, the WP 29 issued assistive guidance in relation to *Google Spain*.

The WP 29 guidance included a list of common criteria for the handling of complaints by European data regulators.[61] Some of these are potentially relevant to this RtbF right stream of the GDPR. The following WP 29 Common Criteria Questions or issues may need to be considered, in particular:

- *Condition 10*:

  In what context was the information published?

  (a)   Was the content voluntarily made public by the data subject?

  (b)   Was the content intended to be made public? Could the data subject have reasonably known that the content would be made public?[62]

- *Condition 11:*

  Was the original content published in the context of journalistic purposes?[63]

This may often be a simple question. However, it can also be more nuanced depending on the circumstances. We may have to distinguish how long a

---

59   *Ibid* para 100(4).
60   See GDPR Arts 68–76. Guidance may also arise from the European Data Protection Supervisor (EDPS); and respective national data protection supervisors.
61   WP 29, guidance list of Common Criteria for the Handling of Complaints by European data protection supervisory authorities. WP 29, *Guidelines on the Implementation of the Court of Justice of the European Union Judgement on 'Google Spain and Inc v Agencia Espanola de Proteccion de Datos (AEPD) and Mario Costeja Gonzalez' C-131/12*, WP 225 (26 November 2014) 12–20.
62   WP 29, guidance list of Common Criteria for the Handling of Complaints 12–20, criteria 10.
63   *Ibid* criteria 11.

journalistic purpose lasts and when it may be considered as spent. At a particular point in time there can be more of a commercial purpose than any current or live journalistic purpose. Also, while there may be an original journalistic purpose, we may have to consider a totally new, much later, secondary purpose of a commercial nature. The point is that we should not make overly broad assumptions.

GDPR RtbF Right 3/Stream 3: Objection

12.19   There is a RtbF where:

> *The data subject objects to the processing pursuant to Article 21(1) [ie right to object] and there are no overriding legitimate grounds for the processing, or the data subject objects to the processing pursuant to Article 21(2) [right to object to marketing processing (including profiling)].*[64]

GDPR

12.20   This right refers to their being an 'objection'. This presumably refers to an objection to the controller from the data subject. It should also mean for or on behalf of the data subject.

Need to Object

12.21   However, the query arises as to whether a notice or filing for erasure, forgetting and takedown under GDPR Article 17 is separate and distinct from an objection under GDPR Article 17. So, for example, must there be a RtbF notice filing and an objection? Are they different or can they be one and the same? This might seem overly analytical, but Google has already argued that the notice, complaint or objection was not a proper filing, complaint or objection and/or was not correctly filed. This argument was made in *NT1* and *NT2*[65] – albeit it ultimately abandoned this argument, at least in that case. It remains to be seen if any service providers will seek to make these types of arguments in future. However, in contrast to such defensive technical arguments, victims and individual data subjects may be denied their rights and remedies if an overly restrictive interpretation were successful. Certain online controllers have also stated that they never received a notice or complaint from an individual, even when online complaint tools were utilised. In addition, it is noted that the provision itself does not specify a particular manner, mechanism or way for objection, etc, thus any reasonable or common sense effort by the individual data subject should, in the main, be sufficient. It is also noteworthy that, in general, the individual data subject is a lay member of the public and not a professional or well-resourced corporate entity well experienced in the strict language and meaning of legal statute documentation.

---

64   GDPR Art 17(1)(c).
65   *NT1 & NT2 v Google LLC* [2018] EWHC 799 (QB) (13 April 2018) Warby J.

Objects

12.22   This right also may suggest a positive act of notice objection by the individual data subject.

RtbF Sub-streams

12.23   The notice objection must, it appears under this provision, be either pursuant to Article 21(1) processing or Article 21(2) processing. This, therefore, suggests two RtbF streams under this provision. That is not to suggest, however, that the notice filing of the individual data subject must expressly state or include reference to provision Article 21(1) or Article 21(2).

Objection Stream One

12.24   Another issue also arises from the above discussion. To the extent that a technical 'objection' is referred to and is meant to be expressly stated (in some manner) by the individual data subject under this right stream, but not under any of the other right streams, one issue that then arises is whether the other right streams are meant to create a positive obligation on controllers to automatically erase, forget and takedown personal data on a rolling forgetting basis even without being asked or contacted by individual data subjects. This might be referred to as a form of forgetting and natural obsolescence of personal data.

Article 21(1) refers to the individual data subject's right to object. It states the individual 'data subject shall have the right to object, on grounds relating to his or her particular situation, at any time to processing of personal data concerning him or her which is based on point (e) or (f) of Article 6(1), including profiling based on those provisions'. When there is such an objection or notice the 'controller shall no longer process the personal data unless the controller demonstrates compelling legitimate grounds for the processing which override the interests, rights and freedoms of the data subject or for the establishment, exercise or defence of legal claims'.

Therefore, there are even further sub-streams, namely, RtbF under (e) and (f) of Article 6 processing.

Article 6(1)(e)

12.25   Article 6(1)(e) states that '[p]rocessing shall be lawful only if and to the extent that … one of the following applies: … processing is necessary for the performance of a task carried out in the public interest or in the exercise of official authority vested in the Controller'.

There will be interesting discussion as to consent and legitimate interest and legitimate ground aspects of processing.

The references to public interest, official authority and vesting suggest some kind of official body and related official type processing – and which is necessary. It is unclear if 'task' and 'purpose' are one and the same or are separate concepts.

Article 6(1)(f)

12.26 Article 6(1)(f) states that '[p]rocessing shall be lawful only if and to the extent that at least one of the following applies: ... processing is necessary for the purposes of the legitimate interests pursued by the controller or by a third party, except where such interests are overridden by the interests or fundamental rights and freedoms of the data subject which require protection of personal data, in particular where the data subject is a child'.

There is an additional provision in relation to erasure, forgetting and takedown pursuant to an objection to Article 21(1) processing. Where the individual data subject objects to the processing pursuant to Article 21(1), the right to erasure, forgetting and takedown needs to be effected by the controller. It refers to a condition that 'there are no overriding legitimate grounds for the processing'. So the Article 21(1) objection erasure, forgetting and takedown will apply as long as there are no other 'overriding legitimate grounds' for (current or continued) processing. Note that the word 'overriding' suggests a higher, more important or superior standard than, for example, 'no *other* legitimate grounds'. If a higher-level standard is applied, this could limit the potential instances where the objection of the individual data subject to Article 21(1) processing could be 'overridden'.

Objection Stream Two

12.27 Where the individual data subject objects to the processing pursuant to Article 21(2), the right to erasure, forgetting and takedown needs to be effected by the controller. There is no additional condition as referred to under the above provision. Therefore, once there is an objection to Article 21(2) processing and erasure, forgetting and takedown is notified, the controller must comply. Note that the provision refers to the separate alternative 'or' and also places a comma before it. This second option to object is absent any inclusion of the reference to 'legitimate grounds'. This would suggest that it does not matter if there is any legitimate ground issue and that the RtbF notice filing must be complied with.

Recitals can often provide further interpretative assistance in relation to the meaning and understanding of the Article legal provisions. Recital 66 of the GDPR states that '[i]n particular, a data subject should have the right to have his or her personal data erased and no longer processed ... where a data subject ... objects to the processing of personal data concerning him or her'.

Charter

12.28 While the DPD 95/46 has now been repealed and replaced by the GDPR, the Charter[66] remains. The Charter was also relevant and relied upon in the

66   Charter of Fundamental Rights of the European Union, 2012/C 326/02.

Google Spain ruling. Parties will, in addition, be required to consider the Charter provisions referred to, namely, Articles 7 and 8.[67] These are set out below.

- *Article 7: Respect for Private and Family Life*

  Everyone has the right to respect for his or her private and family life, home and communications.

- *Article 8: Protection of Personal Data*

  8(1): Everyone has the right to the protection of personal data concerning him or her.

  8(2): Such data must be processed fairly for specified purposes and on the basis of the consent of the person concerned or some other legitimate basis laid down by law. Everyone has the right of access to data which has been collected concerning him or her, and the right to have it rectified.

  8(3): Compliance with these rules shall be subject to control by an independent authority.

These rights and provisions will continue to be relevant in RtbF disputes including this right stream.

DPD 95/46

12.29 The DPD 95/46 Article 12 (prior to the GDPR), entitled 'Rights of access,' provided:

'Member States shall guarantee every data subject the right to obtain from the controller: …

(b) as appropriate the rectification, erasure or blocking of data the processing of which does not comply with the provisions of this Directive, in particular because of the incomplete or inaccurate nature of the data; …'

The DPD 95/46 Article 14 (prior to the GDPR), entitled 'The data subject's right to object,' provided:

'Member States shall grant the data subject the right:

(a) at least in the cases referred to in Article 7(e) and (f), to object at any time on compelling legitimate grounds relating to his particular situation to the processing of data relating to him, save where otherwise provided by national legislation. Where there is a justified objection, the processing instigated by the controller may no longer involve those data; …'

Google Spain

12.30 In terms of the GDPR Article 17 RtbF Right 2/Stream 2 (No Longer Consent), it is also useful to review what the CJEU decided in *Google Spain* (relying on the DPD 95/46 and the Charter).

---

67 See generally Peers, Hervey, Kenner and Ward, *The EU Charter of Fundamental Rights, A Commentary.*

The comments referred to above made in relation to Right 1/Stream 1 and *Google Spain* should be considered in addition to the comments below.

> Article 12(b) and subparagraph (a) of the first paragraph of the DPD 95/46 Article 14 are to be interpreted as meaning that, in order to comply with the rights laid down in those provisions and in so far as the conditions laid down by those provisions are in fact satisfied, the operator of a search engine is obliged to remove from the list of results displayed following a search made on the basis of a person's name links to web pages, published by third parties and containing information relating to that person, also in a case where that name or information is not erased beforehand or simultaneously from those web pages, and even, as the case may be, when its publication in itself on those pages is lawful.'[68]

The above sections of the prior legislation are relevant and reflect the rights relating to rectification, erasure and blocking, and to the right to object. The case confirms that erasure, forgetting and takedown must occur. An issue arises as to whether more is or should also be required per the new GDPR, particularly where consent no longer exists. Restricted processing, such as transaction record-keeping purposes, is limited and would not require or permit web or web results display. (Some jurisdictions do, however, refer to a legal obligation for property sale prices to be available publicly and which may directly or indirectly identify or relate to an individual).

In *Google Spain* it was held that:

> Article 12(b) and subparagraph (a) of the first paragraph of Article 14 of the DPD 95/46 are to be interpreted as meaning that, when appraising the conditions for the application of those provisions, it should inter alia be examined whether the individual data subject has a right that the information in question relating to him personally should, at this point in time, no longer be linked to his name by a list of results displayed following a search made on the basis of his name, without it being necessary in order to find such a right that the inclusion of the information in question in that list causes prejudice to the individual data subject. As the individual data subject may, in the light of his fundamental rights under Charter Articles 7 and 8, request that the information in question no longer be made available to the general public on account of its inclusion in such a list of results, those rights override, as a rule, not only the economic interest of the operator of the search engine but also the interest of the general public in having access to that information upon a search relating to the individual data subject's name. However, that would not be the case if it appeared, for particular reasons, such as the role played by the individual data subject in public life, that the interference with his fundamental rights is justified by the preponderant interest of the general public in having, on account of its inclusion in the list of results, access to the information in question.[69]

Similar to previous comments, the need or imperative for erasure, forgetting, and takedown may increase over time.

---

68   *Google Spain*, ruling, para 100(3).
69   *Ibid* para 100(4).

Official Guidance: WP 29

12.31   It is always important to look at the official guidance which may be issued from time to time on data protection issues. In the European context this is often issued by the EDPB.[70] The EDPB includes representatives from the respective data regulators. However, prior to the GDPR (and the GDPR creation of the EDPB) the previous advisory body, the WP 29 issued assistive guidance in relation to *Google Spain*.

The WP 29 guidance included a list of common criteria for the handling of complaints by European data regulators.[71] Some of these are potentially relevant to this RtbF right stream of the GDPR. The following WP 29 Common Criteria Questions or issues may need to be considered, in particular:

- *Condition 10*:

    In what context was the information published?

    (c)   Was the content voluntarily made public by the data subject?

    (d)   Was the content intended to be made public? Could the data subject have reasonably known that the content would be made public?[72]

GDPR RtbF Right 4/Stream 4: Unlawful

12.32   There is a RtbF where:

> *the personal data have been unlawfully processed.*[73]

GDPR

12.33   One of the issues which arises is whether this refers to unlawful processing under the GDPR or to some activity and processing unlawful under a law separate to the GDPR. Something which might be unlawful outside of the GDPR might be hacked emails or other documents which are uploaded onto the internet. There are potentially at least two acts of criminal wrongdoing in this example.

If the unlawful processing requires or includes some illicit act outside of the GDPR, then the individual data subject may have to be aware of laws other than the GDPR and their rights under it, some of which may involve criminal law. The individual data subject would be expected to know that there are other laws and

---

70   See GDPR Arts 68–76. Guidance may also arise from the European Data Protection Supervisor (EDPS); and respective national data protection supervisors.
71   WP 29, guidance list of Common Criteria for the Handling of Complaints 12–20.
72   *Ibid* criteria 10.
73   GDPR Art 17(1)(d).

that a particular activity or processing amounts to an unlawful breach of some sort under those separate laws.

Even if the 'unlawful' refers to a breach under or also under the GDPR in addition to other laws, the individual data subject still needs to be familiar not just with their rights under the GDPR, but also the nuances of notices and process of application and any possible exceptions or carveouts that may apply.

It will take some time for the general public to become much more familiar with these rights and for data protection supervisory authorities to engage in information transparency campaigns on these specific issues.

Recitals can often provide further interpretative assistance in relation to the meaning and understanding of the main Article legal provisions. Recital 66 of the GDPR states that '[i]n particular, a Data subject should have the right to have his or her personal data erased and no longer processed where ... processing of his or her personal data does not otherwise comply with this Regulation [ie the GDPR]'.

Charter

12.34   While the DPD 95/46 has now been repealed and replaced by the GDPR, the Charter[74] remains. The Charter was also relevant and relied upon in the *Google Spain* ruling. Parties will, in addition, be required to consider the Charter provisions referred to, namely, Articles 7 and 8.[75] These are set out below.

- *Article 7: Respect for Private and Family Life*

  Everyone has the right to respect for his or her private and family life, home and communications.

- *Article 8: Protection of Personal Data*

  8(1): Everyone has the right to the protection of personal data concerning him or her;

  8(2): Such data must be processed fairly for specified purposes and on the basis of the consent of the person concerned or some other legitimate basis laid down by law. Everyone has the right of access to data which has been collected concerning him or her, and the right to have it rectified;

  8(3): Compliance with these rules shall be subject to control by an independent authority.

These rights and provisions will continue to be relevant in RtbF disputes including this right stream.

---

74   Charter of Fundamental Rights of the European Union, 2012/C 326/02.
75   See generally Peers, Hervey, Kenner and A Ward, *The EU Charter of Fundamental Rights, A Commentary*.

DPD 95/46

12.35   The DPD 95/46 Article 12 (prior to GDPR), entitled 'Rights of access' provided:

> Member States shall guarantee every data subject the right to obtain from the controller: ...
>
> (b)   as appropriate the rectification, erasure or blocking of data the processing of which does not comply with the provisions of this Directive, in particular because of the incomplete or inaccurate nature of the data; ...

The DPD 95/46 Article 14 (prior to the GDPR), entitled 'The data subject's right to object' provided:

> Member States shall grant the data subject the right:
>
> (a)   at least in the cases referred to in Article 7(e) and (f), to object at any time on compelling legitimate grounds relating to his particular situation to the processing of data relating to him, save where otherwise provided by national legislation. Where there is a justified objection, the processing instigated by the controller may no longer involve those data; ...

Google Spain

12.36   In terms of the GDPR Article 17 RtbF Right 4/Stream 4 (Unlawful), it is also useful to review what the CJEU decided in the leading *Google Spain* case (relying on the DPD 95/46, and the Charter).

The comments referred to above made in relation to Right 1/Stream 1 and *Google Spain* should be considered in addition to the comments below.

The case held that:

> Article 12(b) and subparagraph (a) of the first paragraph of the DPD 95/46 Article 14 are to be interpreted as meaning that, in order to comply with the rights laid down in those provisions and in so far as the conditions laid down by those provisions are in fact satisfied, the operator of a search engine is obliged to remove from the list of results displayed following a search made on the basis of a person's name links to web pages, published by third parties and containing information relating to that person, also in a case where that name or information is not erased beforehand or simultaneously from those web pages, and even, as the case may be, when its publication in itself on those pages is lawful.[76]

Where the original processing was not lawful, the imperative for erasure, forgetting and takedown increases. This is not an instance of consent, or at least lawful consent. Therefore, there is less opportunity for the search engine controller to resist the application; and equally so the original source controller. It should also be the case that the takedown, erasure and forgetting may have to

---

76   *Google Spain*, ruling, para 100(3).

be more extensive than even referred to the above case, which refers to name, etc. If the original processing, and copying of that data, is unlawful, all such data should be removed, not just such data in a certain search manner.

> Article 12(b) and subparagraph (a) of the first paragraph of Article 14 of the DPD 95/46 are to be interpreted as meaning that, when appraising the conditions for the application of those provisions, it should inter alia be examined whether the individual data subject has a right that the information in question relating to him personally should, at this point in time, no longer be linked to his name by a list of results displayed following a search made on the basis of his name, without it being necessary in order to find such a right that the inclusion of the information in question in that list causes prejudice to the individual data subject. As the individual data subject may, in the light of his fundamental rights under Charter Articles 7 and 8, request that the information in question no longer be made available to the general public on account of its inclusion in such a list of results, those rights override, as a rule, not only the economic interest of the operator of the search engine but also the interest of the general public in having access to that information upon a search relating to the individual data subject's name. However, that would not be the case if it appeared, for particular reasons, such as the role played by the individual data subject in public life, that the interference with his fundamental rights is justified by the preponderant interest of the general public in having, on account of its inclusion in the list of results, access to the information in question.[77]

Similar comments as above arise. Given the original non-legality, there is a question mark over whether any later usage of the data can be lawful – at least from that original source.

Official Guidance: WP 29

12.37   It is always important to look at the official guidance which may be issued from time to time on data protection issues. In the European context this is often issued by the EDPB.[78] The EDPB includes representatives from the respective data protection supervisory authorities. However, prior to the GDPR (and its creation of the EDPB) the previous advisory body, the WP 29 issued assistive guidance in relation to *Google Spain*.

The WP 29 guidance included a list of common criteria for the handling of complaints by European data protection supervisory authorities.[79] Some of these are potentially relevant to this RtbF right stream of the GDPR. The following WP 29 Common Criteria Questions or issues may need to be considered, in particular:

---

77   *Ibid* para 100(4).
78   See GDPR Arts 68–76. Guidance may also arise from the European Data Protection Supervisor (EDPS); and respective national data protection supervisors.
79   WP 29, guidance list of Common Criteria for the Handling of Complaints 12–20.

- *Condition 5*:

  Is the data relevant and not excessive?

  (a) Does the data relate to the working life of the data subject?

  (b) Does the search result link to information which allegedly constitutes hate speech/slander/libel or similar offences in the area of expression against the complainant?

  (c) Is it clear that the data reflects an individual's personal opinion or does it appear to be verified fact?[80]

- *Condition 7*:

  Is the data up to date? Is the data being made available for longer than is necessary for the purpose of the processing?[81]

- *Condition 8*:

  Is the data processing causing prejudice to the data subject? Does the data have a disproportionately negative privacy impact on the data subject?[82]

- *Condition 9*:

  Does the search result link to information that puts the data subject at risk?[83]

- *Condition 10*:

  In what context was the information published?

  (a) Was the content voluntarily made public by the data subject?

  (b) Was the content intended to be made public? Could the data subject have reasonably known that the content would be made public?[84]

- *Condition 12*:

  Does the publisher of the data have a legal power – or a legal obligation – to make the personal data publicly available?[85]

GDPR RtbF Right 5/Stream 5: Legal Erasure

12.38 There is a RtbF where:

the personal data have to be erased for compliance with a legal obligation in Union or Member State law to which the controller is subject.[86]

---

80 *Ibid* criteria 5.
81 *Ibid* criteria 7.
82 *Ibid* criteria 8.
83 *Ibid* criteria 9.
84 *Ibid* criteria 10.
85 *Ibid* criteria 12.
86 GDPR Art 17(1)(e).

GDPR

12.39 Another erasure and forgetting right or example refers to what may be described as legal erasure, forgetting, or takedown. That is, where there is an obligation to erase the data under some law obligation on the controller ('compliance with a legal obligation').

This may suggest a legal obligation under something other than the GDPR, albeit may not be conclusive in that regard. It is also suggestive of quite a strong legal obligation of the controller, possibly more so than a potential lesser compliance-type obligation.

The legal obligation may come from either EU law or from national Member State law.

Recitals can often provide further interpretative assistance in relation to the meaning and understanding of the Article legal provisions. Recital 66 of the GDPR states that '[i]n particular, a data subject should have the right to have his or her personal data erased and no longer processed where … processing of his or her personal data does not otherwise comply with this Regulation [ie the GDPR]'.

Charter

12.40 While the DPD 95/46 is now repealed, and replaced by the GDPR, the Charter[87] remains. The Charter was also relevant and relied upon in the *Google Spain* ruling. Parties will, in addition, be required to consider the Charter provisions referred to, namely, Articles 7 and 8.[88] These are set out below.

- *Article 7: Respect for Private and Family Life*

  Everyone has the right to respect for his or her private and family life, home and communications.

- *Article 8: Protection of Personal Data*

  8(1): Everyone has the right to the protection of personal data concerning him or her.

  8(2): Such data must be processed fairly for specified purposes and on the basis of the consent of the person concerned or some other legitimate basis laid down by law. Everyone has the right of access to data which has been collected concerning him or her, and the right to have it rectified.

  8(3): Compliance with these rules shall be subject to control by an independent authority.

---

87 Charter of Fundamental Rights of the European Union, 2012/C 326/02.
88 See generally Peers, Hervey, Kenner and Ward, *The EU Charter of Fundamental Rights, A Commentary.*

These rights and provisions will continue to be relevant in RtbF disputes including this right stream.

DPD 95/46

12.41   The DPD 95/46 Article 12 (prior to the GDPR), entitled 'Rights of access' provided:

> Member States shall guarantee every data subject the right to obtain from the controller: …

> (b)   as appropriate the rectification, erasure or blocking of data the processing of which does not comply with the provisions of this Directive, in particular because of the incomplete or inaccurate nature of the data; …

The DPD 95/46 Article 14 (prior to the GDPR), entitled 'The data subject's right to object' provided:

> Member States shall grant the data subject the right:

> (a)   at least in the cases referred to in Article 7(e) and (f), to object at any time on compelling legitimate grounds relating to his particular situation to the processing of data relating to him, save where otherwise provided by national legislation. Where there is a justified objection, the processing instigated by the Controller may no longer involve those data; …

Google Spain

12.42   In terms of the GDPR Article 17 RtbF Right 5/Stream 5 (Legal Erasure), it is also useful to review what the CJEU decided in *Google Spain* (relying on the DPD 95/46, and the Charter).

The comments referred to above made in relation to Right 1/Stream 1 and *Google Spain* should be considered in addition to the comments below.

The case held that:

> Article 12(b) and subparagraph (a) of the first paragraph of the DPD 95/46 Article 14 are to be interpreted as meaning that, in order to comply with the rights laid down in those provisions and in so far as the conditions laid down by those provisions are in fact satisfied, the operator of a search engine is obliged to remove from the list of results displayed following a search made on the basis of a person's name links to web pages, published by third parties and containing information relating to that person, also in a case where that name or information is not erased beforehand or simultaneously from those web pages, and even, as the case may be, when its publication in itself on those pages is lawful.[89]

---

89   *Google Spain*, ruling, para 100(3).

Where there is a legal (law) obligation to delete, this would again indicate the widest possible erasure, forgetting and takedown and not just such data in a certain search result manner.

In *Google Spain* it was held that:

> Article 12(b) and subparagraph (a) of the first paragraph of Article 14 of the DPD 95/46 are to be interpreted as meaning that, when appraising the conditions for the application of those provisions, it should inter alia be examined whether the individual data subject has a right that the information in question relating to him personally should, at this point in time, no longer be linked to his name by a list of results displayed following a search made on the basis of his name, without it being necessary in order to find such a right that the inclusion of the information in question in that list causes prejudice to the individual data subject. As the individual data subject may, in the light of his fundamental rights under Charter Articles 7 and 8, request that the information in question no longer be made available to the general public on account of its inclusion in such a list of results, those rights override, as a rule, not only the economic interest of the operator of the search engine but also the interest of the general public in having access to that information upon a search relating to the individual data subject's name. However, that would not be the case if it appeared, for particular reasons, such as the role played by the individual data subject in public life, that the interference with his fundamental rights is justified by the preponderant interest of the general public in having, on account of its inclusion in the list of results, access to the information in question.[90]

Where there is a legal (law) obligation to delete, this would again indicate the widest possible erasure, forgetting and takedown, and not just such data in a certain search result manner. A law obligation to delate may also lean towards original source deletion also.

Official Guidance: WP 29

12.43   It is always important to look at the official guidance which may be issued from time to time on data protection issues. In the European context this is often issued by the EDPB.[91] The EDPB includes representatives from the respective data protection supervisory authorities. However, prior to the GDPR (and its creation of the EDPB) the previous advisory body, the WP 29 issued assistive guidance in relation to *Google Spain*.

The WP 29 guidance included a list of common criteria for the handling of complaints by European data protection supervisory authorities.[92] Some of these are potentially relevant to this RtbF right stream of the GDPR. The following

---

90   *Ibid* para 100(4).
91   See GDPR Arts 68–76. Guidance may also arise from the European Data Protection Supervisor (EDPS); and respective national data protection supervisors.
92   WP 29, guidance list of Common Criteria for the Handling of Complaints 12–20.

WP 29 Common Criteria Questions or issues may need to be considered, in particular:

* *Condition 12*:

  Does the publisher of the data have a legal power – or a legal obligation – to make the personal data publicly available?[93]

GDPR RtbF Right 6/Stream 6: Child Information Society Services Data

12.44   There is a RtbF where:

> *the personal data have been collected in relation to the offer of information society services referred to in Article 8(1) [ie to a child].*[94]

GDPR

Article 8 refers to conditions applicable to a child's consent in relation to information society services. Article 8(1) states: '[w]here point (a) of Article 6(1) applies, in relation to the offer of information society services directly to a child, the processing of the personal data of a child shall be lawful where the child is at least 16 years old. Where the child is below the age of 16 years, such processing shall be lawful only if and to the extent that consent is given or authorised by the holder of parental responsibility over the child.' Individual Member States may set the age at 13 (Article 8(1)).

Article 19 means that the individual data subject has the right to obtain from the controller the erasure of their personal and the controller must erase the personal data where the personal data have been collected in relation to the offer of information society services to a child (referred to in Article 8(1)). It must be erased, forgotten and taken down without undue delay.

This is unconditional and absolute. There are no conditions or carveouts. It is also the case that the parent or guardian of a current child should be able to make the application, or a child once they reach an appropriate age. In the later example, it may be that an adult individual files a notice in relation to images or other personal data of them from the past when they were a child.

Recitals can often provide further interpretative assistance in relation to the meaning and understanding of the main Article legal provisions. Recital 66 of the GDPR states that the 'right is relevant in particular where the data subject has given his or her consent as a child and is not fully aware of the risks involved by the processing, and later wants to remove such personal data, especially on the

---

93   *Ibid* criteria 12.
94   GDPR Art 17(1)(f).

internet. The data subject should be able to exercise that right notwithstanding the fact that he or she is no longer a child'.

Charter

12.45   While the DPD 95/46 is now repealed, and replaced by the GDPR, the Charter[95] remains. The Charter was also relevant and relied upon in the *Google Spain* ruling. Parties will, in addition, be required to consider the Charter provisions referred to, namely, Articles 7 and 8.[96] These are set out below.

- *Article 7: Respect for Private and Family Life*

  Everyone has the right to respect for his or her private and family life, home and communications.

- *Article 8: Protection of Personal Data*

  8(1): Everyone has the right to the protection of personal data concerning him or her;

  8(2): Such data must be processed fairly for specified purposes and on the basis of the consent of the person concerned or some other legitimate basis laid down by law. Everyone has the right of access to data which has been collected concerning him or her, and the right to have it rectified;

  8(3): Compliance with these rules shall be subject to control by an independent authority.

These rights and provisions will continue to be relevant in RtbF disputes including this right stream.

DPD 95/46

12.46   The DPD 95/46 (prior to the GDPR) did not expressly refer to children.

The DPD 95/46 Article 12 (prior to the GDPR), entitled 'Rights of access', provided:

  Member States shall guarantee every data subject the right to obtain from the controller: …

  (b)   as appropriate the rectification, erasure or blocking of data the processing of which does not comply with the provisions of this Directive, in particular because of the incomplete or inaccurate nature of the data; …

The DPD 95/46 Article 14 (prior to the GDPR), entitled 'The data subject's right to object,' provided:

---

95   Charter of Fundamental Rights of the European Union, 2012/C 326/02.
96   See generally Peers, Hervey, Kenner and Ward, *The EU Charter of Fundamental Rights, A Commentary*.

Member States shall grant the data subject the right:

(a) at least in the cases referred to in Article 7(e) and (f), to object at any time on compelling legitimate grounds relating to his particular situation to the processing of data relating to him, save where otherwise provided by national legislation. Where there is a justified objection, the processing instigated by the controller may no longer involve those data; …

Google Spain

12.47 In terms of GDPR Article 17 RtbF Right 6/Stream 6 (Children), it is also useful to review what the CJEU decided in the leading *Google Spain* case (relying on the DPD 95/46, and the Charter).

The comments referred to above made in relation to Right 1/Stream 1 and *Google Spain* should be considered in addition to the comments below.

It was held that:

Article 12(b) and subparagraph (a) of the first paragraph of the DPD 95/46 Article 14 are to be interpreted as meaning that, in order to comply with the rights laid down in those provisions and in so far as the conditions laid down by those provisions are in fact satisfied, the operator of a search engine is obliged to remove from the list of results displayed following a search made on the basis of a person's name links to web pages, published by third parties and containing information relating to that person, also in a case where that name or information is not erased beforehand or simultaneously from those web pages, and even, as the case may be, when its publication in itself on those pages is lawful.[97]

This does not expressly refer to child interests, nor did the previous DPD 95/46. Article 14(a), however, does refer to the right to 'object at any time on compelling legitimate *grounds relating to his particular situation*'. It seems amenable to extend therefore to the particular interests which a child may have and particularly far removed from the original data, content or event. In the current context, it would seem that this right and interest as regards children is more extensive given that these issues are more expressly referred to in the GDPR.

Article 12(b) and subparagraph (a) of the first paragraph of Article 14 of the DPD 95/46 are to be interpreted as meaning that, when appraising the conditions for the application of those provisions, it should inter alia be examined whether the individual data subject has a right that the information in question relating to him personally should, at this point in time, no longer be linked to his name by a list of results displayed following a search made on the basis of his name, without it being necessary in order to find such a right that the inclusion of the information in question in that list causes prejudice to the individual data subject. As the individual data subject may, in the light of his fundamental rights under Charter Articles 7 and 8, request that the information in question no longer be made available to the general public

---

97 *Google Spain*, ruling, para 100(3).

on account of its inclusion in such a list of results, those rights override, as a rule, not only the economic interest of the operator of the search engine but also the interest of the general public in having access to that information upon a search relating to the individual data subject's name. However, that would not be the case if it appeared, for particular reasons, such as the role played by the individual Data subject in public life, that the interference with his fundamental rights is justified by the preponderant interest of the general public in having, on account of its inclusion in the list of results, access to the information in question.[98]

Again, while the previous law did not expressly refer to a child or child's personal data, the above case does refer to matters to be examined as an open list (referring to *'inter alia'*), thus even under *Google Spain* the particular interests of a child can be considered over an adult. The new express reference to children's interest would seem to expand this consideration. In addition, the growing research in relation to children's issues and problem content for children may also become more relevant.

Official Guidance: WP 29

12.48 It is always important to look at the official guidance which may be issued from time to time on data protection issues. In the European context this is often issued by the EDPB.[99] The EDPB includes representatives from the respective data protection supervisory authorities. However, prior to the GDPR, the previous advisory body, the WP 29 issued assistive guidance in relation to *Google Spain*.

The WP 29 guidance included a list of common criteria for the handling of complaints by European data protection supervisory authorities.[100] Some of these are potentially relevant to this RtbF right stream of the GDPR. The following WP 29 Common Criteria Questions or issues may need to be considered, in particular:

- *Condition 3*:

  Is the data subject a minor?[101]

- *Condition 6*:

  Is the information sensitive within the meaning of Article 8 of the Directive 95/46?[102]

- *Condition 7*:

---

98 *Ibid* para 100(4).
99 See GDPR Arts 68–76. Guidance may also arise from the European Data Protection Supervisor (EDPS) and respective national data protection supervisors.
100 WP 29, guidance list of Common Criteria for the Handling of Complaints 12–20.
101 *Ibid* criteria 3.
102 *Ibid* criteria 6.

Is the data up to date? Is the data being made available for longer than is necessary for the purpose of the processing?[103]

- *Condition 8*:

  Is the data processing causing prejudice to the data subject? Does the data have a disproportionately negative privacy impact on the data subject?[104]

- *Condition 9*:

  Does the search result link to information that puts the data subject at risk?[105]

- *Condition 10*:

  In what context was the information published?

  (a)   Was the content voluntarily made public by the data subject?

  (b)   Was the content intended to be made public? Could the data subject have reasonably known that the content would be made public?[106]

- *Condition 11*:

  Was the original content published in the context of journalistic purposes?[107]

GDPR RtbF Right 7/Stream 7: Additional Right – Follow Through

12.49   There is a RtbF as follows:

> Where the controller has made the personal data public and is obliged pursuant to paragraph 1 to erase the personal data, the controller, taking account of available technology and the cost of implementation, shall take reasonable steps, including technical measures, to inform controllers which are processing the personal data that the data subject has requested the erasure by such controllers of any links to, or copy or replication of, those personal data.[108]

GDPR

12.50   There is an additional obligation on the controller where they must comply with an erasure forgetting and takedown right notice.

Where the controller has made the personal data public and is obliged per a notice to erase the personal data, the controller, must 'take reasonable steps, including technical measures, to inform [third party] controllers which are processing the personal data that the data subject has requested the erasure by such controllers

103 *Ibid* criteria 7.
104 *Ibid* criteria 8.
105 *Ibid* criteria 9.
106 *Ibid* criteria 10.
107 *Ibid* criteria 11.
108 GDPR Art 17(2).

of any links to, or copy or replication of, those personal data'. This is provided for in GDPR Article 17(2). The provision aims at achieving follow through erasure, forgetting and takedown where the personal data extends beyond the controller.

The controller can take into account the 'available technology' and the 'cost of implementation', in taking reasonable steps, including technical measures, to inform third-party controllers.

One will recall from the example of access request on websites and on social media, there is an increasing move to resolve some access requests electronically and, where possible, and to use automated tools to do so. The best example of this is Facebook. After Max Schrems initially requested access to his personal data, Facebook developed tools to automate an electronic reply to an access request and allow general access to one's own personal data via online tools. This was quite clever and practical. (However, there remains an ongoing controversy as to whether all fields or signals of personal data are disclosed in the access replies and online tools.)

While there are references to 'available technology', 'cost of implementation' and 'technical measures', these should not be taken to mean that it will be easy for a controller to refuse to engage in notifying third parties or limiting the amount of notification of third parties. What amounts to available technology and technology measures for the time being will always improve and the cost of implementation will constantly reduce. These will not be without difficulty if they are sought to be relied upon by the controller not to do something or reduce the effort or effectiveness of their otherwise required actions. The larger the controller organisation, the more unreasonable it may be to seek to use these terms or criteria as an excuse for not following through under this rights obligation.

Official Guidance: WP 29

12.51   It is always important to look at the official guidance which may be issued from time to time on data protection issues. In the European context this is often issued by the European Data Protection Board (EDPB).[109] The EDPB includes representatives from the respective data protection supervisory authorities. However, prior to the GDPR, the previous advisory body, the Article 29 Working Party (WP 29) issued assistive guidance in relation to *Google Spain*.

The WP 29 guidance included a list of common criteria for the handling of complaints by European data protection supervisory authorities.[110] Some of these are potentially relevant to this RtbF right stream of the GDPR. The following WP 29 Common Criteria Questions or issues may need to be considered, namely:

---

109 See GDPR Arts 68–76. Guidance may also arise from the European Data Protection Supervisor
   (EDPS); and respective national data protection supervisors.
110 WP 29, guidance list of Common Criteria for the Handling of Complaints 12–20.

1   Does the search result relate to a natural person – ie an individual? And does the search result come up against a search on the data subject's name?[111]

2   Does the data subject play a role in public life? Is the data subject a public figure?[112]

3   Is the data subject a minor?[113]

4   Is the data accurate?[114]

5   Is the data relevant and not excessive?

   (a)   Does the data relate to the working life of the data subject?

   (b)   Does the search result link to information which allegedly constitutes hate speech/slander/libel or similar offences in the area of expression against the complainant?

   (c)   Is it clear that the data reflects an individual's personal opinion or does it appear to be verified fact?[115]

6   Is the information sensitive within the meaning of Article 8 of the Directive 95/46?[116]

7   Is the data up to date? Is the data being made available for longer than is necessary for the purpose of the processing?[117]

8   Is the data processing causing prejudice to the data subject? Does the data have a disproportionately negative privacy impact on the data subject?[118]

9   Does the search result link to information that puts the data subject at risk?[119]

10 In what context was the information published?

   (a)   Was the content voluntarily made public by the data subject?

   (b)   Was the content intended to be made public? Could the data subject have reasonably known that the content would be made public?[120]

11 Was the original content published in the context of journalistic purposes?[121]

12 Does the publisher of the data have a legal power – or a legal obligation – to make the personal data publicly available?[122]

---

111 *Ibid* criteria 1.
112 *Ibid* criteria 2.
113 *Ibid* criteria 3.
114 *Ibid* criteria 4.
115 *Ibid* criteria 5.
116 *Ibid* criteria 6.
117 *Ibid* criteria 7.
118 *Ibid* criteria 8.
119 *Ibid* criteria 9.
120 *Ibid* criteria 10.
121 *Ibid* criteria 11.
122 *Ibid* criteria 12.

13   Does the data relate to a criminal offence?[123]

Regulation Guidance

12.52   EU laws are typically divided into what are called 'recitals' and 'Articles'. The Article provides the main legal provisions and measures. The recitals are not legal provisions but rather provide background and guidance on the aims of the legal provisions. They are often used in legal cases helping to assist in interpreting the legal provisions and understanding the intentions of the legislators. The GDPR contains Articles and recitals. Two in particular provide assistance in understanding the main legal Article provisions. There are recital 65 and recital 66.

GDPR Recital 65

12.53   Recital 65 states that an individual 'data subject should have the right to have personal data concerning him or her rectified and a "right to be forgotten" where the retention of such data infringes this Regulation or Union or Member State law to which the Controller is subject'.

Note that it states the right exists where the GDPR is infringed and also where there is a breach or infringement of 'Union or Member State law to which the controller is subject', opening the potential that the rights may be exercised under grounds additional to the GDPR itself. This could also extend to laws separate to data protection laws aimed at implementing the GDPR or aspects of it nationally. Constitutional as well as statute law considerations may potentially arise.

The recital continues it emphasises that '[i]n particular, a data subject should have the right to have his or her personal data erased and no longer processed where the personal data are no longer necessary in relation to the purposes for which they are collected or otherwise processed, where a data subject has withdrawn his or her consent or objects to the processing of personal data concerning him or her, or where the processing of his or her personal data does not otherwise comply with' the GDPR.

In addition, it states '[t]hat right is relevant in particular where the data subject has given his or her consent as a child and is not fully aware of the risks involved by the processing, and later wants to remove such personal data, especially on the internet'.

It also states that '[t]he data subject should be able to exercise that right notwithstanding the fact that he or she is no longer a child'.

In addition, it is stated, '[h]owever, the further retention of the personal data should be lawful where it is necessary, for exercising the right of freedom of

---

123 *Ibid* criteria 13.

expression and information, for compliance with a legal obligation, for the performance of a task carried out in the public interest or in the exercise of official authority vested in the controller, on the grounds of public interest in the area of public health, for archiving purposes in the public interest, scientific or historical research purposes or statistical purposes, or for the establishment, exercise or defence of legal claims'.

GDPR Recital 66

12.54   Recital 66 states that in order '[t]o strengthen [RtbF] in the online environment, the right to erasure should also be extended in such a way that a controller who has made the personal data public should be obliged to inform the controllers which are processing such personal data to erase any links to, or copies or replications of those personal data'.

It is also stated that '[i]n doing so, that controller should take reasonable steps, taking into account available technology and the means available to the controller, including technical measures, to inform the controllers which are processing the personal data of the data subject's request'.

Charter

12.55   While the DPD 95/46 has now been repealed and replaced by the GDPR, the Charter[124] remains. The Charter was also relevant and relied upon in the *Google Spain* ruling. Parties will, in addition, be required to consider the Charter provisions referred to, namely, Articles 7 and 8.[125] These are set out below.

- *Article 7: Respect for Private and Family Life*

    Everyone has the right to respect for his or her private and family life, home and communications.

- *Article 8: Protection of Personal Data*

    8(1): Everyone has the right to the protection of personal data concerning him or her;

    8(2): Such data must be processed fairly for specified purposes and on the basis of the consent of the person concerned or some other legitimate basis laid down by law. Everyone has the right of access to data which has been collected concerning him or her, and the right to have it rectified;

    8(3): Compliance with these rules shall be subject to control by an independent authority.

These rights and provisions will continue to be relevant in RtbF disputes.

---

124 Charter of Fundamental Rights of the European Union, 2012/C 326/02.
125 See generally Peers, Hervey, Kenner and Ward, *The EU Charter of Fundamental Rights, A Commentary*.

DPD 95/46

12.56 DPD 95/45 Article 12 (prior to the GDPR), entitled 'Rights of access' provided:

> Member States shall guarantee every data subject the right to obtain from the controller: …

> (b) as appropriate the rectification, erasure or blocking of data the processing of which does not comply with the provisions of this Directive, in particular because of the incomplete or inaccurate nature of the data; …

The DPD 95/46 Article 14 (prior to the GDPR), entitled 'The data subject's right to object' provided:

> Member States shall grant the data subject the right:

> (a) at least in the cases referred to in Article 7(e) and (f), to object at any time on compelling legitimate grounds relating to his particular situation to the processing of data relating to him, save where otherwise provided by national legislation. Where there is a justified objection, the processing instigated by the controller may no longer involve those data; …

Google Spain

12.57 The *Google Spain* decision does not refer to this new right issue. No doubt this may become a consideration in future cases, and policy.

Official Guidance: WP 29

12.58 It is always important to look at the official guidance which may be issued from time to time on data protection issues. In the European context this is often issued by the EDPB.[126] The EDPB includes representatives from the respective data protection supervisory authorities. However, prior to the GDPR, the previous advisory body, the WP 29 issued assistive guidance in relation to *Google Spain*.

The WP 29 guidance included a list of common criteria for the handling of complaints by European data regulators.[127] Some of these are potentially relevant to this RtbF right stream of the GDPR. The following WP 29 Common Criteria Questions or issues may need to be considered, namely:

1   Does the search result relate to a natural person – ie, an individual? And does the search result come up against a search on the data subject's name?[128]

---

126 See GDPR Arts 68–76. Guidance may also arise from the European Data Protection Supervisor (EDPS); and respective national data protection supervisors.
127 WP 29, guidance list of Common Criteria for the Handling of Complaints 12–20.
128 *Ibid* criteria 1.

2   Does the data subject play a role in public life? Is the data subject a public figure?[129]

3   Is the data subject a minor?[130]

4   Is the data accurate?[131]

5   Is the data relevant and not excessive?

    (a)   Does the data relate to the working life of the data subject?

    (b)   Does the search result link to information which allegedly constitutes hate speech/slander/libel or similar offences in the area of expression against the complainant?

    (c)   Is it clear that the data reflects an individual's personal opinion or does it appear to be verified fact?[132]

6   Is the information sensitive within the meaning of Article 8 of Directive 95/46?[133]

7   Is the data up to date? Is the data being made available for longer than is necessary for the purpose of the processing?[134]

8   Is the data processing causing prejudice to the data subject? Does the data have a disproportionately negative privacy impact on the data subject?[135]

9   Does the search result link to information that puts the data subject at risk?[136]

10   In what context was the information published?

    (a)   Was the content voluntarily made public by the data subject?

    (b)   Was the content intended to be made public? Could the data subject have reasonably known that the content would be made public?[137]

11   Was the original content published in the context of journalistic purposes?[138]

12   Does the publisher of the data have a legal power – or a legal obligation – to make the personal data publicly available?[139]

13   Does the data relate to a criminal offence?[140]

---

129 *Ibid* criteria 2.
130 *Ibid* criteria 3.
131 *Ibid* criteria 4.
132 *Ibid* criteria 5.
133 *Ibid* criteria 6.
134 *Ibid* criteria 7.
135 *Ibid* criteria 8.
136 *Ibid* criteria 9.
137 *Ibid* criteria 10.
138 *Ibid* criteria 11.
139 *Ibid* criteria 12.
140 *Ibid* criteria 13.

7 ADDITIONAL RIGHTS AND GROUNDS

12.59   Bear in mind also GDPR Article 7 which states that '[t]he data subject shall have the right to obtain from the controller the erasure of personal data ... (e) the personal data have to be erased for compliance with a legal obligation in Union or Member State law to which the controller is subject'.

This leaves open that there may be potentially be additional or at least additional nuances provided for in relation to the exercise of RtbF options as and when provided for in Member State law(s). Conceivably, therefore, a Member State may have certain historic references which continue and or carry over post the GDPR. It also leaves open the possibility for a Member State in its own legislation seeking to provide an additional and or more flexible avenue to vindicate certain erasure, forgetting and takedown concerns of an individual data subject. Such potentialities may not be immediately apparent but may be further examined as time goes by. It makes sense, however, that the above more explicit avenues will be of more immediate and direct interest to individual data subjects and to controllers.

8 CONCLUSION: FUTURE RIGHTS AND GROUNDS

12.60   As indicated earlier, it could be a mistake for organisations to think of the GDPR RtbF (and wider interests in RtbF, erasure, forgetting, and takedown) in a simple composite right. This may lead to an organisation missing a deeper necessary consideration of the particular nuances; the different potential avenues to exercising and vindicating an instant RtbF notice; and that there can be both different interests at stake and different temporal urgencies in relation to achieving erasure, forgetting, and takedown as regards particular content and problem content. Furthermore, there may be further RtbFs in future, for example, as further problems, problem content or gaps in existing rules, etc, are identified.

We also see that not all of the WP 29 Common criteria would appear to apply in each of the GDPR RtbF right streams. However, it may be that more than one WP 29 Common Criteria may apply to a given RtbF right or stream.

CHAPTER 13

Additional RtbF Obligations

Article 17

2. Where the controller has made the personal data public and is obliged pursuant to paragraph 1 to erase the personal data, the controller, taking account of available technology and the cost of implementation, shall take reasonable steps, including technical measures, to inform controllers which are processing the personal data that the data subject has requested the erasure by such controllers of any links to, or copy or replication of, those personal data.

I INTRODUCTION

13.1 Some organisations may approach RtbF as an afterthought to its other obligations such as complying with the principles,[1] lawful processing conditions,[2] consent,[3] legitimate processing,[4] data access requests[5] or even data protection security obligations.[6] Worse still, an organisation may leave any dutiful consideration of the GDPR RtbF aside (on the assumption that it does not or will not arise or that it only needs to be looked at if any such notice is received).

An organisation may also envisage RtbF as a simple matter of one less important right and various exemptions or exceptions limiting that right.

All of these approaches would all be less than prudent for an organisation.

Organisations should guard against focusing on the underlying interests of data subjects giving rise to potential RtbF notices as all being identical and linear as well as all RtbF notices as being identical and uniform.

Separate and in addition to the above, organisations should not consider these issues in a blinkered RtbF-only approach. There may, depending on the circumstances, be additional provisions and indeed rights in the GDPR which may have some potential sway and which will need to be considered.

---

1   GDPR Art 5.
2   *Ibid* Art 6.
3   *Ibid* Arts 7 and 8.
4   *Ibid* Art 6(1)(f).
5   *Ibid* Art 15.
6   *Ibid* Arts 32–34.

2 OBLIGATIONS

13.2   The obligation provides that the controller must:

> inform controllers which are processing the personal data that the data subject has requested the erasure by such controllers of any links to, or copy or replication of, those personal data.

The obligations of the controller therefore do not end with its own direct erasure issues. It must examine its systems to see if it assisted others to also make the content available. Where it did, it then needs to appraise these of the notice from the data subject. As yet, it is not clear as to whether this means merely notifying or in addition providing the full basis, etc, of the notice. For example, whether it is permissible to furnish the full notice as received (and any documentation attached or furnished) remains to be seen. Restrictions may need to be applied.

Recital 66 also assists in understanding the reasons, meaning and interpretation associated with this obligation. It states that '[t]o strengthen [RtbF] in the online environment, the right to erasure should also be extended in such a way that a controller who has made the personal data public should be obliged to inform the controllers which are processing such personal data to erase any links to, or copies or replications of those personal data. In doing so, that controller should take reasonable steps, taking into account available technology and the means available to the controller, including technical measures, to inform the controllers which are processing the personal data of the data subject's request.'

Note that it states that the 'controller who has made the personal data public should be obliged to inform the controllers which are processing such personal data' – not just some third-party controller(s) to whom the original controller may have transferred the personal data.

In addition, it clarifies that in relation to the controller and the third-party controller content, the intention and requirement is 'to erase any links to, or copies or replications of those personal data'. The main controller is indicated to be 'obliged to inform the [third party] controllers ... to erase any links to, or copies or replications of those personal data'.

There is an obligation for follow on erasure, forgetting and takedown, in addition to mere notification of the original notice from the data subject.

3 FACTORS

13.3   The provision also provides that:

> Where the controller has made the personal data public and is obliged pursuant to paragraph 1 to erase the personal data, the controller, taking account of available technology and the cost of implementation, shall take reasonable steps, including technical measures ...

The controllers, therefore, may take account of (a) technology; and (b) costs. The cost of sending an email notification to the third parties will be a minimal cost for the controller. The review is likely of its own systems, and some of which may be done online. There is no novelty in having reviews and related work product recorded. However, it would not be surprising if at least some online providers eventually attempt to argue that there is some technology problem in notifying third parties. Systems are already in place in terms of complying with RtbF and the GDPR, and the cost of email notifications and the like are minimal. In many instances, the controller involved will be a very well-resourced multi-national. The extent to which cost arguments may be argued in future may be a double-edged sword. Making a cost of notifying (or other cost) argument may shine a light into other cost areas which the controller may not have anticipated and may not wish to occur.

One can also imagine potential difficulties and retrenchment controller creating difficulties in relation to these layered obligations.

It should also be noted that the two factor considerations raised are a closed list.

While the DPD 95/46 has now been repealed, and replaced by the GDPR, the Charter[7] remains. The Charter was also relevant and relied upon in the *Google Spain* ruling. Charter provisions, particularly, Articles 7 and 8[8] will continue to be relevant in RtbF disputes and may factor in any notice obligation disputes that may arise in addition to the GDPR.

Google Spain

13.4   The *Google Spain*[9] decision does not expressly refer to notification obligations and, in any event, was prior to the GDPR and GDPR RtbF.

4   CONCLUSION

13.5   The issues of damages and compensation will be relevant in a number of contexts. However, it is not immune from consideration in this instance as regards this follow-on obligation.[10] One can contemplate a situation where the controller may have complied with the direct notice, erasure and forgetting issue, yet has not complied with the follow-through obligation at all. Potentially, a compensation and damages issue may arise.

---

7   Charter of Fundamental Rights of the European Union, 2012/C 326/02.
8   See generally S Peers, T Hervey, J Kenner, and A Ward, *The EU Charter of Fundamental Rights, A Commentary* (Beck, Hart and Nomos, 2014).
9   *Google Spain SL, Google Inc v Agencia Española de Protección de Datos (AEPD), Mario Costeja González*, Court of Justice (Grand Chamber), Case C-131/12, 13 May 2014.
10   See also SK Mizrahi, 'Ontario's New Invasion of Privacy Torts: Do They Offer Monetary Redress for Violations Suffered Via the Internet of Things?' *Western Journal of Legal Studies* (2018) (8:1) (COV2) 37.

CHAPTER 14

Exemptions

Article 17

3. Paragraphs 1 and 2 shall not apply to the extent that processing is necessary:

    (a) for exercising the right of freedom of expression and information;

    (b) for compliance with a legal obligation which requires processing by Union or Member State law to which the controller is subject or for the performance of a task carried out in the public interest or in the exercise of official authority vested in the controller;

    (c) for reasons of public interest in the area of public health in accordance with points (h) and (i) of Article 9(2) as well as Article 9(3);

    (d) for archiving purposes in the public interest, scientific or historical research purposes or statistical purposes in accordance with Article 89(1) in so far as the right referred to in paragraph 1 is likely to render impossible or seriously impair the achievement of the objectives of that processing; or

    (e) for the establishment, exercise or defence of legal claims.

I INTRODUCTION

14.1   The exemptions are critically important to understanding the General Data Protection Regulation Right to be Forgotten (GDPR RtbF), its ambit and applicability. These make clear that, depending on the circumstances, there are some RtbF notices which may be stronger than others. The exemptions would also suggest that there are certain circumstances when a given RtbF notice, while otherwise meritorious, may have to be discounted as there is a particular exemption provided.

2 LIMITED EXEMPTIONS

14.2   Perhaps most important to note, however, is that the list of exemptions is a closed list, not an expansive, unlimited or by way of example list of exemptions. If a refusal is to apply it must firmly fit within and comply with one of these specified exemptions.

Rosemary Jay also refers to this by referring to 'grounds on which erasure can be refused' rather than exemptions.[1] She states that:

> It should be noted that the right to erasure and the linking right to a notice of erasure can be refused in some cases but only to the extent that the continued processing is necessary for one or more of the exempt purposes. Therefore, the data controller must act on the request to the extent possible while still meeting the terms of the exemption.[2]

3 COMPLICATIONS

14.3   However, in reviewing the exemptions it is noted that several of them cross-refer to other provisions in the GDPR. Therefore, making immediate sense of the exemptions is not as easy as controllers may wish.

Jay refers to further potential complicating issues and issues of comparison:

> The exemptions repeat some of the general grounds of exemption under which Member States can pass national law but they operate as a stand-alone code. In other words, even if national member State law provides narrow and limited exemptions for any of the heads covered, for example freedom of expression, the ... exemption in art. 17(2)(a)–(e) still applies. It seems inevitable therefore that these will lead, eventually to a consistent standard across the union in these areas, irrespective of variations in national exemptions.[3]

She adds that it also needs to be noted that 'in a couple of areas, the relationship with art. 21 is distinctly convoluted'.[4]

4 ONUS

14.4   Controllers should not make the mistake of assuming that such a complication makes it more difficult for the individual data subject to understand or to make and insist on their RtbF rights. Everyone should be aware of the wide concepts of personal data and data protection,[5] the wide definition of personal data[6] and wide RtbFs.[7] Rather, controllers should consider the perspective that

---

1   R Jay, W Malcolm, E Parry, L Townsend and A Bapat, *Guide to the General Data Protection Regulation, A Companion to Data Protection Law and Practice* (Sweet and Maxwell, 2017) 273. Also note P Lambert, A User's Guide to Data Protection (Bloomsbury, 2020).
2   *Ibid.*
3   *Ibid* at 275–276.
4   *Ibid* at 276.
5   N Purtova, 'The Law of Everything: Broad Concept of Personal Data and Future of EU Data Protection Law' *Innovation and Technology* (2018) (10:1) 40.
6   GDPR Art 4(1).
7   That is not to suggest that there will be no need to recognise further RtbFs or RtbF situations in future.

the rights apply and, in order to refuse, the burden is on the controller to identify and establish that a specific exemption applies and works.

5   LIMITED INTERPRETATION

14.5   Controllers should also be aware of the imperative that all exemptions generally or at least exemptions to fundamental rights such as data protection and including RtbF, must be interpreted strictly and narrowly. Controllers will have difficulty in seeking to extend or apply a loose, extensive interpretation to any given potential exemption it may wish to apply. Unless it is clearly specified as an exemption, it will not apply as an available exemption to a RtbF notice.

6   CERTAIN EXCEPTION ISSUES

14.6   This GDPR right applies except where one of the following grounds applies:

* the personal data are no longer necessary in relation to the purposes for which they were collected or otherwise processed;

* the individual data subject withdraws consent on which the processing is based according to point (a) of Article 6(1), or point (a) of Article 9(2) and where there is no other legal ground for the processing;

* the individual data subject objects to the processing pursuant to Article 21(1) and there are no overriding legitimate grounds for the processing, or the individual data subject objects to the processing pursuant to Article 21(2);

* the personal data have been unlawfully processed;

* the personal data must be erased for compliance with a legal obligation in Union or Member State law to which the Controller is subject; and

* the personal data have been collected in relation to the offer of information society services referred to in Article 8(1).

7 CHARTER

14.7   While the DPD 95/46 has now been repealed and replaced by the GDPR, the Charter[8] remains. The Charter was also relevant and relied upon in the Google Spain[9] ruling. Parties will be required to consider the Charter provisions referred to, namely, Articles 7 and 8.[10] These are set out below.

---

8   Charter of Fundamental Rights of the European Union, 2012/C 326/02.
9   *Google Spain SL, Google Inc v Agencia Española de Protección de Datos (AEPD), Mario Costeja González,* Court of Justice (Grand Chamber), Case C-131/12, 13 May 2014.
10   See generally S Peers, T Hervey, J Kenner, and A Ward, *The EU Charter of Fundamental Rights, A Commentary* (Beck, Hart and Nomos, 2014).

- *Article 7: Respect for Private and Family Life*

  Everyone has the right to respect for his or her private and family life, home and communications.

- *Article 8: Protection of Personal Data*

  8(1): Everyone has the right to the protection of personal data concerning him or her.

  8(2): Such data must be processed fairly for specified purposes and on the basis of the consent of the person concerned or some other legitimate basis laid down by law. Everyone has the right of access to data which has been collected concerning him or her and the right to have it rectified.

  8(3): Compliance with these rules shall be subject to control by an independent authority.

These rights and provisions will continue to be relevant in RtbF disputes (although in the UK issues of Brexit changes, data protection consultation process changes, and potential changes to enhance online safety will need to be considered and reviewed as time progresses).

Exemptions require individualised consideration as appropriate in the circumstances.[11]

8 INDIVIDUALISED CONSIDERATION

14.8   The detail of each notice and of each exemption must be considered however. It should not be considered that an exemption is automatically available or that a given exemption automatically prevails.

It will inevitably be the case that an exemption will apply in certain situations and to certain RtbF notices, but not to others. Even where a given exemption may be sector-specific in focus, individual consideration is also needed and should not be avoided in favour of mere assumptive presumption of an exemption applying or it automatically or always trumping RtbF.

9 NECESSITY

14.9   Article 17(3) provides that, paragraphs 1 and 2 of Article 17 shall not apply to the extent that processing is necessary:

---

11 More generally not commentary such as 'British Library Exempted from "Right to Be Forgotten" Rule' *Information Management Journal* (Nov/Dec 2017) (51:6) 16; Z Kharazian, 'Yet Another French Exception: The Political Dimensions of France's Support for the Digital Right to be Forgotten' *European Data Protection Law Review (EDPL)* (2017) (3:4) 452.

(a)   for exercising the right of freedom of expression and information;

(b)   for compliance with a legal obligation which requires processing by Union or Member State law to which the controller is subject or for the performance of a task carried out in the public interest or in the exercise of official authority vested in the controller;

(c)   for reasons of public interest in the area of public health in accordance with points (h) and (i) of Article 9(2) as well as Article 9(3);

(d)   for archiving purposes in the public interest, scientific or historical research purposes or statistical purposes in accordance with Article 89(1) in so far as the right referred to in paragraph 1 is likely to render impossible or seriously impair the achievement of the objectives of that processing; or

(e)   for the establishment, exercise or defence of legal claims.

This is noteworthy as there is a 'necessity' requirement. This is a precondition or precondition prior to each of the potential exemptions listed below the head paragraph. If it is wishful, but not strictly necessary, it would seem that the exemption may not be available. By specifying 'necessary' it may be setting quite a high standard. This high standard is strict and must also be objective. This may be other than a mere wish or commercial wish list of a given controller. It is suggested that many future disputes may be resolved on this strict necessity point.

10   FREEDOM OF EXPRESSION

14.10

> (a) *for exercising the right of freedom of expression and information.*[12]

The right 'shall not apply to the extent that processing is necessary' 'for exercising the right of freedom of expression and information'.

In the first instance, note that prior to this there is the requirement in the provision that it be 'necessary'. Therefore, this effectively reads in full:

> to the extent that processing is *necessary*: for exercising the right of freedom of expression and information (emphasis added).

If it does not, the exemption would appear not to apply at all.

Recital 65 also adds to this issue. It states '[h]owever, the further retention of the personal data should be lawful where it is *necessary* for exercising the right of freedom of expression and information' (emphasis added).

Jay comments in relation to this issue as follows:

---

12   GDPR Art 17(3)(a).

The importance of the rights of freedom of expression and information are emphasised by their inclusions [in] art.17, there is no definition of the terms … In the case of [*Google Spain*] the CJEU held that the internet search engine was not exercising the right of freedom of expression as the expression was that of the original website, not the search engine and that site had the [potential] benefit of the exemption for journalistic purposes. It remains to be seen whether a broader interpretation will be placed on this new provision.[13]

Therefore, this exception is only available to certain entities, not all entities. It is specific, not general.

No doubt, this will perhaps be one of the more contentious RtbF issues in case law. However, this is a discrete section of overall RtbF notification concerns by data subjects. To reiterate, this may be a niche issue, not a general issue applicable to the majority of RtbF notices.

In fairness, it should also be noted that the above reference also includes the comment that '[t]hey are not limited to journalistic purposes'.[14] This should not be taken to mean that *all* activities of a news organisation are journalistic or contemporary journalism; nor that secondary additional use purposes well after an original news event do not arise, but which may not be journalistic, or wholly journalistic. It is suggested, therefore, that even while this exemption is not available to all entities, it may not be available to all media entities and/or for all media content in all situations (see Chapter 24 below for more commentary in relation to media and freedom of expression issues).

11 LEGAL OBLIGATION BY LAW OR PUBLIC INTERESTS TASK OR OFFICIAL AUTHORITY

14.11

(b) *for compliance with a legal obligation which requires processing by Union or Member State law to which the Controller is subject or for the performance of a task carried out in the public interest or in the exercise of official authority vested in the Controller.*[15]

In the first instance, note that prior to this there is the requirement in the provision that it be 'necessary.' Therefore, this effectively reads in full:

to the extent that processing is *necessary*: for compliance with a legal obligation which requires processing by Union or Member State law to which the controller is subject or for the performance of a task carried out in the public interest or in the exercise of official authority vested in the controller (emphasis added).

13 Jay, Malcolm, Parry, Townsend and Bapat, *Guide to the General Data Protection Regulation, A Companion to Data Protection Law and Practice*, above, at 276.

14 *Ibid.*

15 GDPR Art 17(3)(b).

If it does not, the exemption would appear not to apply at all.

The right 'shall not apply to the extent that processing is necessary' 'for compliance with a legal obligation which requires processing by Union or Member State law to which the controller is subject or for the performance of a task carried out in the public interest or in the exercise of official authority vested in the controller.'

Recital 65 also adds to this issue. It states '[h]owever, the further retention of the personal data should be lawful where it is *necessary* ... for compliance with a legal obligation, for the performance of a task carried out in the public interest or in the exercise of official authority vested in the Controller' (emphasis added).

Jay also comments on this provision, as follows:

> The data controller does not have to comply with a request for erasure which is otherwise justified if the processing is necessary:
>
> * For compliance with a legal obligation which requires processing by Union or Member State law;
>
> * To meet a legal obligation to which the controller is subject; or
>
> * For the performance of a task carried out in the public interest or in the exercise of official authority.
>
> Where the right to erasure follows an objection under art. 21(1) the final point will already have been weighted by the controller in relation to the initial objection. At this later stage, however, it might be a basis to refuse erasure although the right of objection could be met in other ways, for example by restriction of data.[16]

However, a controller should not substitute an action which has not been requested by the data subject in order to refuse the RtbF notice which was actually made.

12 PUBLIC HEALTH INTEREST

14.12

> (c) *for reasons of public interest in the area of public health in accordance with points (h) and (i) of Article 9(2) as well as Article 9(3).*[17]

In the first instance, note that prior to this there is the requirement in the provision that it be 'necessary'. Therefore, this effectively reads in full:

> to the extent that processing is *necessary*: for reasons of public interest in the area of public health in accordance with points (h) and (i) of Article 9(2) as well as Article 9(3) (emphasis added).

---

16 Jay, Malcolm, Parry, Townsend and Bapat, *Guide to the General Data Protection Regulation, A Companion to Data Protection Law and Practice* above at 276.

17 GDPR Art 17(3)(c).

If it does not, the exemption would appear not to apply at all.

The right 'shall not apply to the extent that processing is necessary' 'for reasons of public interest in the area of public health in accordance with points (h) and (i) of Article 9(2) as well as Article 9(3)'.

Recital 65 also adds to this issue. It states '[h]owever, the further retention of the personal data should be lawful where it is *necessary* … on the grounds of public interest in the area of public health' (emphasis added).

Jay comments that 'the exemption is not limited to the special categories but applies to any personal data processed for these purposes'.[18]

Also, one should consider whether this applies more to, or even exclusively, to official organisations or official uses of such data, rather than non-official commercial-type entities.

13 ARCHIVING OR STATISTICS

14.13

> (d) *for archiving purposes in the public interest, scientific or historical research purposes or statistical purposes in accordance with Article 89(1) in so far as the right referred to in paragraph 1 is likely to render impossible or seriously impair the achievement of the objectives of that processing.*[19]

In the first instance, note that prior to this there is the requirement in the provision that it be 'necessary'. Therefore, this effectively reads in full:

> to the extent that processing is *necessary*: for archiving purposes in the public interest, scientific or historical research purposes or statistical purposes in accordance with Article 89(1) in so far as the right referred to in paragraph 1 is likely to render impossible or seriously impair the achievement of the objectives of that processing (emphasis added).

If it does not, the exemption would appear not to apply at all.

The right 'shall not apply to the extent that processing is necessary' 'for archiving purposes in the public interest, scientific or historical research purposes or statistical purposes in accordance with Article 89(1) in so far as the right referred to in paragraph 1 is likely to render impossible or seriously impair the achievement of the objectives of that processing'.

---

18   Jay, Malcolm, Parry, Townsend and Bapat, *Guide to the General Data Protection Regulation, A Companion to Data Protection Law and Practice above at* 276.
19   GDPR Art 17(3)(d).

Recital 65 also adds to this issue. It states '[h]owever, the further retention of the personal data should be lawful where it is *necessary* ... for archiving purposes in the public interest, scientific or historical research purposes or statistical purposes' (emphasis added).

Jay comments that:

> This exemption applies to the extent that the erasure of the data would render impossible or seriously impair the achievement of the objectives. This is quite a high bar and would require clear evidence of the likelihood of the detriment anticipated.[20]

14   LEGAL CLAIMS

14.14

> (c) *for the establishment, exercise or defence of legal claims.*[21]

In the first instance, note that prior to this there is the requirement in the provision that it be 'necessary'. Therefore, this effectively reads in full:

> to the extent that processing is *necessary*: for the establishment, exercise or defence of legal claims (emphasis added).

If it does not, the exemption would appear not to apply at all.

The right 'shall not apply to the extent that processing is necessary' 'for the establishment, exercise or defence of legal claims'.

Recital 65 also adds to this issue. It states '[h]owever, the further retention of the personal data should be lawful where it is *necessary* ... for the establishment, exercise or defence of legal claims' (emphasis added).

Jay comments in this regards that:

> This ground also reflects one of the grounds considered in determining whether a right of objection under art. 21 should be accepted but will need to be re-assessed once erasure is considered. It appears to be quite a wide ground and may well enable data controllers to retain records of erasure requests and responses so that they are able to deal with subsequent claims of non-compliance.[22]

However, a controller may be cautioned against assuming that the legal claim can be new and contemporaneous as compared at the time of collection and original processing.

---

20 Jay, Malcolm, Parry, Townsend and Bapat, *Guide to the General Data Protection Regulation, A Companion to Data Protection Law and Practice above at* 277.
21 GDPR Art 17(3).
22 Jay, Malcolm, Parry, Townsend and Bapat, *Guide to the General Data Protection Regulation, A Companion to Data Protection Law and Practice above at* 277.

Previous Directive

14.15 The DPD 95/46 Article 12 (prior to the GDPR), entitled 'Rights of access' provided:

> Member States shall guarantee every data subject the right to obtain from the controller: ...
>
> (b) as appropriate the rectification, erasure or blocking of data the processing of which does not comply with the provisions of this Directive, in particular because of the incomplete or inaccurate nature of the data; ...

The DPD 95/46 Article 14 (prior to the GDPR), entitled 'The data subject's right to object' provided:

> Member States shall grant the data subject the right:
>
> (a) at least in the cases referred to in Article 7(e) and (f), to object at any time on compelling legitimate grounds relating to his particular situation to the processing of data relating to him, save where otherwise provided by national legislation. Where there is a justified objection, the processing instigated by the Controller may no longer involve those data; ...

So again, there is both history and precedent in this area. That there is an express RtbF, which has internal balancing of interests and provides a fixed exemption list, shows that there is balance in RtbF and suggestions that RtbF is totally abhorrent or that 'There Should Be No Rtbf, Full Stop', is perhaps somewhat off the mark.

Google Spain

14.16 The court in the leading case of *Google Spain* relying on the above Directive, held that:

- Article 2(b) and (d) of Directive 95/46/EC of the European Parliament and of the Council of 24 October 1995 on the protection of individuals with regard to the processing of personal data and on the free movement of such data are to be interpreted as meaning that, first, the activity of a search engine consisting in finding information published or placed on the internet by third parties, indexing it automatically, storing it temporarily and, finally, making it available to internet users according to a particular order of preference must be classified as 'processing of personal data' within the meaning of Article 2(b) when that information contains personal data and, second, the operator of the search engine must be regarded as the 'controller' in respect of that processing, within the meaning of Article 2(d).[23]

- Article 4(1)(a) of Directive 95/46 is to be interpreted as meaning that processing of personal data is carried out in the context of the activities of an establishment of the controller on the territory of a Member State, within

---

23 *Google Spain*, ruling, para 100(1).

the meaning of that provision, when the operator of a search engine sets up in a Member State a branch or subsidiary which is intended to promote and sell advertising space offered by that engine and which orientates its activity towards the inhabitants of that Member State.[24]

- Article 12(b) and subparagraph (a) of the first paragraph of the DPD 95/46 Article 14 are to be interpreted as meaning that, in order to comply with the rights laid down in those provisions and in so far as the conditions laid down by those provisions are in fact satisfied, the operator of a search engine is obliged to remove from the list of results displayed following a search made on the basis of a person's name links to web pages, published by third parties and containing information relating to that person, also in a case where that name or information is not erased beforehand or simultaneously from those web pages and even, as the case may be, when its publication in itself on those pages is lawful.[25]

- Article 12(b) and subparagraph (a) of the first paragraph of Article 14 of the DPD 95/46 are to be interpreted as meaning that, when appraising the conditions for the application of those provisions, it should, *inter alia*, be examined whether the individual data subject has a right that the information in question relating to him personally should, at this point in time, no longer be linked to his name by a list of results displayed following a search made on the basis of his name, without it being necessary in order to find such a right that the inclusion of the information in question in that list causes prejudice to the individual data subject. As the individual data subject may, in the light of his fundamental rights under Charter Articles 7 and 8, request that the information in question no longer be made available to the general public on account of its inclusion in such a list of results, those rights override, as a rule, not only the economic interest of the operator of the search engine but also the interest of the general public in having access to that information upon a search relating to the individual data subject's name. However, that would not be the case if it appeared, for particular reasons, such as the role played by the individual data subject in public life, that the interference with his fundamental rights is justified by the preponderant interest of the general public in having, on account of its inclusion in the list of results, access to the information in question.[26]

It is noted, therefore, that while prior to the GDPR and the above provisions, there is a discrete reference at the very end of the last ruling bullet above, which has potential cross over with the potential exemption (a) above. This will obviously be further explored in future caselaw. However, the above decision makes clear that the freedom of expression and information interests (to the extent that they are the same as referred to in the decision) are a public interest, not a company interest; are not absolute; only provide the carveout as regards clearly public

---

24   *Ibid* para 100(2).
25   *Ibid* para 100(3).
26   *Ibid* para 100(4).

figures; and is not available to all entities, but rather certain entities, and in certain circumstances.

15   TIMING

14.17   Jay also makes the point that timing needs to be considered. The provision refers to compliance 'without undue delay'. She suggests that this may suggest two different time issues. One refers to 'the decision on whether to erase or not'; and the second which 'applies to the technical task of erasing the data'.[27] She adds that:

> All individual rights are subject to the limits set out in art. 12(3). It might be suggested that, in the case of art. 17 the time runs twice: the controller has a month (or two) in which to make the determination and then another month (or two) in which to achieve the erasure. This seems counter-intuitive and it is suggested that it is not intended, but there is no other obvious way to make sense of the repeated use of the terms "without undue delay".'[28]

---

27   Jay, Malcolm, Parry, Townsend and Bapat, *Guide to the General Data Protection Regulation, A Companion to Data Protection Law and Practice above* at 277.
28   *Ibid.*

PART C

OFFICIAL GUIDANCE

CHAPTER 15

The WP 29 Guidance on *Google Spain*

I INTRODUCTION

15.1   The WP 29[1] also refers to RtbF issues as well as *Google Spain*.[2] The Article 29 Working Party (WP 29) was a body made up of representatives of the respective Member State data regulators (data protection supervisory authorities), established under the Data Protection Directive DPD 95/46.[3] Note that this has now been replaced by the European Data Protection Board (EDPB) under the new General Data Protection Regulation (GDPR).[4]

Following the decision in *Google Spain*[5] and possibly because of the resultant publicity,[6] the WP 29 issued a guidance opinion on the case.[7]

---

1   *Google Spain SL, Google Inc v Agencia Española de Protección de Datos (AEPD), Mario Costeja González*, Court of Justice (Grand Chamber) (*Google Spain*), Case C-131/12, 13 May 2014.
2   WP 29, Guidelines on the implementation of the Court of Justice of the European Union judgment on 'Google Spain and Inc v Agencia Española de Protección de Datos (AEPD) and Mario Costeja González' C-131/121; WP 29, Opinion 8/2010 on applicable law (WP 29 adds as follows: 'In its judgment in *Google Spain* the Court of Justice of the European Union decided upon certain matters relating to the territorial scope of Directive 95/46/EC. The WP 29 commenced an internal analysis of the potential implications of this judgment on applicable law and may provide further guidance on this issue during the course of 2015, including, possibly, additional examples.').
3   See, in particular, Directive 95/46/EC of the European Parliament and of the Council of 24 October 1995 on the protection of individuals with regard to the processing of personal data and on the free movement of such data DPD 95/46 Art 29.
4   See, in particular, GDPR Art 68.
5   See *Google Spain*.
6   For example, A Travis *and* C Arthur, 'EU Court Backs "Right to be Forgotten": Google Must Amend Results on Request' *Guardian* (13 May 2014); D Streitfeld, 'European Court Lets Users Erase Records on Web' *New York Times* (13 May 2014); V West/Reuters, 'The Man Who Sued Google to be Forgotten' *Newsweek* (30 May 2014); 'On Being Forgotten' *Economist* (17 May 2014); D Sullivan, 'The Myths and Realities of How the EU's "Right to be Forgotten" in Google Works' *SearchEngineLand.com* (16 May 2014); JP Eckart, 'The Court Case Heard Around the World – *Google Spain SL v Agencia Espanola de Proteccion de Datos* – The Right to Be Forgotten and What It May Mean to the United States' *Dartmouth Law Journal* (2017) (15:1) 42. This is only a very small reflection of the truly international attention the case received.
7   WP 29, Guidelines on the implementation of the Court of Justice of the European Union Judgment on '*Google Spain and Inc v Agencia Española de Protección de Datos (AEPD) and Mario Costeja González*' C-131/12, WP225, 26 November 2014.

It also subsequently issued a separate notice, updating and amending a previous notice: *Update of Opinion on Applicable Law*[8] *in light of the CJEU judgment in Google Spain.*[9]

2   WP 29 GUIDANCE CRITERIA LIST

15.2   It is always important to look at the official guidance which may be issued from time to time on data protection issues. In the European context this is often issued by the EDPB.[10] The EDPB includes representatives from the respective data protection supervisory authorities. However, prior to the GDPR (and the creation of the EDPB) the previous advisory body, the WP 29, issued assistive guidance in relation to *Google Spain*. The WP29 produced a guidance list: Common Criteria for the Handling of Complaints by European Data Protection Authorities.[11] This is contained in the *Google Spain* guidance. The 13 guidance criteria are referred to below.

Criteria Question 1

15.3   This guidance criteria question asks:

> Does the search result relate to a natural person – ie an individual? And does the search result come up against a search on the data subject's name?[12]

The guidance also provides further commentary expanding on this guidance question.

Criteria Question 2

15.4   This guidance criteria question asks:

> Does the data subject play a role in public life? Is the data subject a public figure?[13]

---

8   WP 29, A29 WP Opinion 8/2010 on applicable law (WP179); WP 29, Update of Opinion 8/2010 on Applicable Law in Light of the CJEU Judgment in Google Spain, WP 179 update, 16 December 2015 at fn 1.

9   CJEU judgment of 13 May 2014 in *Google Spain*. This guidance document also briefly discusses some elements of the CJEU judgment of 1 October 2015 in Case C-230/14, *Weltimmosro v Nemzeti Adatvédelmi* és *Információszabadság Hatóság* (*Weltimmo*); WP 29, Update of Opinion 8/2010 at fn 2.

10   See GDPR Arts 68–76. Guidance may also arise from the European Data Protection Supervisor (EDPS) and respective national data protection supervisors.

11   WP 29, guidance list of common criteria for the handling of complaints by European data protection supervisory authorities. WP 29, Guidelines on the Implementation of the Court of Justice of the European Union Judgement on *'Google Spain and Inc v Agencia Espanola de Proteccion de Datos (AEPD) and Mario Costeja Gonzalez'* C-131/12, WP 225 (26 November 2014) 12–20.

12   WP 29, guidance list of common criteria, criteria 1.

13   *Ibid* criteria 2.

The guidance also provides further commentary expanding on this guidance question.

Interestingly, the *NT2*[14] decision appears to suggest that a person can be a public figure by virtue of the crimes which were charged. One would caution against this as a general rule or applying in all instances or indeed perhaps at all. We will need to see how further cases develop on this point. However, the judgment does acknowledge that the public role in that case is not reduced. It also points out that while the claimant was involved in interviews, which referred to the past crimes, this is treated as a 'neutral issue' and was merely an effort to seek to minimise the impact of the problem content.

Perhaps the *GC and Others v CNIL* might be considered somewhat differently.[15] This held that:

- 'The provisions of Article 8(1) and (5) of Directive 95/46/EC [and] the prohibition or restrictions relating to the processing of special categories of personal data ... apply also ... to the operator of a search engine';

- '... the operator of a search engine is in principle required ..., subject to the exceptions provided for by the directive, to accede to requests for de-referencing in relation to links to web pages containing personal data falling within the special categories';

- 'the operator of a search engine is required to accede to a request for de-referencing relating to links to web pages displaying such information, where the information relates to an earlier stage of the legal proceedings in question and, having regard to the progress of the proceedings, no longer corresponds to the current situation, in so far as it is established in the verification of the reasons of substantial public interest referred to in Article 8(4) of Directive 95/46 that, in the light of all the circumstances of the case, the data subject's fundamental rights guaranteed by Articles 7 and 8 of the Charter of Fundamental Rights of the European Union override the rights of potentially interested internet users protected by Article 11 of the Charter.'[16]

Criteria Question 3

15.5   This guidance criteria question asks:

Is the data subject a minor?[17]

---

14   *NT1 & NT2 v Google LLC* [2018] EWHC 799 (QB) (13 April 2018) Warby J at para 210.
15   See *GC and Others v CNIL*, CJEU, C-136/17 (24 September 2019); D De Conca, 'GC et al v CNIL: Balancing the Right to Be Forgotten with the Freedom of Information, the Duties of a Search Engine Operator' *European Data Protection Law Review* (EDPL) (2019) (5:4) 561; C Quelle, 'GC and Others v CNIL on the Responsibility of Search Engine Operators for Referring to Sensitive Data: The End of "Right to be Forgotten" Balancing?' *European Data Protection Law Review* (EDPL) (2019) (5:3) 438; J Globocnik, 'The Right to be Forgotten is Taking Shape: CJEU Judgments in GC and Others (C-136/17) and Google v CNIL (C-507/17)' *GRUR International: Journal of European* (2020) (69:4) 380.
16   *Ibid.*
17   WP 29, guidance list of common criteria, criteria 3.

The guidance also provides further commentary expanding on this guidance question. Interestingly, the judgment in the *NT2*[18] case refers to the age of the individual vis-à-vis being a child, but also to 'capacity' at the relevant time, which may suggest that even adults might be considered in terms of having or not having relevant capacity.

Criteria Question 4

15.6   This guidance criteria question asks:

Is the data accurate?[19]

The court notes in *NT2*[20] that the newspaper data was inaccurate. It adds that the key issue is whether the links should remain given the passage of time, the impact on the claimant, etc.

Criteria Question 5

15.7   This guidance criteria question asks:

Is the data relevant and not excessive?

(a) Does the data relate to the working life of the data subject?

(b) Does the search result link to information which allegedly constitutes hate speech/slander/libel or similar offences in the area of expression against the complainant?

(c) Is it clear that the data reflects an individual's personal opinion or does it appear to be verified fact?[21]

The guidance also provides further commentary expanding on this guidance question.

The court notes in *NT2*[22] that the problem content is not hate speech per se. (Generally, it is noted that online abuse (OA) is wider than hate speech.) In addition, the court states that there is no basis or relevance to justify continued availability and that continued availability would be excessive.

Criteria Question 6

15.8   This guidance criteria question asks:

18 *NT1 & NT2 v Google LLC* at para 211.
19 WP 29, criteria 4.
20 *NT1 & NT2 v Google LLC* at para 212.
21 WP 29, criteria 5.
22 *NT1 & NT2 v Google LLC* at para 213.

Is the information sensitive within the meaning of Article 8 of the Directive 95/46?[23]

The guidance also provides further commentary expanding on this guidance question. The court in *NT2*[24] stated that the data was sensitive. Note that 'sensitive data' as previously referred to under the DPD 95/46 is now referred to as 'special data' under the GDPR.

Criteria Question 7

15.9   This guidance criteria question asks:

Is the data up to date? Is the data being made available for longer than is necessary for the purpose of the processing?[25]

The guidance also provides further commentary expanding on this guidance question.

The court in *NT2*[26] states that this is the main issue or at least an issue for that part of the case.

Criteria Question 8

15.10   This guidance criteria question asks:

Is the data processing causing prejudice to the data subject? Does the data have a disproportionately negative privacy impact on the data subject?[27]

The guidance also provides further commentary expanding on this question. While the court in *NT2*[28] refers to this criterion, potentially it may be misinterpreted as placing an overly high onus on claimants, notwithstanding that in this instance the claimant was successful. It might be suggested that such references including the apparent burden placed on the *NT1* claimant under this criterion should be more restrictive otherwise it has the potential to do mischief with the intention of the express rights provided for in RtbF and may open a Pandora's box to allow certain defendants (or others) to avoid the duty to comply with a valid RtbF notice from a data subject altogether. At least in some (if not more) instances it may be assumed that there is harm or the potential for harm without onerous evidential preconditions being placed on claimants. To the extent that this decision may be interpreted as placing such general hurdles in all instances on claimants, the author would respectfully disagree. Indeed, the CJEU in *Google Spain* refers to

---

23   WP 29, criteria 6.
24   *NT1 & NT2 v Google LLC* at para 214.
25   WP 29, criteria 7.
26   *NT1 & NT2 v Google LLC* at para 215.
27   WP 29, criteria 8.
28   *NT1 & NT2 v Google LLC* at para 216.

the right applying 'without it being necessary in order to find ... that list[ing] causes prejudice'.[29]

Criteria Question 9

15.11   This guidance criteria question asks:

> Does the search result link to information that puts the data subject at risk?[30]

The guidance also provides further commentary expanding on this question. Problem content can indeed put people at various layers and imminence of risk.

Criteria Question 10

15.12   This guidance criteria question asks:

> In what context was the information published?
> (a)   Was the content voluntarily made public by the data subject?
> (b)   Was the content intended to be made public? Could the data subject have reasonably known that the content would be made public?[31]

The guidance also provides further commentary expanding on this question.

Criteria Question 11

15.13   This guidance criteria question asks:

> Was the original content published in the context of journalistic purposes?[32]

The guidance also provides further commentary expanding on this question.

Criteria Question 12

15.14   This guidance criteria questions asks:

> Does the publisher of the data have a legal power – or a legal obligation – to make the personal data publicly available?[33]

The guidance also provides further commentary expanding on this question.

---

29   *Google Spain*, para 4 of decision judgment.
30   WP 29, criteria 9.
31   *Ibid* criteria 10.
32   *Ibid* criteria 11.
33   *Ibid* criteria 12.

Criteria Question 13

15.15   This guidance criteria question asks:

> Does the data relate to a criminal offence?[34]

The guidance also provides further commentary expanding on this question.

It is noted that the court in *NT2*[35] refers under this criterion to this claimant's family being young – unlike the *NT1* claimant. Some might feel that the age of the family is not a deciding factor as to whether there can be prejudice or whether the claim should succeed. The judgment seems to suggest that because of their age, the disclosure of the old conviction is 'capable' of adverse impact. Emphasising this view is the apparent indication that because of the young family, *NT2*'s case on interference with family life is stronger.

Just as OA can and does have adverse effects on children and teenagers, the potential for OA and its adverse effect on others (ie, adults) does not neatly stop at the age of 13 (or even 16). It feels wrong to suggest that the victim of a revenge porn RtbF notification to a search engine and other websites should (or may) fail because their family was all over the age of 13 (or over 16); or that they had no children at all – even if the problem content was circulated to their friends, colleagues and employer.

The point of referring to a young family may be useful, but not to the extent of becoming a block in and of itself to claimants or to allowing a company to raise ever-more complex obstacles and hurdles and to add unnecessary additional days to hearings.

3   LINKED ACTIVITIES AND TAKEDOWN LINKS

15.16   The WP 29 notes that *Google Spain* held that the:

> processing of personal data in question by the search engine operated by Google Inc, a US-based controller, was "*inextricably linked to*" and therefore was carried out "*in the context of the activities*" of Google's establishment in Spain, considering that the advertising and commercial activities of the Spanish subsidiary constituted the "*means of rendering the search engine economically profitable.*"[36]

Therefore, '[o]n these grounds, the CJEU concluded that Spanish law applied to the processing in question'.[37]

---

34   *Ibid* criteria 13.
35   *NT1 & NT2 v Google LLC* at para 222(3).
36   WP 29, Update of Opinion 8/2010 on Applicable Law in Light of the CJEU Judgment in Google Spain, WP 179 update (16 December 2015) 2.
37   WP 29, Update of Opinion 8/2010 at 2.

4 BROAD JUDGMENT ON TERRITORY

15.17 Importantly, the WP 29 indicates that '[t]he implications of the judgment are broader than merely determining applicable law in relation to the operation of the Google search engine in Spain'.[38]

The judgment, for example, 'confirms the broad territorial reach of Article 4(1) (a) of [the DPD 95/46]'.[39] The court 'applies EU law to data processing conducted by a foreign controller established outside the EU, which has a "relevant" establishment in the EU triggering the application of EU data protection law'.[40]

The WP 29 adds that '[h]ow far this broad territorial reach applies, however, raises many questions'.[41] The GDPR is understood to be wider than the DPD 95/46 in this regard.

5 MEMBER STATE LAWS AND DIRECTIVE

15.18 There are, in addition, questions 'as to how to interpret the judgment in cases where the issue is not whether EU law or a foreign law applies, but whether the law of one EU Member State or the law of another Member State applies'.[42] The DPD 95/46 provides that 'where the same controller is established on the territory of several Member States, he must take the necessary measures to ensure that each of these establishments complies with obligations laid down by the national law applicable'.[43]

According to the WP 29, the question this gives rise to is 'whether, and to what extent, companies having a designated "EU headquarters" (acting as a "controller"), need only to comply with one national law within the EU or also with the laws of other EU Member States in which they may also have a "relevant establishment".'[44]

6 RESPONSIBILITY EVEN WITHOUT EU ESTABLISHMENT

15.19 The WP 29 also states that 'it is to be noted that even though the CJEU did not discuss in its judgment whether using a national domain name and/or using robots to collect information from European websites would trigger EU law on the basis of a "use of equipment" test under Article 4(1)(c), the judgment does not by any means exclude the possibility of activities of controllers having

---

38 *Ibid.*
39 *Ibid.* 'This has subsequently also been confirmed by the CJEU in the *Weltimmo* case, see paras 25 and 27; WP 29, Update of Opinion 8/2010 at fn 3.
40 WP 29, Update of Opinion 8/2010 at 2.
41 *Ibid.*
42 *Ibid.*
43 Data Protection Directive 95/46, Art 4(1)(a), second sentence.
44 WP 29, Update of Opinion 8/2010 at 2.

no establishment of any sort within the EU being subject to EU data protection requirements'.[45]

It continues that '[i]ndeed, Article 4 of the [DPD 95/46] makes it clear that this *can* be the case'.[46]

7 UPDATE GUIDANCE

15.20 The WP 29 refers to a previous Opinion on applicable law which it issued, namely, Opinion 8/2010.[47] It now states that that previous Opinion and particular examples therein (and expressly referring to Examples 5 and 11) now needs be read in the light of *Google Spain* as well as the updated guidance document. Effectively, it recognises the need to update in light of legal changes to the environment and case law.

The new guidance document 'explores the first two of these questions, which are both linked to the way the CJEU interpreted the "establishment" test' in Article 4(1)(a) of the DPD 95/46'.[48]

8 ESTABLISHMENT TEST AND 'CONTEXT OF THE ACTIVITIES OF AN ESTABLISHMENT'

15.21 The first question answered in *Google Spain* concerned the 'establishment' test per the DPD 95/46 Article 4. Article 4(1)(a) provides that the DPD 95/46 applies where processing is carried out 'in the context of the activities of an establishment' of the Controller on the territory of a Member State.[49]

The WP 29 recalls that, 'in line with recital 19 of the [DPD 95/46] and the guidance already provided in [the] WP 29 Opinion 8/2010, and as confirmed by the recent *Weltimmo* judgment, the notion of establishment has to be interpreted broadly'.[50]

In paragraph 41 of the *Weltimmo* judgment, the court 'emphasised that if the controller exercises *"a real and effective activity – even a minimal one"* – through *"stable arrangements"* in the territory of a Member State, it will be considered to have an establishment in that Member State'.[51]

---

45   *Ibid.*
46   Emphasis added. WP 29, Update of Opinion 8/2010 on Applicable Law at 2.
47   *Ibid.*
48   *Ibid* at 2–3.
49   *Ibid* at 3.
50   *Ibid.*
51   *Ibid.* See, in particular, para 29 of the *Weltimmo* judgment, 'which emphasizes a flexible definition of the concept of "establishment" and clarifies that "the degree of stability of the arrangements and the effective exercise of activities in that other Member State must be interpreted in the light of the specific nature of the economic activities and the provision of services concerned"; WP 29, Update of Opinion 8/2010 at fn 4.

In *Google Spain*, the Google search engine is provided by Google Inc (a US company). Google does have an office in Spain, namely, Google Spain SL. Google Spain promotes and sells online advertising space. The WP 29 states that the question to be considered, therefore, is whether the personal data processed by the Google search engine index is processed 'in the context of the activities of an establishment' in a Member State because of the activities of Google Spain.[52]

The CJEU held that the DPD 95/46 applies to processing by Google to provide search results in Spain, despite the fact that Google Inc is based in California and that it is Google Inc, rather than Google Spain, which provides search services in Spain.

Google argued that it was not conducting its search activities in Spain and that Google Spain SL was merely a commercial representative for its advertising activities. The court rejected this argument.

The court recalled that Article 4(1)(a) does not necessarily require the processing of personal data in question to be carried out 'by' the relevant establishment itself, rather that it is sufficient if the processing is carried out 'in the context of the activities' of the establishment.[53]

The court 'reasoned that the activities of the operator of the search engine and those of its establishment situated in the Member State concerned are "*inextricably linked*" to the processing carried out by Google Inc's search engine, arguing that the activities of Google Spain SL are the means of rendering the search engine economically profitable'.[54]

So commercial activities cannot be divorced from the other activities.

The WP 29 notes that '[i]t is sufficient that Google Spain SL carries out advertising activities, these being linked to the business model of Google (selling advertising relevant to the results provided by the search engine)'.[55] So, '[i]n other words, without the advertising activities, which are facilitated by Google Spain SL and similar Google subsidiaries across the globe, it would not be economically feasible for Google to offer its search engine services. The search engine activities carried out by Google cannot be separated from the generation of advertising revenue'.[56]

---

52   *Ibid* at 3.
53   See *Google Spain*, para 52, as also confirmed by para 35 in *Weltimmo*; WP 29, Update of Opinion 8/2010 at fn 5.
54   Update of Opinion 8/2010 at 3. See para 56 of the judgment; WP 29, Update of Opinion 8/2010 at fn 6.
55   *Ibid*
56   WP 29, Update of Opinion 8/2010 at 3–4. 'As an additional argument, the CJEU also referred to the fact that the adverts and the search results are displayed on the same page, as further evidence of their inter-dependency'; WP 29, Update of Opinion 8/2010 on Applicable Law at fn 7.

The court, therefore, held that 'the processing of personal data in question is carried out in the context of the commercial and advertising activity of the controller's establishment on the territory of a Member State, in this instance Spanish territory'.[57]

9 ANTI-AVOIDANCE

15.22 There can sometimes be attempts at so-called 'Chinese walls' and responsibility splitting, in an effort to avoid responsibility for carrying out required legal acts.

The court explains that given the objectives of the DPD 95/46, the rules on its scope 'cannot be interpreted restrictively' and that the DPD 95/46 has 'a particularly broad territorial scope'.[58] The court held that 'it cannot be accepted that the processing of personal data carried out for the purposes of the operation of the search engine should escape the obligations and guarantees laid down by [the DPD 95/46], which would compromise the Directive's effectiveness and the effective and complete protection of the fundamental rights and freedoms of natural persons which the [DPD 95/46] seeks to ensure'.[59]

Note reports that there are apparently efforts (in advance of the May 2018 'go live' of the GDPR) of some companies to seek to game plan it to avoid having some group entities having to comply or fully comply with the new GDPR.[60] Since then, however, there have been a number of data protection supervisory authority decisions, other regulator decisions (eg, competition) and court decisions across different EU countries involving multi-national organisations.[61]

10 TARGETING

15.23 The WP 29 states that it is 'important to highlight' that the court ruling[62] 'not only emphasises the fact that "the operator of a search engine sets up in a Member State a branch or subsidiary which is intended to promote and sell advertisement space offered by that engine" but also that this branch or subsidiary "orientates its activity towards the inhabitants of that Member State"'.[63] In

---

57 See para 57 of the judgment; WP 29, Update of Opinion 8/2010 at fn 8. *Ibid* at 4.
58 See paras 53, 54 and 58 of the judgment; WP 29, Update of Opinion 8/2010 at fn 9.
59 *Ibid*.
60 See 'Facebook Shifts 1.5 Billion Users to Avoid GDPR' *PrivacyLaws.com* (26 April 2018); D Ingram, 'Facebook to Put 1.5bn Users Out of Reach of New EU GDPR Privacy Law' *Irish Times* (19 April 2018); A Hern, 'Facebook Moves 1.5 bn Users Out of Reach of New European Privacy Law' *Guardian* (19 April 2018).
61 See eg, E Tannam, 'German Watchdog Orders Crackdown on Facebook's Data Gathering' *Silicon Republic* (7 February 2019); K Lillington, 'German Ruling on Facebook Data Collection Could Finally Protect Consumers' *Irish Times* (14 February 2019); A Hern, 'Facebook Personal Data Use and Privacy Settings Ruled Illegal by German Court' *Guardian* (12 February 2018).
62 See para 60 as well as point 2 of the final holding; WP 29, Update of Opinion 8/2010 at fn 10.
63 *Ibid* at 4.

Google's case this may mean presenting Spanish-orientated advertising alongside the search results.

11 'INEXTRICABLE LINK' BETWEEN EU AND NON-EU ACTIVITIES

15.24 The judgment in *Google Spain* confirms that the activities of a local establishment and data processing activities may be inextricably linked and thereby may trigger the applicability of EU law, even if that establishment is not actually taking any role in the data processing itself. Following the Opinion of its Advocate General[64] the CJEU decided that the sales generated by Google's local establishment in Spain were 'inextricably linked to' the profit generated through the data processing activities –irrespective of where these actually took place –and that this 'inextricable' link was sufficient to trigger the applicability of Spanish law.

12 LOCAL LINK TO PROCESSING ACTIVITIES

15.25 The key point is that even if the local establishment is not involved in any direct way in the processing of data – as was the case here – the activities of that local subsidiary may still bring the data processing within the scope of EU data protection law, as long as there is an 'inextricable link' between the activities of the local establishment and the data processing.

The CJEU's judgment suggests that revenue-raising in the EU by a local establishment, to the extent that such activities can be '*inextricably linked*' to the processing of personal data taking place outside the EU, is sufficient for the DPD 95/46 to apply to such processing by the non-EU controller.[65]

The CJEU ruling was specifically concerned with the question of ad-serving by search engines and with the extent to which a local advertising subsidiary may be considered as a 'relevant' establishment to trigger applicability of EU law. However, companies have many ways to organise themselves and different business models exist. Each scenario must be assessed on its own merits, taking into account the specific facts of the case. It would be a mistake to read the CJEU ruling too broadly and conclude that any and all establishments with the remotest links to the data processing activities will trigger the application

---

64 Opinion of Advocate General Jaaskinen delivered on 25 June 2013 in Case C-131/12. Available at: http://curia.europa.eu/juris/document/document.jsf?docid=138782&doclang=EN. See, in particular, para 64; WP 29, Update of Opinion 8/2010 at fn 11.
65 'This may potentially be the case, for example, for any foreign operator with a sales office or some other presence in the EU, even if that office has no role in the actual data processing, in particular where the processing takes place in the context of the sales activity in the EU and the activities of the establishment are aimed at the inhabitants of the Member States in which the establishment is located'; WP 29, Update of Opinion 8/2010 at fn 12.

of EU law,[66] but equally a mistake to assume automatically that RtbF does not apply. Prudence should dictate that it may well apply. Even where it may not, there may well be other data protection or privacy measures elsewhere which have relevance. Indeed, as indicated elsewhere, the concerns of individuals arising from online information and problem content are not limited to only one territory. Organisations should also be cautious when suggesting EU law does apply on one hand (eg seeking to avail of the limited EU eCommerce defences), but suggest on the other hand that EU law does not apply (eg, RtbF rules).

It also importantly cautions, however, that '[i]t would be equally wrong to read the judgement too restrictively, and merely to apply it to the specific business model of search engine operators'.[67]

13 GENERAL APPLICATION

15.26 In terms of more general applicability, the WP 29 states that '[d]epending on the facts of the case and the role which the local establishment plays, the judgement may apply to other non-EU companies whose business model relies on offering "free services" within the EU, which are then financed by making use of the personal data collected from the users (such as for advertising purposes)'.[68]

Furthermore, 'depending on the facts of each case, it cannot be ruled out that the activities of companies operating under other business models can also fall within the scope of EU law: the activities of foreign companies offering their services in the EU in exchange for membership fees or subscriptions, for example'.[69] By way of further example, this 'may even include organisations seeking donations –where this is done within the context of one or more establishments in the EU'.[70]

14 REVENUE PLANNING

15.27 It is also noted that, 'it may also be relevant that the proceeds from Spanish advertising generated by Google Spain SL are not necessarily used to fund www.google.es or any other European search service and, further, that the advertising contracts are generally entered into with the Google entity in Ireland'.[71]

---

66 'Some commercial activity, for example, may be so far removed from the processing of personal data that the existence of the commercial activity would not bring that data processing within the scope of EU law'; WP 29, Update of Opinion 8/2010 at fn 13.
67 *Ibid* at 5.
68 *Ibid.*
69 *Ibid.*
70 *Ibid.*
71 H Crowther, 'Remember to Forget Me: The Recent Ruling in *Google v AEPD and Costeja*' *Computer and Telecommunications Law Review* (2014) 163; WP 29, Update of Opinion 8/2010 at fn 14. *Ibid* at 5.

This suggests, according to the WP 29 opinion, that 'the necessary economic link between the activities of the local establishment and the data processing activities may not have to be particularly direct to meet the criteria'.[72]

15 LESSON

15.28 The WP 29 summarises that 'if a case by case analysis on the facts shows that there is an inextricable link between the activities of an EU establishment and the processing of data carried out by a non-EU controller, EU law will apply to that processing by the non-EU entity, whether or not the EU establishment plays a role in the processing of data'.[73] This 'confirms' that the DPD 95/46 has a broad territorial reach per Article 4(1).[74] So too will the GDPR.

16 APPLICABLE LAW AND MULTIPLE EU ESTABLISHMENTS

15.29 The WP 29 refers to the question arising in relation to determining which law applies where a company or group of companies operates throughout the EU and has sales offices or other establishments in several Member States and has designated a particular establishment in one EU Member State as its 'EU headquarters' and this establishment is the only one that carries out the functions of a controller in relation to the processing operations in question.[75]

So, the question arises as to whether this means that the controller must comply with the data protection law of only one Member State *or* will it also have to comply with some or all of the laws of the Member States where the company has establishments (which do not necessarily take any role in the processing operations themselves).[76]

The WP 29 puts it as follows, 'would the judgment lead to the application of several national data protection laws if the activities of several establishments of the same controller in the various Member States were "inextricably linked" to the data processing?'[77]

However, it adds that 'the CJEU did not address this issue directly'. The WP 29 states that 'neither did it distinguish its ruling according to whether or not there is an EU establishment which acts as a controller or otherwise plays a role in the processing activities'.[78] Rather, the court judgment added, with what the WP 29 describes as 'general applicability' 'a new interpretation of what "*in the context*

---

72 WP 29, Update of Opinion 8/2010 at 5.
73 *Ibid.*
74 *Ibid.*
75 *Ibid* at 6.
76 *Ibid.*
77 *Ibid.*
78 *Ibid.*

of the activities of an establishment" means: the element of the "*inextricable link*" to the processing activities'.[79]

However, the court did point out that one of the reasons for the approach it took was 'to prevent individuals from being deprived of the protection guaranteed by the [DPD 95/46]'.[80] This argument would, the WP 29 notes, not necessarily apply if a foreign company publicly identifies an EU-based entity as a controller and which, also on the facts of the case, does indeed determine the purposes and means of the processing.[81]

In *Google Spain*, 'EU law would apply in any event'.[82] 'What would be at stake is not whether or not EU data protection law would apply at all. Instead, the question would be, which of the national EU data protection laws would apply' (eg, Irish law, Spanish law or both – the activities of a foreign company headquartered in Ireland but also established in Spain).[83]

'If the company were to be only subject to the data protection law of one Member State, and not also of another, the baselines provided by the [DPD 95/46] would still provide a relatively high level of protection for the individuals concerned.'[84] But, and 'precisely because of the current lack of full harmonisation, it does matter which Member State's law applies'.[85] However, readers will note that the decision as under the DPD 95/46 – and that a directive requires national law implementation. Now the GDPR has been implemented and gone live – and that as a Regulation, it is directly effective and a harmonising measure in itself.

17   'INEXTRICABLE LINK' TEST AS NEW ELEMENT OF '*IN THE CONTEXT OF THE ACTIVITIES*' ANALYSIS

15.30   The WP 29 in its Opinion conclusion states that on the basis of *Google Spain*, 'an additional element should be added to the criteria described in the WP 29 Opinion on applicable law, which may trigger the applicability of EU/ national law' namely, 'the criteria of an "inextricable" (in this specific case economic) "link" between an activity and the data processing'.[86] The court 'identified this "inextricable link" taking into consideration the advertisement-financed business model of free online services, which is currently the most common mode of operating businesses on the internet'.[87] The judgment also 'suggests that other business models, and different forms of activity (including

---

79   *Ibid.*
80   *Ibid.*
81   *Ibid.*
82   *Ibid.*
83   *Ibid.*
84   *Ibid.*
85   *Ibid.*
86   *Ibid* at 7.
87   *Ibid.*

revenue raising) in an EU Member State may also trigger the applicability of EU law, although the assessment must be made on a case-by-case basis'.[88]

It is indicated by WP39 that '[i]rrespective of where the data processing itself takes place, so long as a company has establishments in several EU Member States which promote and sell advertisement space, raise revenues or carry out other activities, and it can be established that these activities and the data processing are *"inextricably linked"*, the national laws of each such establishments will apply'.[89]

The court decision, therefore, 'provides … clarification on two aspects'.[90] The WP 29 refers to the two clarifications on the findings of *Google Spain*, as follows:

- the first clarification that the judgment makes is that it is 'clear that the scope of current EU law extends to processing carried out by non-EU entities with a "relevant" establishment whose activities in the EU are *"inextricably linked"* to the processing of data, even where the applicability of EU law would not have been triggered based on more traditional criteria';[91] and

- the second clarification that the judgment confirms is that 'where there is an *"inextricable link"* –according to Article 4(1)(a) of [the DPD 95/46], there may be several national laws applicable to the activities of a controller having multiple establishments in various Member States'.[92]

18   ONE-STOP SHOP

15.31   The WP 29 notes that the DPD 95/46 'does not create a "one-stop shop" whereby it would only be the law of the Member State of the "EU headquarters" that would apply to all processing of personal data throughout the EU'.[93]

Rather, 'whenever there is an establishment in any EU country, it has to be assessed in each case whether any particular processing activity is carried out in the context of the activities of that establishment. It is not at all uncommon that a company headquartered in one EU Member State and having operations in multiple EU Member States would need to comply with the laws of each of these Member States (perhaps in respect of different parts of its processing operations)'.[94]

The WP 29 gives an example. It refers to 'a bank headquartered in one Member State but offering retail banking services and operating a large number of branch offices throughout the EU must comply with each of these local laws. What

---

88   *Ibid.*
89   *Ibid.*
90   *Ibid.*
91   *Ibid.*
92   *Ibid.*
93   *Ibid* at 6.
94   See also para 28 of the *Weltimmo* judgment; WP 29, *Update of Opinion 8/2010* at fn 17. *Ibid* at 6–7.

applies in the off-line, bricks-and-mortar world, must also apply in the digital world. The contrary could risk encouraging all businesses that are sufficiently mobile, such as many engaged in doing business online, to engage in forum shopping. In turn, this could encourage a regulatory race to the bottom when it comes to data protection'.[95]

One of the original aims of the proposals for the GDPR was to simplify matters by having a one-stop-shop regulator mechanism. This would mean that interested parties would only have to deal with one data protection supervisory authority in the EU, likely that of its main establishment. However, the full one-stop-shop model, while watered down somewhat in the final GDPR, is something which it reasonably favours and is moving towards– with some caveats.[96]

19 GDPR

15.32   Looking forward to the GDPR, the then WP 29 Opinion states that '[t] his broad reach [in the DPD 95/46] is ... to be further extended in the future by the rules set forth in the ... [GDPR][97] which more explicitly relies on the "effects principle" to complement the "territoriality principle" when it comes to the activities of foreign data controllers in the EU'.[98]

20   CONCLUSION

15.33   The guidance points are helpful and will continue to be considered by the courts. The extent to which they act as a line of balance against which divergent

---

95   'In this respect it is useful to refer also to Article 28(6) of the Directive, which provides that each supervisory authority is competent, whatever the national law applicable, to exercise, on the territory of its own Member State, the powers conferred on it in accordance with Article 28(3) of that Directive. Article 28(6) of the Directive also provides that each authority may be requested to exercise its powers by an authority of another Member State and that the supervisory authorities are to cooperate with one another to the extent necessary for the performance of their duties, in particular by exchanging all useful information. With regard to penalties, the CJEU in its judgment in *Weltimmo*, para 60, concluded that a supervisory authority 'cannot impose penalties on the basis of the law of that Member State on the controller with respect to the processing of those data who is not established in that territory, but should, in accordance with Article 28(6) of that Directive, request the supervisory authority within the Member State whose law is applicable to act'; WP 29, Update of Opinion 8/2010 at fn 18. *Ibid* at 7.
96   Note recent cases, referred to in, for example, E Tannam, 'German Watchdog Orders Crackdown on Facebook's Data Gathering,' *Silicon Republic* (7 February 2019); K Lillington, 'German Ruling on Facebook Data Collection Could Finally Protect Consumers,' *Irish Times* (14 February 2019); A Hern, 'Facebook Personal Data Use and Privacy Settings Ruled Illegal by German Court,' *Guardian* (12 February 2018).
97   COM/2012/011 final, Proposal for a Regulation on the protection of individuals with regard to the processing of personal data and on the free movement of such data (General Data Protection Regulation); WP 29, Update of Opinion 8/2010 at fn 15.
98   See also para 56 of the Advocate General's Opinion, which explains that such an approach, attaching the territorial applicability of EU legislation to the targeted public, is consistent with the court's caselaw; WP 29, *Update of Opinion 8/2010* at fn 16. *Ibid* at 5.

cases or points will be viewed remains to be seen. It should also be borne in mind that as forms of problem content develop and change, including issues of urgency, these guidance criteria should also evolve. It is not suggested that the current guidance criteria are designed to capture all forms of problem content that may arise. RtbF is carefully considered, balanced and calibrated to assist data subjects. It should not be overly restricted or perhaps even be restricted at all. Courts should also be reluctant to add new criteria which may act as a hinderance to data subjects and victims (of different forms of online abuse) being able to vindicate their RtbF rights. Rosemary Jay notes, for example, that '[i]t appears obvious that the data subject will have to give the basis on which he or she objects to the processing, for example an allegation that the data have been processed unlawfully, but no more than that appears to be required'.[99] Defendants should not be allowed to introduce discretionary criteria or policies which have an aim or (intended) effect of hindering claims or reducing the number of claims or reducing the number of successfully completed RtbF notices received. The placing of onerous burdens on data subjects in order to file RtbF notices, or to back up notices, beyond that which is reasonably required – particularly overly legal or formalistic criteria – may well step beyond the parameters of the legal obligations of RtbF in an impermissible manner. The EDPB may decide to update the above (WP 29) criteria or add further guidance as further case law develops.

---

99 R Jay, W Malcolm, E Parry, L Townsend and A Bapat, *Guide to the General Data Protection Regulation, A Companion to Data Protection Law and Practice* (Sweet and Maxwell, 2017) at 273. Also note P Lambert, *A User's Guide to Data Protection* (Bloomsbury, 2020).

PART D

EU CASE LAW EXAMPLES

CHAPTER 16

EU Case Law Examples

1 GOOGLE SPAIN: THE GROUND-BREAKING RTBF CASE

16.1   No discussion of RtbF issues would be complete without reference to the ground-breaking RtbF case *Google Spain SL, Google Inc v Agencia Española de Protección de Datos (AEPD), Mario Costeja González Google Spain* dated 13 May 2014.[1] It was decided before the Grand Chamber of the European Court of Justice (ECJ), now called the Court of Justice of the European Union (CJEU). While many aspects were both predicted – and predictable – it did produce a significant amount of surprise in some quarters.

2   DIRECTIVE 95/46: LAW PRE THE GDPR

16.2   It is possible that some individuals may have understood that the General Data Protection Regulation (GDPR) brought in the new RbtF and as such that this right did not exist previously. After all, RtbF was not expressly referred to in the previous Data Protection Directive (DPD) 95/46.[2] To some extent it is understandable as the DPD dates from 1995 – well before the problem issues of the modern internet and social media.[3]

The case was brought under the then current EU laws on data protection and respective national law issues. It is important to point out, therefore, that the case occurred under the existing data protection laws (ie, the DPD 95/46) – even prior to the new GDPR.

---

1   *Google Spain SL, Google Inc v Agencia Española de Protección de Datos (AEPD), Mario Costeja González*, Court of Justice (Grand Chamber), Case C-131/12, 13 May 2014. There is a vast commentary now in relation to this case. See, for example, W Lamik, 'Advancement of the Right to be Forgotten – Analysis of the Judgment of the Court of Justice of the European Union of 24 September 2019 in the Case of Google LLC Versus Commission Nationale de l'Informatique' *European Journal of Privacy Law & Technologies* (EJPLT), Special Issue (2020) 113; J Globocnik, 'The Right to be Forgotten is Taking Shape: CJEU Judgments in GC and Others (C-136/17) and Google v CNIL (C-507/17)' *GRUR International: Journal of European* (2020) (69:4) 380.
2   Directive 95/46, Directive 95/46/EC of the European Parliament and of the Council of 24 October 1995 on the protection of individuals with regard to the processing of personal data and on the free movement of such data (OJ 1995 L 281, p 31).
3   These can range from forgetting, takedown, etc. (see, eg, V Mayer-Schönberger, *Delete, The Virtue of Forgetting in the Digital Age* (Princeton University Press, 2011) to the range of online abuse (see, eg, P Lambert, *International Handbook of Social Media Laws* (Bloomsbury, 2014); P Lambert, *Social Networking, Law, Rights and Policy* (Clarus, 2014). Potential data fine issues can also be considered, see P Lambert, *Data Fines, Understanding the EU Data Fine Rules* (Kortext, 2021).

Readers will note that a directive is an EU legal measure which is required to be implemented in Member States by respective national implementing laws. Hence, the 1995 Directive was implemented via a variety of national laws such as data protection acts. Regulations are EU legal measures which are directly effective in the EU and throughout each of the Member States – without the need for follow-on national implementing legislation. Therefore, the GDPR is directly effective, unlike the previous 1995 Directive.

3   FACTS, HISTORY AND CIRCUMSTANCES

16.3   The CJEU describes the facts and history of the case before it as follows:

> On 5 March 2010, [Mr González], a Spanish national resident in Spain, lodged with the AEPD a complaint against La Vanguardia Ediciones SL, which publishes a daily newspaper with a large circulation, in particular in Catalonia (Spain) (La Vanguardia), and against Google Spain and Google Inc. The complaint was based on the fact that, when an internet user entered Mr González's] name in the search engine of the Google group (Google Search), he would obtain links to two pages of La Vanguardia's newspaper, of 19 January and 9 March 1998 respectively, on which an announcement mentioning [Mr González's] name appeared for a real-estate auction connected with attachment proceedings for the recovery of social security debts.[4]

> By that complaint, [Mr González] requested, first, that La Vanguardia be required either to remove or alter those pages so that the personal data relating to him no longer appeared or to use certain tools made available by search engines in order to protect the data. Second, he requested that Google Spain or Google Inc be required to remove or conceal the personal data relating to him so that they ceased to be included in the search results and no longer appeared in the links to La Vanguardia. [Mr González] stated in this context that the attachment proceedings concerning him had been fully resolved for a number of years and that reference to them was now entirely irrelevant.[5]

> By decision of 30 July 2010, the AEPD rejected the complaint in so far as it related to La Vanguardia, taking the view that the publication by it of the information in question was legally justified as it took place upon order of the Ministry of Labour and Social Affairs and was intended to give maximum publicity to the auction in order to secure as many bidders as possible.[6]

> On the other hand, the complaint was upheld in so far as it was directed against Google Spain and Google Inc. The AEPD considered in this regard that operators of search engines are subject to data protection legislation given that they carry out data processing for which they are responsible and act as intermediaries in the information society. The AEPD took the view that it has the power to require the withdrawal of data and the prohibition of access to certain data by the operators of search engines when it considers that the locating and dissemination of the data are liable to compromise the

4   *Google Spain* para 14.
5   *Ibid* para 15.
6   *Ibid* para 16.

fundamental right to data protection and the dignity of persons in the broad sense, and this would also encompass the mere wish of the person concerned that such data not be known to third parties. The AEPD considered that that obligation may be owed directly by operators of search engines, without it being necessary to erase the data or information from the website where they appear, including when retention of the information on that site is justified by a statutory provision.[7]

Google Spain and Google Inc brought separate actions against that decision before the Audiencia Nacional (National High Court). The Audiencia Nacional joined the actions.[8]

That Court states in the order for reference that the actions raise the question of what obligations are owed by operators of search engines to protect personal data of persons concerned who do not wish that certain information, which is published on third parties' websites and contains personal data relating to them that enable that information to be linked to them, be located, indexed and made available to internet users indefinitely. The answer to that question depends on the way in which [the DPD] 95/46 must be interpreted in the context of these technologies, which appeared after the directive's publication.[9]

Parties

16.4   The main parties to the case were Google (ie, Google Spain and Google Inc) and the Spanish data protection supervisory authority, the Agencia Española de Protección de Datos (AEPD). The AEPD had upheld the original request of the individual to take down (ie, forget) the material in question relating to him.

The original requestor – Mr González – was also represented at the ECJ/CJEU. As is often the case, the EU Commission also made representations.

Given the import of the case representations were made by other interested parties, namely the governments of Spain, Greece, Italy, Austria and Poland.

Issues

16.5   The judgment of the CJEU in the *Google Spain* case makes clear that it considers a number of potential issues as being relevant. These are referred to at the beginning of the ruling as follows:

- personal data;

- protection of individuals with regard to the processing of such data;

- DPD 95/46;

---

7   *Ibid* para 17.
8   *Ibid* para 18.
9   *Ibid* para 19.

- DPD 95/46 Articles 2, 4, 12 and 14;

- material and territorial scope;

- internet search engines;

- processing of data contained on websites;

- searching for, indexing and storage of such data;

- responsibility of the operator of the search engine;

- establishment on the territory of a Member State;

- extent of that operator's obligations and of the individual data subject's rights; and

- the Charter of Fundamental Rights of the European Union (Charter) Articles 7 and 8.

Judgment Issues

16.6   The court indicates that the case more specifically 'concerns the interpretation of':

- Article 2(b) and (d);

- Article 4(1)(a) and (c);

- Article 12(b);

- subparagraph (a) of the first paragraph of Article 14 of the DPD 95/46;[10] and

- Article 8 of the Charter.[11]

The proceedings are between *Google Spain SL (Google Spain), Google Inc and the Agencia Española de Protección de Datos (Spanish Data Protection Agency; the AEPD) and Mr González.*[12]

The case concerns the earlier decision of AEPD which upheld the complaint made by Mr González against those two Google companies and which ordered Google Inc to 'adopt the measures necessary to withdraw personal data relating to [Mr González] from its index and to prevent access to the data in the future'.[13]

---

10   See Directive 95/46/EC.
11   *Google Spain* para 1.
12   *Ibid* para 2.
13   *Ibid.*

4 LEGAL CONTEXT: EUROPEAN UNION LAW

Recitals

16.7 The court notes that Article 1 of the DPD 95/46 has the object of protecting the fundamental rights and freedoms of natural persons, in particular their right to privacy with respect to the processing of personal data and of removing obstacles to the free flow of such data, as stated in recitals 2, 10, 18–20 and 25 in the Directive's preamble.[14] These recitals to the Directive refer as follows:

> (2) ... data-processing systems are designed to serve man; ... they must, whatever the nationality or residence of natural persons, respect their fundamental rights and freedoms, notably the right to privacy, and contribute to ... the well-being of individuals;
>
> ...
>
> (10)... the object of the national laws on the processing of personal data is to protect fundamental rights and freedoms, notably the right to privacy, which is recognised both in Article 8 of the European Convention for the Protection of Human Rights and Fundamental Freedoms [, signed in Rome on 4 November 1950,] and in the general principles of Community law; ... for that reason, the approximation of those laws must not result in any lessening of the protection they afford but must, on the contrary, seek to ensure a high level of protection in the Community;
>
> ...
>
> (18) ... in order to ensure that individuals are not deprived of the protection to which they are entitled under this Directive, any processing of personal data in the Community must be carried out in accordance with the law of one of the Member States; ... in this connection, processing carried out under the responsibility of a Controller who is established in a Member State should be governed by the law of that State;
>
> (19)... establishment on the territory of a Member State implies the effective and real exercise of activity through stable arrangements; ... the legal form of such an establishment, whether simply [a] branch or a subsidiary with a legal personality, is not the determining factor in this respect; ... when a single Controller is established on the territory of several Member States, particularly by means of subsidiaries, he must ensure, in order to avoid any circumvention of national rules, that each of the establishments fulfils the obligations imposed by the national law applicable to its activities;
>
> (20)... the fact that the processing of data is carried out by a person established in a third country must not stand in the way of the protection of individuals provided for in this Directive; ... in these cases, the processing should be governed by the law of the Member State in which the means used are located, and there should be guarantees to ensure that the rights and obligations provided for in this Directive are respected in practice;

14 *Ibid* para 3.

...

(25)... the principles of protection must be reflected, on the one hand, in the obligations imposed on persons ... responsible for processing, in particular regarding data quality, technical security, notification to the supervisory authority, and the circumstances under which processing can be carried out, and, on the other hand, in the right conferred on individuals, the data on whom are the subject of processing, to be informed that processing is taking place, to consult the data, to request corrections and even to object to processing in certain circumstances.[15]

Article 2

16.8   DPD 95/46 Article 2 refers to the definitions or building blocks of the data protection regime. It includes the following definition to which the court refers, namely:[16]

(a) 'personal data' shall mean any information relating to an identified or identifiable natural person (data subject); an identifiable person is one who can be identified, directly or indirectly, in particular by reference to an identification number or to one or more factors specific to his physical, physiological, mental, economic, cultural or social identity;

(b) 'processing of personal data' (processing) shall mean any operation or set of operations which is performed upon personal data, whether or not by automatic means, such as collection, recording, organisation, storage, adaptation or alteration, retrieval, consultation, use, disclosure by transmission, dissemination or otherwise making available, alignment or combination, blocking, erasure or destruction;

...

(d) 'controller' shall mean the natural or legal person, public authority, agency or any other body which alone or jointly with others determines the purposes and means of the processing of personal data; where the purposes and means of processing are determined by national or Community laws or regulations, the controller or the specific criteria for his nomination may be designated by national or Community law; ...[17]

There are also various other definitions to which the court does not refer. For example, there is a definition of what a 'data subject' is. It is not clear why this was apparently omitted, especially given that it was an individual who was most concerned with erasure, forgetting and takedown and who made the original request.

15   *Ibid.*
16   *Ibid* para 4.
17   *Ibid.*

Article 3

16.9   DPD 95/46 Article 3 is entitled 'Scope'. It states in paragraph 1 that:

> This Directive shall apply to the processing of personal data wholly or partly by automatic means, and to the processing otherwise than by automatic means of personal data which form part of a filing system or are intended to form part of a filing system.[18]

Article 4

16.10   DPD 95/46 Article 4 is entitled 'National law applicable'. It provides that:[19]

1.   Each Member State shall apply the national provisions it adopts pursuant to this Directive to the processing of personal data where:

  (a)   the processing is carried out in the context of the activities of an establishment of the controller on the territory of the Member State; when the same controller is established on the territory of several Member States, he must take the necessary measures to ensure that each of these establishments complies with the obligations laid down by the national law applicable;

  (b)   the controller is not established on the Member State's territory, but in a place where its national law applies by virtue of international public law;

  (c)   the controller is not established on Community territory and, for purposes of processing personal data makes use of equipment, automated or otherwise, situated on the territory of the said Member State, unless such equipment is used only for purposes of transit through the territory of the Community.

2.   In the circumstances referred to in paragraph 1(c), the controller must designate a representative established in the territory of that Member State, without prejudice to legal actions which could be initiated against the controller himself.[20]

Article 6

16.11   Section I is entitled 'Principles relating to data quality'. These are referred to as the data protection principles under the directive and the principles under the GDPR. The principles and the obligations and rights contained in the principles are at the core of the data protection regime. Chapter II of DPD 95/46, Article 6 states as follows:[21]

---

18   *Ibid* para 5.
19   *Ibid* para 6.
20   *Ibid*.
21   *Ibid* para 7.

1. Member States shall provide that personal data must be:

    (a) processed fairly and lawfully;

    (b) collected for specified, explicit and legitimate purposes and not further processed in a way incompatible with those purposes. Further processing of data for historical, statistical or scientific purposes shall not be considered as incompatible provided that Member States provide appropriate safeguards;

    (c) adequate, relevant and not excessive in relation to the purposes for which they are collected and/or further processed;

    (d) accurate and, where necessary, kept up to date; every reasonable step must be taken to ensure that data which are inaccurate or incomplete, having regard to the purposes for which they were collected or for which they are further processed, are erased or rectified;

    (e) kept in a form which permits identification of data subjects for no longer than is necessary for the purposes for which the data were collected or for which they are further processed. Member States shall lay down appropriate safeguards for personal data stored for longer periods for historical, statistical or scientific use.

2. It shall be for the controller to ensure that paragraph 1 is complied with.[22]

Article 7

16.12 Section II is entitled 'Criteria for making data processing legitimate'. Chapter II of the DPD 95/46, Article 7 provides that 'Member States shall provide that personal data may be processed only if: …

(f) processing is necessary for the purposes of the legitimate interests pursued by the Controller or by the third party or parties to whom the data are disclosed, except where such interests are overridden by the interests [or] fundamental rights and freedoms of the Data Subject which require protection under Article 1(1).[23]

Article 9

16.13 The DPD 95/46 Article 9 is entitled 'Processing of personal data and freedom of expression'. These are sometimes referred to as legal processing requirements or legal processing conditions. These requirements must be complied with in addition to compliance with the principles. Article 9 provides:

> Member States shall provide for exemptions or derogations from the provisions of this Chapter, Chapter IV and Chapter VI for the processing of personal data carried out solely for journalistic purposes or the purpose of artistic or literary expression only if they are necessary to reconcile the right to privacy with the rules governing freedom of expression.[24]

22 *Ibid.*
23 *Ibid* para 8.
24 *Ibid* para 9.

Article 12

16.14 DPD 95/46 Article 12 is entitled 'Rights of access'. It provides that 'Member States shall guarantee every data subject the right to obtain from the controller' as follows:

'(b) as appropriate the rectification, erasure or blocking of data the processing of which does not comply with the provisions of this Directive, in particular because of the incomplete or inaccurate nature of the data.'[25]

Article 14

16.15 DPD 95/46 Article 14 is entitled 'The data subject's right to object'. It provides:

Member States shall grant the data subject the right: (a) at least in the cases referred to in Article 7(e) and (f), to object at any time on compelling legitimate grounds relating to his particular situation to the processing of data relating to him, save where otherwise provided by national legislation. Where there is a justified objection, the processing instigated by the controller may no longer involve those data.[26]

Article 28

16.16 DPD 95/46 Article 28 is entitled 'Supervisory authority'. It provides as follows:

1. Each Member State shall provide that one or more public authorities are responsible for monitoring the application within its territory of the provisions adopted by the Member States pursuant to this Directive.

   ...

3. Each authority shall in particular be endowed with:

   – investigative powers, such as powers of access to data forming the subject-matter of processing operations and powers to collect all the information necessary for the performance of its supervisory duties,

   – effective powers of intervention, such as, for example, that ... of ordering the blocking, erasure or destruction of data, of imposing a temporary or definitive ban on processing ...

   – ... Decisions by the supervisory authority which give rise to complaints may be appealed against through the courts.

4. Each supervisory authority shall hear claims lodged by any person, or by an association representing that person, concerning the protection of his rights and freedoms in regard to the processing of personal data. The person concerned shall be informed of the outcome of the claim.

---

25 *Ibid* para 10.
26 *Ibid* para 11.

...

6. Each supervisory authority is competent, whatever the national law applicable to the processing in question, to exercise, on the territory of its own Member State, the powers conferred on it in accordance with paragraph 3. Each authority may be requested to exercise its powers by an authority of another Member State. The supervisory authorities shall cooperate with one another to the extent necessary for the performance of their duties, in particular by exchanging all useful information.[27]

These are the provisions of DPD 95/46 which the court expressly refers to in its decision.

Spanish Law

16.17   DPD 95/46 was transposed into law in Spain by the Spanish Organic Law No 15/1999 of 13 December 1999 on the protection of personal data.[28] As indicated above, a directive requires national implementing legislation while the GDPR, as a directly effective Regulation, does not.

5   QUESTIONS AND ISSUES REFERRED

16.18   Cases that reach the ECJ/CJEU operate by way of a Member State court referring a set of specific questions to the EU court.

The questions referred for a preliminary ruling in the *Google Spain* case, are referred by the Audiencia Nacional. It decided to stay the proceedings and to refer the following questions to the Court for a preliminary ruling.

Question 1

16.19   The first question is as follows:

1. With regard to the territorial application of [the DPD 95/46] and, consequently, of the Spanish data protection legislation:

    (a) must it be considered that an "establishment", within the meaning of Article 4(1)(a) of [the DPD 95/46], exists when any one or more of the following circumstances arise:

    – when the undertaking providing the search engine sets up in a Member State an office or subsidiary for the purpose of promoting and selling advertising space on the search engine, which orientates its activity towards the inhabitants of that State,

27 *Ibid* para 12.
28 *Ibid* para 13. Referring to Organic Law No 15/1999, 13 December 1999, BOE No 298 of 14 December 1999, p 43088.

or

– when the parent company designates a subsidiary located in that Member State as its representative and controller for two specific filing systems which relate to the data of customers who have contracted for advertising with that undertaking,

or

– when the office or subsidiary established in a Member State forwards to the parent company, located outside the European Union, requests and requirements addressed to it both by data subjects and by the authorities with responsibility for ensuring observation of the right to data protection, even where such collaboration is engaged in voluntarily?

(b) Must Article 4(1)(c) of [the DPD 95/46] be interpreted as meaning that there is "use of equipment … situated on the territory of the said Member State":

– when a search engine uses crawlers or robots to locate and index information contained in web pages located on servers in that Member State, or

– when it uses a domain name pertaining to a Member State and arranges for searches and the results thereof to be based on the language of that Member State?

(c) Is it possible to regard as a use of equipment, in the terms of Article 4(1)(c) of [the DPD 95/46], the temporary storage of the information indexed by internet search engines? If the answer to that question is affirmative, can it be considered that that connecting factor is present when the undertaking refuses to disclose the place where it stores those indexes, invoking reasons of competition?

(d) Regardless of the answers to the foregoing questions and particularly in the event that the Court … considers that the connecting factors referred to in Article 4 of [the DPD 95/46] are not present:

must [the DPD 95/46] … be applied, in light of Article 8 of the [Charter], in the Member State where the centre of gravity of the conflict is located and more effective protection of the rights of … Union citizens is possible?[29]

Question 2

16.20 The second question is as follows:

2. As regards the activity of search engines as providers of content in relation to [the DPD 95/46] …:

(a) in relation to the activity of [Google Search], as a provider of content, consisting in locating information published or included on the net by third parties, indexing it automatically, storing it temporarily and

---

29 *Google Spain*, para 20.

finally making it available to internet users according to a particular order of preference, when that information contains personal data of third parties: must an activity like the one described be interpreted as falling within the concept of "processing of … data" used in Article 2(b) of [the DPD 95/46]?

(b) If the answer to the foregoing question is affirmative, and once again in relation to an activity like the one described:

must Article 2(d) of [the DPD 95/46] be interpreted as meaning that the undertaking managing [Google Search] is to be regarded as the "controller" of the personal data contained in the web pages that it indexes?

(c) In the event that the answer to the foregoing question is affirmative: may the [AEPD], protecting the rights embodied in [Article] 12(b) and [subparagraph (a) of the first paragraph of Article 14] of [the DPD 95/46], directly impose on [Google Search] a requirement that it withdraw from its indexes an item of information published by third parties, without addressing itself in advance or simultaneously to the owner of the web page on which that information is located?

(d) In the event that the answer to the foregoing question is affirmative:

would the obligation of search engines to protect those rights be excluded when the information that contains the personal data has been lawfully published by third parties and is kept on the web page from which it originates?[30]

Question 3

16.21 The third question is as follows:

3. Regarding the scope of the right of erasure and/or the right to object, in relation to the "derecho al olvido" ([RtbF]), the following question is asked:

Must it be considered that the rights to erasure and blocking of data, provided for in Article 12(b) and the right to object, provided for by [subparagraph (a) of the first paragraph of Article 14] of [the DPD 95/46], extend to enabling the data subject to address himself to search engines in order to prevent indexing of the information relating to him personally, published on third parties' web pages, invoking his wish that such information should not be known to internet users when he considers that it might be prejudicial to him or he wishes it to be consigned to oblivion, even though the information in question has been lawfully published by third parties?[31]

---

30 *Ibid.*
31 *Ibid.*

Q2(a) and (b): Court Consideration of Material Scope of Directive

16.22   The court considered Question 2(a) and (b) concerning the material scope of the DPD 95/46.

The court states that the referring court 'asks, in essence, whether Article 2(b) of [the DPD 95/46] is to be interpreted as meaning that the activity of a search engine as a provider of content which consists in finding information published or placed on the internet by third parties, indexing it automatically, storing it temporarily and, finally, making it available to internet users according to a particular order of preference must be classified as "processing of personal data" within the meaning of that provision when that information contains personal data'.[32]

It continues that '[i]f the answer is in the affirmative, the referring Court seeks to ascertain furthermore whether Article 2(d) of [the DPD 95/46] is to be interpreted as meaning that the operator of a search engine must be regarded as the "controller" in respect of that processing of the personal data, within the meaning of that provision'.[33]

Google

16.23   Google Spain and Google Inc argue that 'the activity of search engines cannot be regarded as processing of the data which appear on third parties' web pages displayed in the list of search results, given that search engines process all the information available on the internet without effecting a selection between personal data and other information'.[34]

It is not clear if the argument is that there is no search engine processing per se, or that the search engine activities do not amount to processing or processing as caught by the DPD 95/46:

> Furthermore, even if that activity must be classified as "data processing", the operator of a search engine cannot be regarded as a "controller" in respect of that processing since it has no knowledge of those data and does not exercise control over the data.[35]

González, Spain, Italy, Austria and Poland

16.24   In contrast to the above, Mr González, the Spanish, Italian, Austrian and Polish governments and the European Commission argued that that activity 'quite clearly involves "data processing" within the meaning of [the DPD 95/46], which

---

32   *Ibid* para 21.
33   *Ibid.*
34   *Ibid* para 22.
35   *Ibid.*

is distinct from the data processing by the publishers of websites and pursues different objectives from such processing. The operator of a search engine is the "controller" in respect of the data processing carried out by it since it is the operator that determines the purposes and means of that processing'.[36]

Greece

16.25 The Greek Government submitted that the activity in question 'constitutes such "processing", but inasmuch as search engines serve merely as intermediaries, the undertakings which operate them cannot be regarded as "controllers", except where they store data in an "intermediate memory" or "cache memory" for a period which exceeds that which is technically necessary'.[37]

Court Position

16.26 The court notes that DPD 95/46 Article 2(b) defines 'processing of personal data' as:

> any operation or set of operations which is performed upon personal data, whether or not by automatic means, such as collection, recording, organisation, storage, adaptation or alteration, retrieval, consultation, use, disclosure by transmission, dissemination or otherwise making available, alignment or combination, blocking, erasure or destruction.[38]

The ECJ/CJEU had previously referred to the internet and related issues in a previous case. The court notes that it 'has already had occasion to state that the operation of loading personal data on an internet page must be considered to be such "processing" within the meaning of Article 2(b) of [the DPD 95/46]'.[39] This is referred to in the *Lindqvist* case (paragraph 25).[40]

The court states that '[s]o far as concerns the activity at issue in the main proceedings, it is not contested that the data found, indexed and stored by search engines and made available to their users include information relating to identified or identifiable natural persons and thus "personal data" within the meaning of Article 2(a) of that Directive'.[41]

Therefore, the court states that:

> it must be found that, in exploring the internet automatically, constantly and systematically in search of the information which is published there, the operator of a search engine "collects" such data which it subsequently

---

36 *Ibid* para 23.
37 *Ibid* para 24.
38 *Ibid* para 25.
39 *Ibid* para 26.
40 *Ibid*. Referring to *Bodil Lindqvist v Åklagarkammaren i Jönköping*, C101/01, EU:C:2003:596, para 25.
41 *Google Spain*, para 27.

"retrieves", "records" and "organises" within the framework of its indexing programmes, "stores" on its servers and, as the case may be, "discloses" and "makes available" to its users in the form of lists of search results. As those operations are referred to expressly and unconditionally in Article 2(b) of [the DPD 95/46], they must be classified as "processing" within the meaning of that provision, regardless of the fact that the operator of the search engine also carries out the same operations in respect of other types of information and does not distinguish between the latter and the personal data.[42]

It might be argued that once something is published online it loses its status as personal data. It is not indicated if this was actually argued in *Google Spain*. (However, Facebook did make that argument in a different case.[43]) The ECJ/CJEU states that '[n]or is the foregoing finding affected by the fact that those data have already been published on the internet and are not altered by the search engine'.[44]

The court notes that it has 'already held that the operations referred to in Article 2(b) of [the DPD 95/46] must also be classified as such processing where they exclusively concern material that has already been published in unaltered form in the media'.[45] The court continues that '[i]t has indeed observed in that regard that a general derogation from the application of [the DPD 95/46] in such a case would largely deprive the directive of its effect'[46] referring to the *Satakunnan Markkinapörssi and Satamedia* case on this point (see paragraphs 48 and 49).[47]

The court states that 'it follows from the definition contained in Article 2(b) of [the DPD 95/46] that, whilst the alteration of personal data indeed constitutes processing within the meaning of the directive, the other operations which are mentioned there do not, on the other hand, in any way require that the personal data be altered'.[48]

Controller Issue

16.27 The court refers to 'the question whether the operator of a search engine must be regarded as the "controller" in respect of the processing of personal data that is carried out by that engine in the context of an activity such as that at issue in the main proceedings. It should be recalled that Article 2(d) of [DPD 95/46] defines "controller" as "the natural or legal person, public authority, agency or

---

42 *Ibid* para 28.
43 This was before the Irish High Court. That was in the case of *McKeogh v Doe and Others* [2012] IEHC 95. Facebook was one of the responding parties.
44 *Google Spain,* para 29.
45 *Ibid* para 30.
46 *Ibid.*
47 *Ibid.* Referring to *Satakunnan Markkinapörssi and Satamedia,* Case C73/07, EU:C:2008:727, paras 48 and 49.
48 *Google Spain,* para 31.

any other body which alone or jointly with others determines the purposes and means of the processing of personal data."'[49]

The court states that '[i]t is the search engine operator which determines the purposes and means of that activity and thus of the processing of personal data that it itself carries out within the framework of that activity and which must, consequently, be regarded as the 'controller' in respect of that processing pursuant to Article 2(d)'.[50]

In the determination of the court, 'it would be contrary not only to the clear wording of that provision but also to its objective – which is to ensure, through a broad definition of the concept of "controller", effective and complete protection of data subjects – to exclude the operator of a search engine from that definition on the ground that it does not exercise control over the personal data published on the web pages of third parties'.[51]

The court points out that 'the processing of personal data carried out in the context of the activity of a search engine can be distinguished from and is additional to that carried out by publishers of websites, consisting in loading those data on an internet page'.[52]

'Moreover', the court states, 'it is undisputed that that activity of search engines plays a decisive role in the overall dissemination of those data in that it renders the latter accessible to any internet user making a search on the basis of the data subject's name, including to internet users who otherwise would not have found the web page on which those data are published'.[53]

In addition, the court states that 'the organisation and aggregation of information published on the internet that are effected by search engines with the aim of facilitating their users' access to that information may, when users carry out their search on the basis of an individual's name, result in them obtaining through the list of results a structured overview of the information relating to that individual that can be found on the internet enabling them to establish a more or less detailed profile of the data subject'[54]

So, therefore, '[i]nasmuch as the activity of a search engine is therefore liable to affect significantly, and additionally compared with that of the publishers of websites, the fundamental rights to privacy and to the protection of personal data, the operator of the search engine as the person determining the purposes and means of that activity must ensure, within the framework of its responsibilities, powers and capabilities, that the activity meets the requirements of [the DPD 95/46] in order that the guarantees laid down by the directive may have full

49   *Ibid* para 32.
50   *Ibid* para 33.
51   *Ibid* para 34
52   *Ibid* para 35.
53   *Ibid* para 36.
54   *Ibid* para 37.

effect and that effective and complete protection of Data Subjects, in particular of their right to privacy, may actually be achieved'.[55]

The court states, 'the fact that publishers of websites have the option of indicating to operators of search engines, by means in particular of exclusion protocols such as "robot.txt" or codes such as "no index" or "no archive", that they wish specific information published on their site to be wholly or partially excluded from the search engines' automatic indexes does not mean that, if publishers of websites do not so indicate, the operator of a search engine is released from its responsibility for the processing of personal data that it carries out in the context of the engine's activity'.[56]

This 'fact does not alter the position that the purposes and means of that processing are determined by the operator of the search engine'.[57]

Furthermore, 'even if that option for publishers of websites were to mean that they determine the means of that processing jointly with that operator, this finding would not remove any of the latter's responsibility as Article 2(d) of [the DPD 95/46] expressly provides that that determination may be made 'alone or jointly with others'.[58]

The court states that:

> [i]t follows from all the foregoing considerations that the answer to Question 2(a) and (b) is that Article 2(b) and (d) of [the DPD 95/46] are to be interpreted as meaning that, first, the activity of a search engine consisting in finding information published or placed on the internet by third parties, indexing it automatically, storing it temporarily and, finally, making it available to internet users according to a particular order of preference must be classified as 'processing of personal data' within the meaning of Article 2(b) when that information contains personal data and, second, the operator of the search engine must be regarded as the "controller" in respect of that processing, within the meaning of Article 2(d). Question 1(a) to (d), concerning the territorial scope of [the DPD 95/46].[59]

Q 1(a) to (d): Applying Data Protection

16.28   The court refers to the questions referred to be answered and that '[b]y Question 1(a) to (d), the referring court seeks to establish whether it is possible to apply the national legislation transposing [the DPD 95/46] in circumstances such as those at issue in the main proceedings'.[60]

---

55 *Ibid* para 38.
56 *Ibid* para 39.
57 *Ibid* para 40.
58 *Ibid*.
59 *Ibid* para 41.
60 *Ibid* para 42.

The court refers to, and presumably relies on the facts as 'established' by the referring court, namely:

- Google Search is offered worldwide through the website "www.google.com". In numerous States, a local version adapted to the national language exists. The version of Google Search in Spanish is offered through the website "www.google.es", which has been registered since 16 September 2003. Google Search is one of the most used search engines in Spain.

- Google Search is operated by Google Inc, which is the parent company of the Google Group and has its seat in the United States.

- Google Search indexes websites throughout the world, including websites located in Spain. The information indexed by its "web crawlers" or robots, that is to say, computer programmes used to locate and sweep up the content of web pages methodically and automatically, is stored temporarily on servers whose State of location is unknown, that being kept secret for reasons of competition.

- Google Search does not merely give access to content hosted on the indexed websites, but takes advantage of that activity and includes, in return for payment, advertising associated with the internet users' search terms, for undertakings who wish to use that tool in order to offer their goods or services to the internet users.

- The Google group has recourse to its subsidiary Google Spain for promoting the sale of advertising space generated on the website "www.google.com". Google Spain, which was established on 3 September 2003 and possesses separate legal personality, has its seat in Madrid (Spain). Its activities are targeted essentially at undertakings based in Spain, acting as a commercial agent for the Google group in that Member State. Its objects are to promote, facilitate and effect the sale of online advertising products and services to third parties and the marketing of that advertising.

- Google Inc designated Google Spain as the Controller, in Spain, in respect of two filing systems registered by Google Inc with the AEPD; those filing systems were intended to contain the personal data of the customers who had concluded contracts for advertising services with Google Inc.[61]

It adds that '[s]pecifically, the main issues raised by the referring Court concern the notion of "establishment" within the meaning of Article 4(1)(a) of [the DPD 95/46] and of "use of equipment situated on the territory of the said Member State", within the meaning of Article 4(1)(c)'.[62]

---

61   *Ibid* para 43.
62   *Ibid* para 44.

Q 1(a): Establishment on Territory

16.29   The court considers Question 1(a) and notes that the referring court asks 'in essence, whether Article 4(1)(a) of [the DPD 95/46] is to be interpreted as meaning that processing of personal data is carried out in the context of the activities of an establishment of the Controller on the territory of a Member State, within the meaning of that provision' when one or more of three conditions are met.[63]

The three questions or conditions are:

–   the operator of a search engine sets up in a Member State a branch or subsidiary which is intended to promote and sell advertising space offered by that engine and which orientates its activity towards the inhabitants of that Member State; or

–   the parent company designates a subsidiary located in that Member State as its representative and controller for two specific filing systems which relate to the data of customers who have contracted for advertising with that undertaking; or

–   the branch or subsidiary established in a Member State forwards to the parent company, located outside the European Union, requests and requirements addressed to it both by data subjects and by the authorities with responsibility for ensuring observation of the right to protection of personal data, even where such collaboration is engaged in voluntarily.[64]

First Condition

16.30   Regarding the first of the three conditions above, the court notes that 'the referring Court states that Google Search is operated and managed by Google Inc and that it has not been established that Google Spain carries out in Spain an activity directly linked to the indexing or storage of information or data contained on third parties' websites'.[65] But '[n]evertheless, according to the referring Court, the promotion and sale of advertising space, which Google Spain attends to in respect of Spain, constitutes the bulk of the Google group's commercial activity and may be regarded as closely linked to Google Search'.[66]

González, Spain, Italy, Austria, Poland and Commission

16.31   Mr González and the Spanish, Italian, Austrian and Polish governments and the Commission submit to the court that, 'in light of the inextricable link between the activity of the search engine operated by Google Inc and the activity of Google Spain, the latter must be regarded as an establishment of the former

---

63   *Ibid* para 45.
64   *Ibid*.
65   *Ibid* para 46.
66   *Ibid*.

and the processing of personal data is carried out in context of the activities of that establishment'.[67]

Google and Greece

16.32   In contrast Google Spain, Google Inc and the Greek government suggest that 'Article 4(1)(a) of [the DPD 95/46] is not applicable in the case of the first of the three conditions listed by the referring Court'.[68]

Court Position

16.33   The court states that 'it is to be noted first of all that Recital 19 in the preamble to [the DPD 95/46] states that "establishment on the territory of a Member State implies the effective and real exercise of activity through stable arrangements" and that "the legal form of such an establishment, whether simply [a] branch or a subsidiary with a legal personality, is not the determining factor"'.[69]

The court points out that it is not disputed in any way that 'Google Spain engages in the effective and real exercise of activity through stable arrangements in Spain'. In addition, 'moreover [it] has separate legal personality, it constitutes a subsidiary of Google Inc on Spanish territory and, therefore, an "establishment" within the meaning of Article 4(1)(a) of [the DPD 95/46]'.[70]

The court addresses the test for meeting this criteria. It states that '[i]n order to satisfy the criterion laid down in that provision, it is also necessary that the processing of personal data by the controller be 'carried out in the context of the activities' of an establishment of the controller on the territory of a Member State'.[71]

Google

16.34   However, it is pointed out that both 'Google Spain and Google Inc dispute that this is the case'.[72] They suggest that 'the processing of personal data at issue in the main proceedings is carried out exclusively by Google Inc, which operates Google Search without any intervention on the part of Google Spain'.[73] The companies argue, therefore, that the 'latter's activity is limited to providing support to the Google group's advertising activity which is separate from its

---

67   *Ibid* para 47.
68   *Ibid*.
69   *Ibid* para 48.
70   *Ibid* para 49.
71   *Ibid* para 50.
72   *Ibid* para 51.
73   *Ibid*.

search engine service'.[74] It is not clear if this was proven, nor if discovery had occurred.

Court Position

16.35 The court responds to this saying that '[n]evertheless … Article 4(1)(a) of [the DPD 95/46] does not require the processing of personal data in question to be carried out "by" the establishment concerned itself, but only that it be carried out 'in the context of the activities' of the establishment'.[75] This is also the position made by the Spanish government and the Commission, according to the judgment.[76]

Furthermore, the court states that 'in light of the objective of [the DPD 95/46] of ensuring effective and complete protection of the fundamental rights and freedoms of natural persons, and in particular their right to privacy, with respect to the processing of personal data, those words cannot be interpreted restrictively'.[77] The court refers 'by analogy' to the *L'Oréal* case (paragraphs 62 and 63).[78]

The court states that it must 'be noted in this context that it is clear in particular from Recitals 18 to 20 in the preamble to [the DPD 95/46] and Article 4 thereof that the European Union legislature sought to prevent individuals from being deprived of the protection guaranteed by the directive and that protection from being circumvented, by prescribing a particularly broad territorial scope'.[79]

The court refers to the objective of the DPD 95/46 and to the wording of Article 4(1)(a). 'In light of that objective of [the DPD 95/46] and of the wording of Article 4(1)(a)' the court states that 'it must be held that the processing of personal data for the purposes of the service of a search engine such as Google Search, which is operated by an undertaking that has its seat in a third State but has an establishment in a Member State, is carried out "in the context of the activities" of that establishment if the latter is intended to promote and sell, in that Member State, advertising space offered by the search engine which serves to make the service offered by that engine profitable'.[80]

The court then states that '[i]n such circumstances' as these 'the activities of the operator of the search engine and those of its establishment situated in the Member State concerned are inextricably linked since the activities relating to the advertising space constitute the means of rendering the search engine at issue

---

74   *Ibid.*
75   *Ibid* para 52.
76   *Ibid.*
77   *Ibid* para 53.
78   *Ibid.* Referring to *L'Oréal and Others* v *eBay International AG and Others* Case C324/09, EU:C:2011:474, paras 62 and 63.
79   *Google Spain*, para 54.
80   *Ibid* para 55.

economically profitable and that engine is, at the same time, the means enabling those activities to be performed'.[81]

The court notes that '[a]s has been stated in paragraphs 26 to 28' of the judgment above, 'the very display of personal data on a search results page constitutes processing of such data. Since that display of results is accompanied, on the same page, by the display of advertising linked to the search terms, it is clear that the processing of personal data in question is carried out in the context of the commercial and advertising activity of the controller's establishment on the territory of a Member State, in this instance Spanish territory'.[82]

The court states that '[t]hat being so, it cannot be accepted that the processing of personal data carried out for the purposes of the operation of the search engine should escape the obligations and guarantees laid down by [the DPD 95/46]'.[83]

That 'would compromise the Directive's effectiveness and the effective and complete protection of the fundamental rights and freedoms of natural persons'.[84] Similar concerns will no doubt arise in relation to the GDPR and RtbF.

The directive seeks to ensure the 'effective and complete protection of the fundamental rights and freedoms of natural persons'.[85] The court refers 'by analogy' to the *L'Oréal* case,[86] 'in particular their right to privacy, with respect to the processing of personal data, a right to which the Directive accords special importance as is confirmed in particular by Article 1(1) thereof and Recitals 2 and 10 in its preamble'. The court refers to a number of cases to this effect, namely, joined cases Österreichischer Rundfunk and Others (paragraph 70); *Rijkeboer* case (paragraph 47); and *IPI* case (paragraph 28 and the cases cited therein).[87]

The court points out that '[s]ince the first of the three conditions listed by the referring Court suffices by itself for it to be concluded that an establishment such as Google Spain satisfies the criterion laid down in Article 4(1)(a) of [the DPD 95/46], it is unnecessary to examine the other two conditions'.[88]

Therefore, '[i]t follows from the foregoing that the answer to Question 1(a) is that Article 4(1)(a) of [the DPD 95/46] is to be interpreted as meaning that processing

81 *Ibid* para 56.
82 *Ibid* para 57.
83 *Ibid* para 58.
84 *Ibid*.
85 *Ibid* .
86 *L'Oréal and Others*, paras 62 and 63.
87 *Google Spain*, para 58. It states 'see, to this effect' Joined Cases C465/00, C138/01 and C139/01 Rechnungshof (*C-465/00*) v *Österreichischer Rundfunk and Others and Christa Neukomm (C-138/01) and Joseph Lauermann (C-139/01)* v *Österreichischer Rundfunk* EU:C:2003:294, para 70; Case C553/07 *College van burgemeester en wethouders van Rotterdam v MEE Rijkeboer* EU:C:2009:293, para 47; and Case C473/12 *Institut professionnel des agents immobiliers (IPI) v Geoffrey Englebert and Others* EU:C:2013:715, para 28 and the case law cited.
88 *Google Spain*, para 59.

of personal data is carried out in the context of the activities of an establishment of the Controller on the territory of a Member State, within the meaning of that provision, when the operator of a search engine sets up in a Member State a branch or subsidiary which is intended to promote and sell advertising space offered by that engine and which orientates its activity towards the inhabitants of that Member State. Question 1(b) to (d)'.'[89]

Q 1(b) and (d): Responsibility of the Search Engine Operator

16.36   So '[i]In view of the answer given to Question 1(a), there is no need to answer Question 1(b) to (d). Question 2(c) and (d), concerning the extent of the responsibility of the operator of a search engine under [the DPD 95/46]'.[90]

Q 2(c) and (d):

16.37   The referring court asks by Question 2(c) and (d) 'in essence, whether Article 12(b) and subparagraph (a) of the first paragraph of Article 14 of [the DPD 95/46] are to be interpreted as meaning that, to comply with the rights laid down in those provisions, the operator of a search engine is obliged to remove from the list of results displayed following a search made on the basis of a person's name links to web pages, published by third parties and containing information relating to that person, also in a case where that name or information is not erased beforehand or simultaneously from those web pages, and even, as the case may be, when its publication in itself on those pages is lawful'.[91]

Google

16.38   It is submitted by Google Spain and Google Inc that 'by virtue of the principle of proportionality, any request seeking the removal of information must be addressed to the publisher of the website concerned because it is he who takes the responsibility for making the information public, who is in a position to appraise the lawfulness of that publication and who has available to him the most effective and least restrictive means of making the information inaccessible'.[92] The court continues '[f]urthermore, to require the operator of a search engine to withdraw information published on the internet from its indexes would take insufficient account of the fundamental rights of publishers of websites, of other internet users and of that operator itself'.[93]

---

89   *Ibid* para 60.
90   *Ibid* para 61.
91   *Ibid* para 62.
92   *Ibid* para 63.
93   *Ibid.*

Austria

16.39   The Austrian Government states, according to the court, that a national data protection supervisory authorities 'may order such an operator to erase information published by third parties from its filing systems only if the data in question have been found previously to be unlawful or incorrect or if the Data Subject has made a successful objection to the publisher of the website on which that information was published'.[94]

González, Spain, Italy, Poland and Commission

16.40   Mr González, the Spanish, Italian, Polish Governments and the Commission submit that the national data protection supervisory authority 'may directly order the operator of a search engine to withdraw from its indexes and intermediate memory information containing personal data that has been published by third parties, without having to approach beforehand or simultaneously the publisher of the web page on which that information appears'.[95] Furthermore, Mr González, the Spanish and Italian Governments and the Commission state that 'the fact that the information has been published lawfully and that it still appears on the original web page has no effect on the obligations of that operator under [the DPD 95/46]'.[96] 'However, according to the Polish [g]overnment that fact is such as to release the operator from its obligations.'[97]

Court Position

16.41   The court states that 'it should be remembered that, as is apparent from Article 1 and Recital 10 in the preamble, [the DPD 95/46] seeks to ensure a high level of protection of the fundamental rights and freedoms of natural persons, in particular their right to privacy, with respect to the processing of personal data'.[98] It also, to this effect, referred to the *IPI* case (paragraph 28).[99]

The court also refers to recital 25 in the preamble to the DPD 95/46. This refers to the principles of protection laid down by the directive reflected, 'on the one hand, in the obligations imposed on persons responsible for processing, in particular regarding data quality, technical security, notification to the supervisory authority and the circumstances under which processing can be carried out, and, on the other hand, in the rights conferred on individuals whose data are the subject of processing to be informed that processing is taking place, to consult the data, to request corrections and even to object to processing in certain circumstances'.[100]

---

94   *Ibid* para 64.
95   *Ibid* para 65.
96   *Ibid*.
97   *Ibid*
98   *Ibid* para 66.
99   *Ibid*. Referring to *IPI* case, para 28.
100 *Google Spain*, above, para 67.

The court notes that it has already held that the provisions of the DPD 95/46, in so far as they govern the processing of personal data liable to infringe fundamental freedoms, in particular the right to privacy, 'must necessarily be interpreted in light of fundamental rights, which, according to settled case-law, form an integral part of the general principles of law whose observance the Court ensures and which are now set out in the Charter'.[101] It refers, in particular, to *P Connolly v Commission* (paragraph 37), and Österreichischer Rundfunk and *Others* (paragraph 68).[102]

Article 7 of the Charter guarantees the right to respect for private life. Article 8 expressly proclaims the right to the protection of personal data. Article 8(2) and (3) specifies that such data 'must be processed fairly for specified purposes and on the basis of the consent of the person concerned or some other legitimate basis laid down by law, that everyone has the right of access to data which have been collected concerning him or her and the right to have the data rectified, and that compliance with these rules is to be subject to control by an independent authority'.[103] 'Those requirements are implemented, inter alia, by [the DPD 95/46] Articles 6, 7, 12, 14 and 28'.[104]

DPD 95/46 Article 12(b) provides that Member States must guarantee every data subject the right to obtain from the controller, as appropriate, the rectification, erasure or blocking of data the processing of which does not comply with the provisions of the DPD 95/46, in particular because of the incomplete or inaccurate nature of the data. 'As this final point relating to the case where certain requirements referred to in Article 6(1)(d) of [the DPD 95/46] are not observed is stated by way of example and is not exhaustive.'[105] Therefore, 'it follows that non-compliant nature of the processing, which is capable of conferring upon the data subject the right guaranteed in Article 12(b) of the Directive, may also arise from non-observance of the other conditions of lawfulness that are imposed by the directive upon the processing of personal data'.[106]

The court states that 'it should be noted that, subject to the exceptions permitted under the DPD 95/46 Article 13, all processing of personal data must comply, first, with the principles relating to data quality set out in Article 6 of the directive and, secondly, with one of the criteria for making data processing legitimate listed in Article 7 of the Directive'.[107] The court refers to Österreichischer Rundfunk

---

101 *Ibid* para 68.
102 *Ibid*. Referring to *Bernard Connolly v Commission*, Case C274/99, EU:C:2001:127 para 37 and Österreichischer Rundfunk and Others para 68.
103 *Ibid* para 69.
104 *Ibid*.
105 *Ibid* para 70.
106 *Ibid*.
107 *Ibid* para 71.

and Others (paragraph 65); joined cases *ASNEF and FECEMD* (paragraph 26); and Worten (paragraph 33).[108]

Under DPD 95/46 Article 6 ('and without prejudice to specific provisions that the Member States may lay down in respect of processing for historical, statistical or scientific purposes'[109]), the controller has the task and duty of 'ensuring that personal data are processed "fairly and lawfully", that they are "collected for specified, explicit and legitimate purposes and not further processed in a way incompatible with those purposes", that they are "adequate, relevant and not excessive in relation to the purposes for which they are collected and/or further processed", that they are "accurate and, where necessary, kept up to date" and, finally, that they are "kept in a form which permits identification of data subjects for no longer than is necessary for the purposes for which the data were collected or for which they are further processed".'[110] In this context, therefore, 'the controller must take every reasonable step to ensure that data which do not meet the requirements of that provision are erased or rectified'.[111]

DPD 95/46 Article 7 refers to legitimisation of processing such as that at issue in the main proceedings carried out by the operator of a search engine, and 'that processing is capable of being covered by the ground in Article 7(f)'.[112]

The court states that 'this provision permits the processing of personal data where it is necessary for the purposes of the legitimate interests pursued by the controller or by the third party or parties to whom the data are disclosed, except where such interests are overridden by the interests or fundamental rights and freedoms of the data subject – in particular his right to privacy with respect to the processing of personal data – which require protection under Article 1(1) of the Directive'.[113] The application of Article 7(f) 'thus necessitates a balancing of the opposing rights and interests concerned, in the context of which account must be taken of the significance of the data subject's rights arising from Articles 7 and 8 of the Charter'.[114]

The court states that '[w]hilst the question whether the processing complies with Articles 6 and 7(f) of [the DPD 95/46] may be determined in the context of a request as provided for in Article 12(b) of the Directive, the data subject may, in addition, rely in certain conditions on the right to object laid down in subparagraph (a) of the first paragraph of Article 14 of the Directive'.[115]

---

108 *Ibid*. The court refers to Österreichischer Rundfunk and Others para 65; joined cases C468/10 and C469/10 *Asociación Nacional de Establecimientos Financieros de Crédito (ASNEF)* (C-468/10) and *Federación de Comercio Electrónico y Marketing Directo (FECEMD) (C-469/10) v Administración del Estado* EU:C:2011:77, para 26; and *Worten–Equipamentos para o Lar SA v Autoridade para as Condições de Trabalho* (ACT) Case C342/12, EU:C:2013:355 para 33.
109 *Google Spain*, para 72.
110 *Ibid*.
111 *Ibid* .
112 *Ibid* para 73.
113 *Ibid* para 74.
114 *Ibid*. The court refers to *ASNEF and FECEMD*, paras 38 and 40.
115 *Ibid* para 75.

Under Article 14(1)(a) of the DPD 95/46, Member States must grant the data subject the right, at least in the cases referred to in Article 7(e) and (f) of the Directive, to object at any time on compelling legitimate grounds relating to his particular situation to the processing of data relating to them, save where otherwise provided by national legislation.[116] The court states that the 'balancing to be carried out under subparagraph (a) of the first paragraph of Article 14 thus enables account to be taken in a more specific manner of all the circumstances surrounding the data subject's particular situation. Where there is a justified objection, the processing instigated by the controller may no longer involve those data.'[117]

Requests under Article 12(b) and Article 14(1)(a) of the DPD 95/46 may be addressed by the data subject directly to the controller,[118] who must then 'duly examine their merits and, as the case may be, end processing of the data in question'.[119] 'Where the controller does not grant the request, the data subject may bring the matter before the supervisory authority or the judicial authority so that it carries out the necessary checks and orders the controller to take specific measures accordingly.[120]

The court states that 'it is to be noted that it is clear from DPD Article 28(3) and (4) of [the DPD 95/46] that each supervisory authority is to hear claims lodged by any person concerning the protection of his rights and freedoms in regard to the processing of personal data and that it has investigative powers and effective powers of intervention enabling it to order in particular the blocking, erasure or destruction of data or to impose a temporary or definitive ban on such processing'.[121]

It is in light of those considerations, the court states, that it is necessary to interpret and apply the provisions of the DPD 95/46 governing the data subject's rights when they lodge with the data protection supervisory authority or judicial authority a request such as that at issue in the main proceedings.[122]

It must be pointed out at the outset that 'as has been found in paragraphs 36 to 38' of the judgment, the processing of personal data, 'such as that at issue in the main proceedings, carried out by the operator of a search engine is liable to affect significantly the fundamental rights to privacy and to the protection of personal data when the search by means of that engine is carried out on the basis of an individual's name, since that processing enables any internet user to obtain through the list of results a structured overview of the information relating to that individual that can be found on the internet':[123]

116 *Ibid* para 76.
117 *Ibid*.
118 *Ibid* para 77.
119 *Ibid*.
120 *Ibid*.
121 *Ibid*, para 78.
122 *Ibid* para 79.
123 *Ibid* para 80.

–   information which potentially concerns a vast number of aspects of [their] private life and which, without the search engine, could not have been interconnected or could have been only with great difficulty;[124]

–   and thereby to establish a more or less detailed profile of [them]. Furthermore, the effect of the interference with those rights of the data subject is heightened on account of the important role played by the internet and search engines in modern society, which render the information contained in such a list of results ubiquitous.[125]

The court states that '[i]n the light of the potential seriousness of that interference, it is clear that it cannot be justified by merely the economic interest which the operator of such an engine has in that processing'.[126] 'However, inasmuch as the removal of links from the list of results could, depending on the information at issue, have effects upon the legitimate interest of internet users potentially interested in having access to that information, in situations such as that at issue in the main proceedings a fair balance should be sought in particular between that interest and the data subject's fundamental rights under Articles 7 and 8 of the Charter.'[127]

Whilst it is true that the data subject's rights protected by those articles also override, as a general rule, that interest of internet users, that balance may however depend, in specific cases, on the nature of the information in question and its sensitivity for the data subject's private life and on the interest of the public in having that information, an interest which may vary, in particular, according to the role played by the data subject in public life.[128]

Following the appraisal of the conditions for the application of Article 12(b) and subparagraph (a) of the first paragraph of Article 14 of [the DPD 95/46] which is to be carried out when a request such as that at issue in the main proceedings is lodged with it, the supervisory authority or judicial authority may order the operator of the search engine to remove from the list of results displayed following a search made on the basis of a person's name links to web pages published by third parties containing information relating to that person, without an order to that effect presupposing the previous or simultaneous removal of that name and information – of the publisher's own accord or following an order of one of those authorities – from the web page on which they were published.[129]

As has been established in paragraphs 35 to 38 of the judgment, 'inasmuch as the data processing carried out in the context of the activity of a search engine can be distinguished from and is additional to that carried out by publishers of websites and affects the data subject's fundamental rights additionally, the operator of the search engine as the controller in respect of that processing must ensure, within

---

124 *Ibid.*
125 *Ibid.* The court refers to the following case to this effect: joined cases *eDate Advertising GmbH and Others v X and Société MGN LIMITED* C509/09 and C161/10, EU:C:2011:685, para 45.
126 *Google Spain*, para 81.
127 *Ibid.*
128 *Ibid.*
129 *Ibid* para 82.

the framework of its responsibilities, powers and capabilities, that that processing meets the requirements of [the DPD 95/46], in order that the guarantees laid down by the directive may have full effect'.[130]

The court adds that '[g]iven the ease with which information published on a website can be replicated on other sites and the fact that the persons responsible for its publication are not always subject to European Union legislation, effective and complete protection of data users could not be achieved if the latter had to obtain first or in parallel the erasure of the information relating to them from the publishers of websites'.[131]

Furthermore, the 'the processing by the publisher of a web page consisting in the publication of information relating to an individual may, in some circumstances, be carried out "solely for journalistic purposes" and thus benefit, by virtue of Article 9 of [the DPD 95/46], from derogations from the requirements laid down by the directive, whereas that does not appear to be so in the case of the processing carried out by the operator of a search engine'.[132] The court states that '[i]t cannot therefore be ruled out that in certain circumstances the data subject is capable of exercising the rights referred to in Article 12(b) and subparagraph (a) of the first paragraph of Article 14 of [the DPD 95/46] against that operator but not against the publisher of the web page'.[133]

The court states, 'it must be stated that not only does the ground, under Article 7 of [the DPD 95/46], justifying the publication of a piece of personal data on a website not necessarily coincide with that which is applicable to the activity of search engines, but also, even where that is the case, the outcome of the weighing of the interests at issue to be carried out under Article 7(f) and subparagraph (a) of the first paragraph of Article 14 of the directive may differ according to whether the processing carried out by the operator of a search engine or that carried out by the publisher of the web page is at issue, given that, first, the legitimate interests justifying the processing may be different and, second, the consequences of the processing for the data subject, and in particular for his private life, are not necessarily the same'.[134]

Indeed, as the court also states 'since the inclusion in the list of results, displayed following a search made on the basis of a person's name, of a web page and of the information contained on it relating to that person makes access to that information appreciably easier for any internet user making a search in respect of the person concerned and may play a decisive role in the dissemination of that information, it is liable to constitute a more significant interference with the data subject's fundamental right to privacy than the publication on the web page'.[135]

---

130 *Ibid* para 83.
131 *Ibid* para 84.
132 *Ibid* para 85.
133 *Ibid*.
134 *Ibid* para 86.
135 *Ibid* para 87.

In light of all the foregoing considerations, the answer to Question 2(c) and (d) is that Article 12(b) and subparagraph (a) of the first paragraph of Article 14 of [the DPD 95/46] are to be interpreted as meaning that, in order to comply with the rights laid down in those provisions and in so far as the conditions laid down by those provisions are in fact satisfied, the operator of a search engine is obliged to remove from the list of results displayed following a search made on the basis of a person's name links to web pages, published by third parties and containing information relating to that person, also in a case where that name or information is not erased beforehand or simultaneously from those web pages, and even, as the case may be, when its publication in itself on those pages is lawful.[136]

Q 3: Scope of the data subject's rights guaranteed by directive

16.42 The court refers to Question 3 of the Spanish court. It summarises that:

the referring Court asks, in essence, whether Article 12(b) and subparagraph (a) of the first paragraph of Article 14 of [the DPD 95/46] are to be interpreted as enabling the data subject to require the operator of a search engine to remove from the list of results displayed following a search made on the basis of his name links to web pages published lawfully by third parties and containing true information relating to him, on the ground that that information may be prejudicial to him or that he wishes it to be "forgotten" after a certain time.[137]

Google, Greece, Austria, Poland and Commission

16.43 Google Spain, Google Inc, the Greek, Austrian and Polish Governments and the Commission consider that this question should be answered in the negative.[138]

They submit in this regard that Article 12(b) and subparagraph (a) of the first paragraph of the DPD 95/46 Article 14 confer rights upon data subjects only if the processing in question is incompatible with the directive or on compelling legitimate grounds relating to their particular situation, and not merely because they consider that that processing may be prejudicial to them or they wish that the data being processed sink into oblivion.[139]

Greece, Austria

16.44 The Greek and Austrian Governments submit that the data subject must approach the publisher of the website concerned.[140]

---

136 *Ibid* para 88.
137 *Ibid* para 89.
138 *Ibid* para 90.
139 *Ibid*.
140 *Ibid*.

González, Spain and Italy

16.45 According to Mr González and the Spanish and Italian Governments, 'the data subject may oppose the indexing by a search engine of personal data relating to him where their dissemination through the search engine is prejudicial to him and his fundamental rights to the protection of those data and to privacy':[141]

– 'which encompass …"[RtbF]"';[142]

– 'override the legitimate interests of the operator of the search engine and the general interest in freedom of information. As regards Article 12(b) of [the DPD 95/46], the application of which is subject to the condition that the processing of personal data be incompatible with the directive, it should be recalled that, as has been noted in paragraph 72 of the present judgment, such incompatibility may result not only from the fact that such data are inaccurate but, in particular, also from the fact that they are inadequate, irrelevant or excessive in relation to the purposes of the processing, that they are not kept up to date, or that they are kept for longer than is necessary unless they are required to be kept for historical, statistical or scientific purposes'.[143]

Court Position

16.46 According to the court, it follows from those requirements laid down in Article 6(1)(c) to (e) of DPD 95/46, that 'even initially lawful processing of accurate data may, in the course of time, become incompatible with the directive where those data are no longer necessary in light of the purposes for which they were collected or processed. That is so in particular where they appear to be inadequate, irrelevant or no longer relevant, or excessive in relation to those purposes and in light of the time that has elapsed'.[144]

Therefore, the court states that 'if it is found, following a request by the data subject pursuant to Article 12(b) of [the DPD 95/46], that the inclusion in the list of results displayed following a search made on the basis of his name of the links to web pages published lawfully by third parties and containing true information relating to him personally is, at this point in time, incompatible with Article 6(1)(c) to (e) of the directive because that information appears, having regard to all the circumstances of the case, to be inadequate, irrelevant or no longer relevant, or excessive in relation to the purposes of the processing at issue carried out by the operator of the search engine, the information and links concerned in the list of results must be erased'.[145]

So far as concerns requests as provided for by Article 12(b) of [the DPD 95/46] founded on alleged non-compliance with the conditions laid down in Article 7(f) of the directive and requests under subparagraph (a) of

141 *Ibid* para 92.
142 *Ibid.*
143 *Ibid.*
144 *Ibid* para 93.
145 *Ibid* para 94.

the first paragraph of Article 14 of the Directive, it must be pointed out that in each case the processing of personal data must be authorised under Article 7 for the entire period during which it is carried out.[146]

In light of the above, the court states that 'when appraising such requests made in order to oppose processing such as that at issue in the main proceedings, it should in particular be examined whether the data subject has a right that the information relating to him personally should, at this point in time, no longer be linked to his name by a list of results displayed following a search made on the basis of his name. In this connection, it must be pointed out that it is not necessary in order to find such a right that the inclusion of the information in question in the list of results causes prejudice to the data subject'.[147]

As the data subject may, in light of their fundamental rights under Articles 7 and 8 of the Charter, request that the information in question no longer be made available to the general public by its inclusion in such a list of results, 'it should be held, as follows in particular from paragraph 81 of the present judgment, that those rights override, as a rule, not only the economic interest of the operator of the search engine but also the interest of the general public in finding that information upon a search relating to the data subject's name. However, that would not be the case if it appeared, for particular reasons, such as the role played by the data subject in public life, that the interference with his fundamental rights is justified by the preponderant interest of the general public in having, on account of inclusion in the list of results, access to the information in question'.[148]

'As regards a situation such as that at issue in the main proceedings, which concerns the display, in the list of results that the internet user obtains by making a search by means of Google Search on the basis of the data subject's name, of links to pages of the on-line archives of a daily newspaper that contain announcements mentioning the data subject's name and relating to a real-estate auction connected with attachment proceedings for the recovery of social security debts, it should be held that, having regard to the sensitivity for the data subject's private life of the information contained in those announcements and to the fact that its initial publication had taken place 16 years earlier, the data subject establishes a right that that information should no longer be linked to his name by means of such a list.'[149] 'Accordingly, therefore, since in the case in point there do not appear to be particular reasons substantiating a preponderant interest of the public in having, in the context of such a search, access to that information, a matter which is, however, for the referring court to establish, the data subject may, by virtue of Article 12(b) and subparagraph (a) of the first paragraph of Article 14 of [the DPD 95/46], require those links to be removed from the list of results.'[150]

---

146 *Ibid* para 95.
147 *Ibid* para 96.
148 *Ibid* para 97.
149 *Ibid* para 98.
150 *Ibid*.

The court states therefore that '[i]t follows from the foregoing considerations that the answer to Question 3 is that Article 12(b) and subparagraph (a) of the first paragraph of Article 14 of [the DPD 95/46] are to be interpreted as meaning that, when appraising the conditions for the application of those provisions, it should inter alia be examined whether the data subject has a right that the information in question relating to him personally should, at this point in time, no longer be linked to his name by a list of results displayed following a search made on the basis of his name, without it being necessary in order to find such a right that the inclusion of the information in question in that list causes prejudice to the data subject'.[151] 'As the data subject may, in light of his fundamental rights under Articles 7 and 8 of the Charter, request that the information in question no longer be made available to the general public on account of its inclusion in such a list of results, those rights override, as a rule, not only the economic interest of the operator of the search engine but also the interest of the general public in having access to that information upon a search relating to the data subject's name.'[152] However, the court states that 'that would not be the case if it appeared, for particular reasons, such as the role played by the data subject in public life, that the interference with [their] fundamental rights is justified by the preponderant interest of the general public in having, on account of its inclusion in the list of results, access to the information in question'.[153]

6   RULING OF COURT

16.47   On the grounds referred to above, the court (Grand Chamber) thereby ruled as follows:

1. Article 2(b) and (d) of [the DPD 95/46] of the European Parliament and of the Council of 24 October 1995 on the protection of individuals with regard to the processing of personal data and on the free movement of such data are to be interpreted as meaning that, first, the activity of a search engine consisting in finding information published or placed on the internet by third parties, indexing it automatically, storing it temporarily and, finally, making it available to internet users according to a particular order of preference must be classified as "processing of personal data" within the meaning of Article 2(b) when that information contains personal data and, second, the operator of the search engine must be regarded as the "controller" in respect of that processing, within the meaning of Article 2(d).[154]

2. Article 4(1)(a) of [the DPD 95/46] is to be interpreted as meaning that processing of personal data is carried out in the context of the activities of an establishment of the Controller on the territory of a Member State, within the meaning of that provision, when the operator of a search engine sets up in a Member State a branch or subsidiary which is intended to promote and sell advertising space offered by that engine and which

151 *Ibid* para 99.
152 *Ibid.*
153 *Ibid.*
154 *Ibid.* Decision ruling para 1.

orientates its activity towards the inhabitants of that Member State.[155]

3.   Article 12(b) and subparagraph (a) of the first paragraph of Article 14 of [the DPD 95/46] are to be interpreted as meaning that, in order to comply with the rights laid down in those provisions and in so far as the conditions laid down by those provisions are in fact satisfied, the operator of a search engine is obliged to remove from the list of results displayed following a search made on the basis of a person's name links to web pages, published by third parties and containing information relating to that person, also in a case where that name or information is not erased beforehand or simultaneously from those web pages, and even, as the case may be, when its publication in itself on those pages is lawful.[156]

4.   Article 12(b) and subparagraph (a) of the first paragraph of Article 14 of [the DPD 95/46] are to be interpreted as meaning that, when appraising the conditions for the application of those provisions, it should *inter alia* be examined whether the data subject has a right that the information in question relating to him personally should, at this point in time, no longer be linked to his name by a list of results displayed following a search made on the basis of his name, without it being necessary in order to find such a right that the inclusion of the information in question in that list causes prejudice to the data subject. As the data subject may, in light of his fundamental rights under Articles 7 and 8 of the Charter, request that the information in question no longer be made available to the general public on account of its inclusion in such a list of results, those rights override, as a rule, not only the economic interest of the operator of the search engine but also the interest of the general public in having access to that information upon a search relating to the data subject's name. However, that would not be the case if it appeared, for particular reasons, such as the role played by the data subject in public life, that the interference with his fundamental rights is justified by the preponderant interest of the general public in having, on account of its inclusion in the list of results, access to the information in question.[157]

In summary, therefore, the case decided that:

- a search engine must be classified as processing personal data and must be regarded as the controller in respect of that processing;[158]

- processing occurs when the search engine sets up a branch or subsidiary in a Member State to promote and sell advertising by the engine and which orientates its activity towards Member State inhabitants;[159]

- a search engine is obliged to remove links to web pages containing information relating to that person, even when publication on those pages is lawful;[160] and

155 *Ibid* para 2.
156 *Ibid* para 3.
157 *Ibid* para 4.
158 *Ibid* para 1.
159 *Ibid* para 2.
160 *Ibid* para 3.

- it is not necessary for the right that the listing causes prejudice. The rights override, as a rule, the economic interest of the search engine and the general public in having access to that information. However, that would not be the case if it appeared for particular reasons, such as the role played by the data subject in public life, that the interference with his fundamental rights is justified by the preponderant interest of the general public.[161]

7 COMMENT ON *GOOGLE SPAIN*

16.48   There has been significant reaction and case commentary[162] in relation to *Google Spain* and analysis[163] of what it many mean more generally for the public, personal data, and public personal data.[164] Attention is also devoted to implications for individuals (such as how they may control their personal data even online[165]) and organisations.[166]

Julia P Eckart correctly described that case as 'the court case heard around the world'. She also comments on its potential implications for the US.[167]

161 *Ibid* para 4.
162 E Frantziou, 'Further Developments in the Right to Be Forgotten: The European Court of Justice's Judgment in Case C-131/12, *Google Spain, SL, Google Inc v Agencia Espanola de Proteccion de Datos' Human Rights Law Review* (2014) (14:4) 761; H Kranenborg, 'Google and the Right to Be Forgotten' *European Data Protection Law Review (EDPL)* (2015) (1:1) 70; C Álvarez Rigaudia, Sentencia Google Spain Y Derecho Al Olvido, *Actualidad Juridica* (2014) (38) (1578-956X) 110; I Cofone, '*Google v Spain*: A Right to Be Forgotten' *Chicago-Kent Journal of International and Comparative Law* (2015) (15:1) 1; O Posykaliuk, 'Scientific Commentary on the Judgment of the Court of Justice of the European Union in the Case of Google Spain SL and Google Inc. v. the Spanish Data Protection Agency (AEPD) and Mario Costeja Gonzalez (Regarding the Right to be Forgotten)' *Law of Ukraine: Legal Journal* (Ukrainian) (2019) (4) 209; D Erdos, 'Disclosure, Exposure and the "Right to be Forgotten" After Google Spain: Interrogating Google Search's Webmaster, End User and Lumen Notification Practices' *Computer Law & Security Review* (2020) (38) 24; S Uncular, 'The Right to Removal in The Time of Post-Google Spain: Myth or Reality Under General Data Protection Regulation?' *International Review of Law, Computers & Technology* (2019) (33:3) 309.
163 D Lindsay, 'The "Right to be Forgotten" by Search Engines under Data Privacy Law: A Legal Analysis of the Costeja Ruling' *Journal of Media Law* (2014) (6:2) 159; A Cheng, 'Forget About the Right to be Forgotten: How About a Right to be Different?' *Te Mata Koi: Auckland University Law Review* (2016) (22) 106.
164 RC Post, 'Data Privacy and Dignitary Privacy: Google Spain, the Right to be Forgotten, and the Construction of the Public Sphere' *Duke Law Journal* (2018) (67:5) 981.
165 O Lynskey, 'Control over Personal Data in a Digital Age: *Google Spain v AEPD and Mario Costeja Gonzalez*,' *Modern Law Review* (2015) (78:3) 522.
166 E Werfel, 'What Organizations Must Know About the "Right to be Forgotten"' (cover story) *Information Management Journal* (2016) (50:2) 30.
167 JP Eckart, 'The Court Case Heard Around the World – *Google Spain SL v Agencia Espanola de Proteccion de Datos* – The Right to Be Forgotten and What It May Mean to the United States' *Dartmouth Law Journal* (2017) (15:1) 42.

Some have questioned the *Google Spain* decision and or RtbF more generally.[168] Others also point to problems with RtbF or its implementation aspects.[169] Some also refer to problems for particular organisations or sectors.[170]

There have also been considerations of the EU RtbF impact on the US, consideration of whether a RtbF should apply in the US[171] and even calls for a RtbF in the US.

There is an increasing industry around both the reputation and RtbF itself.[172]

This will, no doubt, continue to raise issues and dispute in particular circumstances. However, in other situations there should be no dispute at all. It should be noted, for example, that Google (or Alphabet) has a whole range of activities and services. Some of these may also be the focus of RtbF. In addition, search, per se, can involve additional features and applications, such as auto-suggest. These additional activities may also be of concern to individuals in seeking RtbF.

Other issues may also relate to forum shopping and forum splitting, whereby a company may seem to place some activities in one jurisdiction and others in another jurisdiction to try and insulate the latter's activities from the former's rules. Other avoidance-type measures include service splitting (eg, providing a service in one jurisdiction, but billing for that service from another). It remains to be seen how successful these individual efforts may be both as regards the GDPR generally and RtbF more specifically. A given organisation may be more concerned with seeking to limit (if not avoid) the increased penalties and fines regime more so than seeking to avoid RtbF *per se*, but these are issues which will hopefully become clearer over time.

8 SECOND *GOOGLE* EU RTBF CASE

16.49 The is also a second Google RtbF case at CJEU level (the Google France case), originating from France this time.[173]

The Advocat General issued a preliminary recommendation opinion on 10 January 2019. The questions referred from the French court to the CJEU are:

---

168 M Douglas, 'Questioning the Right to Be Forgotten' *Alternative Law Journal* (2015) (40:2) 109.
169 AM Klingenberg, 'Catches to the Right to be Forgotten, Looking From an Administrative Law Perspective to Data Processing by Public Authorities' *International Review of Law, Computers & Technology* (2016) (30:1/2) 67.
170 Klingenberg, 'Catches to the Right to be Forgotten, Looking From an Administrative Law Perspective to Data Processing by Public Authorities' above at 67.
171 B Medeiros, 'The Reputation-Management Industry and the Prospects for a Right to Be Forgotten in the US' *First Amendment Studies* (2017) (51:1) 14.
172 *Ibid.*
173 Case C-507/17. Request for a preliminary ruling from the Conseil d'État (France) lodged on 21 August 2017 – *Google Inc v Commission nationale de l'informatique et des libertés* (CNIL).

1. Must the 'right to de-referencing', as established by the Court of Justice of the European Union in its judgment of 13 May 2014 on the basis of the provisions of Articles 12(b) and 14(a) of Directive [95/46/EC] of 24 October 1995, be interpreted as meaning that a search engine operator is required, when granting a request for de-referencing, to deploy the de-referencing to all of the domain names used by its search engine so that the links at issue no longer appear, irrespective of the place from where the search initiated on the basis of the requester's name is conducted, and even if it is conducted from a place outside the territorial scope of Directive [95/46/EC] of 24 October 1995?

2. In the event that Question 1 is answered in the negative, must the 'right to de-referencing', as established by the Court of Justice of the European Union in the judgment cited above, be interpreted as meaning that a search engine operator is required, when granting a request for de-referencing, only to remove the links at issue from the results displayed following a search conducted on the basis of the requester's name on the domain name corresponding to the State in which the request is deemed to have been made or, more generally, on the domain names distinguished by the national extensions used by that search engine for all of the Member States of the European Union?

3. Moreover, in addition to the obligation mentioned in Question 2, must the 'right to de-referencing', as established by the Court of Justice of the European Union in its judgment cited above, be interpreted as meaning that a search engine operator is required, when granting a request for de-referencing, to remove the results at issue, by using the 'geo-blocking' technique, from searches conducted on the basis of the requester's name from an IP address deemed to be located in the State of residence of the person benefiting from the 'right to de-referencing', or even, more generally, from an IP address deemed to be located in one of the Member States subject to Directive [95/46/EC] of 24 October 1995, regardless of the domain name used by the internet user conducting the search?

The recommendation opinion appears to be based on the earlier DPD 95/45 given the time of filing, notwithstanding that the GDPR is now applicable including the more expressed RtbF thereunder.

The *Google France* case is not seeking to undermine or directly curtail the *Google Spain* decision nor RtbF *per se*. It does ask, however, whether the delisting needs to be on all URLs or domains or merely EU domains. Some might suggest that such restriction (ie, a restriction to EU domains only) would, in fact, act as an indirect delimitation or chipping away at the *Google Spain* decision.

The decision of the full court is still awaited. However, the Advocate General's (AG) opinion report recommends that in this single individual case, the takedown should be limited to the EU URL or domains only – but on a fully EU-wide basis; where this may leave gaps, that geoblocking, etc, techniques must also be implemented. This will be welcomed by the internet company and possibly in other quarters as well. Some critics, however, may see this as an attempt to chip away at *Google Spain* and the RtbF itself.

Given that the problem of online abuse (OA) and other problem content can affect an individual in the EU but originate from almost anywhere or be further distributed outside of the EU it would seem logical that, at least in some instances, the takedown must be global or extend beyond just EU domains to be effective. A revenge porn victim, the victim of a rape which was filmed or someone being blackmailed, would not have an effective remedy if they were limited to only being able to have problem content removed from EU-specific URLs or domains such as .co.uk, .ie, .fr, .de, etc.

One of the problems with the AG opinion is that it does not make clear if it discussed or itself engages with the possibility of EU takedown-only being ineffective to the individual victim nor how the DPD 95/46 (and the GDPR) would be rendered ineffective, if not meaningless, in this regard. Legislation is generally not understood by courts to be toothless in design.

By way of further background, many data protection supervisory authorities agree that at least some erasure, forgetting and takedown must be effected more globally to be effective. The Canadian Supreme Court has also come to the same conclusion.[174] The opinion also does not make clear if the Canadian decision was discussed or considered.

Since the decision in *Google Spain*, it also understood that the companies most concerned have put in place certain procedures to comply with RtbF notices from individuals; in the vast majority of cases, there is little or no controversy and the problem material is taken down.

However, there are a small number of controversial examples in the overall volume of notices made where some dispute may arise. This context is important but appears not to have been considered in the opinion. Just one issue on this point is that there is a danger in setting something in place which may be relevant to a subset of RtbF notices but which, if applied to all RtbF notices, could result in unintended consequences, as well as undermining some significant part of RtbF and the intent of the legislation in the first instance.

While in the vast majority of the uncontroversial cases one would think there should not be any issue with a wide takedown, the issues surrounding a small sub-set of notices may be much more nuanced. One concern is to ensure that the small disputes do not unintentionally adversely impact the cases that are uncontroversial nor remove or limit an important remedy.

It should also be recalled that the legislation is already balanced, so a full rebalancing does not need to be considered in each and every case.

---

174 See *Google Inc v Equustek Solutions Inc*, 2017 SCC 34; [2017] 1 SCR 824 (28 June 2017).

As always, the devil is in the detail. The interim opinion report is not always followed by the court and may not be in this instance. The AG expressly indicates that this recommendation is limited to the facts of this case and, as such, cannot be over-generalised. It would have been useful, therefore, for this caveat to have been carried through to the final paragraph recommendations.

The AG report also states that despite recommending that takedown be limited to the EU (and be EU-wide), 'this does not mean, however, that EU law can never require a search engine operator … to undertake global action' (para 62).

Another problem with the recommendation is that it does not engage with the fact that geoblocking in it is not always effective. It is relatively easy to bypass. Indeed, live expert evidence was presented in the Irish High Court which demonstrated that so-called 'geoblocked' problem content could still be accessed. If geoblocking is ineffective (which might then be considered generally and in the subset of problem cases), there is a separate further reason for erasure, forgetting and takedown to be wider than a limited set of EU URLs or domains. Geoblocking is relevant to the discussion in at least two ways (ie, filling gaps within the EU and also in terms of it being either imperfect or ineffective thus enhancing the need for a wider core global takedown solution). The AG opinion would seem to suggest that geoblocking was only considered in the latter question(s); but it is also relevant, it is suggested, to the first question.

There is another interesting aspect of the AG recommendation. It refers to effectiveness issues and the need for EU-wide protection and geoblocking, but also states that the service provider 'is required to take any measure at [its] disposal to ensure an efficient and complete dereferencing'. Therefore, solutions in addition to geoblocking may have to be used. There are many such other complementary solutions (eg, ContentID). Ironically, this is made available to corporate right holders but appears to be denied to individual victims of OA.

This also raises separate, but interesting, Brexit questions.

To reiterate, the issue is not whether takedown should occur, but rather whether the delisting and takedown must occur both inside and outside Europe or merely inside. RtbF is here to stay. There are many reasons to suggest that, over time, it may need to expand further as problem issues and/or urgency become more pronounced. Despite these disputed cases being of interest, they should not be mistaken (nor be misrepresented) as being representative of the vast majority of RtbF notices – which by all accounts are not controversial. Finally, the decision itself is awaited. In the vast majority of cases. there may be no issue, but there will no doubt continue to be contention and litigation in small but important minority categories. Over time, data protection supervisory authorities will need to assess whether there are more initial refusals in these categories than should be the case; and whether these refusal categories are being represented or misrepresented to the entire universe of RtbF notices. It is suggested that as interesting and important as these subset category refusal disputes may be, the respective legal opinion and decision (where these occur) should make clear that each such decision is dealing with these more niche issues to avoid unintended wider consequences and/or unintentionally reducing or constraining the statute right and a valuable protection for individuals, especially victims of OA.

The Court issued its decision on 24 September 2019.[175] While the court aligns with the view that many RtbFs may not automatically apply outside of the EU – on the basis that the current data law does not expressly state that is should be so applied outside of the EU, it also states that because there is also no ban or prohibition in EU data law on RtbF applying outside of the EU or even worldwide, it is permissible for national data regulators and courts to require international RtbF. In the immediate commentary following the case this later point is often missed.

It states at para 64 that:

'It follows that, currently, there is no obligation under EU law, for a search engine operator who grants a request for de-referencing made by a data subject, as the case may be, following an injunction from a supervisory or judicial authority of a Member State, to carry out such a de-referencing on all the versions of its search engine.'

Paragraph 66 states:

'Regarding the question whether such a de-referencing is to be carried out on the versions of the search engine corresponding to the Member States or only on the version of that search engine corresponding to the Member State of residence of the person benefiting from the de-referencing, it follows from, inter alia, the fact that the EU legislature has now chosen to lay down the rules concerning data protection by way of a regulation, which is directly applicable in all the Member States, which has been done, as is emphasised by recital 10 of Regulation 2016/679, in order to ensure a consistent and high level of protection throughout the European Union and to remove the obstacles to flows of personal data within the Union, that the de-referencing in question is, in principle, supposed to be carried out in respect of all the Member States.'

Paragraph 67 states:

'However, it should be pointed out that the interest of the public in accessing information may, even within the Union, vary from one Member State to another, meaning that the result of weighing up that interest, on the one hand, and a data subject's rights to privacy and the protection of personal data, on the other, is not necessarily the same for all the Member States, especially since, under Article 9 of Directive 95/46 and Article 85 of Regulation 2016/679, it is for the Member States, in particular as regards processing undertaken solely for journalistic purposes or for the purpose of artistic or literary expression, to provide for the exemptions and derogations necessary to reconcile those rights with, inter alia, the freedom of information.'

---

175 *Google LLC v CNIL*, CJEU, Case C-507/17, 24 September 2019.

The decision finds that:

> 'On a proper construction of Article 12(b) and subparagraph (a) of the first paragraph of Article 14 of Directive 95/46/EC of the European Parliament and of the Council of 24 October 1995 on the protection of individuals with regard to the processing of personal data and on the free movement of such data, and of Article 17(1) of Regulation (EU) 2016/679 of the European Parliament and of the Council of 27 April 2016 on the protection of individuals with regard to the processing of personal data and on the free movement of such data and repealing Directive 95/46 (General Data Protection Regulation), where a search engine operator grants a request for de-referencing pursuant to those provisions, that operator is not required to carry out that de-referencing on all versions of its search engine, but on the versions of that search engine corresponding to all the Member States, using, where necessary, measures which, while meeting the legal requirements, effectively prevent or, at the very least, seriously discourage an internet user conducting a search from one of the Member States on the basis of a data subject's name from gaining access, via the list of results displayed following that search, to the links which are the subject of that request.'

In many respects, therefore, much attention will focus on local laws as regards how far the reach should be in individual cases; but the legitimacy of RtbF *per se* is reiterated once more.

PART E

NATIONAL CASE LAW

CHAPTER 17

National Case Law: United Kingdom

1 INTRODUCTION

17.1 The High Court decision in cases *NT1 v Google LLC* and *NT2 v Google LLC*[1] are understood to be the first such RtbF decisions in the UK.[2] The separate cases were argued at the same time before Mr Justice Warby at the High Court and were referred to in the same judgment on 13 April 2018.[3] The claimant NT2 was successful. The claimant in *NT1* was not. It is noted that the names of the claimants were anonymised. Indeed, this is in common in a number of continental EU jurisdictions who seek to protect certain parties when appropriate.[4] In addition, it should be noted that the Information Commissioner was also represented as an intervenor in the proceedings.

It needs to be pointed out, however, that post Brexit, actual EU law, rules, norms, and case law (including the CJEU) are not intended to be directly effective. They may continue to be indirectly influential to a greater or lesser effect. Indeed, it is noted that there is (at least presently, and pending the ultimate result of the current consultation process) an official (UK) view that the Data Protection Act 2018 and UK GDPR are similar and equivalent to EU data laws. Indeed, the EU adequacy decision is (presently) based on this view. Caution is advised, however, to assess to the current legal status for the time being once a particular issue arises.

2 DATA PROTECTION ACT

17.2 The Data Protection Act in these cases is the Data Protection Act 1998 (DPA 1998), ie prior to the current Data Protection Act 2018 (DPA 2018) and UK GDPR (and prior to the European Union (Withdrawal) Act 2018, any data protection consultation process changes as may ensue, and any new online safety protections as may also follow).

---

1   *NT1 & NT2 v Google LLC* [2018] EWHC 799 (QB) (13 April 2018) Warby J, at para 230.
2   Some of general commentary includes eg, A Wills, '*NT1 & NT2 v Google LLC* (Information Commissioner Intervening): Spent Convictions and the Right to be Forgotten' *Entertainment Law Review* (2018) (29:6) 191; I Wilson, '"Right to be Forgotten": High Court Judgment on Delisting' *Computers and Law* (2018) (June–July) 6; P Kirkwood, '*NT1 & NT2 v Google LLC* – The Secretive Case Giving the UK Its First Decision on the Right to Be Forgotten' *European Data Protection Law Review (EDPL)* (2018) (4:3) 384.
3   *NT1 & NT2 v Google LLC*, para 1. The Information Commissioner was also an intervenor party to the proceedings.
4   For example, Germany, France, etc.

3   SUCCESSFUL RTBF CASE: *NT2*

17.3   The successful decision is the *NT2* case, which holds that:

(a)   the delisting claim is not an abuse of the court's process, as alleged by Google;

(b)   the inaccuracy complaint is upheld and an appropriate delisting order will be made;

(c)   the remainder of the delisting claim also succeeds;

(d)   the claim for misuse of private information succeeds; and

(e)   Google was felt to have taken reasonable care and the claimant was not entitled to compensation or damages.[5] (It is not clear what evidence of reasonable care was adduced. This may be more of an issue in future.)

This is discussed in further detail in the following chapters.

4   UNSUCCESSFUL RTBF CASE: *NT1*

17.4   The unsuccessful decision is the *NT1* case, which holds that:

(a)   the delisting claim is not an abuse of the court's process, as alleged by Google;

(b)   the inaccuracy complaint is dismissed. The first article at issue was a substantially fair and accurate report of legal proceedings held in public. The second article at issue was not, but the claimant has failed to prove that the information in the second article was inaccurate in any material respect. Similar conclusions apply to the similar information in the book extract at issue;

(c)   the remainder of the delisting claim is also dismissed;

(d)   the claim for misuse of private information fails; and

(e)   the claims for compensation or damages do not arise – given the above.[6]

This is discussed in further detail in the following chapters.

However, the court also sought to refer to some general principles. These are set out below. It is noted above that this case is under the prior UK law (DPA 1998) and some caution is needed in overinterpreting how it applies currently under the GDPR and GDPR-framed laws. The judge even adds some caution on this point.[7]

---

5   *NT1 & NT2 v Google LLC* at para 230.
6   *Ibid* at para 229. Also see S Mizrahi, 'Ontario's New Invasion of Privacy Torts: Do They Offer Monetary Redress for Violations Suffered Via the Internet of Things?' *Western Journal of Legal Studies* (2018) (8:1) (COV2) 37.
7   See, for instance, *NT1 & NT2 v Google LLC* at para 105.

5   GENERAL PRINCIPLES

17.5   These NT1 and NT2 claims are both about RtbF.[8] The court indicates that these are perhaps more accurately described as the right to have personal information 'delisted' or 'de-indexed' by the operators of internet search engines – which are also referred to as 'ISEs'.[9] (While delisting is indeed correct, the right(s) may be somewhat wider now under the GDPR and the developing need, for various reasons, for erasure, forgetting, takedown and delisting.)

The respective claimants in *NT1* and in *NT2* are two businessmen each of whom were convicted of criminal offences many years ago.[10] The defendant is Google. It operates a website service 'called Search' which returns internet search results that includes links to third-party reports about the claimants' convictions. The two claimants' positions are that the search results conveyed inaccurate information about their offending. They sought orders requiring details about their offending, convictions and sentences to be removed from Google Search results on the basis that such information is:

- old;

- out of date;

- irrelevant;

- of no public interest; and/or

- otherwise an illegitimate interference with their rights.[11]

They also sought compensation for Google's conduct in continuing to return search results disclosing such details after their notice complaints had been made. Google resisted both claims, maintaining that the inclusion of such details in its search results was and remains legitimate.[12]

Claimants' Details Anonymised

17.6   The court indicates that the claimants' details in both cases are anonymised in the judgment 'for reasons which will probably be obvious from this short summary'. The reasons for anonymising are explained in more detail in judgments given in the First PTR Judgment'[13] and the Second PTR Judgment.[14] It was decided that 'anonymity is required to ensure that these claims do not give the information at issue the very publicity which the claimants wish to limit'.[15] In

---

8   *Ibid* at para 1.
9   *Ibid.*
10   *Ibid* at para 2.
11   *Ibid.*
12   *Ibid.*
13   *NT1 & NT2 v Google LLC* [2018] EWHC 67 (QB).
14   *NT1 & NT2 v Google LLC* [2018] EWHC 67 (QB) and [2018] EWHC 261 (QB).
15   *Ibid* at para 3.

addition, '[o]ther individuals and organisations have been given false names in th[e] judgment for the same reason: to protect the identities of the claimants'.[16] (This is interesting given that certain entities have effectively threatened or implied threats against some those seeking erasure eg, of escalating publicity and creating new problem content.)

There is, however, a separate, 'private judgment' in each case containing more identification details which 'tend to identify' the claimants.[17] The private judgments are restricted and may not be published because 'whatever the outcome of these claims, it is not necessary or proportionate for the Court to place on the public record personal data which either is or may at some stage become private, and which in any event is not so generally accessible that the Court should proceed on the basis that its judgment can add nothing to the impact on the claimant'.[18] The issues involved with anonymity[19] generally will become more important to RtbF processes and cases.

Legal Review

17.7 The court acknowledges that the above 'are novel questions, which have never yet been considered in this Court' (ie, the UK High Court). The issues 'arise in a legal environment which is complex and has developed over time'. Indeed, '[m]any of the legislative provisions date back to before the advent of the internet, and well before the creation of ISEs'.[20] The court points out that '[a]s often happens, statute has not kept pace with technical developments'.[21] This reflects the problem of time referred to earlier (see Chapter 1).

Complexities, Agreement and Disagreement

17.8 The decision also continues with an interesting comment referring to where the difference rests between the parties. It states that '[d]uring the trial process some of the complexities that appeared to loom large at the outset have either disappeared, or receded into the background'. 'The trial has ended with quite a large measure of agreement as to the principles I should apply, albeit not as to the answer I should reach by doing so.' The parties 'both submitted that on the facts their respective clients' cases were "overwhelming". I find the matter more finely balanced.'[22]

---

16 *Ibid*.
17 *Ibid* at para 4.
18 See *L v The Law Society* [2010] EWCA Civ 811 para 2 (Sir Anthony Clarke MR). *NT1 & NT2 v Google LLC* at para 4.
19 G Bachmann, P Bialski, and M Hansen, 'The Terms of Anonymity: An Interview With Marit Hansen, German Data Protection Expert' *Ephemera: Theory & Politics in Organization* (2017) (17:2) 421.
20 *NT1 & NT2 v Google LLC* at para 10.
21 *Ibid*.
22 *Ibid*.

Main Issues

17.9   'Stated broadly', the main issues in each of these two cases according to the court, are:

> (1) whether the claimant is entitled to have the links in question excluded from Google Search results either (a) because one or more of them contain personal data relating to him which are inaccurate, or (b) because for that and/or other reasons the continued listing of those links by Google involves an unjustified interference with the claimant's data protection and/or privacy rights; and (2) if so, whether the claimant is also entitled to compensation for continued listing between the time of the delisting request and judgment. Put another way, the first question is whether the record needs correcting; the second question is whether the data protection or privacy rights of these claimants extend to having shameful episodes in their personal history eliminated from Google Search; thirdly, there is the question of whether damages should be paid.[23]

Ten UK Features

17.10   The judgment sets out ten key features of the UK legal framework. These recognise both statute enactments and common law developments.[24] (These may, therefore, be less relevant in civil law continental European countries.) These are the referred to as the:

(1)   European Convention on Human Rights 1951 (Convention).[25] 'Of particular relevance are the qualified rights to respect for private and family life (Article 8) and freedom of expression (Article 10)'.[26]

(2)   European Communities Act 1972 (1972 Act).[27] 'As a result, domestic law has since 1973 been subject to European Union law as contained in Directives and, later on, Regulations of the EU as interpreted by the European Court of Justice, now known as the Court of Justice of the European Union (CJEU). Section 3 of the 1972 Act requires UK Courts to make decisions on matters of EU law "in accordance with … any relevant decision of the [CJEU] …."'[28]

---

23   *Ibid* at para 9.
24   *Ibid* at para 13.
25   The court notes that the UK was an important original founding signatory.
26   *NT1 & NT2 v Google LLC* at para 13(1).
27   By which the UK Parliament decided that the Treaty of Rome (25 March 1957) and other constitutional instruments of what was then the European Economic Community would be given direct legal effect in the UK without further enactment. *NT1 & NT2 v Google LLC* at para 13(2).
28   *Ibid.*

(3) Rehabilitation of Offenders Act 1974 (1974 Act). It provides by sections 1, 4 and 5 that some convictions become 'spent' after the end of a specified rehabilitation period.[29]

(4) DPD 95/46. The purposes of the DPD 95/46 included safeguarding individuals' fundamental rights and freedoms, notably the right to privacy, to an equivalent extent within the EU Member States. Provisions of particular relevance are referred to in the judgment as being contained in Articles 2, 6, 8, 9, 12, 14, 23 and 29.[30]

(5) Data Protection Act 1998 (DPA 1988).[31] Of particular relevance are DPA 1998 sections 1, 2, 4, 10, 13, 14 and 32; the first, fourth, sixth and seventh (data protection) principles in Schedule 1; Schedule 2 paragraph 6; Schedule 3 paragraphs 5, 6(c) and 7A; and paragraph 3 of the Schedule to certain regulations made under DPA 1998 section 10, namely, the Data Protection (Processing of Sensitive Personal Data) Order 2000[32] (2000 Order).[33]

(6) Human Rights Act 1998 (HRA), enacted to ensure Convention rights became directly enforceable before the UK courts.[34] Sections 2 and 6 of the HRA impose duties on the court to interpret and apply domestic legislation in accordance with the Convention Rights, and not incompatibly with the Convention.[35]

(7) 2004 decisions of the *House of Lords in Campbell v MGN*[36] [*Campbell*[37] case] and *In re S (A Child) (Re S)*,[38] 'in which the House recognised the development, under the influence of the HRA, of a common law right to protection against the misuse of private information, and established the methodology to be adopted in reconciling the competing demands of Articles 8 and 10 of the Convention'.[39]

---

29 *Ibid* at para 13(3). The 1974 Act contains provisions specifying the legal effects of a conviction becoming spent. Whether, if and when a conviction becomes spent depends on the length of the sentence. Those effects are subject to certain specified exceptions and limitations. Criminal law issues are also discussed in, for example, M Keiter, 'Criminal Law Principles in California: Balancing a Right to Be Forgotten with a Right to Remember' *California Legal History* (2018) (13) 421.

30 *NT1 & NT2 v Google LLC* at para 13(4).

31 This was enacted on 16 July 1998 to implement the DPD 95/46 in the UK. It has now been replaced by the UK Data Protection Act 2018.

32 SI 2000/417.

33 *NT1 & NT2 v Google LLC* at para 13(5).

34 Enacted on 9 November 1998, by which the rights and freedoms enshrined in the Convention became directly enforceable before the courts of the UK.

35 *NT1 & NT2 v Google LLC* at para 13(6).

36 *Campbell v MGN Ltd* [2004] UKHL 22; [2004] 2 AC 457.

37 J Rowbottom, 'A Landmark at a Turning Point: Campbell and the Use of Privacy Law to Constrain Media Power' *Journal of Media Law* (2015) (7:2) 170.

38 *In re S (A Child)* [2004] UKHL 47; [2005] 1 AC 593.

39 *NT1 & NT2 v Google LLC* at para 13(7).

(8) Charter of Fundamental Rights of the European Union 2000/C 364/01 (Charter).[40] Relevance provisions are Article 7 (respect for private life), Article 8 (protection of personal data), Article 11 (freedom of expression and information), Article 16 (freedom to conduct a business) and Article 47 (right to an effective remedy).[41] Member States must act compatibly with the Charter when implementing EU law.[42] This means, among other things, that the DPD 95/46 must be interpreted and applied in conformity with the Charter rights.[43]

(9) May 2014 decision of the CJEU in *Google Spain SL & another v Agencia Espanola de Proteccion de Datos (AEPD)* and another Case C-131/12 [2014] QB 1022 (*Google Spain*),[44] in which the CJEU interpreted the DPD 95/46 and the Charter as creating a qualified right to be forgotten. The court went on to apply that right to the facts before it, by holding that the individual complainant was entitled to have Google de-list information of which he complained. It is this decision that prompted the original complaints by NT1 and NT2 and hundreds of thousands of other de-listing requests. Google's evidence, contained in a 'Transparency Report', is that between the *Google Spain* decision and 4 October 2017 – a period of some 3½ years – it had been asked to de-list almost 1.9m links or URLs (a detailed analysis of what was and was not in the report does not appear in the case).[45] This may come to be considered in greater detail in future.

(10) GDPR.[46] This is an EU legislative measure with the stated purposes of 'strengthening and setting out in detail the rights of data subjects and the obligations of those who process … personal data …' (recital 11). The GDPR came into force on 25 May 2016 and has direct effect in Member States, including the UK, from 25 May 2018. Article 17 of the GDPR is headed 'Right to erasure ("right to be forgotten").' It is relied upon by Google in its arguments as a 'setting out in detail' of the right and 'which should guide my decision' in these two cases.[47]

6 UK SPENT CONVICTIONS AND THE 1974 ACT

17.11 The issue of spent convictions was not expressly at issue in the *Google Spain* decision. Yet it appears to have become an important issue in each of these cases. It remains to be seen whether this will or should feature in future cases and/

---

40 By which the EU recognised and sought to strengthen the protection for certain fundamental rights resulting from the Convention and from constitutional instruments of the EU.

41 The Charter was proclaimed by the European Parliament in December 2000 but only took full legal effect on the entry into force of the Lisbon Treaty on 1 December 2009.

42 *Rugby Football Union v Viagogo Ltd* [2012] UKSC 55 [2012] 1 WLR 3333 [26–28].

43 Per *Lindqvist v Aklagarkammaren I Jonkoping* (C-101/01) 6 November 2003 [87]; *NT1 & NT2 v Google LLC* at para 13(8).

44 *Google Spain SL, Google Inc v Agencia Española de Protección de Datos (AEPD), Mario Costeja González*, Court of Justice (Grand Chamber), Case C-131/12, 13 May 2014.

45 URLs are Universal Resource Locators. *NT1 & NT2 v Google LLC* at para 13(9).

46 General Data Protection Regulation (EU) 2016/679. Enacted on 27 April 2016.

47 *NT1 & NT2 v Google LLC* para 13(10).

or the extent to which it should (if at all). It does not appear to be as significantly referred to in other RtbF cases.

The purpose of the 1974 Act (prior to the GDPR) is 'to rehabilitate offenders who have not been reconvicted of any serious offence for periods of years'.[48] The nature of the offence is immaterial. The offender age is relevant.[49]

The *NT1* sentence was four years' imprisonment. Legal amendments provide for such a sentence to become spent after seven years.[50] The *NT2* sentence was six months' imprisonment and always qualified as being capable of becoming spent.[51]

Section 4 of the 1974 Act is headed 'Effect of rehabilitation'. It begins as follows:

> (1) Subject to sections 7 and 8 below, a person who has become a rehabilitated person for the purposes of this Act in respect of a conviction *shall be treated for all purposes in law* as a person who has not committed or been charged with or prosecuted for or convicted of or sentenced for the offence or offences which were the subject of that conviction … (original judgment emphasis).[52]

The emphasis 'highlights wording of exceptional breadth that might at first sight be thought to provide a complete and ready answer to these claims'. But none of the arguments suggest this. All the parties (apparently) treat section 4(1) as embodying a legal policy which the court should have regard to in resolving the case. The weight to be given to the policy, however, is more controversial.[53]

Google argues the importance to another express limitation on the statutory right to rehabilitation re defamation actions.[54]

The judgment summarises that a defendant sued for defamation regarding a publication imputing the commission by the claimant of a criminal offence which is the subject of a spent conviction can rely on any reporting privilege that may exist and/or on a defence of truth or honest opinion, unless the publication is proved to have been made with malice.[55] In defamation, a conviction is conclusive

---

48   *Ibid* at para 15. The rehabilitation periods that apply are set out in s 5 of the Act. With one exception they depend on the length of the sentence and take effect from sentence end (see para 16).

49   *Ibid* at para 16. The scheme differs between England & Wales and Scotland

50   *Ibid* at para 16(1). Under the law (England & Wales) as at 10 March 2014, a sentence of more than 30 months was excluded. Amendments in s 139 of the Legal Aid, Sentencing and Punishment of Offenders Act 2012 (LASPO) enlarged the range of sentences that could become spent, to include any sentence of 48 months or less.

51   *Ibid* at para 16(2). Until 10 March 2014, the rehabilitation period for such a sentence was seven years. Amendments in the LASPO reduced that period to two years.

52   *NT1 & NT2 v Google LLC* at para 17.

53   *Ibid*. There was also a discussion in relation to evidence and the admission of evidence in relation to past convictions which are in the nature of spent convictions, see *ibid*, at para 18.

54   Referring to s 8(1) of the 1974 Act referring to defamation. See *NT1 & NT2 v Google LLC* at para 19.

55   *Ibid* at para 21.

proof of guilt against a claimant.[56] In such claims the 'real issue will be malice'.[57] The *NT1* and *NT2* cases are not defamation claims, but 'Google invites me to regard this aspect of the 1974 Act as also embodying an important legal policy to which I should give effect in rejecting' the claims.[58] (The *Google Spain* case did not refer to defamation but rather to data protection.)

The DPD 95/46 and the DPA 1998 impose duties on controllers.[59] Personal data are 'a broad notion, comprising a wide range of information which relates to an individual and is processed by computer'.[60] 'Processing' is also 'very widely defined', 'encompassing almost any dealings with personal data, including holding the data and disclosing it or the information in it.[61] The duty imposed on a controller by the DPA 1998[62] is, subject to section 27(1):

> ... to comply with the data protection principles in relation to all personal data with respect to which he is the data controller.[63]

The principles of data protection (previously the data protection principles)[64] relied on by the claimants are the First, Second, Third, Fourth, Fifth and Sixth (of eight) principles of data protection.[65]

1. Personal data shall be processed fairly and lawfully and, in particular, shall not be processed unless –

   (a) at least one of the conditions in Schedule 2 is met, and

   (b) in the case of sensitive personal data, at least one of the conditions in Schedule 3 is also met.

2. Personal data shall be obtained only for one or more specified and lawful purposes and shall not be further processed in any manner incompatible with that purpose or those purposes.

3. Personal data shall be adequate, relevant and not excessive in relation to the purpose or purposes for which they are processed.

4. Personal data shall be accurate and, where necessary, kept up to date.

5. Personal data processed for any purpose or purposes shall not be kept for longer than is necessary for that purpose or those purposes.

6. Personal data shall be processed in accordance with the rights of data subjects under this Act.[66]

---

56 See the Civil Evidence Act 1968, s 13.
57 Malice, according to the court, appears to mean an irrelevant, spiteful, or improper motive: per *Herbage v Pressdram & Ors* [1984] 1 WLR 1160 (CA).
58 *NT1 & NT2 v Google LLC* at para 21.
59 Controllers are those who make decisions about how and why 'personal data' relating to data subjects is 'processed' *ibid*, para 22.
60 *Ibid*.
61 See DPA 1998, s 1(1). *NT1 & NT2 v Google LLC, ibid* at para 22.
62 *Ibid* s 4(4). *Ibid* at para 22.
63 *Ibid* at para 22.
64 The data protection principles are listed in the then DPA 1988, Sch 1. *Ibid* at para 23.
65 *Ibid* at para 24.
66 *Ibid* at para 23.

The decision refers to sensitive personal data (now referred to as special data or special personal data post the GDPR).[67]

Each claimant stated that by returning against an internet search of their name the URLs complained of, Google is and has been making available to internet users the information contained in the third-party publications and thereby processing the claimant's personal data, and that some or all of which is sensitive (now called special) personal data within the categories set out above.[68] The claimants argue that the processing by Google is in breach of the duty imposed by the DPA 1998[69] because it is not compliant with one or more of the six principles of data protection cited above. The case is that in breach of these principles of data protection the information returned by Google is inaccurate; is 'way out of date'; and is 'being maintained for far longer than is necessary for any conceivable legitimate purpose'.[70]

Google denied the allegations of breach. It also relied on a carve-out from the duty imposed by the DPA 1998.[71] The duty is expressed to be 'subject to s 27(1)', which provides that:

> References in any of the data protection principles or any provision of Parts II and III [of the Act] to personal data or to the processing of personal data do not include references to data or processing which by virtue of [Part III of the DPA 1998] are exempt from that principle or other provision.[72]

One set of exemptions provided for in Part III is found in section 32 (headed 'Journalism, literature and art'). These three activities are defined in the DPA 1998 as 'special purposes'.[73] The judgment refers to section 32 as the 'journalism exemption'. However, note that Google's right to rely on the journalism exemption is contested by the claimants and contested by the ICO.[74] The *Google Spain* case decided that the so called public journalism exemption/ issue did not apply to the search engine.

As indicated previously, the claimants each seek three main remedies:

- an order for the blocking and/or erasure by Google of their personal data;

- an injunction to prevent its further processing; and

- damages.[75]

---

67 Which appears in the First Principle of data protection and is defined by DPA 1998, s 2.
68 *NT1 & NT2 v Google LLC* at para 24.
69 DPA 1998, s 4(4).
70 *NT1 & NT2 v Google LLC* at para 24.
71 DPA 1998 s 4(4).
72 *NT1 & NT2 v Google LLC* at para 25.
73 DPA 1989, s 2. *NT1 & NT2 v Google LLC* at para 25.
74 *Ibid* at para 25.
75 *Ibid* at para 26.

The claims for blocking and/or erasure as referred rely on the DPA 1998.[76] This gives data subjects a right to object to processing that is likely to cause damage or distress and a corresponding right, if the controller does not stop the processing complained of, to seek a court order prohibiting such processing.[77] (Again, this is prior to the more express GDPR RtbF.)

At one stage, Google argued that NT1's 'section 10(1) notice' was not compliant with the statute. However, ultimately Google did not press that point.[78] It is sometimes a feature of cases such as this, that very extensive sets of arguments are raised against parties who take complaints or cases. Some of these may have merit, others less so. This appears to be acknowledged on this point. (That is not to say this or other respondents may not seek to dispute a given notice in future or having received a notice at all despite having so received one).

The court then sets out the provisions relating to its powers:[79]

> If a Court is satisfied, on the application of any person who has given a notice under subsection (1) which appears to the Court to be justified (or to be justified to any extent), that the data Controller in question has failed to comply with the notice, the Court *may* order him to take *such steps* for complying with the notice (or for complying with it to that extent) *as the Court thinks fit* (emphasis added in judgment).[80]

> This wording "must" be interpreted and applied in the light of the corresponding Article of the DPD 95/46, namely, Article 14, granting data subjects the right to object to what may otherwise be lawful processing "on compelling legitimate grounds relating to [their] particular situation," and provides that "[w]here there is a justified objection, the processing ... may no longer involve those data".[81]

Section 14 of the DPA 1998 provides:

> Rectification, blocking, erasure and destruction

> (1) If a Court is satisfied on the application of a data subject that personal data of which the applicant is the subject are inaccurate, the Court may order the data controller to rectify, block, erase or destroy those data and any other personal data in respect of which he is the data Controller and which contain an expression of opinion which appears to the Court to be based on the inaccurate data.[82]

Neither of the claimants seek 'rectification' of any of the data, only its blocking or erasure.[83] This should be noted. (Some entities decide themselves what an individual is seeking and respond via another right which the individual or notice

---

76 DPA 1998, ss 10 and 14. *NT1 & NT2 v Google LLC* at para 27.
77 *Ibid*, s 10. *Ibid*.
78 *NT1 & NT2 v Google LLC* at para 27.
79 Which are contained in DPA 1998, s 10(4). *Ibid*.
80 *Ibid*.
81 *Ibid*.
82 *Ibid* at para 28.
83 *Ibid*.

has not activated at all. This is problematic. Effectively, the RtbF right and notice is ignored and not vindicated properly or at all.)

The court states that the wording of section 14 'would seem to be narrower in scope than that of the corresponding Article of the' DPD 95/46.[84] Article 12(b) requires Member States to guarantee every data subject the right to obtain 'as appropriate the rectification, erasure or blocking of data the processing of which does not comply with the provisions of this Directive, *in particular* because of the *incomplete* or inaccurate nature of the data' (emphasis added in judgment).[85] However, the court feels that any discrepancy appears to be 'immaterial' for present purposes, 'as Google takes no point on it'.[86] (This is not the first time that there has been a disparity between a national data protection law and the DPD 95/46, indeed as the case acknowledges. Given that the new GDPR is directly effective, however, it should be that such disparity is in general reduced in future). (In the Brexit and post-Brexit context, it remains to be seen whether disparity issues may arise, and what additional complexity such issues may potentially lead to. Additional consideration of any new online safety rules or consultation process changes would also need to be considered carefully.)

7 DAMAGES

17.12   The claims for compensation rely on section 13 of the DPA 1998. This provides:

> 13. Compensation for failure to comply with certain requirements
>
> (1) An individual who suffers damage by reason of any contravention by a data controller of any of the requirements of this Act is entitled to compensation from the data controller for that damage.
>
> (2) *An individual who suffers distress by reason of any contravention by a data controller of any of the requirements of this Act is entitled to compensation from the data controller for that distress if –*
>
> > (a) *the individual also suffers damage by reason of the contravention, or*
> >
> > (b) *the contravention relates to the processing of personal data for the special purposes.* [Original emphasis in judgment.]
>
> (3) In proceedings brought against a person by virtue of this section it is a defence to prove that he had taken such care as in all the circumstances was reasonably required to comply with the requirement concerned.[87]

The judgment places section 13(2) in italics because, as the Court of Appeal held in *Vidal-Hall v Google Inc*,[88] the sub-section 'fails effectively to implement

---

84   *Ibid* at para 29.
85   *Ibid*.
86   *Ibid* at para 29.
87   *Ibid* at para 30.
88   *Vidal-Hall v Google Inc* [2015] EWCA Civ 311 [2016] QB 1003.

Article 23 of the DPD 95/46, and has to be disapplied because it is incompatible with the Charter'.[89]

'Accordingly,' therefore, 'compensation is recoverable under the DPA [1998] for non-material damage, as well as material loss'.[90] The Court sets out the steps in the Court of Appeal's conclusion in the *Vidal-Hall* case:

> 79. ... Article 23 of the Directive does not distinguish between pecuniary and nonpecuniary damage. There is no linguistic reason to interpret the word "damage" in article 23 as being restricted to pecuniary damage. More importantly, for the reasons we have given such a restrictive interpretation would substantially undermine the objective of the Directive which is to protect the right to privacy of individuals with respect to the processing of their personal data.
>
> ...
>
> 84. .... if interpreted literally, section 13(2) has not effectively transposed article 23 of the Directive into our domestic law. It is in these circumstances that the question arises whether it is nevertheless possible to interpret section 13(2) in a way which is compatible with article 23 so as to permit the award of compensation for distress by reason of a contravention of a requirement of the [DPA 1998] even in circumstances which do not satisfy the conditions set out in section 13(2) (a) or (b).
>
> ...
>
> 94. We cannot ... interpret section 13(2) compatibly with article 23.
>
> 95. Mr Tomlinson and Ms Proops [Counsel for the claimants and the ICO] submit that section 13(2) should be disapplied on the grounds that it conflicts with the rights guaranteed by articles 7 and 8 of the Charter. We accept their submission. ...
>
> 96. Article 47 of the Charter provides: "Right to an effective remedy and to a fair trial. Everyone whose rights and freedoms guaranteed by the law of the Union are violated has the right to an effective remedy before a tribunal in compliance with the conditions laid down in this article."
>
> 97. Article 7 provides that: "Everyone has the right to respect for his or her private and family life, home and communications." Article 8(1) (as we have earlier noted) provides that: "Everyone has the right to the protection of personal data concerning him or her."
>
> 98. As this Court stated in the *Benkharbouche* case[91] ... (i) where there is a breach of a right afforded under EU law, article 47 of the Charter is engaged; (ii) the right to an effective remedy for breach of EU law rights provided for by article 47 embodies a general principle of EU law; (iii) (subject to exceptions which have no application in the present case) that general principle has horizontal effect; (iv) in so far as a provision of national law conflicts with the requirement for an effective remedy in article 47, the domestic Courts can and must disapply the conflicting

---

89 *NT1 & NT2 v Google LLC* at para 31.
90 *Ibid.*
91 *Benkharbouche & Anor v Embassy of the Republic of Sudan (Rev 1)* [2016] QB 347, paras 69–85.

provision; and (v) the only exception to (iv) is that the Court may be required to apply a conflicting domestic provision where the Court would otherwise have to redesign the fabric of the legislative scheme.[92]

Note also that damages and compensation, expressly referred to as rights in the GDPR will be a point of interest in future cases. Just as fines and penalties have increased, it may be that damages and compensation will come to rise also. As with all litigation cases, some cases may have stronger compensation claims than others. This case appears to have taken an overly restrictive view, insofar as the judgment does not seem to identify the facts and factors upon which the defendant respondent was felt to have acted reasonably. Without singling any website out, there are ample reports across jurisdictions that there is often no response to online abuse (OA) reports to a website and, in many cases, where there is action, it is not always prompt. It is suggested that, in future, courts in a variety of cases, including RtbF cases, will have to go into more detail in assessing the actual policies on-site and internally, website, design and actual actions of given websites and companies. It should not be blindly assumed in all instances that a company or website acts reasonably – without further scrutiny. Websites can also adopt policies aiming to reduce the number of reports it received, or the number of reports that will be successfully auctioned (from the user's perspective). If there is deliberation, calculation and policy design to minimise or reduce the full vindication of individual rights on a given website, some may suggest that there is an element of unreasonableness and that this may impact consideration of damage and compensation issues, and other remedies. These areas have only begun to be considered in a court setting. It is predicted that such considerations will increase.

There is also wider discussion in relation to internet torts, compensation and redress.[93] The caveat, however, is that there may be differences between European common law jurisdictions and civil law jurisdictions. Note also the recent UK report raising concerns for the rights of individuals and the effects of certain online activity, and the action and inaction of certain service providers (referring for instance to 'digital gangsters' and misleading testimony).[94] There is also discussion in relation to new internet protections for individuals eg a possible new Digital Safety Commissioner (DSC) in Ireland.

Google Spain

17.13   The judgment summarises what happened in *Google Spain*. The claimant was a Spanish individual who wished to remove two links on Google Search, linking to an auction notice posted on a Spanish newspaper's website, regarding his previous bankruptcy. He complained that the auction notice was many years

---

92 *NT1 & NT2 v Google LLC* at para 31.
93 In relation to Canada, for example, see Mizrahi, 'Ontario's New Invasion of Privacy Torts: Do They Offer Monetary Redress for Violations Suffered Via the Internet of Things?' at 37.
94 *8th Report – Disinformation and 'fake news': Final Report,* Digital, Culture, Media and Sports Committee (UK) (18 February 2019).

out of date. He also complained that it was no longer relevant. The newspaper and Google refused to remove the links to the notice. He complained to the Spanish data protection supervisory authority against the newspaper, Google, and Google Spain SL (Google's Spanish subsidiary). The CJEU held that Google was bound by the DPD 95/46 because it had set up a subsidiary in an EU Member State which was intended to promote and sell advertising space offered by 'Google Search' and which 'orientated' or targeted its activity towards the inhabitants of that state.[95]

The CJEU held as follows:

(1) In making available information containing personal data published on the internet by third parties an entity operating an ISE is processing personal data for the purposes of the [DPD 95/46], and is a data controller in respect of that processing, with an obligation to ensure "within the framework of its responsibilities, powers and capabilities", that the data subject's rights are protected in accordance with the' DPD 96/46.[96]

(2) There is a "right to be forgotten": a data subject's fundamental rights under articles 7 and 8 of the Charter entitle them to request that information no longer be made available to the general public by means of a list of results displayed following a search made by reference to their name, and their rights may override the rights and interests of the ISE and those of the general public. It is unnecessary for the data subject to show that the inclusion of the information in the search results caused prejudice.[97]

(3) Upon application by a data subject a national authority or court can therefore, in an appropriate case, order the operator under Article 12(b) and/ or 14(1)(a) of the [DPD 95/46] to remove, from search results displayed following a search made on a person's name, links to web pages published by third parties containing information relating to that person; this may be so, even if that name or information has not been erased beforehand or simultaneously from those web pages, and even where the publication of the information on those web pages is lawful.[98] [There is also a paragraph 4 in the decision.]

Warby J states that '[i]t is worthy of note that the Court drew distinctions between the processing of information for journalistic purposes on the one hand, and its processing by ISEs on the other, suggesting that the rights of data subjects will vary accordingly'.[99]

The following features of the court's reasoning are outlined by Warby J as important:

---

95 *NT1 & NT2 v Google LLC* at para 32.
96 The court refers, in particular, to paras 28, 33–34 and 38.
97 The court refers, in particular, to paras 94 and 96.
98 The court refers, in particular, to paras 81, 85, 94, 99. *NT1 & NT2 v Google LLC* at para 32.
99 *Ibid* at para 33.

(1) The impact of processing by an ISE will tend to have a more significant impact on the privacy and data protection rights of individuals than other forms of processing. Such processing

> ... is liable to affect significantly the fundamental rights to privacy and to the protection of personal data when the search by means of that engine is carried out on the basis of an individual's name, since that processing enables any Internet user to obtain through the list of results a structured overview of the information relating to that individual that can be found on the Internet – information which potentially concerns a vast number of aspects of his private life and which, without the search engine, could not have been interconnected or could have been only with great difficulty – and thereby to establish a more or less detailed profile of him. Furthermore, the effect of the interference with those rights of the data subject is heightened on account of the important role played by the Internet and search engines in modern society, which render the information contained in such a list of results ubiquitous: see to this effect *eDate Advertising GmbH v X* ...[100] ([80]).

(2) ISEs did not appear to the court to be processing information "solely for journalistic purposes", so as to benefit from the privileges enjoyed by the latter:

> ... *the processing by the publisher of a web page consisting in the publication of information relating to an individual may, in some circumstances, be carried out 'solely for journalistic purposes' and thus benefit, by virtue of Article 9 of [the DPD 95/46], from derogations from the requirements laid down by the Directive, whereas that does not appear to be so in the case of the processing carried out by the operator of a search engine.* It cannot therefore be ruled out that in certain circumstances the data subject is capable of exercising the rights referred to in Article 12(b) and subparagraph (a) of the first paragraph of Article 14 of [the DPD 95/46] against that operator but not against the publisher of the web page.[101]

(3) A delisting request relating may therefore be made, and upheld, in respect of "links to web pages published lawfully by third parties and containing true information in relation to him personally ..." if the inclusion of those links in the list of search results returned by the ISE nonetheless appears, having regard to all the circumstances of the case, to be inadequate, irrelevant or no longer relevant, or excessive *in relation to the purposes of the processing at issue carried out by the operator of the search engine* ([94], emphasis added [in judgment]).

(4) A delisting request should be assessed by reference to the circumstances which obtain at the time when the request is made: [94], [96].[102]

---

100 *eDate Advertising GmbH v X* (Joined Cases C509/09 and C-161/10) [2012] QB 654; [2011] ECR I-10269, para 45.
101 *Ibid* at para 85. Emphasis added in judgment.
102 *NT1 & NT2 v Google LLC* at para 33.

The CJEU held that the seriousness of the potential effects of listing by an ISE meant that it 'cannot be justified by merely the economic interest which the operator of such an engine has in that processing'. That was referring to Google's rights under Article 16 of the Charter.[103]

The validity of a delisting notice should be determined, said the CJEU, by striking 'a fair balance' between 'the legitimate interest of internet users potentially interested in having access' to the information and 'the data subject's fundamental rights under articles 7 and 8 of the Charter'.[104] At paragraph 81, and again at paragraph 97, the CJEU observed that the latter rights would 'as a general rule' override not only 'the economic interest of the operator of the search engine but also the interest of the general public in finding that information on a search relating to the data subject's name'. Whether it did so in an individual case would depend on such factors as 'the nature of the information in question and its sensitivity for the data subject's private life and on the interest of the public in having that information, an interest which may vary, in particular, according to the role played by the data subject in public life ...' That role may be a reason for concluding 'that the interference with his fundamental rights is justified by the preponderant interest of the general public in having, on account of inclusion in the list of results, access to the information in question'.[105]

The information complained of in the *Google Spain* case was initially published 16 years earlier. It was drawn from the online archives of a part of the newspaper containing official announcements. On the facts, the CJEU held that having regard to the sensitivity of the data and since there did not appear to be 'particular reasons substantiating a preponderant interest of the public' in having access to that information 'in the context of such a search'. Articles 12 and 14 of the DPD 95/46 required the removal of the links from the list of results.[106]

8 ARTICLE 29 WORKING PARTY GUIDELINES

17.14 The court also refers to the Article 29 Working Party[107] (WP 29) guidelines. Note, however, that post Brexit, EU bodies will not be as directly influential in the UK, including the WP 20 and its replacement, namely, the European Data Protection Board (EDPB). In the immediate future, at least in the UK, much attention will be paid to the ICO and its guidance.

---

103 *Ibid* at para 34.
104 *Google Spain*, CJEU, para 81.
105 *NT1 & NT2 v Google LLC* at para 34.
106 *Google Spain*, CJEU, at para 98. *NT1 & NT2 v Google LLC* at para 35. The WP 29 membership includes a representative from the data protection supervisory authority of each Member State. The functions of the WP 29 are described in DPD 95/46 Arts 29 and 30 and Directive 2002/58 Art 15, in summary, to examine and make recommendations on matters relating to data protection in the EU and to have 'advisory status'.
107 DPD 95/46 Art 29 established a Working Party on the Protection of Individuals with regard to the Processing of Personal Data (WP 29).

On 26 November 2014 the WP 29 published 'Guidelines on the Implementation of [Google Spain].' The guidance comprises:

- An executive summary;

- Part I 'Interpretation of the CJEU judgment'; and

- Part II 'List of common criteria for the handling of complaints by European data protection authorities'.[108]

The court advises that the WP 29 Executive Summary is helpful. It identifies four salient features from *Google Spain*:

1. Search engines as data controllers. The ruling recognises that search engine operators process personal data and qualify as data controllers within the meaning of Article 2 of [the DPD 95/46]. The processing of personal data carried out in the context of the activity of the search engine must be distinguished from, and is additional to that carried out by, publishers of third-party websites.

2. A fair balance between fundamental rights and interests In the terms of the Court, "in the light of the potential seriousness of the impact of this processing on the fundamental rights to privacy and data protection, the rights of the data subject prevail, as a general rule, over the economic interest of the search engine and that of internet users to have access to the personal information through the search engine". However, a balance of the relevant rights and interests has to be made and the outcome may depend on the nature and sensitivity of the processed data and on the interest of the public in having access to that particular information. The interest of the public will be significantly greater if the data subject plays a role in public life.

3. Limited impact of de-listing on the access to information. In practice, the impact of the de-listing on individuals' rights to freedom of expression and access to information will prove to be very limited. When assessing the relevant circumstances, [data protection supervisory authorities] will systematically take into account the interest of the public in having access to the information. If the interest of the public overrides the rights of the data subject, de-listing will not be appropriate.

4. No information is deleted from the original source. The judgment states that the right only affects the results obtained from searches made on the basis of a person's name and does not require deletion of the link from the indexes of the search engine altogether. That is, the original information will still be accessible using other search terms, or by direct access to the publisher's original source.[109]

Point 2 above highlights and Warby J indicates the fact that the CJEU regarded the sensitivity of the data in question as an important element in striking the balance.[110]

---

108 *NT1 & NT2 v Google LLC* at para 36.
109 *Ibid* at para 37.
110 *Ibid* at para 38.

Point 4 'explains why it may be misleading to label the right asserted by these claimants as the "right to be forgotten." They are not asking to "be forgotten". The first aspect of their claims asserts a right not to be remembered inaccurately. Otherwise, they are asking for accurate information about them to be "forgotten" in the narrow sense of being removed from the search results returned by an ISE in response to a search on the claimant's name.'[111] A successful claim against Google would be applied to and by other ISEs.[112]

However, Warby J states that it 'does not follow that the information at issue would have to be removed from the public record, or that a similar request would have to be complied with by a media publisher on whose website the same information appeared'.[113] The *NT* claimants are not asking for any such remedy.[114]

It is also worth noting, Warby J indicates, that a successful delisting request or order in respect of a specified URL will not prevent Google from returning search results containing that URL; it only means that the URL must not be returned in response to a search on the claimant's name.[115] (It remains to be seen if this is the case in all instance; and also if this will be the case post the GDPR. For example, a pseudonym or avatar name may, depending on the circumstances, be of such a nature as to easily identify the individual if searched for. The jurisprudence thus far appears focused on text-based content, as opposed to image content and image searches, which may have more distinct issues to consider).

Part II of the WP 29 Guideline sets out 13 'common criteria' and commentary for the handling of complaints by national data protection supervisory authorities.

The parties to the *NT* cases are agreed that this Part of the Guidelines are important to the court in assessing these claims.[116] The judge states that not all the 'common criteria' are relevant to the present cases, but most of them have 'at least some relevance'. They explain the status and role of these criteria as follows:

> the list of common criteria which the [national data protection supervisory authorities] will apply to handle the complaints, on a case-by-case basis … should be seen as a flexible working tool which aims at helping [the national data protection supervisory authorities] during the decision-making processes. The criteria will be applied in accordance with the relevant national legislations. No single criterion is, in itself, determinative. The list of criteria is non-exhaustive and will evolve over time, building on the experience of [the national data protection supervisory authorities].[117]

111 *Ibid.*
112 *Ibid.*
113 *Ibid.*
114 *Ibid.*
115 *Ibid.*
116 *Ibid* at para 39.
117 *Ibid.*

Part II of the Guidelines further explain the criteria as based on 'a first analysis of the complaints so far received from data subjects whose delisting requests were refused by the search engines'. (It may have to be expanded or evolved further over time as new issues, additional jurisprudence, arise, and as problem content and the nuances come to be better understood). It states that:

> In most cases, it appears that more than one criterion will need to be taken into account in order to reach a decision. In other words, no single criterion is, in itself, determinative.

> Each criterion has to be applied in the light of the principles established by the CJEU and in particular in the light of the "the interest of the general public in having access to [the] information".[118]

9   GDPR

17.15   The court also refers to Article 17 of the GDPR and is encouraged by Google to follow or adopt the GDPR, notwithstanding that at the time of the decision the GDPR was not yet live.[119]

10   MISUSE OF PRIVATE INFORMATION

17.16   A second cause of action is relied on in the *NT* cases, namely, the misuse of private information. As appears from, among other cases, *Campbell, McKennitt v Ash*[120] and *Vidal-Hall*[121] [*Campbell*[122] case] this is a tort which emerged from the equitable wrong of breach of confidence under the influence of the Human Rights Act 1998. (This may be a further point or difference with continental European jurisdictions.) It has two essential ingredients:

(1)   the claimant must enjoy a reasonable expectation of privacy in respect of the information in question; if that is established, the second question arises;

(2)   in all the circumstances, must the Article 8 rights of the individual yield to the right of freedom of expression conferred on the publisher by Article 10?[123]

The latter inquiry is, the court states, commonly referred to as 'the balancing exercise'. It is undertaken in the way set out by Lord Steyn in the *Re S* case at paragraph 17:

> First, neither article has as such precedence over the other. Secondly, where the values under the two articles are in conflict, an intense focus on the comparative importance of the specific rights being claimed in the individual

---

118 *Ibid* at para 40.
119 *Ibid* at para 41.
120 *Campbell, McKennitt v Ash* [2006] EWCA Civ 1714; [2008] QB 73, para 11.
121 *Vidal-Hall v Google Inc* [2015] EWCA Civ 311; [2016] QB 1003.
122 Rowbottom, 'A Landmark at a Turning Point: Campbell and the Use of Privacy Law to Constrain Media Power' above at 170.
123 *NT1 & NT2 v Google LLC* at para 42.

case is necessary. Thirdly, the justifications for interfering with or restricting each right must be taken into account. Finally, the proportionality test must be applied to each. For convenience I will call this the ultimate balancing test.[124]

The authorities provide numerous illustrations of this balancing process, which is, of course, highly fact sensitive.[125] The relationship between the laws of misuse of private information and data protection have been discussed on occasion. They are 'often' considered to lead to the same conclusion, for much the same reasons[126] (but not always[127]). In this case, it is agreed (by the parties) that both deserve consideration.[128]

11   CONVICTIONS, CONFIDENTIALITY AND PRIVACY

17.17   Criminal trials take place in public. Criminal verdicts and sentences are also public. Historically, it has been lawful to report these matters at the time and subsequently with the benefit of either absolute or qualified immunity from liability as regards defamation and contempt of court. Laws provide reporting restrictions in certain circumstances – to protect privacy interests (eg, the Sexual Offences Amendment Act 1992); due administration of justice (eg, the Contempt of Court Act 1981).[129] Subject to laws or orders of this kind, however, privileges or immunities for fair and accurate reports have existed for some time.[130]

The question of whether and if so when information about a conviction can count as an item of confidential information and/or an aspect of an individual's private or family life, the use or disclosure of which may be actionable, has been considered on a number of occasions.[131] It has not so far, according to the court, been held capable of being confidential information. It is only recently that there has been an acknowledgment that information of this kind can fall within the ambit of an individual's private life.[132]

Elliott v Chief Constable of Wiltshire[133] struck out a claim in breach of confidence, describing the suggestion that a conviction announced in open court could be confidential as 'absurd'. *R (Pearson) v DVLA*[134] rejected a submission that continued reference to a spent conviction on the paper driving licence of

---

124 *Ibid.*
125 *Ibid* at para 43.
126 See, for instance, the *Campbell v MGN Ltd* litigation, *Murray v Express Newspapers plc* [2007] EWHC 1908 (Ch) [2007] EMLR 22.
127 See *Mosley v Google Inc* [2015] EWHC 59 (QB) [2015] EMLR 11 [8]–[9] (Mitting J).
128 *NT1 & NT2 v Google LLC* at para 43.
129 See eg, the Sexual Offences Amendment Act 1992, s 2 and the Contempt of Court Act 1981, s 4(2).
130 They have existed for some time, at common law, under the Defamation Act 1952, the Defamation Act 1996, as well as under the 1981 Act, s 5. The 1974 Act (on rehabilitation), s 8 is an example of a qualified privilege or immunity. *NT1 & NT2 v Google LLC* at para 44.
131 It has been considered on a number of occasions in the UK courts since 1974
132 *NT1 & NT2 v Google LLC* at para 45.
133 *Elliott v Chief Constable of Wiltshire*, Sir Richard Scott V-C, *The Times* (5 December 1996).
134 *R (Pearson) v DVLA* [2002] EWHC 2482 (Admin) Maurice Kay J.

a professional lorry driver represented an interference with his rights under Article 8(1) of the Convention. The Judge held that Article 8 was not even engaged (and that if it was, the applicable regime was justified in pursuit of the legitimate public policy aim of enhancing the efficiency and effectiveness of sentencing in respect of repeat offences). The 1974 Act was held to create no more than 'a limited privilege, provided not under the Convention but by domestic legislation'.[135]

L v Law Society[136] rejected the argument that the protection afforded by the 1974 Act renders details of spent convictions confidential. It rejected a submission that the proceedings should be held in private to protect the appellant against disclosure of his 'private life' within the meaning of Article 8 of the Convention.[137] As to confidentiality, agreeing with *Pearson*, Sir Anthony Clarke MR held that the Act:

> does not attempt to go beyond the grant of those limited privileges to provide a right of confidentiality in respect of spent convictions. While the 1974 Act in some respects may place an individual with spent convictions in the same position as someone with no convictions, it does not do so by rendering the convictions confidential; it does so simply by putting in place a regime which protects an individual from being prejudiced by the existence of such convictions.[138]

However, a number of public law cases decided over recent years have recognised that a conviction may, with the passage of time, so recede into the past 'as to become an aspect of an individual's private life'. Particular cases in the Supreme Court, the Northern Ireland Court of Appeal, and in the Court of Appeal of England and Wales are referred to by the court.[139] These are referred to below.

Case I

17.18 *R (L) v Comr of Police for the Metropolis (L)*[140] was a case about cautions. Lord Hope suggested (obiter)[141] that Strasbourg authority showed that information about convictions 'which is collected and stored in central records can fall within the scope of private life within the meaning of Article 8(1), with the result that it will interfere with the applicant's private life when it is released'. Although in one sense public information because the convictions took place in public '[a]s it recedes into the past, it becomes a part of the person's private life which must be respected'.[142]

---

135 *NT1 & NT2 v Google LLC* at para 46.
136 *L v Law Society* at paras 24–25.
137 *Ibid* at paras 37–44.
138 *NT1 & NT2 v Google LLC* at para 47.
139 *Ibid* at para 48.
140 *R (L) v Comr of Police for the Metropolis (Secretary of State for the Home Dept intervening)* [2009] UKSC 3; [2010] 1 AC 410 (L).
141 *Ibid* at para 27.
142 *NT1 & NT2 v Google LLC* at para 48(1).

Case 2

17.19   *R (T) v Chief Constable of Greater Manchester Police*[143] was also about cautions. It did 'not relate to the disclosure of a spent conviction that will have been imposed in public'.[144] But it referred to Lord Hope's observation in L and adopted the suggestion of Liberty (an intervenor), that 'the point at which a conviction … recedes into the past and becomes part of a person's private life will usually be the point at which it becomes spent under the 1974 Act'. The other Justices[145] agreed.[146]

Case 3

17.20   In *Gaughran v Chief Constable for the Police Service of Northern Ireland*,[147] the majority held that 'the fact that a conviction may become spent is a potentially relevant but by no means decisive factor in considering where the balance lies' between the convicted person's privacy rights and the public policy justifications for retaining biometric data.[148]

Case 4

17.21   In *CG v Facebook Ireland*,[149] the Northern Ireland Court of Appeal (NICA) referred to T and agreed that with the passage of time the protection of an offender by prohibiting the disclosure of previous convictions may be such as to outweigh the interests of open justice. On the facts, that information, in conjunction with other information, did give rise to a reasonable expectation of privacy.[150]

The court held, however, that the open justice principle and the public's right to know about convictions and have information about what happened in open court could 'only be outweighed in the most compelling circumstances' by the Article 8 rights of the individual in freedom from intrusion. It is right to mention, Warby J states, that this was a case about disclosures on Facebook in 2013 of convictions for sexual offending in 2007 for which the claimant had been sentenced to 10 years' imprisonment. The rehabilitation regime was not in play as an issue in that case.[151]

---

143 *R (T) v Chief Constable of Greater Manchester Police* [2014] UKSC 35; [2015] AC 49 (T).
144 Lord Wilson, *ibid*, at para 18.
145 *Ibid* at para 158.
146 *NT1 & NT2 v Google LLC* at para 48(2).
147 *Gaughran v Chief Constable for the Police Service of Northern Ireland* [2015] UKSC 29; [2016] AC 345 at para 37.
148 *NT1 & NT2 v Google LLC* at para 48(3).
149 *CG v Facebook Ireland Ltd* [2016] NICA 54; [2017] EMLR 12 at para 44.
150 *NT1 & NT2 v Google LLC* at para 48(4).
151 *Ibid*.

Case 5

17.22 In *R (P) v Secretary of State for the Home Department*,[152] the Court of Appeal considered the lawfulness of the scheme for the disclosure of convictions, in its revised form following the Supreme Court's decision in T. It held that the vice identified by the Supreme Court was that the scheme required the indiscriminate disclosure of convictions, without proper safeguards to allow adequate examination of the proportionality of the interference with Article 8 rights that it involved.[153] The balance required was identified by the Court of Appeal as the 'balance between the rights of individuals to put their past behind them, and what is necessary in a democratic society'.[154] Factors identified as relevant in striking that balance included: 'the nature of the offence, the disposal in the case, the time which has elapsed since the offence took place, or the relevance of the data to the employment sought'.[155]

Warby J then states '[s]o much for the potential for information about convictions to be or become confidential or private'.[156] The question of whether the common law of misuse of private information should afford reporting privileges akin to those established by the common law and extended by law, in defamation and contempt of court, has been discussed in at least one text, which has suggested that the law would be likely to follow the same contours.[157] Some cases have come close to addressing the question,[158] but the issue has never arisen directly for decision by the courts in a context such as the present cases.[159]

12 THE E-COMMERCE DIRECTIVE AND REGULATIONS

17.23 The Court of Appeal also refers to the E-Commerce Directive[160] and corresponding national implementing legislation (in the UK, the E-Commerce Regulations[161]) – 'if only to clear it out of the way for the record'.[162]

Note of course, that now in the post-Brexit environment direct EU laws will be not effective in the UK in general. However, there may be certain retained EU law in the UK in certain circumstances, and in addition there may be UK laws which replicate the effect of the measures referred to in the original EU

---

152 *R (P) v Secretary of State for the Home Department* [2017] EWCA Civ 321; [2017] 2 Cr App R 12.
153 *NT1 & NT2 v Google* at para 48(5).
154 *Ibid* at para 63.
155 *Ibid* at para 41. *NT1 & NT2 v Google LLC* at para 48(5).
156 *Ibid* at para 49.
157 See M Tugendhat and I Christie, *The Law of Privacy and the Media* (OUP, 2016) at para 11.64ff.
158 See not only *CG* but also *Crossley v Newsquest (Midlands South) Ltd* [2008] EWHC 3054 (QB) [58] (Eady J), citing *R v Arundel Justices ex parte Westminster Press* [1985] 1 WLR 708.
159 *NT1 & NT2 v Google LLC* at para 49.
160 Directive 2000/31/EC on certain legal aspects of information society services, in particular electronic commerce, in the Internal Market, of 8 June 2000.
161 The Electronic Commerce (EC Directive) Regulations 2002 (SI 2002/2013).
162 *NT1 & NT2 v Google LLC* at para 50.

measures. Indeed, in time it remains to be seen if new UK laws will seek to mirror to some extent new EU laws, such as, for example, the proposed Digital Markets Act or proposed Digital Services Act. Careful review will be needed in particular instances.

Google's position at the start of the case was that the activities undertaken by Google Search amount to 'caching' – by which it would then be entitled to a potential exemption from any obligation to pay compensation unless and until the underlying material had been removed from the third-party website or the court had ruled on the issue, pursuant to Directive Article 13 (and the corresponding UK Regulation 18).[163] That was disputed by the claimants and also disputed by the ICO.[164]

However, after hearing the ICO's submissions on this issue, Google withdrew its argument and reliance on caching 'in this case'. It is unclear if Google is seeking to reserve and or argue this point at a later time in another case. It is noted that this so-called 'caching' argument, has been sought to be used in an earlier case by Google in a different jurisdiction, but the case ultimately settled.[165]

The court describes that Google 'explained that whilst the company still considered the argument to be correct in law, it had considered in particular the submissions of [the ICO] as to the burden of regulatory oversight which Google's legal analysis would place on the ICO'.[166] Google 'decided that it should give further consideration to the issue, and in particular the relationship between these provisions of the E-Commerce Directive and Regulations and s 13 of the [DPA 98]'.[167]

It can also be commented that the suggestion that the search and public listing function as appears in Search (ie, search engine search results) amounting caching (as widely understood and as referred to in eCommerce legislation) is untenable. That is not to say non-public activities other than search may amount to caching depending on the circumstances. One can understand the intention to fall within caching, but to suggest Search is caching would appear to be in the nature of moonshot litigation. It would be more correct to describe Search as hosting. The search provider is undoubtedly a host as referred to under eCommerce legislation. However, to the extent that hosting refers to third party content on or via Search, it is clear that certain content and problem content is not third party (eg, materials and content generated and created by a Search service provider itself and not created by a third party). There are, therefore, certain activities and content which may not even fall to be described as hosted content (as envisaged under eCommerce defence rules). No doubt these nuances will be areas of future jurisprudential discussion – and wider discussion.

---

163 *Ibid.*
164 *Ibid.*
165 This was sought to be argued in *McKeogh v Doe & Others* [2012] IEHC 95.
166 *NT1 & NT2 v Google LLC* at para 50.
167 *Ibid.*

CHAPTER 18

Successful UK RtbF Case – *NT2*

I INTRODUCTION

18.1 This is the first successful RtbF case to come before the UK High Court.[1] The court describes RtbF as 'more accurately' being 'the right to have personal information "delisted" or "de-indexed" by the operators of internet search engines'. Internet search engines are referred to by the court as 'ISEs'.[2] There is a public judgment and also a more detailed 'private judgement' – to help keep the identity of the claimant and his personal details private.

Now however, attention also needs to be paid to the Data Protection Act 2018 and UK GDPR in the UK, and indeed any additional legal changes, such as may ensure from the data protection consultation process of 2021 and 2022, and any new online safety measures.[3]

2 DESCRIPTION

18.2 The facts of NT2's case are distinct and separate from those of NT1.[4] The only similarities are some similar factual 'contours' and issues of principle raised. The cases were heard one after the other with the same legal representation.[5]

NT2 was involved in a controversial business which had received public opposition due to its environmental practices. Over ten years ago he had pleaded guilty to two counts of conspiracy regarding the business, receiving a short custodial sentence.[6]

1　See general commentary such as A Wills, '*NT1 & NT2 v Google LLC* (Information Commissioner Intervening): Spent Convictions and the Right to be Forgotten' *Entertainment Law Review* (2018) (29:6) 191; I Wilson, '"Right to be Forgotten": High Court Judgment on Delisting' *Computers and Law* (2018) (June–July) 6; P Kirkwood, '*NT1 & NT2 v Google LLC* – The Secretive Case Giving the UK Its First Decision on the Right to Be Forgotten' *European Data Protection Law Review (EDPL)* (2018) (4:3) 384.
2　*NT1 & NT2 v Google LLC* [2018] EWHC 799 (QB) (13 April 2018) Warby J, at para 1; *NT1 v Google LLC* [2018] FSR 22: 659.
3　Note the following assistive guidance texts, namely, P Lambert, The UK GDPR Annotated (Kortext, 2021); P Lambert, 5 Essential GDPR Content Lists (Koretext, 2021); and Essential GDPR Index (Kortext, 2021).
4　*Ibid* at para 7.
5　*Ibid.*
6　*Ibid.*

There were simultaneous local and national media reports of the conviction and sentence. He served six weeks in custody before being released on licence. The sentence came to an end over ten years ago. The conviction became 'spent' several years ago.[7]

The reports remained online and the link hits continued to be returned by Google Search. *NT2*'s original conviction and sentence were mentioned in some more recent publications on other matters. Two of these were reports of interviews by *NT2*.[8]

NT2 requested that Google remove the links.[9] The first de-listing request was submitted (by *NT2*'s solicitors) on 14 April 2015 (ie, prior to the GDPR go-live). It related to eight links. Google responded 'promptly' by e-mail on 23 April 2015.[10]

Google declined to de-list the links stating that the requested links 'relate to matters of substantial public interest to the public regarding [*NT2*'s] professional life'.[11] (Note that the decision in *Google Spain* referred rather to the 'preponderant interest of the general public in having, on account of its inclusion in the list of results, access to the information in question'. Some will suggest that 'preponderant public interest' may be a higher standard than 'substantial public interest').

On 24 June 2015, *NT2*'s solicitors sent a claim letter in respect of the same eight links originally complained of. Proceedings issued on 2 October 2015. During the proceedings, a further three links were added to the claim. Thus, there were eleven links in total.[12]

NT2 claims the same heads of relief as *NT1*.[13]

The claimant seeks orders requiring details about their offending, convictions and sentences to be removed from Google Search results. This is on the basis that such information is:

- old;

- out of date;

- irrelevant;

- of no public interest; and/or

- otherwise an illegitimate interference with their rights.[14]

---

7   *Ibid.*
8   *Ibid.*
9   *Ibid.*
10 *Ibid* at para 8.
11 *Ibid.*
12 *Ibid.*
13 *Ibid.*
14 *Ibid* at para 2.

It also seeks compensation for Google's conduct in continuing to return search results disclosing such details after complaints had been made. Google resisted both claims, maintaining that the inclusion of such details in its search results was and remains legitimate.[15]

Intervenor

18.3   In addition to the parties NT1 and NT2, and Google, the Information Commissioner (ICO), was also present and presented at the case. The judge permitted the ICO to intervene in the case.[16]

Witnesses

18.4   Some internet and social media cases operate based on the documentation generated between the parties and, obviously, the legal arguments presented by the respective legal representatives in court on their feet (so to speak).

The judge heard factual evidence from *NT2* directly.[17]

The court also heard from Ms SC from Google. She was described as a 'legal specialist' at Google. She is not, however, a lawyer. It was described that '[h]er primary responsibility is to assess or oversee the assessment of de-listing requests'. The witnesses gave oral evidence and each was cross-examined. Ms C gave evidence once (*NT1*) and this oral evidence also stands as her evidence in the *NT2* case.[18] There were also two witness statements (undisputed), in addition to a large amount of documentary evidence.[19]

3   MAIN ISSUE

18.5   The main issues, 'stated broadly' by the court are:

(1) whether the claimant is entitled to have the links in question excluded from Google Search results either,

(a) because one or more of them contain personal data relating to him which are inaccurate, or

(b) because for that and/or other reasons the continued listing of those links by Google involves an unjustified interference with the claimant's data protection and/or privacy rights; and

---

15 *Ibid.*
16 See the second PTR judgment at paras 9–11, *NT1 & NT2 v Google LLC.*
17 *NT1 & NT2 v Google LLC* at para 11.
18 This was by agreement.
19 *NT1 & NT2 v Google LLC* at para 11.

(2) if so, whether the claimant is also entitled to compensation for continued listing between the time of the delisting request and judgment. Put another way, the first question is whether the record needs correcting; the second question is whether the data protection or privacy rights of these claimants extend to having shameful episodes in their personal history eliminated from Google Search; thirdly, there is the question of whether damages should be paid.[20]

The issues in this case are, with minor modifications, the same as those in *NT1*.[21] This claimant complains of links to eleven source publications, though it seems that two had been taken down since the claims were made. There is one inaccuracy complaint, which relates to an item in a national newspaper of relatively recent date. That item and the URLs that link to the other remaining sources, are relied on in support of this claimant's *Google Spain*[22] delisting claim. This concerns information about the claimant's crimes, his conviction and his sentence ('the crime and punishment information').[23]

The court heard oral evidence from *NT2* himself, who was cross-examined. Witness statements from two other witnesses were filed on behalf of *NT2* and taken as read because their contents were undisputed: a Mr H, a director of a number of the claimant's companies and Mr W. Ms C's [of Google] two witness statements did not call for cross-examination, her answers in the *NT1* case being taken as her evidence in this action. The court had four lever arch files of documentary material.[24]

The court found the claimant to be an honest and generally reliable witness. The court accepted his evidence on most of the points of dispute.[25]

4 ABUSE OF PROCESS

18.6   The court explains below Google's argument that the *NT1* case is an abuse of process and also outlines the court's reasons for rejecting it (see Chapter 19).[26] The same submissions were advanced by Google in respect of NT2's claim. They failed for the same reasons in this case[27] (see Chapter 19 below for further details).

20 *Ibid* at para 9.
21 See paras 54–57 above in judgment.
22 *Google Spain SL, Google Inc v Agencia Española de Protección de Datos (AEPD), Mario Costeja González*, Court of Justice (Grand Chamber), Case C-131/12, 13 May 2014.
23 *NT1 & NT2 v Google LLC* at para 174.
24 *Ibid* at para 175.
25 *Ibid* at para 176
26 See paras 58–65. *NT1 & NT2 v Google LLC* at para 177.
27 *Ibid*.

5   DATA PROTECTION

Facts: Delta and the conspiracies

18.7   NT2 started his career in the property business. By the early years of this century he had become a senior executive and a shareholder in Delta, a company engaged in a controversial business that was the subject of public opposition over its environmental practices. There were protests by individuals, local authorities became involved as did a national regulator. Delta's business was the subject of some nuisance-making interventions, together with some criminal conduct. NT2 received death threats.[28]

He formed the view that this was all associated with the campaigns against the company. With the support of Delta's board, he engaged an investigations firm to find out who was engaged in hostile activity. He did not initially expect the firm to engage in unlawful activity for that purpose, but when it identified unlawful methods that it planned to use, *NT2* agreed and authorised it to do so. The firm used phone tapping and computer hacking.[29]

At some stage thereafter, the claimant moved abroad. Some months later, Delta was sold to XRay, for a very large sum. The claimant received some tens of millions of pounds for his share in the business. The court rejects Google's case that *NT2*'s authorisation of the investigations firm was motivated by concern that the protests might scupper or hinder the sale of the business to XRay.[30]

The hacking and phone tapping were later discovered by the authorities and prosecutions followed. *NT2* pleaded guilty at a relatively early stage. Some three years after he instructed the investigations firm, he was sentenced together with several others, including Mr R, another Delta executive. The claimant's sentence was six months' imprisonment.[31]

The court's starting point for a sentence after the trial was 12 months. This was as a deterrent sentence. The court reduced it, to account for the plea of guilty and some personal mitigation. This did not involve any allegations of financial gain. The present court finds that this was not industrial espionage directed at competitors or customers. *NT2* had a commercial motivation: to protect the business of which he owned a share. But he made no direct personal gain from his crime. The court also rejects Google's case that *NT2* was motivated by a desire to prevent legitimate protest. It accepted his evidence that he wished to identify and take action against the perpetrators of the activities outlined above.[32]

The claimant did not seek to appeal against sentence.[33]

---

28   *Ibid* at para 178.
29   *Ibid* at para 179.
30   *Ibid* at para 180.
31   *Ibid* at para 181.
32   *Ibid* at para 182.
33   See para 16(2) above. *NT1 & NT2 v Google LLC* [2018] EWHC 799 (QB) (13 April 2018) Warby J, at para 183.

Facts: Zodiac

18.8   After he moved abroad, NT2 took financial advice from Zodiac, a financial firm based in that country.[34]

6   THE PROBLEM URLS

18.9   Details of the eleven URLs complained of are set out in the private judgment. Their nature can be fairly summarised by reference to three categories. Five are contemporary reports in the national and local news media of the claimant's conviction and sentencing, and the underlying offending. There are two interviews given by the claimant, over seven years ago, about his conviction and his business plans. Then there are four other articles, spanning a decade, which refer to his offending, conviction, and sentence.[35]

7   INACCURACY

The National Newspaper Article

18.10   The one article or item which the claimant complains was inaccurate was not a contemporary report of the conviction or sentencing. It first appeared in a national newspaper a few years ago, over eight years after the claimant was sentenced. The item was a small component of one part of a more substantial article or feature, with a financial theme, which referred to other individuals and companies, including Zodiac and ran to several pages. It is difficult to deal with this part of the case in anything other than these broad terms, in this public judgment. Full details of the item complained of and the feature of which it formed part are to be found in the private judgment.[36]

The Complaint

18.11   The gist of the complaint is that the item is misleading as to the nature and extent of the claimant's criminality and it suggests that he made criminal proceeds from it with which, with the aid of Zodiac, he dealt dishonestly and sought to shield from creditors.[37]

Evidence and Submissions

18.12   NT2's evidence is that he made no profit or proceeds from his crime and engaged in no such dishonest dealings as the item suggested. NT2 suggests

---

34   *NT1 & NT2 v Google LLC* at para 184.
35   *Ibid* at para 185.
36   *Ibid* at para 186.
37   *Ibid* at para 187.

that the claimant has found himself, quite inappropriately, portrayed as one of a rogues' gallery of serious criminals. Google accepts that the item did convey serious imputations against 'suspected criminals' but these parts of the item would not have been taken to refer to NT2. Google has not sought to accuse the claimant of dishonest dealings with any proceeds of any crime or attempts to shield assets from creditors.[38]

Assessment

18.13 The court applies the principles identified at paragraphs 80–87 of the judgment. In this case there is a further issue, namely whether the words complained of in the newspaper article refer or would be understood to refer to the claimant. That is the language of defamation law. Data protection law applies to data that relates to an identifiable individual. In this case, the claimant's case on reference or identifiability is built simply on the content of the offending item. There seems to me to be no material difference, at least for the purpose of this case, between defamation and data protection. Nobody has suggested any such difference. A person is referred to, or identifiable, if the words complained of would be taken by the reasonable reader of the article or item as a whole to refer to the claimant.[39]

The court finds that the article complained of is inaccurate,[40] in that it gives a misleading portrayal of the claimant's criminality and conveys imputations to the effect of which he complains.[41]

Remedies

18.14 In the light of these conclusions the court makes an appropriate delisting order, in respect of the URL for the national newspaper article, in its current form, on the grounds that the article is inaccurate, contrary to the Fourth Principle of data protection, so that continued processing by Google would represent a breach of duty under section 4(4) of the DPA 1998. Curiously, the court adds that '[o]f course, if the underlying article were at any stage amended so as to remove the subsection which leads to the complaint, the need for any relief might disappear.'[42] This later point remains to be seen, and whether it is correct or indeed practical in terms of vindicating rights and the GDPR RtbF.

The court deals separately with the question of compensation or damages.[43]

---

38 *Ibid* at para 188.
39 *Ibid* at para 189.
40 For reasons set out in detail in the separate private judgment at paras 49–53.
41 *Ibid* at para 190.
42 *Ibid* at para 191.
43 *Ibid* at para 192.

8   PRIVACY ISSUES

18.15   The arguments in NT2's case also give rise to the Exemption Issue and the Structure Issue. The court has already set out its conclusions on those matters, all of which apply equally to the present case.[44] On the DPA Compliance Issue in this case, the reasoning in NT1 applies,[45] though there is one difference, in that two of the articles complained of were published with the claimant's consent; it is that which satisfies a DPA 1998 Schedule 3 requirement. That leaves the *Google Spain* issue.[46]

Google Spain Legal Principles

18.16   Everything that the court has said about the applicable legal principles when dealing with the case of *NT1*, applies to the present case also. That includes the legal discussion between paragraphs 136 and 164, in relation to the WP 29 criteria.[47]

Further Facts

18.17   Google relies on some further facts, in support of its case that the personal data contained in the third-party publications accessible via the URLs complained of remain adequate and relevant, their continuing availability serves a legitimate purpose and is in the public interest. The facts relied on fall into two main categories:

(1)   facts about additional business activities in which he has engaged since his conviction and sentence; and

(2)   public statements made by the claimant.[48]

Additional Business Activities

18.18   The claimant's uncontradicted evidence is that, since selling his stake in Delta, he has not been involved in the same controversial industry. He has been involved in other business activities, to which Google maintains the crime and punishment information in his case is relevant. Those activities have been undertaken through a corporate vehicle, Echo and companies in the Echo group. Google's case concerns the Echo group's role in turning around struggling

---

44   *Ibid*. See paras 95–102, and 103–105.
45   *Ibid*. See paras 106–116.
46   *Ibid* at para 193.
47   *Ibid* at para 194.
48   *Ibid* at para 195.

businesses; in the letting and sale of property; and in a sports marketing company, which is involved in sponsorship and large-scale property development.[49]

It is Google's case that those who were or might become involved or concerned in or affected by such business activities 'should readily be able to find out the truth about the claimant's previous business activities *including* [the crime and punishment information], *including* by carrying out searches on search engines such as' Google's Search service (court emphasis).[50]

Public Statements

18.19   Google relies on two press interviews given by the claimant over seven ago, in which he discussed the crime and punishment information. Google says that the claimant has thereby 'since the conviction became spent' discussed it and the criminal proceedings leading to it in interviews with the national media. Google's case is that these 'were clearly intended to be used to exculpate any damage caused to the claimant's reputation by his conviction and guilty plea' and to create favourable publicity for himself and his business interests.[51]

Google also relies on the fact that the claimant has in other ways sought – and continues to seek – to promote himself as a successful businessman with (according to Google) 'a particular emphasis on his alleged experience in financial investment and corporate environmental policies'. Reliance is placed on the claimant's personal website, a blog he ran over seven years ago and four instances of online news reports of similar vintage.[52]

Google's case is that it is 'plainly in the public interest' that current clients of the claimant's businesses or potential clients and various other categories of person 'should readily be able to find out [the crime and punishment information], including being able to find it by carrying out a search on search engines' such as Google Search.[53]

Assessment

18.20   There is one general point to make about these aspects of Google's case: that their formulation in the defence is in part over-broad and rather woolly. The court is not concerned with the merits of people being able to find out 'the truth about the claimant's business activities including ...[54] his role in the conspiracies of 2004, his sentence or other aspects of the crime and punishment information.

---

49   *Ibid* at para 196.
50   *Ibid* at para 197.
51   *Ibid* at para 198.
52   *Ibid* at para 199.
53   *Ibid* at para 200.
54   Judgment emphasis.

It is the crime and punishment information that is at issue'.[55] (*Google Spain* refers to wider information, as does the GDPR.)

As indicated above,[56] the fact that a delisting order would or might make other relevant information unavailable to those searching for the claimant's name would be a material consideration when exercising a discretion. But the fact that a publication at a given URL might contain some relevant information about the claimant cannot confer relevance on the crime and punishment information that it would not otherwise possess. Much of the cross-examination was tied to this unduly vague and blurred version of the case. That is understandable, given that this is the way the case was pleaded. However, (a) as Google acknowledged, the court is not bound by admissions extracted in cross-examination on issues which are for the court to determine; (b) as it is, some apparent concessions extracted as a result of this broad-brush approach seem to the court to be near valueless.[57]

The nature of the conviction seems to me to be a significant factor in the court's evaluation. It is a conviction for invasion of privacy, not for any form of dishonesty. The claimant did not contest the charges but pleaded guilty. The court's conclusions as to the claimant's state of mind are also relevant. If he acted in good faith, believing the company's business to have been targeted by malign actors, that reduces his culpability and the impact on his integrity. If his principal motivation was, as the court finds, to identify those responsible for trespass, criminal damage and death threats and to take action against them, then the case for suggesting that his past crimes undermine his present environmental credentials, or his more recent claims about his commitment to environmental principles, is threadbare. The claimant's current attitude to his criminality is also material. In oral evidence he said 'It was a cataclysmic mistake, for which I pleaded guilty and took full responsibility for. I do not know what else I can say about it.' He does not cavil; his attitude is one of remorse, which the court assesses as genuine.[58]

In the separate private judgment, the matters the court has outlined above are further detailed, considered and evaluated. The court has concluded that the relevance of the crime and punishment information to any decisions that might need to be made by investors in, staff or customers of the businesses referred to by Google is 'slender to non-existent'.[59]

As for the claimant's public statements, the changes in the Legal Aid, Sentencing and Punishment of Offenders Act 2012 (LASPO) have – perhaps understandably – caused some difficulty. Retrospective changes in the law are unusual and can be confusing. The interviews were given as a result of advice, at a time when the claimant's convictions were *not* spent.[60] It was only later that they became

---

55 *NT1 & NT2 v Google LLC* at para 201.
56 *Ibid.*
57 *Ibid* at para 202.
58 *Ibid* at para 203.
59 *Ibid* at para 204.
60 Judgment emphasis.

spent, with effect from an earlier date. *NT2*'s interviews were given in that context, to give his own account of events. That is understandable and not a matter for condemnation. It seems to the court that Mr Tomlinson (counsel or the claimant(s)) is right to submit that, having mentioned the conviction, *NT2* cannot be accused of seeking to conceal it from the public. The position has now changed as the conviction is spent – and would have become spent even if LASPO had not changed the law. The claimant's consent has been withdrawn. In his interviews, he did not seek to evade or escape from the factual basis of his conviction. He sought to put that in context.[61]

As for the website and blog, the content relied on was also published before the claimant's conviction became spent. The claimant's evidence is that the purpose was not to promote new business, but rather, on advice, to counter the numerous references to his conviction that appeared in prominent webpages in Google Search results against his name. The court accepts his evidence on this point. To that extent, his case resembles that of *NT1*.[62]

Unlike *NT1*, however, this claimant made no claims that were inconsistent with the evidence or findings against him or extravagantly beyond what might have been justified by reference to the principle of rehabilitation. *NT2* had admitted, the prosecution allegations. Neither his postings nor his interviews made false claims to have or to deserve a long-standing reputation for integrity.[63]

The court accepts *NT2*'s submission that the evidence in this case does not support Google's case that the claimant's business activities or his public statements mean that any of the categories of people identified *should* (as Google maintains)[64] 'readily have been able to find out the truth' about the crime and punishment information or that this ought to be the case in the future. The case on relevance is a weak one at best.[65]

Application of the Law to Facts

18.21 The court then refers to the WP 29 criteria.[66]

Q1: Does the information come up on a search on the claimant's name?

18.22 The court answers yes.[67]

61 *NT1 & NT2 v Google LLC* at para 205.
62 *Ibid* at para 206.
63 *Ibid*.
64 Judgment emphasis.
65 *NT1 & NT2 v Google LLC* at para 207.
66 *Ibid* at para 208.
67 *Ibid* at para 209.

Q2: Public life, public figure?

18.23   NT2's position is akin to that of NT1 in this respect. He was a public figure, with a role in public life, as a result of his crimes. That public role is now much reduced, but not wholly eliminated. The fact that he referred to his conviction and sentence in his interviews is neutral, because it was motivated by a desire to minimise the impact of the crime and punishment information.[68]

Q3: Maturity/capacity

18.24   The claimant was not a minor nor did he lack capacity at any relevant time. He was a mature adult at all material times, in full possession of his faculties.[69]

Q4: Accuracy

18.25   The national newspaper article was inaccurate in the respects specified above and in the private judgment. Otherwise, it is not alleged by the claimant that any of the data were inaccurate. The court proceeds on the footing that the publications at the other URLs were, as Google asserts, substantially accurate accounts of events as far as the claimant is concerned. The key issue is whether it remains legitimate for Google to return links to the source publications, given the passage of time, the impact on the claimant and other material considerations.[70]

Q5: Relevance

18.26   The data do not amount to hate speech, nor – with the possible exception of the newspaper article – do they represent 'offences' against the claimant 'in the area of expression'. To a limited extent, the data reflect opinions, but the gist of the complaint concerns those parts that appear to be verified fact. With the exception, again, of the newspaper article, they are verified fact. The court has dealt with relevance above and in the separate private judgment. It may not be necessary to reach any further conclusions about the relevance of the newspaper article, given the court's finding of inaccuracy and the relief that will follow. If necessary, however, the court would find that the article in its current form – that is, including the sub-section at which the complaint is directed – lacks any or any sufficient relevance to justify its continued accessibility in response to a search on the claimant's name. The continued availability of the data via Google is excessive.[71]

---

68   *Ibid* at para 210.
69   *Ibid* at para 211.
70   *Ibid* at para 212.
71   *Ibid* at para 213.

Q6: Sensitivity

18.27   The personal data are sensitive data (now known as special data). The points made in this regard when dealing with the claim of NT1 hold good in the present context also.[72]

Q7: Made available for longer than necessary?

18.28   This is the main issue on this part of the case. This criterion, the court states, does not add anything of value in the present context.[73]

Q8: Prejudicial/harmful? and/or dangerous?

18.29   Clearly, the continued accessibility of the data is not dangerous; it does not expose the claimant to a risk of personal injury. (Obviously this may be different in certain instances of online abuse (OA)). As to other prejudice or harm, NT2's case is that the availability of the data has had 'a profound adverse impact on the claimant and his business and personal life, including on members of his close family and school-age children'. His evidence is that he has frequently been called on to give explanations about his conviction and has had difficulty with finding banking facilities. This is corroborated by the unchallenged evidence of his witnesses. It has not been challenged.[74]

For reasons given above, the claimant's relationship with his grown-up children is not relevant, save marginally; he gives no detailed evidence about it. He has not established any impact on a family life enjoyed with his adult children. He has a second family, with school-age children. The impact on that family is material, but the court indicated that it had hardly any evidence about it. As with *NT1*, a lot of the evidence is about the impact of the information on the claimant's business. He says: 'I feel that I am put at a disadvantage in securing banking facilities or business opportunities as a consequence of the information about me that is accessible through Google Search, and I believe this will simply continue unless Google "delists" the links about which I have complained.' His supporting witnesses corroborate that.[75]

His evidence does go beyond this, to an extent. He says, 'members of my close family have told me that they have been questioned about their association with me, which I have found very distressing. Some people just ask me straight out what it was like in prison'. This is vague and lacking in detail. There are no statements from the family members nor any explanation of why. Nonetheless, it does go rather beyond the evidence in the case of *NT1*.[76] It may be suggested that

---

72   *Ibid* at para 214.
73   *Ibid* at para 215.
74   *Ibid* at para 216.
75   *Ibid* at para 217.
76   *Ibid* at para 218.

this may be too high a bar to require; also, that this is not so specified in *Google Spain* itself.

Q10: Context/consent and journalistic purposes?

18.30   The position differs in relation to the three categories of publication. Like NT1, this claimant did not consent to the contemporaneous reporting of the criminal proceedings against him, but such reporting was a natural, probable and foreseeable consequence of his offending and those elements of the information in question have been placed in the public domain as a result of steps deliberately taken by the claimant. So was subsequent fair and accurate reporting of the same information, in the context of the remaining publications.[77]

The two interviews which *NT2* now seeks to delist were given and published with his consent. That consent has now been withdrawn. It is not suggested that there is any legal obstacle to the claimant validly revoking his consent for the future such as a contractual obligation, an estoppel or the like. The claimant's evidence is that he gave the interviews on advice to limit the impact of other reports of the conviction. No other circumstances have been identified which would make it legitimate to continue processing personal data which the claimant once put into the public domain, but now wishes to withdraw from that context, to the extent of having it delisted by Google.[78]

Q12: Legal power or obligation to make the data publicly available?

18.31   None of the publishers has any obligation, the court suggests. (This may be referred to further in future cases.) Whether any of them has the power has not been debated. The court proceeds on the basis that – with the exception of the sub-section of the national newspaper article that refers to this claimant – the source publishers have the legal right to make the data available.[79] This may be an area of contention in future cases.

Q13: Do the data relate to a criminal offence?

18.32   The answer given is yes. As in the case of *NT1*, the court regards this as the most important criterion. A number of distinctions arise.[80]

(1)   *NT2*'s conviction was always going to become spent. It was firmly within the scheme of the 1974 Act, as originally enacted. Although the sentence would have been longer but for personal mitigation, it would still have been

---

77   *Ibid* at para 219.
78   *Ibid* at para 220.
79   *Ibid* at para 221.
80   *Ibid* at para 222.

a sentence capable of becoming spent. The LASPO changes came in a matter of months before it would have been spent anyway.[81]

(2) Much of *NT2*'s case is about business reputation, as opposed to private or family life. However, unlike *NT1*, he has given credible detail in support of the case on damage to business.[82]

(3) Unlike *NT1*, this claimant has a young family and the impact of disclosure of his old conviction is capable of having an adverse impact on them. His case on interference with family life is stronger.[83] (It remains to be seen if this is a requirement or if it will be required in future cases.)

(4) As to relevance, the conviction in this case was not one involving dishonesty and it was based on a plea of guilty. This claimant acknowledges his guilt and expresses genuine remorse. The court also sees considerable force in *NT2*'s submission, that his conviction did not concern actions taken by the claimant in relation to 'consumers, customers or investors' but rather in relation to the invasion of the privacy of third parties. There is no plausible suggestion nor is there any solid basis for an inference that there is a risk that this wrongdoing will be repeated by the claimant. The information is of scant (if any) apparent relevance to any business activities that he seems likely to engage in.[84]

9 OVERALL COURT ASSESSMENT

18.33 The court's key conclusions in respect of NT2's delisting claim are that the crime and punishment information has become out of date, irrelevant and of no sufficient legitimate interest to users of Google Search to justify its continued availability, so that an appropriate delisting order should be made.[85]

The conviction was always going to become spent and it did so in March 2014, though it would have done so in July of that year in any case. *NT2* has frankly acknowledged his guilt and expressed genuine remorse. There is no evidence of any risk of repetition. His current business activities are in a field quite different from that in which he was operating at the time. His past offending is of little if any relevance to anybody's assessment of his suitability to engage in relevant business activity now or in the future. There is no real need for anybody to be warned about that activity.[86]

---

81   *Ibid* at para 222(1).
82   *Ibid* at para 222(2).
83   *Ibid* at para 222(3).
84   *Ibid* at para 222(4).
85   *Ibid* at para 223.
86   *Ibid*.

10 MISUSE OF PRIVATE INFORMATION

Q1: A Reasonable Expectation of Privacy?

18.34 Some of this may differ as between common law and civil law jurisdictions.

As in *NT1*'s case, the information is essentially public, not private. But the position has changed. With the passage of time and in all the circumstances, Article 8 is now engaged, and the presence of a young family in this claimant's life is a distinguishing factor. The court accepts that the claimant enjoys a reasonable expectation of privacy in respect of the information, for the reasons given below.[87]

Q2: A 'Misuse' of the Information?

18.35 Google submits that proof of misuse is a separate and independent requirement of this tort. The argument did not go far on this issue, but I am not persuaded. The court is content to deal with the case on the conventional two-stage test.[88]

Q3: Striking the Balance

18.36 The impact on the claimant is such as to engage Article 8. The business prejudice does not suffice for that purpose, but there is just enough in the realm of private and family life to cross the threshold. (This position may be different in other cases. In future cases this may be seen as being overly restrictive and other than is intended in *Google Spain* or the GDPR RtbF. In *Google Spain*, one of the harms indeed did relate to business or commercial type harm.) The existence of a young, second family is a matter of some weight. Even so, the evidence does not, for the court, demonstrate a grave interference. But it is enough to require a justification. Google's case on relevance is very weak. The claimant's evidence suggests that he has acknowledged his past error. His current and anticipated future business conduct does not make his past conduct relevant to anybody's assessment of him or not significantly so. Continued accessibility of the information complained of is hard to justify. The factors that go to support that view are weak, by comparison with those that weigh in favour of delisting.[89]

---

87 *Ibid* at para 224.
88 *Ibid* at para 225.
89 *Ibid* at para 226.

11   REMEDIES

18.37   A delisting order is appropriate, the court finds.[90]

As to compensation or damages, the main issue would seem to be the conduct of Google. Was it reasonable and, if so, does that excuse the company from liability for damages? These are difficult issues, the court acknowledges. The court also states that it only reached a conclusion after a trial of several days. It would be hard to say, by reference to the terms of DPA 1998 section 13(3), that Google failed to take 'such care as in all the circumstances was reasonably required' to comply with the relevant requirements.[91] However, it is suggested that more may have to be asked of policies, processes, design, etc, in future, as there can, in certain circumstances, be such deliberate calculation as that a user or ordinary person would say that there is an unreasonableness on the part of the website. These will be issues for future cases.

Consider further that these cases put what might be considered a high onus and some may suggest an unnecessarily high onus on the claimants in certain respects but does not appear to place any onus on the defendant to establish that it did, in fact, act reasonably. It may not be appropriate for a court to merely assume without evidence on the point that a company has acted reasonably, or reasonably in all pertinent issues.

'True it is', the Court states, 'that the burden of proof lies on Google'.[92] However, it is somewhat unclear what, if any, evidence was furnished on these reasonableness issue(s).

NT2 makes the point that Ms C's [from Google] evidence is hearsay. She was not directly involved in the relevant decision making and it was suggested that her evidence be treated as worthless. But Ms C had credibly explained Google's processes, and the court accepted her evidence on this issue, so far as it goes. This is an enterprise that the court accepts 'is committed' to compliance with the relevant requirements. (It remains to be seen if this will always be the case (nor indeed how it may have been demonstrated in this instance. A recent official parliamentary report has been highly critical of certain internet service providers, going so far as to refer to 'digital gangsters' and untruthful answers.[93]) In a number of respects, however, representative bodies and users (and policymakers) in various jurisdictions would take issue with the helpfulness, reasonableness and compliance of certain websites – in particular in relation to dealing with report issues. In the 'current legal environment', the court states that 'it would be harsh to say that it had failed to take reasonable care to do so'. For similar reasons, the court concludes that no damages are payable for misuse of private

90   *Ibid* at para 227.
91   *Ibid.*
92   *Ibid* at para 228.
93   *8th Report – Disinformation and 'Fake News': Final Report*, Digital, Culture, Media, Sports and Committee (UK) (18 February 2019).

information.[94] This will no doubt be a matter of future contention in cases. One cannot be assured that this will be the final say on the damage and compensation issues, and the respective nuances. More detailed examinations may well occur in future.

12   OVERALL CONCLUSIONS OF NT2

18.38   The court's conclusions in the NT2 case are as follows:

(1)   the delisting claim is not an abuse of the court's process, as alleged by Google;

(2)   the inaccuracy complaint is upheld, and an appropriate delisting order will be made, its terms to be the subject of argument;

(3)   the remainder of the delisting claim also succeeds. An appropriate order will be made, in terms to be the subject of argument;

(4)   the claim for misuse of private information succeeds; but

(5)   Google took reasonable care and the claimant is not entitled to compensation or damages.[95]

---

94   *Ibid.*
95   *Ibid* at para 230.

CHAPTER 19

Unsuccessful UK RtbF Case – *NT1*

I INTRODUCTION

19.1   This RtbF case, *NT1 & NT2 v Google LLC*, was ultimately not successful.[1] There is a public judgment and also a more detailed 'private judgment' – to help keep the identity of the claimant and his personal details private.[2] While this case was unsuccessful, it is more extensive in its discussion than the successful *NT2* case.

On occasion there can be misunderstanding and misrepresentation of RtbF cases. For example, while this instant case was unsuccessful from the individual's perspective, it may be misrepresented and (over) generalised. That this applicant was unsuccessful does not mean that all applicants will be refused or will be unsuccessful. Nor does it undermine the basis or necessity of the wider RtbF. Cases such as this should not be taken to represent all instances where previous criminal convictions is the problem content sought to be taken down.

At the same time, successful RtbF cases, even those relating to the successful takedown of problem content should not be misrepresented as necessarily bad, inherently bad or that 'RtbF is Bad, Full Stop'. The wider contextual interest and concerns of individuals and society should also be understood.

The policy remains, regardless of individual refusals which may occur because of particular circumstances.

2 DESCRIPTION

19.2   NT1 was involved with a controversial property business dealing with the public (late 1980s and early 1990s) when in his thirties. In the late 1990s, in his forties, he was convicted in a criminal conspiracy trial connected with his business activities and was imprisoned.[3] The case was reported in the media at

---

1   *NT1 & NT2 v Google LLC* [2018] EWHC 799 (QB) (13 April 2018) Warby J, at para 1; *NT1 v Google LLC* [2018] FSR 22: 659.
2   For some of the general commentary, see for example, A Wills, '*NT1 & NT2 v Google LLC* (Information Commissioner Intervening): Spent Convictions and the Right to be Forgotten' *Entertainment Law Review* (2018) (29:6) 191; I Wilson, '"Right to be Forgotten": High Court Judgement on Delisting' *Computers and Law* (2018) (June–July) 6; P Kirkwood, '*NT1 & NT2 v Google LLC* – The Secretive Case Giving the UK Its First Decision on the Right to Be Forgotten' *European Data Protection Law Review (EDPL)* (2018) (4:3) 384.
3   He was accused of but not tried for a separate conspiracy with the same business. Some former staff were convicted of this separate issue. *NT1 & NT2 v Google LLC* at para 5.

that time. Links to the reports were made available by Google Search. Other links, including some to information on a parliamentary website, were also provided.

NT1 was released early on licence.[4] The sentence came to an end and it eventually became a 'spent' conviction.[5]

The reports remained available online, and links and hits continued to be returned by Google Search.[6] Ultimately, *NT1* requested Google to remove these links from its website search service.[7]

The first 'de-listing' request was submitted to Google on 28 June 2014, requesting that six links be removed. Google replied on 7 October 2014.[8]

Google agreed to block one link but declined to block the other five.[9] *NT1* asked Google to reconsider, but it maintained its refusal regarding the five links. *NT1*'s solicitors wrote to Google on 26 January 2015 requiring them to 'cease processing' links to two media reports.[10]

In April 2015 Google replied, again by way of a refusal.[11]

On 2 October 2015, *NT1* issued proceedings, seeking:

- orders for the blocking and/or erasure of links to these two media reports;

- an injunction to prevent Google from continuing to return such links; and

- financial compensation.[12]

Sometime in December 2017, *NT1* expanded the claim to cover a third link, relating to a book extract covering the same subject matter, in similar reliefs as above.[13]

The claim sought orders requiring details about their offending, conviction and sentences to be removed from Google Search results on the basis that such information is:

(1) old;

(2) out of date;

(3) irrelevant;

---

4   After serving half his custodial sentence. *NT1 & NT2 v Google LLC* at para 5.
5   *Ibid.*
6   *Ibid* at para 5.
7   *Ibid.*
8   *Ibid* at para 6.
9   *Ibid.*
10   *Ibid.*
11   *Ibid.*
12   *Ibid.*
13   *Ibid.* In this regard, the court also refers to *L v The Law Society* [2010] EWCA Civ 811 [2] (Sir Anthony Clarke MR).

(4) of no public interest; and/or

(5) otherwise an illegitimate interference with their rights.[14]

It also sought compensation for Google's conduct in continuing to return search results disclosing such details after complaints had been made to it. Google resisted both claims, maintaining that the inclusion of such details in its search results was and remained legitimate.[15]

Intervenor

19.3 In addition to the parties NT1 and NT2, and Google, the Information Commissioner (ICO), was also present and presented at the case. The judge permitted the ICO to intervene.[16]

Witnesses

19.4 Some internet and social media cases operate based on the documentation generated between the parties and obviously the legal arguments presented by the respective legal representatives in court.

Here, the judge heard factual evidence from *NT1* directly.[17]

The court also heard from Ms SC from Google. She was described as a 'legal specialist' at Google. She was not, however, a lawyer; rather '[h]er primary responsibility is to assess or oversee the assessment of de-listing requests'. The three witnesses gave oral evidence and each were cross-examined. Ms C gave evidence once (*NT1*), but her oral evidence also stands in the *NT2* case.[18] There were also two witness statements (undisputed), in addition to a large amount of documentary evidence.[19]

3 MAIN ISSUES

19.5 The main issues 'stated broadly' are described by the court as:

(1) whether the claimant is entitled to have the links in question excluded from Google Search results either,

(a) because one or more of them contain personal data relating to him which are inaccurate, or

---

14 *Ibid* at para 2.
15 *Ibid*.
16 See the Second PTR Judgment at paras 9–11, *NT1 & NT2 v Google LLC*.
17 *NT1 & NT2 v Google LLC* at para 11.
18 This was by agreement.
19 *NT1 & NT2 v Google LLC* at para 11.

(b) because for that and/or other reasons the continued listing of those links by Google involves an unjustified interference with the claimant's data protection and/or privacy rights; and

(2) if so, whether the claimant is also entitled to compensation for continued listing between the time of the delisting request and judgment. Put another way, the first question is whether the record needs correcting; the second question is whether the data protection or privacy rights of these claimants extend to having shameful episodes in their personal history eliminated from Google Search; thirdly, there is the question of whether damages should be paid.'[20]

Data Protection

19.6   The claim contends that the Google Search facility operates in such a way as to return the offending URLs such that Google is a controller of information that is personal data relating to the claimant and is processing such personal data within the meaning of the DPD 95/46 and the Data Protection Act (DPA) 1998. Accordingly, Google owes him the duty provided for in section 4(4) of the DPA 1998.[21]

Google admits that its presentation of search results as a consequence of a search being carried out on the name of the data subject involves the processing of personal data of which it is the controller.[22]

Google admits that it owes this statutory duty in respect of such processing.[23]

However, Google makes no admissions in respect of any operations prior to presentation of search results, such as finding or indexing information.[24]

For the purposes of this case, and the claim of *NT2*, it is 'unnecessary to go further'.

Nor is it necessary to determine another issue raised by Google (ie, the processing of sensitive personal data (now referred to as special personal data)). Google admits that the offending URLs contain information that falls within the categories of sensitive personal data and that its post-notification activities involve the processing of such data. Subject to the journalism exemption, Google accepts

---

20   *Ibid* at para 9.
21   *Ibid* at para 48.
22   *Ibid* at para 53.
23   *Ibid*.
24   *Ibid*.

that upon receipt of a delisting request it is obliged to conduct the balancing exercise prescribed by *Google Spain*.[25]

The issue that did arise as to the formal or substantive validity of *NT1*'s original request under s 10 of the DPA 1998 has fallen away.[26]

Data Protection Liability

19.7   The main issues as to liability in relation to the data protection claims are defined under two headings, as follows:

(1)   *Inaccuracy issues*

Is there information in any of the three third-party publications which is inaccurate, in breach of the Fourth Data Protection Principle, in a way or to an extent that requires or should lead the court to grant the blocking, erasure and injunctive remedies sought?

(2)   *Privacy issues*

The arguments give rise to four inter-related questions, as follows:

(a)   Is Google entitled to rely on the journalism exemption? (*Exemption Issue*).

(b)   At what point in the legal analysis should the court assess the compatibility of Google's processing of the offending links with the principles in the *Google Spain* case (*Structure Issue*)? (There are three competing arguments on this question.)

(c)   Does Google's processing comply with its obligations under section 4(4) of the DPA 1998 (*DPA Compliance Issue*)?

(d)   Does Google's processing comply with the requirements of *Google Spain* (*Google Spain Issue*)?[27]

Misuse of Private Information

19.8   The judgment summarises the issues in respect of the Misuse Issues:

(1)   Does the claimant enjoy a reasonable expectation of privacy in respect of any of the information at issue?

(2)   If so, how, on the particular facts of the case, should the balance between the rights of privacy and freedom of expression be struck?[28]

---

25   *Google Spain SL, Google Inc v Agencia Española de Protección de Datos (AEPD), Mario Costeja González,* Court of Justice (Grand Chamber), Case C-131/12, 13 May 2014. *NT1 & NT2 v Google LLC* at para 53.
26   *NT1 & NT2 v Google LLC* at para 53.
27   *Ibid* at para 54.
28   *Ibid* at para 55.

Damages

19.9   If the claim succeeds on liability in respect of the inaccuracy and/or privacy issues, and/or misuse of private information, the question then arises as to what damages or compensation should be awarded (damages issue).[29]

4   ABUSE

19.10   Google argues that NT1's claims are an abuse of the court's process. It argues that they 'amount in substance to claims for damage to reputation which are intended to outflank the limits on reputation claims in the law of defamation and section 8' of the 1974 Act. This is argued as a 'further reason' for dismissing the claims. Warby J feels 'it is in reality a threshold issue'. If the argument is sound, it 'should' result in the dismissal of the claims.[30]

Google's argument is that the claims are 'in essence' complaints about the damage caused to *NT1*'s reputation by the continued availability of the URLs complained of. It is argued that a claimant such as *NT1* has no right to bypass the protections which the law of defamation affords to the right of freedom of expression by framing his case in a cause of action other than defamation, and using this as a vehicle for 'recovering essentially the same relief' on the same grounds. In support of its argument, Google relies on some of the jurisprudence in this area.[31]

Google argues that the Supreme Court twice recently warned against using torts other than defamation to obtain relief that would not be available in that tort. In *O (A Child) v Rhodes,*[32] Lord Neuberger cautioned against attempts to 'extend or supplement' defamation law by resorting to a different tort.[33]

One could query the similarity between the tort of the intentional infliction of psychological harm, in the above case, and the EU and statute law of personal data protection as referred to in the above argument.

---

29   *Ibid* at para 56. Sarit K Mizrahi, 'Ontario's New Invasion of Privacy Torts: Do They Offer Monetary Redress for Violations Suffered Via the Internet of Things?' *Western Journal of Legal Studies* (2018) (8:1) (COV2) 37.
30   *Ibid* at para 58.
31   Which jurisprudence includes *Woodward v Hutchins* [1977] 1 WLR 760; *Gulf Oil v Page* [1987] Ch 327; *Lonrho v Al Fayed (No 5)* [1993] 1 WLR 1489; *Service Corporation International plc v Channel Four Television* [1999] EMLR 83, 89; *McKennitt v Ash* at para 42; *Terry (previously LNS) v Persons Unknown* [2010] EMLR 16 at para 95 and *Tillery Valley Foods Ltd v Channel Four Television Corp* [2004] EWHC 1075 (Ch) at para 21. *NT1 & NT2 v Google LLC* [2018] EWHC 799 (QB) (13 April 2018) Warby J at para 59.
32   *O (A Child) v Rhodes* [2015] UKSC 32; [2016] AC 219 at para 111.
33   In that case, the tort of the intentional infliction of psychological harm. This may be necessary post Brexit, however. See S Aidinlis, 'The Right To be Forgotten as a Fundamental Right in the UK After Brexit' Communications Law (2020) (25:2) 67.

In *Khuja v Times Newspapers Ltd*,[34] Lord Sumption took the point further. He emphasised the need for 'coherence' in the law. The claimant, anonymised as 'PNM', sought to prevent publication of information disclosed in open court at a criminal trial. He relied on the tort of misuse of private information, emphasising the impact that publication would have on private and family life, in particular, the effect on his immediate family. The Supreme Court upheld the decision of the judge at first instance and the Court of Appeal to refuse an injunction. Giving the judgment of the majority, Lord Sumption states:[35]

> A party is entitled to invoke the right of privacy to protect his reputation but, as I have explained, there is no reasonable expectation of privacy in relation to proceedings in open Court. The only claim available to PNM is based on the adverse impact on his family life which will follow indirectly from the damage to his reputation. It is clear that in an action for defamation no injunction would issue to prevent the publication of a fair and accurate report of what was said about PNM in the proceedings. It would be both privileged and justified. In the context of the publication of proceedings in open Court, it would be incoherent for the law to refuse an injunction to prevent damage to PNM's reputation directly, while granting it to prevent the collateral impact on his family life in precisely the same circumstances.[36]

Warby J is 'not persuaded that these high authorities, or the earlier cases I have cited, provide a justification for dismissing the claims of *NT1* as an abuse of process'.[37] As a 'general rule' it 'is legitimate for a claimant to rely on any cause of action that arises or may arise from a given set of facts'. This is not ordinarily an abuse just because one or more other causes of action might arise or be pursued instead of, or in addition to, the claim that is relied on. The Supreme Court did not hold that Mr Khuja's application was an abuse of process.[38] His own reputation could not, in that context, support his claim to enjoy a reasonable expectation of privacy; although the impact on his family life could serve that purpose, it could not suffice. As Lord Sumption said at paragraph 34(2):

> [PNM] … is entitled to rely on the impact which publication would have on his relations with his family and their relations with the community in which he lives. I do not underestimate that impact … But … the impact on PNM's family life of what was said about him at the trial is no different in kind from the impact of many disagreeable statements which may be made about individuals at a high profile criminal trial … the collateral impact that this process has on those affected is part of the price to be paid for open justice and the freedom of the press to report fairly and accurately on judicial proceedings held in public.[39]

34   *Khuja v Times Newspapers Ltd* [2017] UKSC 49; [2017] 3 WLR 351.
35   *NT1*, at para 34(3).
36   *NT1 & NT2 v Google LLC* at para 60.
37   *Ibid* at para 61.
38   Rather it failed because he could offer nothing that would outweigh the importance of free reporting of proceedings in open court.
39   *NT1 & NT2 v Google LLC* at para 61.

Warby J speculates that '[t]hese are powerful considerations that might have provided an overwhelming answer to the present claims if they lacked their defining characteristic, namely that *NT1*'s conviction is spent'.[40]

But even these considerations would still 'not' have rendered the present claims as an abuse of process.[41] The touchstone for identifying this kind of abuse was well described by Buxton LJ in the *McKennitt* case (a breach of confidence claim). The defence referred to abuse as the court had held the information in question was false. At paragraph 79, Buxton LJ said as follows:

> 79 If it could be shown that a claim in breach of confidence was brought *where the nub of the case* was a complaint of the falsity of the allegations, and that that was done *in order to avoid the rules of the tort of defamation*, then objections could be raised in terms of abuse of process. That might be so at the interlocutory stage in an attempt to avoid the rule in *Bonnard v Perryman* ...[42]: a matter, it will be recalled, that exercised this Court in *Woodward v Hutchins* ...[43]
>
> 80 That however is not this case. ...[44]

The judge accepts that the protection of reputation is a significant and substantial element of *NT1*'s claim – and the motivation for the case.[45] This conclusion is 'inevitable' on the pleadings and testimony as to the damage which concerns him.[46] Paragraph 12.1 of *NT1*'s Final Amended Particulars of Claim state that he 'has been and continues to be treated as a pariah in his personal, business and social life. He lives in fear that anyone he meets will find the URLs on Google 'and ... as a result shun him'. This is 'the classic language of reputational harm'. However, it is 'wrong to draw too sharp a distinction between the protection of reputation on the one hand and private life on the other'. The case law shows that injury to reputation can engage the protection of Article 8 of the Convention.[47]

The protection of reputation is not the claimant's only objective. He relies on factors which go beyond mere reputation and cross over into areas of private life distinct from matters of reputation. 'I do not find that *NT1* is seeking to exploit data protection law or the tort of misuse of private information to "avoid the rules" – to get round the obstacles that defamation law would place in his way.' 'He is relying on the new law pronounced by the CJEU' – incidentally with the same party opponent. Mr Tomlinson submits that the court should not

---

40   *Ibid* at para 63.
41   *Ibid.*
42   *Bonnard v Perryman* [1891] 2 Ch 269.
43   *Woodward v Hutchins* [1977] 1 WLR 760. NT judgment emphasis.
44   *NT1 & NT2 v Google LLC* at para 62.
45   *Ibid* at para 63.
46   *Ibid.*
47   See, eg, *McKennitt*, para 80; *Gulati v MGN Ltd* [2015] EWHC 1482 (Ch), para 168 (Mann J) (appeal dismissed, [2015] EWCA Civ 1291); and *Khuja v Times Newspapers Ltd* at para 61. *NT1 & NT2 v Google LLC* [2018] EWHC 799 (QB) (13 April 2018) Warby J, at para 63.

be too liberal in its labelling of prejudice as 'injury to reputation' which would undermine the *Google Spain* regime.[48]

Also, 'in my judgment it is possible and legitimate to take account in other ways of the fact and extent of the reputational concerns that feature so prominently in *NT1*'s case'. 'I believe they can properly be brought into account when assessing the *Inaccuracy Issues*, the *Google Spain Issue*, and the *Misuse Issues*.' This applies equally to the impact of section 8 of the 1974 Act and the policy that underpins that provision. These are factors to which the court can have regard, as appropriate, when determining the liability issues.[49]

5   INACCURACY

Essential Facts

19.11   The facts are described in summary in the judgment – but not in detail to avoid identification.[50]

In the 1980s, *NT1* and Mr S established a company, Alpha, offering services and credit to consumers and companies for property. Together, they successfully exploited that opportunity. They had equal shares in the business. *NT1* moved abroad. His evidence was that he left Mr S in charge. Within a matter of months *NT1* became aware of problem' issues (eg, press reports of problems with sales practices, Trade Association fines and complaints). *NT1* returned to the UK.[51]

Large payments were made by Alpha to offshore companies of *NT1*. These were queried by the Inland Revenue regarding tax evasion. *NT1* (and a Mr F) were charged with participation in conspiracy. Both pleaded not guilty but were convicted.[52]

During the false accounting conspiracy, *NT1* bought out Mr S. He thereby became the sole owner of Alpha.[53]

There was second conspiracy and Alpha's customers were the victims. *NT1* and others were charged in respect of this conspiracy. The prosecution did not proceed, but the charge remained on file.[54]

Consumer complaints were made to Alpha, a trade body, and to regulators about its business conduct. Civil claims were brought. Subsidiaries of Alpha were subjected to regulatory sanctions. Alpha's offices and *NT1*'s home were raided

---

48   *NT1 & NT2 v Google LLC* at para 64.
49   *Ibid* at para 65.
50   *Ibid* at para 66.
51   *Ibid* at para 67.
52   *Ibid* at para 68.
53   *Ibid* at para 69.
54   *Ibid* at para 70.

by the police. Alpha was then subject to a compulsory winding-up order. Some of these events were the subject of Parliamentary comment.[55]

NT1 was arrested and charged. His assets were frozen by the Crown Prosecution Service. The Inland Revenue's claims were settled and *NT1* was prosecuted. Reporting restrictions were imposed under s 4(2) of the 1981 Act. *NT1* was sentenced to four years' imprisonment and disqualified from holding the position of a company director.[56]

The trial judge found *NT1* to have been the boss and therefore mostly responsible for the dishonest conspiracy. The judge made clear that a personal mitigation matter meant that the sentence was less than would otherwise have been imposed.[57]

Link Publications

19.12 The first media report of the sentencing was a headline and 16 text paragraphs. This (first article) was published in the financial pages of a national newspaper within a few weeks of sentencing. The second publication (second article) appeared months later in a national newspaper. It was an item within a longer article on consumer affairs. It consisted of a headline and 13 text paragraphs.[58]

NT1 appealed unsuccessfully against his sentence. The Court of Appeal accepted the trial judge's view of the role of *NT1* and found he had been the principal actor in the false accounting conspiracy.[59]

The third URL complained of by *NT1* is a book extract (book extract), first published some two years after the Court of Appeal's decision. This comprised a headline and six paragraphs of text.[60]

A recent Google search shows a snippet from each of the first article, the second article and the book extract. The article snippets appear as items one and two on the first search page. The book extract snippet is item eight on page two. As the complaint is one of inaccuracy in the underlying publications, not the snippets, 'I do not consider it would be right to assess the snippets'.[61]

It may be that inaccuracy issues may arise in other cases and factual situations.

---

55   *Ibid* at para 71.
56   *Ibid* at para 73.
57   *Ibid* at para 74.
58   *Ibid* at para 75.
59   *Ibid* at para 76.
60   *Ibid* at para 77.
61   *Ibid* at para 78.

The Complaints

19.13   Six inaccuracy complaints are made (eg, some word(s) or phrase(s) were picked out and it was stated that: 'The claimant did not "[QUOTE WORD(S)/ PHRASE(S)]".' The pleadings do not identify which URLs contains the alleged inaccuracy. No particulars of inaccuracy are provided. 'This is not especially transparent or helpful.' It has required the judge to carry out an analysis of where the alleged inaccuracies were.[62]

The judge's analysis suggests that there are three complaints about the first article, five about the second article (three of which relate to that article only), and two about the book extract. The claimant's approach also seems to beg the question of what sense a given word or phrase bears, when read in its context: 'I cannot help feeling that in a context such as the present – where the claimant sues in respect of media publications – he should be expected to specify the meaning(s) he attributes to particular words or phrase, and which he says is inaccurate.' 'A claimant should also give particulars of inaccuracy' according to the judge.[63] The judge continues that '[i]t is after all *NT1* who alleges inaccuracy, and so the burden of proof rests on him, as Mr Tomlinson [for the claimants] accepts'.[64]

The Right Approach in Principle

19.14   NT1's case is that there have been breaches of the first part of the fourth principle of data protection: the requirement that personal data 'shall be accurate'.[65]

The requirement that data be 'kept up to date' does not, according to the judgment, have any application in this context of the case. [66]

There has been some dispute about how to decide whether a published article is 'inaccurate' for the present purpose. Two sources of law have been addressed in the case.[67]

The first is from data protection law itself. Section 70(2) of the DPA 1998 contains a 'supplementary definition' which states that: 'For the purposes of this Act, data are inaccurate if they are incorrect or misleading as to any matter of fact.' This does not take the matter much further, the judge feels, but the reference to fact emphasises that this principle of data protection is 'not concerned with matters

---

62   *Ibid* at para 79.
63   Those are well-established requirements of a statement of case in a defamation or malicious falsehood claim, which the judge says are 'surely' appropriate in this context for the same reasons. Warby J, at para 79.
64   *NT1 & NT2 v Google LLC* at para 79.
65   *Ibid* at para 80.
66   *Ibid*.
67   *Ibid*.

of comment, opinion or evaluation'. The reference to 'misleading' is stated to indicate that the court should not adopt too narrow and literal an approach.[68]

The WP 29 comments on its criterion 4 are indicated in the judgment to be helpful. It states:

> In general, "accurate" means accurate as to a matter of fact. There is a difference between a search result that clearly relates to one person's opinion of another person and one that appears to contain factual information.

> In data protection law the concepts of accuracy, adequacy and incompleteness are closely related. [Data protection supervisory authorities] will be more likely to consider that de-listing of a search result is appropriate where there is inaccuracy as to a matter of fact and where this presents an inaccurate, inadequate or misleading impression of an individual. When a data subject objects to a search result on the grounds that it is inaccurate, the [data protection supervisory authorities] can deal with such a request if the complainant provides all the information needed to establish the data are evidently inaccurate.[69]

A second source of 'possible guidance is the domestic law of defamation'. Although the DPD 95/46 (and now the GDPR) 'must be given an autonomous interpretation' the judge feels that 'it may be legitimate to draw on national legal traditions when implementing the broad principles established by European law'.[70]

The court follows the analogy of defamation. It states that:

> [i]n a libel action, where truth is in issue, the court will first determine the single natural and ordinary meaning which the words complained of would convey to the ordinary reasonable reader. It is that which the defendant must then prove to be true.[71]

The court adds that:

> A claim for libel cannot be founded on a headline or other matter, read in isolation from the related text; the court must identify the single meaning of a publication by reference to the response of the ordinary reader to the entire publication.[72]

The claimant initially submitted that the position is different presently. Unlike the position in a libel case, the court looks not at the 'natural and ordinary meaning' of the article read as a whole, but at each discrete 'item of information' it contains. The argument is that any factual statement in the articles or book extract must be read in its proper context, and that any complaint of inaccuracy must be assessed

---

68 *Ibid* at para 81.
69 *Ibid.*
70 *Ibid* at para 82.
71 *Ibid.*
72 *Charleston v News Group Newspapers Ltd* [1995] 2 AC 65; *NT1 & NT2 v Google LLC* at para 82.

in the light of the ordinary and natural meaning of which the offending statement is a part.[73]

The judge notes that, by the end of the case, the claimants moved in this direction, 'accepting that words must be read and interpreted in context' but still resisted the introduction of the defamation principles as to meaning, suggesting that they contained 'artificial' restrictions.[74]

The judge preferred Google's submissions. 'I do not regard the principles identified in *Charleston* as artificial. Nor do I think them inapposite' to the case. [75]

The defamation principles were developed over centuries in cases involving issues arising from the publication of words and their impact on reputation. Google's submissions have two other virtues. They have support in domestic case law. In *Lord Ashcroft v AG*,[76] Gray J held it arguable that ostensibly innocent words might convey a secondary, inferential meaning which embodied sensitive personal data (now called special personal data under the GDPR) about an individual to the effect that he was involved in money laundering.[77] In *Quinton v Peirce*,[78] Eady J applied the single meaning rule when assessing whether data were inaccurate within the meaning of the fourth principle of data protection. In addition, the defamation rules seem well-adapted to testing whether the words satisfy the WP 29 criterion of giving 'an inaccurate, inadequate or misleading impression of an individual'.[79]

The judge also refers to the 'repetition rule' in defamation law, which recognises that an accurate report of what a third party has said about a person may convey an inferential defamatory meaning which is false.[80]

The ordinary meaning of the statement, 'the prosecutor alleged that the defendant had defrauded the Revenue' is, according to the judgment, that the claimant is guilty of fraud. That could turn out to be untrue. The same is true of the statement that 'the Jury found him guilty of fraud'.[81]

The policy of defamation law holds, the judgment indicates, that the publisher responsible for the inferential meaning, whilst protecting those who report accurately on court proceedings, and on certain other kinds of proceeding or statement such as Parliamentary proceedings, even if the report conveys a false or

---

73   *Ibid.*
74   *Ibid* at para 83.
75   *Ibid.*
76   *Lord Ashcroft v Attorney-General* [2002] EWHC 1122 (QB) [22] Gray J.
77   See N Moreham and M Warby *Tugendhat & Christie, The Law of Privacy and the Media* (OUP, 2016) at para 7.25.
78   *Quinton v Peirce* [2009] EWHC 912 (QB) [2009] FSR 17, at paras 27–29, 92.
79   *NT1 & NT2 v Google LLC* at para 83.
80   *Ibid* at para 84.
81   *Ibid.*

inaccurate inferential meaning. The protection is absolute or qualified, according to the context. Some accurate reports are privileged 'subject to explanation or contradiction'. The interpretative provisions contained in Schedule 1 Part II of the DPA 1998 contain some 'apparently' relevant provisions for qualified exemption from the strict requirements of accuracy.[82] They state:

> 7. The fourth principle [of data protection] is not to be regarded as being contravened by reason of any inaccuracy in personal data which accurately record information obtained by the data controller from the data subject or a third party in a case where
>
>   (a) having regard to the purpose or purposes for which the data were obtained and further processed, the data controller has taken reasonable steps to ensure the accuracy of the data, and
>
>   (b) if the data subject has notified the data controller of the data subject's view that the data are inaccurate, the data indicate that fact.[83]

It is noteworthy the judgment states, that the remedial provisions of the DPD 95/46 and DPA 1998 afford the court a discretion, and 'considerable latitude'. Section 10(4) of the DPA 1998 gives the court a discretion to require a controller to take 'such steps … as the Court thinks fit'. Section 14 also provides that if the court is satisfied that personal data are inaccurate it 'may' order the controller to rectify, block, erase or destroy those data. Sections 14(2) and (3) contain further provisions. Some of these build on the requirements of Schedule 1 Part II paragraph 7 referred to above, namely:

> (2) Subsection (1) applies whether or not the data accurately record information received or obtained by the data controller from the data Subject or a third party but where the data accurately record such information, then –
>
>   (a) if the requirements mentioned in paragraph 7 of Part II of Schedule 1 have been complied with, the court may, instead of making an order under subsection (1), make an order requiring the data to be supplemented by such statement of the true facts relating to the matters dealt with by the data as the court may approve, and
>
>   (b) if all or any of those requirements have not been complied with, the court may, instead of making an order under that subsection, make such order as it thinks fit for securing compliance with those requirements with or without a further order requiring the data to be supplemented by such a statement as is mentioned in paragraph (a).
>
> (3) Where the court –
>
>   (a) makes an order under subsection (1), or
>
>   (b) is satisfied on the application of a data subject that personal data of which he was the data subject and which have been rectified, blocked, erased or destroyed were inaccurate,

---

82 *Ibid.*
83 *Ibid.*

it may, where it considers it reasonably practicable, order the data controller to notify third parties to whom the data have been disclosed of the rectification, blocking, erasure or destruction.[84]

This makes clear that 'even where data are found to be inaccurate the court has a toolbox of discretionary remedies that can be applied' according to the case circumstances. The court may grant a remedy 'even if' by virtue of Schedule 1 Part II paragraph 7 the data are not found to be inaccurate.[85]

At one extreme, the court may deem it appropriate to order a controller both to block and erase data, and to tell third parties to whom the data have been disclosed that this has been done. At the other extreme, the court may conclude that no order should be made.[86]

Between those two extremes lies a variety of options.[87]

The court order will need to be 'tailored to the circumstances, having regard to the effect a particular remedy would have on the parties and on the wider public'. Some of the options might be excessive. For example, '[i]f a long article on a matter of public interest containing a substantial amount of information about the claimant was found to contain one inaccuracy, of a relatively minor nature, the knock-on effects of blocking access via an ISE such as Google might make it hard to justify the grant of that remedy'.[88] Rectification, or an order under section 14(2) may be more appropriate. Such an option may not be available on the facts of a given case. It could be, for example, that an ISE lacked the technical ability to add to an individual search result or snippet an indication of 'the data subject's view that the data are inaccurate' or 'a supplementary statement of "the true facts"'.' The evidence in this case does not tell the judge anything about that, 'probably because the claimants have not sought rectification or any lesser remedy than blocking and erasure'.[89]

The court suggests that it 'seems' legitimate to have regard 'in this context' also to English defamation law. Defamation law always allows a 'generous latitude' to those reporting to court or parliament.[90] 'It would be wrong to treat the two branches of the law as co-terminous, as they not only have different origins but also serve different purposes. It is possible to give more weight to literal accuracy in the context of data protection law, with its broader aims and its wider and more flexible range of remedies. It is appropriate, however, to bear in mind domestic principles to ensure, as far as possible, that the law has the "coherence" to which Lord Sumption referred in *Khuja*'.[91]

---

84 *Ibid* at para 85.
85 *Ibid* at para 86.
86 *Ibid*.
87 *Ibid*.
88 *Ibid*.
89 *Ibid*.
90 It goes so far as to permit reporting which conveys the 'impression' of the journalist, see, eg, *Cook v Alexander* [1974] 2 QB 279, CA.
91 *NT1 & NT2 v Google LLC* at para 87.

The Evidence

19.15 Google's case depends on documentary evidence and such support as it can derive from replies under cross-examination. The hearsay rule has been abolished for civil proceedings so there is no difficulty, generally, about reliance on statements of fact contained in third-party documents. The documents relied on include transcripts of the judge's sentencing remarks and of the Court of Appeal's judgment dismissing the NT1 appeal. Discussion queried whether Google's case was limited by Hollington v F Hewthorn.[92] Nobody doubts that convictions are admissible as evidence of guilt.[93] Nor is there room for doubt that judgments or sentencing remarks (which are a form of judgment) are admissible as hearsay evidence of the facts of the case, subject always to the requirements of section 4 of the Civil Evidence Act 1995 regarding the evaluation of hearsay.[94] Section 11(2) of the Civil Evidence Act 1968 plainly contemplates that evidence can be adduced of the facts on which a conviction is based. But I wondered whether Hollington v Hewthorn might be an impediment to reliance on the court's conclusions or findings on contested issues of fact, whether made at first instance or on appeal, if those go beyond the facts leading to the conviction. In the end I do not think this is a problem.[95]

As Tugendhat J pointed out in *Director of Assets Recovery Agency v Virtosu*,[96] *Hollington v Hewthorn* is distinguishable where, as here, the previous judgment can be linked with the conduct proved by the previous court and the issue for consideration is identical. As further pointed out in *Virtosu* at paragraph 41, it has been held by the Court of Appeal that *Hollington v Hewthorn* 'does not purport to be an authority' on the matter of 'raising in a civil action the identical question that had already been decided in a criminal court of competent jurisdiction'. It is fair to mention that the claimant did not seek to exclude reliance on the sentencing remarks in *Hollington v Hewthorn*, perhaps in part because his client's case relies in part on findings made by the courts, which are said to exculpate *NT1*. Further, it is for the claimant to prove inaccuracy. I agree with Google that, on the face of it, an attempt to do so in reliance on a proposition contrary to the findings of a criminal court of competent jurisdiction would be an abuse of process.[97]

It is not an inherently easy task to determine the truth of statements published nearly 20 years ago about events that were older still, following two lengthy trials. 'The evidence I have to help me in that task is limited and far, far less than was before the trial Court or the Court of Appeal.' *NT1* has chosen, as is his right, to place relatively little evidence before the court on the inaccuracy issues. The documents all come from Google. *NT1*'s witness statement is less

---

92 *Hollington v F Hewthorn & Co Ltd* [1943] KB 587.
93 Section 11 of the 1968 Act provides for that.
94 See *Hourani v Thomson* [2017] EWHC 432 (QB) paras 21–22.
95 *NT1 & NT2 v Google LLC* at para 88.
96 *Director of Assets Recovery Agency v Virtosu* [2008] EWHC149 (QB) [2009] 1 WLR 2808, paras 39–40.
97 See *Hunter v Chief Constable of West Midlands Police* [1982] AC 529. *NT1 & NT2 v Google LLC* at para 89.

than comprehensive in its explanation of why the offending publications are inaccurate. It deals with the articles in two relatively short paragraphs. It does not mention the book extract at all. Granted, those two paragraphs of the witness statement are preceded by an account of the factual background, but that itself is fairly superficial and the two elements are not clearly linked. Moreover, aspects of the inaccuracy complaint are not addressed by the statement. As a result, much of the claimant's response to the documents relied on by Google emerged for the first time under cross-examination.[98]

NT1 did not perform well and made a bad impression on the judge. He began by giving long-winded and elaborate answers to simple questions, showing a tendency to make speeches rather than give answers. He tended to 'evade, to exaggerate, to obfuscate, and worse'.[99]

The court found part of the claimant's evidence 'most unconvincing': 'I regard the claimant's unreliable evidence about the undertakings as a factor that undermines his credibility.'[100]

Some of the evidence given by the claimant in relation to other parts of the case further undermined his credibility.[101] 'Overall, I find myself unable to accept much of the claimant's evidence on the inaccuracy issue and, as a rule, where that evidence conflicts with contemporary documents, and the inferences that can fairly be drawn from those documents, I accept the latter.'[102] The judge also found *NT1* somewhat quarrelsome.[103]

Assessment of the Six Complaints

19.16   The court rejected all six complaints of inaccuracy, for the following reasons.[104]

Complaint 1

19.17   The main complaint is that the headline of the first article suggests the claimant was convicted of the second conspiracy. The Google amended defence admitted this alleged inaccuracy, but said it was immaterial. In written opening submissions, Google argued that the offence of which NT1 was actually convicted was so 'very closely connected' to the other offence and so serious, that 'the said inaccuracies would have no greater adverse impact on the claimant's reputation than the true facts summarised in the content'.[105]

---

98 *NT1 & NT2 v Google LLC* at para 90.
99 *Ibid* at para 91(5).
100 *Ibid* at para 91(6).
101 See in particular para 123 in judgment (*NT1 and 2*).
102 *NT1 & NT2 v Google LLC* at para 92.
103 *Ibid* at paras 92(1)–92(2).
104 *Ibid* at para 93.
105 *Ibid*.

That argument is redolent of the somewhat complex statutory provisions of s 2(3) of the Defamation Act 2013 and 'I would have had to think hard before accepting it'. *NT1*s oral argument and closing put his case rather differently, submitting that this article is not capable of bearing the meaning complained of and that (having regard to the s 4(2) order postponing reporting) the first article was 'a classic contemporary Court report'. 'I broadly agree with that.'[106]

NT1's argument depends on 'taking the headline out of context in a way that is contrary to principle'. Even if that was wrong, I would still not exercise my discretion to grant an order for the blocking or erasure of the URLs on this ground alone. The 'most that could be justified, assuming either to be practicable, would be a limited order for rectification or the addition of a notation'. But neither of those remedies has been claimed.[107]

In so far as this complaint applies to the second article and/or the book extract, these also fail for essentially the same reasons. Both were felt, 'when read as a whole' to give a clear enough account of what it was that the claimant was convicted of.[108]

Complaint 2

19.18   The second complaint is that the first article and book extract give a false impression of the claimant's role in the management of Alpha. The claimant has not established that these publications are inaccurate in this respect. If this complaint is meant to include a claim that the publications falsely implicated him in the second conspiracy, 'he has not adequately pleaded that case' and in addition 'he has failed to persuade me that the publications were inaccurate in this respect'.[109]

Complaint 3

19.19   The third complaint relates to an assertion about Alpha's fate in both articles and the book extract. The claimant's case is that this is inaccurate as Alpha 'was placed temporarily in administration, the only creditor was then paid in full and the company was reinstated'. The court did not accept that account of events and rejected the complaint on the further grounds that the information 'is not personal data of the claimant'; the court states that the claimant 'has fallen a long way short of showing that the wording used was, in context, inaccurate or misleading'; for the reasons given at complaint 1 above, the court says that it 'would not have ordered blocking or erasure anyway, as a matter of discretion'.[110]

106 *Ibid* at para 93(1).
107 *Ibid*.
108 *Ibid*.
109 On this complaint point 2, the judgment also advises looking at complaint points 4–6 below. *NT1 & NT2 v Google LLC* at para 93(2).
110 *NT1 & NT2 v Google LLC* at para 93(3).

Complaints 4, 5 and 6

19.20 Complaints 4 to 6 are taken together. They all relate only to the second article. Each complaint asserts that specific wording contained in that article was inaccurate. The complaints have a common underlying theme, namely that the second article 'meant that the claimant was guilty of the second conspiracy'. The court 'agree[s] that it did'. The second article 'made it clear to any reasonable reader that the claimant was convicted of the false accounting conspiracy, and not convicted or even tried for the second conspiracy. But it implied that he was guilty of that crime, and that he had got away with the proceeds of that crime'. That was 'certainly not accurate Court reporting'.[111] The question is one of substance. The claimant did not persuade the court 'that the second article was inaccurate in any of these respects'. He was not convicted of participating in the second conspiracy 'but nor was he acquitted'. He was charged. The CPS considered it had a realistic prospect of securing a conviction. He was not tried, but for reasons that have no bearing on his guilt or innocence. Interestingly, the court states that '[t]he absence of a conviction does not tilt the balance in his favour'. The court finds that NT1 had sufficient control of Alpha's affairs to cause millions to be transferred to his offshore companies commencing shortly after his return from abroad. The second conspiracy was already under way at that time, which makes it more likely than not that the funds that went to the offshore companies included the proceeds of fraud and continued for a long while afterwards. The claimant's increased shareholding after the buy-out of Mr S gave NT1 legal and, in the court's judgment, practical control of Alpha. That view is supported by the conclusions reached by the sentencing Judge and the Court of Appeal, which were considered both admissible and reliable for present purposes. The business carried on after NT1 took control of it. 'I do not accept the claimant's case that in this period others were doing the dirty work, without his knowledge or involvement, whilst he tried to clean up behind the scenes.' An important element, according to the court, is the undertakings NT1 gave, and the court's assessment of their significance and the claimant's evidence about them. The court also see merit in Google's point, namely, that it should draw an adverse inference against the claimant from his repeated failures over the years to take the opportunity to challenge allegations made against him. He made no representations to the regulator, despite the gravity of the steps being taken or threatened, he put in no evidence in response to the serious allegations made in the winding-up proceedings, he elected to remain silent at his criminal trial and in response to the Revenue.[112]

The judge in summarising the decision on these points quotes the WP 29 in saying that *NT1* has failed to 'provide … all the information needed to establish the data are evidently inaccurate'.[113]

---

111 Within DPA 1998 Sch 1 Part II para 7.
112 *NT1 & NT2 v Google LLC* at para 93(4), (5) and (6).
113 *Ibid* at para 94.

6 PRIVACY

Exemption

19.21 The domestic provision relied on by Google is the so-called 'Journalism exemption' (per DPA 1998 s 32). The exemption in fact applies to processing for what are called the 'special purposes', a rather broader notion encompassing 'journalism, literature and art'. This type of exemption is 'authorised by' the DPD 95/46 (per Art 9). This is headed 'Processing of personal data and freedom of expression' and provides as follows:

> Member States shall provide for exemptions or derogations from the provisions of this Chapter, Chapter IV and Chapter VI for the processing of personal data carried out solely for journalistic purposes or the purpose of artistic or literary expression only if they are necessary to reconcile the right to privacy with the rules governing freedom of expression.[114]

Section 32(1) of the DPA 1998 provides that:

> Personal data which are processed only for the special purposes are exempt from any provision to which this subsection relates if –
>
> (a) the processing is undertaken with a view to the publication by any person of any journalistic, literary or artistic material,
>
> (b) the data controller reasonably believes that, having regard in particular to the special importance of the public interest in freedom of expression, publication would be in the public interest, and
>
> (c) the data controller reasonably believes that, in all the circumstances, compliance with that provision is incompatible with the special purposes.'[115]

The provisions to which section 32(1) relates (ie, the requirements from which exemption may be claimed) include all the principles of data protection with which this action is concerned, as well as section 10 (the right to prevent processing) and section 14 (the right to blocking, erasure, etc).[116]

The first question is whether section 32 is engaged at all. Put another way, the court asks if the personal data at issue been processed or will it be processed 'only for the special purposes'? Closely associated with that question is the question of whether processing by Google is undertaken 'with a view to' publication for journalistic purposes. In the court's judgment, 'Google's case on the *Exemption Issue* fails at this threshold stage'. The court could accept the starting point of Google's argument, that the concept of journalism in EU law is a broad one. 'The concept extends beyond the activities of media undertakings and encompasses other activities, the object of which is the disclosure to the

---

114 *Ibid* at para 95.
115 *Ibid* at para 96.
116 *Ibid* at para 97.

public of information, opinions and ideas.'[117] Importantly, however, it adds that 'the concept is not so elastic that it can be stretched to embrace every activity that has to do with conveying information or opinions. To add the label that all such activity is '"journalism" would be to elide the concept of journalism with that of communication'. The two are 'plainly' not the same thing and the court expressly states that it does 'not consider that Google's own activity can be equated with journalism'.[118]

Nor can the court agree with the narrower version of Google's submission. It asserts that the concept of journalism is apt to cover, at least in the present cases, the purpose of the service provided to internet users 'by Google's search engine'. It is submitted that the process of making search results available is 'for the purpose of' enabling users to access third-party publishers' content which discloses information, opinions and ideas. Google 'is quick to emphasise that it is not a publisher' of the content at the URLs; and that it is 'only a facilitator'.[119] But Google also points out, 'fairly' that this is not in itself an obstacle to its reliance on section 32. The court states that the scope of the exemption is not confined to processing which consists of journalistic publication by the person relying on the exemption. It also extends to processing 'undertaken with a view to the publication *by any person*' of any journalistic material (emphasis added in judgment). The argument is that the information available at the URLs complained of consist of journalistic material published by third parties and Google's role is undertaken 'with a view to' such publication, facilitating publication by the third parties.[120]

The court states that this 'narrower argument can be characterised, without meaning to disparage it, as parasitic'.[121] The argument depends upon the character of the underlying publication. It can 'only' be relied on where that publication is 'for purposes properly characterised as journalism, or for one of the other special purposes'.[122]

The court adds generally that much material that people will want to have delisted will not be within those particular confines.[123]

The court states that there may be a *range*[124] of support or ancillary activities that are undertaken by those who are not themselves publishers, but which involve

---

117 See, eg, *Tietosuojavaltuutettu v Satakunnan Markkinapörssi Oy*, Case C-73/07 [2010] All ER (EC) 213 [61]. *NT1 & NT2 v Google LLC* at para 98.
118 *Ibid* at para 98.
119 See *Metropolitan International Schools Ltd v Designtechnica Corp* [2009] EWHC 1765 (QB); [2011] 1 WLR 1743.
120 *NT1 & NT2 v Google LLC* at para 99.
121 *Ibid*.
122 *Ibid*.
123 *Ibid*.
124 Author's emphasis.

processing the sole and exclusive purpose of which is to enable third parties to publish journalistic material.[125]

The court refers to the example of processing by a printer to which a newspaper has outsourced its production. (The court does not consider that this can fairly be said of an ISE such as Google.) Its activities are not exclusively subsidiary, subservient, or ancillary to those of any publisher. The reality, according to the court, as is clear from the evidence of Ms C (from Google) and common knowledge, is that the processes of obtaining, indexing, storing, and making available information that are engaged in by an ISE are automated and governed by computer-based algorithms.[126]

The so called 'All' search function is carried out indiscriminately, in the sense that the search criteria have no regard to the nature of the source publications. Searches for 'news' content may target a narrow range of sources. But whatever the nature of the search in question, when Google responds to a search on an individual's name by facilitating access to journalistic content about that individual, this is 'purely accidental, and incidental to its larger purpose of providing automated access to third party content of whatever nature it may be, that it has identified and indexed and meets the search criteria specified by the user.'[127]

That is, the court states, a *commercial purpose* which, however valuable it may be, is not undertaken for any of the special purposes, or 'with a view to' the publication by others of journalistic material.[128] Such processing is undertaken for Google's own purposes which are of a separate and distinct nature.[129]

In the court's judgment, 'both versions of the argument would fail on the alternative ground that the processing involved when Google Search makes available third-party content that happens to be of a journalistic nature is not properly regarded as processing undertaken "solely" or "only" for journalistic purposes, as required by Article 9 and s 32'.[130]

In *Google Spain*, the Grand Chamber indicates[131] that it did not consider an ISE would process solely for journalistic purposes, and although that was not an integral part of the court's reasoning the instant court considers that this is true.[132]

The court also accepts the argument of the ICO that Google's approach to the journalism exemption is to be resisted because it would have consequences that cannot have been intended by the legislators.[133]

---

125 *NT1 & NT2 v Google LLC* at para 100.
126 *Ibid*.
127 *Ibid*.
128 Within s 32(1)(a).
129 *NT1 & NT2 v Google LLC* at para 100.
130 *Ibid* at para 101.
131 *Google Spain*, at para 85.
132 *NT1 & NT2 v Google LLC* at para 101.
133 *Ibid*.

The ICO's argument is that sections 3, 45 and 46 of the DPA 1998 impose severe constraints on the its powers of enforcement where data are processed for special purposes. If Google's activities were to fall within that description, it would be able to 'operate' the 'right to be forgotten regime' *without regulatory oversight and control*.[134] The court considers that its conclusions 'to be consistent with' the Article 9 stricture,[135] that Member States may provide for journalistic exemptions '*only if* they are necessary to reconcile ... privacy with ... freedom of expression'.[136]

The court adds that, in any event, it would have rejected Google's argument on the *Exemption Issue*, for the following reasons. Each of section 32(1)(b) and (c) has a subjective and an objective element: the data controller must establish that it held a belief that publication would be in the public interest, and that this belief was objectively reasonable; it must establish a subjective belief that compliance with the provision from which it seeks exemption would be incompatible with the special purpose in question, and that this was an objectively reasonable belief. That is the ordinary and natural meaning of the words used (and of the somewhat similar provisions of section 4 of the Defamation Act 2013[137]). There is no evidence that anyone at Google ever considered the public interest in continued publication of the URLs complained of, at any time before *NT1* complained. It was part of the process of assessment that Google undertook, as described by Ms C. Thus far, there might be something in Google's argument, that it should be exempt if the view it took on the public interest was a reasonable one. But it would still have to go on to show that it held a reasonable belief that it would be incompatible with the special purposes for its continued processing of the data to be carried out in compliance with the DPA 1998. There is no evidence of that at all.[138]

Google's RtbF assessment process is 'not designed or adapted for that purpose'. That may be because it has not considered until recently that the journalism exemption might be available. It certainly did not suggest this in *Google Spain*.[139]

Therefore, according to the court, Google's reliance on section 32 would have failed at the section 32(1)(b) stage.[140]

Structure

19.22   There are three competing arguments on this question.[141]

---

134 Author's emphasis.
135 DPD 95/46 Art 9.
136 Emphasis added in judgment. *NT1 & NT2 v Google LLC* at para 101.
137 Discussed in *Economou v de Freitas* [2016] EWHC 1853; [2017] EMLR 4 para 136 and paras 139(2), (3).
138 *NT1 & NT2 v Google LLC* at para 102.
139 *Ibid*.
140 *Ibid*.
141 *Ibid* at para 103.

NT1 submits that the *Google Spain* balance falls to be struck at the remedial stage, after a conclusion has been reached on liability.[142]

Google argues that the court should adopt a staged approach, deciding first whether there is a *prima facie* obligation to the erasure of personal data and then, if so, considering whether the obligation is avoided because the processing is necessary for the exercise of the right of freedom of expression. Google submits that 'the lack of a lawful basis for the processing of sensitive personal data merely gives rise to the qualified right to be forgotten'. Google relies on the structure of GDPR Article 17, which it submits is, in this respect, a 'setting out' of the law as declared by the CJEU in *Google Spain*, and that it should be applied by this instant court.[143]

The ICO rejects these approaches as both 'wrong' and 'unprincipled'. It contends that the issue is a straightforward question of liability, which necessitates a decision on whether Google has complied with its duties under the DPA 1998, as interpreted in the light of the DPD 95/46 and the Charter. The ICO argues, however, that for this purpose the requirement of the first principle of data protection, that the processing comply with at least one condition in Schedule 3, should be disapplied, if the circumstances are such that, on an application of the *Google Spain* criteria, the balance tips against delisting. The basis for disapplication would be the same as that adopted by the Court of Appeal in the *Vidal-Hall* case.[144]

This last argument betrays the fact that the various approaches adopted by the parties are all at least partly driven by a view (on the part of the ICO and the claimants) and/or a concern (on the part of Google) that on a straightforward application of the DPA 98 and/or the DPD 95/46, Google is, or may be, unable to demonstrate that any Schedule 3 condition is met.[145]

On the face of it, that would lead 'inevitably' to a conclusion that it is in breach of statutory duty.

All parties agree that this is not a tenable approach. The reasoning process involved would be too 'mechanistic' to be compatible with the requirements of the Charter and the Convention. It would afford no recognition to the fact, acknowledged by the CJEU in *Google Spain*, that there may be free speech justifications for disclosing sensitive personal information (now called special personal data), even if the data subject does not consent.[146]

---

142 *Ibid.*
143 *Ibid.*
144 *Vidal-Hall v Google* [2015] EWCA Civ 311 at para 32. *NT1 & NT2 v Google LLC* at para 103.
145 *NT1 & NT2 v Google LLC* at para 104.
146 *Ibid.*

The court states that '[t]hese are not easy questions'[147] and then comments that '[n]ow that I have resolved the *Exemption Issue* against Google, I am not sure that the answers matter, either for this case or more generally'.[148]

The court notes that the parties agree that it must address the *Google Spain* balancing exercise 'at some point' and 'with due regard to the [WP 29] criteria'.[149]

In addition, the instant case is being determined in the 'twilight' of the DPD 95/46 regime, with the 'first light' of the GDPR regime already visible on the horizon. As such, the court postulates that it may be 'unlikely that my decision will have an impact on other cases'.

However, in part 'recognising that this case may be considered by another Court' the court states its conclusions, with brief reasons.[150]

19.23   The court came to the following conclusions.

(1)   The court rejects Google's submission. It is 'unable to identify any principled basis' upon which it can use the GDPR as an aid to the interpretation of *Google Spain* or to the identification of the legal principles that apply to these events, some of which occurred before the enactment of the GDPR, and all of which ('so far'[151]) have taken place before the GDPR has effect. 'I do not myself detect such an approach as explicit or implicit in *Google Spain*.'[152]

(2)   The Court also rejects *NT1*'s approach. As indicated, when dealing with the *Inaccuracy Issue*, the court does consider the flexibility of the remedies provided for by the DPA 1998 and the DPD 95/46 to be an 'important' feature of the law in this area. But this 'would be unsatisfactory'. The Court thinks that the ICO is right to say it is 'unprincipled' to leave so much to its discretion.[153]

(3)   The solution that 'fits best' with the structure of the law and the decision of the CJEU is, in the instant court's judgment, that advocated by the ICO. However, the court is reluctant to take the 'radical step of disapplying' any part of the DPA 1998. There is a 'powerful argument' that the scheme of the DPA 1998 is incompatible with fundamental rights, as it fails to recognise any possibility of a free speech justification for the processing of sensitive personal data (now called special personal data) without consent. The same would seem to be true of the DPD 95/46 which, in this respect, the DPA 1998 merely mirrors.[154]

---

147 *Ibid* at para 105.
148 *Ibid*.
149 *Ibid*.
150 *Ibid*.
151 Possibly alluding to the option for appeals in the instant case, which would give temporal issues likely reach into the GDPR go-live horizon.
152 *NT1 & NT2 v Google LLC* at para 105(1).
153 *Ibid* at para 105(2).
154 *Ibid* at para 105(3).

The CJEU did not need to confront this issue in *Google Spain*, as the data in that case, though 'sensitive' in the 'colloquial sense' as they concerned personal financial matters, were not 'special category data' within Article 8 of the DPD 95/46. In the instant court's judgment, it is 'not necessary' to go as far as the ICO contends it should. On the facts of this instant case, at least, the court feels that it 'need not confront the question of disapplication'. The court considers that a Schedule 3 condition is met.[155]

DPA Compliance

The first principle of data protection

19.24 On the facts of the instant case, the general requirements of this principle of data protection, that processing be 'fair and lawful' add nothing to the requirement, that processing comply with at least one Schedule 2 condition and, if the data are sensitive personal data (now special personal data), at least one condition in Schedule 3. Most of the personal data with which the court is concerned are sensitive (now special) personal data. The court starts with Schedule 3.[156]

Schedule 3

19.25 The court rejects most of Google's arguments that its processing was compliant with Schedule 3. The processing of NT1's data by making them available to those who search on his name was not, nor is it, 'necessary for the purposes of exercising legal rights' within Condition 6(c) of Schedule 3.[157] The rights relied on those of internet users under Convention Article 10 and Charter Articles 8 and 11, as well as the Article 16 freedom of Google to conduct a business. I do not consider that broad interpretation can stand. As the ICO and NT1 submit, this condition must be applied in conformity with Article 8.2(e) of the DPD 95/46, which uses the terms 'legal claims'; its 'focus is on the protection of underlying rights'.[158]

Google's argument on paragraph 7A of Schedule 3 is 'close to unarguable'. That condition applies to processing of information 'disclosed by an anti-fraud organisation'. It is argued that this paragraph should be given a wide interpretation, encompassing both public and private sector organisations concerned with exposing and preventing wrongdoing. The court saw nothing to

---

155 *Ibid.*
156 *Ibid* at para 106.
157 DPA 1998, Condition 6(c) of Sch 3.
158 *R (British Telecommunications plc) v Secretary of State for Culture, Olympics, Media and Sport* [2012] EWCA Civ 232; [2012] *Bus Law Review* 1766 [74]; *NT1 & NT2 v Google LLC* at para 107.

warrant such a broad interpretation of wording which on its face is specific and relatively narrow in ambit.[159]

Nor can Google rely on Schedule 3 Condition 10 and paragraph 3 of the Schedule to the Sensitive Personal Data Order.[160] That condition is, in substance, a narrower version of section 32 of the DPA 1998. It lays down a set of requirements which are cumulative.[161] Among the requirements are that the processing in question is 'for the special purposes' and 'with a view to the publication of ... data by any person'. Whatever else might be said about the application of this condition to the facts of this case, the existence of those two requirements means that Google's argument is unsound, for the reasons the court has given in deciding the *Exemption Issue*.[162]

The Schedule 3 condition that the court does find satisfied is Condition 5: that 'the information contained in the personal data has been made public as a result of steps deliberately taken by the data subject'. In reaching that conclusion the Court follows a path already trodden by Stephens J in *Townsend v Google Inc*[163] and a principle that seems to be logical, and well-established in domestic and European law. In *Townsend*, Stephens J refused an application for leave to serve proceedings on Google in California, claiming remedies under the DPA 1998 in respect of the processing of information about the convictions of a prolific offender.[164] One of Stephens J's conclusions was that Schedule 3 Condition 5 was so clearly satisfied that there was no triable issue. He reasoned, at paragraph 62, that 'legally as a consequence of the open justice principle by committing an offence [the offender] is deliberately taking steps to make the information public'. *NT1* quarrels with this analysis. He argues that the claimant took no steps, deliberate or otherwise, to 'make the information contained in the data' public. Condition 5, he says 'requires some act of dealing with information'. An offender such as *NT1*, who commits an offence in private, is by no means deliberately making his conduct public. The instant court does not believe this reasoning is sound.[165]

First, the wording of condition 5 'is important'. It does not require a deliberate decision or 'step' by the individual data subject 'to make' the information public, but rather (a) the taking by him of a deliberate step or steps, as a result of which (b) the information is 'made public'. A person who deliberately conducts himself in a criminal fashion runs the risk of apprehension, prosecution, trial, conviction and sentence. Publicity for what happens at a trial is the ordinary consequence of the open justice principle:

159 *NT1 & NT2 v Google* at para 108.
160 Data Protection (Processing of Sensitive Personal Data) Order 2000 (SI 2000/417). This was made by the Secretary of State pursuant to Condition 10.
161 See *Campbell v MGN Ltd* [2002] EWHC 499 (QB) para 121 (Morland J).
162 *NT1 & NT2 v Google LLC* at para 109.
163 *Townsend v Google Inc* [2017] NIQB 81, Stephens J.
164 By the age of 24 the plaintiff had accumulated 74 convictions, of which only two were spent.
165 *NT1 & NT2 v Google LLC* at para 110.

An important aspect of the public interest in the administration of criminal justice is that the identity of those convicted and sentenced for criminal offices should not be concealed. Uncomfortable though it may frequently be for the defendant that is a normal consequence of his crime.[166]

The same must be true of the details of the offending and other information disclosed in open court, including information about himself which a criminal reveals at a trial or in the course of an application. The European Court of Human Rights was making a related point, the court feels, in *Axel Springer AG v Germany*.[167] The applicant complained of sanctions imposed for reporting information about a celebrity's arrest, conviction, and sentence for possession of cocaine. Finding a violation of Article 10, the Court observed that, whilst reputation is protected by Article 8 of the Convention, it 'cannot be relied on in order to complain of a loss of reputation which is the *foreseeable consequence of one's own actions* such as, for example, the commission of a criminal offence ...'.[168]

The argument in favour of the application of Condition 5 would be stronger, if one was dealing with a person who committed a crime in public; someone who does that has 'placed himself in public view'.[169] But it would be wrong, as well as impracticable, to draw a distinction of principle for these purposes between information about crimes committed in public and those committed in private. The place for drawing that distinction is in weighing up the competing considerations of privacy and publicity.[170]

NT1 is entitled to point to the wording Article 8.2(e) of the DPD 95/46 from which DPA 1998 Schedule 3 condition 5 derives. Article 8.2(e) exempts the processing of 'special category data' from the general prohibition in Article 8.1 where it 'relates to data which are *manifestly* made public *by the data subject*.'[171] This, however, is rather obscure language. The court does not think it provides a sufficient reason to depart from the ordinary meaning of condition 5 itself. It attaches weight to the fact that a narrow interpretation would tend towards the unacceptable conclusion discussed above. The court sees a good deal of force in the point made by Google, that if this condition were not available in respect of processing of this nature it is hard to see how ordinary members of the public could lawfully discuss online the convictions (whether recent or historic) of those appearing before the courts.[172]

---

166 *Re Trinity Mirror plc* [2008] EWCA Crim 50; [2008] QB 770 para 32 (Sir Igor Judge P).
167 *Axel Springer AG v Germany* 32 BHRC 493 para 83.
168 Emphasis added in judgment. *NT1 & NT2 v Google LLC* at para 111.
169 See *In re JR38* [2015] UKSC 42, [2016] AC 1131 [32], citing Higgins LJ (sitting in the Divisional Court of the Queen's Bench Division in Northern Ireland).
170 *NT1 & NT2 v Google LLC* at para 112.
171 Emphasis in judgment.
172 *NT1 & NT2 v Google LLC* at para 113.

Schedule 2

19.26   The fact that a Schedule 3 condition is satisfied means that it is not necessary to consider the disapplication of that part of section 4(4) that requires this to be so. It is by no means the end of the matter, of course. A Schedule 2 condition must also be met. This is referred to below. It is agreed by all the parties that, in principle, the Schedule 2 condition 6(1) is capable of application to this case. It reads as follows:

> The processing is necessary for the purposes of legitimate interests pursued by the data controller or by the third party or parties to whom the data are disclosed, except where the processing is unwarranted in any particular case by reason of prejudice to the rights and freedoms or legitimate interests of the data subject.[173]

Generally speaking, Google plainly has a legitimate interest in the processing of third-party data in pursuit of its business as an ISE and third parties have a legitimate interest in receiving information via Google or other ISEs. These obvious propositions are bolstered by the authority of the CJEU which, in paragraphs 73–74 of *Google Spain*, agreed with the Advocate General's submissions on the point. The AG had said that internet intermediaries 'act as bridge builders between content providers and internet users ...' playing a role that '... has been considered as crucial for the information society'.[174] The vital questions are whether, on the facts of this case, the particular processing at issue is 'necessary' for the purposes of such interests or is 'unwarranted' for any of the reasons specified in condition 6(1). This condition clearly calls for the conduct of a balancing exercise. The court states that the authority to date is that the exercise it must undertake in this context is an assessment of proportionality,[175] involving essentially the same Article 8/Article 10 'ultimate balancing test'.[176] It must form part of the balancing process mandated by *Google Spain*. Indeed, as the ICO points out, the CJEU's analysis was heavily reliant on Article 7(f) of the DPD 95/46, which is the analogue of condition 6(1).[177]

The Second to Sixth Principles

19.27   The court states that it has already dealt with NT1's case under the fourth principle of data protection. Otherwise, in the court's judgment, the question of whether Google's processing of the claimant's personal data was in breach of or in compliance with these principles is subsumed by or, in Google's phrase, 'collapses into' the *Google Spain* balancing exercise. It does not require separate consideration.[178]

---

173 *Ibid* at para 114.
174 *Ibid* at para 36.
175 See *Morland J in Campbell v MGN Ltd* (above) paras 116–117.
176 As prescribed by *In re S (Murray v Express Newspapers)* [2007] EWHC 1908 (Ch); [2008] 1 FLR 704 [76] (Patten J).
177 *NT1 & NT2 v Google LLC* at para 115.
178 *Ibid* at para 116.

7 GOOGLE SPAIN

Facts

19.28 The facts the court needs to consider for this purpose are not only those of and surrounding NT1's conviction, but also the other matters that have already been examined when dealing with the inaccuracy issue. Google contends that NT1's business career since his imprisonment and his social media profile both support its case that the processing complained of was and is compliant with Google's statutory duty under the DPA 1998, and its obligations under *Google Spain*.[179]

The court then summarises this part of the case and its findings.[180]

NT1's Subsequent Business Career

19.29 Google relies on publicly available documents relating to business activities of NT1, which it describes as 'indicative of the nature of his ongoing business activities'. The documentation evidences a variety of business ventures stretching over some 15 years, as well as a demand made by the Inland Revenue for information about NT1's affairs, a High Court ruling on the validity of that demand and a decision by the OFT refusing an application by NT1 for a consumer credit licence. NT1 was cross-examined about these documents, and what they did or did not show about his behaviour.[181]

NT1 obstructed an Inland Revenue investigation into his tax affairs by steadfastly refusing to provide any of the information that had been requested. When the Revenue made a statutory demand for that information,[182] *NT1* mounted a flimsy and deservedly unsuccessful legal challenge. A High Court Judge dismissed six grounds of challenge advanced on a renewed judicial review application. The Judge held that *NT1* had put forward any possible pretext to avoid giving the information within his reach. Warby J stated: 'In his evidence to me, *NT1* sought to distance himself from the conduct of the legal proceedings. I was not persuaded that he had left this to his lawyers. He put forward additional reasons to justify his failure to provide the information. The instant Court did not accept those reasons, which I regard as unconvincing and unmeritorious.' The court accepted the earlier Judge's assessment.[183]

After his release from prison, *NT1* made an application to the OFT for a Consumer Credit Licence. But he did so without disclosing his previous association with a credit licensee whose licence was revoked. The application was refused on

179 *Ibid* at para 117.
180 *Ibid*.
181 *Ibid* at para 118.
182 Taxes Management Act 1970 s 20.
183 *NT1 & NT2 v Google LLC* at para 119.

the grounds that he was not fit to hold such a licence, because of his conviction (which was not 'spent' at that time) and because of his failure to declare the previous association. In his evidence to me, *NT1* described the reasons for refusal as 'somewhat disingenuous'. He claimed that it was the fact of his association with a business that had a consumer credit licence revoked that had led him to make the application in the first place and that, if he had not made reference to the prior association in the written application, he had done so orally. The instant court did not accept *NT1*'s evidence on this aspect of the case. It accepts and adopts the findings of the OFT.[184]

NT1's post-prison business career has included lending money to business and individuals over the last 15 years or so. This money came from the profits of Alpha. *NT1* had 'siphoned off' several million pounds in the false accounting conspiracy and had taken a further £3 million by way of the funds frozen in Switzerland. This much *NT1* accepted in cross-examination. He did not accept that any of the money he lent represented the proceeds of fraud. The instant court did, however, conclude that this was the case. The court accepted *NT1*'s case, that Alpha's business was not fraudulent from the outset. It also accepted that the scale of the fraud was modest in comparison to the number of transactions undertaken by companies in the Alpha group. The Court of Appeal also made that observation. But the scale of the fraud was 'not negligible' and it was 'profitable' and on the balance of probabilities the profits contributed to the sums that *NT1* took out of the business.[185]

Google relies on lending activities involving three companies[186] and a group of companies owned or controlled by a Mr T, his family or associates (T Companies). Google also relies on a number of other, smaller loan transactions. This activity started in the early years of the present century, shortly after the expiry of *NT1*'s prison sentence but at a time when he was disqualified from acting as a company director. The court's findings as to the lending activity undertaken during this period are set out and explained in detail in the private judgment. The main findings are these.[187]

(1) Between his release from prison and about 2015 *NT1* used the monies above to engage in substantial commercial lending activities. Some of this was done via a Bahamian company, Charlie Ltd. The court rejects Google's argument that there was a related Swiss company called Charlie AG or similar and that *NT1* engaged in consumer lending. His lending was to businesses. The court does not accept Google's case that Charlie AG or Charlie Ltd lent at 'extremely high rates of interest'. The 'scant evidence' on the point is insufficient to support that case.[188]

---

184 *Ibid* at para 120.
185 *Ibid* at para 121.
186 Oscar Ltd, Charlie Ltd, and Victor plc.
187 *NT1 & NT2 v Google LLC* at para 122.
188 *Ibid* at para 122(1).

(2) Charlie took a stake in an English company (Bravo), to which it lent about £300,000. At the same time, *NT1* entered into a 15-year consultancy agreement with Bravo, by which he was to provide up to three days a month of consultancy services for a fee. That was to increase by 10 per cent each year. Within two years it had reached £66,000 per annum, which greatly exceeded the remuneration due to any director of the company. By that time, Charlie's stake in Bravo had increased to about a quarter of the issued share capital. The court did not accept *NT1*'s evidence that the consultancy fee was not paid. Having considered other possibilities, it accepts Google's case that *NT1* was acting as a shadow director of Bravo during this period.[189]

(3) However, the court does not accept Google's argument that there were serious failures of disclosure about *NT1*, when Oscar Ltd issued a prospectus for the takeover of Bravo and the listing of the business on the London Stock Exchange. The plan was for Oscar Ltd to acquire the entire issued share capital in Bravo, then change its name to Bravo plc, which would be the listed entity. Google's argument is that the representations in paragraph 7.6 of the prospectus were false because they said that none of the 'Directors expected nor any of the Proposed Directors' had any unspent convictions in relation to indictable offences, had been a director of a company that had been placed in compulsory liquidation, been criticised by any regulator or disqualified from acting in the management or conduct of the affairs of a company. *NT1* had acted as a shadow director of Bravo. If he thereby counted, or should have been counted, as one of the 'Directors' or 'Proposed Directors' those representations would have been false or misleading. Google's argument is that he did. It states the quoted terms referred to 'the directors of [Bravo] or proposed directors of [Bravo plc]'. The court does not agree.[190]

(4) The term 'Directors' was defined on page 4 of the prospectus to mean the directors of 'the Company', which was in turn defined to mean Oscar Ltd (Bravo plc, as it was to become). The prospectus went further and identified the directors as those named on page 3. The names that appeared there were those of directors of Oscar Ltd. The term 'Proposed Directors' was also defined in the prospectus, to mean six named individuals. These were men whom, it was proposed, would become directors of the listed company. It arguably might have been better, perhaps, if disclosure had been made about *NT1*, because he was a significant figure in the business of Bravo. But he was not a director or shadow director of Oscar Ltd. His role as an active 'consultant' to, and shadow director of Bravo did not make him so. The court is not persuaded by his evidence that he had nothing to do with the prospectus. The court doubts that is true. But given the court's conclusions on the allegations of misrepresentation it does not matter.[191]

---

189 *Ibid* at para 122(2).
190 *Ibid* at para 122(3).
191 *Ibid* at para 122(4).

(5) More than eight years after its flotation, Bravo plc raised some £16 million in various tranches. It eventually went into insolvent administration with a deficiency of over £14 million.[192]

(6) Charlie lent a six-figure sum to Victor plc, under a short-term loan agreement which provided for interest and a substantial 'repayment premium'. Less than a year later, the parties agreed to convert this premium into equity, as a result of which Charlie owned over a quarter of the issued share capital of Victor plc, as well as being owed the amount of the original loan and interest. The evidence about this transaction is scant and unclear. The transaction documents themselves are not available, only descriptions of them. The court states that '[i]t is hard to know what to make of' Google's argument that the loan involved a 'repayment premium' that was equal to the amount of the loan. It concludes that this was the case. The probable explanation is that the loan was a very high-risk transaction, undertaken without any valuable security, to fund a speculative property development opportunity. The court was not persuaded by Google's argument that this was an investment transaction on the part of Charlie. It took an equity stake because the property transaction did not come to fruition, Victor plc had no funds available and to swap debt for equity made the best of a bad job.[193]

(7) *NT1*, via corporate vehicles, lent seven-figure sums to Mr T, a former bankrupt, via the T Companies, which were property development businesses selling to consumers and investors. The main purpose of the loans was to fund the buy-out of someone who had been a partner of Mr T in the businesses. The court was not persuaded by Google that this activity was investment as opposed to lending. *NT1* took a stake in the main corporate vehicle of the T Companies' business, but that was by way of security for a relatively short period. Nor did the court accept Google's argument that these business activities involved *NT1* in some way in the conduct of a business similar to that of Alpha, which engaged in comparable sales practices towards consumers and investors. His role was as a lender not a participant in the business. A sales brochure for one of the T Companies that was put to *NT1* in an attempt to support that case post-dated his involvement with the businesses and did not support the comparison other than in a very broad fashion.[194]

(8) Other loans. Google has not established out its case that *NT1* made other loans to consumers. Google referred to the activities of three companies, Zebra Ltd, Tango Ltd and Uniform Ltd, in or between June 2011 and May 2015. Google had little information about these companies, relying on what *NT1* fairly described as 'generic descriptions that are so often provided in … accounts … when filed'. In this regard, the court accepts *NT1*'s evidence about the activities of the three companies, and that they were not dealing or proposing to deal with consumers.[195]

192 *Ibid* at para 122(5).
193 *Ibid* at para 122(6).
194 *Ibid* at para 122(7).
195 *Ibid* at para 122(8).

The court refers to a finding at this, as it goes to credibility. *NT1* initially said that Charlie Ltd was owned by a family trust of which he was a beneficiary, which may be correct. He was asked, 'It is a company controlled by you as well as owned by your family trust?' His prompt answer was 'No. The arrangements with the family trust do not allow me control'. Shortly afterwards, he admitted that he was able to use the company as his lending vehicle and accepted that his earlier point had been 'in that context … an artificial point'. This is taken by the court as an illustration of two more general features of the his evidence. It is unreliable on quite important points of detail, despite the emphatic way was is given; and his reluctance to make an unequivocal concession. His 'patent unreliability' according to the court in this regard is obviously relevant when assessing his evidence about the control of Alpha, and about his role in respect of Bravo.[196]

NT1's Online Profile

19.30 For a period, over recent years, NT1 caused online postings to be made which spoke positively about his business experience, standing and integrity. Google describes these online postings – now removed – as 'boasts', saying they included claims that are 'thoroughly misleading [and] dishonest' and which need to be corrected by the correct information which is and for this reason should remain available at the URLs complained of.[197]

The principal vehicle for these postings was a WordPress blog, though a variety of social media were also used. On the blog and at least one of the social media websites, claims were made that *NT1* had gained recognition for his flawless professional integrity, few being better known for this characteristic. The social media websites also stated that *NT1* had earned recognition for his business expertise gained over 25 years in the consulting business.[198] It clearly promotes the idea that *NT1* is a man of unblemished integrity, with a longstanding reputation.[199]

All this material came to be published as a result of instructions given by *NT1* to a reputation management business, called Cleanup. He had heard of adverse Google Search results being successfully removed by organisations such as Cleanup, whom he retained 'in order to create material online that would detract from the negative postings'. The aim was to 'demote' the negative material.[200]

NT1 equivocated about his personal responsibility for the published content. In his witness statement he said that the postings were 'material I have authorised to be published about me' but went on to say that the sites were 'designed and

196 *Ibid* at para 123.
197 *Ibid* at para 124.
198 The actual wording used is set out in the private judgment.
199 *NT1 & NT2 v Google LLC* at para 124.
200 *Ibid* at para 125.

written by [Cleanup] with no input from me save that I approved the content and supplied the background information that they had requested from me'. He was questioned about this account. At first, he claimed never to have seen a blog. Later, he conceded that he had been sent the wording to be posted online, but he never unequivocally admitted that he had read and approved any such wording.[201]

The true position 'emerges with tolerable clarity' from the documents. By e-mail dated 22 May 2014, Ms AF of Cleanup sent *NT1* a questionnaire to obtain information about him on which to base the content which Cleanup was to prepare. He was urged to provide as much information as possible, including 'achievements, accolades, ...' The plan that AF set out in this e-mail was for 'our journalists' to use the questionnaire to create content which would then be sent back to *NT1* 'for approval'. The e-mail made clear that 'I will always make sure to send you all and any content before we put it live on the internet'. When this e-mail was put to him, *NT1* started by answering evasively: 'She doesn't actually say it is for me to approve.' When shown the full wording of the e-mail again, he eventually agreed that it did say the wording was to be sent to him for approval but qualified his admission by saying that it was a URL that was sent. That may be true. The papers include an undated progress report with URLs linking to the blog and to postings at Smore and Live journal. But the court has no doubt the links were sent to *NT1* before the posts went live, as well as afterwards. It is not credible that *NT1* failed to follow those links on either occasion. He must have read what was to be posted and approved it in both the formal and the substantive sense. The evidence suggests to me that the wording is in part standard form, 'boilerplate', rather than tailored to the specific facts and circumstances of *NT1*'s career. But the court has no doubt that it was put together in reliance on information provided by *NT1* in response to Cleanup's questionnaire and that he both knew of and approved the wording before it was posted.[202]

NT1 did ultimately accept that he had omitted from these blogs – or allowed to be omitted from them – any reference to a criminal conviction. Leaving aside for the present any question of rehabilitation, it seems to the court indisputable that the quoted statements about *NT1*'s integrity and reputation are false or at best highly misleading. The fact of his conviction for criminal dishonesty involving a £3.3 million fraud is enough to falsify the assertions of integrity. There is, however, a good deal more that casts a long and dark shadow over his integrity, as set out in this judgment above. Moreover, it is his own case that his reputation has been injured by reporting of his conviction, and by reporting connecting him with the business of Alpha. The claims on the blog and social media are inconsistent with his own evidence in this case which, in this respect, the court believes to be true. The court also finds that the blogs and social media presented a misleading picture of his business career, taken as a whole.[203]

201 *Ibid* at para 126.
202 *Ibid* at para 127.
203 *Ibid* at para 128.

NT1's case is not that these representations about him, his character, conduct and reputation were true. He denies, however, that the public was misled. He was not seeking to attract business or work, or otherwise addressing the public. He denounced as 'disingenuous and dishonest' any suggestion that he was marketing himself. His evidence is that he was just seeking to demote the harmful information in the URLs complained of, by putting other positive information 'out there'. His case is that he was justified in the attempt. *NT1*'s counsel describes this as 'an attempt at self-help' which did not work.[204]

The court had no evidence as to the extent of publication of the blog or the social media posts, but the more important question is whether they were aimed at the public. It is obvious that they were. It may well not have mattered to *NT1* whether he gained business, but that is not really the issue; it was not put to him that he was marketing himself. His objectives could only be achieved by putting out messages about himself on public platforms which were then picked up by Google's web crawlers. He was content to do this using messages he knew to be false and misleading.[205]

That is, however, subject to: the court recognising a risk that Google's criticisms are 'circular'. If harmful information about a person is being made available to the public in a way that is unlawful, it might be unjust – without more – to criticise that person for using self-help methods of removing that information from the public domain by demoting it in ISE search results.

The claimant's dealings with Cleanup began two months after his conviction became retroactively spent. Whether, paying due regard to the principle of rehabilitation, the claimant is still to be criticised for making these representations is a matter the court must address in its overall assessment of where the balance lies.[206]

Law

19.31   Two further points of dispute about the nature of the balancing exercise are addressed before carrying out that exercise:[207]

- the first concerns the state of the scales 'at the outset'. Are they tilted in favour of the individual data subject, as a matter of principle, as *NT1* submits?

- the second point concerns the boundaries to be observed in making my assessment.[208]

Google relies on a number of factors that are not, or not in terms to be found in the WP 29 criteria:

---

204 *Ibid* at para 129.
205 *Ibid* at para 130.
206 *Ibid*.
207 *Ibid* at para 131.
208 *Ibid*.

- the nature of the third-party publishers;

- the public availability of the information;

- the nature of the information and the alleged inaccuracies;

- the claimant's business activities and their relationship with the information published at the URLs complained of; and

- the claimant's own online descriptions of himself.[209]

Counsel for *NT1* derides this as 'a process' of Google 'inventing its own criteria'. He argues that:

- those factors partly overlap with the WP 29 criteria;

- but also go beyond them;

- that some are irrelevant, or of little weight; and

- that the exercise is 'unhelpful'.[210]

In the court's judgment, the balancing process in any individual delisting case is ordinarily, as a matter of principle, to be entered into with the scales in equal balance as between delisting on the one hand and continued processing on the other. The court refers to the basis that such cases will ordinarily engage the rights protected by Convention Articles 8 and 10 and, for as long as European law is part of UK domestic law, their counterparts under the Charter, as well as the right to freedom of information contained in Charter Article 11. Accordingly, with appropriate adaptation, the *In re S* case approach must be followed: neither privacy nor freedom of expression 'has as such precedence over the other'; the conflict is to be resolved by an 'intense focus on the comparative importance of the specific rights being claimed in the individual case'.[211]

The court does not read *Google Spain* as being inconsistent with this. What the CJEU was saying, in the passages at [81] and [97] on which *NT1* relies, is that in the majority of cases of this kind, the facts will be such that the factors in favour of delisting will outweigh those in favour of the continued availability of the data, via an ISE. The 'general rule' to which the court was referring was descriptive, not prescriptive. One factor in that conclusion was that the economic interests of an ISE are not of equal inherent weight or value to the privacy or data privacy rights of an individual. 'But the Court was not saying the same thing about the rights of the public to receive information and opinions. That would seem to be at odds with principle and authority.'[212]

NT1 does not cite any authority to support the two propositions of law which he offers by way of explanation: that the right to receive information is inherently

209 *Ibid.*
210 *Ibid.*
211 *Ibid* at para 132.
212 *Ibid* at para 133.

less weighty than the right to impart it; and that Google's activities do not even involve the exercise of the right to freedom of expression.[213]

The second of these propositions would appear to be 'at odds' with *Google Spain* in which, the CJEU[214] agreed with the suggestion made by the Advocate General[215] that the legitimate interests pursued by ISEs include, '(i) making information more easily accessible for Internet users; and (ii) rendering dissemination of the information uploaded on the Internet more effective' which 'relate respectively to ... fundamental rights protected by the Charter, namely freedom of information and freedom of expression (both in Article 11)'. The court would regard the CJEU's references to a 'general rule' and its observation that a claim to delist sensitive or other private information may be defeated by a 'preponderant' interest of the general public in having access to that information, as descriptions of how cases of this kind are most likely to work out in practice; but not as tantamount to a declaration that the public's interest in access to information is inherently of lesser value than the individual's privacy rights. The court notes that the WP 29 commentary seems consistent with the its own assessment. It suggests that 'in determining the balance ... the jurisprudence of the [ECtHR] is especially relevant'.[216]

Regarding the criteria relied on by Google, some may go 'a little outside' the WP 29 criteria. However, there is nothing wrong in principle there. The criteria were created over three years ago, within seven months of the *Google Spain* decision based on the early experience of the new regime. They are expressed to be flexible, non-exhaustive and liable to 'evolve' over time on the basis of experience.[217]

The factors relied on by Google in this case all seem to the court to have some bearing on the issue for decision, and in particular on the question of whether the data remain 'relevant,' or are 'excessive,' or have been 'kept for longer than is necessary' within the third and fifth principles of data protection. The court indicates that it seeks to weave its consideration of Google's points into its review of the 13 WP 29 criteria.[218]

Application of Law to Facts

Q1: Does the search result relate to a natural person – ie, an individual? Does the search result come up against a search on the data subject's name?

19.32 The court answers yes. This is the starting point 'without which no delisting claim would be viable'.[219]

213 *Ibid* at para 134.
214 CJEU, at paras 73–74.
215 AG at para 95.
216 *NT1 & NT2 v Google LLC* at para 134.
217 *Ibid* at para 135.
218 *Ibid*.
219 *Ibid* at para 136.

Q2: Does the data subject play a role in public life? Is the data subject a public figure?

19.33   NT1 has never been in politics, held any public office or played a role in public affairs. Nor has he been a sportsman, entertainer or engaged in other highly public areas of life. He has always been in business. But the WP 29 on this criterion suggests a broader meaning for the term 'public figures': 'individuals who, due to their functions/commitments, have a degree of media exposure'. The criterion of 'playing a role in public life' is broader still. The WP 29 offers illustrations which include 'business-people and members of the (regulated) professions', explaining that the key factor is the potential relevance of information about the individual: 'A good rule of thumb is to try to decide where the public having access to the particular information – made available through a search on the data subject's name – would protect them against improper public or professional conduct.'[220]

By these standards, *NT1* was a public figure with a role in public life. He was reasonably well-known to the public at large as a person who played a leading role in a controversial property business, who had been tried, convicted and sentenced for criminal conspiracy in connection with that business and charged but never tried for another conspiracy. His name appeared in public statements, such as from the regulator and in reports of the criminal proceedings. The 'rule of thumb' would have favoured the continued availability of accurate information about his conduct and, in particular, his misdeeds. Since he left prison over a decade ago, he has played a role in business, but he has not been a public figure. Counsel for *NT1* accepts that he has 'played a role in public life' for present purposes but describes this as 'extremely limited'. 'That is a fair point. *NT1*'s business role has not been a leading or prominent one.' His social media postings are misleading in that respect, the court feels. The court states that 'Plainly, the argument that the public needs to know about his past to guard against impropriety has gradually weakened over time'.[221]

However, as the WP 29 comment on this criterion makes clear, the degree of privacy that attaches to the information is also a relevant factor.[222]

Another WP 29 'rule of thumb' is that 'if applicants are public figures, and the information in question does not constitute genuinely private information, there will be a stronger argument against de-listing'. Counsel for *NT1* reminds the court in this context of the well-known passage in *von Hannover (No 1)*,[223] which identifies a 'fundamental distinction ... between reporting facts capable of contributing to a debate in a democratic society and reporting details of the private life of an individual who does not exercise such functions'.

---

220 *Ibid* at para 137.
221 *Ibid* at para 138.
222 *Ibid* at para 139.
223 *von Hannover v Germany (No 1)* (2005) 40 EHRR 1 at [63].

This passage is cited by the WP 29. *NT1* argues that there is no current debate to his past behaviour has any relevance. That may be true. But the court states that the criterion does not require an extant debate; the test is whether the information is 'capable of contributing' to a debate of the kind referred to. More importantly, the principle is concerned with 'details of the private life of an individual'.

Google argues that the information in this case is not of that kind or at least that most of it is not. It relates wholly or mainly to the claimant's criminal conduct in a public role in the management of a company selling services to the public, not to his private or personal life. He invites comparison with *Yeo v Times Newspapers*[224] and *Axon v Ministry of Defence.*[225] In the former case, the same Judge as in the instant case held that information about a politician's offer to help a company by using his public office was of such a nature that it fell outside the ambit of his private or personal life.[226] In the latter case,[227] Nicol J reached a similar conclusion about information relating to the events leading to the removal of a Royal Navy warship commander from that role.[228]

The court agrees with Google. The information here includes some about *NT1*'s health (health information). This is 'intrinsically private' in nature but it is vague, historic and it was made public in the course of the proceedings. For those reasons and others the court could not justify a stand-alone delisting claim.

The rest of the information (crime and punishment information) is 'sensitive' but it is not intrinsically private in nature. The criminal behaviour has a private aspect in that it was undertaken in secret and was not intended for public view. But it was not intimate or even personal. It was business conduct, and it was criminal. Having been identified and then made the subject of a public prosecution, trial and sentence, it all became essentially public. The authorities do show that information that begins as public may become private and that Article 8 may be engaged by dealings with information, of whatever kind, that have a grave impact on the conduct of a person's private life – for instance by undermining their 'personal integrity' – or by interfering with their family life.[229] But the essential nature of the crime and punishment information in this case was public, not private. The claimant did not enjoy any reasonable expectation of privacy during the process of trial, conviction and sentencing. If the right to respect for private or family life interest had been engaged at that time there is no room for doubt that the open justice principle would have roundly trumped it for the reasons given in

---

224 *Yeo v Times Newspapers Ltd* [2015] EWHC 3375 (QB); [2017] EMLR 1.
225 *Axon v Ministry of Defence* [2016] EWHC 787 (QB); [2016] EMLR 20.
226 Held in that case at para 147.
227 Held in that case at paras 41–49.
228 *NT1 & NT2 v Google LLC* at para 139.
229 See the discussion in *Yeo v Times Newspapers Ltd* at paras 141–146. Warby J, at para 140.

CG v Facebook,[230] *Khuja*,[231] and *Re Trinity Mirror*[232] (above).[233] One key question in this case is how that position is affected by the passage of time.[234]

Q3: Is the data subject a minor?

19.34 The court answers no. NT1 was and has remained at all material times a mature adult with full capacity.[235]

Q4: Are the data accurate?

19.35 The court does not consider that the information has been shown to be inaccurate in any material way.[236]

Q5: Are the data relevant and not excessive? (a) Do the data relate to the working life of the data subject? (b) Does the search result link to information which is allegedly constitutes hate speech/slander/libel or similar offences in the area of expression against the complainant? (c) Is it clear that the data reflect an individual's personal opinion or do they appear to be verified fact?

19.36 The crime and punishment information is neither hate speech nor libel. It does relate to the claimant's working life and appears to be (and is) factual. The sub-questions do not, however, exhaust the factors that have a bearing on whether data are relevant or excessive. On the facts of this case, the court does not believe that anything turns on the requirement that data be not 'excessive'. No fine distinctions are to be drawn. When it comes to relevance, the question arises, 'relevant to what?' The WP 29 commentary identifies the 'overall purpose of these criteria'. It is 'to assess whether the information contained in a search result is relevant or not according to the interest of the general public in having access to the information'.[237] Relevance is 'closely related' to the age of the data, so that 'depending on the facts of the case, information that was published a long time ago eg 15 years ago, might be less relevant that information that was published 1 year ago'. The WP 29 commentary goes on to observe that:

> Data protection – and privacy law more widely – are primarily concerned with ensuring respect for the individual's fundamental right to privacy (and to data protection). Although all data relating to a person is personal data, not all data about a person is private. There is a basic distinction between a person's private life and their public or professional persona. The availability

---

230 *CG v Facebook Ireland Ltd* [2016] NICA 54; [2017] EMLR 12 [44].
231 See *Khuja v Times Newspapers Ltd*.
232 *Re Trinity Mirror plc* n 167 above at para 32 (Sir Igor Judge P).
233 See *CG v Facebook* n 231 above at para 49(4); *Khuja v Times Newspapers Ltd* at para 61 and *Re Trinity Mirror* at n 233 above at para 111.
234 *NT1 & NT2 v Google LLC* at para 140.
235 *Ibid* at para 141.
236 *Ibid* at para 142.
237 Emphasis added in judgment.

of information in a search result becomes more acceptable the less it reveals about a person's private life.[238]

Both the example and the statement of principle are pertinent in this case. The information was in the main not private, and it was relevant; its relevance has faded, but the essentially public character of most of the information has not altered. One factor is whether (as the Working Party put it) the individual data subject is 'still engaged in the same professional activity'. *NT1* is not, but he is still in business. Customers and others are affected by his activities but not consumers. His impact on the world of business and that of consumers is much reduced from what it was. Again, attention is directed to what has changed with the passage of time.[239]

Google argues two further factors in support of its case on relevance:

(i) it is said that those who deal or might deal with companies associated with *NT1* need to know about his business background, including his conviction and sentence; and

(ii) *NT1*'s social media profile shows that there is a need to correct the record. I shall return to these points when I consider criterion 13.[240]

Q6: Is the information sensitive in the meaning of Article 8 of the Directive?

19.37   The reference is to data in 'special categories' for which 'sensitive' is the English term. For practical purposes, all the information qualifies as sensitive. The significance of this is explained in the WP 29 commentary:

> As a general rule, sensitive data … has a greater impact on the data subject's private life than "ordinary" personal data. A good example would be information about a person's health, sexuality or religious beliefs.[241]

The health information in this case is not of any great weight, however it is 'out of date'. But that does not of itself demand de-listing. Not all disclosures of health data call for the same treatment. As Lady Hale said in *Campbell v MGN Ltd*,[242] [*Campbell*[243] case] 'The privacy interest in the fact that a public figure has a cold or a broken leg is unlikely to be strong enough to justify restricting the press's freedom to report it. What harm could it possibly do?' The health information in this case is different, but the same can be said. *NT1*'s evidence contains no complaint of any separate or distinct harm that is said to result from the disclosure of that information, which would surely not have been complained of in isolation. It is an incidental but integral part of the overall story.

---

238 *NT1 & NT2 v Google LLC* at para 143.
239 *Ibid*.
240 *Ibid* at para 144.
241 *Ibid* at para 145.
242 *Campbell v MGN Ltd* [2004] UKHL 22; [2004] 2 AC 457, para 157.
243 J Rowbottom, 'A Landmark at a Turning Point: Campbell and the Use of Privacy Law to Constrain Media Power' *Journal of Media Law* (2015) (7:2) 170.

It is the crime and punishment information about which there is a real issue. If the balance is struck in favour of delisting that information, it will disappear from search results and the health information will disappear with it. But the reverse would plainly be unjustifiable.[244]

Q7:Are the data up to date? Are the data being made available for longer than is necessary for the purpose of the processing?

19.38 The WP 29 identifies the objective of this criterion as ensuring that 'information that is not reasonably current and that has become inaccurate because it is out-of-date is de-listed'. The health information is out of date and in that sense inaccurate; but it is an accurate picture of the historic position and does not purport to be anything more. Its disclosure is trivial. All the crime and punishment information is historic, but it is not inaccurate. Whether that information is being made available for longer than necessary is the main issue in the case. This criterion offers no separate guidance.[245]

Q8: Is the data processing causing prejudice to the data subject? Do the data have a disproportionately negative privacy impact on the data subject?

19.39 The CJEU made clear in *Google Spain* that the claimant in a delisting case does not need to prove prejudice (or harm, as the court calls it). But it is not controversial that, as the WP 29 commentary puts it, 'where there is evidence that the availability of a search result is causing prejudice to the data subject, this would be a strong factor in favour of de-listing'. WP 29 identifies the criterion for justified objection that appears in the DPD 95/46 Article 14(a) (origin of the DPA 1998 s 10): 'compelling legitimate grounds relating to his particular situation'. An example is given, which does not fit the present case, but has 'some relevance':

> The [processing of the] data might have a disproportionately negative impact on the Data Subject where a search result relates to a trivial or foolish misdemeanour which is no longer – or may never have been – the subject of public debate and where there is no wider public interest in the availability of the information.[246]

The instant court adds the words in brackets, as they 'must be implied'. It adds that '[i]nformation does not harm a person, only what is done with it'.[247]

The claimant's case on harm is pleaded in paragraph 12 of his particulars of claim and the evidence of harm is to be found in his witness statement.[248]

244 *NT1 & NT2 v Google LLC* at para 145.
245 *Ibid* at para 146.
246 *Ibid* at para 147.
247 *Ibid*.
248 *Ibid* at para 148.

There are no other statements, nor is there any other evidence of harm.[249]

The evidence does not reveal how many searches have been or are being made using the claimant's name.[250]

No allegation as to the extent of disclosure was made in the particulars of claim and nobody seems to have thought of investigating the issue.[251]

Paragraph 12 of the particulars of claim alleges that the processing has caused the claimant 'substantial damage and distress' under three main headings.[252]

(1)   Treatment as a pariah in his personal, business and social life with a consequent significant effect on his previously outgoing personality. He is said to live 'in fear that anyone he does meet will inevitably look him up using the defendant's search engine and subsequently and as a result shun him'[253];

(2)   Threats made in public places by 'people referring to the content still linked by the defendant's search engine and seeking to extract money from him in consequence'[254];

(3)   Disruption of his family life by the effect of the defendant's search engine results. *NT1* says that his wife has become withdrawn and insecure and faced questions from her friends about the search results. 'This in turn has affected adversely the quality of the claimant's personal, private and family relationships with each of his children and his wife.'[255]

Some further information is provided in the confidential schedule to the particulars of claim. This reiterate the above and provide some elaboration. As counsel for *NT1* points out, none of this was challenged in cross-examination, but that does not prevent the court from making its own assessment of the evidence. Adopting the criterion specified in the DPD 95/46 Article 14(a), the court finds that the claimant's case on harm is for the most part legitimate, though not entirely so; it is not, overall, particularly compelling.[256]

There are causation issues. The relevant harm is that which is being or will be caused by the processing which the claimant seeks to prevent. He cannot place any great weight on harm which would result in any event. So this, it seems to me, is one context in which the court needs to consider Google's 'public domain' argument: the issue of harm needs to be considered in light of the fact that the information in question will continue to be available on the source websites and

---

249 *Ibid.*
250 *Ibid.*
251 *Ibid.*
252 *Ibid* at para 149.
253 *Ibid* at para 149(1).
254 *Ibid* at para 149(2).
255 *Ibid* at para 149(3).
256 *Ibid* at para 150.

in a number of other locations on the internet. The court is not overly impressed by this argument. Accessibility is not the same thing as actual access. The CJEU was surely right to point out in *Google Spain* that information distribution via ISEs is inherently different from and more harmful than publication via source websites. The reality is that few are likely to locate the crime and punishment information otherwise than through a search engine.[257]

That raises the question of what a Google search on the claimant's name would look like if the three URLs complained of were removed. Nobody has led evidence on that issue.[258]

However, the court infers from a search in mid-February 2018 that are in evidence, that the other third-party websites would not feature on the first two pages of a search. That said, it is also true that *NT1* cannot rely on any harm that results from legitimate processing in the past. His witness statement concedes 'up to a point the fact of my conviction is to blame' for the harm to personal and professional relationships of which he complains. It is not just that his own conduct is one cause of that harm. Many will have got to know the crime and punishment information as a result of earlier, legitimate, communication via Google or otherwise, at a time when the conviction was not spent. This is particularly true of pre-existing contacts, both business and personal.[259]

This is, according to the court, pertinent when it considers the evidence in support of the pleaded complaint of 'threats'. The only evidence relates to incidents when *NT1* was in prison, serving his sentence and some incidents shortly after he was released. This is all significantly more than 15 years ago, well over a decade before *NT1*'s first complaint, and over seven years before his conviction became spent. This is significant harm, the court states, but it cannot count as harm that resulted from any illegitimate processing by Google.[260]

Nor, the court states, can the only specific incident recounted by *NT1* in which a business deal was expressly hindered by the counterparty's knowledge of his conviction. This was some nine years ago and, as *NT1* acknowledges, this was before the conviction became spent. There is evidence that two bank accounts were closed in 2013. *NT1*, in a single sentence, attributes this to the availability of information about the conviction. That may be so, but the bank did not say so, there has been no disclosure nor any other evidence about the matter, and I am unable to draw that inference. The other evidence of business harm is vague. There are no names, dates, or details. *NT1*'s evidence is that he has not been offered employment since he left prison. But he does not say that he has applied for employment and the court does not consider that it would be justified in drawing the inference that his lack of an employed job, as opposed to self-employment, is due to processing by Google since the conviction became spent.

---

257 *Ibid* at para 151.
258 *Ibid*.
259 *Ibid*.
260 *Ibid* at para 152.

The court would accept that knowledge of the claimant's conviction has affected his business life to some degree, and the continued availability of the crime and punishment information since the conviction may have had some impact. In the end, it is really impossible to reach a conclusion on the evidence before me that this aspect of his life has been significantly prejudiced by the continued availability of the crime and punishment information via Google search in recent years.[261]

The court turns to the claimant's private and family life. The evidence that he has been 'treated as a pariah' in his social life is entirely general in nature. It amounts to little more than a reiteration of the pleaded case. No specific incidents of any kind are recounted, despite the lengthy period with which we are concerned. The position is similar so far as the claimant's evidence about the impact on his family life is concerned. Indeed, it is less satisfactory. No specific mention is made of the claimant's wife, so the evidence falls short of the pleading. The evidence consists largely of generalities about the impact on the claimant's adult children, and the effect on him of their distress. Details of specific incidents or even of the nature of the impact are lacking. As counsel for *NT1* acknowledges, impacts on relationships with adult children who are not part of the claimant's household do not engage 'family life' within Article 8; in this context, '… neither blood ties nor the concern and affection that ordinarily go with them are, by themselves or together, in my judgment enough to constitute family life'.[262] The impact on the rights of persons other than the claimant is a legitimate consideration, when assessing the legitimacy of a communication. The claimant's distress at the impact on others or 'reflexive' distress is also a legitimate head of harm, properly to be considered under the heading of interference with his private life. But the absence of statements from any of the family members themselves is surprising. It is well established that where a party seeking to restrain freedom of expression wishes the court to give weight to the impact on others, he will generally be expected to adduce evidence from those others or explain why such evidence is not before the court.[263]

Standing back from the detail, a substantial part of the claimant's evidence and, in my judgment, a major part of his concern, about the continued availability of this information is business related. But much of this is of some age; the evidence is for the most part general; and there are real causation issues. The court accepts that the continued availability of the information via Google Search in recent years has had some impact on the claimant's private life. But much of that impact will inevitably have been felt as a result of earlier, legitimate communications.[264]

As for the present and future, the impact appears to be mainly consequential on the impact on the feelings of the claimant and his family of the fact that the crime

---

261 *Ibid* at para 153.
262 *Kugathas v Secretary of State for the Home Department* [2003] EWCA Civ 31 para 19 (Sedley LJ) paras 30–31 (Simon Brown LJ).
263 *YXB v TNO* [2015] EWHC 826 (QB) para 18; *NT1 & NT2 v Google LLC* at para 154.
264 *NT1 & NT2 v Google LLC* at para 155.

and punishment information is 'out there', available to anybody who searches for the claimant's name. There is clearly a real concern that the claimant and his family will be shunned and avoided by those who, now and in the future, come to learn via Google of his crime and punishment. That is a 'natural and reasonable concern' given the nature of the information. It can easily be inferred that some adverse impact of that kind will result. However, the fact remains that there is nothing concrete to which the claimant can point. There is no corroborative evidence from the family members whom the claimant prays in aid; and there are again causation issues.[265]

In short, the instant case is not closely comparable to the illustration given by the WP 29 and the evidence of harm or 'prejudice' does not add great weight to the case in favour of delisting.[266]

Q9: Does the search result link to information that puts the data subject at risk?

19.40   The court answers no.[267]

Q10: What context was the information published? (a) Content voluntarily made public by the data subject? (b) Intended to be made public? Could data subject have reasonably known the content would be made public?

19.41   The WP 29 commentary on this criterion focuses on consent, suggesting that if this was the only justification for the original processing, revocation may make delisting appropriate. Those considerations are not directly relevant in the instant case. The claimant did not consent and the initial publication had a different justification. But it is relevant that the information was published in the national media, in substantially fair and accurate reporting of legal proceedings held in public and related reporting which has not been shown to be inaccurate. Both the legal proceedings and their media coverage were both foreseeable results of the dishonest criminal conduct in which the claimant deliberately engaged. Again, one is brought back to the question of what has changed with the passage of time.[268]

One factor that the court expressly does not consider this claimant can legitimately argue is any legitimate expectation of rehabilitation, enjoyed when he left prison. His witness statement asserts that 'When I left prison, I looked towards completing my rehabilitation and being able to start over. I understood that the law recognises this, in that my conviction would eventually become "spent" (which it did on …) …' He was not challenged about this, but it cannot be true – unless he misunderstood the law or had a crystal ball. As explained above if the law had remained as it stood when *NT1* left prison, his conviction would

---

265 *Ibid.*
266 *Ibid.*
267 *Ibid* at para 156.
268 *Ibid* at para 157.

never have become spent. He cannot have had any legitimate expectation that this would occur until the changes wrought by LASPO came into effect, which was well over a decade after he left prison.[269]

Q11: Was the original content published in the context of journalistic purposes?

19.42   Yes, though NT1 submits that the Book Extract is for advertising purposes. This issue has received little attention and I treat the information as journalistic in its origin and at least predominantly journalistic in its overall character. 'The fact that information is published by a journalist whose job is to inform the public is a factor to weigh in the balance' states the WP 29 commentary.[270]

It is a factor of some weight, the court states, in particular because of the subject-matter: crime and related legal proceedings. The fact that the information is a media report of that kind is not of itself enough, because *Google Spain* 'clearly distinguishes between the legal basis for publication by the media, and the legal basis for search engines to organise search results based on a person's name'.[271]

Q12: Does the publisher of the data have a legal power – or a legal obligation – to make the personal data publicly available?

19.43   There is no obligation, according to the court. The question of whether the publishers have a legal power to continue publishing has not been debated. It is no part of NT1's case that it does not. A delisting claim does not require a claimant to advance or establish such a contention. That is clear from *Google Spain*. It is common ground in the instant case that the newspaper publisher has received and rejected a complaint and that no proceedings have been brought against it. It is to be assumed that the publisher will continue to make the information publicly available on its website and would be entitled to do so. The court also takes into account that access to the information is and will continue to be available via a number of other websites.[272]

Q13: Do the data relate to a criminal offence?

19.44   This, in the court's view, is the single most important criterion in the present case.

The WP 29 commentary states as follows:

> EU Member States may have different approaches as to the public availability of information about offenders and their offences. Specific legal provisions may exist which have an impact on the availability of such information over time. [Data protection supervisory authorities] will handle such cases in

269 *Ibid* at para 158.
270 *Ibid* at para 159.
271 *Ibid*.
272 *Ibid* at para 160.

accordance with the relevant national principles and approaches. As a rule, [data protection supervisory authorities] are more likely to consider the de-listing of search results relating to relatively minor offences that happened a long time ago, whilst being less likely to consider the de-listing of results relating to more serious ones that happened more recently. However, these issues call for careful consideration and will be handled on a case-by-case basis.[273]

A review of the rehabilitation laws of Member States conducted by Google's solicitors, Pinsent Masons, was presented before the court. It suggests that there is a diversity of approach across the EU. The existence of a rehabilitation law of some kind would appear to be universal, but there seem to be a variety of methods and criteria for establishing when a given conviction should become spent, and some differences in the consequences when it does. The methods include rehabilitation based on sentence, the passage of time and individual judicial assessment. The review is at a high level of generality and has been subject to some mild criticism by *NT1*'s counsel. It is not admissible evidence of foreign law. What is clear, however, is that the WP 29 considered it to be consistent with *Google Spain* for individual jurisdictions to apply their own domestic rehabilitation laws, even if these diverge from those of other Member States. That is consistent with the margin of appreciation afforded to states when implementing the DPD 95/46, the Convention and Charter. National laws must be interpreted and applied consistently with those instruments. But no party in the instant case suggests that there is any single, transnational, rule or set of rules to which resort can be had to provide an answer in this context. With that in mind, the court suggests following WP 29's guidance by identifying the relevant domestic principles and applying them to the particular facts of this case.[274]

The starting point, the court indicates, must be the 1974 Act. The high point of the claimant's case, as presented by counsel, is couched in the language of section 4 of the 1974 Act. In the opening it was submitted that the claimant 'is entitled to be treated for all purposes as a person who has not committed or been charged with or prosecuted for or convicted of or sentenced for the offence or offences which were the subject of' the conviction. *NT1* must be right when he relies on section 4 to show that there is a strong public policy in favour of the rehabilitation of criminal offenders. The ICO offers some support for that approach, submitting that the public policy principle underpinning the Act is that 'once a criminal has served his or her time, it is important that the ability of that individual to rehabilitate themselves is not unduly prejudiced'. But the ICO does not go all the way with *NT1*'s opening submission.[275]

In the ICO submission, in a delisting case involving a spent conviction, it would be wrong automatically to assume that the balance tips in favour of continued indexation or alternatively in favour of de-indexation.[276]

---

273 *Ibid* at para 161.
274 *Ibid* at para 162.
275 *Ibid* at para 163.
276 *Ibid*.

Rather, the ICO suggests, each case must turn on its own individual facts, albeit that 'the fact that the conviction is spent ought generally to weigh heavily in the balance in favour of de-indexing the relevant website'. By the end of the trial, *NT1* had adopted that line of argument. His case is that 'the fact that a conviction is spent is not determinative' but it is weighty.[277]

Google acknowledges that the fact that the claimant's conviction is spent is a relevant factor. But it argues that for a variety of reasons it carries relatively little weight on the particular facts of the case. As a fall-back from its 'abuse of process' argument,[278] Google relies on section 8 of the 1974 Act as an important statement of Parliamentary policy which points in the opposite direction from section 4 and, it argues, is weighty in this instant case. That submission is resisted by *NT1* and the ICO, on the basis that section 8 is irrelevant given that this is not a claim for libel or slander (defamation).[279]

Behind the competing submissions lie some 'obvious difficulties'. It is not a simple matter of applying section 4 of the 1974 Act without regard to other factor or considerations. Such a hard-edged approach would be incompatible with human rights jurisprudence and the fact-sensitive approach that is 'required'. The argument for the ICO, and the argument with which *NT1* ended up, acknowledge that much.[280]

The court's task according to the judgment is to:

- interpret and apply the will of Parliament as expressed in a statute passed some 25 years before the advent of the internet, to a set of facts of a kind that Parliament cannot then have foreseen;

- to do so consistently with the will of Parliament as expressed via the HRA in 1998; and

- to do so in the light of the fact that it was not until 2004 that the courts identified the existence of the common law tort of misuse of private information;

- the conclusions arrived at then have to be fitted into the scheme of RtbF, first authoritatively recognised in a CJEU judgment of 2014 by which this court is bound, by reason of the 1972 Act.[281]

Without attempting to be exhaustive, the court arrived for the purposes of these instant cases, at the following 'reconciliation':

(1) The right to rehabilitation is an aspect of the law of personal privacy. The rights and interests protected include the right to reputation and the right to respect for family life and private life, including unhindered social

---

277 *Ibid*.
278 At paras 58–60 of the judgment above.
279 *NT1 & NT2 v Google LLC* [2018] EWHC 799 (QB) (13 April 2018) Warby J, at para 164.
280 *Ibid* at para 165.
281 *Ibid*.

interaction with others. Upholding the right also tends to support a public or societal interest in the rehabilitation of offenders. But the right is not unqualified. It will inevitably come into conflict with other rights, most notably the rights of others to freedom of information and freedom of expression. It is not just legitimate but clearly helpful for Parliament to lay down rules which clearly prescribe the point at which a given conviction is to be treated as spent. But such rules, depending simply on the offender's age and the nature and length of the sentence, can only afford a blunt instrument. Parliament has legislated for exceptions, but these cannot be treated as necessarily exhaustive of the circumstances in which information about a spent conviction may be disclosed. More subtle tools are needed, if the court is to comply with its duty under the HRA to interpret and apply the law compatibly with the Convention. Section 4 of the 1974 Act must be read down accordingly as expressing a legal policy or principle;[282]

(2) The starting point, in respect of information disclosed in legal proceedings held in public, is that a person will not enjoy a reasonable expectation of privacy.[283] But there may come a time when they do. As a general rule (or 'rule of thumb,' to adopt the language of the WP 29), the point in time at which Parliament has determined that a conviction should become spent may be regarded as the point when the convict's Article 8 rights are engaged by any use or disclosure of information about the crime, conviction, or sentence.[284] But this does not mean that in 1974 Parliament enacted a right to confidentiality or privacy from that point on.[285] Still less does it follow that the convict's Article 8 rights are of preponderant weight, when placed in the balance. As a matter of principle, the fact that the conviction is spent will normally be a weighty factor against the further use or disclosure of information about those matters, in ways other than those specifically envisaged by Parliament. The starting point, after all, is the general policy or principle in favour of that information being 'forgotten' as expressed in section 4 of the 1974 Act. That policy has if anything become weightier over time. It is likely that in many cases the particular circumstances of the individual offender will support the application of that general principle to his or her case. But the specific rights asserted by the individual concerned will still need to be evaluated and weighed against any competing free speech or freedom of information considerations, or other relevant factors, that may arise in the particular case;[286]

(3) Part of this balancing exercise will involve an assessment of the nature and extent of any actual or prospective harm. If the use or disclosure causes, or is likely to cause, serious or substantial interference with private or family life that will tend to add weight to the case for applying the general rule. But where the claim relies or depends to a significant extent upon harm to

---

282 *Ibid* at para 166(1).
283 *Khuja v Times Newspapers Ltd* at para 61 above.
284 See *T*, para 49(2) above.
285 *L v The Law Society*, [2010] EWCA Civ 811 [2] (Sir Anthony Clarke MR) paras 47–48.
286 *Ibid* at para 166(2).

reputation, the court is in my judgment bound to have regard to section 8 of the 1974 Act. It is possible to identify a public policy that underlies that section, and which qualifies the public policy that underpins section 4. It is that offenders whose convictions are spent should not be able to obtain remedies for injury to their reputation (or consequent injury to feelings) resulting from the publication in good faith of accurate information about the spent conviction, or the related offending, prosecution or sentence. It is not a satisfactory answer to this point to say that the causes of action relied on are not libel or slander, but data protection and/or misuse of private information. That is too narrow and technical an approach, which ignores the fact that neither course of action was known to Parliament when it legislated. The fact that, as the court accepts, reputational harm can support a claim under those causes of action tends, in fact, to undermine the force of that argument. I therefore do not accept that the policy that underlies s 8 falls to be disregarded merely because the claim is not framed in defamation. Again, there can be no bright line, because Convention jurisprudence shows that reputational harm can be of such a kind or severity as to engage Article 8;[287] but subject to considerations of that kind I would consider that this statutory policy or principle falls to be applied by the court;[288]

(4) Another aspect of the proportionality assessment will be the nature and quality of the societal benefits to be gained in the individual case by the use or disclosure in question. Freedom of expression has an inherent value, but it also has instrumental benefits which may be weak or strong according to the facts of the case. The fact that the information is, by its very nature, old will play a part at this stage also;[289]

(5) Most, if not all, of these points about spent convictions are likely to be relevant in more than one context. Where a spent conviction is the subject of a de-listing claim, the court will need to weave its evaluation according to domestic principles into the overall *Google Spain* balancing exercise. The WP 29 criteria are a key tool for this purpose. One matter that the ICO rightly identifies as needing due weight at this stage is fact that de-indexation does not *per se* remove the source websites containing the relevant data from the online environment. It merely makes that data harder for the public to find.[290]

In this case, the following factors from the domestic legal context would appear to be of some importance. First, *NT1*'s case lies at the very outer limit of the statutory scheme. Thanks to the LASPO amendments, since March 2014 his case has been positioned on the very cusp of the scheme. His sentence was such that, if it had been one day longer under the law as it stood from 1974 to 2014, it would never have become spent. Moreover, the fact that the sentence qualifies for rehabilitation is advantageous? The sentencing remarks make clear that the sentence would have been longer but for a matter of personal mitigation, which

287 *Yeo v Times Newspapers Ltd* at para 140.
288 *NT1 & NT2 v Google LLC* at para 166(3).
289 *Ibid* at para 166(4).
290 *Ibid* at para 166(5).

had no bearing on culpability and no longer applies. Secondly, *NT1*'s case on harm is not especially compelling. It is largely to do with harm to reputation. The policy of the 1974 Act militates against granting a remedy to prevent harm of that kind. There is, of course, no question of Google acting maliciously. Factors that might prevail over the statutory policy are absent. Much of the evidence of harm is to do with harm to business reputation and business activity. This does not engage Article 8. The claimant's case on interference with family life is very weak; his case on interference with private life is not strong.[291]

On the other side of the equation, the court would accept Google's argument on relevance, to this extent. For a period of time after the date on which *NT1*'s conviction is to be treated as spent, it has been of some relevance to a limited number of people with whom this claimant had business dealings to know about his dishonest criminal past; there were people who had a legitimate interest in having that knowledge in order to make informed decisions about dealing with him. His criminal past was also relevant, during that period, to anybody who read or might read the blog and social media postings which the claimant, via Cleanup, put out about himself. Those postings were false or misleading. It was quite unnecessary, to achieve the claimant's stated objective of demoting the offending URLs, to put forward such clear and gross misrepresentations of his business history and his actual or reputed integrity. The fact that the claimant took down the posts after Google served a defence relying on the misrepresentations they contained, is telling. The inference the court draws is that he was reacting to what, having taken legal advice, he saw as a criticism of some merit. His attempts to offer other explanations were unconvincing. The continued accessibility of substantially fair and accurate information to the contrary served the legitimate purpose of correcting the record. These purposes might perhaps have been served by means other than making the information available via Google or another ISE, but it is not easy to see how.[292]

That said, *NT1* has a point when he argues that, if there was ever any need for anyone to know these matters for these reasons, it has been met, because HMRC know about it all, and the information has been available to others via Google. The issue that is relevant to the delisting claim is whether, even if the information ever was relevant in these ways, its relevance has now been exhausted. *NT1* argues that it has. I am not so sure. A number of factors seem to me in combination to make the crime and punishment information of some continuing relevance to the public's assessment of the claimant. His conviction was for serious dishonesty, on a substantial scale. He has very obvious difficulties in acknowledging his guilt, as opposed to the fact of his conviction. The court's assessment is that he does not consider himself to have been guilty and that the conviction and the sentence both still rankle with him. He has not persuaded me that it was inaccurate to implicate him in the further fraud of which others were convicted. In recent years, he has engaged in crude attempts to re-write history, via his blog and social media postings. The content was clearly misleading, and he approved it. He was initially

291 *Ibid* at para 167.
292 *Ibid* at para 168.

evasive and at all times quite unapologetic about this. The court found him to be an unreliable witness, whose evidence was not always honest. He remains in business, dealing with large sums. He is not, in that respect, by any means a recluse. It may be that delisting would not present a risk to the public revenue but the dangers do not in my judgment end there. The court accepts Google's submission that the claimant's conduct, including his evasive and dishonest conduct in the witness box, demonstrates that he cannot be trusted to provide an accurate account of his business background or credentials to those with whom he comes into contact in the course of business now and in the future.[293]

Overall Assessment

19.45   The court refers to the key conclusions it has reached.

Around the turn of the century, *NT1* was a public figure with a limited role in public life. His role has changed such that he now plays only a limited role in public life as a businessman not dealing with consumers. That said, he still plays such a role. The crime and punishment information is not information of a private nature. It was information about business crime, its prosecution and its punishment. It was and is essentially public in its character. *NT1* did not enjoy any reasonable expectation of privacy in respect of the information at the time of his prosecution, conviction and sentence.[294]

The court's conclusion is that he is not entitled to have it delisted now. It has not been shown to be inaccurate in any material way. It relates to his business life, not his personal life. It is sensitive information and he has identified some legitimate grounds for delisting it. But he has failed to produce any compelling evidence in support of those grounds. Much of the harm complained of is business-related and some of it pre-dates the time when he can legitimately complain of Google's processing of the information. His Article 8 private life rights are now engaged, but do not attract any great weight. The information originally appeared in the context of crime and court reporting in the national media, which was a natural and foreseeable result of the claimant's own criminal behaviour. The information is historic and the domestic law of rehabilitation is engaged. But that is only so at the margins. The sentence on this claimant was of such a length that at the time he had no reasonable expectation that his conviction would ever be spent. The law has changed, but if the sentence had been any longer, the conviction would still not be spent. It would have been longer but for personal mitigation that has no bearing on culpability. His business career since leaving prison made the information relevant in the past to the assessment of his honesty by members of the public. The information retains sufficient relevance today. He has not accepted his guilt, has misled the public and this court, and shows no remorse over any of these matters. He remains in business, and the information serves the purpose of minimising the risk that he will continue to mislead, as he has in the

293 *Ibid* at para 169.
294 *Ibid* at para 170.

past. Delisting would not erase the information from the record altogether, but it would make it much harder to find. 'The case for delisting is not made out.'[295]

8 THE *MISUSE ISSUES*

A Reasonable Expectation of Privacy?

19.46   The court's conclusion on this and the next issue have already been substantially identified. The information at issue is public not private in nature. At the time of his prosecution, conviction and sentence Article 8 was not engaged and the claimant had no reasonable expectation of privacy. That has changed with the passage of time, the fact that recent amendment of the 1974 Act has made his conviction spent and the impact on his private life of the continued accessibility of the crime and punishment information.[296]

Although the claimant's main concern is reputation, and primarily business reputation, there is enough to engage Article 8. Whether the claimant enjoys a reasonable expectation of privacy in respect of the information is, the court believes, a separate question, which it would answer in the negative. The reasons are said to come into play at the next stage.[297]

Striking the Balance

19.47   The court continues and suggests that assuming that it is wrong in the conclusion just stated above, it finds that the result of the In *re S* balancing process is the same as that of the *Google Spain* process. The impact on the claimant's business reputation of the continued accessibility of the crime and punishment information is not such as to engage Article 8. The evidence fails to establish any material interference with his right to respect for family life. The court is not persuaded that there is anything more than a modest interference with his private life. The information has been legitimately available for many years. It continued to be relevant to the assessment of the claimant by members of the public, after the conviction became spent, by reason of his business activities. The information has continued relevance in view of the claimant's continued role in business, in conjunction with his past dishonesty, failure to acknowledge guilt, and his misstatements to the public and this court.[298]

Delisting would very significantly impede, even if it would not altogether block, public access to that information in respect of an untrustworthy businessman who poses some risk to the public.[299]

---

295 *Ibid.*
296 *Ibid* at para 171.
297 *Ibid.*
298 *Ibid* at para 172.
299 *Ibid.*

The Article 8 factors do not have sufficient weight to make that interference a proportionate response. Looked at from the opposite perspective, the interference with Article 8 that continued processing by Google represents is justified by, and proportionate to, the factors that favour the Article 10 right to receive information in this case. Having reached these conclusions it is not necessary to address, in this context, Google's submission that the processing complained of does not qualify as a 'misuse' of private information.[300]

9 DAMAGES

19.48 Since the court has found Google's continued processing to be justified according to the *Google Spain* test, 'there is no basis for any award of compensation under [the DPA 1998] s[ection] 13'. No damage has been suffered 'by reason of any contravention … of this Act'. It is not necessary to evaluate Google's defence under section 13(3). The court suggests that in that connection that it might have found Ms C's (of Google) evidence helpful. Nor can any question arise of damages for misuse of private information.[301]

There is growing discussion as regards internet torts, remedies, liability and monetary redress.[302]

10 OVERALL CONCLUSIONS IN *NT1*

19.49 The conclusions in the NT1 case are that:

(1) The delisting claim is not an abuse of the court's process, as alleged by Google.

(2) The inaccuracy complaint is dismissed. The first article was a substantially fair and accurate report of legal proceedings held in public. The second article was not, but the claimant has failed to prove that the information in the second article was inaccurate in any material respect. Similar conclusions apply to the similar information in the book extract.

(3) The remainder of the delisting claim is also dismissed.

(4) The claim for misuse of private information fails.

(5) The claims for compensation or damages do not arise.[303]

While this decision is much more extensive, one wonders whether it will receive critical review over time, in light of the decision in *Google Spain*, the GDPR RtbF and whether it was overly critical and set too high a bar for the claimant. For

300 *Ibid.*
301 *Ibid* at para 173.
302 Mizrahi, 'Ontario's New Invasion of Privacy Torts: Do They Offer Monetary Redress for Violations Suffered Via the Internet of Things?' above at 37.
303 *NT1 & NT2 v Google LLC* at para 229.

example, RtbF is already part of a rebalancing given the growing power and potential of permanence and global reach. Some may query whether some or all of the decision against the claimant was fully fair on all points or introduced additional legal hurdles (such as defamation) to RtbF considerations which may not have been considered part of *Google Spain*. A further consideration may be the strong reliance in the decision on strong evidence of family-type harm, which was not apparently required in *Google Spain*. Significant emphasis was placed on the spent convictions legislation – which is complex in and of itself.[304] However, there may be merit in suggesting that it may have been overanalysed and that RtbF matters can proceed without or regardless of such consideration. For instance, a very old conviction referred to online should be, at least in some instances, amendable to a successful RtbF notice (and order) regardless of any spent convictions legislation. This point would seem to be even stronger the more minor the conviction in question. Claimants may also query whether there was an overly strict interpretation referred to in terms of requiring harm or actual harm, what harm is sufficient to ground a successful RtbF ruling and what harm is not sufficient.

It has been indicated that '[t]he intention of [the] decision in not allowing NT1 the de-listing order … was that the claimant was still putting out false and misleading statements in his business dealings, that he had remained in the same business as before, that he had failed to acknowledge his guilt and above all, that he had not shown sufficient remorse'.[305]

On balance, it remains to be seen how much can be generalised from the unsuccessful *NT1* decision. In any event, the GDPR RtbF has gone live since the decision was announced. It should also be noted that this also relates to criminal convictions, as opposed to non-criminal matters or other legal matters. It may also be that RtbF notices of this nature are a smaller subset of the total number of notices filed – the majority of which may be successful – without the need for contentious litigation. The majority of notices will not depend on how one comes across in a witness box.

Also, '[t]he judgments in *NT1*, *NT2* and *AR*[306] reveal inconsistencies in police practices and the interpretation of the Rehabilitation of Offenders Act 1974 in relation to what should and should not be disclosed after a person has been acquitted or whether a conviction has been spent. For the time being the right to be forgotten on internet search engines remains unclear and open to many legal challenges'.[307]

---

304 See, eg, discussion in U Smartt, 'The Three Rs: Remorse, Rehibilitation, Right to be Forgotten: How De-listing is Left Up to the Courts in *NT1* & *NT2* and *AR v Chief Constable of Greater Manchester*' European Intellectual Property Review (2018) (40:12) 803.

305 *Ibid*, at 808.

306 *AR v Chief Constable of Greater Manchester* [2018] UKSC 47 (on appeal from [2016] EWCA Civ 490).

307 Smartt, 'The Three Rs: Remorse, Rehibilitation, Right to be Forgotten: How De-listing is Left Up to the Courts in *NT1* & *NT2* and *AR v Chief Constable of Greater Manchester*' above at 810.

CHAPTER 20

ICO and the RtbF

I INTRODUCTION

20.1   The Information Commissioner's Office (ICO) has issued guidance in relation to RtbF and also dealt with a number of complaint cases where individuals have not been satisfied with the response from the respective service providers. As we can see from the *NT1* and *NT2* cases, we also know that the ICO became an intervenor in the cases and made submissions to the court and rebutted some of the assertion or claims of the respective online search provider.

2 GUIDANCE

20.2   The ICO has issued guidance for organisations to consider. This includes a checklist (see below). The guidance[1] summarises matters as follows:

- the GDPR introduces a right for individuals to have personal data erased;

- the right to erasure is also known as 'the right to be forgotten';

- individuals can make a request for erasure verbally or in writing;

- an organisation will have one month to respond to a request;

- the right is not absolute and only applies in certain circumstances; and

- this right is not the only way in which the GDPR places an obligation on you to consider whether to delete personal data.[2]

The guidance advises that individuals have the right to have their personal data erased if:

- the personal data is no longer necessary for the purpose which it was originally collected or processed it for;

- the company is relying on consent as its lawful basis for holding the data, and the individual withdraws their consent;

---

1   ICO, Right to Erasure. Available at: https://ico.org.uk/for-organisations/guide-to-data-protection/guide-to-the-general-data-protection-regulation-gdpr/individual-rights/right-to-erasure/.
2   *Ibid.*

- the company is relying on legitimate interests as its basis for processing, the individual objects to the processing of their data, and there is no overriding legitimate interest to continue this processing;

- the company is processing the personal data for direct marketing purposes and the individual objects to that processing;

- the company has processed the personal data unlawfully (ie, in breach of the lawfulness requirement of the first principle of data protection);

- the company must do it to comply with a legal obligation; or

- the company has processed the personal data to offer information society services to a child.[3]

3 CHILDREN

20.3   The guidance states that:

> There is an emphasis on the right to have personal data erased if the request relates to data collected from children. This reflects the enhanced protection of children's information, especially in online environments, under the GDPR.

> Therefore, if you process data collected from children, you should give particular weight to any request for erasure if the processing of the data is based upon consent given by a child – especially any processing of their personal data on the internet. This is still the case when the data subject is no longer a child, because a child may not have been fully aware of the risks involved in the processing at the time of consent.[4]

Note also that the court in *NT1* and *NT2* referred to the possibility of capacity or incapacity of an adult as also being a relevant factor.

The ICO also refers to RtbF when it refers to the rights of children in relation to their data.[5]

---

3   *Ibid.*
4   *Ibid.*
5   'What Rights Do Children Have,' ICO, at https://ico.org.uk/for-organisations/guide-to-data-protection/guide-to-the-general-data-protection-regulation-gdpr/children-and-the-uk-gdpr/what-rights-do-children-have/. Also 'How Does The Right to Erasure Apply to Children?' ICO, at https://ico.org.uk/for-organisations/guide-to-data-protection/guide-to-the-general-data-protection-regulation-gdpr/children-and-the-uk-gdpr/how-does-the-right-to-erasure-apply-to-children/.

The ICO also refers to RtbF when referring to the following, namely, consent issues,[6] right of access,[7] the ADISA asset recovery standard,[8] technology issues,[9] right to have data deleted,[10] and right to erasure.[11]

4 ONWARD NOTIFICATIONS

20.4 In terms of follow on notification, the guidance states that:

> The GDPR specifies two circumstances where you should tell other organisations about the erasure of personal data:
>
> • the personal data has been disclosed to others; or
>
> • the personal data has been made public in an online environment (eg, on social networks, forums or websites).
>
> If you have disclosed the personal data to others, you must contact each recipient and inform them of the erasure, unless this proves impossible or involves disproportionate effort. If asked to, you must also inform the individuals about these recipients.
>
> The GDPR defines a recipient as a natural or legal person, public authority, agency or other body to which the personal data are disclosed. The definition includes controllers, processors and persons who, under the direct authority of the controller or processor, are authorised to process personal data.
>
> Where personal data has been made public in an online environment reasonable steps should be taken to inform other controllers who are processing the personal data to erase links to, copies or replication of that data. When deciding what steps are reasonable, you should take into account available technology and the cost of implementation.[12]

5 BACKUPS

20.5 The ICO also comments on whether companies must delete back-up data. It states that:

6   'Why Is Consent Important?' ICO, at https://ico.org.uk/for-organisations/guide-to-data-protection/guide-to-the-general-data-protection-regulation-gdpr/consent/why-is-consent-important/.

7   'Right of Access / Subject Access Requests and Other Rights,' ICO, at https://ico.org.uk/for-organisations/sme-web-hub/frequently-asked-questions/right-of-accesssubject-access-requests-and-other-rights/.

8   At   https://ico.org.uk/for-organisations/sme-web-hub/frequently-asked-questions/right-of-accesssubject-access-requests-and-other-rights/.

9   'Technology, Trust and Slippers With Torches,' ICO, at https://ico.org.uk/about-the-ico/news-and-events/trust-technology-and-slippers-with-torches/.

10 'Your Right to Get Your Data Deleted,' ICO, at https://ico.org.uk/your-data-matters/your-right-to-get-your-data-deleted/.

11 'Right to Erasure,' ICO, at https://ico.org.uk/for-organisations/guide-to-data-protection/guide-to-the-general-data-protection-regulation-gdpr/individual-rights/right-to-erasure/.

12 *Ibid.*

If a valid erasure request is received and no exemption applies, then you will have to take steps to ensure erasure from backup systems as well as live systems. Those steps will depend on your particular circumstances, your retention schedule (particularly in the context of its backups) and the technical mechanisms that are available to you.

You must be absolutely clear with individuals as to what will happen to their data when their erasure request is fulfilled, including in respect of backup systems.

It may be that the erasure request can be instantly fulfilled in respect of live systems, but that the data will remain within the backup environment for a certain period of time until it is overwritten.

The key issue is to put the backup data "beyond use", even if it cannot be immediately overwritten. You must ensure that you do not use the data within the backup for any other purpose (ie, that the backup is simply held on your systems until it is replaced in line with an established schedule). Provided this is the case it may be unlikely that the retention of personal data within the backup would pose a significant risk, although this will be context specific. For more information on what we mean by "putting data beyond use" see our old guidance under the 1998 Act on deleting personal data (this will be updated in due course).[13]

ICO CHECKLISTS

20.6   The ICO checklist content is set out below.[14]

Preparing for RtbF notices

1	Confirm the company knows how to recognise a request for erasure and we understand when the right applies.	
2	Confirm the company has a policy for how to record requests we receive verbally.	
3	Confirm the company understands when we can refuse a request and are aware of the information we need to provide to individuals when we do so.	

Complying with RtbF requests

1	Confirm the company has processes in place to ensure that we respond to a request for erasure without undue delay and within one month of receipt.	

---

13 *Ibid.*
14 Also see House of Lords European Union Committee, *EU Data Protection Law: A 'Right to be Forgotten'* (Stationery Office UK, 2014); LA Bygrave, 'A Right to Be Forgotten?' *Communications of the ACM* (2015) (58:1) 35 [UK]. In addition, note Data Protection Act 2018, UK GDPR, and P Lambert, The UK GDPR Annotated (Kortext, 2021).

2	Confirm the company is aware of the circumstances when we can extend the time limit to respond to a request.	
3	Confirm the company understands that there is a particular emphasis on the right to erasure if the request relates to data collected from children.	
4	Confirm the company has procedures in place to inform any recipients if we erase any data we have shared with them.	
5	Confirm the company has appropriate methods in place to erase information.	

CHAPTER 21

UK Law

I INTRODUCTION

21.1   The UK has enacted a new Data Protection Act 2018 and otherwise introduced the UK GDPR, comprising the core of UK data protection law. This refers to particular variations from the General Data Protection Regulation (GDPR). It also refers to variations and exemptions. Thus, these changes need to be examined to see the potential impact, if any, as regards RtbF.[1]

2 CHANGES FROM GDPR

21.2   Section 8 of the Data Protection Act 2018 (DPA 2018) refers to lawfulness of processing, public interest, etc. It states that:

> In Article 6(1) of the GDPR (lawfulness of processing), the reference in point (e) to processing of personal data that is necessary for the performance of a task carried out in the public interest or in the exercise of the controller's official authority includes processing of personal data that is necessary for –
>
> • the administration of justice;
>
> • the exercise of a function of either House of Parliament;
>
> • the exercise of a function conferred on a person by an enactment or rule of law;
>
> • the exercise of a function of the Crown, a Minister of the Crown or a government department; or
>
> • an activity that supports or promotes democratic engagement.

In relation to child's consent for information society services (internet services), the UK changes the age of consent in the GDPR (16 years of age) to 13 years of age (DPA 2018, s 9).

The Information Commissioner's Office (ICO) (the data protection supervisory authority) in the UK is required to produce a guide for individuals on how to seek redress, including in relation to data protection (DPA 2018, s 177). The ICO will also review journalism practices and compliance with the data protection legislation (DPA 2018, s 178).

---

1   Note that the UK GDPR is not an Act as such and there is no single authoritative official statute text. It is introduced into law via a circuitous legislation route. It is important, therefore, to look at all of the law routes used to introduce and structure the UK GDPR. See P Lambert, The UK GDPR Annotated (Kortext, 2021).

The GDPR applies in the UK and Article 17, which refers to the erasure, forgetting and takedown right, is directly effective in the UK. However, the DPA 2018 does provide several variations and exemptions. Schedule 2 refers to 'exemptions etc from the GDPR' and refers to 'GDPR provisions to be adapted or restricted' known as 'the listed GDPR provisions'. Schedule 2, Part 1(1)(a)(v) refers to 'Article 19(1) and (2) (right to erasure)'.

GDPR Article 16 (right to rectification);[2] Article 18(1) (restriction of processing);[3] and Article 19 (notification obligation regarding rectification or erasure of personal data or restriction of processing)[4] are also included in Schedule 2.

Immigration

21.3   The first exemption is for the purposes of immigration: 'The GDPR provisions listed [below] do not apply to personal data processed for any of the following purposes – (a) the maintenance of effective immigration control, or (b) the investigation or detection of activities that would undermine the maintenance of effective immigration control, to the extent that the application of those provisions would be likely to prejudice any of the matters mentioned in paragraphs (a) and (b).' The items exempted in relation to the provisions of the GDPR (the rights and obligations in which may be restricted by virtue of Article 23(1) of the GDPR) include:

- Article 17(1) and (2) (right to erasure)[5]; and

- Article 18(1) (restriction of processing).[6]

GDPR Articles 16 (rectification) and 19 (notification) are not exempt for immigration purposes.

Information to be disclosed by law etc or in connection with legal proceedings

21.4   In addition, the 'listed GDPR provisions do not apply to personal data consisting of information that the controller is obliged by an enactment to make available to the public, to the extent that the application of those provisions would prevent the controller from complying with that obligation'.[7]

Also, the 'listed GDPR provisions do not apply to personal data consisting of information that the controller is obliged by an enactment to make available to

---

2   Data Protection Act (DPA) 2018, Sch 2, Pt 1(1)(a)(iv). Also, see Lambert, *The UK GDPR Annotated*, above.
3   *Ibid* Pt 1(1)(a)(vi).
4   *Ibid* Pt 1(1)(a)(vii).
5   *Ibid* Sch 2, Pt 1(4)(2)(d).
6   *Ibid* Sch 2, Pt 1(4)(2)(e).
7   *Ibid* Sch 2, Pt 1(5)(1).

the public, to the extent that the application of those provisions would prevent the controller from making the disclosure'.[8]

In addition, the

listed GDPR provisions do not apply to personal data where disclosure of the data –

(a) Is necessary for the purpose of, or in connection with, legal proceedings (including prospective legal proceedings),

(b) Is necessary for the purpose of obtaining legal advice, or

(c) Is otherwise necessary for the purposes of establishing, exercising or defending legal rights.

to the extent that the application of those provisions would prevent the controller from making the disclosure.[9]

Functions designed to protect the public, etc

21.5　　GDPR Articles 17(1) and (2), 16, 18(1) and 19 are also exempt in relation to certain functions designed to protect the public. These are official functions appointed to protect:

- the public against certain types of financial loss;[10]

- the public from dishonesty and similar activities;[11]

- charities;[12]

- certain health and safety situations;[13]

- the public from official maladministration and failures;[14] and

- the public from certain adverse business activities and anti competitive activities.[15]

Audit functions

21.6　　GDPR Articles 17(1) and (2), 16, 18(1) and 19 are also exempt in relation to certain audit function activities.[16]

8　*Ibid* Sch 2, Pt 1(5)(2).
9　*Ibid* Sch 2, Pt 1(5)(3).
10　*Ibid* Sch 2, Pt 1(7), Table (1).
11　*Ibid* Sch 2, Pt 1(7), Table (2).
12　*Ibid* Sch 2, Pt 1(7), Table (3).
13　*Ibid* Sch 2, Pt 1(7), Table (4).
14　*Ibid* Sch 2, Pt 1(7), Table (5).
15　*Ibid* Sch 2, Pt 1(7), Table (6).
16　*Ibid* Sch 2, Pt 1(8).

Bank of England

21.7 GDPR Articles 17(1) and (2), 16, 18(1) and 19 are also exempt in relation to certain Bank of England activities.[17]

Regulatory functions re legal services, health service and children's services

21.8 GDPR Articles 17(1) and (2), 16, 18(1) and 19 are also exempt in relation to certain regulatory functions.[18] These are:

- the Listed Services Board;

- function of complaints under Part 6 of the Legal services Act 2007;

- certain functions under the NHS Redress Act 2006;

- certain parts of the Health and Social Care (Community Health and Standards) Act 2003, or Part 2A of the Public Services Ombudsman (Wales) Act 2005; and

- certain complaints under the Social Services and Well-being (Wales) Act 2014.

Regulatory functions of certain other persons

21.9 GDPR Articles 17(1) and (2), 16, 18(1) and 19 are also exempt in relation to discharging certain additional situations in the listed table where it would be likely to prejudice the proper discharge of the function. The persons in the second table are the Commissioner, Scottish Information Commissioner, Pensions Ombudsman and a list of other official office holders.[19]

Parliamentary privilege

21.10 GDPR Articles 17(1) and (2), 16, 18(1) and 19 are also exempt in relation to certain parliamentary privilege activities.[20]

Judicial appointments

21.11 GDPR Articles 17(1) and (2), 16, 18(1) and 19 are also exempt in relation to certain judicial related activities.[21]

---

17 *Ibid* Sch 2, Pt 1(9).
18 *Ibid* Sch 2, Pt 1(10).
19 *Ibid* Sch 2, Pt 1(11).
20 *Ibid* Sch 2, Pt 1(13).
21 *Ibid* Sch 2, Pt 1(14).

Crown honours, etc

21.12   Articles 17(1) and (2), 16, 18(1) and 19 are also exempt in relation to certain crown and related activities.[22]

Journalism

21.13   Part 5 of the DPA 2018 refers to exemptions, etc, based on GDPR Article 85(2) for reasons of freedom of expression and information. In relation to journalistic, academic, artistic and literary purposes, Part 5, section 26 refers to 'special purposes' and lists one of these as 'the purposes of journalism'.[23] The listed provisions for this paragraph (s 26) include:

- GDPR Article 17(1) and (2) (right to erasure);

- GDPR Article 16 (right to rectification);

- GDPR Article 18(1)(a), (b) and (d) (restriction of processing);

- GDPR Article 19 (notification obligation regarding rectification or erasure of personal data or restriction of processing); and

- GDPR Article 21 (objections to processing).[24]

> The listed GDPR provisions do not apply to the extent that the controller reasonably believes that the application of those provisions would be incompatible with the special purposes.'[25] This exclusion of the application of the listed GDPR provisions 'applies to the processing of personal data carried out for the special purposes if—
>
> (a) the processing is being carried out with a view to the publication by a person of journalistic, academic, artistic or literary material, and
>
> (b) the controller reasonably believes that the publication of the material would be in the public interest.[26]
>
> In determining whether publication would be in the public interest the controller must take into account the special importance of the public interest in the freedom of expression and information.[27]

In addition, '[i]n determining whether it is reasonable to believe that publication would be in the public interest, the controller must have regard to any of the codes of practice or guidelines listed in sub-paragraph (6) that is relevant to the publication in question'.[28] These are the BBC Editorial Guidelines, the Ofcom

---

22   *Ibid* Sch 2, Pt 1(15).
23   *Ibid* Pt 5, s 26(1)(a).
24   *Ibid* s 26(9).
25   *Ibid* s 26(3).
26   *Ibid* s 26(2).
27   *Ibid* s 26(4).
28   *Ibid* s 26(5).

Broadcasting Code and the IPSO Editors' Code of Practice.[29] They may be amended or added to by the Secretary of State by way of regulations.[30]

3 DEROGATIONS FOR RESEARCH, STATISTICS AND ARCHIVING

21.14 Part 6 refers to derogations etc based on Article 89 for research, statistics and archiving.

Research and Statistics

21.15 The listed GDPR provisions for this section do not include Article 17, but do include Article 16, Article 18(1), and Article 21(1).

Archiving in the public interest

21.16 The listed GDPR provisions for this section do not include Article 17, but do include Article 16, Article 18(1), Article 19 and Article 21(1).

Health, social work, education and child abuse data

21.17 This is referred to In Schedule 3, Part 1. One of the listed GDPR provisions to be exempted is GDPR Article 17. The listed provisions include:

- Article 17(1) and (2) (right to erasure);
- Article 16 (right to rectification);
- Article 18(1) (restriction of processing); and
- Article 21 (objections to processing).[31]

Health data is referred to in Schedule 3, Part 2. Social work data is referred to in Schedule 3, Part 3. Education data is referred to in Schedule 3, Part 4. Child abuse data is referred to in Schedule 3, Part 5.

4 CONCLUSION

21.18 A note of caution is needed as laws can continue to change, and it is particularly possible after a major event such as Brexit. Changes should be anticipated for many years. In addition to these types of changes, there is presently an official consultation process which may result in further possible changes during 2022 and thereafter. Review will be needed to assess to what extent there may be an express proposed change regarding RtbF.

29 *Ibid* s 26(6).
30 *Ibid* s 26(7).
31 *Ibid* Sch 3, Pt 1, s 1.

CHAPTER 22

Post-Brexit Change

I INTRODUCTION

22.1   The path to Brexit will be the subject of historical analysis for generations.[1] However, there are many questions in relation to understanding Brexit, Brexit rules, and what post-Brexit change issues more generally mean in practice,[2] what it may mean for data protection,[3] and in particular, commercial imperatives such as the ability to continue data transfers. The factors which were key in the *NT1 & NT2*[4] case, while obviously pertinent therein, also need to be considered in the context of Brexit and the post-Brexit environment. While there has been a variety of general official guidance,[5] this is mostly of a general data protection nature (and more recently looking at transfers) as opposed to specifically on Brexit and RtbF. There are no specific assurances as regards data subject rights under RtbF and certainty for controllers. While there was often some level of confusion during the process of political Brexit, there will remain some level of query if not uncertainty for some time.[6] The below is not a definitive guide to post-Brexit issues, but rather a flavour of the level of uncertainty which necessitated changing and updating of official advices both during and after Brexit. Often the attention was on Brexit per se, UK data protection laws, and issues of data transfers – rather than other issues such as RtbF. While Brexit has now been achieved, and the new UK law is contained in the Data Protection Act 2018 (DPA 2018) and UK GDPR,[7] and the adequacy decision for data transfers,

---

1   As well as perhaps counter-intelligence interests (eg, in relation to live elections and ongoing lesson learned).

2   D Allen Green, *Brexit* (OUP, 2019); S Peers, 'Brexit: The Legal Dimension' in C Barnard, and S Peers, *European Union Law* (OUP, 2014) at 815.

3   P Lambert, 'Data Protection and Brexit Threats – Will Adequacy Work?' *Communications Law* (2018) (23)(4) 1; W RM Long, and F Blythe, 'Data Protection and Post-Brexit Issues' *International Journal for the Data Protection Officer, Privacy Officer and Privacy Counsel (IDPP)* (2018) (2:9) 8; W Ashford, 'Security Industry Welcomes Planned UK Data Protection Bill as EU's GDPR Looms' *Computer Weekly* (15 August 2017) 4; V Mitsilegas, 'European Criminal Law After Brexit' *Criminal Law Forum* (2017) (28:2) 219; ZA Lewis, 'A Dramatic Brexit? Why the United Kingdom's EU Referendum Vote Could Send the UK Film Industry "Reeling"' *Syracuse Journal of International Law* (2017) (45:1) 83.

4   *NT1 & NT2 v Google LLC* [2018] EWHC 799 (QB) (13 April 2018) Warby J.

5   See, eg, Department for Digital, Culture, Media & Sport, 'Data Protection if There is No Brexit Deal – Official Position,' *International Journal for the Data Protection Officer, Privacy Officer and Privacy Counsel (IDPP)* (2018) (2:9) 16.

6   S Anderson, 'Brexit Data Confusion,' *International Journal for the Data Protection Officer, Privacy Officer and Privacy Counsel (IDPP)* (2018) (2:9) 10. Also see S Aidinlis, 'The Right to be Forgotten as a Fundamental Right in the UK After Brexit' *Communications Law* (2020) (25:2) 67.

7   See P Lambert, *The UK GDPR Annotated* (Kortext, 2021).

the clear potential for changes to UK and related UK data protection laws means that these issues will continue to vex practitioners. Stability and certainty are welcomed by industry as well as practitioners. The new consultation process foreboding potentially wide and significant change during 2022 and 2023 will no doubt further complicate matters.

Practitioners will need to be familiar with the General Data Protection Regulation (GDPR),[8] the DPA 2018,[9] and the new UK GDPR[10] – and a variety of additional proposed measures. Less understood, however, is the impact of post-Brexit data protection and change on RtbF issues. Perhaps, unfortunately, great care will also be needed to monitor on an ongoing bases where a potential roster of ongoing changes will individually and collectively impact RtbF rights and considerations. The least that can be said is that assessing these issues will be more onerous outside the EU than would otherwise have been the case.

2   OFFICIAL POSITIONS

22.2   This section is not meant as a definitive listing of all official commentary and guidance but more to serve to demonstrate that even officially these issues are recognised as complex and important, and that already there have been changes over even a short space of time. One point is that more changes can still occur, and are likely to occur.

ICO

22.3   There was a flurry of official guidance during and immediately after Brexit. The Information Commissioner's Office (ICO) published many comments and guidance documents. These included guidance on Brexit and even the form of Brexit that might occur (including the possibility of a 'No Deal' Brexit at one stage).

Some of the official ICO documentation included:

- 'Six Steps to Take' guide;

- 'Broader' guidance document on leaving EU if no withdrawal agreement;

- Overview FAQs guidance;

- Official blog posts; and

- press statements.

8   Regulation (EU) 2016/679 of the European Parliament and of the Council of 27 April 2016 on the protection of natural persons with regard to the processing of personal data and on the free movement of such data and repealing Directive 95/46/EC (General Data Protection Regulation). OJ L 119, 4.5.2016, pp 1–88.
9   Data Protection Act 2018. 2018 c12. Enacted 23 May 2018. Available at: www.legislation. gov. uk/ukpga/2018/12/ contents/enacted.
10   See UK GDPR and Lambert, *The UK GDPR Annotated* ; and also P Lambert, *5 Essential GDPR Content Lists* (Kortext, 2021); P Lambert, *Essential GDPR Index* (Kortext, 2021).

ICO blog post

22.4   An ICO blog post stated that the 'Government has made clear that the [GDPR] will be absorbed into UK law at the point of exit, so there will be no substantive change'. While that may have been the case at the time, critics might query the legal nature and status of the ultimate UK GDPR (as it is not an official independent legislative act on its own); and now given the consultation and other political pronouncements, how long equivalence and adequacy may last.

ICO Six-step Guide

22.5   The ICO six-step assistance guide also states that '[i]f you operate in the EEA, you may need to comply with both the UK data protection regime and the EU regime after the UK exits the EU. You may also need to appoint a representative in the EEA'.

1.   Continue to comply;

2.   Transfers to the UK;

3.   Transfers from the UK;

4.   European operations;

5.   Documentation;

6.   Organisational awareness.

Point 1 (Continue to comply) states, *inter alia*, that:

> The [DPA 2018] will remain in place. The government intends to bring the GDPR directly into UK law on exit, to sit alongside it. There will be some technical adjustments to the UK version of the GDPR so that it works in a UK-only context – for example, amending provisions referring to EU law and enforcement cooperation.

Point 2 (Transfers to the UK) states, *inter alia*, that organisations need to:

> Review your data flows and identify where you receive data from the EEA, including from suppliers and processors. Think about what GDPR safeguards you can put in place to ensure that data can continue to flow once we are outside the EU.

It continues that this 'means the sender needs to make sure there are adequate safeguards in place, or one of the exceptions listed in the GDPR'.

It also refers to the importance of the adequacy decision issue.

The ICO also advises that '[y]ou may want to consider putting standard contractual clauses (SCCs) in place if you are receiving data from the EEA'.

Point 3 (Transfers from the UK) refers to transfers from the UK to the EU and also to transfers from the UK to countries outside the EEA. In terms of the latter, the guidance states, *inter alia*, '[w]e expect the UK government to confirm that the UK will reflect existing EU adequacy decisions, approved EU SCCs and BCRs'. It then cross-refers to the more detailed guidance. Readers will note that this is descriptive of some future governmental and legal decisions and rules. It was unclear specifically what this refers to or when.

Point 4 (European operations) states, *inter alia*, that '[i]f you operate across Europe, you should review your structure, processing operations and data flows to assess how the UK's exit from the EU will affect the data protection regimes that apply to you'.

It also refers to data protection regimes and reiterates that organisations may need to comply with the EU and the UK data protection regimes, highlighting the need for dual compliance exercises. Issues of branches and establishments within the post-Brexit EU need to be considered. A further consideration is having to deal with the UK and one or more respective data protection authorities.

The need to appoint a representative located in the EU is also highlighted.

Point 6 (Organisational awareness) reiterates the need for training and internal awareness raising processes. This is needed generally, but also needs to be utilised as Brexit-related data changes arise, as well as engagement and consultation to identify these issues in advance and make appropriate preparations. Reference is also made to the need for organisations to have a risk register and to update this as appropriate.

'Broader' ICO Guidance

22.6   The ICO also issued a broader Brexit transfer guidance. It highlights that the (various) guidance is particularly relevant to organisations which:

•   operate in the EEA (which includes the EU); or

•   send personal data outside the UK; or

•   receive personal data from the EEA.

It is also indicated to be relevant where the following apply to the organisation:

•   the Privacy and Electronic Communications (EC Directive) Regulations 2003 (PECR);

•   the Network and Information Systems Regulations 2018 (NIS); or

•   Regulation (EU) 910/2014 on electronic identification and trust services for electronic transactions in the internal market (eIDAS).

The guidance refers to the DPA 2018. It points out that it came into force at the same time as the GDPR and covers four data protection regimes, namely:

- Part 2, Chapter 2: General processing – the GDPR – 'this chapter supplements the GDPR so that it operates in a UK context'.

- Part 2, Chapter 3: Other general processing – 'this chapter applies a UK version of the GDPR (the "applied GDPR") to those areas outside the scope of EU law, such as defence'.

- Part 3: Law enforcement processing – 'this chapter brings into UK law the EU Data Protection Directive 2016/680 (the Law Enforcement Directive)'.

- Part 4: Intelligence services processing.

ICO Overview FAQs Guidance

22.7   The ICO frequently asked questions (FAQs) guidance refers to various data protection issues in the new environment.

3   THE EUROPEAN UNION (WITHDRAWAL) ACT 2018

22.8   The DPA 2018 did not implement the GDPR in the UK given the then current direct effect of the GDPR.[11] Hence the ultimate need for the UK GDPR being adopted.

One of the main aims was to maintain pre-existing EU law already applicable in the UK after Brexit. There is also power for various ministerial changes in future.

The European Union (Withdrawal) Act 2018 (EUWA) received Royal Assent on 26 June 2018. The following are relevant to consider. Section 20 of the EUWA 2018 offers an interpretation of the following terms:

- Charter of Fundamental Rights (the Charter of Fundamental Rights of the European Union of 7 December 2000, as adapted at Strasbourg on 12 December 2007');

- 'Exit day' ('29 March 2019 at 11.00 pm ...');

- 'EU regulation' ('a regulation within the meaning of Article 288 of the Treaty on the Functioning of the European Union');

- 'EU directive' (a directive within the meaning of Article 288 of the Treaty on the Functioning of the European Union');

- 'Retained direct EU legislation' ('any direct EU legislation which forms part of domestic law by virtue of section (as modified by or under this Act or by other domestic law from time to time, and including any instruments made under it on or after exit day'); and

- 'Withdrawal agreement' ('an agreement (whether or not ratified) between the United Kingdom and the EU under Article 50(2) of the Treaty on European Union which sets out the arrangements for the United Kingdom's withdrawal from the EU').

11   See Lambert, *The UK GDPR Annotated*.

Section 20(4) of the EUWA 2018 provides that 'A Minister of the Crown may, by regulations –

    (a) amend the definition of "exit day" in subsection (1) to ensure that the day and time specified in the definition are the day and time that the Treaties are to cease to apply to the United Kingdom; and

    (b) amend subsection (2) in consequence of such amendment.

Section 9(1) provides that:

> A Minister … may by regulation make such provision as the Minister considers appropriate for the purposes of implementing the withdrawal agreement if the Minister considers that such provision should be in force on or before exit day, subject to the prior enactment of a statute by Parliament approving the final terms of withdrawal of the United Kingdom from the EU.

Note that 'regulations under this section may not … amend, repeal or revoke the Human Rights Act 1998 or any subordinate legislation made under it' (s 9(3)(e)). Also '[n]o regulations may be made under this section after exit day' (s 9(4)).

Section 2 refers to 'Saving for EU-derived domestic legislation'. It includes the following:

> EU-derived domestic legislation, as it has effect in domestic law immediately before exit day, continues to have effect in domestic law after exit day.

This potentially includes DPA 2018.

Section 3, however, may be more pertinent. It states that:

> Direct EU legislation, so far as operative immediately before exit day, forms part of domestic law on and after exit day (s 3(1)).

This should seem to include an EU regulation – which may then include the GDPR. However, there remains some uncertainty, not least as then organisations may have to refer to the DPA 2018, the EUWA, any Ministerial legislation and any other legislation that may also ensue plus the withdrawal agreement itself. Subject to an adequacy decision being issued, that may also be referred to.

> A definition of 'direct EU legislation' is contained within section 3(2)(a). This refers to 'any EU regulation …'.

Section 4 refers to a saving for rights, powers, liabilities, obligations, restrictions, remedies and procedures which were in effect immediately before exit day. These are to continue after exit day.

There are also provisions in relation to exceptions for saving and incorporations (s 5). This refers to the principle of supremacy of EU ceasing for laws after exit day (s 5(1)). However, it may apply to 'relevant' issues of interpretation (see s 5(2)).

The Charter 'is not part of domestic law on or after exit day' (s 5(4)). (This may have the potential to interact with issues of a future transfer adequacy decision assessment process.) However, note that section 5(5) states:

> Subsection (4) does not affect the retention in domestic law on or after exit day in accordance with this Act of any fundamental rights or principles which exist irrespective of the charter (and references to the Charter in any case law are, so far as necessary for this purpose, to be read as if they were references to any corresponding retaining fundamental rights or principles).

Section 6 refers to interpretation of 'retained EU law'. This section confirms that courts are not bound by 'any principles laid down, or any decision made, on or after exit day by the European Court' (s 6(1)). UK courts cannot continue to refer matters to the European Court (s 6(6(1)(b)). Having said that, UK courts 'may have regard to anything done on or after exit day by the European court, another EU entity or the EU so far as it is relevant to any other matter before the court' (s 6(2)).

The Supreme Court and High Court are 'not bound' by any retailed EU case law (see s 6(4)). 'In deciding whether to depart from any retained EU case law, the Supreme Court or the High Court … must apply the same test as it would apply in deciding whether to depart from its own case law' (s 6(5)).

Definitions for 'retained case law', 'retained EU law', 'retained general principles of EU law' amongst others are set out in section 6(7).

Section 7(1) refers to status of retained EU law. It provides that:

> Anything which –
>
> (a) was, immediately before exit day, primary legislation of a particular kind, subordinate legislation of a particular kind or another enactment of a particular kind,
>
> (b) continues to be domestic law as an enactment of the same kind.

Under section 7(2) of the EUWA 2018, retained direct principal EU legislation cannot be modified other than as specified.

Section 7(5)(f) refers to the Human Rights Act, while section 7(6) defines 'retained direct principal EU legislation'.

EUWA Official Explanatory Commentary

22.9   Detailed explanatory notes are available with the EUWA 2018. The Overview indicates that the EUWA 'repeals the European Communities Act 1972 (ECA) on the day the United Kingdom leaves the European Union' and ends the supremacy of EU law.

The 'principal purpose of the Act is to provide a functioning statute book on the day [31 January 2020] the UK leaves the EU'. 'As a general rule, the same rules and laws apply on the day after exit as on the day before. It will then be for Parliament and, where appropriate, the devolved legislatures to make any future changes' ((explanatory note (EN)10).

It adds that:

> The approach in the act to preserving EU law is to ensure that all EU laws which are directly applicable in the UK and all laws which have been made in the UK in order to implement our obligations as a member of the EU are converted into domestic law on the day the UK leaves the EU, subject to some limited exceptions (EN 48).

Section 1 repeals the European Communities Act 1972 (EN 74). EU legislation is 'given legal effect in the UK via section 2(1) of the ECA 1972, which described how such legislation is to have effect "in accordance with the EU treaties". It is this which ensures that, for example, EU regulations are directly applicable and fully binding in all member states' (EN 81).

The guidance adds that 'Section 3 ... convert[s] "direct EU legislation' into domestic legislation at the point of exit' (EN 82). 'Subsection (1) therefore provides for the conversion into domestic law of this direct EU legislation' (EN 83).

> Subsection (2)(a) converts EU regulations, certain EU decisions and EU tertiary legislation (now known as delegated and implementing acts), as they have effect immediately before exit day. These terms are defined at section 20. Section 20 and Schedule 6 provide that certain instruments are exempt EU instruments. These exemptions reflect that certain EU instruments did not apply to the UK because the UK did not adopt the Euro, or because the UK did not participate in certain aspects of the EU acquis, in the area of freedom, security and justice. EU decisions which are addressed only to a member state other than the UK are also not converted into domestic law. Additionally, so far as EU-derived domestic legislation under section 2 reproduces the effect of an EU regulation, decision or tertiary legislation, these instruments are not converted under this section. This is to avoid duplication on the statute book after exit' (EN 84).

Data Transfers

22.10 Perhaps understandably the issue of data transfers and the continued ability for data transfers attracted most of the Brexit and post-Brexit commentary in the data protection field. Transfers of personal data outside of the EU are prohibited *per se*. This is a longstanding bedrock position in data protection rules. Therefore, on Brexit day the potential remained for data transfers to the UK to cease – at least pending some additional official arrangements.[12]

---

12 See generally, Lambert, 'Data Protection and Brexit Threats – Will Adequacy Work? above at 1.

General Principle on Transfers

22.11 Article 44 of the GDPR sets out the general principle for transfers within the EU under the data protection regime. The rule provides that:

> Any transfer of personal data which are undergoing processing or are intended for processing after transfer to a third country or to an international organisation shall take place only if, subject to the other provisions of this Regulation, the conditions laid down in this Chapter are complied with by the controller and processor, including for onward transfers of personal data from the third country or an international organisation to another third country or to another international organisation. All provisions in this Chapter shall be applied in order to ensure that the level of protection of natural persons guaranteed by this Regulation is not undermined.

Therefore 'any' transfer to a third country outside of the EU or EEA[13] may 'take place only if' certain conditions are met. So, the default position is that external transfers should not occur. Only if specified conditions are satisfied by way of exemption from the default rule might the transfer become permissible.

With Brexit, the UK is no longer an EU or an EEA member country. The default rule kicks in and post-Brexit transfers, by default, are no longer permitted between the EU and UK.

Exceptions

22.12 There are a limited number of exceptions to the EU transfer ban. One of these is that the EU has made a determination called an 'adequacy decision' permitting such data transfers to a named country from the EU on the basis that the recipient jurisdiction has an adequate level of protection and rights in relation to personal data at least equivalent to those in the EU.

Adequacy Exception

22.13 One of the provided exceptions is known as the adequacy exception or condition. Article 45 of the GDPR provides as follows:

1. A transfer of personal data to a third country or an international organisation may take place where the Commission has decided that the third country, a territory or one or more specified sectors within that third country, or the international organisation in question ensures an adequate level of protection. Such a transfer shall not require any specific authorisation.

2. When assessing the adequacy of the level of protection, the Commission shall, in particular, take account of the following elements:

---

13 The EEA is the European Economic Area, which currently comprises the EU countries plus Iceland, Liechtenstein, and Norway.

(a) the rule of law, respect for human rights and fundamental freedoms, relevant legislation, both general and sectoral, including concerning public security, defence, national security and criminal law and the access of public authorities to personal data, as well as the implementation of such legislation, data protection rules, professional rules and security measures, including rules for the onward transfer of personal data to another third country or international organisation which are complied with in that country or international organisation, case-law, as well as effective and enforceable data subject rights and effective administrative and judicial redress for the data subjects whose personal data are being transferred;

(b) the existence and effective functioning of one or more independent supervisory authorities in the third country or to which an international organisation is subject, with responsibility for ensuring and enforcing compliance with the data protection rules, including adequate enforcement powers, for assisting and advising the data subjects in exercising their rights and for cooperation with the supervisory authorities of the Member States; and

(c) the international commitments the third country or international organisation concerned has entered into, or other obligations arising from legally binding conventions or instruments as well as from its participation in multilateral or regional systems, in particular in relation to the protection of personal data.

3. The Commission, after assessing the adequacy of the level of protection, may decide, by means of implementing act, that a third country, a territory or one or more specified sectors within a third country, or an international organisation ensures an adequate level of protection within the meaning of paragraph 2 of this Article. The implementing act shall provide for a mechanism for a periodic review, at least every four years, which shall take into account all relevant developments in the third country or international organisation. The implementing act shall specify its territorial and sectoral application and, where applicable, identify the supervisory authority or authorities referred to in point (b) of paragraph 2 of this Article. The implementing act shall be adopted in accordance with the examination procedure referred to in Article 93(2).

4. The Commission shall, on an ongoing basis, monitor developments in third countries and international organisations that could affect the functioning of decisions adopted pursuant to paragraph 3 of this Article and decisions adopted on the basis of Article 25(6) of [the DPD 95/46].

5. The Commission shall, where available information reveals, in particular following the review referred to in paragraph 3 of this Article, that a third country, a territory or one or more specified sectors within a third country, or an international organisation no longer ensures an adequate level of protection within the meaning of paragraph 2 of this Article, to the extent necessary, repeal, amend or suspend the decision referred to in paragraph 3 of this Article by means of implementing acts without retroactive effect. Those implementing acts shall be adopted in accordance with the examination procedure referred to in Article 93(2).

On duly justified imperative grounds of urgency, the Commission shall adopt immediately applicable implementing acts in accordance with the procedure referred to in Article 93(3).

6. The Commission shall enter into consultations with the third country or international organisation with a view to remedying the situation giving rise to the decision made pursuant to paragraph 5.

7. A decision pursuant to paragraph 5 of this Article is without prejudice to transfers of personal data to the third country, a territory or one or more specified sectors within that third country, or the international organisation in question pursuant to Articles 46 to 49.

8. The Commission shall publish in the *Official Journal of the European Union* and on its website a list of the third countries, territories and specified sectors within a third country and international organisations for which it has decided that an adequate level of protection is or is no longer ensured.

9. Decisions adopted by the Commission on the basis of Article 25(6) of [the DPD 95/46] shall remain in force until amended, replaced or repealed by a Commission Decision adopted in accordance with paragraph 3 or 5 of this Article.

This should not be thought of as an exception but rather a mechanism by which to seek an exception from the default transfer ban.

It should also be noted that while there are other exceptions or mechanisms, the adequacy mechanism refers not to what each individual company might seek to do but operates on a national or nation-state basis. The adequacy mechanism applies to the UK *per se*, not company by company. (Individual organisations would benefit to the extent that they were located in the UK.)

This data transfer prohibition, and the associated problems for the UK, were ultimately overtaken by the issuance of an EU adequacy decision for the UK. (Note, however, that such decisions are officially reviewed and assessed over time; and where clear changes occur, and some would argue that the UK has already announced potential changes which may amount to significant change or departure from EU equivalent norms, such decision can be paused or event terminated). Thus, presently the UK is deemed to satisfy EU data transfer rules and therefore overcoming the default transfer ban rule.

UK Adequacy Decision

22.14 Substantial discussion, if not concern, surrounded whether the EU would agree to an adequacy decision for UK data transfers. Despite some scepticism, an adequacy decision was granted on 28 June 2021 for the UK.[14] This is entitled the Decision on the Adequate Protection of Personal Data by the United Kingdom

14 Press Release, 'EU Adopts "Adequacy" Decisions Allowing Data to Continue Flowing Freely to the UK,' *Department for Digital, Culture, Media & Sport* (28 June 2021).

– General Data Protection Regulation.[15] While this predominantly relates to data transfer issues, it is relevant also to RtbF insofar as it is a moment in time assessment that UK data protection laws – and by implication UK RtbF laws – are deemed by the EU to be adequate and equivalent.

Close attention is needed, however, as a consultation process was launched in 2021 with an intention to make quite wide ranging changes to UK data protection laws.[16] Such changes, if and when finalised, hold potential implications for whether the deemed adequacy will be breached.

If it is challenged by third parties or otherwise reviewed by the EU on foot of new law changes, the adequacy decision may be suspended or halted. This backdrop will need to me considered by policymakers as well as interested commercial entities.

The current RtbF DPA 2018 statute version states as follows:

Rights to rectification and erasure (DPA 2018)

(1) If a court is satisfied on the application of a data subject that personal data relating to the data subject is inaccurate, the court may order the controller to rectify that data without undue delay.

(2) If a court is satisfied on the application of a data subject that the processing of personal data relating to the data subject would infringe any of sections 86 to 91, the court may order the controller to erase that data without undue delay.

(3) If personal data relating to the data subject must be maintained for the purposes of evidence, the court may (instead of ordering the controller to rectify or erase the personal data) order the controller to restrict its processing without undue delay.

(4) If—

    (a) the data subject contests the accuracy of personal data, and

    (b) the court is satisfied that the controller is not able to ascertain whether the data is accurate or not,the court may (instead of ordering the controller to rectify or erase the personal data) order the controller to restrict its processing without undue delay.

(5) A court may make an order under this section in relation to a joint controller whose responsibilities are determined in an arrangement under section 104 only if the controller is responsible for carrying out the rectification, erasure or restriction of processing that the court proposes to order.

(6) The jurisdiction conferred on a court by this section is exercisable by the High Court or, in Scotland, by the Court of Session.

---

15 Decision on the Adequate Protection of Personal Data by the United Kingdom – General Data Protection Regulation, European Commission (28 June 2021), available at https://ec.europa.eu/info/files/decision-adequate-protection-personal-data-united-kingdom-general-data-protection-regulation_en.

16 'Open Consultation, Data: A New Direction' *Department for Digital, Culture, Media & Sport* (10 September 2021). The consultation response deadline closed on 19 November 2021.

4   UK GDPR

22.15   There is at least an initial attempt to have an equivalent of the EU RtbF in the UK.

RtbF in the UK is recognised and referred to in section 100 of the DPA 2018.

Research and/or case law may come to assess whether differences arise as between the GDPR text and the DPA 2018 text regarding RtbF issues, and if and how substantial these many be.

The proposed Digital Safety Bill which is aimed at online safety issues, may in that regard also supplement the development of digital rights and aspects of RtbF rights in the UK.

RtbF has already been recognised in UK courts, for example, in *NT1 v Google LLC* and *NT2 v Google LLC*.[17] These also expressly referred to EU rules, caselaw, and rights. There is additionally the concept of UK retained EU law which is intended to continue even after Brexit.

A note of caution (if one was needed on foot of concerns for adequacy if adverse changes are made to UK data laws), is raised by Stergios Aidinlis[18] where he discusses potential effects of Brexit on RtbF issues. He suggests that there may be few changes or (adverse) effects on RtbF in the short term in the UK post Brexit. However, he does suggest that longer term, there may indeed be adverse effect changes to RfbF in the UK and that a UK-RfbF may diverge and become more restrictive than the EU GDPR.

This would be potentially problematic in relation to digital rights and RtbF, but may have further ripple effects in terms of adverse consequences for adequacy.

It should also be pointed out that while Aidinlis[19] may be somewhat comforted in terms of RtbF remaining the same in the UK (at least in the immediate term), this assessment is made without knowledge of the now announced changes per the consultation process of 2021, some of which appear to be significant. He also highlights how greater reliance on torts may occur for vindication of RtbF rights in the UK.[20]

For example, there are changes which would at least initially appear to impinge upon the critical independence of the ICO as a fully independent data regulator.

---

17   *NT1 & NT2 v Google LLC* [2018] EWHC 799 (QB) (13 April 2018) Warby J, at para 230.
18   S Aidinlis, 'The Right to be Forgotten As A Fundamental Right in the UK After Brexit,' *Communications Law* (2020) (25:2) 67.
19   *Ibid.*
20   *Ibid.*

The assessment of potential effects on RtbF need to be reviewed once more detail and the suggested text of the data law changes are made available.[21]

5 THE *NT1* & *NT2* CASE

22.16   It also needs to be recalled what occurred in the *NT1* & *NT2*[22] case(s).

To any extent that there is a non-equivalence, whether in law, statute or case law

NT1 & *NT2*[23] refers to ten key legal features of the existing legal framework, including enactments and corresponding common law developments.[24] These ten features are:

(1)   The European Convention on Human Rights 1951 (Convention) of which the United Kingdom was a founding signatory. Of particular relevance are the qualified rights to respect for private and family life (Article 8) and freedom of expression (Article 10).[25]

(2)   The European Communities Act 1972 (1972 Act), by which the United Kingdom Parliament decided that the Treaty of Rome (25 March 1957) and other constitutional instruments of what was then the European Economic Community should be given direct legal effect in the UK without further enactment. As a result, domestic law has, since 1973, been subject to European Union law as contained in Directives and, later on, Regulations of the EU as interpreted by the European Court of Justice, now known as the Court of Justice of the European Union (CJEU). Section 3 of the 1972 Act requires UK Courts to make decisions on matters of EU law 'in accordance with … any relevant decision of the [CJEU]…'.[26]

(3)   The Rehabilitation of Offenders Act 1974 (1974 Act) which provides by sections 1, 4 and 5 that some convictions become 'spent' after the end of a specified rehabilitation period. Whether a conviction becomes spent and, if so, when, depends on the length of the sentence. The 1974 Act contains provisions specifying the legal effects of a conviction becoming spent. Those effects are subject to certain specified exceptions and limitations.[27]

---

21   The possibility of adverse impacts from official changes on the independence of the ICO are highlighted by P Lambert, *Data Regulators: ICO in a Time of Change* (Bloomsbury Professional, 2021); 'UK Data Protection Regulator's Independence Under Threat,' *PrivSec*, 25 March 2022; and interview by the new Information Commissioner in *Politico* reiterating that independence must be maintained, 'UK Data Chief Rejects Claims Country is Ditching Privacy Rights as "Bullshit"', *Politico*, 22 March 2022. If the ICO's independence is compromised, it would seem that all bets are off in terms of the UK be deemed equivalent to EU rules and norms. This would affect considerations of RtbF, as well as other data protection issues.
22   *NT1 & NT2 v Google LLC* [2018] EWHC 799 (QB) (13 April 2018) Warby J.
23   *Ibid.*
24   *Ibid* at para 13.
25   *Ibid* at para 13(1).
26   *Ibid* at para 13(2).
27   *Ibid* at para 13(3).

(4) The DPD 95/46 on the protection of individuals with regard to the processing of personal data and on the free movement of such data of 24 October 1995. The purposes of the DPD 1995 included safeguarding individuals' fundamental rights and freedoms, notably the right to privacy, to an equivalent extent within the Member States of the EU. Provisions of particular relevance are contained in Articles 2, 6, 8, 9, 12, 14, 23 and 29.[28]

(5) The DPA 1998 was enacted on 16 July 1998 to implement the DPD 95/46. Of particular relevance are DPA 1998 sections 1, 2, 4, 10, 13, 14 and 32; the first, fourth, sixth and seventh principles of data protection in Schedule 1; Schedule 2 paragraph 6; Schedule 3 paragraphs 5, 6(c) and 7A; and paragraph 3 of the Schedule to certain regulations made under DPA 1998 section 10, namely the Sensitive Personal Data Order[29] (2000 Order).[30]

(6) The Human Rights Act 1998 (HRA 1998), enacted on 9 November 1998, by which the rights and freedoms enshrined in the Convention became directly enforceable before the courts of the UK. sections 2 and 6 of the HRA 1998 impose on the court duties to interpret and apply domestic legislation in accordance with the Convention Rights, and not to act incompatibly with the Convention.[31]

(7) The 2004 decisions of the House of Lords in the *Campbell v MGN* case[32] [*Campbell*[33] case] and *In re S*,[34] in which the House recognised the development, under the influence of the HRA 1998, of a common law right to protection against the misuse of private information and established the methodology to be adopted in reconciling the competing demands of Articles 8 and 10 of the Convention.[35]

(8) The Charter of Fundamental Rights of the European Union 2000/C 364/01 (Charter), by which the EU recognised and sought to strengthen the protection for certain fundamental rights resulting from the Convention and from constitutional instruments of the EU. Of relevance are Articles 7 (respect for private life), 8 (protection of personal data), 11 (freedom of expression and information), 16 (freedom to conduct a business) and 47 (right to an effective remedy).[36] Member States are required to act compatibly with the Charter when implementing EU law.[37] This means,

---

28 *Ibid* at para 13(4).
29 Data Protection (Processing of Sensitive Personal Data) Order 2000 (SI 2000/417).
30 *NT1 & NT2 v Google LLC* at para 13(5).
31 *Ibid* at para 13(6).
32 *Campbell v MGN Ltd* [2004] UKHL 22 [2004] 2 AC 457.
33 J Rowbottom, 'A Landmark at a Turning Point: Campbell and the Use of Privacy Law to Constrain Media Power' *Journal of Media Law* (2015) (7:2) 170.
34 *In re S (A Child)* [2004] UKHL 47 [2005] 1 AC 593.
35 *NT1 & NT2 v Google LLC* at para 13(7).
36 The Charter was proclaimed by the European Parliament in December 2000, but only took full legal effect on the entry into force of the Lisbon Treaty on 1 December 2009.
37 *Rugby Football Union v Viagogo Ltd* [2012] UKSC 55 [2012] 1 WLR 3333 at [26]–[28].

among other things, that the DPD 95/46 must be interpreted and applied in conformity with the Charter rights.[38]

(9) The May 2014 decision of the CJEU in the *Google Spain*[39] case and another Case C-131/12 [2014] QB 1022 (*"Google Spain"*), in which the CJEU interpreted the DPD 95/46 and the Charter as creating a qualified RtbF. The court went on to apply that right to the facts before it, by holding that the individual complainant was entitled to have Google de-list information of which he complained. This decision prompted the original complaints by *NT1* and *NT2*, and hundreds of thousands of other de-listing requests. Google's evidence, contained in a 'Transparency Report' is that between the *Google Spain* decision and 4 October 2017 – a period of some 3½ years – it had been asked to de-list almost 1.9 million links or URLs (Universal Resource Locators).[40]

(10) The GDPR.[41] This is a legislative measure of the EU enacted on 27 April 2016, with the stated purpose, among others, of 'strengthening and setting out in detail the rights of data subjects and the obligations of those who process ... personal data ...'[42] The GDPR came into force on 25 May 2016 and had direct effect in Member States, including the UK, from 25 May 2018. Article 17 of the GDPR is headed 'Right to erasure ("[RtbF]")' and is relied on by Google as a 'setting out in detail' of the right, which should guide the court's decision.[43]

6 CONCLUSION

22.17 The above discussion highlights the complexities of recent changes to UK data protection. A variety of further changes are expected, and not least from the 2021–2022 consultation process. Significant concern and attention must be directed to assessing any and all such changes and their impact on takedown and RtbF issues. There can also be potential for such impacts to be direct or indirect, and intentional and unintentional. This in itself adds to the complexity. Over time we should also expect more attention to be paid to the many takedown and RtbF data protection issues. Recent official hearings in relation to online issues signify that the issues of online activities, harms, and ultimately takedown and RtbF, are beginning to receive more of the warranted attention that they deserve.

---

38 *Lindqvist v Aklagarkammaren I Jonkoping* (C-101/01) 6 November 2003 at para 87. *NT1 & NT2 v Google LLC* at para 13(8).
39 *Google Spain SL, Google Inc v Agencia Española de Protección de Datos (AEPD), Mario Costeja González,* Court of Justice (Grand Chamber), Case C-131/12, 13 May 2014.
40 *NT1 & NT2 v Google LLC* at para 13(9).
41 Regulation (EU) 2016/679 (aka the General Data Protection Regulation (GDPR)).
42 *Ibid* recital 11.
43 *NT1 & NT2 v Google LLC* at para 13(10).

The above discussion also highlights how there is little official guidance on RtbF issues in the context of the post-Brexit landscape. There is also little commentary.[44]

While previously there may have been little consideration of onward transfers or disclosure from the UK of data coming from the EU, these now need to be considered in terms of an impacts or conflicts with EU RtbF rules (as well as more generally). While EU compatible RtbF rules should be expected in the UK, concerns would arise if, for example, these rights or controls were lost to data that is transferred to some third county. Where such transfers may be permitted, if that is the case, there need to be considerations, legally and practically, of how to carry through and maintain takedown and RtbF in the recipient third country.

While the anticipated Online Safety Bill is welcome, we should also consider any impact on RtbF considerations to ensure no diminishment or impediments occur unintentionally.

As government comments have frequently referred to a variety of changes to international trade and data protection rules, and which will occur in a variety of manners, one would hope that impact assessments occur for these rolling changes on the potential impacts on takedown, RtbF, and safety issues.

As potential changes may be occurring for some time to come, it does not seem possible that the level of monitoring required for RtbF impacts will lessen any time soon.

---

44 One exception is C Dibene, 'Sir, the Radar Sir, It Appears to Be … Jammed: The Future of "The Right to Be Forgotten" in a Post-Brexit United Kingdom' *San Diego International Law Journal* (2017) (19:1) 161. The RtbF is still often more the subject of general discussion as opposed to Brexit discussion. See eg, LA Bygrave, 'A Right to Be Forgotten?' *Communications of the ACM* (2015) (58:1) 35. It remains to be seen whether the discussion by the House of Lords will help or hinder this general discussion. It does not seem to have featured in the *NT1* and *NT2* cases. See House of Lords, 'EU Data Protection Law: A "Right to be Forgotten"' *House of Lords European Union Committee* (Stationery Office, 2014).

PART F

ADDITIONAL CASES

CHAPTER 23

Additional Cases

1 INTRODUCTION

23.1 There are also developing cases apart from the *Google Spain*[1] decision. Some of these are at the level of data protection supervisory authorities, when individuals are dissatisfied with the response from the controller. Others are at national and international court level. Bear in mind also that even though the General Data Protection Regulation (GDPR) go-live is only months old, countries outside the European Union are developing legislation which is similar or includes similar elements. The GDPR is easily the most influential data protection law thus far and it is still early days.

The below are provided as indicative of a growing number of RtbF cases and not suggested as providing the latest RtbF jurisprudential situation in each respective jurisdiction,

2 SWEDEN

23.2 The Swedish data protection supervisory authority (Datainspektionen) received a complaint in relation to a RtbF notice to Google. The subject matter related to a report about purported crimes by a named individual in approximately 2006. The issue was whether the problem content was to be taken down locally or globally. Ultimately, the supervisory authority indicated that the results should be taken down globally, commenting that:

> There may be situations where search results must be deleted also when searches are made from other countries. This may be the case if there is a specific connection to Sweden and to the data subject, for example if the information on the webpage which is linked to is written in Swedish, addressed to a Swedish audience, contains information about a person that is in Sweden or if the information has been published on the Swedish domain se.[2]

Google took the matter to court. The Stockholm Administrative Court took a different view and indicated that global takedown was not required in this

---

1 *Google Spain SL, Google Inc v Agencia Española de Protección de Datos (AEPD), Mario Costeja González*, Court of Justice (Grand Chamber), Case C-131/12, 13 May 2014.
2 Datainspektionen, 'Press Release, The Right to Be Forgotten May Apply All Over the World' (4 May 2017). Available at: www.datainspektionen.se/press/nyheter/the-right-to-be-forgotten-may-apply-all-over-the-world/. Archived at: https://perma.cc/NT8D-42Z3.

instance.[3] Google won a partial victory. The data protection supervisory authority is reported to be appealing this court decision.[4]

In another Swedish case, the data protection supervisory authority refers to what may potentially be online abuse (OA) on a xenophobic website. It appears that Google refused to address the OA or to fully assist in the matter. The data protection supervisory authority comments as follows:

> A third complaint refers to a person who had set up an organization for unaccompanied minors seeking asylum in Sweden and who wanted to delete search results to a xenophobic webpage that published information about him/her in a derogatory way. Google considers that the web page contains political criticism of the complainant and that his/her role in public life is of general interest. The DPA, however, concludes that the search result must be deleted since it refers to information of a personal nature which is irrelevant for the criticism made towards the person in capacity of representative of the organisation.[5]

3 FRANCE

23.3 In *Google v CNIL*, the French data protection supervisory authority (Commission Nationale de l'Informatique et des Libertés (CNIL)) required that Google delist all domain searches worldwide subsequent to a successful notice for erasure, forgetting and takedown, rather than just in EU domains (eg, Google. fr) Google appealed this case to the European Court of Justice (ECJ) (now the Court of Justice of the European Union (CJEU) effectively seeking to reduce the effect of the *Google Spain* decision and territoriality scope issues.[6] Google was also fined €100,000 by CNIL for failure to implement the decision.

The case was eventually referred to the CJEU[7]. The questions addressed to the CJEU from the French court are as follows:

1. Must the 'right to de-referencing', as established by the Court of Justice of the European Union in its judgment of 13 May 2014 on the basis of the provisions of Articles 12(b) and 14(a) of Directive [95/46/EC] of 24 October 1995, be interpreted as meaning that a search engine operator is required, when granting a request for de-referencing, to deploy the de-referencing to all of the domain names used by its search engine so that the links at issue no longer appear, irrespective of the place from where

---

3   *Ibid.* Also see report and comment at N Malovic, 'Swedish Court Holds That Google Can Only Be Ordered to Undertake Limited Delisting in Right to be Forgotten Cases' *IPKitten* (5 May 2018).

4   'Swedish Data Watchdog Appeals After Google Partly Wins Case on Right to be Forgotten' *TelecomPaper.com* (30 May 2018). Available at: www.telecompaper.com/news/swedish-data-watchdog-appeals-after-google-partly-wins-case-on-right-to-be-forgotten--1246391.

5   Datainspektionen, 'Press Release, The Right to Be Forgotten May Apply All Over the World'.

6   See, for instance, M Finck, 'Google v CNIL Defining the Territorial Scope of European Data Protection, *OBLB* (16 November 2018). Available at: www.law.ox.ac.uk.

7   See M Scott, 'French Court Refers Google Privacy Case to EC,' *Politico.eu* (19 July 2017).

the search initiated on the basis of the requester's name is conducted, and even if it is conducted from a place outside the territorial scope of Directive [95/46/EC] of 24 October 1995?

2. In the event that Question 1 is answered in the negative, must the 'right to de-referencing', as established by the Court of Justice of the European Union in the judgment cited above, be interpreted as meaning that a search engine operator is required, when granting a request for de-referencing, only to remove the links at issue from the results displayed following a search conducted on the basis of the requester's name on the domain name corresponding to the State in which the request is deemed to have been made or, more generally, on the domain names distinguished by the national extensions used by that search engine for all of the Member States of the European Union?;

3. Moreover, in addition to the obligation mentioned in Question 2, must the 'right to de-referencing', as established by the Court of Justice of the European Union in its judgment cited above, be interpreted as meaning that a search engine operator is required, when granting a request for de-referencing, to remove the results at issue, by using the 'geo-blocking' technique, from searches conducted on the basis of the requester's name from an IP address deemed to be located in the State of residence of the person benefiting from the 'right to de-referencing', or even, more generally, from an IP address deemed to be located in one of the Member States subject to Directive [95/46/EC] of 24 October 1995, regardless of the domain name used by the internet user conducting the search?[8]

Note also that the parties also generally get an opportunity to shape the questions and may even offer an initial draft to be approved by the court.

The Advocate General (AG) issued what some may see as a somewhat controversial opinion, effectively suggesting that the erasure, forgetting, and takedown may be limited to the EU only and not otherwise. This suggestion, some may feel, ignores the point that harm can occur from content located outside of the EU and that such a limitation, in particular circumstances, can leave the individual or victim without a remedy or an effective remedy. The opinion appears to rely, in part, on the point that the service provider in addition to being ordered to ensure erasure, forgetting, and takedown for the EU, should also be ordered to ensure geoblocking. Unfortunately, geoblocking is not perfect and is (in many instances) easy to circumvent. The AG's opinion did not engage with the problems of geoblocking. The opinion also does not consider that many people avail of international travel and by so doing there is a great risk to the individual or victim that an EU-limited order may leave large gaps and be ineffective. Geoblocking can also be circumvented from ordinary users inside the EU. The Irish High Court, for example, was shown a live demonstration

---

8 *Google Inc v Commission Nationale de l'Informatique et des Libertés (CNIL)*, CJEU, case C-507/17.

from experts of the limitations of geoblocking and how EU geoblocked problem content was still accessible and available. Ultimately, that later case was settled and no decision was made on this point. In future, however, courts dealing with RtbF matters will, on occasion, have to delve into some of the more technical, design and policies issues of the respective service provider(s) than has occurred to date.

The ultimate court decision states that:

- 'currently, there is no obligation under EU law, for a search engine operator who grants a request for de-referencing made by a data subject, as the case may be, following an injunction from a supervisory or judicial authority of a Member State, to carry out such a de-referencing on all the versions of its search engine' (para 64);

- 'it should be emphasised that, while, as noted in paragraph 64 above, EU law does not currently require that the de-referencing granted concern all versions of the search engine in question, it also does not prohibit such a practice. Accordingly, a supervisory or judicial authority of a Member State remains competent to weigh up, in the light of national standards of protection of fundamental rights (see, to that effect, judgments of 26 February 2013, Åkerberg Fransson, C-617/10, EU:C:2013:105, paragraph 29, and of 26 February 2013, *Melloni*, C-399/11, EU:C:2013:107, paragraph 60), a data subject's right to privacy and the protection of personal data concerning him or her, on the one hand, and the right to freedom of information, on the other, and, after weighing those rights against each other, to order, where appropriate, the operator of that search engine to carry out a de-referencing concerning all versions of that search engine' (para 72);

- 'On a proper construction of Article 12(b) and subparagraph (a) of the first paragraph of Article 14 of Directive 95/46/EC ..., and of Article 17(1) of Regulation (EU) 2016/679 ... (General Data Protection Regulation), where a search engine operator grants a request for de-referencing pursuant to those provisions, that operator is not required to carry out that de-referencing on all versions of its search engine, but on the versions of that search engine corresponding to all the Member States, using, where necessary, measures which, while meeting the legal requirements, effectively prevent or, at the very least, seriously discourage an internet user conducting a search from one of the Member States on the basis of a data subject's name from gaining access, via the list of results displayed following that search, to the links which are the subject of that request' (decision).

While many commentators focus on the aspect of the case referring to erasure being viewed as limited to the EU in terms of the law not expressly stating so, the commentators often overlook the fact that the Court also said that local jurisdictions and data regulators *can* require erasure outside of the EU also. EU data law 'does not prohibit such a practice' of requiring RtbF outside of the EU also.

It states that '[a]ccordingly, a supervisory or judicial authority of a Member State remains competent to weigh up, in the light of national standards of protection of fundamental rights ..., a data subject's right to privacy and the protection of personal data concerning him or her, on the one hand, and the right to freedom of information, on the other, and, after weighing those rights against each other, *to order*, where appropriate, the operator of that search engine to carry out a *de-referencing* concerning *all versions* of that search engine' (emphasis added). Global RtbF remain possible. Or indeed RtbF in certain specified versions or countries in addition to the EU.

It is suggested, therefore, that there will be further jurisprudence in respective Member States where EU plus other versions or countries may be applied.

It remains to be seen, however, what approach will ensue in a post Brexit UK.

4 CANADA

23.4   In between the *Google Spain* case and the go live of the GDPR, the Canadian Supreme Court also dealt with the issue of worldwide takedown. Again, the case involved Google. While the issues were commercial, between commercial parties and involved the infringement of intellectual property rights, the Supreme Court acknowledged the need and essential requirement for worldwide takedown to have an effective remedy. In *Google Inc v Equustek Solutions Inc*, it was held that:

> *Per* McLachlin CJ and Abella, Moldaver, Karakatsanis, Wagner, Gascon and Brown JJ: The issue is whether Google can be ordered, pending a trial, to globally deindex D's websites which, in breach of several court orders, is using those websites to unlawfully sell the intellectual property of another company.
>
> The decision to grant an interlocutory injunction is a discretionary one and entitled to a high degree of deference. Interlocutory injunctions are equitable remedies that seek to ensure that the subject matter of the litigation will be preserved so that effective relief will be available when the case is ultimately heard on the merits. Their character as "interlocutory" is not dependent on their duration pending trial. Ultimately, the question is whether granting the injunction is just and equitable in the circumstances of the case.
>
> The test for determining whether the court should exercise its discretion to grant an interlocutory injunction against Google has been met in this case: there is a serious issue to be tried; E is suffering irreparable harm as a result of D's ongoing sale of its competing product through the Internet; and the balance of convenience is in favour of granting the order sought.
>
> Google does not dispute that there is a serious claim, or that E is suffering irreparable harm which it is inadvertently facilitating through its search engine. Nor does it suggest that it would be inconvenienced in any material way, or would incur any significant expense, in deindexing D's websites. Its arguments are that the injunction is not necessary to prevent irreparable harm

to E and is not effective; that as a nonparty it should be immune from the injunction; that there is no necessity for the extraterritorial reach of the order; and that there are freedom of expression concerns that should have tipped the balance against granting the order.

Injunctive relief can be ordered against someone who is not a party to the underlying lawsuit. When nonparties are so involved in the wrongful acts of others that they facilitate the harm, even if they themselves are not guilty of wrongdoing, they can be subject to interlocutory injunctions. It is common ground that D was unable to carry on business in a commercially viable way without its websites appearing on Google. The injunction in this case flows from the necessity of Google's assistance to prevent the facilitation of D's ability to defy court orders and do irreparable harm to E. Without the injunctive relief, it was clear that Google would continue to facilitate that ongoing harm.

Where it is necessary to ensure the injunction's effectiveness, a court can grant an injunction enjoining conduct anywhere in the world. The problem in this case is occurring online and globally. The Internet has no borders – its natural habitat is global. The only way to ensure that the interlocutory injunction attained its objective was to have it apply where Google operates – globally. If the injunction were restricted to Canada alone or to google.ca, the remedy would be deprived of its intended ability to prevent irreparable harm, since purchasers outside Canada could easily continue purchasing from D's websites and Canadian purchasers could find D's websites even if those websites were deindexed on google.ca.

Google's argument that a global injunction violates international comity because it is possible that the order could not have been obtained in a foreign jurisdiction, or that to comply with it would result in Google violating the laws of that jurisdiction, is theoretical. If Google has evidence that complying with such an injunction would require it to violate the laws of another jurisdiction, including interfering with freedom of expression, it is always free to apply to the British Columbia courts to vary the interlocutory order accordingly. To date, Google has made no such application. In the absence of an evidentiary foundation, and given Google's right to seek a rectifying order, it is not equitable to deny E the extraterritorial scope it needs to make the remedy effective, or even to put the onus on it to demonstrate, country by country, where such an order is legally permissible.

D and its representatives have ignored all previous court orders made against them, have left British Columbia, and continue to operate their business from unknown locations outside Canada. E has made efforts to locate D with limited success. D is only able to survive – at the expense of E's survival – on Google's search engine which directs potential customers to D's websites. This makes Google the determinative player in allowing the harm to occur. On balance, since the worldwide injunction is the only effective way to mitigate the harm to E pending the trial, the only way, in fact, to preserve E itself pending the resolution of the underlying litigation, and since any countervailing harm to Google is minimal to nonexistent, the interlocutory injunction should be upheld.[9]

9 *Google Inc v Equustek Solutions Inc*, 2017 SCC 34 [2017] 1 SCR 824. Available at: https://scc-csc.lexum.com/scc-csc/scc-csc/en/item/16701/index.do.

This is noteworthy for being a Superior Court decision, its worldwide nature, and the fact that it was recognised that effective remedies are needed. A further point and comparison to be made is that the errant party involved was persistent and uncooperative. The same can be said about many online abusers. The victims of OA need not just a remedy, but a remedy which works, is effective and is unobstructed.

5 ELSEWHERE

23.5 There have also been RtbF cases in the Netherlands[10] and Romania.[11] Worldwide there have been RtbF cases in South America and Japan. Further research is recommended to collate the various RtbF decision and trends worldwide.

6 CONCLUSION

23.6 No doubt the number of RtbF cases both within and outside the EU will continue to increase. So too will calls for both a federal privacy law and an express RtbF in the US. It is noted also that there are certain deletion or erasure provisions contained in the California Consumer Privacy Act (CDPA). Indeed, it is noted that recent criminal justice reform aimed, *inter alia*, at reducing incarceration, and extended incarceration, and more release, will quite possibly create an additional need for RtbF there.

---

10 S Kulk and F Zuiderveen Borgesius, 'Freedom of Expression and Right to Be Forgotten Cases in the Netherlands after *Google Spain' European Data Protection Law Review (EDPL)* (2015) (1:2) 113.
11 S-D Şchiopu, 'An Example of Romanian Case Law on the Digital Right to be Forgotten' *Bulletin of the Transilvania University of Braşov: Series VII: Social Sciences, Law* (2018) (11:60:1) 175.

PART G

MEDIA ISSUES

CHAPTER 24

Media

I INTRODUCTION

24.1 The area of media law and interests has a distinguished legal pedigree and literature.[1] Some of this literature refers to defamation and privacy issues and comparisons;[2] increasingly issues of media, data protection and privacy;[3] and even data protection and privacy media injunctions.[4] There are related areas such as confidentiality (eg, professional confidentiality[5] or confidentiality and personality[6]) and freedom of information (FOI).[7]

Some RtbF issues will be uncontroversial. Journalism, however, in some instances is one of the interesting RtbF zones of interest. Some have argued against a RtbF from the perspective that it might interfere with journalism rights or interests.[8] Some may feel that there is a required balance to be undertaken,[9] which may not favour so-called journalistic interests and/or that a RtbF may sometimes trump perceived journalistic claims. It has also been argued that there is an unjustified

---

1   D Rolph, M Vitins, J Bannister and D Joyce, *Media Law* (OUP, 2015); P Keller, *European and International Media Law* (OUP, 2011); R Caddell and H Johnson, *Blackstone's Statutes on Media Law* (OUP, 2013); M Dodd and M Hanna, *McNae's Essential Law for Journalists* (OUP, 2020); K Donders Caroline Pawwels and J Loisen, *The Palgrave Handbook of European Media Policy* (Palgrave Macmillan, 2014).
2   AT Kenyon, *Comparative Defamation and Privacy Law* (CUP, 2018); Chapter 8, for example, refers to defamation and privacy issues, in NA Moreham, and Sir Mark Warby, *Tugendhat and Christie, The Law of Privacy and the Media* (OUP, 2016) at 349; M Collins, *Collins on Defamation* (OUP, 2014); D Erdos, 'Data Protection and the Right to Reputation: Filling the "Gaps" After the Defamation Act 2013' *Cambridge Law Journal* (2014) (73:3) 536.
3   Moreham, and Warby, *Tugendhat and Christie, The Law of Privacy and the Media*; G Robertson, and A Nicol, *Robertson and Nichol on Media Law* (Sweet and Maxwell, 2007); A Etzioni, *Privacy in a Cyber Age: Policy and Practice* (Palgrave Macmillan, 2015); D Bloy, *Media Law* (Sage, 2006); M McGonagle, *Media Law* (Round Hall, 2018).
4   I Goldrein, *Privacy Injunctions and the Media: A Practice Manual* (Hart, 2012).
5   R Pattenden and D Sheehan, *The Law of Professional-Client Confidentiality* (OUP, 2016).
6   E Christie Reid, *Personality, Confidentiality and Privacy in Scots Law* (W Green/Thomson Reuters, 2010).
7   J Macdonald and R Crail, *Macdonald on the Law of Freedom of Information* (OUP, 2016).
8   M Santín, 'The Problem of the Right to be Forgotten from the Perspective of Self-Regulation in Journalism' *El Profesional de la Información* (2017) (26:2) 303.
9   O Pollicino and G De Gregorio, 'Privacy or Transparency: A New Balancing of Interests for the Right to Be Forgotten of Personal Data Published in Public Registers' *Italian Law Journal* (2017) (3:2) 647.

interference via the RtbF with freedom of expression and the right to freedom of expression.[10]

Some literature refers to the media interests as being freedom of expression related.[11] Other literature refer to freedom of information (apparently in an access context).[12] The literature can also refer to media issue in the context of a right to know.[13] There are also references to a right to right to inform.[14]

There is also increasing consideration of media-related RtbF issues in different jurisdictions, such as in the Netherlands,[15] Germany,[16] Scotland,[17] Brazil[18] and the US.[19]

Often, initial commentary from the sector itself was initially narrowly cast in terms of criticising RtbF from a sometimes knee-jerk reaction perceiving that it was impinging or restricting news journalism. This is not strictly correct as

---

10 S Vlachopoulos, 'Freedom of Expression in the Internet the Example of the "Right to be Forgotten"' *European Review of Public Law* (2018) (30:1) 113.

11 See for example B Muçi and E Muçi, 'Defining the Right to be Forgotten and its Relationship With Freedom of Expression' *European Journal of Economics, Law and Social Sciences* (2020) (4:1) 26; K Faisal, 'Balancing Between Right to be Forgotten and Right to Freedom of Expression in Spent Criminal Convictions' *Security* (2021) (4:4) 1; S-D Şchiopu, 'Some Aspects of the Right to be Forgotten from the Perspective of Balancing the Freedom of Expression with the Respect for Private Life in the Online Environment' *Jus et Civitas: A Journal of Social and Legal Studies* (2019) (6:1) 27; R Matefi, 'The Balance Between the Right to Freedom of Expression and the Protection of the Personality Rights From the Jurisprudence Perspective' *Jus et Civitas: A Journal of Social and Legal Studies* (2019) (6:1) 1.

12 I Jiménez-Castellanos Ballesteros, 'The Conflict Between the Right to be Forgotten of the Criminal History and Freedom of Information: Digital Newspaper Archives (In this respect the Spanish Constitutional Court Judgment of June 4, 2018 and the European Court of Human Rights' Judgment in the M.L. and W.W. vs. Germany case, June 28, 2018)' *Revista de Derecho Político* (2019) (1:106) 137; S De Conca, 'GC et al v CNIL: Balancing the Right to be Forgotten With the Freedom of Information, the Duties of a Search Engine Operator (C-136/17 GC et al v CNIL)' *European Data Protection Law Review* (EDPL) (2019) (5:4) 561.

13 F Zufall, 'Challenging the EU's Right to be Forgotten: Society's Right to Know in Japan' *European Data Protection Law Review* (EDPL) (2019) (5:1) 17.

14 F Sergio, 'The Right to be Forgotten: The Regulatory-Jurisprudential Evolution of the Right to Be Forgotten and the Relations with the Right to Inform in a Constitutionally Oriented Purpose' *European Journal of Privacy Law & Technologies* (EJPLT) (2020) (1) 177.

15 S Kulk and F Zuiderveen Borgesius, 'Freedom of Expression and Right to Be Forgotten Cases in the Netherlands after *Google Spain*' *European Data Protection Law Review (EDPL)* (2015) (1:2) 113.

16 C Kodde, 'Germany's "Right to be Forgotten" – Between the Freedom of Expression and the Right to Informational Self-Determination' *International Review of Law, Computers* (2016) (30:1/2) 17.

17 Christie Reid, *Personality, Confidentiality and Privacy in Scots Law*.

18 M Viola de Azevedo Cunha and G Itagiba, 'Between Privacy, Freedom of Information and Freedom of Expression: Is there a Right to be Forgotten in Brazil?' *Computer Law & Security Review* (2016) (32:4) 634.

19 A Gajda, 'Privacy, Press and the Right to be Forgotten in the United States' *Washington Law Review* (2018) (93:1) 201.

RtbF is a retrospective tool and does not impact real-time journalistic activities at all.

More recent media sector comments are less entrenched, and even recognise that there can be a need for RtbF. Some media entities now consider the many details and interests involved with media RtbF issues and even adopt specific policies, including for past crime stories, eg *Boston Globe*; *Cleveland.com*; and the news agency *Associated Press* (AP). It is increasingly evident that there can be many nuances issues involved in RtbF generally, and also specifically in the media RtbF area, and that there can be legitimate RtbF type interests which can be appropriate in the media sector.[20]

2 BALANCE

24.2 Some have referred to a so-called right to remember.[21] In some instances there is analysis, in others comparison[22] and in still others suggestions that the right to remember should always trump RtbF or indeed that there should not be RtbF. One nuance in the latter suggestion is not that there is no need and basis for RtbF, but rather that it should not exist simpliciter.

Others put this issue in a more nuanced state and ask what it is that should, or must, be remembered.[23] There is also commentary on even more specific issues such as RtbF and right to remember and, balancing these issues, in the context of the criminal law in California.[24]

There is increasing detailed consideration of the RtbF, the interests and concerns of individuals that are being vindicated, the right as it exists under GDPR statute (regulation) law. There is also consideration of RtbF as a 'human right to be forgotten',[25] protection and self determination.

20 Generally, see E Corcione, 'The Right to be Forgotten, Between Web Archives and Search Engines: Further Steps at the European Court of Human Rights' *European Data Protection Law Review* (EDPL) (2019) (5:2) 262; A Right to be Forgotten: Largest American News Agency Changes Policy For Crime Reporting To Do Less Harm' https://www.milwaukeeindependent. com/, 21 September 2021;
21 S Wechsler, 'The Right to Remember: The European Convention on Human Rights and the Right to Be Forgotten, Columbia. *Journal of Law & Social Problems/Paul and Katie Law Review* (2015) (49:1) 135; C Rees and D Heywood, 'The "Right to be Forgotten" or the "Principle That Has Been Remembered,"' *Computer Law & Security Review* (2014) (30:5) 574.
22 Wechsler, 'The Right to Remember: The European Convention on Human Rights and the Right to be Forgotten' *above* at 135.
23 K Stewart, 'Looking Backward, Moving Forward: What Must Be Remembered When Resolving the Right to Be Forgotten' *Brooklyn Journal of International Law* (2017) (42:2) 843.
24 M Keiter, 'Criminal Law Principles in California: Balancing a Right to Be Forgotten with a Right to Remember' *California Legal History* (2018) (13) 421.
25 A Neville, 'Is It a Human Right to Be Forgotten? Conceptualizing The World View' *Santa Clara Journal of International Law* (2017) (15:2) 157.

While there has been criticism,[26] some unjustified, of RtbF, there is equally more considered commentary on issues of balance, practical implementation and the like.[27]

3 PROBLEMS AND SOLUTIONS

24.3   Others recognise the need for solutions to the problem issues which can be assisted by having a RtbF. On its strictest interpretation (the original Jimmy Wales argument of No RtbF 'Full Stop' approach), many legitimate concerns can be ignored or left unaided. Victims of revenge porn can be left with no ability or right, to seek takedown of problem images online which were maliciously posted by a third party. There is also a middle or centre ground, one example of which may include solutions for dealing with particularly old news on search engines.[28] This area will no doubt continue to garner research as well as comment – and argument from interested parties.[29]

4 RANGE OF MEDIA RTBF ISSUES

24.4   As the consideration of RtbF increases, we will see a range of potential media and RtbF issues. In the first instance readers should note that when we refer to the media we are generally talking about the newspaper and broadcast media. The media are the vehicle for the exercise of public rights or rights of the public. *Google Spain*, for example, in the final part of the decision refers to the 'interest of the public in having, on account of its inclusion in the list of results, access to the information in question'.[30]

Just some of the specific media RtbF issues, which can be quite nuanced issues, include:

---

26   For example, see K Byrum, *The European Right to be Forgotten: The First Amendment Enemy* (Lexington, 2018).
27   See, eg, S Singleton, 'Balancing a Right to be Forgotten with a Right to Freedom of Expression in the Wake of *Google Spain v AEPD*' *Georgia Journal of International* (2015) (44:1) 165; P Jonason, 'The Right to be Forgotten: The Balance Between the Right to Privacy and Freedom of Expression' *European Review of Public Law* (2018) (30:1) 213; CE Carbone, 'To Be or Not to be Forgotten: Balancing the Right to Know with the Right to Privacy in the Digital Age' *Virginia Journal of Social Policy & the Law* (2015) (22:3) 525; J Abramson, 'Searching for Reputation: Reconciling Free Speech and the Right to Be Forgotten' *North Carolina Journal of Law & Technology* (2015/6) (17:1) 1; Keiter, 'Criminal Law Principles in California: Balancing a Right to Be Forgotten with a Right to Remember' at 421.
28   HL Cook, 'Flagging the Middle Ground of the Right to Be Forgotten: Combatting Old News with Search Engine Flags' *Vanderbilt Journal of Entertainment & Technology Law* (2017) (20:1) 1.
29   M Xue, G Magno, E Cunha, V Almeida and KW Ross, 'The Right to be Forgotten in the Media: A Data-Driven Study' *Proceedings on Privacy Enhancing Technologies* (2016) (4) 389.
30   Emphasis added. *Google Spain SL, Google Inc v Agencia Española de Protección de Datos (AEPD), Mario Costeja González*, Court of Justice (Grand Chamber), Case C-131/12, 13 May 2014 at para 4.

- RtbF and outdated newspaper news reports;[31]

- RtbF and outdated newspaper reports and content which are not news reports;

- Rtbf and outdated broadcast news reports;[32]

- RtbF and outdated broadcast reports and content which are not news reports;

- RtbF and newspaper archives;[33]

- RtbF and newspaper news archives;[34]

- RtbF and newspaper non-news archives;

- RtbF and newspaper archives offline;

- RtbF and newspaper archives online;[35]

- RtbF and broadcaster archives;

- RtbF and broadcaster news archives;

- RtbF and broadcaster non-news archives;

- RtbF and broadcaster archives offline;

- RtbF and broadcaster archives online;

- traditional offline data protection and privacy;

- online data protection and privacy;

- journalism, own content, content sources, official data or officially posted data and request to take it down or otherwise restrict access;[36]

- adults, media and RtbF;

- online amplification, online permanence, online (and offline) chilling, and effects;

- memory and forgetting;[37]

- lost and diminished data protection and privacy;

---

31 Cook, 'Flagging the Middle Ground of the Right to Be Forgotten: Combatting Old News with Search Engine Flags' at 1.
32 *Ibid.*
33 A Salarelli, 'Right to be Forgotten and Online Newspapers Archives: Some Considerations on Social Memory in Our Times' *JLIS.it* (2013) (5:1) 1.
34 *Ibid.*
35 *Ibid.*
36 E Carava, 'Personal Data Kept in Companies Registers: The Denial of the Right to Be Forgotten' *European Data Protection Law Review (EDPL)* (2017) (3:2) 287.
37 Salarelli, 'Right to be Forgotten and Online Newspapers Archives: Some Considerations on Social Memory in Our Times' at 1; V Mayer-Schönberger, *Delete: the Virtue of Forgetting in the Digital Age* (Princeton, 2009).

- rebalancing and 'regaining' data protection and privacy;[38]

- news, newsworthiness and non-news;[39]

- informational self-determination;[40]

- media reporting, identification restrictions, anonymity – rules and policies;

- children, media and RtbF;

- children with adults; and adults with children and RtbF;

- media interests, public interests and interests;

- balance and conflict;[41]

- freedom of expression, and data protection, erasure and forgetting;[42]

- RtbF, media, 'tension and conflict';[43]

- RtbF, regulation and self regulation in journalism;[44]

- how and who in media decide what is forgotten under RtbF, and any implications;[45]

- where, how and why media criticism of RtbF arisies;[46]

- RtbF and media representative bodies;

- RtbF, different media, different standards; different interests;

- interactions between media with search engines and other online service providers – on individual RtbF notices;

- interactions between media with search engines and other online service providers – on general RtbF policy;

- recognising rights – including the RtbF – in real time;[47] and

---

38 F Brimblecombe and G Phillipson, 'Regaining Digital Privacy: The New Right to Be Forgotten and Online Expression' *Canadian Journal of Comparative and Contemporary Law* (2018) (4) 1.

39 JE McNealy, 'The Emerging Conflict Between Newsworthiness and the Right to be Forgotten' *Northern Kentucky Law Review* (2012) (39:2) 119.

40 Kodde, 'Germany's "Right to be Forgotten" – Between the Freedom of Expression and the Right to Informational Self-Determination' above at 17.

41 E Lee, 'The Right to Be Forgotten v Free Speech' *I/S: A Journal of Law and Policy for the Information Society* (2015) (12:1) 85.

42 J Barnes, 'Data Protection and the Article 10 Right to Freedom of Expression' in Moreham and Warby, *Tugendhat and Christie, The Law of Privacy and the Media* at 301.

43 *Ibid*, at section 7.05 in Chapter 7.

44 Santín, 'The Problem of the Right to be Forgotten from the Perspective of Self-Regulation in Journalism' above at 303.

45 P Sanchez Abril and JD Lipton, 'The Right to be Forgotten: Who Decides What the World Forgets?' *Kentucky Law Journal* (2015) (103:3) 363.

46 D Erdos, 'European Union Data Protection Law and Media Expression: Fundamentally Off Balance' *International & Comparative Law Quarterly* (2016) (65:1) 139.

47 E Lee, 'Recognizing Rights in Real Time: The Role of Google in the EU Right to Be Forgotten' *UC Davis Law Review* (2016) (49:3) 1017.

- the need to deal with certain situations swiftly and in real time, viral online abuse, viral attacks, etc; RtbF and realtime forgetting, etc).[48]

5 GDPR

24.5   There is obvious media interest in the GDPR, the *Google Spain* case and RtbF itself for its societal implications. There is, in addition, media self-interest at play, especially insofar as there is a potential for media content to be the subject of RtbF notices from individual data subjects.

In terms of the latter, this interest will focus less on the right and more on the exemptions. RtbF rights referred to in GDPR Article 17(1) and (2) can potentially be exempt. The provision that media organisations will naturally look to most will be the provision stating that there can be an exemption:

> to the extent that the processing is necessary:
>
> (a)   for exercising the right of freedom of expression and information.[49]

In the first instance, it must be appreciated that this potential exemption (and with the other exemptions) has a necessity requirement. It must be 'necessary' to be able to apply. That it is a possibility, a potential, a wish list, is not necessary, is not a requirement, is not required, can be achieved by other means, has other more proportional means available, etc, mitigate the potential to be able to utilise this exemption.

Being 'necessary' can also be interpreted as being strictly necessary.

The second main issue to note is that this is a freedom of expression interest at play. This is normally understood not as a media interest or media right per se, but rather as a public right. The media is the vehicle (or one of the vehicles) through which the public right to freedom of expression can be achieved or vindicated.

While the words 'and information' are added to the freedom of expression reference, it is not fully clear what this will mean in practice for RtbF considerations, or disputes. It may be understood as the flip side of the expression coin (eg, public right to express information/public right to receive information).

It may be, however, that in some future case an entity other than a genuine newspaper media entity may seek to argue that 'expression' and 'information' are not conjoined and that 'information' is detached and separate and creates a wider (exemption) right which included wider recipient entities other than traditional media.

---

48   *Ibid.*
49   GDPR Art 17(3)(a).

A further issue which will no doubt arise, will be the issue of freedom of expression in relation to news reporting and news journalism. Issues then arise as to other content. Other issues will relate to new reporting content being judged at the conjunction of the news event. News eventually recedes and arguably some will suggest that must be taken to mean that journalists' interests recede over time. Indeed, this issue is acknowledged in both the official guidance and in case law. The older, less newsworthy and aged the news content, the stronger are RtbF notices from individual data subjects.

A further issue arising is that of new uses and secondary purposes. The further the new activities are from the news event or original publication, and the further removed from any current news issue, the more likely it will be that data subjects will use these points when seeking to restrict, prevent or erase content from susceptibility to these new uses. They will also argue that the original purpose is spent and that there cannot be a justifiable new modern use.

6 GOOGLE SPAIN

24.6   The *Google Spain* case acknowledges that RtbF and such interests can trump not only the search engine interest (including search engine commercial interests), but also potential media interests (as reflecting the public interest).

It refers to RtbF rights of the data subject and that 'those rights override, as a rule … the economic interest of the operator of the search engine'.

It also refers to RtbF rights of the data subject and that 'those rights override, as a rule … the interest of the general public in having access to that information upon a search'.

These must be taken, therefore, as the default position in circumstances such as the *Google Spain* case. It is noted that in this case, the problem content at issue was old news references or reports.

This just goes to show that news media organisations should not assume that necessary (news media) interest in the freedom of expression has no temporal limitations or that its interest in the freedom of expression is in any way absolute.

This raises the issue of RtbF requests to third parties (indirect) and to the new organisation itself (direct). It may be relatively easy for a news organisation to have, or to take, an absolutist (or principled) view and to refuse all RtbF notices from data subjects. Such a strict policy may not be the most considered in light of the actual express right(s) of RtbF and also given that the above exemption should not be taken to be an absolute answer to all RtbF notices received. It is suggested that news organisations need to have a more considered, wide-eyed review of RtbF – also recognising that the interests and policies of different news organisations are not always the same.

7 WP29

24.7   As indicated elsewhere, the WP29 issued guidance following the *Google Spain* case. Included in this guidance was a list of 13 issues to be considered when dealing with RtbF notification issues.

One of the suggested criteria[50] asks whether the relevant data or content is 'relevant and not excessive'. It might be suggested that, again, there is a temporal element, being that the content is currently relevant, or not, at the time of the RtbF notification; and that it can either be currently proportionate or currently disproportionate on a temporal basis at the time of the RtbF notification. These would appear relevant issues to consider in relation to news organisation content.

Another criterion asks whether 'the data is up to date'? Is the data being made available for longer than is necessary for the proposed of the processing'.[51] Again, if one of the temporal issues is the age of the data and the purpose means the original news purpose at the time of publication, this leans against some of the arguments that a media organisation may have wished to make.

Of particular interest is criterion 11. This asks whether 'the original content [was] published in the context of journalistic purposes'. This may well be argued by data subjects to again refer to temporal issues, the point in time being the original publications data and the purpose and journalistic purpose being again taken at the time of the original publication.

8   PUBLIC FIGURE

24.8   *Google Spain* also makes clear that, in those circumstances, the balance and interest clearly lies in favour of takedown, erasure and forgetting – even viz a vis the interests of media and journalistic organisations.

The carveout or exception from the above, as provided in *Google Spain* itself, is where the individual is a public figure. Potentially there may be other circumstances, as it refers to 'such as'. The language used is: '[h]owever, that would not be the case if it appeared, for particular reasons, such as the role played by the individual data subject in public life'.[52]

There is no definition, however, of public figure.

Debate may arise perhaps as to what a public figure is; whether the individual must be a public figure prior to the news event referring to the individual; or whether the news event raises the individual up to the level of a public figure. As many social media would-be internet stars will testify, it can take a lot to

---

50   WP29, criterion 5.
51   *Ibid* criterion 7.
52   *Google Spain* para 100(4).

become famous, yet once attained, the moment of fame can be fleeting. So even if someone is a public figure today, it does not mean that they are the same public figure next week, still less in a given number of years from now. Nostalgia, too, does not make a contemporary (newsworthy) public figure. Fame is fleeting; so too is whatever the 'public' element of 'public figure' may be.

An issue which may not have much attention is the right of public figure individuals to have details erased or forgotten of their history under a different gender.[53]

9 PREPONDERANCE

24.9   Regardless of who is or is not a public figure, when it is public and when it becomes not public, media and journalistic organisations have a further associated hurdle to consider. *Google Spain* states that:

> However, that would not be the case if it appeared, for particular reasons, such as the role played by the individual data subject in public life, that the interference with his fundamental rights is justified by the preponderant interest of the general public in having, on account of its inclusion in the list of results, access to the information in question.[54]

So, when seeking to rely on a person being a public figure as an exception basis from RtbF obligations, such interest must be predicated on 'the preponderant interest of the general public in having … access to the content'.

This should not be assumed to mean that the media interest (ie, the public interest) is per se predominant. That would suggest that in all instance the media (public) interest is always superior – which is not the case. A better reading is that the media public interest can, in some instances, become predominant. They are not automatically predominant. That would be too wide a view.

On this basis, a mere interest or mere claim may be insufficient in the circumstances. Rather, it must be the single 'preponderant interest'. This will not be easy to establish in all cases and may not be possible in most cases. In addition, where the data subject can refer to their having the preponderant interest, competing interest or equal interest, RtbF notice should proceed. The onus would appear to be clearly on the media or journalistic organisation to establish the preponderance, in order then to avail of the carveout or exemption. A mere interest is not a preponderant interest. Therefore, media entities should not assume that there is a general easily and widely available exemption per se.

---

53 H Iannucci, '"Erasing Transgender Public Figures" Former Identity with the Right to Be Forgotten' *Federal Communications Law Journal* (2021) (73:2) 259.
54 *Ibid.*

10   NEW DIGITAL MEDIA AND JOURNALISM

24.10   What was once hardcopy, traditional media and news journalism is now expanding online in the internet era, such as the *Washington Post*, *New York Times*, and *Guardian* online versions.

In addition, however, whole new forms of digital media and digital journalism are arising which is only based online. Examples of the latter include *Politico*, *Mother Jones*, *Punchbowl News*, and *TheJournal*.

While the above concentrate on news and journalism, other entities are more concerned with entertainment, sport, gossip, or other genres.

Separate to the above organisational entities, there is also a wide variety of so-called individual journalists who push videos, stories, and other content online.

More recently, there are a range of individuals also pushing online content as so-called 'influencers' – in contrast to more dedicated news or journalism. Notwithstanding that, some of these individuals still have comparatively large audiences (sometimes referred to as (dedicated) followers).

There are also other forms of online media being created on an almost regular basis.

RtbF issues will apply to these as they do to other entities, and to other more established media forms. However, it may be that some of these new digital media entities or individuals might have difficulty in an instant case in establishing that they are 'media' or that they are 'journalists' in the traditional sense. The result being that where there may be some exemption, media right, or other accommodation in law benefiting established media in some way, it may not be also available to one of the new digital media promoters.

There may be serious arguments and issues as to whether freedom of expression,[55] media reporting defences,[56] and now RtbF media accommodations[57] can be availed of when a problem arises for one of these new digital media enterprises or individuals.[58] On the other side of the coin, more traditional media and journalistic entities while being able to avail of certain legal accommodations, will also have to comply with the requirements of such accommodations, media ethics rules, and relevant industry codes.[59]

---

55   A Koltay, *New Media and Freedom of Expression* (Oxford Hart Publishing, 2019); P Coe, 'New Media and Freedom of Expression: by András Koltay, Oxford Hart Publishing' Review, *Journal of Media Law* (2019) (11:2) 163.
56   A Koltay and P Wragg (eds), *Comparative Privacy and Defamation* (Elgar, 2020).
57   'Digital Media and the Right to be Forgotten' *Lawyer* (18 May 2020) 1-1.
58   SA Eldridge II and B Franklin (eds), *The Routledge Handbook of Developments in Digital Journalism Studies* (Routledge, 2019); U Smartt, *Media & Entertainment Law* (Taylor and Francis, 2019); A Sehl, R Fletcher and RF Picard, 'Crowding Out: Is there Evidence that Public Service Media Harm Markets? A Cross-National Comparative Analysis of Commercial Television and Online News Providers' *European Journal of Communication* (2020) (35:4) 389.
59   LT Price, K Sanders and WN Wyatt (eds), *The Routledge Companion to Journalism Ethics* (Routledge, 2021).

PART H

ADDITIONAL SOLUTION
OPTIONS TO CONSIDER

CHAPTER 25

Potential Additional Solutions

1 INTRODUCTION

25.1 There are also other solution issues to the aforementioned problem issues to consider in the GDPR. These include right to rectification; right to restriction of processing; privacy by design (PbD) and data protection by design (DPbD) and default;[1] data protection impact assessments (DPIAs); and prior consultations with data protection supervisory authorities; and not least issues of damages and compensation. (While there are also other solution issues and policy to consider in addition to the GDPR and GDPR RtbF, these are not the core focus of the current discussion.)

2 RIGHT TO RECTIFICATION

25.2 Chapter III, Section 3 of the GDPR is headed '[r]ectification and erasure'. This was already an important and topical issue and is now even more important as a result of the *Google Spain*[2] case (see below) and also issues such as online abuse (OA).

The individual data subject has the right to obtain from the controller without undue delay the rectification of inaccurate personal data concerning them. Taking into account the purposes of the processing, the individual data subject shall have the right to have incomplete personal data completed, including by means of providing a supplementary statement.[3]

There are also additional rights options available to the individual data subject apart from the right to erasure and forgetting provided pursuant to Article 17.

Article 16 provides the right to rectification to the individual data subject. The individual data subject has the right to obtain from the controller the rectification of inaccurate personal data concerning him or her. The rectification must occur without undue delay.

---

1   JE Giannakakis, '"Privacy By Design (PbD) and Transparency Requirements Under the General Data Protection Regulation (GDPR) as Fraud Prevention Tools' *International Journal for the Data Protection Officer, Privacy Officer and Privacy Counsel (IDPP)* (2017) (1:2) 8.
2   *Google Spain SL, Google Inc v Agencia Española de Protección de Datos (AEPD), Mario Costeja González*, Court of Justice (Grand Chamber), Case C-131/12, 13 May 2014.
3   GDPR Art 16.

A separate right also arises. The Article provides that the individual data subject has the right to have incomplete personal data completed.

This right to have incomplete data completed also includes providing, or by means of providing, a supplementary statement. It is important to note that the right and discretion of the individual data subject – not at the choice or discretion of the controller ('*the data subject shall have the right to* have incomplete personal data completed, including by means of providing a supplementary statement').

The right to have incomplete personal data completed, including by means of providing a supplementary statement, raises the issue of what amounts to 'incomplete' and what must be included to make particular data 'completed'.

In terms of considering a 'supplementary statement', the issue arises as to who drafts the statement; if and where that might be the controller, if a draft must be furnished in advance to the individual data subject, and whether the individual data subject is required to agree same before it goes live.

Recital 65 also adds to this issue. It states that '[a] data subject should have the right to have personal data concerning him or her rectified and ... where the retention of such data infringes this Regulation or Union or Member State law to which the controller is subject'.

The DPD 95/46 Article 12 (prior to the GDPR), entitled 'Rights of access' provided:

> Member States shall guarantee every data subject the right to obtain from the controller: ...
>
> (b) as appropriate the rectification ... of data the processing of which does not comply with the provisions of this Directive, in particular because of the incomplete or inaccurate nature of the data; ...'

The DPD 95/46 Article 14 (prior to the GDPR), entitled 'The data subject's right to object,' provided:

> 'Member States shall grant the data subject the right:
>
> (a) at least in the cases referred to in Article 7(e) and (f), to object at any time on compelling legitimate grounds relating to his particular situation to the processing of data relating to him, save where otherwise provided by national legislation. Where there is a justified objection, the processing instigated by the controller may no longer involve those data; ...'

The court in the leading case of *Google Spain* relying on the above Directive, held that:

- Article 12(b) and subparagraph (a) of the first paragraph of Article 14 of [the DPD 95/46] are to be interpreted as meaning that, in order to comply with the rights ... a search engine is obliged to remove from the list of results displayed following a search made on the basis of a person's name links to web pages, published by third parties and containing information relating to that person, also in a case where that name or information is not erased beforehand or simultaneously from those web pages, and even, as the case may be, when its publication in itself on those pages is lawful;

- Article 12(b) and subparagraph (a) of the first paragraph of Article 14 of [the DPD 95/46] are to be interpreted as meaning that, when appraising the conditions for the application of those provisions, it should, inter alia, be examined whether the individual data subject has a right that the information in question relating to him personally should, at this point in time, no longer be linked to his name by a list of results displayed following a search made on the basis of his name, without it being necessary in order to find such a right that the inclusion of the information in question in that list causes prejudice to the individual data subject. As the individual data subject may, in the light of his fundamental rights under Articles 7 and 8 of the Charter, request that the information in question no longer be made available to the general public on account of its inclusion in such a list of results, those rights override, as a rule, not only the economic interest of the operator of the search engine but also the interest of the general public in having access to that information upon a search relating to the individual data subject's name. However, that would not be the case if it appeared, for particular reasons, such as the role played by the individual data subject in public life, that the interference with his fundamental rights is justified by the preponderant interest of the general public in having, on account of its inclusion in the list of results, access to the information in question.

3   RESTRICTION OF PROCESSING

25.3   Article 18 also provides a right to restriction of processing of personal data to the individual data subject. The individual data subject has the right to obtain from the controller the restriction of processing of their personal data.

This restriction of processing right arises where one of a number of scenarios are met. These are listed as follows:

(a)   the accuracy of the personal data is contested by the individual data subject, for a period enabling the controller to verify the accuracy of the personal data;

(b)   the processing is unlawful and the individual data subject opposes the erasure of the personal data and requests the restriction of their use instead;

(c)   the controller no longer needs the personal data for the purposes of the processing, but they are required by the individual data subject for the establishment, exercise or defence of legal claims;

(d)   the individual data subject has objected to processing pursuant to Article 21(1) pending the verification whether the legitimate grounds of the controller override those of the individual data subject.

The restriction in relation to 'the accuracy of the personal data is contested by the data subject, for a period enabling the controller to verify the accuracy of the personal data' suggests a temporary restriction – 'for a period'; 'for ... enabling ... verif[ication] [of] accuracy'.

It is not stated what happens next under ground (a). If there is verification of inaccurate data, what happens? What is the obligation? Once would assume that inaccurate personal data would be corrected or deleted. However, it might be considered that the requesting individual data subject may prefer one rather than the other. Another point of consideration is whether the decision is entirely left to the controller.

Ground (b) raises some queries. If processing is unlawful, how might it become lawful – even by the individual data subject opposing erasure? Does the act of opposing erasure amount a consent, express or otherwise?

In terms of ground (c), this would seem to require some notification and request to the controller from the individual data subject. However, the potential for this ground to apply should not be without temporal limit. The time after which potential action might arise would seem to be the time limit after which this ground would become no longer available.

The ground under (d) above also appears to be envisages as being temporary in nature.

Where the processing has been restricted under paragraph 1, such personal data shall, with the exception of storage, only be processed:

* with the individual data subject consent; or

* for the establishment, exercise or defence of legal claims; or

* for the protection of the rights of another natural or legal person; or

* for reasons of important public interest of the Union or of a Member State.

A further obligation arises for the controller. An individual data subject who has obtained restriction of processing must be informed by the controller before the restriction of processing is lifted. While no notice period is specified, it must be interpreted to mean that the individual data subject has sufficient time to receive the notice and to be able to respond to the controller on any issue that the individual data subject considers important or relevant.

The DPD 95/46 Article 12 (prior to the GDPR), entitled 'Rights of access' provided:

> Member States shall guarantee every data subject the right to obtain from the controller: ...
>
> (b) as appropriate the rectification, erasure or blocking of data the processing of which does not comply with the provisions of this Directive, in particular because of the incomplete or inaccurate nature of the data; ...

The DPD 95/46 Article 14 (prior to the GDPR), entitled The data subject's right to object, provided:

> 'Member States shall grant the data subject the right:
>
> (a) at least in the cases referred to in Article 7(e) and (f), to object at any time on compelling legitimate grounds relating to his particular situation to the processing of data relating to him, save where otherwise provided by national legislation. Where there is a justified objection, the processing instigated by the controller may no longer involve those data; ...'

The court in the leading case of *Google Spain*[4] relying on the above Directive, held that:

- Article 12(b) and subparagraph (a) of the first paragraph of the DPD 95/46 Article 14 are to be interpreted as meaning that, in order to comply with the rights laid down in those provisions and in so far as the conditions laid down by those provisions are in fact satisfied, the operator of a search engine is obliged to remove from the list of results displayed following a search made on the basis of a person's name links to web pages, published by third parties and containing information relating to that person, also in a case where that name or information is not erased beforehand or simultaneously from those web pages, and even, as the case may be, when its publication in itself on those pages is lawful;

- Article 12(b) and subparagraph (a) of the first paragraph of the DPD 95/46 Article 14 are to be interpreted as meaning that, when appraising the conditions for the application of those provisions, it should, inter alia, be examined whether the individual data subject has a right that the information in question relating to him personally should, at this point in time, no longer be linked to his name by a list of results displayed following a search made on the basis of his name, without it being necessary in order to find such a right that the inclusion of the information in question in that list causes prejudice to the individual data subject. As the individual data subject may, in the light of his fundamental rights under Charter Articles 7 and 8, request that the information in question no longer be made available to the general public on account of its inclusion in such a list of results, those rights override, as a rule, not only the economic interest of the operator of the search engine but also the interest of the general public in having access to that information upon a search relating to the individual data subject's name. However, that would not be the case if it appeared, for particular reasons, such as the role played by the individual data subject in public life, that the interference with his fundamental rights is justified by the preponderant interest of the general public in having, on account of its inclusion in the list of results, access to the information in question.

---

4   *Google Spain SL, Google Inc v Agencia Española de Protección de Datos (AEPD), Mario Costeja González.*

4 NOTIFICATION TO THIRD PARTIES

25.4 Article 19 of the GDPR relates to a notification obligation regarding rectification or erasure of personal data or restriction of processing.

The controller must communicate any rectification or erasure of personal data or restriction of processing of personal data (per Articles 16, 17(1) or 18) to each recipient to whom the personal data have been disclosed.

This communication obligation on the controller applies unless this proves 'impossible or involves disproportionate effort'. It may be difficult to justify or prove that it is impossible, at least from a technical or process perspective. However, it may be that in certain, even exceptional, circumstances there may be no way to contact a particular recipient (eg, no contact details are listed or available for an individual recipient). This will not be available to the controller in most instances. Even where the controller may not have maintained records as regard contact details for a recipient, it is still possible for the controller to investigate contemporary details for the recipient.

Even where it is impossible to contact a particular recipient, in instances where there are a number of recipients, is very unlikely that it will be impossible to contact all of them.

A more likely avenue that a Controller may wish to seek to avail of is the possibility of there being 'disproportionate effort'. However, it must be reasonable and justifiable in the circumstances to avail of this ground. As technology expands, the ease of creating new avenues of compliance continues, and the cost continues to lessen, it may be more difficult to justify this ground that might initially have appeared. The more resources the organisation has, the more difficult it may be to suggest that the effort is disproportionate. Even where large numbers of individuals may be needed, it may be suggested that these are still normal internal resources and are not disproportionate.

It is also possible that 'disproportionate' needs to be considered in terms of the right and need of the individual data subject, and even a very large effort is still necessary to vindicate the needs and right of the individual data subject making the request. The view of the damage and legitimate interests of the individual data subject cannot or should not be ignored when considering what effort is fair and required and what factors are to be considered when looking at the parameters of 'disproportionate effort'.

Article 16 refers to the right of rectification belonging to the individual data subject.

Article 17(1) refers to the erasure and forgetting right belonging to the individual data subject.

Article 18 refers to the right to restriction of processing belonging to the individual data subject.

The controller must also inform the individual data subject about those recipients if the individual data subject requests it. It will be up to the individual data subject to make the request. It may be, therefore, that the individual data subject may have to make two requests: one for the original rectification or erasure of personal data or restriction of processing; and the second requesting the recipient's details.

5 DATA PROTECTION BY DESIGN AND BY DEFAULT

25.5   Article 25 refers to data protection by design and by default. Note also the related concept of Privacy by Design (PbD). In some ways PbD is the impetus or precursor for the current DPbD rules.

Taking into account the state of the art and the nature, scope, context and purposes of the processing as well as the risks of varying likelihood and severity for rights and freedoms of natural persons posed by the processing, the controller shall, both at the time of the determination of the means for processing and at the time of the processing itself, implement appropriate technical and organisational measures, such as pseudonymisation, which are designed to implement data protection principles, such as data minimisation, in an effective way and to integrate the necessary safeguards into the processing to meet the requirements of the GDPR and protect the rights of individual data subjects.[5]

The controller shall implement appropriate technical and organisational measures for ensuring that, by default, only personal data which are necessary for each specific purpose of the processing are processed. That obligation applies to the amount of data collected, the extent of their processing, the period of their storage and their accessibility. Such measures will ensure that personal data are not made accessible by default, without the individual's intervention to an indefinite number of natural persons.[6]

An approved certification mechanism pursuant to Article 42 may be used as an element to demonstrate compliance with the requirements set out in Article 25(1) and (2).[7]

There is significant interest in design type issues coming from a variety of areas.[8] The relationship with the rights and interests of data subjects, such as in relation to RtbF, will also need to be considered further.

---

5   GDPR Art 25(1).
6   *Ibid* Art 23(2).
7   *Ibid* Art 25(3).
8   John E Giannakakis refers to Privacy by Design (PbD) and transparency requirements under the GDPR, and in relation to it application as fraud prevention tools. JE Giannakakis, "'Privacy By Design (PbD) and Transparency Requirements Under the General Data Protection Regulation (GDPR) as Fraud Prevention Tools' *International Journal for the Data Protection Officer, Privacy Officer and Privacy Counsel (IDPP)* (2017) (1:2) 8.

6 DATA PROTECTION IMPACT ASSESSMENT

25.6   Chapter IV, section 3 of the GDPR refers to Impact Assessments and Prior Consultations. Where a type of processing using new technologies and taking into account the nature, scope, context and purposes of the processing is likely to result in a high risk for the rights and freedoms of natural persons, the controller shall, prior to the processing, carry out an assessment of the impact of the envisaged processing operations on the protection of personal data. A single assessment may address a set of similar processing operations that present similar high risks.[9]

The controller shall seek the advice of the DPO, where designated, when carrying out a data protection impact assessment.[10]

A data protection impact assessment referred to in Article 35(1) will be required in the case of:

- a systematic and extensive evaluation of personal aspects relating to natural persons which is based on automated processing, including profiling, and on which decisions are based that produce legal effects concerning the natural person or similarly significantly affect the natural person;

- processing on a large scale of special categories of data referred to in Article 9(1), or of personal data relating to criminal convictions and offences referred to in Article 10; or

- a systematic monitoring of a publicly accessible area on a large scale.[11]

The supervisory authority shall establish and make public a list of the kind of processing operations which are subject to the requirement for a data protection impact assessment pursuant to Article 35(1). The supervisory authority shall communicate those lists to the EDPB.[12]

The supervisory authority may also establish and make public a list of the kind of processing operations for which no data protection impact assessment is required. The supervisory authority shall communicate those lists to the EDPB.[13]

Prior to the adoption of the lists referred to in Article 35(4) and (5) the competent supervisory authority shall apply the consistency mechanism referred to in Article 63 where such lists involve processing activities which are related to the offering of goods or services to individual data subjects or to the monitoring of their behaviour in several states, or may substantially affect the free movement of personal data within the EU.[14]

---

9   GDPR Article 35(1).
10   *Ibid* Art 35(2).
11   *Ibid* Art 35(3).
12   *Ibid* Art 35(4).
13   *Ibid* Art 35(5).
14   *Ibid* Art 35(6).

The assessment shall contain at least:

- a systematic description of the envisaged processing operations and the purposes of the processing, including where applicable the legitimate interest pursued by the controller;

- an assessment of the necessity and proportionality of the processing operations in relation to the purposes;

- an assessment of the risks to the rights and freedoms of individual data subjects referred to in Article 35(1); and

- the measures envisaged to address the risks, including safeguards, security measures and mechanisms to ensure the protection of personal data and to demonstrate compliance with the GDPR taking into account the rights and legitimate interests of individual data subjects and other persons concerned.[15]

Compliance with approved codes of conduct referred to in Article 40 by the relevant controllers or processors shall be taken into due account in assessing the impact of the processing operations performed by such controllers or processors for the purposes of a data protection impact assessment.[16]

Where appropriate, the controller shall seek the views of individual data subjects or their representatives on the intended processing, without prejudice to the protection of commercial or public interests or the security of the processing operations.[17]

Where the processing pursuant to Article 6(1)(c) or (e) has a legal basis in EU law or the law of the state to which the controller is subject, that law regulates the specific processing operation or set of operations in question, and a data protection impact assessment has already been carried out as part of a general impact assessment in the context of the adoption of this legal basis, Article 35(1)–(7) shall not apply, unless states deem it necessary to carry out such assessment prior to the processing activities.[18]

Where necessary, the controller shall carry out a review to assess if the processing is performed in compliance with the data protection impact assessment at least when there is a change of the risk represented by the processing operations.[19]

7 PRIOR CONSULTATION

25.7   The controller shall consult the supervisory authority prior to the processing where a data protection impact assessment as provided for in

---

15 *Ibid* Art 35(7).
16 *Ibid* Art 35(8).
17 *Ibid* Art 35(9).
18 *Ibid* Art 35(10).
19 *Ibid* Art 35(11).

Article 33 indicates that the processing would result in a high risk in the absence of measures taken by the controller to mitigate the risk.[20]

Where the supervisory authority is of the opinion that the intended processing referred to in Article 36(1) would infringe the GDPR, in particular where the controller has insufficiently identified or mitigated the risk, it shall, within a period of up to eight weeks of receipt of the request for consultation, provide written advice to the controller and, where applicable the processor and may use any of its powers referred to in Article 58. That period may be extended for six weeks, taking into account the complexity of the processing. The supervisory authority shall inform the controller, and where applicable the processor of any such extension within one month of receipt of the request for consultation together with the reasons for the delay. Those periods may be suspended until the supervisory authority has obtained any information it has requested for the purposes of the consultation.[21]

When consulting the supervisory authority pursuant to Article 36(1), the controller shall provide the supervisory authority with:

- where applicable, the respective responsibilities of controller, joint controllers and processors involved for processing within a group of undertakings;

- the purposes and means of the intended processing;

- the measures and safeguards provided to protect the rights and freedoms of individual data subjects pursuant to the GDPR;

- where applicable, the contact details of the DPO;

- the data protection impact assessment provided for in Article 35; and

- any other information requested by the supervisory authority.[22]

States shall consult the supervisory authority during the preparation of a proposal for a legislative measure to be adopted by a national parliament or of a regulatory measure based on such a legislative measure, which relates to the processing.[23]

Notwithstanding Article 36(1), states' law may require controllers to consult with, and obtain prior authorisation from, the supervisory authority in relation to the processing by a controller for the performance of a task carried out by the controller in the public interest, including processing in relation to social protection and public health.[24]

---

20 *Ibid* Art 36(1).
21 *Ibid* Art 36(2).
22 *Ibid* Art 36(3).
23 *Ibid* Art 36(4).
24 *Ibid* Art 36(5).

8 DAMAGES AND COMPENSATION

25.8 One of the most important developing issues is the ability of individuals to sue for damages for breach of their data protection rights. Arguably, a perceived inhibitor on such litigation is not so much that there have been no instances where an infringement has taken place, but rather that some have felt it difficult to show – or show sufficient – monetary damages.

Cases such as *Vidal-Hall v Google*[25] (even though eventually settled) and the extended damages provisions in the GDPR may change this perception. In addition to dismissing the frequent jurisdictional objection, the Court of Appeal made it easier for individuals to make data protection damages claims. The decision means that a claim for monetary damages is possible independent of showing financial loss by virtue of the data protection infringement.

A cautionary note might be that the brokered settlement in the US of $19 million was rejected as not being sufficient. This relates to the Target data breach incident.

An additional cautionary example is a data protection fine against the government for an error relating to a single letter. The fine was £8 million. This is even prior to the DPA 2018 and the GDPR.

Indeed, damages and compensation in general apart from RtbF is a growing focus both inside and outside the UK[26] and EU.[27] The prospect for group or class actions has also increased post the GDPR.

---

25 [2015] EWCA Civ 311.
26 Particularly after *Google Inc v Vidal-Hall* [2015] EWCA Civ 311 (27 March 2015).
27 For example, SK Mizrahi, 'Ontario's New Invasion of Privacy Torts: Do They Offer Monetary Redress for Violations Suffered Via the Internet of Things?' *Western Journal of Legal Studies* (2018) (8:1) (COV2) 37.

PART I

IMPACT, COMMENTARY AND FUTURE

CHAPTER 26

Conclusion: Impact and Future

I INTRODUCTION

26.1 New technologies 'permit easy dissemination and using of information. Current ICT allows individuals to share (sometimes unwittingly) their personal preferences and behaviour information on an unprecedented scale. This could lead to people losing control of personal information'.[1] What are the implications?[2] One issue is the impact of personal data online and how this can become available to others for longer than might otherwise be the case in the past; or indeed in a whole host of new ways that would not have occurred in the past. There is increasing evidence that some of this may even occur without full transparency and knowledge on the part of the individual to whom the data relates. Research is increasingly identifying these concerns and *Google Spain*, which was discussed throughout the world, shines a light on these particular concerns and some of the problem issues. The General Data Protection Regulation Right to be Forgotten (GDPR RtbF) further develops how the legal regime will seek to deal with these important issues.

Data protection and privacy for personal data are increasing issues for organisations, individuals, society and policymakers[3] – from RtbF, problem content, use of the internet to vet and screen job applicants,[4] monitoring employees[5] students and users, profiling users, targeting users, and aggregating and linking increasing amounts of data from different sources which are able to identify individuals in ways which did not occur previously.

---

1   T Stanimir, 'Personal Data Protection and the New Technologies' *Proceedings of the International Conference on Information Technologies* (2011) 333.
2   S Nelson, J Simek, and J Foltin, 'The Legal Implications of Social Networking' *Regent University Law Review*, (2009–2010) (22) 1. Also, P Viscounty, J Archie, F Alemi and J Allen, 'Social Networking and the Law,' *Business Law Today* (2008–09) (58) 18.
3   See, eg, P Roth, 'Data Protection Meets Web 2.0: Two Ships Passing in the Night' *UNSW Law Journal* (2010) (33) 532. NJ Slabbert, 'Orwell's Ghost: How Teletechnology is Reshaping Civil Society' *CommLaw Conspectus* (2007–2008) (16) 349.
4   C Brandenburg, 'The Newest Way to Screen Job Applicants: A Social Networker's Nightmare' *Federal Communications Law Journal* (2007–2008) (60) 597; D Gersen, 'Your Image, Employers Investigate Job Candidates Online More than Ever. What can You Do to Protect Yourself?' *Student Law* (2007–2008) (36) 24; I Byrnside, 'Six Degrees of Separation: The Legal Ramifications of Employers Using Social Networking Sites to Research Applicants' *Vanderbilt Journal of Entertainment and Technology Law* (2008) (2) 445.
5   AR Levinson, 'Industrial Justice: Privacy Protection for the Employed' *Cornell Journal of Law and Public Policy* (2009) (18) 609.

2 AWARENESS

26.2   Increasingly potential employers, schools and universities use online information to assess applications. Unfortunately, this sometimes has adverse consequences for individuals.[6] In addition, many users, particularly those of a younger age, do not (fully) appreciate that their online activities can have major consequences. These consequences can be current, or many years in the future.

Data laws, data regulators, and courts will increasingly have to consider issues of future harms and future risks for individuals.

There is arguably more to be done by social media in terms of informing and appraising users of the issues which can arise, particularly where children and teenagers are concerned. Some of these concerns were at least in part the reason why a new social media project targeting children was cancelled, or at least paused, by Facebook (Meta). A separate photo facial recognition capability has also been cancelled by Facebook (Meta).[7]

Developing literature is also helping to shed light on how harm and risk of harm can be quite different to what might have originally been envisaged when the GDPR RtbF was drafted. Consider, for example, the recent controversy relating to the whistleblower release of internal research from Facebook (Meta) which indicated that the use of Instagram can be harmful to young girls. Obviously, there are much more details to this research and its parameters. However, there have already been congressional and parliamentary hearings in the US, UK, and EU. One such whistleblower also spoke at the Lisbon Web Summit. The point here is that harm and risk of harm can be more nuanced than say a specific comment or specific article referring to an individual. Harms can come from micro-data (micro-data harms). To appreciate this, we need to understand that much modern social media utilises hundreds, if not thousands, of different data points or data signals. Each data signal stream or collection point will cumulatively amass a significant data pool. Some have suggested that there is a lack of transparency from social media companies as to the full list of data signals that are being collected, and how the resulting data pools are used.

As the public (and also politicians and data regulators) come to better understand the existence and nature of data signal collections, and their uses, individuals in future may begin to file new types of RtbF notices – not to delete or delist an article – but rather to delete specific data signal collections, and also to delete associated data pools that have previously been collected. So, someone may wish to remain on Facebook (Meta), Instagram, etc, but be concerned to use RtbF (and other data rights) to prevent data signals being linked to harm propensities eg suicide, self harm, unhealthy diet, etc.

---

6   See Edwards and Waelde above at 481.
7   D Ingram, 'Facebook to Delete 1 Billion People's "Facial Recognition Templates,"' *NBCNews. com*, 2 November 2021.

The potential argument that this is burdensome or not technically possible is undermined when we learn more of how new signal collections are created, developed, and operationalised. It is also undermined by the fact that already Facebook (Meta), to take as an example, has agreed to discontinue the use of certain sensitive signals.[8]

While it has been announced that data in relation to facial recognition technology is to be deleted, it is not immediately clear if the cancelled signals data will also be deleted.

So, the capabilities of RtbF tools may come to be applied in very new ways. Importantly, as new risks arise, and also our knowledge of previously unknown harms grows, the need for RtbF is enhanced still further.

A separate development in RtbF should be the use of RtbF tools by parents on behalf of their young children. This aspect of the potential of RtbF tools is underappreciated. Recent developments and disclosures regarding risks bring this new application of RtbF data laws and data rights a step closer.

The WP 29 in its Opinion regarding social media, previously recognised the dangers arising from apps.[9] Compliance with data laws must be ensured. There is also a UK Home Office Good Practice Guidance for the Providers of Social Networks.[10] Arguably, these could be updated. This is an area where significant ongoing research is needed. Indeed, presently there is a push to introduce a new digital safely law in the UK. Subject to its being adopted, and its exact content, this may be influential more internally also. It will certainly be impactful in the UK.

In addition, it should be noted that social media companies have also recognised that their own awareness and preparedness needs to increase following the revelations surrounding the attacks on US elections and the ongoing ripples from the Cambridge Analytica scandal.[11]

3   DISCRETION

26.3   RtbF is a useful tool for individuals when seeking to deal with problem content issues. There is also an important element of individual discretion. An individual does not have to identify that there has been a revenge porn incident, demands, blackmail, etc, to avail of the GDPR RtbF. Individuals are able to have content taken down for more discretionary, subjective and personal reasons.

---

8   E Roth, 'Facebook Removes Pseudoscience and Targetting Category' *VentureBeat.com*, 23 April 2020; 'Facebook and Instagram will Delete "Sensitive" Ad Targeting Groups Linked to Race, Politics' *TheVerge.com*, 9 November 2021.

9   WP 29, Opinion 5/2009 on online social networking. Available at: http://ec.europa.eu/justice/policies/privacy/docs/wpdocs/2009/wp163_en.pdf.

10   Available at: www.gov.uk/government/uploads/system/uploads/attachment_data/file/251456/industry_guidance_social_networking.pdf.

11   The UK ICO also investigated the latter events, as well as specific entities and individuals.

The content to be removed does not have to be wrong. There is a risk that an organisation may set too high a bar when it is establishing processes for dealing with RtbF notices. It would be incorrect to establish procedures which are only responsive to inaccurate content or content of the most egregious sexual nature. RtbF operates on an individual discretionary basis also. There are increasing examples where individuals have had to engage data regulators when an individual company applies its compliance with RtbF too restrictively.

4   ONE SOLUTION

26.4   The GDPR RtbF offers a valuable tool for individuals who wish to have more control over their data and those who perceive that they may wish or need to regain more control over their personal data.

This is apt as more evidence arises demonstrating that individuals, and especially younger individuals, may not be immediately aware of all of the uses of their data and how some use may result in obvious and less obvious harms.

The issue of problem content online (and different forms of such problem content, which are increasing) is increasingly recognised. (Some may also suggest that more appreciation, understanding, and concern is also warranted for particular problems.) The GDPR RtbF is a valuable tool to help individuals tackle problem content online.

However, the GDPR RtbF is not the only solution to (a) the issue of control of personal data; or (b) the issue of problem content online. The control issue must also be looked at via the prism of enhanced emphasis on consent, transparency, trust, ethics, pre-problem solving, data protection by design and default; impact assessments; consultations), etc. Additional solution aspects to the problem content issue, in addition to the RtbF, include criminal legislation. Design, responsibility, education, etc also need to be considered.

The discussion of RtbF to date is also generally focused on a single individual being the person seeking to exercise RtbF data laws. There is increasing momentum suggesting that more than one person may be interested to exercise RtbF tools, in particular the parents of a younger person.

The prior understanding of RtbF tools applying only to the end published online content may well come to be reappraised with additional focus to intermediary stages such as signal data collection tools and signal data collection points; and also the pools of signal data that has been collected.

While RtbF is indeed one solution amongst a number of different solution tools, it may well come to be seen as dynamic and applicable to more problem (and discretionary) situations than commentators might have initially assessed.[12]

---

12   That is not to say that some problems or situations may be found where the RtbF tool does not (fully) alleviate the issue in question. It may be that in relation to certain issues or problems, additional or expanded RtbFs will be called for in future.

5   INVESTIGATIONS

26.5   Problem internet issues are increasingly being looked at by policymakers. The UK Digital, Culture, Media and Sport (DCMS) Committee has been investigating internet disinformation and fake news issues and recommends more detailed internet regulation.

Internet organisations can be officially investigated and audited much like any other. One audit,[13] for example, reviewed certain specific aspects of social media data protection compliance. This arose after a number of complaints regarding specific aspects of an organisation. The following issues were looked at: privacy policies; advertising; access requests; retention; cookies/social plug-ins; third-party apps; disclosures to third parties; facial recognition/tag suggest; data security; deletion of accounts; friend finder; tagging; posting on other profiles; credits; pseudonymous profiles; abuse reporting and compliance management/governance.[14] It is noted that this was prior to the Cambridge Analytica controversy. There have also been investigations and litigation in the US regarding privacy and internet issues[15] and investigations are ongoing.

These are controversial and evolving issues in terms of both data protection compliance as well as take downs and liability for material on (and via) websites. This is a critical area of contention in litigation (and policy discussion) and it will continue to expand. Sony has been fined £250,000 by the ICO and Google was sued by UK Apple users.[16] Facebook has been fined £500,000 by the ICO regarding Cambridge Analytica. There was also a significant US fine regarding this same issue.

While these investigations are also in some way crossing with problems, problem activities and RtbF, it may be that specific investigations may occur in future solely or predominantly devoted to RtbF issues, how it is being implemented and how it may need further amendment or enhancement, etc. The more that

---

13   Data Protection Commissioner, 'Facebook Ireland Limited, Report of Re-Audit' (21 September 2012).

14   The Europe Against Facebook group also point out that there are particular issues and complaints outstanding. Available at: www.europe-v-facebook.org/EN/en.html. There was also a group created in the US by MoveOn.org called 'Petition: Facebook, Stop Invading My Privacy', similarly objecting to certain practices of the social media website. A Morganstern, 'In the Spotlight: Social Network Advertising and the Right of Publicity' *Intellectual Property Law Bulletin* (2007–2008) (1) 181; R Podolny, 'When "Friends" Become Adversaries: Litigation in the Age of Facebook' *Manitoba Law Journal* (2009) (33) 391; Y Hashemi, 'Facebook's Privacy Policy and Its Third-party Partnerships: Lucrativity and Liability' *BU Journal of Science & Technology Law* (2009) (15) 140. P Nyoni and M Velempini, 'Data Protection Laws and Privacy on Facebook' *SA Journal of Information Management* (2015)(17:1) 1.

15   The Beacon advertising feature. See appeal and lower court in the case of *McCall v Facebook*. The appeal case is *McCall v Facebook*, US Court of Appeals for the Ninth Circuit. Available at: http://cdn.ca9.uscourts.gov/datastore/opinions/2012/09/20/10–16380.pdf. See, eg, W McGeveran, 'Disclosure, Endorsement, and Identity in Social Marketing' *Illinois Law Review* (2009) (4) 1105.

16   See *Google Inc v Vidal-Hall* [2015] EWCA Civ 311 (27 March 2015).

data regulators, policymakers, and society learn of how new tech harms can arise (separate to beneficial uses), more attention will focus on the need for new solutions. RtbF is an important and central consideration in the array of solutions.

6 TRANSFERS, PROCESSORS, THIRD PARTIES

26.6   Organisations may quite legitimately need to engage third parties or outsource particular tasks. However, it is not always clear that the organisation will have ensured that both an appropriate written contract and appropriate security measures are in place with the outsourced processor as regards the personal data received and processed by it. Users should also be informed of such outsourcing and be reassured as to security measures. Consent, transparency, and prior information are equally important compliance issues. In the present context, where RtbF occurs, these processors (and other third parties) should be notified in terms of the RtbF as appropriate to ensure follow through takedown.

7 NEW RISKS

26.7   New problems and risks will continue to develop. YouTube has had to react after it was revealed that paedophiles were using secret coded comments in the comment sections to videos on YouTube which featured young people. While certain actions, deletions, etc, may have occurred on YouTube, it may be that some of these videos or images were copied to other internet locations. It may be that examples may arise where the data subject of one of these wishes to have their image taken down and forgotten.

Significant takedown and or deletions of facial images were undertaken by Facebook (Meta). While RtbF notices could have been directed to some of these specific images, there also appear to be policy and risk justifications for ceasing facial recognition activities, and deleting the appropriate data.

The deletion of certain sensitive data signals, again by Facebook (Meta), is also due in part to increasing awareness and scrutiny of the existence and application of these particular signal risks. (Some may suggest that there may also be additional data signal risks which should be discontinued.)

The DPD 95/46 recital 53 stated that certain processing operations are likely to pose specific risks to the rights and freedoms of individual data subjects by virtue of their nature, their scope or their purposes, such as that of excluding individuals from a right, benefit or a contract, or by virtue of the *specific use of new technologies*; it is for states, if they so wish, to specify such risks in their legislation.

Recital 54 of the DPD 95/46 stated that with regard to all the processing undertaken in society, the amount posing such specific risks should be very limited. States must provide that the data regulator check such processing prior to it being carried out. Following this prior check, the data regulator may, according to its national law, give an opinion or an authorisation regarding the processing. Such checking may equally take place in the course of the preparation either of a measure of the national parliament or of a measure based on such a legislative measure, which defines the nature of the processing and lays down appropriate safeguards.

The GDPR also continues this trajectory with the obligations to proactively examine risk and gap issues, and to carry out audits and assessments. While most organisations will have engaged in the GDPR (and UK GDPR in the UK) compliance exercises leading up to go-live, it must be stressed that data protection compliance is an ongoing exercise. In addition, there is a new emphasis in being able to record and demonstrate compliance, as opposed to merely making statements without appropriate backup. Complying with RtbF notices is required. But it is also necessary to be able to demonstrate such compliance through documentation, processes, and procedures.

This goes to show that the environment in which RtbF will operate will not remain static and constant. Ongoing review will be required by organisations, as well as other interested parties.

8   GDPR RTBF

26.8   The individual has the right to obtain the erasure and forgetting of personal data concerning them without undue delay. The controller has the obligation to erase personal data without undue delay.[17] As indicated in earlier chapters, this may require detailed understanding of the issues, concerns and nuances of RtbF. However, it may be a mistake to seek to ignore RtbF notices or categories of such notices. It must be borne in mind that there is a legislative intention to provide a right and remedy and that there are indeed issues, and sometimes problems, that need to be addressed and which RtbF tools seek to do. No doubt the full contours of the GDPR RtbF will be examined further in future case law.

9   RIGHT TO RECTIFICATION

26.9   There is a right to obtain from the controller without undue delay the rectification of personal data concerning them. The individual has the right to obtain completion of incomplete personal data completed, including by means of providing a supplementary statement.[18] However, organisations should not decide for themselves that this is what they will do once they receive a RtbF notice, particularly as this was not requested and is not reflective of the rights, interests and concerns of the data subject where they have pursued their RtbF.

17   GDPR Art 17(1).
18   GDPR Art 16.

This may be viewed as a tactical misapplication of rights and required responses by the controller.

10 PREVENTING PROCESSING FROM CAUSING DAMAGE OR DISTRESS

26.10 Individuals have a right to prevent processing likely to cause damage or distress. This may also need to be considered and how it may cross with RtbF rights.

11 COMPENSATION AND DAMAGES

26.11 Individual data subjects are entitled to damages and compensation for failure to comply with certain requirements, particularly where there is material or non-material damage. This can be relevant to RtbF cases and will no doubt be developed further over time. Where RtbF rights are refused – or frustrated – data fines from data regulators, or compensation and damages via data litigation, may follow. Similarly, so where appropriate safety and related tools are absent or inadequate.[19] Tools must be present and effective, and data rights viewed from an effective and purposeful perspective.[20] Rights, protections, fines, compensation, damages, etc, must be effective – or else be set at nought.[21]

12 CHILDREN

26.12 Processing of children's personal data are referred to in GDPR recital 38. Article 8 of the GDPR makes provisions in relation to conditions for children's consent for information society services. Where Article 6(1)(a) applies, in relation to the offer of information society services directly to a child, the processing of personal data of a child shall be lawful where the child is at least 16 years old. Where the child is below the age of 16, such processing shall be lawful only if and to the extent that such consent is given or authorised by the holder of parental responsibility over the child.[22] (States may provide by law

---

19 A White, 'Google ets Record Belgian Privacy Fine Over "Right to be Forgotten"' *Bloomberg.com* (14 July 2020); P Lambert, *Understanding the New EU Data Fine Rules* (Kortext, 2021).

20 Data laws set out clear data rights that cannot be ignored nor reduced just because that may suit a given company. Data fines are also expressly required to be 'effective, proportionate and dissuasive' (GDPR Art 83(1)).

21 J Ausloos, *The Right to Erasure in EU Data Protection Law: From Individual Rights to Effective Protection* (OUP, 2020); P Lambert, 'The AG Opinion in Google France, An Adequate Remedy?' *International Journal for the Data Protection Officer, Privacy Officer and Privacy Counsel* (IDPP) (2019) (3:3); J Kaganoff, 'Send the Word Over There: An Offshore Solution to the Right to be Forgotten' *Northwestern Journal of International Law & Business* (2021) (41:2) 245; KG Vazquez, 'The Right to be Forgotten does not Apply Outside the European Union: A Proposal for Worldwide Application' *Southwestern Journal of International Law* (2021) (27:1) 146; Lambert, *Understanding the New EU Data Fine Rules*.

22 GDPR Art 8(1).

for a lower age for those purposes provided that such lower age is not below 13 years (Article 8(1)) – as the UK has done (DPA 2018, s 9).The controller shall make reasonable efforts to verify in such cases that consent has been given or authorised by the holder of parental responsibility over the child, taking into consideration available technology.[23] This shall not affect the general contract law of states such as the rules on the validity, formation or effect of a contract in relation to a child.[24] These additional concerns and potential problem issues (including online abuse (OA)) will require particular attention when considering the RtbF and how to comply.

13   DATA ACCESS RIGHTS

26.13   The individual data subject has the right to obtain from the controller confirmation as to whether personal data concerning them are being processed. Where that is the case, they have the right to access the personal data and the following information.[25]

These access rights must be read in light of the GDPR RtbF (eg, whether individuals may seek to use an access right to assist or further map out the details being the focus of a RtbF notice). In addition, an access request may arise after a RtbF notice has been successfully processed to see if there may be other additional information which the individual may need to consider.

14   IDENTIFICATION RIGHTS

26.14   In the context of OA or other attacks, it may be necessary for a victim to seek court assistance to help identify the attacker. This may include tracing or identification-type orders (eg, Norwich Pharmacal orders). Such orders and the related disclosure can, in particular circumstances, assist on (further) focusing takedown and RtbF notices.

15   NOTIFICATION RECTIFICATION, ERASURE OR RESTRICTION

26.15   Article 18 of the GDPR refers to the right to restriction of processing. The individual data subject has the right to obtain from the controller the restriction of the processing where certain circumstances apply.[26]

It may be that restrictions may have to apply immediately or may be requested on an immediate basis, pending the full resolution of the RtbF notice. These issues may be considered further.

---

23   GDPR Art 8(2).
24   GDPR Art 8(3).
25   GDPR Art 15(1).
26   GDPR Art 18(1).

The controller must communicate any rectification, erasure, or forgetting of personal data or restriction of processing carried out in accordance with GDPR Articles 16, 17(1) and 18 to each recipient to whom the personal data have been disclosed. The controller must inform the individual data subject about those recipients if the individual data subject requests it.[27] It needs to be considered whether individuals need to be informed of this right and also to ensure that this obligation is implemented and has appropriate advance processes and procedures to do so, as opposed to waiting for RtbF notices in the first instance.

16   A RIGHTS, PROTECTION, OR SAFETY ISSUE, OR ALL?

26.16   Does the RtbF needs to be considered in isolation as a specific defined solution or should it be viewed as part of a suite of potential solutions available to data subject when dealing with particular online problem content issues? There will no doubt be further discussion and research on this issue.

17   ONLINE ABUSE

26.17   Cyberbullying is one facet of OA. Online abuse can range from threats to defamation to harassment to stalking to grooming to cyberbullying to breach of privacy and data protection. Revenge porn is an increasingly commented upon example of OA. There are also overlaps. The cyberbullying of children can involve harassment, threats, verbal abuse, defamation or, in the case of Amanda Todd, data protection and privacy breaches later expanding to threats. There may also be elements of deliberation and planning involved. The required solutions are multifaceted. RtbF is one of these, and an important one.

No matter how many 'RtbF report buttons' are on websites (assuming they are transparent and easy to find, which is not uniformly the case) they can be useless without protocols, policies, and procedures to follow through on reports that are made. Notice reports and complaints are also meaningless unless there are enough people to deal with and investigate the notice reports.

It would be interesting to examine and compare the number of people employed in RtbF investigation teams on various websites. Should there be a minimum number of such employees required per number of users? Should there be a minimum number of such employees per amount of notice reports made on a given website? Some RtbF problems may be more urgent. Some may be more important to deal with immediately on an urgent basis. Other factors may also be relevant.

Some would suggest that websites can not only be unhelpful but can also be positively obstructive. It remains to be seen how many RtbF notices are refused unjustly. These may vary across sectors and websites.

---

27   GDPR Art 19.

18   FUTURE AND ADDITIONAL RTBFS

26.18   *Google Spain*, while largely predictable, was received with some surprise. The GDPR RtbF is also relatively new. No doubt there will be issues that we have not yet considered that will need to be discussed and also some which may come to be litigated.

It may be that there are already different Rights to be Forgotten (RtbFs). Furthermore, there may be identified future risks, interests, rights, and problems which need new or addition express RtbFs. It may be that some aspects of current RtbF routes may need to be more express and pronounced. These issues will come to develop over time, as will associated research and policy discussion.

While there is discussion in terms of a 'generic' RtbF[28] there is already recognition that there is a need for at least some more individual RtbF interest specifity. The GDPR refers to children in both general and specific terms. This nuance and differentiation may need to expand further in future. We are arguably only coming to appreciate that there are many new risks of particular technologies for children. Recent disclosures regarding Instagram and young girls are an example.

There is discussion on relation interest balancing. *Google Spain* included balancing; indeed there is already balance in the drafting of the GDPR and GDPR RtbF. It is not the case that every application must start from the beginning when deciding balance issues in such a manner as would seek to undermine RtbF entirely.

However, it is interesting to consider the balance issue in conjunction with temporal aspects. For example, the balance changes in favour of forgetting the older the content in question.[29]

We need to also consider if there should be a greater balance in favour of RtbF where children and risks to children are involved.

There is also an argument to be made that the younger a person is and the longer that particular content can pose damage to them as they have more life effects ahead of them, the more we should lean into RtbF.

This may seem counter to many people's understanding of the *Google Spain* RtbF which references older and outdated content. However, it appears *Google Spain* while correctly recognising the need for RtbF for content as it gets older, does not go into detailed consideration of the associated age of the individual in

---

28   T Hale-Kupiec, 'Immortal Invasive Initiatives: The Need for a Genetic Right to Be Forgotten' *Minnesota Journal of Law, Science and Technology* (2016) (17:1) 441. Also see W Gregory Voss, and Celine Castets-Renard, 'Proposal for an International Taxonomy on the Various Forms of the 'Right to be Forgotten': A Study on the Convergence of Norms' *Colorado Technology Law Journal* (2016) (14:2) 281.

29   Generally, see eg, Giovanni Sartor, 'The Right to Be Forgotten: Balancing Interests in the Flux of Time' *International Journal of Law and Information Technology* (2015) (24:1) 72.

question ... and that the risk can be elongated due to the person being younger in age (including college students and young adults).

Gregory W Voss also refers to the ongoing evolution on data protection law in light of contemporary changes.[30] This perhaps anticipates that while the law cannot stand still in a world of ongoing change, RtbF may need to expand in future. Various authors are now identifying the potential need for additional RtbFs, whether for additional specific problem issues, such as genetic personal data,[31] or in jurisdictions which do not have a GDPR equivalent (eg, the federal US). There are also some consideration in terms of RtbF after death.[32]

Just as contemporary challenges are emerging to data protection and privacy[33] it is guaranteed that future challenges will also arise, some of which we can predict but many more which we cannot yet envisage or anticipate.

A further example of the nuance of RtbF is the real imperative to achieve certain RtbF in a rapid manner (eg, in the context of real time, viral online abuse). There is an urgency which may not exist in some other instances of RtbF notices. This does not yet appear to be reflected in the online forms for filing RtbF notices and will need further consideration.[34]

While certain balance issues arise in in the context of media and news content, as RtbF and the objects of RtbF and associated risk issues become more developed, the application of RtbF and RtbF processes may become more segmented and streamed.[35]

---

30 GW Voss, 'After Google Spain and Charlie Hebdo: The Continuing Evolution of European Union Data Privacy Law in a Time of Change' *Business Lawyer* (2015/2016) (71:1) 281.

31 T Hale-Kupiec, 'Immortal Invasive Initiatives: The Need for a Genetic Right to Be Forgotten' *Minnesota Journal of Law, Science and Technology* (2016) (17:1) 441.

32 J Kall, 'A Posthuman Data Subject: The Right to Be Forgotten and Beyond' *German Law Journal* (2017) (18:5) 1145.

33 N Witzleb, D Lindsay, M Paterson and S Rodrick, *Emerging Challenges in Privacy Law: Comparative Perspectives* (CUP, 2014).

34 More generally see L Edward, 'Recognizing Rights in Real Time: The Role of Google in the EU Right to be Forgotten' *UC Davis Law Review* (2016) (49:3) 1017; Nadezhda Purtova, 'The Law of Everything: Broad Concept of Personal Data and Future of EU Data Protection Law' *Innovation and Technology* (2018) (10:1) 40.

35 Even in terms of current used of RtbF and compliance with RtbF, there is a developing discussion on some of the frameworks and elements. See for instance, H Yaish, 'Forget Me, Forget Me Not: Elements of Erasure to Determine the Sufficiency of a GDPR Article 17 Request' *Journal of Law, Technology & the Internet* (2019) (10:1) 1; N Voiculescu and M-B Berna, 'Analytical Issues of the Right to be Forgotten – Between Theoretical Landmarks and Practical Expectations' *Law Annals from Titu Maiorescu University* (2020) 11; S Duffy, 'Dereferencing and the Right to be Forgotten in Practice: Some Practical Tips on How to Get Google to Dereference Content' *Computers and Law* (2019) 30; MR Leiser, '"Private Jurisprudence" and the Right to be Forgotten Balancing Test' *Computer Law & Security Review* (2020) 39; S De Conca, 'GC et al v CNIL: Balancing the Right to Be Forgotten with the Freedom of Information, the Duties of a Search Engine Operator (C-136/17 GC et al v CNIL)' *European Data Protection Law Review (EDPL)* (2019) (5:4) 561; 'Better In Than Out: When Constitutional Courts Rely on the Charter' *European Constitutional Law Review* (2020) (16:1) 1; J-M Chenou and R Radu, 'The "Right to be Forgotten": Negotiating Public

Even while certain areas that may be considered somewhat understood and established in the RtbF field, such as RtbF and new media, there may also be developments and issues that surprise. Regardless of jurisdictional issues, and focusing on issues and individual interests the case of Britney Spears may assist. Her long suffering conservatorship has been ended. The following suggest the need for further consideration of the nuances of media and RtbF issues. Many articles, comments, and other materials will have been posted during the period of the conservatorship, and previously. She was not in a legal position to exercise RtbF (again we are speaking at an interests and headline level, not jurisdictionally). Now she is in a position to do so. Prior to the conservatorship, she was the subject of intense media attention. Much of this appeared in entertainment type publications as opposed to what we would consider mainstream news media. At least some stores might be contested for accuracy. Recently, some individuals involved in the original media circus have actually apologised to Britney. While some entities may have control to take down some old inaccurate and tasteless content, RtbF type issues arise even for someone as well-known as Britney Spears where inaccuracies arise and where significant health issues have been referred to. Ms Spears might refer to her trauma and ill health at the original time as being added reasons for RtbF, and inaccuracy or untruth where this applies also. In addition, she can also refer to her current and future health and wellbeing as reasons favouring RtbF. This is notwithstanding that she is a famous figure. This is to suggest that media RtbF issues can develop more contours than might have originally been considered.

Sometimes circumstances may conspire to make public personal opinions of an individual which they may not have intended to be published or posted online. At the time of the GDPR RtbF much discission was deliberately focused on media news issues in light of RtbF, but ignoring that many non-media RtbF issues also exist. However, over time we may come to consider that addition rights issues also arise (separate to data protection, privacy, and freedom of expression media interests) and which may not have been considered. One example may be right to freedom of conscience,[36] especially where posting and continuance of personal opinions and issues of conscience are maintained online which were not intended to ever be there. Continuing to maintain it online, could prevent an individual's

---

and Private Ordering in the European Union' *Business* (2019) (58:1) 74; OJ Gstrein, 'Right to be Forgotten: European Data Imperialism, National Privilege, or Universal Human Right?' *Review of European Administrative Law* (2020) (13:1) 125; C Quelle, 'GC and Others v CNIL on the Responsibility of Search Engine Operators for Referring to Sensitive Data: The End of "Right to be Forgotten" Balancing?' *European Data Protection Law Review (EDPL)* (2019) (5:3) 438; C Kwak, L Lee and H Lee, 'Could You Ever Forget Me? Why People Want to be Forgotten Online' *Journal of Business Ethics* (2021) (February) 1; R Matefi, 'The Balance Between The Right to Freedom of Expression and the Protection of the Personality Rights From the Jurisprudence Perspective' *Jus et Civitas* (2019) (6:1) 1; S-D Şchiopu, 'Some Aspects of the Right to be Forgotten From the Perspective of Balancing the Freedom of Expression with the Respect for Private Life in the Online Environment' *Jus et Civitas: A Journal of Social and Legal Studies* (2019) (6:1) 27.

36 J Valciukas, 'Right to Freedom of Conscience in the West: Forgotten Right?' *Logos-Vilnius* (2020) (103) 108.

autonomy to think independently and maintain their ability to maintain private thoughts and ideas of conscience.

We are increasingly all too aware of the problem of bad actor attacks and data breaches.[37] Ransomware attacks are even focusing on hospitals and vital societal infrastructure (eg Colonial Pipeline). A frequent feature of these attacks, when successful, is that large quantities of personal data is stolen. In some of these instances, this personal data is subsequently released online. While there are developing services branded as reputation protection and fraud type alerts, these can be costly and are not all encompassing. Sometimes the controller entity from where the data is stolen may fund these third-party services for its customer – but generally limited to 12 months only. So, there is a new risk for individuals after 12 months. These services are not a complete solution. It is therefore helpful to have RtbF tools separate and in addition to commercial services to deal with some of the data breach posting issues.

To date most RtbF notices relate to text content (eg articles, postings), and sometimes additionally photographs which may be associated with the above text content. However, as more audio recordings and video recordings are being posed online, it will be inevitable that RtbF will also come to focus on these types of content for removal.[38]

A growing debate will centre on the need and justifications for taking down police arrest images from the internet, and even prison images of individuals.[39] RtbF will come to play a part in this debate.

Many offices, especially in the software development and tech sectors, operate multi-access or shared access for multiple individuals to the same stored databases and files. There will be examples where errant employees or ex-employees[40] publish information on the internet from those shared files and which may contain personal data. The individuals the subject of such data may wish to consider RtbF issues. It may also come to be considered whether a concerned company may seek to claim or exercise RtbF interests on behalf of its employees when seeking to get material taken down as promptly as possible. Alternatively, a company may seek to facilitate some sort of group RtbF claims by or in conjunction with its employees.

---

37 T Bailey, R Isenberg, C Lewis and D Ware, 'Building Security into the Customer Experience' *McKinsey Insights* (29 June 2020); H Tuttle, '2020 Cyberrisk Landscape' *Risk Management* (2020) (67:1) 18.

38 I Ilin and A Kelli, 'The Use of Human Voice and Speech for Development of Language Technologies: The EU and Russian Data-protection Law Perspectives' *Juridica International* (2020) (29) 71.

39 AJ Pitts, 'Challenging the Carceral Imaginary in a Digital Age: Epistemic Asymmetries and the Right to Be Forgotten' *International Journal of Political Philosophy / Las Torres de Lucca* (2021) (10:19) 3.

40 The Morrisons cases arose as a result of an errant ex-employee stealing employee record details and posting these online.

There has been some speculation in the UK, for example, of the potential increase of class actions in the data rights field. This has also included the issue of professional litigation funding companies. A recent Google case may be viewed by some as restricting the scope for some of these actions.[41] Bear in mind, however, that RtbF is focused more on a solution outcome as opposed to being more money (damages, compensation, etc) orientated. There is a basis for suggesting that RtbF – and even group RtbF – may be outside the scope of the recent decision. Indeed, the GDPR expressly provides for representation entities for individuals.[42]

While sophisticated social media sites will collect large amounts of data and signals, news devices in the home may be less obvious sources of (large scale) data collection. This includes personal devices and virtual assistants.[43] In efforts to personalise[44] almost everything an individual does when walking, exercising, driving, or relaxing at home, enormous new data signal collection opportunities arise – but with arguably less concern than individuals have in relation to their social media data. Increasingly, large swathes of such data is stored online in the cloud.[45] Who has it, who can access it, and where it is will become tricking issues for RtbF to tackle.

There is a significant marketplace now in relation personal activity, exercise, and health recording devices. All of these seek to collect significant amounts of personal data.[46] It is not always clear how the data may be used, by whom, and

41   This is a recent case and will need further analysis. The case is *Lloyd (Respondent) v Google LLC (Appellant)*, UK Supreme Court, 11 November 2021. The case involved jurisdiction issues, and arises under the prior DPA 1998, not the UK GDPR nor DPA 2018.
42   See GDPR Article 80.
43   CD Stoian, 'Affecting the Right of a Private Life Through the Use of the Virtual Assistance' *Journal of Humanistic & Social Studies* (2019) (10:2) 135.
44   J Boudet, B Gregg, K Rathje, E Stein and K Vollhardt, 'The Future of Personalization -- and How to Get Ready For It' *McKinsey Insights* (18 June 2019).
45   M Kelly, E Furey and J Blue, 'GDPR Article 17: Eradicating Personal Identifiable Information & Achieving Compliance in a Hybrid Cloud' 2019 30th Irish Signals and Systems Conference (ISSC) (1-6 June 2019).
46   M Correia, G Rego and R Nunes, 'The Right to be Forgotten Versus the Right to Disclosure of Gamete Donors' ID: Ethical and Legal Considerations' *Acta Bioéthica* (2021) (27:1) 69; E Balistri, F Casellato, C Giannelli and C Stefanelli, 'BlockHealth: Blockchain-Based Secure and Peer-to-Peer Health Information Sharing With Data Protection and Right to be Forgotten' *ICT Express* (2021) (7:3) 308; M Correia, G Rego, R and R Nunes, 'Gender Transition: Is There a Right to be Forgotten?' *Health Care Analysis* (2 May 2021) 18; H Iannucci, '"Erasing Transgender Public Figures" Former Identity with the Right to be Forgotten' *Federal Communications Law Journal* (2021) (73:2) 259; S Suzuki, K Mizoguchi, H Watanabe, T Nakamura and Y Deguchi, 'Privacy-Aware Data-Lifetime Control NAND Flash System for Right to be Forgotten with In-3D Vertical Cell Processing' 2019 IEEE Asian Solid-State Circuits Conference (A-SSCC) (2019) (November) IEEE, 231; G Scocca and F Meunier, 'A Right to be Forgotten for Cancer Survivors: A Legal Development Expected to Reflect the Medical Progress in the Fight Against Cancer' *Journal of Cancer Policy* (2020) 25; C Llaneza, 'An Analysis On Biometric Privacy Data Regulation: A Pivot Towards Legislation Which Supports The Individual Consumer's Privacy Rights in Spite of Corporate Protections' *St Thomas Law Review* (2020) (32:2) 177; M JS Beauvais and BM Knoppers, 'Coming Out to Play: Privacy, Data Protection, Children's Health, and COVID-19 Research' *Frontiers in Genetics* (2021)

where. RtbF issues are clearly relevant, but as yet, not actively engaged. There are even efforts to get inside our heads to access our mind data and thoughts.[47] That will be a whole new level of complexity for RtbF matters, as well as data ethics and medical health ethics. In the future there will be more emphasis paid to issues of RtbF and data ethics.[48]

The Covid-19 epidemic had led data regulators and health officials to have to think swiftly of data protection issues involving largescale vaccination databases.[49] While we are still in the midst of the pandemic, it is quite conceivable that some individuals may wish to seek to access, vet, or delete some of the vaccine data relating to them. RtbF in those circumstances will be sought to be used.

The way in which people learn and engage with educational platforms and apps (whether at university (academic) or at home, eg home language learning) can lead to the creation of new data statistics and other personal data relating to each individual.[50] This raises a host of data protection compliance issues. RtbF is one of these.

One interesting issue is the experiment by some companies to let employees know how much other employees earn.[51] Some refer to this as 'radical transparency'.[52] If some of these details make their way online, and an employee later leaves that

---

(11); M Tsirintani, M Serifi and S Binioris, 'Digital Oblivion (The Right to be Forgotten): A Big Challenge for the Public Hospital Management in Greece' *Studies in Health Technology and Informatics* (2019) 91; C Cicchini, M Mazzeo, D Livoli, A Simone, V Valeriano and F Pugliese, 'The Right to be Protected, the Right to be Forgotten: The European General Data Protection Regulation 679/2016 in Emergency Medicine' *Italian Journal of Emergency Medicine* (2020) (9:1) 41.

47 P Lambert, 'Who Owns What's Inside Your Head?: Thoughts, Mind Data, Ownership and Future Battles Ahead' *European Intellectual Property Review* (EIPR) (2020) (42:3) 174.

48 EU Commission, *Ethics and Data Protection* (14 November 2018); CR La Roche, 'The "Right to be Forgotten": An Ethical Dilemma' *Journal of Leadership, Accountability & Ethics* (2020) (17:3) 36; CE Clark, KK Chang and SP Melvin, *Business and Society: Ethical, Legal, and Digital Environments* (Sage, 2020); G Aitchison and S Meckled-Garcia, 'Against Online Public Shaming: Ethical Problems With Mass Social Media' *Social Theory* (2021) (47:1) 1; A Trites, 'Black Box Ethics: How Algorithmic Decision-Making is Changing How we View Society and People: Advocating for the Right for Explanation and the Right to be Forgotten in Canada' *Global Media Journal: Canadian Edition* (2020) (12:1) 18; A Olteanu, J Garcia-Gathright, M de Rijke and M Ekstrand, 'FACTS-IR: Fairness, Accountability, Confidentiality, Transparency, and Safety in Information Retrieval' *SIGIR Forum* (2019) (53:2) 20.

49 M Correia, G Rego and R Nunes, The Right to be Forgotten and Covid-19: Privacy Versus Public Interest' *Acta Bioéthica* (2021) (27:1) 59; C Stupp, 'Virus Tech Draws Scrutiny From European Privacy Advocates' *Wall Street Journal* (8 March 2021).

50 E Mougiakou, S Papadimitriou and M Virvou, 'Synchronous and Asynchronous Learning Methods Under the Light of General Data Protection Regulation' 2020 11th International Conference on Information, Intelligence, Systems and Applications (IISA) (1–7 July 2020).

51 Indeed, there is one Scandinavian country which publishes the earnings or taxes of everyone. This is almost unique, however, in the wider European context, and certainly jars with data rights, data protection, and privacy.

52 See K Morgan, 'How Much "Radical Transparency" in a Workplace Is Too Much?' *BBC*, 17 November 2021,

company, they may decide that they do not wish their data to remain online and may seek to use RtbF tools to achieve this.

Developments in software and blockchain raise issues, on the one hand, of how to improve and better implement data protection and data security.[53] On the other hand, however, there are issues in relation to personal data being embedded in a permanent or semi-permanent manner where subsequent users may be able to see personal details.

While the breadth of misinformation and inauthentic content is wide, a portion of this can include the images of individual in doctored content.[54] These individuals may seek to look at RtbF options.

While the internet has brought many benefits, there is an increasing expansion in new ways to hate, threaten others, dox or identify individuals in as public a manner as possible when the individual was seeking to maintain their privacy (eg posting the real name, address, contact details, etc, and sometimes inviting others to attack the individual via the newly public details), and other forms of shaming.[55] These examples while not exhaustive demonstrate that there is an expanding need for solutions and tools. RtbF can be one of these.

53   D Armstrong and P Schwartfeger, 'Blockchain: The Right to be Forgotten (or Not); How Organisations Can & Should Respond to Erasure Request on Blockchain' *New Law Journal* (2021) (171:7946) 13; E Balistri, F Casellato, C Giannelli and C Stefanelli, 'BlockHealth: Blockchain-Based Secure and Peer-to-Peer Health Information Sharing With Data Protection and Right to be Forgotten' *ICT Express* (2021) (7:3) 308; A Rieger, J Lockl, N Urbach, F Guggenmos and G Fridgen, 'Building a Blockchain Application that Complies with the EU General Data Protection Regulation' *MIS Quarterly Executive* (2019) (18:4) 263; J Butler, 'Living in Digital Harmony: Immutable Blockchains Conflict With the Right to be Forgotten' *Law Institute Journal* (2019) (93:10) 69; G Maria Riva, 'What Happens in Blockchain Stays in Blockchain. A Legal Solution to Conflicts Between Digital Ledgers and Privacy Rights' *Frontiers in Blockchain* (2020) (3).
54   TL Thompson, 'No Silver Bullet: Fighting Russian Disinformation Requires Multiple Actions' *Georgetown Journal of International Affairs* (2020) (21) 182.
55   G Aitchison and S Meckled-Garcia, 'Against Online Public Shaming: Ethical Problems with Mass Social Media' *Social Theory* (2021) (47:1) 1; LMJ Cooper, 'Social Media and Online Persecution' *Georgetown Immigration Law Journal* (2021) (35:3) 749; P Billingham and T Parr, 'Online Public Shaming: Virtues and Vices' *Journal of Social Philosophy* (2020) (51:3) 371; J Israel, *Living With Hate in American Politics and Religion: How Popular Culture Can Defuse Intractable Differences* (Columbia University Press, 2019); I Down and KJ Han, 'Far Right Parties and "Europe": Societal Polarization and the Limits of EU Issue Contestation' *Journal of European Integration* (2021) (43:1) 65; D Nash, 'Politics of Humiliation – How do We Save Us From Our Liberal Selves?' *Cultural History* (2021) (10:2) 275; K Haley, 'Sharenting and the (Potential) Right to be Forgotten,' *Indiana Law Journal* (2020) (95:3) 1005; P Billingham and T Parr, 'Online Public Shaming: Virtues and Vices,' *Journal of Social Philosophy* (2020) (51:3) 371; M Odlanicka-Poczobutt and A Szyszka-Schuppik, 'The Right to be Forgotten as an Element of the Personal Data Protection System in the Organisation' *Organization & Management Quarterly* (2020) (51:3) 57; N Hodge, 'Getting Smart About Artificial Intelligence: How Can Companies Avoid the Risks and Regulatory Pitfalls of Artificial Intelligence-Based Technology?' *Risk Management* (2021) (68:8) 20; H Tuttle, '2020 Cyberrisk Landscape' *Risk Management* (2020) (67:1) 18; M Goldmann, 'As Darkness Deepens: The Right to Be Forgotten in the Context of Authoritarian Constitutionalism' *German*

19 CONCLUSION

26.19   All organisations need to become very familiar with the GDPR RtbF, and also not forgetting the *Google Spain* RtbF. It reflects the growing recognition that there can be content and problem content online which should be taken down, and also reflects the new and expanded EU data protection regime. (This is in addition to discretionally no-fault RtbF.) Organisations must continually adopt best practice around data protection compliance. While these tools are actively being used as intended, we will continue to need to measure effects,[56] effectiveness,[57] and seek to measure effects of current risk, and identify new developing risks as quickly as possible after they develop. As we come to understand how wide the range of problem issues are, we may need to consider different frames or streams of RtbF as solutions for discrete problem issues.[58] RtbF may also be coupled with the growing concern for online safety. RtbF is one, but certainly not the only tool, for dealing with harm, risk, and safety issues.

Over time data laws can be set to be reviewed to assess where they are working best, where improvements may be suggested, and also to identify new issues that may not have been encompassed but which need to be.[59] The GDPR has scheduled reviews. The recent Brexit adequacy decision has a scheduled review period. The GDPR RtbF will no doubt be reviewed for improvements and gaps issues from

---

Law Journal, Special Issue (2020) (21) 45; T Reed, 'Indigenous Dignity and the Right to Be Forgotten' *Brigham Young University Law Review* (2021) (4) 1119.

56   G Aleksandra, 'Can the Internet Forget? – The Right to be Forgotten in the EU Law and its Actual Impact on the Internet. Comparison of the Approaches Towards the Notion and Assessment of its Effectiveness,' *Wroclaw Review of Law, Administration and Economics* (2020) (9:1) 86.

57   A Gebuza, 'Can the Internet Forget? – The Right to be Forgotten in the EU Law and its Actual Impact on the Internet. Comparison of the Approaches Towards the Notion and Assessment of its Effectiveness' *Wroclaw Review of Law, Administration* (2019) (9:1) 86; S Duffy, 'Dereferencing and the Right to be Forgotten in Practice: Some Practical Tips on How to Get Google to Dereference Content' *Computers and Law* (2019) (December) 30; J Ausloos, *The Right to Erasure in EU Data Protection Law: From Individual Rights to Effective Protection* (OUP, 2020); P Lambert, 'The AG Opinion in Google France, An Adequate Remedy?' *International Journal for the Data Protection Officer, Privacy Officer and Privacy Counsel* (IDPP) (2019) (3:3); J Kaganoff, 'Send the Word Over There: An Offshore Solution to the Right to Be Forgotten' *Northwestern Journal of International Law & Business* (2021) (41:2) 245; KG Vazquez, 'The Right to Be Forgotten Does Not Apply Outside the European Union: A Proposal for Worldwide Application' *Southwestern Journal of International Law* (2021) (27: 1) 146; Lambert, *Understanding the New EU Data Fine Rules*.

58   C Brewer, 'Do Companies Have the Right Tools to Make Proactive Safety Decisions?' *Hydrocarbon Processing* (2021) (100:1) 19; A O'Connell and K Bakina, 'Using IP Rights to Protect Human Rights: Copyright for "Revenge Porn" Removal' *Legal Studies* (2020) (40:3) 442.

59   O Lynskey, 'Delivering Data Protection: The Next Chapter' *German Law Journal* (2020) (21:1) 80.

time to time.[60] Wider GDPR issues will be considered[61]; and new problem issues that RtbF can be a solution for will also be considered.[62] The GDPR RtbF was a progression from the *Google Spain* RtbF,[63] There will be further progressions and improvements over time. While a variety of interests and perspectives were and are already considered within the data laws, GDPR and the GDPR RtbF, we should always remember that it is an individual data right and should be a user centric right and effective tool. We should never lose sight of the reasons why individuals use and feel the need to have to use RtbF tools.[64]

A significant area of future development for RtbF, and which may not require any immediate law changes, is the locus of the data which is the subject of RtbF. Until recently most of the focus has been on online articles, materials, and related content – whether text-based or photographical-based.[65] There is increasing discussion internationally of the need for data regulators and or other entities to be able to get access to the algorithms developed by (certain) social media companies.[66] Such calls are escalated on foot of official hearings and increasing

---

60   A Bobić, 'Developments in The EU-German Judicial Love Story: The Right To Be Forgotten II' *German Law Journal* (2020) (Supplement) (21) 31; J Globocnik, 'The Right to Be Forgotten is Taking Shape: CJEU Judgments in GC and Others (C-136/17) and Google v CNIL (C-507/17)' *GRUR International: Journal of European* (2020) (69:4) 380; M José Reymond, 'The Future of the European Union "Right to be Forgotten"' *Latin American Law Review* (2019) (2) 81; S Atalar, 'Does GDPR Cover The Expectations After DPD?' *Law* (2019) (10:19) 55; CC Goldfield, 'The "Right to be Forgotten" and its Unintended Consequences to Intelligence Gathering' *Florida Journal of International Law* (2020) (32:2) 183; D Erdos, 'Disclosure, Exposure and the "Right to be Forgotten" After Google Spain: Interrogating Google Search's Webmaster, End User and Lumen Notification Practices' *Computer Law & Security Review* (2020) (38) 24.

61   'Better In Than Out: When Constitutional Courts Rely on the Charter' *European Constitutional Law Review* (2020) (16:1) 1; D Erdos and K Garstka, 'The "Right to be Forgotten" Online Within G20 Statutory Data Protection Frameworks' *International Data Privacy Law* (2020) (10:4) 294; J Ausloos, *The Right to Erasure in EU Data Protection Law: From Individual Rights to Effective Protection* (OUP, 2020); P Lambert, 'The AG Opinion in Google France, An Adequate Remedy?' *International Journal for the Data Protection Officer, Privacy Officer and Privacy Counsel* (IDPP) (2019) (3:3); J Kaganoff, 'Send the Word Over There: An Offshore Solution to the Right to Be Forgotten' *Northwestern Journal of International Law & Business* (2021) (41:2) 245.

62   CD Stoian, 'Affecting the Right of a Private Life Through the Use of the Virtual Assistance' *Journal of Humanistic & Social Studies* (2019) (10:2) 135; CT Bavitz, 'The Right to be Forgotten and Internet Governance: Challenges and Opportunities' *Latin American Law Review* (2019) (2) 1; Oksana Vasylivna Kiriiak, 'The Right to be Forgotten: Emerging Legal Issues' *Review of European and Comparative Law* (2021) (46:3) 27.

63   A Satariano and E Bubola, 'Europe's Law to Aid Privacy Gathers Force' *New York Times* (23 September 2019).

64   C Kwak, J Lee and H Lee, 'Could You Ever Forget Me? Why People Want to be Forgotten Online' *Journal of Business Ethics* (2021) (February) 1.

65   As indicated earlier, this may soon expand to audio recordings, and to video records, beyond just text and still images.

66   'Professor Calls for Access to Facebook Algorithms and Data' *Yahoo! Finance*, 6 October 2021, referring to Sinan Aral, David Austin Professor of Management at the MIT Sloan School of Management and MIT Initiative on Digital Economy. Also see generally, TD Grant and DJ Wischik, 'Show Us the Data: Privacy, Explainability, and Why the Law Can't Have Both' *George Washington Law Review Arguendo* (2020) (88:6) 1350; T Sérgio Cabral, 'Forgetful AI: AI and the Right to Erasure under the GDPR' *European Data Protection Law Review* (EDPL)

evidence that some social media activities can be more harmful than previously understood from the outside, and that sometimes evidence (eg, research) exists internally which can confirm these harms. There is also related discussion in terms of things like data ethics, and a right of explanation.[67]

In terms of RtbF, attention may focus on getting more details on each category-type of personal data that exists in relation to an individual, what signal data collection points exist, and where that data is stored. Interest may also focus on who can access or otherwise benefit from such data. Individuals may be surprised at the extent, or greater extent, of this hidden data relating to them. Data regulators and others will be interested to understand the relationship, escalation loops, and feedback loops, between this hidden data and data more visible online. While it may not be plain sailing initially, individuals will be increasingly concerned to use RtbF (and other tools) to delete and take down this hidden data and hidden data systems as it relates to and affects them.

While data ethics is an increasing discussion issue in relation to data protection more generally, there is less specific data ethics literature directed especially to RtbF. Such specific attention is overdue. It may be useful in that context to also consider recent discussions in terms algorithms and if and when access may be required, for example, to consider and improve online safety (and what corporate safeguards may be needed). Once there is discussion of access to algorithms – and also the wide array of data signal captures – the discussion will also encompass issues of computer software design, website design, app design, marketing appeal and design, and related design issues.[68]

(2020) (6:3) 378; M Odlanicka-Poczobutt and A Szyszka-Schuppik, 'The Right to be Forgotten as an Element of the Personal Data Protection System in the Organisation' *Organization & Management Quarterly* (2020) (51:3) 57; N Hodge, 'Getting Smart About Artificial Intelligence: How Can Companies Avoid the Risks and Regulatory Pitfalls of Artificial Intelligence-Based Technology?' *Risk Management* (2021) (68:8) 20; I Jiménez-Castellanos Ballesteros, 'The Conflict Between the Right to be Forgotten of the Criminal History and Freedom of Information: Digital Newspaper Archives (In this respect the Spanish Constitutional Court Judgment of June 4, 2018 and the European Court of Human Rights' Judgment in the M.L. and W.W. vs. Germany case, June 28, 2018)' *Revista de Derecho Político* (2019) (1:106) 137; A Trites, 'Black Box Ethics: How Algorithmic Decision-Making is Changing How We View Society and People: Advocating for the Right for Explanation and the Right to be Forgotten in Canada' *Global Media Journal: Canadian Edition* (2019) (11:2) 18; HJ Watson, 'Avoid Being Creepy in the Use of Personal Data and Algorithms' *Business Intelligence* (2019) (24:2) 5; I Pilving and M Mikiver, 'Kratt as an Administrative Body: Algorithmic Decisions and Principles of Administrative Law,' *Juridica International* (2020) (29) 47; A Kesa and T Kerikmäe, 'Artificial Intelligence and the GDPR: Inevitable Nemeses?' *TalTech Journal of European Studies* (2020) (10:3) 67; C Wendehorst, 'Strict Liability for AI and Other Emerging Technologies' *Journal of European Tort Law* (2020) (11:2) 150; Quang-Vinh Dang, 'Right to Be Forgotten in the Age of Machine Learning,' chapter in *Advances in Digital Science* (ICADS, 2021) 403.

67   A Trites, 'Black Box Ethics: How Algorithmic Decision-Making is Changing How We View Society and People: Advocating for the Right for Explanation and the Right to be Forgotten in Canada' *Global Media Journal: Canadian Edition* (2019) (11:2) 18.

68   On some of these wider design considerations, see W Hartzog, *Privacy's Blueprint, The Battle to Control the Design of New Technologies* (Harvard University Press, 2018); DJ Solove and W Hartzog, 'The FTC and the New Common Law of Privacy' *Columbia Law Review* (2014) (114:3) 583; W Hartzog, 'Are Privacy Laws Deficient?' *International Journal for the Data*

The discussions in relation to a proposed Online Safety Bill in the UK, and UK and international hearings in relation digital harms, online safety, and particular service providers may also come to directly (eg if there are specific changes impacting directly on RtbF rules) or indirectly (eg even if only re-emphasising the issues of online information, harms, and general need for remedies and tools more generally) influence the ongoing practice of dealing with RtbF.

Further still, practitioners will need to consider general changes in this space, whether national, European or international, including, for example, consultation change proposals, proposed Digital Services Act and proposed Digital Markets Act, and the UK reaction to these new laws. President Biden also hints at new internet child safety changes in the 2022 State of the Union Speech.

In conclusion, there is more than a clear need for RtbF, and indeed separate RtbFs as the needs can differ. It is unfortunate, however, that as beneficial and brilliant as the internet is, the small number of areas where there is a demonstrated need for RtbF are growing as bad actions and bad actors are increasing. It is unfortunate too that bad actions are not limited to bad actors.

Protection Officer, Privacy Officer and Privacy Counsel (IDPP) (2018) (2:10) 17; N Richards and W Hartzog, 'Taking Trust Seriously in Privacy Law' *Stanford Technology Law Review* (2016) (19:3) 431; G Gunasekara, 'Enforcement Design for Data Privacy: A Comparative Study' *Singapore Journal of Legal Studies* (2021) (March) 19; DW Linna Jr and WJ Muchman, 'Ethical Obligations to Protect Client Data When Building Artificial Intelligence Tools: Wigmore Meets AI' *Professional Lawyer* (2020) (27:1) 27; I Jiménez-Castellanos Ballesteros, 'The Conflict Between the Right to be Forgotten of the Criminal History and Freedom of Information: Digital Newspaper Archives (In this respect the Spanish Constitutional Court Judgment of June 4, 2018 and the European Court of Human Rights' Judgment in the M.L. and W.W. vs. Germany case, June 28, 2018)' *Revista de Derecho Político* (2019) (1:106) 137; N Hodge, 'Getting Smart About Artificial Intelligence: How Can Companies Avoid the Risks and Regulatory Pitfalls of Artificial Intelligence-Based Technology?' *Risk Management* (2021) (68:8) 20; A Trites, 'Black Box Ethics: How Algorithmic Decision-Making is Changing How We View Society and People: Advocating for the Right for Explanation and the Right to be Forgotten in Canada' *Global Media Journal: Canadian Edition* (2020) (12:1) 18.

Index